BEYOND EAGLE AND SWASTIKA

German Nationalism Since 1945

VOLUME II

BEYOND EAGLE AND SWASTIKA

German Nationalism Since 1945

By KURT P. TAUBER

VOLUME II

WESLEYAN UNIVERSITY PRESS

Middletown, Connecticut

Library of Congress Catalog Card Number: 67–15231

Manufactured in the United States of America

FIRST EDITION

Table of Contents

VOLUME II

NOTES AND REFERENCES

Advice to the Reader

The gathering of all bibliographical notes here permits a simplification which will be found useful. As is customary, all sources are shown with full data at their first appearance. Thereafter, the form "Smith (XI/237)" means "For full data, see the first citation of this source, which is at Chapter XI, note 237." Thus there are no blind-alley *op. cits.* or *loc. cits.* to contend with.

The same method is used for simple cross references to notes in this book; e.g., See above, VII/13.

Preface

1. Julius Deussen, "Streiflicher [*sic*] und Entscheidungen," in Werner Deubel, ed., *Deutsche Kulturrevolution* ([Berlin: Verlag für Zeitkritik,] 1931), cited in Harry Pross, ed., *Die Zerstörung der deutschen Politik, Dokumente 1871–1933* ([Frankfurt:] Fischer Bücherei, [c. 1959]), pp. 176–177.

Chapter I. The Antiliberal Tradition

1. As the facts underlying the generalizations in the following introductory historical sketch are widely known, the text has, with few exceptions, not been burdened with detailed bibliographical references. Instead, we list here those works which the author found especially useful in writing this chapter: Ralph F. Bischoff, *Nazi Conquest through German Culture* (Cambridge: Harvard University Press, 1942); William T. Bossenbrook, *The German Mind* (Detroit: Wayne State University Press, 1961); Martin Broszat, "Die völkische Ideologie und der Nationalsozialismus," *Deutsche Rundschau,* LXXXIV, 1 (January, 1958), 53–68; Walter Bussmann, "Politische Ideologien zwischen Monarchie und Weimarer Republik," *Historische Zeitschrift,* CXC (1960), 55–77; Rohan D'O. Butler, *The Roots of National Socialism 1783–1933* (New York: Dutton, 1942); Eugen Fischer-Baling, *Besinnung auf uns Deutsche* (Düsseldorf: Politische Bildung, 1957); Otto Flake, *Die Deutschen: Aufsätze zur Literatur und Zeitgeschichte* (Hamburg: Rütten & Loening, [c. 1963]); Otto H. von der Gablentz, *Die Tragödie des Preussentums* (Munich: Hanfstaengl, 1948); Walter Gerhard, *pseud.* [i.e., Waldemar Gurian], *Um des Reiches Zukunft* (Freiburg i. Br.: Herder, [1932]); Friedrich Glum, *Philosophen im Spiegel und Zerrspiegel. Deutschlands Weg in den Nationalismus und Nationalsozialismus* (Munich: Isar, 1954); Wolfgang Herrmann, *Der neue Nationalismus und seine Literatur* (Breslau: Städtische Volksbüchereien, 1933); H. Stuart Hughes, *Consciousness and Society; The Reorientation of European Social Thought 1890–1930* (New York: Macmillan, 1958); Klemens von Klemperer, *Germany's New Conservatism: Its History and Dilemma in the Twentieth Century* (Princeton: Princeton University Press, 1957); Hans Kohn, *German History: Some New German Views* (Boston: Beacon, 1954) and *The Mind of Modern Germany* (New York: Scribner's, 1960); Leonard Krieger, *The German Idea of Freedom* (Boston: Beacon, 1957); Alfred Kruck, *Geschichte des Alldeutschen Verbandes, 1890–1939* (Wiesbaden: Steiner, 1954); Walter Z. Laqueur, *Young Germany: A History of the German Youth Movement* (London: Routledge & Kegan Paul, 1962); Robert W. Lougee, *Paul de Lagarde 1827–1891: A Study of Radical Conservatism in Germany* (Cambridge: Harvard University Press, 1962); Paul W. Massing, *Rehearsal for Destruction: A Study of Political Anti-Semitism in Imperial Germany* (New York: Harper, 1949); Henry C. Meyer, *Mitteleuropa in German Thought and Action 1815–1945* (The Hague: Nijhoff, 1955); Armin Mohler, *Die Konservative Revolution in Deutschland 1918–1932* (Stuttgart: Vorwerk,

1950); Jean F. Neurohr, *Der Mythos vom Dritten Reich* (Stuttgart: Cotta, 1957); Ernst Nolte, *Der Faschismus in seiner Epoche* (Munich: Piper, [1963]); Emil Obermann, *Soldaten, Bürger, Militaristen. Militär und Demokratie in Deutschland* (Stuttgart: Cotta, 1958); Helmut Plessner, *Die verspätete Nation. Über die politische Verführbarkeit des bürgerlichen Geistes* (3d ed.; Stuttgart: Kohlhammer, 1959); Adolf Rapp, *Der deutsche Gedanke* (Bonn: Schroeder, 1920); Hermann Rauschning, *The Conservative Revolution* (New York: Putnam, 1940) and *The Revolution of Nihilism: Warning to the West,* [trans. by E. W. Dickes] (New York: Alliance Book, Longmans, Green, [c. 1939]); Eva G. Reichmann, *Hostages of Civilization* (Boston: Beacon, 1951); Hans Joachim Schoeps, *Das andere Preussen* (Stuttgart: Vorwerk, 1952); Franz Schonauer, *Deutsche Literatur im Dritten Reich* (Olten, Freiburg i. Br.: Walter, 1961); Otto-Ernst Schüddekopf, *Die deutsche Innenpolitik im letzten Jahrhundert und der konservative Gedanke* (Braunschweig: Limbach, 1951) and *Linke Leute von rechts: Die revolutionären Minderheiten und der Kommunismus in der Weimarer Republik* (Stuttgart: Kohlhammer, [c. 1960]); Hans-Joachim Schwierskott, *Arthur Moeller van den Bruck und der revolutionäre Nationalismus in der Weimarer Republik* (Göttingen: Musterschmidt, 1962); Friedrich C. Sell, *Die Tragödie des deutschen Liberalismus* (Stuttgart: Deutsche Verlags-Anstalt, 1953); Louis L. Snyder, *German Nationalism: The Tragedy of a People* (Harrisburg, Penna.: Stackpole, 1952); Kurt Sontheimer, *Antidemokratisches Denken in der Weimarer Republik* (2d ed.; [Munich:] Nymphenburg, [1964, c. 1962]); Fritz Stern, *The Politics of Cultural Despair: A Study in the Rise of the Germanic Ideology* (Berkeley, Los Angeles: University of California Press, 1961); Samuel D. Stirk, *The Prussian Spirit* (London: Faber & Faber, 1941); Peter Viereck, *Metapolitics: The Roots of the Nazi Mind* (New York: Capricorn Books, 1961); Robert G. L. Waite, *Vanguard of Nazism: The Free Corps Movement in Postwar Germany 1918–1923* (Cambridge: Harvard University Press, 1952).

After completion of this chapter two other pertinent books have appeared: Hermann Glaser, *Spiesser-Ideologie. Von der Zerstörung des deutschen Geistes im 19. und 20. Jahrhundert* (2d ed.; Freiburg: Rombach, [c. 1964]); George L. Moss, *The Crisis of German Ideology. Intellectual Origins of the Third Reich* (New York: Grosset & Dunlap, [c. 1964]).

2. "Das Deutsche Reich. Deutschland?/ Aber wo liegt es?/ Ich weiss das Land nicht zu finden./ Wo das Gelehrte beginnt, hört das Politische auf." Johann Christoph Friedrich von Schiller, "Xenien (Musenalmanach für das Jahr 1797)," in Julius Petersen and Gerhard Fricke, eds., *Schillers Werke, Nationalausgabe* (Weimar: Böhlaus, 1943). I (*Gedichte 1776–1799*), 320. See also Sell (I/1), pp. 46–47.

3. H. S. Reiss, ed., *Political Thought of the German Romantics 1793–1815* (Oxford: Blackwell, 1955), p. 3.

4. The Carlsbad Decrees, devised by the Austrian Chancellor Klemens von Metternich, acquiesced in by Frederick William III of Prussia, and thus imposed on the German *Bund* on September 20, 1819, were aimed at the radical nationalist student movement of the Burschenschaften, after one of its members, Karl Ludwig Sand, had assassinated the reactionary poet

and journalist August von Kotzebue. The Decrees provided for rigid censorship and for the suppression of subversion through the close supervision of universities and schools. The Burschenschaften were dissolved. Cf. below, X/231, 236, 237.

5. Walther Rathenau aptly and harshly castigated this development: "The spiritual treason of the upper bourgeoisie, which disavowed its background and responsibility, which not only dammed up the springs of democracy but poisoned them—for the price of a reserve lieutenancy, for membership in a student corps, for a patent of nobility, a seat in the House of Lords, and the title of a Commercial Councillor—which was so venal, cowardly, and fat as to place (through its instrument, the National Liberal Party) Germany's fate into the hands of reaction: this was the treason which destroyed Germany, which destroyed the monarchy, and which has made us contemptible in the eyes of all nations." *Der Kaiser; eine Betrachtung* (Berlin, 1918), p. 65. Quoted in Obermann (I/1), pp. 197–198.

6. The irrationalist, vitalist attack upon liberalism and traditionalist conservatism was a *fin de siècle* phenomenon not limited to Germany. Though it was probably more deeply rooted in Germany than anywhere else and certainly reached its greatest virulence in German intellectual circles, the mere mention of such names as Feodor Dostoevski, Georges Sorel, Maurice Barrès, Charles Maurras, Vilfredo Pareto, Knut Hamsun, D. H. Lawrence, Giulio Evola, G. K. Chesterton, Lothrop Stoddard, and Madison Grant suggests the existence of the movement in other lands.

7. For a not very persuasive attempt to deny the importance of the idea of *Reich* in nineteenth-century German historical and political thought, see Wilhelm Mommsen, "Zur Bedeutung des Reichsgedankens," *Historische Zeitschrift,* CLXXIV (1952), 385–415. In that essay Mommsen continues the argument of Arnold Berney's "Reichstradition und Nationalstaatsgedanke (1789–1815)," *ibid.,* CXL (1929), 57–86.

8. The notion of a Third Reich goes back to the second-century Christian sect of Montanists, according to whom three different dispensations in three distinct historical periods would successively manifest the three persons of the Trinity. The realm of God the Father (Old Testament) was superseded by the realm of the Son (New Testament), which in turn was expected to yield soon to the third realm, that of the Holy Ghost. We find this notion again as the Third or Eternal Gospel in the work of the twelfth-century Joachim of Flora and as the "Third Rome" (Moscow), after the destruction of the "Second Rome" (Byzantium) by the Turks, in the writings of a Slavic monk. This trinitarian basis is still in evidence in corrupted form in the writings of such a revolutionary conservative as Arthur Moeller van den Bruck, who speaks of a third party which will surmount the contradiction between the party of progress and the forces of conservation. The third party will unleash a truly conservative revolution: it will create the Third Reich.

9. An analogy of this sort is dangerous, as it is likely to conceal crucial differences in the origins, structures, and dynamics of the sociocultural movements concerned. Nevertheless, it helps to fix certain inescapable similarities which provide useful clues for further analysis. Of the beatnik,

Edwin H. Powell writes: "The beatnik is neither reactionary nor revolutionary; he is simply an anarchist in waiting. Existing society is a sham; . . . his reaction to it is a kind of passive resistance. He 'opts out,' he plays it cool, he disaffiliates: . . . the beat affiliates with a new community in order to validate his disaffiliation from a larger society." "Beyond Utopia: The 'Beat Generation' as a Challenge for the Sociology of Knowledge," in Arnold M. Rose, ed., *Human Behavior and Social Processes* (Boston: Houghton Mifflin, [c. 1962]), p. 366. According to Norman Podhoretz, the bohemianism of the nineteen-fifties "is hostile to civilization; it worships primitivism, instinct, energy, 'blood.' To the extent it has any intellectual interests at all, they run to mystical doctrines, irrationalist philosophies." "The Know-Nothing Bohemians," *Partisan Review* (Spring, 1958), pp. 308–309. And John C. Holmes sees in the beatniks' rejection of conventional morality "a return to an older, more personal code of ethics which includes the inviolability of comradeship, the respect for confidences, and an almost mystical regard for courage—all of which are the ethics of the tribe, rather than the community; the code of a small, compact group living in an indifferent or a hostile environment which it *seeks not to conquer or change, but only to elude*." "The Philosophy of the Beat Generation," in Seymour Krim, ed., *The Beats* (Greenwich, Conn.: Fawcett Publications, 1960), p. 22. The sense of cultural discontinuity which animates the Beat Generation has also been identified as a key element in the cultural climate which bred the Conservative Revolution and Nazism in Germany. Max Picard characterized that mood as follows: "I am totally alone; nowhere is there a pulse, a life around me, and beyond me there is nothing but nothingness. . . . In this world of discontinuity the ego is not even the center of a destroyed world; it merely is like some projection on the empty screen of a cinema." *Hitler in Ourselves,* trans. by Heinrich Hauser (Chicago: Regnery, 1947), p. 184. Cf. also the remaining essays in Krim, *The Beats,* and in Gene Feldman and Max Gartenberg, eds., *The Beat Generation and the Angry Young Men* (New York: Citadel, [1958]). For a good, short bibliography see Powell, "Beyond Utopia," pp. 373–377.

10. Like all generalizations, this one is not without exceptions. There arose early persuasive voices within the Wandervogel, warning against excessive romantic enthusiasm at the expense of present reality. Alfred Thon, one of the leaders of the original Steglitz Wandervogel, recalls an article in the official Wandervogel journal which sternly reminded the romantic youngsters: "Whoever is incapable of accepting the image of the Rhine with four railroad tracks running alongside and with belching smokestacks in the lowlands beyond has not yet learned to perceive clearly (*unbefangen*)." "Geburt und Jugend des Wandervogel," in Will Vesper, ed., *Deutsche Jugend. 30 Jahre Geschichte einer Bewegung* (Berlin: Holle, 1934), p. 30.

11. "The atmosphere (*Geist*) of the *Materialschlacht* and of trench warfare, which were contested more uncompromisingly, more wildly, more brutally than any previous [battles], produced men the likes of whom the world had hitherto never seen. It was an entirely new race—energy incarnate, loaded with enormous power (*höchster Wucht*). Lithe, lanky, sinewy

bodies, chiseled features, and underneath the helmet, eyes which thousands of horrors had turned to stone. They were conquerors (*Überwinder*), men of steel, sent into the fray in its most gruesome form. Their sprint across the torn landscape was the ultimate triumph of a fantastic dread (*Grausen*). Jugglers of death, masters of explosives and flame throwers, magnificent beasts of prey, thus they leaped through the trenches. In the moment of confrontation they were the quintessence of the most elemental combat instinct which can exist in this world, the keenest unification of body, intelligence, will, and senses." Ernst Jünger, *Der Kampf als inneres Erlebnis* (Berlin: Mittler, 1940), pp. 33–34, quoted in Pross (Pref./1), p. 79. Four years after completion of this chapter a good analysis of nationalist-folkish literature of the interwar years became available—unfortunately too late to be here taken into account: Rolf Geissler, *Dekadenz und Heroismus. Zeitroman und völkisch-nationalsozialistische Literaturkritik,* Schriftenreihe der Vierteljahrshefte für Zeitgeschichte, no. 9 (Stuttgart: Deutsche Verlags-Anstalt, [c. 1964]), pp. 76–103.

12. *Betrachtungen eines Unpolitischen* (Berlin: Fischer, 1919), p. xxxiii. For the problem of Mann's early antidemocratic views, see Kurt Sontheimer, "Thomas Mann als politischer Schriftsteller," *Vierteljahrshefte für Zeitgeschichte,* VI, 1 (January, 1958), 1–44.

13. These sobering considerations, however, together with the incipient pacifism of a section of the Youth Movement, had been quickly swept away by the enthusiasm of the first months of the war.

14. See, for instance, Jünger (I/11), p. 18. "But Germany had to lose the war, even if it had won the battle of the Marne and the U-boat war." And Franz Schauwecker categorically declares in the motto of his war novel *Aufbruch der Nation*: "We had to lose the war in order to gain the nation." Geissler (I/11), p. 94.

15. Mann (I/12), p. 28.

16. The non- and antimonarchist nature of radical nationalism after the First World War is frequently overlooked. See, for example, the otherwise useful book of Walter H. Kaufmann, *Monarchism in the Weimar Republic* (New York: Bookman Associates, 1953).

17. Oswald Spengler, *Preussentum und Sozialismus* (Munich: Beck, 1920), p. 4.

18. Mohler (I/1), pp. 12–13.

19. Mohler's analogy does not apply to those nationalist revolutionaries and *bündisch* youth groups who, though distinctly non-Hitlerites, argued that National Socialism and the Nazi Third Reich were a necessary step toward the ultimate goal of a Fourth Reich—the folkish, supranational, pacifist, communist-Christian, universal realm under the leadership of the Germans. See, for example, Kurt van Emsen, *pseud.* [i.e., Karl Strünkmann, M.D.], *Adolf Hitler und die Kommenden* (Leipzig: Lindner, 1932).

20. Characteristically, Rudolf Pechel provided the Conservative Revolutionaries with the watchword, "Join the smallest group!" See "Das Wort geht um," in A. Moeller v.d. Bruck, H. von Gleichen, and M. H. Boehm, eds., *Die neue Front* (Berlin: Paetel, 1922), p. 75.

21. This is the title of one of the earliest works in the English language devoted to the political and social thought of the Conservative Revolution. Aurel Kolnai, *The War Against the West,* pref. by Wickham Steed (London: Gollancz, 1938).

22. This much was admitted by the Young Conservative Edgar J. Jung, who was later to fall victim to Hitler's murder squads in the Blood Purge of 1934. In 1932 he wrote: "We not only rejoice [at the growth of National Socialism] but we have done our bit to bring it about. In untold work on a small scale, especially among the educated classes, we created the prerequisites for the day when the German people would give its votes to the National Socialist candidates." "Neubelebung von Weimar? Verkehrung der Fronten," *Deutsche Rundschau,* CCXXXI (June, 1932), 159, quoted in Stern (I/1), p. 297. Four years earlier Baldur von Schirach, then Nazi student leader, had warned a Nazi student group of Jung: "Dr. Edgar Jung, half Jew, who likes to call himself a '100% revolutionary,' has nothing to do with the NSDAP. I personally consider him one of the worst enemies of the movement. . . . He seems to be obsessed by great ambition and probably would like to become a leader of academic youth. However, it is also possible that he has been given the job by certain circles to collect the students around him, to prevent their joining Hitler. In any case: Announce at every occasion, also in public, that this gentleman has nothing to do with us." (Von Schirach's letter of November 20, 1928, reproduced in Pross [Pref./1], p. 367.)

Chapter II. The Twilight of the Gods: The Second World War and the Occupation

1. On January 22, 1943, Ulrich von Hassel, German Ambassador to Italy until 1938, noted in his diary: "One cannot yet say definitely that the war is lost, but it is certain that it cannot be won." *Vom anderen Deutschland* (Zurich: Atlantis, 1946), p. 292. On May 15, 1943, Goebbels confided to his diary: "Morale among the masses is so low as to be rather serious. Even people of good will are now worried about further developments. The man in the street no longer sees any way out of the military dilemma." Louis P. Lochner, ed., *The Goebbels Diaries, 1942–1943* (New York: Doubleday, 1948), p. 380.

2. From a confidential eyewitness account of the meeting at Grenzhotel Herzogau near Furth im Wald, held between April 20 and April 23, 1945.

3. In contrast to the Werewolf's failure in the Reich, it managed to develop considerable militancy and more than annoying activity in the Sudeten territory of Czechoslovakia. The blowing up of factories in Ustí nad Labem (Aussig), maintenance of a secret radio transmitter in the frontier town of Dečin, assassinations of Czech officers, and attempted liberation of Germans from internment camps testify to the undaunted spirit of Nazi enthusiasts. Joseph B. Schechtman, *Postwar Population Transfers in Europe,*

1945–1955 (Philadelphia: University of Pennsylvania Press, 1962), p. 65. What role in this noticeably greater activism was played by the last Reich training chief of the Hitler Youth, Gottfried Griesmayr, is not clear. For Griesmayr's preparations for such a role, see below, V/39.

4. As late as October, 1954, no more than 42 per cent of the population believed that foreign troops would remain in Germany only temporarily (up to another ten years). Eleven per cent thought they would remain forever. Elisabeth Noelle and Erich Peter Neumann, eds., *Jahrbuch der öffentlichen Meinung 1947–1955* (2d ed.; Allensbach/Bodensee: Verlag für Demoskopie, [c. 1956]), p. 204.

5. For a history tracing the development of Allied policy toward Germany in the course of the war, see John L. Snell, *Wartime Origins of the East-West Dilemma over Germany* (New Orleans: Hauser, 1959). Cf. Rudolf Wildenmann's excellent *Macht und Konsens als Problem der Innen- und Aussenpolitik* (Frankfurt, Bonn: Athenäum, 1963), pp. 25–43.

6. An indication of that marginality was the doubt about the legitimacy of opposition to a totalitarian dictatorship. This can be gleaned both from the high percentage of people who still blame the loss of the war on the men of July 20, 1944, and insist that overt resistance is always evil (see below, Chapter VIII, Section E) and from the results of an opinion poll in October, 1954, which asked whether emigrants who fled from Hitler's regime and who worked with the Allies during the war should be barred from high public office in the Bonn Republic. Thirty-nine per cent of the respondents thought that former emigrants should be barred from high public office, while only 13 per cent agreed that high office should be accessible to them; 26 per cent believed that the answer depended on the situation in each individual case, and 22 per cent were undecided. Noelle and Neumann (II/4), p. 139. The shameful campaign methods employed against the top SPD candidate, Willy Brandt, a former *émigré,* in the course of the 1961 election seem to indicate that popular attitudes in these matters change only slowly.

7. For a minority dissent from this view, see Eugene Davidson, *The Death and Life of Germany* (New York: Knopf, 1959), p. 50. On the other hand, Harry Pross, sensitive student of recent German history and one of the finest minds among the gifted young postwar generation of editors and journalists, argues that the tragedy of Military Government activity consisted in "resuscitating precisely that element in German political thought which had been undermined through Nazi corruption, namely, the bureaucratic mentality. When we speak today of collapse, we do not refer by that suspect word to the collapse of megalomania, but rather to the chaos of the few unadministered weeks during which anarchy reigned under the aegis of an undecided military bureaucracy. The denazification [process] and the reconstruction of an indigenous administration which had to allocate scarce materials again re-established the administration as an important political element in German thought. It has remained that ever since." *Vor und nach Hitler. Zur deutschen Sozialpathologie* (Olten: Walter, 1962), pp. 155–156.

8. Control Council Directive No. 24 of January 12, 1946, entitled "Removal from Office and from Positions of Responsibility of Nazis and of

Persons Hostile to Allied Purposes," left no doubt as to the official requirements, at least with regard to top administrative personnel. Paragraph 13 contains the following unambiguous order: "It is essential that the head executive German officials at the levels of Provinz, Regierungsbezirk and Kreis should be confirmed anti-Nazis even if this entails the employment of persons less well qualified to discharge their administrative duties." Beate Ruhm von Oppen, ed., *Documents on Germany under Occupation 1945–1954* (London: Oxford University Press, 1955), p. 107.

9. Among the readily accessible American discussions of this problem are (in the order of their publication): Harold Zink, "The American Denazification Program in Germany," *Journal of Central European Affairs,* VI, 4 (October, 1946), 227–240; Elmer Plischke, "Denazification Law and Procedure," *The American Journal of International Law,* XLI (October, 1947), 807–827; John H. Herz, "The Fiasco of Denazification in Germany," *Political Science Quarterly,* LXII (December, 1948), 569–594; Joseph F. Napoli, "Denazification from an American's Viewpoint," *Annals of the American Academy of Political and Social Science,* no. 264 (July, 1949), pp. 115–123; Lucius D. Clay, *Decision in Germany* (New York: Doubleday, 1950); William E. Griffith, *The Denazification Program in the United States Zone of Germany* (Ph.D. dissertation, Harvard University, 1950); Edward H. Litchfield *et al., Governing Postwar Germany* (Ithaca, N.Y.: Cornell University Press, 1953); Guenther Roth and Kurt H. Wolff, *The American Denazification of Germany* (Columbus, Ohio: Ohio State University, Department of Sociology and Anthropology, 1954); John D. Montgomery, *Forced to Be Free* (Chicago: University of Chicago Press, 1957); Harold Zink, *The United States in Germany 1944–1955* (Princeton: Van Nostrand, 1957), Chapter 11; Lewis J. Edinger, "Post-Totalitarian Leadership in the German Federal Republic," *American Political Science Review,* LIV, 1 (March, 1960), 58–82; John Gimbel, "American Denazification and German Local Politics, 1945–1949: A Case Study in Marburg," *ibid.,* pp. 83–105, and his later *A German Community under American Occupation* (Stanford: Stanford University Press, 1961). See also Raul Hilberg's magisterial *The Destruction of the European Jews* (Chicago: Quadrangle, 1961), pp. 699–701, for summary tables and statistics.

10. How widespread falsification of the document was among those who had something to hide will never be known. In the autumn of 1962 the main defendant in the Coblenz mass-murder trial, former SS Captain Georg Heuser, who had become, after the war, chief of the intelligence section of the Rhineland-Palatinate police, estimated in court that about 80 per cent of all Germans gave false answers to the questionnaire. *Manchester Guardian,* October 16, 1962.

11. Article 2, Section 2, and Articles 59, 60. See the discussion by Wilhelm Högner in "Besprechung neo-nazistischer Erscheinungen im politischen Leben," in Bayerischer Landtag, *Stenographischer Bericht über die Verhandlungen des Bayerischen Landtags* (137th public session), V, 137 (January 17, 1950), 447.

12. Article 1, Section 1; Articles 24–28; Article 35, Section 4.

13. Article 2, Section 1; Article 4.

14. Article 34.

15. Article 3.

16. *Frankfurter Rundschau,* September 1, 1948.

17. See Hessisches Ministerium für Politische Befreiung, *Amtsblatt* (Wiesbaden), I, 5 (February 6, 1947), 2.

18. In this connection, see Bayerisches Statistisches Landesamt, *Statistisches Jahrbuch für Bayern 1947,* XXIII ([Munich, 1948]), Tables 4, 7, 8, 10, and 12 on pp. 278, 279, 281, and 282.

19. See *Badische Neueste Nachrichten* (Karlsruhe), July 9, 1949. In the entire U.S. Zone, 30 per cent of all officials of all grades were chargeable under the law at the end of 1947. See Zentralamt der U.S. Militärregierung, *Bericht über die Auswirkung des Entnazifizierungs- und Entmilitarisierungsgesetzes bei Behörden und in Privatunternehmen.*

20. This was, of course, particularly true of those who were held in internment camps for months, and sometimes even years, pending their final denazification. These people, in fact, hardly ever appealed the initial Spruchkammer decisions, since that would have meant continued internment until the slowly grinding wheels of the appeals procedure finally settled their cases.

21. [Club republikanischer Publizisten,] *CrP-Information,* June, 1957, p. 54.

22. Letter (dated March 9, 1952) from Albert Friehe, of Bückeburg, to Jan Blankemayer, of Hildesheim, an equally incorrigible Nazi who included in the newspaper announcement of his wife's death, in spring 1957, reference to her former eminence, "BdM-Führerin und Frauenschaftsleiterin der Kampfzeit," and said in the obituary that "the sorrow over the collapse of the Reich through treason and traitors within the country shortened her life." In 1959 Blankemayer was fined DM 50 for having laid a wreath on the grave of Otto Ohlendorf, who had been executed in 1951 for the murder of ninety thousand people. The inscription on the wreath read: "To our faithful comrade—The former *Standarte* Garbolzum." The law mentioned in the letter was passed pursuant to a decision taken by the Ministers of Justice of the several states at a conference in Rothenburg o. d. Tauber on November 5, 1949.

23. See Walter Spengemann, "Die missglückte Entnazifizierung," *Norddeutsche Zeitung* (Hanover), September 7, 1948.

24. See Paul Wilhelm Wenger, "Entnazifizierung am Ende," *Rheinischer Merkur* (Koblenz), April 2, 1949. For Blunck's literary activity in Nazi Germany and thereafter, see below, Chapter XI, Section B/VII.

25. See Friedrich M. Reifferscheidt, "1945 bis 1950: Triumph des Hindenburg-Deutschen," *Frankfurter Hefte,* VI, 2 (February, 1951), 95–96.

26. Fritz Erler, "Über den Nazismus," *Neuer Vorwärts* (Hanover), November 23, 1951.

27. In August, 1948, a public-opinion survey revealed that only 4 per cent of the respondents thought that "denazification was necessary and has accomplished its task." Another 10 per cent agreed that denazification had its faults but had on the whole accomplished its task. As against this 14 per

cent in support, there were 39 per cent who held that denazification had been bungled, however necessary it might have been; another 31 per cent refused to acknowledge even the program's necessity, and 9 per cent thought denazification was little more than a piece of chicanery of the occupation powers. Seven per cent alleged not to have a view on this subject. Noelle and Neumann (II/4), p. 142.

28. Alfred Grosser, *Western Germany from Defeat to Rearmament,* trans. by R. Rees (London: Ahern & Kerwin, 1955), p. 36.

29. *Ibid.,* p. 37.

30. See, for instance, Hessisches Ministerium für Politische Befreiung, "Rundverfügung Nr. 72, Bescheinigung für Amnestierte und Nichtbetroffene," *Amtsblatt* (Wiesbaden), I, 7 (February 3 [*sic*], 1947), 25.

31. The bulk of the Spruchkammern were soon to be dissolved. See *ibid.,* II, 46 and 47 (July 24 and August 13, 1948).

32. The so-called *Überführungsgesetz* of January 15, 1948. See *ibid.,* II, 38 (March 20, 1948), 151–152. For a graphic description of the informal boycott, see Peter Miska, "Wir sind schon wieder so weit," *Frankfurter Rundschau,* April 26, 1950, p. 4.

33. For a lively account of the difficulties and accomplishments of the British denazification effort, see Raymond Ebsworth, *Restoring Democracy in Germany* (London: Steven; New York: Praeger, 1960), pp. 8–15. For the problems and vagaries of denazification in the French Zone, see F. Roy Willis, *The French in Germany, 1945–1949* (Stanford: Stanford University Press, 1962), pp. 147–163.

34. In August, 1948, it will be remembered (see above, II/27), 79 per cent of all respondents opposed denazification—as necessary but bungled (39 per cent), not necessary and bungled (31 per cent), and merely an arbitrary chicanery of the occupiers (9 per cent). In November, 1953, these figures respectively were 63, 23, 26, 14. Noelle and Neumann (II/4), p. 142.

35. For a short but excellent review of the trials, see Hilberg (II/9), pp. 684–698.

36. It might be salutary to recall here Gerald Reitlinger's dry comment: "It seems to be a common habit, not confined to Germany, to regard any *idée fixe* as idealism, particularly if it is a cruel one." *The SS, Alibi of a Nation, 1922–1945* (2d ed., rev.; London: Heinemann, 1957), p. 32. Cf. also Thilo Koch, "Idealismus—ein deutsches Missverständnis," *Deutsche Rundschau,* LXXX, 4 (April, 1954), 362–365.

37. Article 3.

38. Probably a large majority of educated Germans would today agree with Admiral Karl Dönitz' defense counsel, the ultranationalist Navy Judge Advocate Otto Kranzbühler, when he said (in a debate on "The Merits and Demerits of Historical Trials," organized by the Catholic Academy in Munich in November, 1961) that the Nuremberg trials "undermined faith in the rule of law by showing how easily it can be corrupted by the political abuse of historic trials." Indeed, one participant at the conference sadly admitted that "those who continue to brand Hitler's criminal and predatory

incursions as aggressive war are being increasingly looked upon as traitors." *Frankfurter Rundschau,* November 21, 1961.

39. Cf. Grosser (II/28), pp. 68–70. That this is, of course, not so—and was not the case in Nazi Germany—is attested to by many witnesses. See, for example, the sworn deposition of former Legation Counselor Reinhard Henschel, Document CXXVa-100 of the archives of the Centre de Documentation Juive Contemporaine (Paris), reproduced in Léon Poliakov and Josef Wulf, *Das Dritte Reich und seine Diener, Dokumente* (Berlin-Grunewald: arani, 1956), p. 149. Cf. also "Introduction to Clemency Board Report Regarding Applications for Clemency for War Criminals Convicted by U.S. Tribunal at Nuremberg," as reproduced in U.S. Department of State, Office of the High Commissioner for Germany, *6th Quarterly Report on Germany, January 1—March 31, 1951,* pp. 111–112.

40. This point was made (without avail) by the Minister Presidents of the German Länder in the British and American Zones in a unanimous statement addressed to the Control Council on March 26, 1946. On October 5, 1946, the heads of the Länder and city governments of the British and American Zones at the Bremen Conference again passed a resolution incorporating the views expressed in their March statement. See Ruhm von Oppen (II/8), pp. 167–168.

41. For a review of the post-World War II experience with German prosecutions of "the perpetrators of destruction," see Hilberg (II/9), pp. 702–704. The drive against Nazi criminals failed, argues Hilberg, "because there was so much sympathy for these men" (p. 703). Hilberg, however, neither discusses nor even mentions the Central Office of Preparation and Coordination for the Prosecution of Concentration Camp and War Crimes, set up in Ludwigsburg. For a fair though skeptical summary of the German reaction to, and handling of, war crimes prosecutions, see Alistair Horne, *Return to Power: A Report on the New Germany* (New York: Praeger, 1956). Cf. below, Chapter XVIII, Section E.

42. For an early but entirely valid view, see Hans Speier, " 'Reeducation,' the U.S. Policy," in his *Social Order and the Risks of War* (New York: Stewart, 1952), pp. 397–414.

43. Helmut Hammerschmidt, "Ist der Nationalsozialismus tot?" [Club republikanischer Publizisten,] *CrP-Information,* April, 1957, p. 37.

44. The well-known commentator of the South German Broadcasting Corporation, Walter von Cube, has called it a moral and historical necessity. *Ich bitte um Widerspruch* (Frankfurt: Frankfurter Hefte, 1952), p. 11.

45. See Karl Jaspers, *The Question of German Guilt,* trans. by E. B. Ashton (New York: Dial, 1947), *passim.*

Chapter III. The First Stirrings: 1945–1948

1. See Lewis Hertzmann, *DNVP, Right-Wing Opposition in the Weimar Republic, 1918–1924* (Lincoln, Nebr.: University of Nebraska Press, 1963), pp. 124–164; and Werner Liebe, *Die Deutschnationale Volkspartei 1918–1924* (Düsseldorf: Droste, 1956), pp. 61–73. See also Hanns Hubert Hofmann, *Der Hitlerputsch: Krisenjahre deutscher Geschichte 1920–1924* (Munich: Nymphenburg, 1961), p. 72. Cf. Sigmund Neumann, *Die deutschen Parteien* (Berlin: Junker und Dünnhaupt, 1932), p. 62. Wulle's fellow leaders were Albrecht von Gräfe, Wilhelm Henning, and Count Ernst von Reventlow. Wulle had been editor in chief and political director of the monarchist, Prussomanic pan-German paper *Deutsche Zeitung* from 1918 to 1920. For Wulle's break with the Pan-German League, see Alfred Kruck, *Geschichte des Alldeutschen Verbandes, 1890–1939* (Wiesbaden: Steiner, 1954), pp. 149–150.

2. August Abel, "Reinhold Wulle zum Gedächtnis," *Der Informationsbrief* (July, 1950), p. 8. Cf. Kaufmann (I/16), p. 118.

3. Bureau des Reichstags, *Reichstags Handbuch, II. Wahlperiode, 1924* (Berlin, 1924). The new party gathered almost two million votes and sent thirty-two deputies to the Reichstag.

4. According to Ludendorff's version, the decision to participate in the election had been his, but only after Hitler had refused to give a clear yes or no answer to Ludendorff's question in that regard. See Erich Ludendorff, *Vom Feldherrn zum Weltrevolutionär und Wegbereiter deutscher Volksschöpfung* (*Meine Lebenserinnerungen von 1919 bis 1925*) (Munich: 1940), I, p. 328, cited in Winfried Martini, *Die Legende vom Hause Ludendorff* (Rosenheim: Inngau, Lang, 1949), pp. 59–60.

5. See Goebbels' diary entries of October 21 and November 10, 1925, and March 21, 1926, in Helmut Heiber, ed., *Das Tagebuch von Joseph Goebbels 1925/26* (Stuttgart: Deutsche Verlags–Anstalt, [1961]), pp. 36, 41, 66. In the third number of *Nationalsozialistische Briefe* (November 1, 1925) Goebbels wrote an open letter to Wulle under the title "Das traurige Ende einer Kampfansage." It concluded as follows: "Now we are facing you as a political opponent and say [the things] that must be said—openly, honestly, without beating around the bush. And [we] see in you that bourgeois opposition against [your] own bourgeois state, the opposition that would want to, but is not able, [to oppose]—the opposition of the saver (*Sparer*), pensioner, and *petit bourgeois,* which treats itself good-naturedly and with moderation to a bit of hostility toward this damned expensive state and, whenever necessary, warms its feet [at our fire]." The enmities in the camp of the nationalist-folkish extremists provoked one of the chief spokesmen of the Deutschvölkische Freiheitspartei, Count Reventlow, to the following outburst of exasperation: "He who knows the organizational life of Germany and . . . especially the folkish [area] knows also how busy *invidia et stultitia* [envy and stupidity] are being kept, how quickly the not exactly most exalted passions are inflamed, how readily the most unbelievable nonsense gains credence and the most infamous suspicions are expressed and accepted. If all

this isn't thoroughly changed, it will be unthinkable that the folkish movement should ever become a political power that can even remotely be led." Quoted from Reventlow's *Reichswart* in Hermann Martin, *Demokratie oder Diktatur?* (Berlin: Politik und Wirtschaft, 1926), p. 205.

6. See von Ostau's *curriculum vitae,* prepared by the Forschungsgemeinschaft des "Anderen Deutschlands" (Hanover), May 18, 1948. Cf. the typescript of a contribution to the organ of the conservatives of Schleswig-Holstein, edited by Colonel Eldor Borck, undated, but most likely April or May, 1947. (Between 1925 and 1933 Borck was DNVP deputy in the Prussian diet.)

7. Julius Friedrich, *Wer spielte falsch? Hitler, Hindenburg, der Kronprinz, Hugenberg, Schleicher* (Hamburg: Laatzen, no date, but probably October, 1949), p. 13. Karl Dietrich Bracher's characterization of the brochure and its reliability is apt: "[a] participant observer's sloppy journalistic account in which apt, intimate glimpses are paired with wild combinations and many unproved quarter-truths." *Die Auflösung der Weimarer Republik* (2d ed.; Stuttgart, Düsseldorf: Ring, 1957), p. 459, note 56.

8. Friedrich (III/7), p. 74.

9. *Ibid.,* pp. 36–37. In view of the character of the source, caution and even a measure of reserve are called for. Cf. von Ostau's lecture "Der Irrweg der deutschen Parteien" (delivered before a University of Bonn audience on January 27, 1948), p. 6. This lecture permits a clear estimate of the proximity of von Ostau's political thought to Otto Strasser's "solidarism," as he is pleased to call his brand of corporativism.

10. For von der Schulenburg's part in the Resistance, see Eberhard Zeller, *Geist der Freiheit* (3d ed.; Munich: Rinn, [1956]), pp. 105–114. Von der Schulenburg was later slated as Minister for Internal Affairs in the government which was to have been established after the planned assassination of Hitler in July, 1944.

11. Of Wulle, Friedrich writes: "This former folkish radical had only slowly overcome Schleicher's skepticism and had become an important driving force of his plans." (III/7), p. 37.

12. Deutsche Aufbau Partei, Hauptvorstand, der 1. Vorsitzende, *Rundschreiben,* no. 3 (end of February, 1946).

13. The truth of this allegation is drawn into doubt by an official document of September 12, 1938, in which the executive secretary of the Reich Chamber of Literature, Wilhelm Ihde, demands Wulle's exclusion from the chamber and the close investigation of his publishers. (Reproduced in Josef Wulf, *Literatur und Dichtung im Dritten Reich* ([Gütersloh:] Mohn, [c. 1963], pp. 186–190). Of course, it is conceivable that the Chamber of Literature had not been informed of Wulle's arrest.

14. See Wulle's letter to the defense counsel of the former Reich Minister of the Interior, Wilhelm Frick, in International Military Tribunal, *Trial of the Major War Criminals* (Nuremberg: 1949), XL, Document Frick–37 (Exhibit Frick–10), 165–167.

15. Deutsche Aufbau Partei (III/12).

16. *Ibid.,* no. 2 (January, 1946), p. 5.

17. This fact, too, is in doubt in view of the document cited above, III/13.

18. Reinhold Wulle, *Geschichte einer Staatsidee* (Berlin: NBD—Nationaler Bücherdienst, 1935), pp. 8, 29.

19. *Ibid.* pp. 40, 41, 43.

20. *Ibid.* pp. 98, 118.

21. *Ibid.* p. 168.

22. Wulle, "Höre Herr . . . ," (unpublished typescript, no date), p. 9.

23. "Whatever is called freedom in a democracy is nothing but a fraudulent euphemism for the dictatorship of an artificially created, so-called public, opinion. Whoever is not in jail may move around freely if he has the leisure to do so. Beyond that, the law of having-to-live (*Gesetz des Lebensmüssens*) prescribes for everyone his movements. If this is done out of a consciousness of duty, then it contains the ethic of obedience which ennobles human activity. There simply is no freedom in the sense in which this term is often understood. Freedom exists only in God." *Ibid.*, p. 11.

24. "Is this not precisely the racial characteristic (*Arteigene*) of the Nordic race, when it is not swamped by foreign influence (*überfremdet*)? To feel one's integrity within the All is the inextinguishable longing of the North. . . . Christianity has been grasped in its depth only by the Teutons." *Ibid.*, p. 12.

25. Wulle, "Christliches Abendland: Vergangenheit oder Aufgabe" (unpublished manuscript, no date), p. 15.

26. *Ibid.* p. 33.

27. Wulle, "Betrachtungen eines Unpolitischen" (unpublished manuscript, beginning of July, 1946), p. 23.

28. Wulle, *Die Grossen 5—Aufstand gegen Versailles,* "Das abc des NBD" Series, no. 1 (Berlin: NBD—Nationaler Bücherdienst, no date).

29. Wulle (III/18), p. 167.

30. Wulle, "Betrachtungen eines Unpolitischen. (B.) Das Weltbild Europas (Fortsetzung)" (unpublished manuscript, mimeographed, August, 1946), p. 3.

31. For expressions of the ideas summarized in these two paragraphs, see Wulle (III/25), pp. 12 ff., 16, 18, 25, and Wulle (III/27), pp. 1, 9, 10. In his identification of democracy with the rise of the masses, with the rise of Hitler as its necessary consequence, Wulle is joined by a roster of highly respectable, irreproachably non-Nazi conservative historians, such as Rosemarie von dem Hagen, "Rousseau und die Problematik der Demokratie," *Deutsche Rundschau,* LXXVI, 3 (1950), 157–166; Ernst von Hippel, "Rousseaus Staatslehre als Mystik des Materialismus," *Neues Abendland,* VI, 7 (1950), 337–345; and Gerhard Ritter, *Europa und die deutsche Frage* (Munich: Münchner Verlag [Graph. Kunstanstalt], 1948), "The Historical Foundations of the Rise of National Socialism," in Maurice Baumont *et al.*, eds., *The Third Reich* (New York: Praeger, 1955), pp. 381–416, and "The Military and Politics in Germany," *Journal of Central European Affairs,* XVII, 3 (October, 1957), 259–271. For a general discussion and additional bibliography, see Andrew G. Whiteside, "The Nature and Origins of Na-

tional Socialism," *Journal of Central European Affairs,* XVII, 1 (April, 1957), 48–73, but especially 69–72. For a trenchant critique of Ritter's notions, see Robert G. L. Waite's review essay in *American Historical Review,* LXI, 1 (October, 1955), 129 ff. On the ideologically conditioned differential understanding of the concept "democracy," see Arne Naess, Jens A. Christophersen, and Kjell Kvalø, *Democracy, Ideology and Objectivity: Studies in the Semantics and Cognitive Analysis of Ideological Controversy* (Oslo: Oslo University Press; Oxford: Blackwell, 1956).

32. These appear to have included elements from Claus Heim's old Conservative Revolutionary Landvolkbewegung in Schleswig-Holstein. See Sopade *Informationsdienst,* no. 837 (August 1, 1949).

33. Under the pseudonym Junius Alter, Sontag published in 1930 his well-known biographical sketches of Conservative Revolutionaries, traditionalist conservatives, and National Socialists, *Nationalisten. Deutschlands nationales Führertum der Nachkriegszeit* (Leipzig: Koehler, 1930). (See Deutsche Aufbau Partei [III/12].) From 1914 to 1917 Sontag had been the editor in chief of the Pan-German League's weekly *Alldeutsche Blätter.*

34. Letter to *Vorbereitender Werbeausschuss* (British Zone) *für die DKP, z. Hd. des Landesgerichtrats a. D. Dr. Ohlsen,* April 22, 1946. The letter was signed by Ewers (Lübeck), Schultz (Eutin), Dockhorn (Salzgitter), Schüler (Alfeld), Grübmeier (Wesermünde-Stadt), Wientzen (Segeberg-Lauenburg), Hauenschild (Göttingen), Barnowitz (Wolfenbüttel), Beyer (Burgdorf-Northeim-Uelzen), von Ostau (Ahaus-Burgsteinfurt), Kellinghusen (Hamburg), Kuhl (Emden), and Sanders (Hanover).

35. Deutsche Aufbau Partei (III/12), no. 2 (January, 1946), p. 3.

36. See, for example, Otto Schmidt-Hannover, "Vernebelung" (unpublished article, no date), p. 3, or his "Persilschein" for his old party colleague, Lothar Steuer (1925–1933, DNVP Member of the Prussian Land diet; 1933–1938, deputy in the Nazi Reichstag), dated April 25, 1946; cf. also "Redeverbot für Schmidt-Hannover" (mimeographed, no date, but probably March, 1947). The full argument can be found in his general apologia for the conservative-nationalist opposition to the Weimar Republic, *Umdenken oder Anarchie: Männer-Schicksale-Lehren* ([Göttingen:] Göttinger Verlagsanstalt, [1959]). Schmidt-Hannover occupies an ideological position which can be characterized by the following quotations from his book: "What we call 'order' in today's liberal-socialist constitutions is only inadequately camouflaged and temporarily bridled anarchy" (p. 11). "Those powers which formed an alliance for the annihilation of the imperial power of Germany and Austria, and which placed upon encircled, bled-white, and revolutionized Germany the burden of the war-guilt taint, initiated the crisis of the twentieth century. The imperial Western powers, aided by supranational centers of high finance, of the armament industry, and of the Allies' fraternal lodges—together with the revolutionary forces which are pushing for a 'universal republic'—have spun the threads of the web of fate behind which the transformations between the Atlantic and Pacific Oceans are today being carried out" (p. 12). According to Schmidt-Hannover, the Nazi revolution—the product of Versailles, economic de-

pression, and multiparty parliamentarism—was "misguided and misused by ambitious and dilettante Jacobins" (p. 33). He sees the NSDAP as a Leftist, not Rightist, party and concludes that "Communism and social democracy prepared the way for Hitler's National Socialism" (p. 33). Schmidt-Hannover's attempt to whitewash the non-Nazi wing of Weimar's extreme Right had been anticipated by his friend Josef Borchmeyer, Hugenberg's counsel. Borchmeyer edited a collection of defense documents under the title *Hugenbergs Ringen in deutschen Schicksalsstunden: Tatsachen und Entscheidungen in den Verfahren zu Detmold und Düsseldorf, 1949–50* (Detmold: Maximilian, 1951). Two years earlier the same publisher brought out *Hugenberg und die Hitler Diktatur* which consisted of (1) "Ein Beitrag zur Verteidigung von Alfred Hugenberg in dem Entnazifizierungsverfahren vor dem Berufungsausschuss Detmold," by Lothar Steuer with the assistance of Otto Meesmann, which Borchmeyer submitted to the tribunal, and (2) "Weitere Beiträge zum Entnazifizierungsverfahren." Borchmeyer's and Schmidt-Hannover's apologetics should be read alongside Karl Dietrich Bracher's magisterial works: *Die Auflösung der Weimarer Republik* (III/7), and, with coauthors Wolfgang Sauer and Gerhard Schulz, *Die nationalsozialistische Machtergreifung: Studien zur Errichtung des totalitären Herrschaftssystems in Deutschland 1933/34* (Cologne, Opladen: Westdeutscher Verlag, 1960). See also Friedrich Freiherr Hiller von Gaertringen's excellent chapter on the DNVP in Erich Matthias and Rudolf Morsey, eds., *Das Ende der Parteien 1933* (Düsseldorf: Droste, 1960), pp. 543–652.

37. Schmidt-Hannover's speech at the convention of conservatives of Schleswig-Holstein held in the Stadthalle of Rendsburg on April 30, 1946.

38. Memorandum of Schmidt-Hannover, dated December 13, 1946, anent article in *Flensburger Tageblatt,* no. 72, p. 1. This represented a considerable change for Schmidt-Hannover, who in 1928–1929 had fought bitterly against the attempt of "Tory democrats" like Georg Quabbe, Walther Lambach, Gottfried R. Treviranus, and eventually Count Kuno Westarp to move the radical, extremist Hugenberg wing of the DNVP (to which he belonged) into co-operation with the Weimar Republic. See Bracher (III/7), pp. 309–330.

39. According to the Deutsche Reichs-Partei leader and former Bundestag deputy, Adolf von Thadden, the program had been initially drafted by Hans Zehrer. No substantiating evidence for this claim has come to the author's attention.

40. It is not without irony that this argument continues to receive support from extreme Western Germanophobes, like the late Lord Vansittart. Here, too, illegitimate pseudo theories of historical inevitability, or even racial theories, are invented to show how the entire history of the Germans, or their racial characteristics, *necessarily* led to the rise of Nazism.

41. Its members were the chairmen of the five Land organizations: Jäger (Rhineland), von Ostau (Westphalia), Ziegeler (Hamburg), Harckensee (Schleswig-Holstein), and Sanders (Lower Saxony). To them were added two other members from each of the Land organizations: Sontag, Bierbrauer (Rhineland); Klingspor, Martin (Westphalia); Borck, Ewers

(Schleswig-Holstein); Jacobi, Kellinghusen (Hamburg), Behr, Hauenschild (Lower Saxony).

42. It consisted of Sontag, Jäger and von Ostau. Sontag agreed to serve as chairman.

43. Unpublished minutes of Delegates' Convention, June 27, 1946, p. 3. According to Schmidt-Hannover's memorandum (III/38), p. 2, von Ostau's suggestion had been Deutsche Rechts-Partei (Konservative Sammlung), and it was only upon his own strenuous warning that "Sammlung" was too reminiscent of the various " 'Eintopf'-, 'Knochen'- usw.-Sammlungen der Nazizeit" that the zonal founding committee changed the "Sammlung" to "Vereinigung"—without, incidentally, any mandate from the delegates.

44. The prerequisites for Military Government approval of party organizations on the district level had assured that none of the original (founding) members of the district executive committees was a former Nazi Party member. This was reinforced by a stern warning from von Ostau in his letter to the district organizations of June 5, 1946. Members of district executive committees who assumed their positions after the founding of the district party organization were not subject to British "precensorship." If they had been members of the Nazi party or any of its affiliated organizations or appeared politically unreliable on other grounds, they were, of course, subject to removal at the discretion of the military control officer.

45. The results of this first free election in Germany in thirteen years were carefully, even anxiously, analyzed by the occupation authorities. Yet, to the question "Which way had the former Nazis voted?" no clear answer could be given. One member of the administration and local government section of the British Control Commission for Germany came to this conclusion: "On the whole, districts where there had formerly been a strong Nazi vote returned a higher proportion of FDP and NLP candidates, but undoubtedly many ex-Nazis voted for the center and left parties. Perhaps they went deliberately over to the opposite camp out of disillusionment." Ebsworth (II/33), p. 59.

46. Interview, August 3, 1958.

47. For the nature and history of the Stahlhelm under Weimar and Bonn, see below Chapter IX, Section A.

48. "Protokoll der Delegiertentagung" (typescript, November 23–24, 1946), pp. 2–3.

49. *Rundschreiben,* no. III/47 (March 24, 1947). Identical charges are also contained in a letter from Klingspor to all district organizations of North Rhine–Westphalia, March 31, 1947.

50. See Deutsche Rechts-Partei (Konservative Vereinigung), *Rundbrief —Mitteilungsblatt der DRP(KV)*, no. 8/47 (April 30, 1947). Cf. handbill announcing the formation of the von Ostau splinter under the name Nationale Einheitspartei Deutschlands, "Delegiertentagung in Bad Godesberg," April 17, 1947.

51. DRP(KV), Landesverband Nordrhein-Westfalen, "Resolution" (typescript), April 24, 1949. See also DRP(KV) (III/50).

52. DRP(KV) (III/50).

53. Schmidt-Hannover, "Redeverbot" (III/36).

54. Interview, August 3, 1958.

55. DRP(KV) (III/50), p. 2, and Statistisches Landesamt, "Wahlen und Abstimmungen," *Statistisches Handbuch für Schleswig-Holstein* (Kiel-Wik: 1950 [?]), p. 535.

56. There is a very large body of information, of varying reliability, on Schlüter's past which appeared in connection with the sensational reaction inside and outside of Germany to his appointment in May, 1955, to the position of Minister of Education in Lower Saxony. For some of the best summaries, see "Ein Feuer soll lodern," *Der Spiegel,* IX, 24 (June 15, 1955), 12–24, and the following issues of *Feinde der Demokratie* (Nordmark), IV, 5 (May–June, 1955), 31–40; IV, 6 (June 1, 1955); IV, 9 (August–September, 1955), 35–43; and V, 4/5 (January–March, 1956), 29–34. See also Deutscher Gewerkschaftsbund, Landesbezirk Niedersachsen, *Der Fall Schlüter,* Presseübersicht, I and II (May 31 and June 6, 1955); *Du und Dein Landtag, Parlamentsberichte der SPD Fraktion im Niedersächsischen Landtag,* no. 20 (July, 1955), pp. 20–30, and 22 (February, 1956), pp. 23–32; and Niedersächsischer Landtag, Dritte Wahlperiode, "Bericht des 6. Parlamentarischen Untersuchungsausschusses des Niedersächsischen Landtages, betreffend die Vorgänge, die zur Berufung des Abg. Schlüter zum Niedersächsischen Kultusminister am 26. Mai 1955 führten," *Landtagsdrucksache Nr. 177* (February, 1956), pp. 660–669. For a statement in defense of Schlüter, see *Die grosse Hetze. Der niedersächsische Ministersturz. Ein Tatsachenbericht zum Fall Schlüter* ([Göttingen:] Göttinger Verlagsanstalt, [1958]); the anonymous author is rumored to be Otto Schmidt-Hannover.

57. "Der Fall Schlüter," *Deutsche Universitäts–Zeitung,* X, 11 (June 8, 1955), 3–4.

58. DRP(KV), *Rundschreiben,* no. V/48 (May 3, 1948). Cf. "Aus dem Parteileben. Bericht über den Delegiertentag der Deutschen Rechten," *Der Konservative Bote* (Hamburg) II, 4/5 (May 15/31, 1948), 10–11.

59. *Wolfsburger Nachrichten,* no. 147 (June 28/29, 1948).

60. Cf. the unpublished manuscript on the sociological structure of Wolfsburg by Josef Schmidt, of Hanover. (Copy in the author's possession.) See also J. Engel, "Wer hat Angst vor dem bösen Wolf–sburg?" *Die Neue Zeitung* (Munich), September 2, 1949.

61. *Deutscher Presse Dienst* (Hamburg), December 6, 1948.

62. *Der Spiegel,* III, 11 (March 12, 1949), 7.

63. *Ibid.*

64. Schmidt (III/60).

65. For the PORO survey results, see Sopade *Informationsdienst,* no. 837 (August 1, 1949), pp. 8-9.

66. *Deutscher Presse Dienst* (Hamburg), December 6, 1948.

67. *Ibid.*

68. Letter of Adolf von Thadden to Hermann Klingspor, January 10, 1949. Cf. "Im Zeichen des Erfolges," *Rechts heran! DRP-Nachrichten,* February 7, 1949, p. 3.

69. From a *curriculum vitae* supplied by Herr Leuchtgens, dated June

7, 1948. For the relation of the Farmers and Peasants Party to Nazism, to which its members deserted in droves, see Eugen Schmahl, *Entwicklung der völkischen Bewegung* (Giessen: Roth, [1933]), and especially the annex, Wilhelm Seipel's "Entwicklung der nationalsozialistischen Bauernbewegung in Hessen."

70. Schmahl (III/69), pp. 153-154, 156-157, 159, 163-164, 166.

71. Heinrich Leuchtgens, "Der Entwurf einer Verfassung des Deutschen Reiches" (Draft Constitution), typescript, n.d. (probably summer, 1945). Articles 9, 10; Article 12, Section 2; Articles 25, 58, 81, 88.

72. Leuchtgens persisted in his attempts to sell himself to the Americans, despite his disappointing experiences. As late as 1949 he still struggled to persuade American officials in Bonn that he was "Germany's Senator Taft" and that their indifference to his schemes was sheer lunacy. See, for example, Charles W. Thayer, *The Unquiet Germans* (New York: Harper, [1957]), p. 147. However, in fairness to the memory of the late Heinrich Leuchtgens, it should be mentioned that some of his policy proposals, unrealistic though they appeared in 1945, were fully vindicated by subsequent events. Thus, for instance, Leuchtgens urged closest German-American collaboration in opposition to Russia and even called for a German military contribution to an integrated Western defense system.

73. "Programm der Nationaldemokratischen Partei Deutschlands," Friedberg, October 18, 1945. Published under Military Government Information Control License No. US-W-2061.

74. For the June elections the NDP distributed widely an "Erklärung" (dated Friedberg, June 21, 1946) in which its inability to present its own candidates was mentioned in connection with the refusal of the Americans to license the NDP on the Land level, and in which electors and members of the NDP were urged to vote for those candidates who would be certain to stress the supreme importance of reunification, the freedom and independence of the individual personality, the protection of private property, and the unconditional maintenance of private initiative.

75. Cf. *Telegraf* (Berlin), August 24, 1948, cited in Sopade *Informationsdienst,* no. 603 (October 19, 1948).

76. From a handwritten note of Leuchtgens, bearing the date April 30, without giving the year, but most likely 1948.

77. The urban districts were Giessen-Stadt, Marburg-Stadt, and Wiesbaden. The rural districts were Alsfeld, Büdingen, Lauterbach, Wetzlar, Giessen-Land, and Marburg-Land.

78. See *Frankenpost* (Hof), January 29, 1947. Cf. Sopade *Informationsdienst,* no. 495 (June 14, 1948), and *Neues Deutschland* (Berlin), February 4, 1947.

79. "Aufruf an die Beamten und Behördenangestellten," *Der Nationaldemokrat* (Friedberg), no. 1 (February, 1948), p. 2.

80. "An die deutschen Arbeiter," *ibid.*, no. 9 (June, 1948), p. 1.

81. Col. James R. Newman, director of OMGUS in Land Hesse, cited in *Nordwestdeutsche Rundschau* (Wilhelmshaven), April 29, 1948.

82. *Ibid.* Cf. *Rhein-Neckar Zeitung* (Heidelberg), May 4, 1948.

83. *Rhein-Neckar Zeitung* (Heidelberg), May 9, 1948.

84. Interview with the late Karl-Heinz Priester in Wiesbaden on May 19, 1957.

85. *Ibid.*

86. In 1932, Priester had taken over the Presse-Schulung section of the Hitler Youth Bann of Hesse–Nassau Süd. In 1933 he became chief of the equivalent section of Oberjungbann I. In 1935–1939, Priester was executive director of Strength through Joy; and in 1939, having been rejected by the SS, he joined the army, where he rose to the rank of first lieutenant.

87. Hessisches Statistisches Landesamt, "Die Kommunalwahlen in Hessen am 25. April 1948," *Staat und Wirtschaft in Hessen. Statistische Mitteilungen,* IV, 1 (February 1, 1948 [*sic; recte* 1949]), 22. Fifteen of the twenty candidates put up by the NDP in Wiesbaden were elected to the city council, capturing exactly one-quarter of its seats.

88. See *Rhein-Neckar Zeitung* (Heidelberg), May 4, 1948.

89. *Die Welt* (Hamburg), May 4, 1947; cf. *Die Zeit* (Hamburg), May 6, 1948.

90. Alsfeld, Büdingen, Friedberg, Giessen, and Lauterbach.

91. *Die Zeit* (Hamburg), May 6, 1948.

92. Cf. *Telegraf* (Berlin), August 24, 1948, quoted in Sopade *Informationsdienst,* no. 603 (October 19, 1948).

93. *Die Neue Zeitung* (Munich), April 29, 1948.

94. See *Die Welt* (Hamburg), May 4, 1948.

95. *Ibid.*

96. Viktor H. Weinland, "Wiedergeburt des Nationalsozialismus?" *Echo der Woche* (Munich), III, 76 (January 7, 1949), 2.

97. *Telegraf* (Berlin), July 17, 1948; cf. also Sopade *Informationsdienst,* no. 602 (October 18, 1948), and a number of draft memoranda of Leuchtgens to General Lucius Clay, in the author's possession.

98. *Der Spiegel,* II, 31 (August 4, 1948).

99. See *Der Nationaldemokrat* (Friedberg), II, 8 (July, 1949): "Entschliessung" (p. 1) and "Parteidiktatur!" and "Zur Bundestagswahl!" (p. 2).

100. See "Zusammenschluss der deutschen Rechten," *Der Konservative Bote* (Hamburg), II, 6/7 (June 15/30, 1948), 1.

101. The agreement to the contrary notwithstanding, an NDP founding committee was organized in Kiel (Schleswig-Holstein) under the leadership of Robert Brede, who presented the new party to the public on November 27, 1948. In his first public announcement, Brede described the NDP as a "center party" which rejected parliamentary democracy in favor of an "authoritarian democracy." At the same time, Brede called for a new German army, which alone would be capable of giving to young men "the experience of their lives" and which would be a means for the inculcation of *Kameradschaft.* See *Die Neue Zeitung* (Munich), November 27, 1948. Cf. Weinland (III/96).

102. See *Interpress* (Hamburg), February 11, 1949.

103. *Deutscher Presse Dienst* (Hamburg), August 5, 1948.

104. *Darmstädter Echo,* August 11, 1948.

105. Will Hayne in a private intelligence report of January, 1949. Cf. *Interpress* (Hamburg), February 11, 1949, and Sopade *Informationsdienst,* no. 760 (April 30, 1949).

106. *Telegraf* (Berlin), November 10, 1948.

107. *Frankfurter Rundschau,* November 22, 1948; but see Leuchtgens' denial in *Die Welt* (Hamburg), January 13, 1949.

108. "In memoriam Pestbeule," *Der Nationaldemokrat* (Friedberg), II, 3 (April 1, 1949), 1.

109. The losses benefited mostly an *ad hoc* independent-voters alliance which represented primarily the refugees and expellees and those who had been bombed out. "Zum Wahlsieg in Alsfeld," *Der Nationaldemokrat* (Friedberg), II, 5 (beginning of May, 1949), 1.

110. *Der Nationaldemokrat* (Friedberg), II, 4 and 5 (April 15 and beginning of May, 1949).

Chapter IV. The Rising Tide: 1949

1. U.S. Department of State, *Bulletin,* XX, 511 (April 17, 1949), 500.

2. "Charter of the Allied High Commission for Germany, June 20, 1949," *ibid.,* XXI, 523 (July 11, 1949), 25–28, 38.

3. See Peter Furth, "Ideologie und Propaganda der SRP," in Otto Büsch and Peter Furth, *Rechtsradikalismus im Nachkriegsdeutschland* (Berlin: Vahlen, 1957), p. 208.

4. See letter of Lt. Col. E. G. Brown, MBE, KRO HQ SK & LK Bonn, CCG (BR) BAOR, to Wolfgang Kölpin, Bad Godesberg–Muffendorf, July 10, 1947.

5. See von Ostau's letter to General B. H. Robertson, November 17, 1947.

6. Letter of Wolfgang Kölpin to HQ 210 Mil. Gov. Det., Bonn (Att.: Col. Brown), of March 15, 1948; the *Kreis* officer's answer of March 17, 1948 (Ref. 210/5/7); and the final rejection of Kölpin's request "in pursuance of its [the Military Government's] policy not to authorize the formation of splinter parties" on May 25, 1948. See also the refusal to authorize the Deutscher Block, a new party formation consisting of von Ostau's own followers from North Rhine–Westphalia, Karl Meissner's Deutscher Block (Bavaria), and Erich Brazel's Neue Partei (Württemberg-Baden), in letter of Lt. Col. E. G. Brown, SCO, KRO, 210 HQ CCG, SK & LK Bonn, BAOR 19, to Wolfgang Kölpin, Bad Godesberg, July 16, 1948. In this connection, cf. von Ostau's broadsides "Mitteilung!" of June 14, 1948, and "Mitteilung an alle Gesinnungsfreunde" of July 16, 1948. Cf. *Die Neue Zeitung* (Munich), July 1, 1948, and von Ostau's "Offene Antwort" (reprinted as flier, no date).

7. For details on Canon Goebel, see "Geistlicher Rat teuer," *Der Spiegel,* III, 11 (March 12, 1949), 9–11. Cf. Max Hildebert Boehm, "Gruppenbildung und Organisationswesen," in Eugen Lemberg and Friedrich

Edding, eds., *Die Vertriebenen in Westdeutschland: Ihre Eingliederung und ihr Einfluss auf Gesellschaft, Wirtschaft, Politik und Geistesleben* (Kiel: Hirt, 1959), II, esp. 533 ff. See below, VIII/53.

8. At a meeting in Lippstadt on November 16, 1948.

9. See the accusations of "Dr." Walter Kniggendorf, alias Walter H. Bergmann, in *Deutscher Informationsdienst*, no. 224 (November 18, 1952). Cf. *Neuer Vorwärts* (Hanover), October 29, 1949, and the statement of Schlüter as reported in *Hessische Nachrichten* (Kassel), September 10, 1949.

10. Bundesverfassungsgericht (Erster Senat), ["Urteil] in dem Verfahren über den Antrag der Bundesregierung auf Feststellung der Verfassungswidrigkeit der Sozialistischen Reichspartei," 1 BvB 1/51, October 23, 1952, p. 31. Cf. Niedersächsischer Landtag, Zweite Wahlperiode, *Landtagsdrucksache Nr. 735*, October 30, 1952, p. 1268.

11. See "Wo steht heute der alte Marschierer?" (no date, probably summer, 1951), published by Volksbund für Frieden und Freiheit, Landesleitung Niedersachsen, p. 3. Cf. also *Der Spiegel*, III, 44 (October 29, 1949), 9.

12. See letters of von Ostau to the members of the founding committee, November 30 and December 20, 1948, and to the members of the Arbeitsausschuss, January 8, 19, and 25, 1949. For the programmatic and ideological content of the Emergency Association, see Notgemeinschaft des deutschen Volkes (NDV), "Aus der Vergangenheit lernen: Was will die 'Notgemeinschaft des deutschen Volkes (NDV)'? Zur vorbereitenden Tagung am 5. Februar 1949 in Goslar," printed broadside, February 1, 1949, and von Ostau's working draft "Was bezweckt die NDV?" typescript (no date, but probably January, 1949).

13. Beratungsstelle für die Aufstellung unabhängiger Kandidaten, "Merkblatt für die Aufstellung unabhängiger Kandidaten bei der Bundestagswahl am 14. August 1949."

14. "Wahlgesetz zum ersten Bundestag und zur ersten Bundesversammlung der Bundesrepublik Deutschland von 15. Juni 1949," *Bundesgesetzblatt*, p. 21, supplemented by "Gesetz zur Ergänzung und Abänderung des Wahlgesetzes . . . vom 5. August 1949." The relevant sections are Paragraph 11, Section 1, and Paragraph 14, Section 3.

15. Gerhard Krüger, "Wichtige nachträgliche Mitteilung," Bisperode, July 8, 1949.

16. These details emerge from a letter of von Thadden dated September 22, 1949; the addressee's name has been removed from the copy in the author's possession. The Electoral Law provided that approximately 60 per cent of the parliamentary seats were to be filled by the plurality elections of candidates in the several single-member electoral districts (Paragraph 9). The other 40 per cent of the seats were to be filled by the following method (Paragraph 10, Sections 1–2): "(1) All votes cast in a Land for each of the parties . . . will be added up; from them will be computed by the maximum-number method (d'Hondt) the mandates which are due to each party. . . . (2) The number of mandates won in the [single-member] electoral districts by [each party] will be subtracted from the number of deputies which has

been computed for each party by the above method. The seats which accrue to it [i.e., the difference between the total number of seats which a party was found to have earned on the basis of its proportional strength and the number of seats gained through plurality victories in single-member electoral districts] will be filled from the Land Supplementary List in accordance with its sequence."

17. Press conference in Hamburg, July 28, 1949, reported in Sopade *Informationsdienst*, no. 837, August 1, 1949.

18. Only six days before the election did Brigadier John Lingham see fit to remove the political-activities ban from Schlüter. Schlüter saw in this an attempt to create the false impression that German politics could be carried on freely under Allied control. To dramatize the hypocrisy of this move and to underscore his contention that the belated lifting of the ban had effectively destroyed all possibility of freely realizing his political aims, Schlüter resigned from the chairmanship of the Land organization and from the district organization of Göttingen, as well as from his position as deputy chairman of the Zonal party organization. (Schlüter to his Land deputy chairman, Heinrich Rathert, August 12, 1949.) Wolfgang Falck's activities ban of April 12, 1949, was also not lifted in time to permit either his re-election to the chairmanship of the district organization Gifhorn (the suspension of which had been quite unexpectedly ended in late June or early July) or his candidacy for the DRP in the general elections. In Falck's place a former major and bearer of the Knight's Cross, Helmut Hillebrecht, a radical nationalist and "German socialist," was elected chairman of the district Gifhorn and placed on the Supplementary List in the eleventh position. *Die Welt* (Hamburg), July 16 and July 23, 1949.

19. Richter had also applied to the CDU, FDP, and DP, but these parties were unwilling to offer him any but relatively minor posts. See *Politisches Archiv* (Berlin-Grunewald), WRP/012. Cf. *Der Spiegel,* III, 44 (October 29, 1949), 9.

20. Photostat of Richter's handwritten "Lebenslauf," dated February 12, 1947.

21. See *Der Spiegel,* III, 32 (August 4, 1949), 9–10.

22. In May, 1952, Rössler was found guilty on charges of using an unauthorized alias, imposture, breach of the electoral laws, and forgery, and was sentenced to eighteen months in prison.

23. Quoted from the *Neue Presse* (Coburg) in *Der Spiegel,* III, 27 (June 30, 1949), 6. Cf. *ibid;* III, 49 (December 1, 1949), 7. For an expert assessment of Remer's role on July 20, 1944—at variance with the estimate of the Hitler regime, the *Neue Presse,* and Remer's followers—see Col. (i.R.) Wolfgang Müller, "Geschichtliches Gutachten: War Major Remer schon am 20. Juli 1944 als Führer ein Drückeberger?" (typescript), June 1, 1952. Critical appraisals of Remer as person and as military leader are presented in Walter Kniggendorf, "Otto Ernst Remer: Das Problem des Untertan," *Florett* (no date), and in Vorstand der SPD, *Ich bin Generalmajor Remer* (no date). Remer's own estimate of his role can be found in his *20. Juli 1944* (Hamburg: Deutsche Opposition, 1951).

24. See von Thadden's letter (IV/16).

25. Quoted in *Nordwest Zeitung* (Oldenburg), August 13, 1949.

26. Quoted in *Der Spiegel,* III, 49 (December 1, 1949), 8.

27. Quoted in G. Paulus, "Remer beschloss Politiker zu werden," *Braunschweiger Zeitung,* September 6, 1959, p. 8.

28. *Ibid.*

29. *Lüneburger Landeszeitung,* August 26, 1949.

30. Paragraph 14, Section 3, of the Electoral Law stipulated that "Land Supplementary Lists may be submitted only by those political parties which have been licensed (*zulassen*) in the Land on a Land-wide scale."

31. For the definition of *Heimatvertriebene, Zugewanderte,* and *Zugezogene* as well as for the detailed figures on which this analysis is based, see Niedersächsisches Amt für Landesplanung und Statistik, *Die Bevölkerung Niedersachsens nach den Ergebnissen der Volkszählung am 13. September 1950,* Zählung der Bevölkerung, Gebäude, Wohnungen und nichtlandwirtschaftlichen Arbeitsstätten 1950, Ser. F, vol. 15, no. 1. A. Textteil (Hanover, 1955), especially Chapter II, pp. 15–19. See also Günther Franz, *Die politischen Wahlen in Niedersachsen 1867 bis 1949,* with an appendix, "Die Wahlen 1951 bis 1956" (3d. ed., enl.; Bremen-Horn: Dorn, 1957).

32. That Schleswig-Holstein, with its 45 per cent of new population, gave a dismal 2 per cent of its total vote to the DKP-DRP is not in itself overwhelming evidence of the absence of a direct relationship between the two. Here a very special condition accounted for the disaster: the wholesale and corporative desertion of the DKP to the German Party in 1947. The DKP was never able to recoup these losses. Lübeck, for instance, had been a stronghold of the DKP before 1947, when over 10 per cent of its residents voted for that party; in 1949 it gave the DKP a mere 2.8 per cent of the valid votes, while 14 per cent voted for the DP. (In this connection, it is well to remember the disparity in character of the Lower Saxon DP and its Schleswig-Holstein branch. In Lower Saxony the DP was still strongly tied to the nativist, conservative-monarchist Guelph element. In Schleswig-Holstein the DP could, and did, readily compete in terms of unrestrained nationalist demagogy, invoking the memories of the Conservative Revolutionary *Landvolk* movement.)

33. The distribution of the votes for so-called independent candidates, who in most instances represented the expellee organizations in Lower Saxony, shows a good inverse correlation with DRP vote concentrations. This supports the view that it was the middle-German refugee, rather than the expellee, who favored the DRP.

34. Wilhelmshaven, Gifhorn, Emden, Hameln, Salzgitter, Helmstedt, Soltau, Hildesheim, Friesland, Braunschweig (Land), Leer, Celle (Land), Harburg, Braunschweig (Stadt), Neustadt/R., Ammerland, Münden, Göttingen (Stadt), Hameln-Pyrmont, Wittmund, and Celle (Stadt).

35. In Lower Saxony the major parties received the following percentages of votes (for the sake of comparison, the percentages for the entire Federal Republic are added in parentheses): SPD, 33.4 (29.2); CDU, 17.6

(31); DP, 17.8 (4); FDP, 7.5 (11.9); KPD, 3.1 (5.7); Center Party, 3.4 (3.1); others, 9.1 (13.3).

36. In the city of Emden, where the DRP received over 26 per cent of all votes to become the second largest party, the FDP lost over 52 per cent of its 1948 votes. In the city of Hameln, Krüger's home district, the DRP also became the second largest party, here at the expense of the DP, which lost 36 per cent of its 1948 support, and the FDP, which again lost almost 53 per cent. In Salzgitter, where the DRP was second only to the SPD, almost half of its votes came from the CDU, which had lost 44 per cent of its 1948 electoral support. The same was true of the district Helmstedt, where the DRP had become the second largest party, with over one-fifth of all votes cast, by virtue of a successful raid on the CDU, which lost over half of its 1948 votes. In the traditionally nationalist district Celle (Land), where as early as 1924 the radical folkish elements gathered almost 16 per cent of the votes and where the enormously large pluralities of the conservative-monarchist Guelphs had melted away under the impact of Nazism, the CDU lost 56 per cent of its votes, largely to the DRP. In the city district of Celle, the FDP and CDU suffered 55 and 33 per cent losses, respectively, at least partly to the benefit of the DRP.

37. Though not conclusive, available evidence strongly supports the view that it was not the status as expellees but the economic hardships which a disproportionate number of expellees suffered that determined their preference for the DRP. Areas of high employment and relatively high concentrations of expellees show a much lower positive correlation than districts with relatively fewer expellees but high unemployment.

38. In this connection, it may be instructive to recall that even before 1933, about 10 per cent of Nazi Party votes in Lower Saxony came from the Marxist Left. This was especially true of the rural areas, where social democracy had made surprisingly deep inroads after 1918. The SPD proved unable, however, to strike deep enough roots in those districts to hold its followers against the onslaught of Hitler's demagogy. See Franz (IV/31), pp. 62–65.

39. For massive corroborative evidence, see *ibid.*, pp. 27–68, 277–286.

40. See above, IV/16.

41. The five deputies-elect were von Thadden, "Richter" (actually Rössler), Dorls, Herwart Miessner of Hannover-Kleefeld, former official in the corporate tax division of the Lower Saxon Oberfinanzpräsidium, and Heinz Frommhold, of Alfeld.

42. Engel (III/60).

43. Von Thadden's letter (IV/16).

44. Especially by the Hamburg organization under Carl Schlumbohm. See von Thadden's letter of complaint to the Parteileitung of May 6, 1949; and cf. DRP, Interessenvertretung für das Land Niedersachsen, *Rundschreiben,* no. VII/49 (April 25, 1949).

45. For example, in a letter which had fallen accidentally into the hands of Anton Mainzer, a member of the anti-Dorls-Krüger faction, Krüger had

urged one of his followers in the Hildesheim district to ensure his own election as delegate to the forthcoming conference, at which the Dorls-Krüger group proposed to take over the party apparatus. See *Der Spiegel,* III, 44 (October 29, 1949), 10.

46. *Die Welt* (Hamburg), August 30, 1949.

47. Von Thadden's letter (IV/16), p. 1.

48. Quoted in Walter H. Bergmann (pseudonym for Kniggendorf), "Rechtsradikales Kabarett," *Das Freie Wort* (Düsseldorf) August 23, 1952, p. 5.

49. See above, IV/41.

50. The election of the officers and members of the executive committee reflected the feeling of the delegates. "Richter" was given the first chairmanship, and Miessner was made deputy chairman and public information chief. Hillebrecht, the radical chairman of the Volkswagen Workers' Council, was put in charge of labor and social problems. Falck, another Wolfsburg veteran, was placed on the executive committee to organize a youth movement; and Johannes Guth, of Brunswick, was made general secretary of the party. The district chairman of Göttingen (city), H. C. Narten, a member of the Parteileitung, was voted onto the executive committee to take charge of the party's economic policies. The radical chairman of Salzgitter, Rolf Nehring, a close friend of Guth, was also elected to the committee. The journalist Friedrich Ehrhardt was asked to take over the as yet nonexistent party press. Finally, the executive committee was rounded out with the election of two "moderates," von Thadden and the chairman of the district Hildesheim-Marienburg, Anton Mainzer, to whom the treasury was turned over.

51. Of the twelve people who appeared at the Wuppertaler Hof, eight represented North Rhine–Westphalia; three, Lower Saxony; and one, Schleswig-Holstein. Hamburg was not represented at all. The twelve were Klingspor, Baron von Lüninck, Steuer, Borchmeyer, Pfestorf, Piepenbrink, Martin, and Schwecht for North Rhine–Westphalia; von Thadden, Miessner, and Narten for Lower Saxony; and Harckensee for Schleswig-Holstein. (Minutes of the meeting, typescript, September 1, 1949.)

52. That the conflict between "conservatism" and "Nazism" within the DRP was generally recognized as such, emerges from a letter of Reinhold Wulle to Wolfgang Müller, October 12, 1949.

53. These forces were under the local leadership of the district chairman of Hameln-Pyrmont, Heinz Billig, a former SA Obersturmführer. See report of Billig's speech at Bad Pyrmont on September 4, 1949, in *Deutsche Presse Agentur* (*dpa*) (*Landesdienst Niedersachsen*), September 4, 1949.

54. Letter of von Thadden to Klingspor, September 7, 1949.

55. Letter of von Thadden to Klingspor, September 19, 1949.

56. See *Norddeutsche Zeitung* (Hanover), September 9, 1949, and *Hessische Nachrichten* (Kassel), September 10, 1949. The accusation of Strasserism referred, of course, to Dorls, who had indeed come from the "Left" wing of the Nazi Party and who after 1945 maintained contact with the exiled Strasser. The rumors, however, that Dorls was Strasser's lieutenant,

charged with making the necessary political preparations for the return of the master, were without foundation of fact.

57. *Der Nationaldemokrat* (Friedberg), II, 8 (July, 1949), 1.

58. Hessisches Statistisches Landesamt, "Die Bundestagswahlen in Hessen am 14. August 1949," *Staat und Wirtschaft in Hessen. Statistische Mitteilungen,* IV, 5 (October 1, 1949), 132.

59. Other NDP candidates appeared in the places numbered 13, 17, 22, 31, and 36 on the List.

60. See, for example, the mouthpiece of the U.S. Military Government, *Die Neue Zeitung* (Munich), V, 87 (July 12, 1949).

61. From the minutes of the meeting of the Zonal Parteileitung in Wuppertal-Barmen, September 1, 1949 (typescript).

62. "Abrechnung mit Herrn Euler!" and "Zur Auflösung der LDP," *Der Nationaldemokrat* (Friedberg), II, 3 (April 1, 1949), 2. "Wirrwarr in den deutschen Parteien!" *ibid.*, II, 4 (April 15, 1949), 2. "Wer lügt—Leuchtgens oder Euler?" *ibid.*, II, 5 (beginning of May, 1949), 2.

63. *Die Neue Zeitung* (Munich), V, 87 (July 12, 1949).

64. *Der Nationaldemokrat* (Friedberg), II, 9 (middle of August, 1949), 1.

65. *Die Neue Zeitung* (Munich), September 13, 1949. Cf. *Die Welt* (Hamburg), September 15, 1949.

66. "Zum Bonner Grundgesetz," *Der Nationaldemokrat* (Friedberg), II, 2 (March, 1949), 1.

67. "Atlantik Pakt," *Der Nationaldemokrat* (Friedberg) II, 3 (April 1, 1949), 1. "Deutschland zwischen Ost und West" and "Der Atlantik Pakt und wir!" *ibid.*, II, 4 (April 15, 1949), 1–2. "Eine Schlacht für den Frieden!" *ibid.*, II, 5 (beginning of May, 1949), 2.

68. "Entschliessung," *Der Nationaldemokrat* (Friedberg), II, 8 (middle of July, 1949), 1.

69. For the quotations from Priester, see his *Die 12 Punkte-Forderung der NDP an die deutsche Bundesregierung und die Herren Oberkommissare und ihre Begründung. Originalbericht über die Wiesbadener NDP-Versammlung am 27. Oktober, 1949 in der Bose Aula zu Wiesbaden* (n.p., n.d.), pp. 8, 10, 16.

70. For details on the inner party struggles, see *Norddeutsche Zeitung* (Hanover), December 23, 1949; *Offenbacher Post,* December 30, 1949; *Frankfurter Rundschau,* December 30, 1949; *Die Welt* (Hamburg), January 6, 1950; *Neuer Vorwärts* (Hanover), January 20, 1950; and "Nationaldemokraten: Auch die sind uns recht," *Der Spiegel,* IV, 3 (January 19, 1950), 10.

71. See report of an anti-Nazi speech made in Munich three days after the Harzburg meeting: Regierungsrat Weintz, "Die illegale monarchistische Bewegung in Bayern," Geheime Staatspolizei, Polizeistelle München (Munich: October, 1939), p. 184. Partially reproduced in *Deutscher Informationsdienst,* no. 294 (August 4, 1953), p. 5. The Gestapo document is in the hands of the family of Father Siegfried Huber, of Prien am Chiemsee,

Bavaria. A copy of Weintz's report was sent to the German consulate in Zurich, since one of the Bavarian monarchist "conspirators," Father Huber, had escaped to Switzerland just one step ahead of the Gestapo. After the war, Father Huber returned to Bavaria and brought the document with him. See James Donohoe, *Hitler's Conservative Opponents in Bavaria 1930–1945* (Leiden: Brill, 1961), pp. 130–143.

72. In the summer of 1939, Loritz, under the name Dr. Lederer, made contact with the conservative, Catholic, Bavarian, monarchist Resistance circle around Adolf Freiherr von Harnier. *Ibid.*, p. 143. After the war, Loritz claimed for himself the authorship of the well-known Beer Hall Cellar attempt on Hitler's life in November, 1939. Despite the fact that American military intelligence sources have at one time or another supported Loritz' version of the story, it is well to treat this claim with greatest reserve.

73. Loritz wanted to call his party the German Reconstruction Association, but the American control officer refused permission for so provocative a label. *Der Informationsdienst,* no. 115 (September 26, 1951), p. 1.

74. Bayerisches Statistisches Landesamt (II/18), pp. 316–325, 327–345.

75. See *Telegraf* (Berlin), August 31, 1947. The question of Loritz' financial sources was constantly discussed in the press. See, for example, *Offenbacher Post,* July 24, 1947; *Berliner Zeitung,* April 27, 1947; *Südost Kurier* (Bad Reichenhall), July 12, 1947; *Frankenpost* (Hof), July 12, 1947; and *Hamburger Echo,* July 25, 1947.

76. These sanguinary—if psychotic—plans were made public by his former party colleague Julius Höllerer on the floor of the Bavarian diet, years after they were first laid. See Bayerischer Landtag (II/11), pp. 456–457.

77. See the accounts in *Münchener Mittag,* June 23, 1947, and *Hochland Bote,* June 24, 1947.

78. According to reports, Loritz, who denied that the delegates had any right to take such action, made frantic efforts to prevent the meeting from taking place. He even promised some of the opposition leaders who were organizing the meeting lucrative jobs in his ministry if they would desist. When that failed, he tried vainly to get the Military Government to prohibit the meeting.

79. Interview with Karl Meissner, Hamburg, April 17, 1957.

80. *Südost Kurier* (Bad Reichenhall), July 16, 1947.

81. For some of Loritz' almost unbelievable antics, see *Informationsblatt der Wirtschaftlichen Aufbau–Vereinigung,* II, no. 2, as quoted in Bayerischer Landtag (II/11), II, 37 (November 28, 1947), 241–242. Also cf. *Politisches Archiv* (Berlin-Grunewald), WRP/043.

82. See *Donau Kurier* (Ingolstadt), October 28, 1947, and *Telegraf* (Berlin), November 1, 1947. One of the triumvirs, the deputy Alfred Noske, refused to accept his own election on the ground that he could not share office with a fugitive from justice and with a man whose political notions included some kind of Danubian federation. That ancient Bavarian particularist conception had always received considerable support from Bavarian

monarchists and from some French circles. It envisages the destruction of the German Reich and the creation of a federation of states extending from the French border to Hungary. The persistent linking of Loritz to the notion of a Danubian federation was probably largely due to the facts that Loritz had very likely been working for the French intelligence service, that he possessed a French passport, and that his older brother, Johann Loritz, who had fled to Paris in the first months of the Hitler regime, had favored an independent Bavaria in close alliance with France, as well as the disruption of Prussia–Germany. See Johann Loritz' letters to the former French Ambassador Count Vladimir d'Ormesson of June 8, 1933, as quoted in Weintz (IV/71). See also the newspaper *Der Allgäuer,* as quoted in the *Berliner Zeitung,* April 27, 1947, where the question of a Danubian federation was publicly raised in connection with Loritz.

83. These accusations were turned over to the Attorney-General, who asked the Landtag to revoke Meissner's parliamentary immunity. This was done. See Bayerischer Landtag (II/11), II, 37 (November 28, 1947), 240, 246. See also Meissner's press conference in Straubing, as reported in the *Niederbayrische Nachrichten* (Straubing), November 7, 1947; cf. *Telegraf* (Berlin), November 8, 1947, and *Süddeutsche Zeitung* (Munich), September 26, 1947.

84. Interview with Meissner, April 17, 1957.

85. Bayerischer Landtag (II/11), II, 37 (November 28, 1947), 245.

86. See, in this regard, the remarks of Deputy Jean Stock (SPD): "It is shameful for the Bavarian Landtag that such a thing should occur at all. Furthermore, it is shameful that a part of the people of Bavaria elect such people [Deputies Meissner, Noske, and Josef Klessinger] to the Landtag. (*Quite so! and applause.*) How often do we have to listen to having these things rubbed in, in Bonn . . . so that one almost has to be ashamed of being a Bavarian Landtag deputy! It can't go on like that. At long last, we'll have to get some probity into the Bavarian Landtag. (*Quite so!*)" *Ibid.* IV, 112 (June 1, 1949), 246.

87. *Der Kurier* (Berlin), December 4, 1947.

88. *Süddeutsche Zeitung* (Munich), November 30, 1948.

89. Interview with Meissner, April 17, 1957.

90. See above, IV/6. Before this, negotiations were carried on among Meissner, Wolfgang Leck, chairman of the Hesse Land organization of the DB, and Leuchtgens (NDP). See *Rhein-Neckar Zeitung* (Heidelberg), May 4, 1948.

91. The leaders of the secessionist district organizations of Hamburg and Neumünster, Carl Belz and K. G. Schrödter, were made co-chairmen of the British Zonal council of the DB. Keen rivalry between them led to Schrödter's resignation from the DB. He went over to the German Union (Deutsche Union, DU), together with his following and, on his suggestion, some of the Bavarian DB members who, like Noske, had become restive under the radical and dictatorial leadership of Meissner. Belz, who had been arrested by the British on suspicion of being the leader of an underground movement, was himself expelled from the DB by Meissner and replaced by

the former Hitler Youth leader and radical anti-Semite, Günther Bardey. The Zonal affairs of the party were given over to one Major Otto Martens, of Dithmarschen. (Enno Manns' confidential informations on the DB, January, 1949.) Meissner is convinced that both Belz and Schrödter were in the pay of foreign intelligence services, Belz in the East's, Schrödter in the West's. (Interview, April 17, 1957.)

92. Bayerischer Landtag (II/11), III, 93 (December 1, 1948), 300.

93. According to Meissner, the campaign of violence against the DB came to an abrupt end only after his goons succeeded in sending 95 per cent of the opposition into the hospital in the course of a fracas in Wunsiedel in March, 1950.

94. *SPD Pressedienst*, P/IV/102 (August 29, 1949).

95. Report of the Land convention at Vohenstraus/Oberpfalz on June 21, 1949.

96. *SPD Pressedienst*, P/IV/102 (August 29, 1949).

97. Hacker was later expelled from the DB and formed the totally insignificant Republican Reconstruction Party of Germany (Republikanische Aufbaupartei Deutschlands). See *Der Informationsdienst*, no. 27 (November 13, 1950).

98. Quoted by Landtag Deputy Franz Haas (SPD) in Bayerischer Landtag (II/11), V, 128 (November 9, 1949), 166.

99. Cited in Bayerischer Landtag (II/11), V, 136 (December 16, 1949), 432.

100. *Ibid.* Cf. *ibid.*, V, 137 (January 17, 1950), 457–458.

101. *Ibid., V,* 136 (December 16, 1949), 441: "Ladies and gentlemen, five minutes ago you threw a man down the stairs, and it was well done. . . ." Cf. *Weser-Kurier* (Bremen), December 17, 1949.

102. Bayerischer Landtag (II/11), V, 137 (January 17, 1950), 459.

103. *Der Tagesspiegel* (Berlin), April 30, 1949. Cf. *Stuttgarter Zeitung,* May 4, 1949, and *Deutsche Presse Agentur (dpa)*, *Inf.* 163 (November 2, 1949).

104. *Neuer Vorwärts* (Hanover), December 8, 1950.

105. Reported in the *Münchener Abendblatt,* December 16, 1949, as quoted by Deputy Andreas Kurz (CSU) in Bayerischer Landtag (II/11), V, 136 (December 16, 1949), 441. See also *ibid.*, 137 (January 17, 1950), 458.

106. See *Deutsche Presse Agentur (dpa)*, *Inf.* 62 (October 22, 1949), *Inf.* 28 (October 23, 1949), and *Inf.* 37 (October 23, 1949).

107. Interview with Meissner, April 17, 1957. Tentative discussions between a former SS officer, Reiter (Worms), and the former chairman of Priester's delegation in the Wiesbaden city council, Max Keding, with a view toward organizing the DB in Worms, came to naught.

108. For a fair, if critical, account see Karl O. Paetel's "Otto Strasser und die 'Schwarze Front,'" *Politische Studien,* VIII, 92 (December, 1957), 269–281. Yet much more revealing are Strasser's *Hitler and I* (Boston: Houghton Mifflin, 1940), *History in My Time* (London: Cape, [1941]), and *Exil* (Munich: Deutsche Freiheit, 1958). See also Douglas Reed's two biogra-

phies, *Nemesis? The Story of Otto Strasser* (Boston: Houghton Mifflin, 1940) and *The Prisoner of Ottawa: Otto Strasser* (London: Cape, 1953). The brief biographical sketch by Otto's brother, the Benedictine priest Bernhard Strasser—*Gregor and Otto Strasser* (Külsheim/Baden: Stössel, June, 1954)—though, of course, totally uncritical, is useful. Cf. also Georg Jentsch's brief biographical sketch reproduced in Otto Strasser's pamphlet *Deutschland und der 3. Weltkrieg* (Munich: Deutsche Freiheit, 1961), pp. 5–8. Reed's books must be read with the kind of caution that befits an author who is capable of bringing out in 1952 a new version of Kurt van Emsen's Teutomaniac occultism. Reed called his version *Der grosse Plan der Anonymen* (Zurich: Thomas, 1952) and succeeded in getting some distribution within Germany by having it published by a Swiss firm.

109. Their "German socialism" is said to have received the first "socialist" impulse from the national socialism of Thomas Garrigue Masaryk, the father of Czechoslovakia, and from the neoconservatism of Arthur Moeller van den Bruck. In a remarkable intellectual biography of Masaryk—*Europa von Morgen: Das Ziel Masaryks* (Zurich: Weltwoche, 1939)—Otto Strasser sets the great democrat, humanitarian, and Christian an almost baroque monument. Uncritically enthusiastic, at times fulsome in his adulation, Strasser not only celebrates Masaryk's religiously based, unshakable faith in democracy and his ethical (non-Marxist) socialism and humanitarian nationalism but also appears to accept Masaryk's scathing condemnation of "Prussianism" and especially of the baneful role of Prussian militarism (pp. 145–146, 186 ff., 191). In some other respects, Strasser tries hard to make it appear that Masaryk shared his biographer's disdain for political parties and his preference for corporatism and that Masaryk's political thought contained elements of racial and folkish theories (pp. 126 ff., 131 ff., 142). Unlike his hero Otto Strasser has, in the course of his tempestuous political life, not always clung so fervently to either democratic or humanitarian values nor always condemned authoritarianism and racial anti-Semitism. For Strasser's relation to the thought of Moeller van den Bruck, see Strasser's open letter to General Lucius D. Clay, reproduced in *Deutscher Presse Dienst* (Hamburg), February 26, 1949. See also Strasser's testimony in the case of Mrs. Anna Margarethe von Flotow before the Munich *Amtsgericht* on March 1, 1956 (AZ II/221/56), reproduced in *Deutscher Informationsdienst,* no. 598 (October 5, 1956), p. 3; *Die Brücke,* III, 3 (April, 1956), 10-11.

110. For Strasser's famous final talk with Hitler, see Appendix in Strasser's *Aufbau des deutschen Sozialismus* (2d ed.; Prague: Grunov, [pref. 1936]). Exactly what Strasser's relations were to Hitler and the Nazi Party after 1930 became an important postwar question to many former members of the Black Front. On the answer to it depended their being officially accorded the status of victims of the Nazi regime and thus acquiring legal rights to restitution and compensation. Radically divergent answers can reasonably be given. Cf., for example, the enthusiastic defense of Strasserism as basically opposed to all the main tenets of Hitlerism in Wolfgang Abendroth, "Das Problem der Widerstandstätigkeit der 'Schwarzen

Front,'" *Vierteljahrshefte für Zeitgeschichte*, VIII, 2 (April, 1960), 181–187, with the hostile (if superficial) treatment in Alfred Werner, "Trotzky of the Nazi Party," *Journal of Central European Affairs*, XI, 1 (January–April, 1951), 39–46. German courts have so far refused to recognize the Black Front as a principled, nontotalitarian opposition to Nazism.

111. Such as Bund Oberland, Bündische Reichsschaft, the Werwolf circle, the Young German Order, the revolutionary Landvolk movement, and the *Tat* circle. The former NSDAP members under Otto Strasser's leadership formed themselves into a Fighting Fellowship of Revolutionary National Socialists (Kampfgemeinschaft revolutionärer Nationalsozialisten, KGRNS). Between June and September, 1931, the KGRNS collaborated with Captain Walter Stennes' rebellious SA groups, which called themselves the National Socialist Fighting Movement of Germany (Nationalsozialistische Kampfbewegung Deutschlands, NSKBD). The unified Strasser-Stennes group was called the National Socialist Fighting Fellowship of Germany (Nationalsozialistische Kampfgemeinschaft Deutschlands, NSKD). See Schüddekopf (I/1), pp. 317–331. For the relationship of the Young German Order to the Black Front movement, see Klaus Hornung, *Der Jungdeutsche Orden* (Düsseldorf: Droste, 1958), pp. 111, 125.

112. "The banner of all its [the Black Front's] members is the black banner of Moeller [van den Bruck], who is its great teacher and whose book, *Das Dritte Reich*, is the basic book of the Black Front." Richard Schapke, *Die Schwarze Front: Von den Zielen und Aufgaben und vom Kampfe der deutschen Revolution*, preface by Otto Strasser (Leipzig: Lindner, 1932), p. 77, quoted in Stern (I/1), p. 265.

113. For the espionage and counterespionage scandals in which Strasser became involved during his Czech exile, see *Deutscher Informationsdienst*, no. 598 (August 24, 1956).

114. Kurt Singer in New York, Bruno Fricke in Buenos Aires, Helmut Hütter in Rio de Janeiro, and Hugo Efferoth in La Paz. See G. Tabor, "Übersee Deutschtum und deutsche Politik," *Kölnische Rundschau*, December 13, 1948, p. 3.

115. Strasser had always stressed—this was characteristic of many of the national revolutionaries—that political tactics were not the result of merely pragmatic considerations, but rather the specific manifestations of larger ideological and theoretical principles. All the major national revolutionaries authored more or less complex, more or less abstruse theoretical tracts which were celebrated by their followers as "target books" (*Zielbücher*). The Black Front boasted several of these, prominent among them Otto Strasser's *Germany Tomorrow*, trans. by Eden and Cedar Paul (London: Cape, [1940]). Part III of this book contains, in effect, almost all of Strasser's earlier *Aufbau des deutschen Sozialismus* (IV/110). In 1946 Strasser brought his program up to date with a second *Zielbuch, Germany's Renewal* (*Deutschlands Erneuerung* [Buenos Aires: Trenkelbach, (1946)].) Of equal importance for an understanding of the ideological orientation of the Black Front is Schapke (IV/112). Schapke, incidentally, was executed by the Nazis.

116. Undoubtedly, Spann's most influential work has been *Der wahre Staat* (Leipzig: Quelle & Meyer, 1921). It was that book, more than any other, which earned him widespread recognition as "the philosopher of the Christian corporative state." Spann's "universalist" neoconservatism was given wide circulation through a large number of disciples.

117. Donohoe (IV/71), p. 18, suggests that Strasser's dramatic abandonment of radical anticlericalism might have been due to the influences of his sojourn in London or the Spanish monastery.

118. See Strasser's letters to Kurt Sprengel of May 15, June 2, June 23, and July 11, 1949, quoted in "Zum ewigen Frieden," *Der Spiegel*, III, 36 (September 1, 1949), 8. Under the circumstances, it was characteristic that an official request to the U.S. Military Government authorities of Württemberg-Baden for a party license should be made, only to be withdrawn at Strasser's request. *Telegraf* (Berlin), November 17, 1947, and *Interpress* (Hamburg), November 26, 1948.

119. See Sopade *Informationsdienst*, no. 649 (December 14, 1948).

120. See Sopade *Informationsdienst*, Sonderdienst, no. 263 (April 11, 1949). For the history and high lights of the Cologne group's differences with their erstwhile master, see Peter Thoma's "Dr. Otto Strasser, die neutralistische Idee und der Neutralismus," *Die Sammlung* (Rundbrief der Sammlung zur Tat), no. 38 (no date, but very likely January or February 1961), pp. 9–12.

121. The Reich President, for instance, would not only have life tenure but would also have the power to appoint members to the Reich Council. As the Strasser constitution provided for the passage and ratification of laws by the approval of any two of the three coequal branches of government, (the Reich Estate Chamber, the Reich Council, and the Reich Presidency), absolute veto power and even legislative power would thus lie in the hands of the President.

122. Sopade *Informationsdienst* (IV/120).

123. See *SPD Pressedienst*, spd/III, 145 (November 29, 1948). Cf. Sopade *Informationsdienst* (IV/119) and *Das Volk* (Freiburg i. Br.), November 25, 1948.

124. Sopade *Informationsdienst* (IV/220).

125. *Deutscher Presse Dienst* (Hamburg), January 22, 1949.

126. The first to join Bauer was the Hessian chairman, Rudolf Knochenhauer. Others followed. Even Hans Giessen, the Land chairman of North Rhine–Westphalia, wanted to quit because of the incessant intriguing and infighting.

127. On April 22, 1949, the *Echo der Woche* (Munich) called these "theses" meaningless generalizations, a judgment shared by Bauer and his friends. (Letter of Thoma to Steinfeld, April 27, 1949.)

128. It proclaimed such high-flown nonsense as "the synthesis of state, society, and individual through a combination of liberalism (individualism) and socialism (collectivism) as the basis of a new bourgeois-proletarian social order" and the replacement of "liberal individualism" by "social individualism" and of "collective socialism" by "individual socialism" to create

a "social socialism." More seriously, the document ended with a frank appeal to unreasoned action: "The solution of the social question never emerges from theory but exclusively from practice, from deed. . . . Man, awaken! People, arise! Into action!"

129. The Cologne group criticized the various program and bylaw drafts as "somewhat romantic. You in the French Zone, of all people, have provided a draft which has strong mystical tendencies. We would like to see . . . a bit more Latin *ratio* instead." (Letter of Bauer, Thoma, and Karl E. Naske to Steinfeld and Draeger, April 30, 1949.) Cf. also Thoma's strongly worded criticism in his letter to Steinfeld, April 27, 1949. Even Draeger agreed: "Don't be put off by pamphlet No. 1 [*People, Arise for Action*]. . . . I immediately rejected it as worthless. . . . The same is true of the platform. I fully agree with you!" (Letter of Draeger to Bauer, May 3, 1949.) In another letter to Bauer (May 7, 1949), Draeger is equally critical of the bylaws: "The Villingen bylaws are not only romantic; they are useless. They too were drafted before my time. After I read them for the first time, I put them aside and just laughed."

130. Letters of Steinfeld to Bauer, March 28 and 30, 1949.

131. Letter of Steinfeld to Bauer, April 14, 1949. At a meeting of the Action Committee of the SzT in Cologne on May 8, 1949, the feasibility of such a holding company was debated at length. Steinfeld saw the possibility of bringing into the SzT (insofar as they did not already constitute its membership) the Working Association of Free Electors (Baden), the Party of Free Electors (Munich), the New Party (Stuttgart), the Oppositional Socialists (Rhineland-Palatinate), the Religious Socialists, the Central Association of Returnees (CDH), the Young Socialists of Cologne, the Group for an All-German Constitution, the Organization for Refugees, the International Peace League (Augsburg), and possibly the Deutsche Union (DU), with whose general secretary, Günther Scholz, talks were being held. The expellee spokesman, Friedrich Kopatschek, saw insuperable difficulties in embracing so varied a group of political associations—all the more so since a mass organization such as the CDH, with its half-million members, could easily outvote all the rest of the groups put together. The CDH representative, Fritz Geisbauer, also reminded Steinfeld that the corporative group membership in SzT would be impossible for the CDH, since many of its members already belonged to a party. It was decided that the SzT would have to be a party with individual membership.

132. Mimeographed letter of Bauer, Naske, and Thoma to their political friends, April 15, 1949.

133. Hessisches Statistisches Landesamt (III/87).

134. Letter (IV/132). Even the political busybody and marginal Strasserite, Joachim von Ostau, cautiously inquired about possible collaboration. To the Cologne group he represented blackest reaction, and they warned that any organization which featured von Ostau was more than likely to be banned by the occupation authorities. (Letters of Bauer to Steinfeld, May 22 and July 25, 1949. Also mimeographed letter of Bauer, Naske, and Thoma to their political friends, August 8, 1949.) Steinfeld, how-

ever, thought that von Ostau had "in our opinion very good ideas on political reconstruction" and, in any case, "certainly has useful friends." Reactionary or no, "we believe that we will be able to steer Herr von Ostau onto the right track." (Letter of Steinfeld to Eduard Sauer, May 24, 1949.)

135. The program was identical with that which Rossaint had worked out with Bauer, Thoma, and Kopatschek and which he presented to the provisional section committee of the SzT at its Cologne meeting of May 8, 1949. The ten points were: (1) reunification; (2) complete sovereignty of the reunified Reich; (3) federalization of all European peoples and Germany's participation in that federal union; (4) neutralization of Germany; (5) land and home for everyone; (6) *Betriebsgemeinschaften*, that is, a socially owned economy, freed from all state controls, which is administered by the several syndicalist plant associations; (7) a German office for currency control; (8) just distribution of the burdens and sacrifices made necessary by the loss of the war and its aftermath; (9) legal and social equality of women; and (10) rejection of all political parties and their replacement by self-administered organizations in industry, art, science, culture, youth, social welfare, etc.

136. Ruth Fischer, the recognized leader of the German Communist Party (KPD) in the early twenties and one of its Reichstag deputies until 1928, was expelled from the KPD on grounds of "deviationism."

137. Rossaint, who in the late nineteen-twenties and early thirties had been one of the leaders of the Catholic youth group Sturmschar, became the center of a mammoth show trial staged by the Nazis in March, 1937, in an effort to break the opposition of the illegally persisting parts of the Youth Movement. Charged with illegal collaboration with the underground Communist Party and the national-revolutionary forces of the Black Front, Rossaint was convicted and sentenced to eleven years' imprisonment. The trial, incidentally, illumined the entire area of anti-Nazi collaboration of Catholic, Communist, "autonomous," and even *bündisch* youth groups. See below, Chapter X, Section D.

138. Van Emsen (I/19). Dr. Strünkmann died in 1953.

139. In the following year Kampf joined the chairman of the extremist League of Front-Line Soldiers (Bund der Frontsoldaten, BdF), Otto Silber, in founding the League of Former German Soldiers (Bund ehemaliger deutscher Soldaten, BedS), which they later renamed the Anti-War Movement of Germany (Antikriegs-Bewegung Deutschlands, ABD). It remained without influence on the development of either the rapidly growing veterans' organizations or the equally rapidly growing neutralist movement.

140. This was possible because French authorities had suddenly reversed their inflexible nonlicense policy, for reasons which are still quite inexplicable, and granted the SzT a license for Württemberg-Hohenzollern as well as for Baden.

141. See *Informations- und Pressedienst der SzT*, no date, p. 3.

142. Letter of Draeger to the members of the Action Committee of the SzT, August 4, 1949.

143. In the French Zone, the SzT came out with only one campaign

poster. It bore the heading: "The old parties have failed!" See *Informations- und Pressedienst der SzT*, no date, p. 2.

144. In the Bundestag, Ott attached himself first to Loritz' WAV and later to the Union of Expellees and Victims of Injustice (Bund der Heimatvertriebenen und Entrechteten, BHE). In 1952, Deputy Ott, the then forty-two-year-old ex-priest, surprised in the act of making obscene propositions to strange women over his office telephone, resigned his parliamentary seat. This, however, did not prevent him from later becoming chairman of a local Catholic-welfare organization or from teaching religion in a vocational high school in Aschaffenburg. See *Der Spiegel*, XVII, 43 (October 23, 1963), 126.

145. For Götzendorff's later activity, see *Der Informationsdienst*, no. 22 (October 31, 1950), p. 2, and no. 30 (November 23, 1950), p. 2. See also *Bulletin on German Questions* (London), IX, 199/200 (November 5, 1957). See below, XIV/47.

146. See Otto Stolz, "Neo-Nazis schaffen Querverbindungen," *Neue Zeitung* (Munich), October 14, 1949.

Chapter V. New Patterns of Leadership: Cadre Formations 1949–1953

1. This expression stems from Werner Naumann's "Wo stehen die ehemaligen Nationalsozialisten?" reprinted in his *Nau-Nau gefährdet das Empire?* (Göttingen: Plesse, 1953), p. 159.

2. A typical example of this attitude was provided by Naumann when he strongly advised the Nazi heroes, General H. B. Ramcke and Colonel Hans-Ulrich Rudel, against participating at a meeting of Meissner's DB in Lübeck on December 15, 1952. At that time he told Rudel, "I'm afraid you'd be exploited by that little group. In my opinion, you are too good for that. I'd like to keep you for a much larger framework and not for such a little thing as that." British intelligence report (V/12), par. 18.

3. See below, Chapter VIII, Section C.

4. See below, Chapter VII, Section D.

5. See below, VI/220.

6. See below, Chapter XV, Section C.

7. See below, VIII/67.

8. Together with Richard Schapke, a lieutenant of Strasser, Franke organized the National Socialist Workers' and Farmers' Youth. See Schüddekopf (I/1), p. 496, note 25.

9. Strasser, *Exil* (IV/108), p. 80. See also letter of Strasser's friend Otto Loerbroks to the editors of the *Frankfurter Neue Presse*, February 24, 1950.

10. See Douglas Reed's biographies (IV/108), *Nemesis? The Story of Otto Strasser*, pp. 172–176, and *The Prisoner of Ottawa: Otto Strasser*, pp. 142–147. Cf. *Deutsche Presse Agentur* (*dpa*), *Inf.* 319 (March 9, 1950), and *Deutscher Informationsdienst*, no. 598 (August 24, 1956).

11. The professional anti-Communist vigilante, Friedrich Victor Risse, reported on Franke's return to the Nazis and the SS as follows: "During this Czech period, he received from Heydrich safe conduct to Berlin in order to close a deal with the SD chief for his rehabilitation at the RSHA [Reich Security Main Office] so that he could become SS captain, executive officer (lc) in a *Totenkopf* division, and department chief in the SS personnel office—[all] at the price of betraying the personnel and . . . connections of the Strasser emigration." ("Im Zwielicht des geteilten Vaterlandes," *Deutsche Soldaten–Zeitung* [Munich], VII, 2 [February, 1957], 5.) According to SS Major Harald Milde, one of Franke's former colleagues in the personnel division of the SS, who had been instrumental in obtaining for him the position of personal assistant to the personnel chief, Adolf Katz, Franke had within a year managed to acquire a villa by corrupt means (*erschoben*) and then promptly betrayed the anti-Himmler group. (Letter of Ernst Riggert to Colonel Wolfgang Müller, November 26, 1951. See below, VI/62.) Despite efforts by the state attorney's office in Bielefeld and considerable circumstantial evidence presented by former Black Front members, the fact of Franke's betrayal could not be established by legally unimpeachable proof. See Otto Giessler's deposition, reprinted in *Deutsche Presse Agentur* (*dpa*), *Inf.* 1104 (September 6, 1950) and *Inf.* 339 (March 8, 1951). See also notices in *Die Neue Zeitung* (Munich), October 8 and December 7, 1951. For further "evidence," see letter of Dr. B. Fleiss to Ernst Buchrucker, November 17, 1950, reprinted in *Vertrauliche Information,* no. 56 (December 16, 1950), p. 2. Important in this connection is Otto Strasser's letter to *Der Spiegel,* March 8, 1950, and the article on Franke in *Stuttgarter Nachrichten,* April 4, 1950. See also letter of Strasser's friend Werner Dietz to Kriminalpolizei, Hamburg–Blankenese, June 22, 1950 (copy in the author's possession).

12. From a confidential British intelligence report that was widely rumored to have provided the basis for the arrest in January, 1953, of leading members of the so-called Naumann or Gauleiter circles. Shortly thereafter *Der Spiegel* (VII, 20 [May 13, 1953], 5–6) obtained a copy of that memorandum and attributed its authorship to F. W. Read-Jahn, then a political officer on the staff of the British Land Commissioner of North Rhine–Westphalia. In a communication to the author of May 5, 1966, Mr. Read-Jahn asserts that he "certainly had nothing to do with any report of this nature," and that *Der Spiegel*'s use of his name in this connection was "pure speculation and completely unfounded." (Cf. below, V/89 and XVII/66. A mimeographed copy of the report is in the author's possession.)

13. Initially the Bruderrat consisted of only four men: Beck, Franke, von der Milbe, and Eugen Achenbach. (From a confidential report of Fritz Zietlow, April 17, 1951.) During the Third Reich, Achenbach had been a leading functionary of the German Association of Manufacturers and the director of its Adolf Hitler Fund. After the war, he became a contractor in Hamburg with continued excellent contacts with big business. (He must not be confused with Ernst Achenbach, erstwhile political adviser to Nazi Ambassador Otto Abetz in Paris and, after the war, one of the leaders of the

FDP in North Rhine–Westphalia and its chief liaison to the Naumann circle.) The secrecy of the Bruderschaft inspired a flurry of unsubstantiated rumors concerning its ideological orientation and its leadership personnel. According to one widespread if unreliable account, the Bruderrat was to have included Generals Hasso von Manteuffel and Oldwig von Natzmer, and Count Hans Christoph von Stauffenberg, cousin of the hero of the Twentieth of July. (See Joachim Joesten, "The Menace of Neo-Nazism," *New Germany Reports*, no. 15 [September, 1950], pp. 16–17.) Von der Milbe, who had never become particularly active, soon died, leaving a Bruderrat of three members. Later, in the fall of 1950, it was enlarged to six members by co-opting (1) former SS Lieutenant Colonel Horst Nolte of Celle, a close relative of the East Zonal General Martin Lattmann, German correspondent for *Nordisk Kamp* (Malmö), the official journal of a radical Swedish Nazi organization, the National Socialist Fighting League, under the anti-Engdahl extremist Göran Assar Oredsson, and an active organizer of militarist-nationalist youth groups; (2) Schott von der Howen, of Bremen, a former adjutant of Goebbels; and (3) K. G. Schrödter, of Neumünster, a Silesian farmer and expellee. (Cf. above, IV/91.)

14. Axmann, centrally involved in the organization of a postwar Nazi underground movement, was arrested in December, 1945. In May, 1949, the Nuremberg denazification tribunal placed him in Group I, "Major Offenders," and imposed on him a prison sentence of three and a quarter years, the forfeiture of all property above DM 3,000, and a ban on political activity. It would appear that the prison sentence was considered served by his previous internment.

15. A perfectly loyal, if archconservative, supporter of the Bonn Republic and the FDP's foremost military expert in Parliament, von Manteuffel publicly denied ever having had anything to do with the Bruderschaft. However, the evidence to the contrary appears quite persuasive, if not by any means conclusive. (See, for example, Basil Davidson, "The Manteuffel Plan," *The New Statesman and Nation*, XL, 1008 [July 1, 1950], 6.) Von Manteuffel later became a member of the DP and chairman of its North Rhine–Westphalian Land organization. He resigned from it in the fall of 1959, when he was charged with manslaughter for having ordered the execution of one of his soldiers. Convicted on the charge, he was sentenced to eighteen months in prison.

16. General Stumpff also left the Bruderschaft to attach himself to one of the so-called bourgeois parties. In his case, it was Chancellor Adenauer's CDU.

17. Hans Jürgen von Arnim and Kurt Dittmar are also often mentioned as having belonged to the inner circle of the Bruderschaft. These reports, however, cannot be regarded as reliable evidence.

18. See Hans Fritzsche's testimony at Nuremberg. International Military Tribunal, *Trial of the Major War Criminals* (Nuremberg: 1947), XVII, 230. Cf. below, VIII/42.

19. For brief discussions of the June Club's political orientation, membership, and influence, see von Klemperer (I/1), pp. 102–111; Stern (I/1), Chapter 13; and Mohler (I/1), pp. 92–93.

20. Otto H. Hess, one of the DU's founders (not to be confused with Otto Hess the later functionary and leader of the Deutsche Reichs Partei, who—to compound confusion—was for several years one of the leading personalities of the DU), characteristically located the sickness of the times in pervasive party hatred and party struggle. He felt certain that its cure could be effected by a "rally movement" which would press for "un-doctrinaire politics," i.e., the absolute separation of politics from Weltanschauung. (From a confidential report of the founding meeting at Brunswick, January 24, 1949.)

21. Most prominent in the early Berlin meetings were Günther Scholz, political editor of the French-licensed newspaper *Der Kurier* and former member of the Deutsche Freischar "Stamm grosser Jäger"; Otto H. Hess, publisher of the influential student paper *Colloquium* and important organizer of the Free University in West Berlin; Peter Lorenz, chairman of the CDU's Junge Union in Berlin; Herbert H. Geisler, publisher of *Der Wegweiser* and local FDP politician; Jürgen Reiss, an editor of the American-licensed *Der Tagesspiegel;* and the East Zonal Liberal Democratic editor Harold Esche. Esche made a name for himself by his anti-Soviet activity (shortly after the war, he published a monograph on *Die Ausplünderung des deutschen Ostens* [Rosenheim: Inngau, Lang, no date]) and by his initial membership in Rainer Hildebrandt's notorious Fighting League against Inhumanity (Kampfgruppe gegen Unmenschlichkeit, KgU), the West-financed, anti-Communist sabotage, espionage, and propaganda outfit, of which Geisler also was a charter member.

22. See Sopade *Informationsdienst*, no. 705 (February 22, 1949).

23. See below, Chapter VI, Section B. The editor in chief of *Christ und Welt* is Giselher Wirsing, the former publisher of *Die Tat*, whose activity for the SS and SD made him appear, in the eyes of his employers, an "eager, diligent, and extraordinarily valuable co-worker." (Quoted in Léon Poliakov and Josef Wulf, *Das Dritte Reich und seine Denker* [Berlin: arani, 1959], p. 478.) Editor in chief of the *Münchener Neueste Nachrichten* under the Nazis, staff contributor to the *Völkischer Beobachter,* SS major, and anti-Semitic ideologist, Wirsing predicted in 1942 in a virulent anti-American book that "Jewish predominance . . . is far too blatant and far too triumphant to fail to lead . . . to a revulsion and to attract general hatred, as it has done in almost all European countries." In 1944 he counseled that "the emasculation of the Jewish spirit can come only by withdrawing from it the fertile soil [on which it battens] . . . in a scientific age." (Quoted in "Auch ein Korrespondent," *Vorwärts* [Bad Godesberg], May 11, 1956.) For Wirsing's part in the gala opening of Rosenberg's Institute for Research on the Jewish Question (Frankfurt), see Max Weinreich, *Hitler's Professors: The Part of Scholarship in Germany's Crimes against the Jewish People* (New York: Yiddish Scientific Institute—YIVO, 1946), pp. 99, 107. On that auspicious occasion, the topic of Wirsing's paper was "The Jewish Question in the Near East."

24. Ernst A. Hepp, editor in chief of *Christ und Welt* in 1948/1949, had been press attaché at the German embassy in Washington before the war. There he was engaged in spreading German propaganda among Ger-

manophiles, isolationists, native Fascists, and German-Americans. Wolfgang Höpker, his deputy at *Christ und Welt,* had been Giselher Wirsing's right-hand man at the *Münchener Neueste Nachrichten,* an important Nazi paper. In 1956 he became editor in chief of the conservative *Hannoversche Allgemeine Zeitung.* For further details see *Hannoversche Presse,* February 10, 1949.

25. In the nineteen-twenties, Boehm was appointed director of the Institut für Grenz- und Auslandsstudien and became chairman of the German Association for Nationality Law. Typical of his "scientific" activity is the influential book *Die deutschen Grenzlande* (Berlin: Hobbing, 1925), with its folkish and bitterly irredentist message. Boehm's most influential works were *Das eigenständige Volk* (Göttingen: Vandenhöck & Ruprecht, 1933) and *Ruf der Jungen: Eine Stimme aus dem Kreise von Moeller van den Bruck* (3d ed.; Freiburg i. Br.: Urban, 1933). Boehm published voluminously throughout the twelve-year period of the Nazi Reich. This did not prevent the Bonn government from inviting him to serve as co-editor of a three-volume work about the influence of expellees on West German society, economy, politics, and intellectual life. This appointment did not lack a certain piquancy: it had been, after all, Boehm and his ilk whose irredentist, folkish twaddle was not a little responsible for the forceful expulsions after 1945.

26. In the last stages of the war, Majewski edited the *Nord-West Front Soldaten-Zeitung,* in which he urged German soldiers to a last-ditch defense. Majewski also edited the first DU publication, *Deutsche Wirklichkeit.*

27. For an assessment of Hoetzsch, his institute, and their relation to the anti-Communist ideologues around Goebbels and Rosenberg, see Walter Laqueur, *Russia and Germany: A Century of Conflict* (London: Weidenfeld and Nicolson, [c. 1965]), pp. 179–180.

28. A description of this group, which never was defined and permanent enough to be properly called a circle, was provided by Mehnert himself and published by the *Deutscher Presse Dienst* (Hamburg) (no date, but very likely autumn or winter 1948). Mehnert, who initially sympathized with the Strasser wing of neoconservatism, was later said to have published a loyalist Nazi paper in the Far East even after the fall of the Third Reich.

29. Materials on the Laupheim Circle, from a confidential report of its meeting at Bad Wimpfen on July 21, 1951, by Henning Wilcke and a further unpublished, confidential report of a meeting between the working committees of the DU and the Laupheim group in Ulm on February 4–5, 1949. Great hopes were set in one August Heinrichsbauer, who had played the role of fund raiser for radical-nationalist groups during Weimar and was now expected to do the same for the DU. In the postwar period, Heinrichsbauer, who till 1950 was the press chief of the Federation of German Industry, evidently had the task of collecting and distributing funds to those parties and groups whose politics German big business wished to support. (See Bundestag, *Bericht des Untersuchungsausschusses* [44. Ausschuss], *Verhandlungen des Deutschen Bundestages,* 1. Wahlperiode, Anlagen, *Drucksache Nr. 2274,* and *Verhandlungen des deutschen Bundestages,*

1. Wahlperiode, *Stenographische Berichte*, 148. Sitzung [June 7, 1951], pp. 5897–5898, and 149. Sitzung [June 8, 1951], pp. 5961–5962. See below, VII/166.)

Heinrichsbauer is the author of books on the Ruhr industry (see, for example, his *Der Ruhrbergbau in Vergangenheit, Gegenwart und Zukunft* [Essen: Glückauf, 1948]) and on the role of big business in the rise of Nazism (*Schwerindustrie und Politik* [Essen: West, 1948]).

30. Haussleiter, a Franconian journalist and, later, a war correspondent during the Nazi regime, and veteran of a number of disagreements with Julius Streicher, emerged from private life in 1946 when he headed a Bourgeois and Farmers' Alliance to oppose the SPD and KPD candidates in his electoral district. The Alliance, having gained an absolute majority in the local elections of 1946, corporatively joined the CSU. There Haussleiter represented the antistates-rights wing. The Landtag's credential committee at first refused to seat him, on the ground that his war diary clearly marked him as a militarist. In responding to the invitation to collaborate in the founding of the DU, Haussleiter was primarily interested in gaining adherents in his running battle against the CSU's Catholic wing under Josef Donsberger and Alois Hundhammer. During the "democratic" phase of his early postwar career, Haussleiter was not beyond describing himself and his friends as on the fringes of the conspiracy of July 20, 1944—a fact which, if true, he would carefully conceal from his later associates and followers. See his notarized deposition on behalf of his friend Karl Arthur Weller, reproduced in *Deutscher Informationsdienst*, no. 286 (July 3, 1953), pp. 2–3. For sheer contrast, see "Sonderdruck aus dem Informationsdienst 'Die Deutsche Gemeinschaft,' " dealing with "Die Wahrheit über Landsberg" (1951), and "Wer ist August Haussleiter?" *Die Deutsche Gemeinschaft* (Munich), VIII (1st August ed., 1957), 3.

31. See below, Chapter VI, Section E.

32. Persistent rumors even linked one of the leading Socialist politicians, Carlo Schmid, and the Bavarian CSU Minister President, Hans Ehard, with the DU. However, they publicly denied these rumors. Spiecker, a former government commissar for Upper Silesia, had had considerable connections with revolutionary nationalism after the First World War. Called as a witness in one of the last great *Feme* murder trials, he evaded the central issue, presumably because he feared exposure of the fact that he, the Prussian government, and the Reich government had had full knowledge of the *Feme* murders and had tacitly approved. This, at least, is the interpretation of Friedrich Wilhelm von Oertzen in his panegyric on the Free Corps: *Die Deutschen Freikorps 1918–1923* (6th ed.; Munich: Bruckmann, 1939), pp. 472–473. In 1931 Spiecker became "Special Commissioner of the Reich in the Reich Ministry of the Interior for the Fight against National Socialism."

33. This revulsion did not prevent Mende from attempting to establish himself in the CDU and its youth organization, the Young Union. Only when he tried to lead the Young Union corporatively into the DU did he run into massive opposition. In the spring of 1949, Mende also participated

in a meeting of youth leaders at Ludwigstein Castle in honor of Karl O. Paetel, the former *bündisch,* national-Bolshevik, anti-Hitler Conservative Revolutionary, who emigrated to the United States in the nineteen-thirties and has lived and worked there ever since.

34. The founding of the DU had been preceded by sensational and inaccurate press reports on the mysterious new political organization *in spe.* See, for example, *Badische Zeitung* (Freiburg), January 8, 1949; *Wirtschafts–Zeitung* (Stuttgart), January 12, 1949; *Das Andere Deutschland* (Hanover), January 14, 1949; *Rheinischer Merkur* (Koblenz), January 15, 1949; *Bremerhavener Zeitung,* January 15, 1949; *Südost Kurier* (Bad Reichenhall), January 19, 1949; and *Deutscher Presse Dienst* (Hamburg), January 7 and 10, 1949. The Brunswick meeting itself received a wide and highly skeptical press. See, for example, *Hannoversche Presse,* January 25, 1949; *Westdeutsche Allgemeine Zeitung* (Bochum), January 25, 1949; *SPD Pressedienst,* January 24, 1949; *Die Neue Zeitung* (Bremen), January 28, 1949; *Offenbach Post,* January 27, 1949; *Nordsee Zeitung* (Bremerhaven), January 28, 1949; and *Schwäbische Landeszeitung* (Augsburg), January 28, 1949.

35. Leaflets "Was will die Deutsche Union?" "Grundsätze der Deutschen Union," and "Resolution," all undated.

36. Conversation reported by Gert P. Spindler to Günther Draub, published by Willi Knothe, Frankfurt, in *Der Informationsdienst*, March 25, 1950.

37. See confidential Laupheim Circle report on the Ulm meeting (see above, V/29).

38. The internal struggles began even before the DU was officially founded. (Confidential eyewitness account of the founding meeting, dated January 24, 1949). Anxious to get total control over the organizational machinery of the DU, Haussleiter chafed under the constant opposition from his two cochairmen, von Stauffenberg and Otto H. Hess. See *Die Sammlung*, Mitteilungsblatt der deutschen Volksbewegung Sammlung zur Tat (Cologne), January, 1950, p. 4.

39. Griesmayr had been a member of Reichsleiter Martin Bormann's staff and a speech writer for Hitler. As he had devoted himself almost exclusively to the study of Nazi ideology, in 1940 he was assigned to the Hitler Youth to supervise their indoctrination. Eager to develop the ideological firmness of the Hitler Jugend, Griesmayr planned an eight-year program with monthly topics or ideological themes. In addition, he introduced a catechism in which Nazi slogans were invested with religious affects. See *Unser Glaube. Bekenntnis eines jungen Deutschen* (Berlin: Nordland, [1941]). The same purpose was also served by new rituals, such as "The Pledging of the Youth," which, he hoped, would eventually displace confirmation and first communion as milestones in the young person's emotional-religious life. In short, Griesmayr aimed at nothing less than providing Germany's youth with a new Nazi religion. Nothing, however, characterizes the virulence of his fanaticism so clearly as his proclamation, following Hitler's death, of a new Nazi party whose ten-point program was built

"on the pure teachings of the Führer." He made preparations to "preserve the *Volkssubstanz*" by sending armed Hitler Youths into the woods of the as-yet-unoccupied parts of the Sudetenland. He himself was to take charge of their "spiritual education." They were not to surrender to U.S. forces or go into occupied territory. (From an interview with N. J. Ryschkowsky.) At the same time, it is important to stress that the thirty-page brochure which Griesmayr wrote for the DU, *The Political Road of the War Generation* (*Der politische Weg der Kriegsgeneration*, Schriftenreihe der Deutschen Union [Berlin: Hess, 1950]) was a bitter disappointment to revolutionary irreconcilables. They saw in it essentially an acknowledgment of the irreversibility of the events since 1945, a "capitulation before the Western victors," and writhed at Griesmayr's profession to democracy and rejection of illegal, revolutionary means to reverse the results of 1945. Also, Griesmayr's demand for a united Europe was totally unacceptable to the ultras, who saw in it an abandonment of the sacred concepts *Nation* and *Reich*. In the eyes of those who were plotting and waiting for "the day," who had fortified themselves behind an indomitable all-or-nothing position, Griesmayr had gone over to the enemy. For a good example of this attitude, see F. Schwarzenborn's book review in *Der Weg*, VI, 3 (March, 1952), 222.

40. For Kiefer's other political activity see below, VI/79; VI/219; and VII/162.

41. See Horst Voigt, "Bruderschaft und Deutsche Union," *Die Bruderschaft* (Hanover), August, 1950, p. 11. Voigt is a former Hitler Youth leader (Jungvolk).

42. "Um die Bruderschaft," *Vertrauliche Information* (typescript, no date, but very likely end of August, 1950). Cf. *Die Bruderschaft* (Hanover), January, 1950, p. 27.

43. Voigt, "Die Bruderschaft—Gesinnungsgemeinschaft und Orden," *Die Bruderschaft* (Hanover), January, 1950, pp. 2, 18. For the "elite" conception of the Nazis, see Joachim H. Knoll, *Führungsauslese im Liberalismus und Demokratie* (Stuttgart: Schwab, 1957), pp. 195–205; and for the elitism of the Conservative Revolution, see Sontheimer (I/1), pp. 240–280.

44. Voigt (V/43), pp. 2, 19.

45. Franke-Gricksch in a letter to Konrad Adenauer and Jakob Kaiser, reprinted in *Deutsche Presse Agentur* (*dpa*), *Inf.* 1657 (December 11, 1950), pp. 1–3.

46. *Ibid.*, p .3.

47. Franke-Gricksch, quoted in *Neue Presse* (Coburg), November 16, 1950.

48. Helmut Beck-Broichsitter, *Informationsdienst der Kriegsgeneration*, no. 2 (June, 1951).

49. Quoted in *Deutsche Presse Agentur* (*dpa*), *Inf.* 1366 (September 18, 1951).

50. Letter of September 9, 1952, quoted in *Deutsche Presse Agentur* (*dpa*), *Inf.* 1658 (September 22, 1952), p. 5.

51. The name was clearly meant to suggest the famous Herrenklub of Weimar days. As the successor of the June Club, and under the leadership

of Heinrich von Gleichen and Count Hans Bodo von Alvensleben, that Herrenklub became the center of neoconservative activity. Despite its mere five thousand members, the club exerted an enormous influence on the intellectual life of the Conservative Revolution and on the entire Right. The thought of Franz von Papen and of his political secretary, the Munich lawyer Edgar J. Jung, may be taken as typical of the venomously antidemocratic, antiliberal, antiparliamentarian, Christian-authoritarian romanticism which the Junkers—and the barons of pit, rolling mill, and counting house—mistook for responsible conservatism.

52. Among these were Countess Lili Hamilton, the late Carl E. Carlberg, and Colonel A. G. Nordenswan. See Gunnar Berg, "Brücke der Liebe," *Nation Europa,* IV, 6 (June, 1954) 61–64; and Carl E. Carlberg, "Dreizehn Thesen," *ibid.,* 12 (December, 1954), 42–43. See *Deutscher Informationsbrief,* no. 6 (March 16, 1951). On Nazism in Sweden, especially on the Swedish SS volunteers, see Armas Sastamoinen, *Hitlers svenska förtrupper* (Stockholm: Federatius, 1947). For Carlberg see below, XII/43.

53. The *Archiv für publizistische Arbeit* (Intern. Biogr. Archiv), August 24, 1944: "He found the way to the Führer, as far as his convictions were concerned (*gesinnungsmässig*), when he was still in junior high school (*Tertianer*), and despite his youth he soon became one of the most eager and intrepid champions of National Socialist ideology (*Gedankengut*)."

54. See, for example, "Das anspornende Vorbild des Führers," *Nord-West Front Soldaten-Zeitung,* no. 79 (April 27, 1945).

55. "Das politische Testament Adolf Hitlers vom 29. April 1945," in Hans-Adolf Jacobsen, ed., *1939–1945: Der zweite Weltkrieg in Chronik und Dokumenten* (5th ed.; Darmstadt: Wehr und Wissen, 1961), p. 532.

56. Herbert S. Lucht, the owner of the firm Combinel, had been *Kulturreferent* in the Goebbels ministry.

57. *Final Report to the Secretary of the Army on the Nuremberg War Crimes Trials under Control Council Law No. 10,* Washington, D.C., 1949, pp. 47–48, quoted in Hilberg (II/9), p. 694. Cf. also Nuremberg Document NG–4895 on the conference of February 28, 1941, in which Achenbach, Otto Abetz, Theodor Dannecker, and Carltheo Zeitschel participated.

58. In February, 1952, Achenbach's organization published an appeal for a general amnesty, which was signed by, among others, Friedrich Middelhauve, chairman of the North Rhine–Westphalian FDP; Carl Spiecker, the former Center Party leader; and Friedrich Grimm, an expert on "political trials" and later the defense counsel for Naumann. (Vorbereitender Ausschuss zur Herbeiführung der Generalamnestie, "Aufruf zur Unterstützung der überparteilichen Aktion zur Herbeiführung der Generalamnestie" [Essen, February, 1952].)

59. The Boxheim document was a carefully worked-out plan for a Nazi coup d'état which fell into the hands of the Hessian police in 1931. As the admitted author of the plot, Best was tried for high treason, but the proceedings were discontinued when the court gave credence to his story that he had intended to make use of his plan only in the face of an imminent Communist coup. The plan and the official handling of the case became

famous for the light they threw both on the sincerity of the Nazis' assurances of legality and on the state of the German judiciary when Rightist radicals stood in the dock. (See Walter Wagner, "Politische Justiz in der Weimarer Republik," *Politische Meinung,* VI, 58 [1961], 50–63, and 60 [1961], 48–61.) For Best's early exploits in the Third Reich, see the apparently authoritative account of Heinrich Orb, *pseud., Nationalsozialismus: 13 Jahre Machtrausch* (2d ed.; Olten: Walter, 1945), pp. 73–80. Best, who had been convicted of war crimes and sentenced to fifteen years' imprisonment, was freed in 1951. After some years as Achenbach's office manager, he became legal counsel in 1955 of the giant Hugo Stinnes works in Mühlheim. See *Deutsche Presse Agentur* (*dpa*), *Inf.* 35/55 (March 25, 1955).

60. In 1948, Six was sentenced at Nuremberg to twenty years' imprisonment, but he regained his freedom four years later. One cannot be certain whether it was as former head of the ideological research office of the SS Reich Security Main Office (*Amt* VII) or as chief of the "Advance Commando Moscow" of the Mobile Killing Unit "B"—or, indeed, as former head of the Foreign Office's cultural policy division—that Six was selected to direct police action in Great Britain after the successful Nazi invasion and occupation. (See *The Wiener Library Bulletin* [London], XII, 1–2 [1958], 32.) Six, the former dean of the faculty for foreign countries at Berlin University, passed his apprenticeship in the mobile-unit murder apparatus in Smolensk, where he appeared to have ferreted out Soviet commissars for subsequent extermination. (See the Nuremberg Military Tribunal's findings on Six, *Trials of War Criminals before the Nuernberg Military Tribunals Under Control Council Law No. 10,* October, 1946–April, 1949 [Case 9, "The *Einsatzgruppen* Case"] IV, 521–526.) For his activity in selling radical anti-Semitism to other countries, see the Transcript of the Minutes of the Krummhübel Conference on the Jewish Question (April 3–4, 1944), Document 3319-PS, International Military Tribunal, *Trial of the Major War Criminals* (Nuremberg: 1948), XXXII, 163–175. For a summary, see Joseph Tenenbaum, *Race and Reich* (New York: Twayne, 1956), pp. 41–46. See also *Parlamentarisch–Politischer Pressedienst,* June 24, 1955, pp. 2–3.

61. From Naumann's diary, as quoted in Freie Demokratische Partei (FDP), "[Vertraulicher Bericht an] den Gesamtvorstand der Bundespartei über die Lage im Landesverband Nordrhein-Westfalen . . . ," Bonn, June 5, 1953. (Confidential Report of the [three-man] Committee of Inquiry [Federal Minister of Justice Thomas Dehler, Federal Minister of Home Construction Fritz Neumayer, and Bundestag Deputy Alfred Onnen] to the enlarged executive board of the FDP.) (Copy of copy.) Naumann brazenly insisted that he never kept a diary and that all the talk about confidential diary entries, which kept the German press in breathless suspense for weeks on end, was pure, unadulterated British lies. See his *Nau-Nau* (V/1), pp. 63–65.

62. FDP (V/61), p. 3.

63. In 1944 Hunke was selected to address a very exclusive and high-level anti-Jewish Congress which Rosenberg, Goebbels, and von Ribbentrop were planning. Hunke's topic was to have been "The Jew in the Economic

Life of the Nations." He never had a chance to deliver this speech, as the whole idea of the congress had to be abandoned. On the congress, see Weinreich (V/23), pp. 219–235. See also below, V/107.

64. In the light of all this, see Naumann's signally unconvincing attempt to minimize the significance in postwar Germany of meetings made up exclusively of high Nazi officials, in his *Nau-Nau* (V/1), *passim,* but especially pp. 120–153. (Cf. also "Dr. Werner Naumann an den NWDR," *Das Ziel* [Hanover] II, 10 [July 25, 1953], 3.) Though the publisher alleged that the book was authored by Naumann, it is actually largely the work of Karl Heinrich Peter, a confidant of the Naumann circle. Naumann himself, in fact, disagreed with some details in the book, such as the unkind words about the radical Nazi Bundestag deputy Wolfgang Hedler, which were put in Naumann's mouth. (From a discussion among Naumann; the former SRP leader, Werner Körper; the Stahlhelm leader, Karl Smets; and two others, October 21, 1953.) In 1961, Peter caused an outcry of indignation in the German press and official circles when he published his edition of Gestapo Chief Ernst Kaltenbrunner's secret report to Hitler on the conspiracy of July 20, 1944. (Archiv Peter für historische und zeitgeschichtliche Dokumentation, ed., *Spiegelbild einer Verschwörung. Die Kaltenbrunner Berichte an Bormann und Hitler über das Attentat vom 20. Juli 1944.* Geheime Dokumente aus dem ehemaligen Reichssicherheitshauptamt [Stuttgart: Seewald, 1961].)

65. Quoted in Fried Wesemann, "Die Totengräber sind unter uns (I)," *Frankfurter Rundschau,* June 9, 1953, p. 5.

66. With regard to retail merchants' associations, the case of the EDEKA (Einkaufsgenossenschaft deutscher Kolonialwarenhändler—Purchasing Association of German Grocers), with over 40,000 members, is instructive. The Naumann thesis in personnel management is remarkably demonstrated in the publishing house associated with that organization. The director of the house was Walfried Mayer, who had been the executive director of a Nazi business association and had remained a convinced Nazi. His deputy and closest confidant was Alfred Salat, charter member of Dr. Scheel's Herrenklub and former member of the board of directors of the official Nazi publishing house Eher Verlag, whom Ernst Wiechert in his autobiography called one of the Nazi regime's most dangerous and unscrupulous cat's-paws. ("Jahre und Zeiten. Erinnerungen 1945/1946," in Ernst Wiechert, *Sämtliche Werke* [Munich, Vienna, Basel: Desch, (1957)], IX, 679.) Salat retained his EDEKA position, despite having been placed in Group II by the denazification authorities, and saw to it that EDEKA's magazine opened its pages to Nazi authors, such as Hanns Johst, Hermann Claudius, and Heinrich Zillich. Scheel himself was EDEKA's company physician. When Scheel was arrested, Salat fled to the south to avoid sharing the same fate. Under the pressure of events, both he and Scheel were dismissed, but no sooner had the wind blown over than the Nazis consolidated their hold on the organization. A former Hitler Youth leader became secretary to Mayer; another was made secretary to the association's director; a former high civil servant was made a department chief in the publishing

house. An EDEKA department chief, the former General Georg Benthack, had been prosecuted for his part in the execution of four German soldiers after the capitulation. EDEKA also employed in a leading position the former undersecretary of the Reich Ministry of Nutrition. During Scheel's arrest, his boss at the Rautenberg Sanatorium and intimate of the group of Hamburg incorrigibles, Dr. Heinrich Kunstmann (later chairman of the DRP), became company physician at the EDEKA. See report in *Feinde der Demokratie* (Nordmark), no. 6 (August 20, 1953), pp. 21–22.

67. Prosecution Document A 38 (part of an unpublished, mimeographed compilation of documents). From Naumann's speech of November 1, 1952 in Düsseldorf.

68. Naumann, "Wo stehen die ehemaligen Nationalsozialisten?" reprinted in Naumann (V/1), p. 159.

69. Quoted in Wesemann (V/65). Also Prosecution Document B 5.

70. Naumann (V/68).

71. "He said, he knew from experience that whenever three men sat together, one of them was sure to be from the AVS." (Confidential report of a conversation with Naumann, October 21, 1953.)

72. Naumann's diary carries the following entry for August 26, 1950: "Naturally I agree that Adenauer is not the worst solution for us, for the time being. A people in our situation, without national sovereignty, governed by High Commissioners, needs [leaders of Stresemann's type (*Stresemänner*)]." FDP(V/61), p. 2.

73. Report (V/71).

74. Quoted in Wesemann (V/65), p. 6.

75. Naumann (V/68), pp. 159–160.

76. Quoted in Wesemann (V/65).

77. Prosecution Document A 36.

78. Quoted in Wesemann (V/65).

79. From Naumann's confidential speech of November 19, 1952, in Hamburg, reproduced in Prosecution Document B 30.

80. Prosecution Document E 30.

81. In his confidential speech of November 19, 1952, Naumann said: "We must act when time indicates that the right minute has arrived. Time must not command us; we must order the time." Reproduced in Prosecution Document C 5.

82. Wesemann (V/65), June 12, 1953, p. 7.

83. Quoted *ibid.*

84. Prosecution Document A 49. Regarding the atrocities perpetrated by the totalitarian regime, Naumann felt that it was nonsensical "to condemn as crimes against humanity what was in reality nothing but the fulfillment of a historical duty." (Prosecution Document E 93.)

85. FDP (V/61), p. 1. The court that discontinued the proceedings against Naumann and his friends and set them free came to a similar conclusion in regard to Naumann's political orientation, albeit without conjecturing on his subjective sense of predestination. "He who—like Dr. Naumann, above all—has eagerly and emphatically approved of National

Socialism for some time, and after years tries to play once again a role in political life without unambiguously rejecting [those parts] of National Socialist ideology that are irreconcilable with the existing constitutional order, opens himself to the well-founded suspicion that . . . by his reappearance on the political stage he merely wishes to pursue the old goals. Every other interpretation would fly in the face of experience (*lebensfremd*) and be unrealistic." Reproduced in Friedrich Grimm, *Unrecht im Rechtsstaat. Tatsachen und Dokumente zur politischen Justiz, dargestellt am Fall Naumann* (Tübingen: Deutsche Hochschullehrer-Zeitung, 1957), pp. 226–227, and Manfred Jenke, *Verschwörung von rechts?* (Berlin: Colloquium, [c. 1961]), pp. 437–439.

86. Quoted in Prosecution Document B 4. Achenbach, as will be seen, held very similar views on this matter.

87. Quoted in Wesemann (V/65), p. 5. Also Prosecution Document A 34.

88. Letter of Frau Dr. Mehringer of June 17, 1952. Prosecution Document Z 5.

89. The arrests were made in the night of January 14/15, 1953, in Hamburg, Düsseldorf, and Solingen. The persons affected were Naumann, Scheel, Zimmermann, Haselmeyer, Siepen, and Scharping. On the fifteenth, Kaufmann was arrested. Bornemann could not be found; he remained in hiding until the case was turned over to German authorities, to whom he surrendered voluntarily. The fullest treatment of the Naumann case is partly in the form of an apologia by Naumann's defense counsel, Friedrich Grimm (V/85). The other secondary materials, especially in newspapers, on this sensational case are, of course, multitudinous. Only a few additional ones can be cited here: *Feinde der Demokratie* (Nordmark), no. 4 (February 12, 1953), pp. 1–14; "Nau-Nau!" *Der Spiegel,* VII, 4 (January 21, 1953), 5–8; "Der Mufti lässt grüssen," *ibid.* VII, 5 (January 28, 1953), 5–6; "Verschwörung wider den Geist," *ibid.*, VII, 20 (May 13, 1953), 5–6; "Angebot der CDU," *ibid.*, VII, 32 (August 5, 1953), 6; *Feinde der Demokratie* (Lower Saxony), II, nos. 3, 4, 5, 7, 8, 10 (January–August, 1953); and *Deutsche Presse Agentur* (*dpa*), *Infs.* 2038 (November 17, 1952), 92 (January 19, 1953), 97 (January 20), 105 (January 21), 209 (February 5), 862 (June 10), 1136 (July 30), p. 2, 1144 (August 3), p. 2, and 1269 (September 2), p. 3.

90. Wilke had been a high Hitler Youth leader and editor in chief of the Hitler Youth house organ, *Wille und Macht.* After the war he was employed by the Hugo Stinnes Corporation. Wilke died suddenly in 1952. See *Deutsche Presse Agentur* (*dpa*), *Inf.* 35/55 (March 25, 1955).

91. See FDP (V/61), p. 5.

92. In the style of resigned understatement which is so typical of the FDP "Confidential Report" (V/61), the new party newspaper is characterized as follows: "The position (*Haltung*) of the . . . weekly newspaper *Die Deutsche Zukunft* is unclear and erratic (*uneinheitlich*). In part, and especially in the beginning, a restorative tendency was represented" (p. 14).

93. *Ibid.*, p. 5.

94. *The Wiener Library Bulletin* (London), VI, 1–2 (January–April

1952), 7. See also Radomír Luža, *The Transfer of the Sudeten Germans. A Study of Czech-German Relations, 1933–1962* ([New York:] New York University Press, 1964), p. 65, footnote 11.

95. See below, text near VIII/63.

96. FDP (V/61), pp. 8–9. Also cf. the confidential letter of Wolfgang Sarg, chairman of the anti-Semitic, Nazi intelligence network, Natinform, to his deputy, June 30, 1953. Döring, who was later to become the FDP's deputy leader, died in January, 1963, at the age of forty-three. The so-called German Program was the frankly nationalist platform of the now radicalized FDP Land organization. It was to form the program of the "national rally" and as such was designed, by its blatant nationalism, to entice those who could still be aroused by unscrupulous appeals to their resentments and residual nostalgia for the past.

97. Fritzsche died on September 27, 1953.

98. It has also been alleged that the German Program was coauthored by Werner Best. See SPD, *Das wahre Gesicht der FDP* (Bonn: n. pub., July, 1953), p. 8.

99. Conversation of January 11, 1952, reproduced (from wire-tap tapes) in Wesemann (V/65), June 11, 1953, p. 5.

100. Conversation of January 17, 1952. *Ibid.*

101. FDP (V/61), p. 12.

102. *Ibid.*, pp. 11–12.

103. In the Ennepe-Ruhr District, the ex-Nazi mayor and SS Colonel August Düsterloh was elected to the county council on the FDP list. In Wesel, the former Nazi mayor of Breslau and NSDAP Reich Speaker Josef Schönwälder was elected to the city council on the FDP ticket. Similarly in Cologne, the Nazi city treasurer, Oskar-Wilhelm Türk; in Rheydt, the SS special judge, Rudolf Gahlen; in Neheim-Hüsten, former NS Local Group Leader Heinrich Beckschäfer; in Brilon, Nazi Landrat Schramm, Local Group Leader Görge, and Nazi Mayor Wespers; and in Plettenberg, Gau Propaganda Speaker Alfred Steuer. See SPD (V/98), p. 25.

104. For the developments in Lower Saxony, see the detailed account in *Feinde der Demokratie* (Lower Saxony), II, 8 (May–June, 1953), and 9 (July, 1953). The office manager was Günther Schwägermann, once Goebbels' adjutant. The business manager was the former Nazi mayor of Kattowitz, Hans Tiessler, who headed the fund-raising Society for the Promotion of the Lower Saxon Economy. The director of organization was the former NSKK leader, Friedrich G. Brinkmann. Hitler Youth Leader Gustav Ernst, of Northeim, a cold fanatic who had been the representative of the party chancellery at the staff of the Supreme Commander West, became FDP district secretary and a member of the Land executive board. The chairmanship of the agricultural committee of the Land organization was turned over to the SRP man, Ernst Ostermann. The SRP member of the Land diet, Heinz Knoke, was also placed on that committee. Such other former SRP functionaries as Werner Bänsch, an old Nazi district leader, and the former SRP District Leaders Hans Meise and Kurt Rediges also found a congenial haven in the FDP. For a more complete list see *Parlamentarisch-Politischer Pressedienst*, 90/55 (August 8, 1955), item 7.

105. Wesemann (V/65), June 13, 1953, p. 7.

106. See below, XVII/62–65. The most humorous comment on the bitter intraparty struggles in the FDP was made by one of the nationalists, Landtag deputy Winfried Hedergott, at the Land convention of the Lower Saxon FDP on August 1–2, 1953, at Northeim: "Good Lord, everyone here, after all, is for Naumann—some for Friedrich, the others for Werner." (Friedrich Naumann [1860–1919], the great progressive, nationalist liberal, was one of the founders of the German Democratic Party [DDP] and thus an ancestor of the liberal-democratic wing of the FDP.)

107. After the war, Hunke became secretary general of the Academy for Spacial (*Raum*) Research and Planning, an organization, located in Hanover, which enjoys some public financial subvention through the Lower Saxon Ministry of the Interior. In the course of a change of the Lower Saxon government, subsequent to the Land election of 1955, the BHE, one of the coalition partners, on whose ticket Hunke had been elected to the Land parliament, insisted that he be given the post of state secretary in the Ministry for Social Security. This caused considerable discussion in the cabinet, most of it apparently on the question of Hunke's professional qualification for the post, not on his political qualifications. He finally came into the ministry in the rank of ministerial councillor. Later he became vice-chairman of the BHE's Land organization. *Feinde der Demokratie* (Lower Saxony), IV, 9–10 (August–September, 1955), 36. See also above, V/63; and below, VIII/88; text near XVII/143.

108. See Wesemann (V/105).

109. See below, Chapter XV, Section C.

110. Quoted in Wesemann (V/65).

111. Quoted in Wesemann (V/82).

112. British intelligence report (V/12), paragraphs 43–46. A former "intelligence agent" of the Bruderschaft formulated it this way: "Kaufmann and Scheel . . . maintained far-flung political contacts; thus, e.g., to [Waldemar] Kraft who sought advice — especially from Kaufmann — regarding the build-up of the then newly founded BHE." (From a confidential report, September, 1966.)

113. See above, V/1.

Chapter VI. Nationalist Neutralism and Soviet Policy

1. U.S. Department of State, Office of the High Commissioner for Germany, *2nd Quarterly Report on Germany, January 1–March 31, 1950,* p. 42. The exact number of "neutralists" in Germany at that time is difficult to establish, since much depends on the definition of neutralism and on identifying the kind of neutralism which a particular survey instrument measures. For instance, in July, 1950, a randomized sample of 1,500 to 1,800 adults was asked: "What is your personal position: in today's world conflict [do you stand] on the side of the West or of the East, or would you say that you are neutral, that is, neither for the East nor for the West?" In response, 64 per cent opted for the West, 2 per cent for the East; 26 per cent considered

themselves neutral; 8 per cent were indifferent or undecided. A year later a similar sample was asked: "What do you personally consider most important: that we Germans make friends with the Americans, that we make friends with the Russians, or that we assume a position of neutrality between the two?" In this instance, only 29 per cent thought that close relations with America were important; 1 per cent were for friendship with Russia; 60 per cent thought neutrality most important; and 10 per cent were undecided. Again, in March, 1951, a cross-sample of adults was asked: "Do you favor German participation in the defense of Western Europe, or are you for the neutralization of Germany?" This time 39 per cent favored participation; 36 per cent, neutralization; and 25 per cent were undecided. Noelle and Neumann (II/4), pp. 332, 353.

2. This does not mean that reunification was at that time widely considered the most important problem, worthy of any degree of sacrifice. In July, 1952, an opinion survey asked: "If you had to decide, what is at this time more important to you: security vis-à-vis Russia, or the unity of Germany?" Fifty-one per cent preferred safety to unity, 33 per cent, unity to safety; and 16 per cent were undecided. *Ibid.*, p. 315. When a Soviet offer suggested reunification of the four Zones at the price of renouncing all claims to the Eastern territories under Polish and Soviet administration, only 12 per cent of the respondents were willing to accept the offer (and even then with major qualifications), while 75 per cent rejected renunciation as the price for reunification. *Ibid.*, p. 317.

3. In January, 1952, 52 per cent of a national sample expected reunification through peaceful negotiation, while 43 per cent saw no hope for reunification on that basis. *Ibid.*, p. 315.

4. The importance and nature of the nationalist neutralist's virulently anti-Western affect are cleverly presented in the form of a fictitious conversation in Roland Klaus, "Nicht gestern, Freund, morgen!" *Aus Politik und Zeitgeschichte,* supplement of *Das Parlament* (Bonn), December 28, 1958.

5. For a very brief summary of these measures and of the activity which allegedly justified them, see U.S. Department of State, Office of the High Commissioner for Germany, "Communist Campaign against German Defense," *7th Quarterly Report on Germany, April 1–June 30, 1951,* pp. 57–62. For a cautious defense of the German record on the full protection of civil liberties, see C. R. Foster and George Stambuk, "Judicial Protection of Civil Liberties in Germany," *Political Studies,* IV (1956), 190–194. Heinrich Hannover's vigorous indictment, *Politische Diffamierung der Opposition im freiheitlich-demokratischen Rechtsstaat* (Dortmund-Barop: Pläne, 1962), written from the point of view of the democratic Left, came to my attention too late to be incorporated in my remarks, but the evidence cited by Hannover amply supports my critical view of the Adenauer regime's activity in the vital area of freedom of expression and association.

6. Taubert had been head of Division (*Referat*) Pro. II in the Goebbels ministry. As such he had been in charge of "1. Propagandistic struggle against political opponents (particularly Jewry, Communism, Freemasonry, reactionaries, etc.). 2. Church policies . . . 9. Supreme guidance of the 'Anti-Semitic Action' and of the 'Institute for Scientific Research on the

Soviet Union,' as well as political direction of the publishing house 'Nibelungen' and of the periodical *Die Aktion.*" In 1941, Gobbels named Taubert (who had become known as "Dr. Anti-") "general division head for all questions of the Eastern-European space within my scope, and plenipotentiary in the Rosenberg commissariat." In 1933, Taubert had founded the equally anti-Jewish General Association of German Anti-Communist Societies and prided himself on being the wirepuller behind the Anti-Comintern. In November, 1936, he organized "the first confidential international anti-Communist conference in Feldafing near Munich," which fulfilled the objectives of "unflinching continuation of anti-Bolshevik and anti-Jewish propaganda" and of creating "friendly organizations in every country of the world." After the invasion of Poland, his fertile brain "conceived the idea of a colossal film that would once and for all unmask 'the eternal Jew.' " Weinreich (V/23), pp. 113–115, 133, 284. In the postwar period, Taubert claimed to have revised his views on the Jews and recanted his anti-Semitism and to be "fighting most sharply against every form of a return to totalitarianism and anti-Semitism." See Taubert's brief in his libel suit against *Der Weg* (Buenos Aires), reproduced in *Deutscher Informationsdienst,* no. 545 (March 6, 1956), pp. 2–3.

7. Countless articles have been written on the rigidity and self-defeating sterility of Adenauer's Eastern policies. Among recent efforts are Melvin Croan, "Reality and Illusion in Soviet-German Relations," *Survey,* no. 44/45 (October, 1962), pp. 12–28, and Fritz René Allemann's "Adenauer's Eastern Policy," *ibid.,* pp. 29–36. A not uninteresting recent contribution, by a conservative Lower Saxon Guelph who through the years appeared to have supported Adenauer's inflexible orientation to the West, is Wolf Christian von Harling, *Deutschland zwischen den Mächten* (Hamburg: Holsten, 1962).

8. By far the most complete account of the so-called national-revolutionary wing of the Conservative Revolution is provided by Schüddekopf (I/1). My discussion, however, goes beyond specific national-revolutionary conceptions, to convey the notion of German socialism as it was used by all strands of the Conservative Revolution, including the Young Conservatives. For a brief, but very skillful, American account of National Bolshevism, see von Klemperer (I/1), pp. 139–150, and his much earlier "Kommt ein Viertes Reich? Zur Geschichte des Nationalbolschewismus in Deutschland," *Dokumente,* VIII, 2 (1952), 129–144. (This is a translation of an article entitled "Toward a 4th Reich? The History of National Bolshevism," *Review of Politics,* XIII, 2 [April, 1951], 191–210.) In addition, see Abraham Ascher and Guenter Lewy, "National Bolshevism in Weimar Germany: Alliance of Political Extremes against Democracy," *Social Research,* XXIII, 4 (Winter, 1956), 450–480; Stern (I/1), pp. 246–253; and Arthur Spencer, "National Bolshevism," *Survey,* no. 44/45 (October, 1962), pp. 133–152.

9. Nor did Eastern influence in Germany. In the words of Friedrich Wilhelm Foerster: "Mais l'Asie ne commence pas en Prusse orientale; elle a rayonné bien au delà de cette province sur le monde allemand tout entier —et tout d'abord par l'intermédiaire de l'Ordre Teutonique, qui avait repris la tradition totalitaire de Bysance et avait essayé de la réaliser dans son

oeuvre de colonisation en Allemagne orientale et de la répandre à partir de là. Ainsi la plus grande tragédie allemande a été que l'Asie et l'Europe se sont heurtées en plein milieu de l'Allemagne." "La position de l'Allemagne entre l'Est et l'Ouest. Les dangers de la reconstitution de l'armée allemande," *L'Année Politique et Economique,* XXX, 137 (June–July, 1957), 213.

10. Koppel S. Pinson, *Modern Germany* (New York: Macmillan, 1954), p. 39.

11. See Herbert Helbig, *Die Träger der Rapallo Politik* (Göttingen: Vandenhöck & Ruprecht, 1958); and on the German army's relation to the Soviet Union, see (among many others) Edward Hallett Carr, *German-Soviet Relations between the Two World Wars, 1919–1939* (Baltimore: Johns Hopkins Press, 1951); F. L. Carsten, "The Reichswehr and the Red Army 1920–1933," *Survey,* no. 44/45 (October, 1962), pp. 114–132; Gordon A. Craig, *The Politics of the Prussian Army, 1640–1945* (Oxford: Clarendon, 1955); Otto Gessler, *Reichswehrpolitik in der Weimarer Zeit* (Stuttgart: Deutsche Verlags-Anstalt, 1958); Harold J. Gordon, *The Reichswehr and the German Republic 1919–1926* (Princeton: Princeton University Press, 1957); G. W. F. Hallgarten, "General Hans von Seeckt and Russia 1920–1922," *The Journal of Modern History,* XXI, 1 (March, 1949), 28–34; Gustav Hilger and Alfred G. Meyer, *The Incompatible Allies: A Memoir-History of German-Soviet Relations, 1918–1941* (New York: Macmillan, 1953); and Hans Speidel, "Reichswehr und Rote Armee," *Vierteljahrshefte für Zeitgeschichte,* I, 1 (January, 1953), 9–45.

12. See Hans W. Gatzke, "Russo-German Military Collaboration during the Weimar Period," *American Historical Review,* LXIII, 3 (April, 1958), 565–597. Cf. also Foerster (VI/9), p. 213: "La République de Weimar elle-même n'a nullement signifié un retour résolu de l'Allemagne à la civilisation occidentale. Elle a édifié une façade démocratique, mais seulement dans le but de tromper l'Occident. Derrière cette façade, elle a collaboré avec la Russie pour réaliser le réarmament allemand et pour pouvoir un jour annuler le traité de Versailles."

13. See Neurohr (I/1), pp. 116–139, 202–219; and more recently Kurt Sontheimer's excellent *Antidemokratisches Denken* (I/1), pp. 341–359. On "German socialism" it might now be useful to consult Herman Lebovics, *A Socialism for the German Middle Classes: The Social Conservative Response to Industrialism 1900–1933* (Ph.D. dissertation, Yale University, 1965). Unfortunately it came to the attention of the present author too late to enable him to apply Lebovics' findings to this chapter.

14. For the historical antecedents to these theories of social imperialism, see Franz Neumann, *Behemoth: The Structure and Practice of National Socialism 1933–1944* (New York: Oxford University Press, 1944), pp. 104–107, 184–210.

15. Spengler (I/17), p. 29.

16. *Ibid.,* p. 30. Cf. Mann (I/12), pp. xxxiv ff., for a violent diatribe on the incompatibility of Teutonism and Romanism. See also Neumann (VI/14), pp. 197–198.

17. Spengler (I/17), pp. 41, 42.

18. E. Günther Gründel, *Die Sendung der Jungen Generation, Versuch einer umfassenden revolutionären Sinndeutung der Krise* (Munich: Beck, 1932), pp. 239–243, 247. Cf. Arthur Moeller van den Bruck, *Das Dritte Reich* (4th ed.; Hamburg: Hanseatische Verlagsanstalt, 1931), p. 65. Incidentally, a very similar syndrome appears in Joseph Goebbels prior to his surrender to Hitler. See his diary entries from August 12, 1925, to July 23, 1926, in Heiber (III/5). Gründel's judgments would, of course, not be shared by the more radical national-Bolshevik thinkers.

19. Gründel (VI/18), pp. 227–229.

20. *Ibid.*, p. 230.

21. On the "anticapitalist longing" of the threatened and radicalized middle classes in Weimar Germany, see Wolfgang Hock, *Deutscher Antikapitalismus. Der ideologische Kampf gegen die freie Wirtschaft im Zeichen der grossen Krise,* pref. by Heinrich Rittershausen, Veröffentlichungen des Instituts für Bankwirtschaft und Bankrecht an der Universität Köln, Wirtschaftswissenschaftliche Reihe, no. 9 (Frankfurt: Knapp, [1960]).

22. *Die Tat* itself summarized the main demands of its editors: "An end to international trade, the authoritarian state, a planned economy, autarchy, South-East policies, and the necessity for a synthesis of nationalism and socialism, Right and Left, into a new folk community." "Der Weg der Tat," *Die Tat,* XXIV, 6 (September, 1932), 517, cited in Bracher (III/7), p. 355, note 85.

23. See the perceptive essay on Moeller in Stern (I/1), pp. 183–267, and, above all, Schwierskott (I/1).

24. It would be instructive to trace the connections between the social and political thought of the Conservative Revolution in Europe, specifically in Germany, and the post-World War II nationalist-socialist ideologies in the developing countries, especially Nasserism. The history of the world-wide movement of nationalist anticapitalism has yet to be written.

25. Especially from Moeller van den Bruck's *Das Recht der jungen Völker* (Munich: Piper, 1919) and from his essays, which later were collected by Hans Schwarz in the quite different *Das Recht der jungen Völker: Aus dem politischen Nachlass* (Berlin: Der Nahe Osten, 1932) and in *Sozialismus und Aussenpolitik* (Breslau: Korn, 1933).

26. Cf. Kurt Sontheimer, "Der Tatkreis," *Vierteljahrshefte für Zeitgeschichte,* VII, 3 (July, 1959), 229–260.

27. Zehrer is currently editor in chief of the important newspaper *Die Welt* (Hamburg). Another leading member of the *Tat* Circle, Ferdinand Fried (pseudonym for Friedrich Zimmermann), is also on the staff of *Die Welt.* Indeed, two of the three remaining initial chief collaborators on *Die Tat,* Ernst Wilhelm Eschmann and Giselher Wirsing, also hold prominent positions in German postwar journalism. (Cf. above, V/23). For Zehrer's radical elitism in his *Tat*-years see Walter Struve, "Hans Zehrer as a Neoconservative Elite Theorist," *American Historical Review,* LXX, 4 (July, 1965), 1035-1057. Wildenmann (II/5) demonstrates the startling persistance of strongly authoritarian features in Zehrer's thought by comparing Zehrer's editorial in *Die Welt* of February 6, 1960, with his *Tat* article of October,

1931 (p. 122). For Fried's lustrous career in the immediate vicinity of Heinrich Himmler, Reinhard Heydrich, and Richard-Walther Darré in the first years following the Nazi seizure of power, see his own *curriculum vitae,* reproduced in Poliakov and Wulf (V/23), p. 368. In this connection it is instructive to compare Fried's *Der Aufstieg der Juden* (Goslar: Blut und Boden, [c. 1937]) and his *Die soziale Revolution. Verwandlung von Wirtschaft und Gesellschaft* (Leipzig: Goldmann, [c. 1942]) with *Der Umsturz der Gesellschaft* (Stuttgart: Deutsche Verlags–Anstalt, [1950]) and *Das Abenteuer des Abendlandes* ([Düsseldorf, Cologne:] Diederichs, [c. 1950]). In his postwar books, Fried's earlier, primitive anti-Semitism and preference for the authoritarian state have been deleted, his arrogance, medievalist romanticism, and amateurish historicism have remained.

28. For an account of his collaboration, with emphasis on the national–Communists, see Spencer (VI/8).

29. See, for instance, Beck-Broichsitter's interview with the *Deutsche Presse Agentur* (*dpa*), *Inf.* 279 (March 1, 1950), p. 4.

30. Franke-Gricksch, "Europa, Aufmarsch- oder Kraftfeld," *Die Bruderschaft* (Hanover), January, 1950, p. 4.

31. *Ibid.,* p. 11.

32. *Ibid.,* p. 21.

33. *Ibid.,* pp. 21–22.

34. The confidential report which quotes Franke is unsigned. Neither the accuracy of the information nor the reliability of the informant could be established. For a brief survey of Communist tactics in the summer of 1950, see U.S. Department of State, Office of the High Commissioner for Germany, "New Phase of Communist Tactics in Germany," *4th Quarterly Report on Germany, July 1–September 30, 1950,* pp. 35–41.

35. Letter to General Hasso von Manteuffel, an associate of the Bruderschaft in its early and secret stages of development, dated July 31, 1950.

36. Beck, "Der Kernpunkt," *Die Bruderschaft (Rundschreiben an den Freundeskreis Hannover),* August, 1950, pp. 2–5.

37. See interview with Colonel Detlev von Platen, anti-Hitler General Staff officer, who was the information and intelligence chief of the Bruderschaft, *Deutsche Presse Agentur (dpa), Inf.* 1066 (August 20, 1950).

38. Franke-Gricksch (V/45).

39. Beck's signing of the Stockholm "Peace Petition" was announced by the SED Press Service. In an interview with *Deutsche Presse Agentur (dpa),* Beck denied having signed the document. *Inf.* 929 (August 8, 1950), p. 1.

40. In 1930, Scheringer had been expelled from the Reichswehr for Nazi activities and sent to prison. A few months later he created a sensation when he announced from his jail cell that he had resigned from the NSDAP and joined the Communist Party.

41. S-r, "Bruderschaft in West und Ost," *Frankfurter Rundschau,* March 3, 1951.

42. Gerhardt Boldt is the author of an eyewitness account, *Die letzten Tage der Reichskanzlei* (Hamburg: Rowohlt, 1947).

43. Affidavit ("Eidesstattliche Erklärung"), a typescript by Fritz Zietlow, dated April 15, 1951. From the information contained in this document, the possibility cannot be excluded that both Boldt and Beck were, in fact, agents of either the Office for the Protection of the Constitution (Verfassungsschutzamt) or an American intelligence agency. Rumors to that effect have consistently hovered around these two men. It has also been said, on equally unsubstantiated grounds, that Franke and Colonel Detlev von Platen were in the pay of the British Secret Service. Only one thing is certain: the Bruderschaft was thoroughly infiltrated, not only by the intelligence services of all the occupying powers, but also by the Verfassungsschutzämter of both the federal government and some of the Länder.

44. See S-r (VI/41). Cf. also *Hannoversche Presse,* February 24, 1951, and Josef Schmidt, "Bruderzwist in der Bruderschaft," *Süddeutsche Zeitung* (Munich), no. 48 (February 27, 1951).

45. A photostat of a copy of the document is in the writer's possession.

46. See below, X/14.

47. Unfortunately, no primary documents have as yet been obtainable to indicate how the Soviet authorities reacted to this memorandum. All we know with reasonable certainty is that Boldt followed up his first trip to East Berlin, at the end of November, with a second visit on December 15–16, 1950. Reports of probably fair accuracy would have us believe that the mediation through the Soviet Zonal News Service, ADN, was not working smoothly and that the Soviet negotiators expressed a merely guarded, formal interest in the entire enterprise. They apparently listened courteously to the Bruderschaft propositions without giving undue encouragement, let alone firm agreement. It is certain that Boldt undertook a third trip to the Eastern sector of Berlin on December 28, 1950, and that he was unable on that occasion to meet any of his previous interlocutors, supposedly because they were on vacation. It is also said that this time Soviet authorities failed even to reimburse Boldt for his travel expenses. It is not at all beyond the range of possibility that Russian caution was due to the fact that they had found out or suspected that Beck and Boldt were working for American Intelligence or were paid *agents provocateurs.* In any event, in the summer of 1951, East German Communist sources called the Bruderschaft "agents of the occupation powers in West Germany" and an important element in Western remilitarization plans. See, for example, German Democratic Republic, National Front of Democratic Germany, National Council, *White Book on the American and British Policy of Intervention in West Germany and the Revival of German Imperialism* (n.p., [1951]), especially pp. 101–102, 151.

48. S-r (VI/41).

49. Cf., for example, interview with Franke-Gricksch, *Deutsche Presse Agentur (dpa), Inf.* 1240 (September 23, 1950).

50. Letter of Beck-Broichsitter to H. L. Rose, September 22, 1950.

51. Letter to H. L. Rose of October 11, 1950. Beck sent a carbon copy to Wilhelm Moll of HiCOG's political affairs division.

52. Cf. below, VIII/43.

53. This familiar national-revolutionary conception is strongly reminiscent of Ernst Niekisch' Resistance Movement (Widerstandsbewegung), whose programmatic motto was "Sparta-Potsdam-Moscow" and which symbolized its characteristic ideology in the form of a Prussian eagle, a sword, a hammer, and a sickle. Cf., J. A. Elten, "Die Brüder von der 'Bruderschaft,' " *Süddeutsche Zeitung* (Munich), no. 216 (September 19, 1950).

54. Grünberg, an intimate of former Gauleiter Erich Koch, and (later) rector of the University of Königsberg, was a member of the Naumann circle and is now prominently associated with the NPD.

55. Gerd Voigt, "Otto Hoetzsch—eine biographische Skizze," *in* Leo Stern, ed., *Der Antikommunismus in Theorie und Praxis des deutschen Imperialismus* ([Halle: Martin-Luther-Universität Halle-Wittenberg,] 1963), pp. 142–156.

56. A photostat of this letter is in the writer's possession.

57. See Beck's complaint about this "probably accidental oversight" in his letters of January 23 and January 29, 1951.

58. *Welt am Sonntag* (Hamburg), no. 7 (February 18, 1951), p. 2.

59. Letter to Bruderrat and to former SS General Georg Ebrecht, district leader of Bruderschaft in Lindau, January 29, 1951.

60. *Deutsche Presse Agentur (dpa), Inf.* 299 (February 26, 1951).

61. Letter of Beck-Broichsitter to one of his political friends, middle of February, 1951. Cf. also Schmidt (VI/44).

62. In actual fact, the split in the Buderschaft into the Beck and Franke factions involved weeks of organizational maneuvering, mutual exclusions, and parliamentary manipulation. According to one testimony, former SS Major Milde, who had worked under SS Colonel Adolf Katz in the personnel division of the SS and who had been instrumental in appointing Franke as Katz's personal assistant, was the driving force behind Franke's exclusion from the Bruderschaft. Milde had learned to hate Franke, whom he accused of having betrayed the anti-Himmler clique in the RSHA, of having worked in the postwar period for the Russians and other intelligence services, of being "dangerous, absolutely unscrupulous," and—like Heydrich—of being adept at making friends with his opponents in order to destroy them, ultimately, all the more effectively. (Letter of Ernst Riggert to Colonel Wolfgang Müller, November 26, 1951. See above, V/11.) In October, 1951, Franke disappeared in East Berlin. He was never heard from again. His wife followed him into the East Zone and likewise disappeared. In 1955, Frau Franke returned to West Germany on the last transport from the Soviet Union. Only then did it become known that she and her husband had been tried in 1952 by a Russian military court on charges of pro-Western intelligence and anti-Soviet propaganda activity. Franke had been condemned to death; his wife received a twenty-five-year sentence. In 1957 the Soviet Red Cross informed the search service of the German Red Cross that Franke–Gricksch had died in a camp in August, 1953. See *Reichsruf* (Hanover), VI, 19 (May 11, 1957), 6.

63. See, for example, a mimeographed letter from the Land organization

Hamburg of the Bruderschaft Deutschland, April, 1952, in which the aim is defined as follows: "We conceive it to be our task to bring together a German elite stratum."

64. Erich P. Neumann and Elisabeth Noelle, eds., *Antworten* (2d ed; Allensbach/Bodensee: Verlag für Demoskopie, 1955), pp. 132, 161. See also the extensive list of polls with suspiciously high antirearmament results in "Was denkt das Volk über den 'Verteidigungsbeitrag'?" Der Führungsring ehemaliger Soldaten, *Rundbrief,* no. 7 (May, 1952), pp. 5–6.

65. Beck-Broichsitter, ed., *Bruderschaft Deutschland* (Hamburg), no. 13 (January, 1952), p. 4.

66. Bruderschaft Deutschland, Land Hamburg, letter of invitation to a meeting, May 29, 1952.

67. Report in *Hannoversche Presse,* February 24, 1951. Cf. also Schmidt (VI/44).

68. See *Deutsche Presse Agentur (dpa), Inf.* 336 (March 7, 1951).

69. In June, 1952, Beck-Broichsitter, who had been borrowing ever more blatantly from the vocabulary and theatrical art of the Nazi movement, finally joined (together with many of his followers) the Socialist Reich Party.

70. Schenke maintains he left the Hitler Youth in 1937, when he could no longer reconcile the "democratic socialism" for which he allegedly stood with the *Führer* principle, which gained ascendancy at that time(!) in the organization. From an interview with Schenke, Hamburg, July 26, 1957.

71. Cf. Helmut Bohn, "Die patriotische Karte in der sowjetischen Deutschlandpolitik (III)," *Ost-Probleme,* VII, 42 (October 21, 1955), 1607. The Hitler Youth Leaders circle's immediate liaison man to the Communists was Wolfgang Plat, former Antifa leader in a Russian prisoner-of-war camp and son of Martin Plat, executive secretary of the Hamburg Free Democratic Party and chairman of the League of Nazi Victims (Bund der Verfolgten des Naziregimes, BVN). Wolfgang was in charge of the "all-German" activity of a Communist-front organization, with special responsibility for liaison to the Hitler Youth Leaders circle. See also Hermann Werdau, "Die Jünger der braunen und roten Diktatur," *PZ-Archiv,* February 5, 1952, pp. 38 ff.

72. The publisher of this paper was Schmitz; the editor in chief was the former *Angriff* editor, Zantke; the managing editor was Jurzeck; and the business manager, the former Hitler Youth official, Georg Beschoner. Cf. below, VI/211.

73. See, for example, "Schluss jetzt," "Auf uns kommt es an," "Wo steht der deutsche Soldat?" *Deutscher Beobachter* (Hamburg), I, 1 (June 8, 1951), 1–2; "Vertrauen zu wem?" *Ibid.,* I, 2 (June 22, 1951), 1–2; "Gleichberechtigung im Sterben!" and " 'Preussens Gloria' auf US-Schalmeien!" *Ibid.,* I, 3 (June 27, 1951), 2. In contrast to the scathing sarcasm and bitterness which characterized the *Beobachter's* handling of all things Western, especially the relationship between the so-called war generation and the Bonn administration, we find this description of the relationship of youth in the Soviet Zone to its government: "The sorry complaint of the West German coalition parties . . . that the war generation cannot be approached is discredited by the

fact that in East Germany, cooperation has in a large measure been achieved. To be sure, that was hardly accomplished by the Western method of merely asking for 'young legs' for the parties, whose 'heads' intended to continue to keep things under their control, or of attempting to capture the political will of the war generation with a 'grocery store' or 'some other well-paid position.' " *Ibid.,* I, 1 (June 8, 1951), 1. It is worthy of special note that the *Deutscher Beobachter* referred to the Soviet Zone as East Germany. No one does that in Germany who does not wish to imply that he has written off what is really East Germany; namely, the Eastern provinces under Polish and Russian administration. Invariably, West Germans refer to the Soviet Zone as Central Germany. Only Ulbricht and the Soviet Zonal Communists have renounced all claims to the territories east of the Oder-Neisse line.

74. For the policies propounded by the Nauheim circle and characterizations of its leading members, see Wilhelm Cornides, "Die Neutralitätslehre des Nauheimer Kreises," *Politisches Archiv,* VI, 8 (April 20, 1951), 3879–3892.

75. The Second European Congress of the European National (in Malmö, Sweden, May 12–16, 1951) at which Priester played a very prominent role, accepted unanimously the report of its program committee which contained the following: "The Congress is of the opinion that it will be important in the future to follow closely the splinter movements within Stalinist Communism and to take up contact with those who have not compromised themselves by collaboration with reactionary democracy. . . ." (VII/20).

76. See *Deutsche Presse Agentur (dpa), Inf.* 95 (January 17, 1951).

77. Erwin Mebus, Hans D. Duelfer, Helmut Schudnat, and Bruno Fricke, Otto Strasser's erstwhile confidant.

78. See below, VI/130 and nearby text. *Deutsche Presse Agentur (dpa), Inf.* 80 and 95 (January 15 and 17, 1951).

79. A former activist in the nationalist-neutralist movement, J. F. G. Grosser (in a letter to the author of June 9, 1961), suggests that Heinemann's refusal to sign the proclamation was due also to his dislike for Gereke. Heinemann, Mrs. Helene Wessel, the former chairman of the Center Party, and other democratic pacifists were under constant pressure to broaden their political organizations by acknowledging their "duty toward the Right." That meant, in short, the construction of an anti-Adenauer coalition across all existing shadings of political opinion (except for the official opposition party, the SPD, which was rejected as mere "sham opposition"), including the extreme nationalists. Heinemann resisted this pressure at first. Throughout the summer of 1952, negotiations for such an all-encompassing opposition bloc were carried on. The aim of men like Theodor Kögler was to persuade Heinemann and Mrs. Wessel to include in the leadership group of their prospective party a nationalist general, a former Nazi who had not been criminally implicated, and a nationalist of more subdued opinions. The names suggested to Heinemann were General Student, former Staatsrat Wilhelm Meinberg, and the Zeppelin pioneer, Hugo Eckener. When the All-German People's Party (Gesamtdeutsche Volkspartei, GVP) was

founded on November 30, 1952, without nationalists and Nazis in the top leadership, disappointment was great. Nonetheless, in the electoral campaign of 1953, the word was passed by radically anti-West nationalists and national-Bolsheviks to vote for the Heinemann-Wessel party. (This whole development is succinctly described in a letter of Theodor Kögler to Wilhelm Benning, December 12, 1952.) For the attitude of East-oriented nationalists, the following is characteristic: "Teich told me today that for the next election it is of utmost importance to deliver the votes for the All-German People's Party of Dr. Heinemann. Another party would be out of the question. The SRP is banned; the DB and DG would soon follow. The DRP is merely a sham opposition. . . . Helene Wessel . . . to be sure, is a bitch (*Mistvieh*), but she is useful." (Letter of informant of March 9, 1953.) After the outlawry of the SRP in October, 1952, its Land chairman of Rhineland-Palatinate, Werner Körper, was said to have "negotiated" with Heinemann and Mrs. Wessel. The Land leader of the DU, Otto Hess, was also reported to have had private talks with them. (From an interview with Körper and Miss Albrecht, Körper's fiancée, December 2, 1952.) In 1954, Heinemann participated in the meetings of the Foreign Policy Association (Gesellschaft für Aussenpolitik), which embraced the political spectrum from the notorious Left-neutralist pastor, Professor Helmut Gollwitzer, to such radical ex-Nazis and nationalists as the former Bruderschaft and DU leaders Gottfried Griesmayr and Wilhelm Kiefer. At that time Heinemann also welcomed into his Aktionskreis the ultranationalist Parachute General Student, SS Major Fritz Brehm (cf. below, VI/217), and Schenke. Rumor had it that the Aktionskreis also enjoyed the patronage of such prominent SPD members as the Bundestag deputies Herbert Wehner and Fritz Erler. For additional details on the Foreign Policy Association, see below, VI/219. See *Deutscher Informationsdienst,* no. 548 (March 13, 1956), p. 3, and Werner Kugler, "Angstpsychose von 'links bis rechts'?" *Die Brücke,* II, 6 (June 10, 1955), 1.

80. For a complete list of the signatories of the "Call to Peace," see Cornides (VI/74), pp. 3891–3892.

81. Cf. Ekkehard Genz, "Politische Träumer an Bonner Tischen," *Welt am Sonntag* (Hamburg), September 30, 1951, and the letter to the editor of October 2, 1951, by Theodor Voss. Voss was one of the participants, together with Noack, Kögler, Schenke, Erich Arp, and others, of a planning conference for neutralist tactics, discussed in the article by Genz.

82. See *Der Informationsdienst,* no. 51 (February 10, 1951), pp. 1–2.

83. For an East German account of this and subsequent neutralist activities, see German Democratic Republic (VI/47), pp. 167–193, especially pp. 182–183. This source places the number of delegates at the Essen conference at 1700. Cf. also Cornides (VI/74), p. 3887.

84. U.S. Department of State (VI/5), p. 58.

85. See *Der Informationsdienst,* no. 59 (March 11, 1951). East German Foreign Minister Ernst Dertinger sent his secretary, Mrs. Ilsa Bubener, under a false name, as an observer. From an interview with Schenke, Hamburg, July 26, 1957; see also Cornides (VI/74), p. 3887.

86. See, for example, his romantic, historical verse dramas, "Heinrich

von Kleists Tod," "Im Schatten des Kaisers," and "Der Weg zum Vesuv," contained in Rudolf Jungnickel, *Gewissen und Gewalt* (Coburg: Veste, 1954). In 1946–1947, Jungnickel was Dramaturg at the Stadttheater in Nordhausen (Thuringia). Before that, he had taught school at Gotha where he resigned in January, 1946, because he thought it immoral to teach under conditions of foreign occupation. From an interview with Jungnickel, Bonn, May 26, 1957.

87. "Rudolf Jungnickels 'Papenheim'-Briefe und das 'Deutsche Manifest,' " *Die Brücke,* II, 3 (March, 1955), 5.

88. Jungnickel, *Ich will euch sagen was Not tut. Rede eines jungen Deutschen* (Frankfurt am Main: Hilbert, 1948), p. 3: "Und mit hitzigem Eifer begann ich alsdann, den Krebs des mephistophelischen Intellekts, jenes materialistische Denken einer verlogenen Intelligenz, aufzuspüren und dawider zu handeln!" Jungnickel insists that his opposition to the parties had its source not in resentment against the parliamentary or democratic order, but in his conviction that supporting them was tantamount to furthering the fatal tendencies toward "ideologization" and "totalitarianization."

89. *Das Flugblatt,* January 15, 1949. Prior to 1948, Jungnickel's efforts were exclusively in the nonpolitical intellectual area. Anxious not to be pushed into a political engagement before the cultural and intellectual unity of Germany had been clearly established, Jungnickel sought "to awake the spiritual consciousness of youth" and to arm it in "defense against spiritual alienation." Jungnickel found the root of all evil in the "ideologization of Germany's intellectual life," which, he felt, was bound to result in the destruction of Germany's "spiritual unity."

90. See Jungnickel's brochure, *Sammlung der Jugend* (n.p., n.d).

91. The aim and organizational plan of this enterprise can be gleaned from a throwaway addressed to "Deutsche Männer! Deutsche Jugend!" and dated "Christmas 1950, New Year 1951." While still insisting on waging the battle on the "spiritual" level, Jungnickel now no longer saw his task in the total spiritual regeneration of the personality. He had furthermore reconciled himself to the necessity of traditional organization, painful as it was to borrow pages from the book of bureaucratic rationalism. A few hours prior to the opening of the German Congress, the Peace Corps West held a meeting in Frankfurt's St. Paul's Church. There Jungnickel was said to have argued that the People's Police of the Soviet Zone constituted no danger to peace and that if, despite the Soviet Union's peaceful intentions, the Federal Republic should nonetheless be occupied, the thing to do was to permit oneself to be "run over." Sentiments such as these prompted Cornides to call the Peace Corps West a Communist-front organization. Cornides (VI/74), p. 3892.

92. The outrage of the Hitler Youth Leader circle at Priester's indiscretion was massive. See "Der Weg der Nationalen Opposition," *Deutscher Beobachter* (Hamburg), I, 2 (June 22, 1951), 12.

93. See *Der Informationsdienst,* no. 117 (October 2, 1951).

94. The hope was to corral the votes of the younger generation in the labor unions, on the farms, and in the religious organizations. Discussions

were carried on also with such unregenerate folkish radicals as Reinhold Kriszat and Karl-Heinz Heubaum. Kriszat was the editor and Heubaum the publisher of a blatantly folkish-*bündisch* youth magazine, *Widerhall,* which was apparently to be used as the core publication of the new undertaking. See the editorial "Realer Wille zur Not-Wende," *Widerhall,* II, Sonderfolge (end of September/beginning of October, 1951), 1–2. Note there also the neutralist poem "Ode of a German," signed "J.", but most likely by Jungnickel. Heubaum, incidentally, was later convicted twice for distributing anti-Semitic literature and after his third conviction evaded jail by fleeing into the East Zone. (See *Deutscher Informationsdienst,* no. 604 [October 29, 1956].) For Kriszat, see below, VII/33, X/93 and nearby text.

95. Letter of Karl–Heinz Heubaum to W. Schulz von Thun, May 15, 1952. The program of the party had been worked out by the publisher of the *Informationsbrief der Dritten Front,* Alexander Braun. It called for armed neutrality. (Program draft of November 1, 1951, and accompanying letter of Braun of November 2, 1951.)

96. For details on Brüning's and Rauschning's speeches, see *Deutscher Informationsdienst,* no. 359 (April 2, 1954), pp. 1–2; no. 367 (May 5, 1954), pp. 2–3; no. 382 (May 29, 1954), pp. 1–6. See also Hermann Rauschning's *Deutschland zwischen West und Ost* (Berlin: Christian, [1950]); *Ist Friede noch möglich?* (Heidelberg: Vowinckel, 1953), and *Mitten ins Herz* (Berlin: Henssel, 1955). Cf. also Heinrich Brüning, *Die Vereinigten Staaten und Europa. Ein Vortrag gehalten im Rhein-Ruhr-Klub, Düsseldorf* (Stuttgart: Deutsche Verlags–Anstalt, [1954]).

97. See *Deutscher Informationsdienst,* no. 421 (November 12, 1954); no. 424 (November 29, 1954); no. 434 (January 5, 1955); no. 437 (January 14, 1955); no. 439 (January 22, 1955); and no. 453 (March 16, 1955).

98. See below, VI/226.

99. Colonel Bogislav von Bonin was later to denounce the newspaper as a cat's-paw for Soviet Russian interests. For von Bonin's own foreign political and strategic views, see his lecture before the Arbeitsgemeinschaft Sozialdemokratischer Akademiker as reported in *Vorwärts* (Bad Godesberg), July 1, 1955, p. 5. Von Bonin's background, strategic views, and eventual public insubordination are described in some detail in Hans Speier, *German Rearmament and Atomic War* (Evanston, Ill.: Row, Peterson, 1957), pp. 75–83.

100. Hermann Schaefer had left the "national-Bolshevik" weekly, *Die Nation,* to put out the *Rheinisch-Westfälische Nachrichten.* About developments in Schaefer's new paper see *Deutscher Informationsdienst,* no. 539 (February 12, 1956), pp. 1–4; no. 552 (March 3, 1956), p. 1; no. 553 (April 9, 1956), pp. 1–6; no. 563 (May 18, 1956); no. 702 (November 13, 1957), pp. 3–4; no. 743 (May 29, 1958), pp. 1–2.

In 1958 Schaefer, under the pseudonym Hans-Georg Hermann, published a defense of Viktor Agartz entitled *Verraten und Verkauft* (Fulda: Fuldaer Verlagsanstalt), which was a good deal more than mere defense. It was an understandably bitter attack against the narrowness and vindictiveness which had characterized Adenauer's confrontation with ideas and policies that did not fit into his personal scheme of things. Even beyond that, Schaefer depicts persuasively a climate of anti-Communist hysteria which those who experienced the McCarthy period in the United States are able to appreciate.

101. See *Deutscher Informationsdienst,* no. 751 (July 11, 1958), pp. 2–5, and below, VI/211.

102. The advertising manager of the *Nationale Rundschau,* Karl-Robert Schöpflin, an old Nazi, had been regional chairman of the outlawed SRP. Other former members of the Strasbourg Hitler Youth and Gau Leadership who now worked on the *Nationale Rundschau* were Hans Günter Henn and Hans Lossnitzer. Both Schöpflin and Henn became members of Haussleiter's German Community (DG). Henn was later to be an active participant in an anti-Haussleiter *Fronde* which sought to organize a large nationalist-neutralist rally under the ostensible aegis of the DRP. Cf. below, XVI/73 and nearby text.

103. The subscriber list of the *Nationale Rundschau* was taken over by Gerhard Bednarski's *Der Ruf,* whose editorial policy was almost identical.

104. See, for example, "Ein Wort zur Versöhnung," *Neue Politik,* I, 43/44 (December 24, 1956), 3–4; or the entire issue, II, 3 (January 21, 1957).

105. "Jenseits der Ideologien," *ibid.,* II, 21 (May 25, 1957), 13–14.

106. "Volksstaat oder Parteienstaat?" *Ibid.,* II, 10 (March 9, 1957), 3–4.

107. Schenke sees Germany's task in the replacement of the outworn liberalistic social order by an "order which stresses the community without jeopardizing, of course, personal freedom." Opposed to the influence of ideologies on policy formulation, Schenke insists that the state must once again become a neutral agent above the struggle of conflicting interests, and not the tool of one of these interest blocs. To achieve this elevation of the state above the din of political battle, Schenke suggests radical changes in the electoral laws. At present, he argues, free elections in Germany are a fiction, as only a few can afford to vote their convictions. All the rest vote according to the slogans which powerful propaganda machines have hammered into their heads. Only with the abolition of direct elections can the present mass democracy be converted into an "order of freedom." From an interview with Schenke, Hamburg, July 26, 1957.

108. Schenke organized in September, 1957, a German-China Society (not to be confused with the German-Chinese Society founded in February, 1957, by the CDU Bundestag deputy Ernst Majonica to foster relations with Formosa) which made it its business to promote trade and the relations with the People's Republic. The initial executive board (with Schenke as chairman) consisted of Hjalmar Schacht, Hermann Schwann, and former Ambassador Werner-Otto von Hentig, among others. (See *Deutscher Informationsdienst,* no. 828 [n.d., probably September, 1959], pp. 1–11.)

109. The rebels consisted mostly of the Land organization of Berlin, under the leadership of Paul Hofmann, and small BHE splinters from Lower Saxony, Bavaria, and the Saar.

110. Hinder's activity in nationalist-neutralism goes back a good many

years. In the early nineteen-fifties he worked closely with Erich Teich and Wilhelm Wesemeyer, two key men in the East-financed Leadership Circle of Former Soldiers (FeS). From a report of a discussion with Teich and Wesemeyer in Bad Godesberg, April 14, 1953.

111. On the question of armaments, the Hinder-Jentsch wing of the GU—in opposition to the wishes of the Berliners behind Paul Hofmann—went beyond the Russian peace proposals of 1957–1958 which recognized the need for armed neutrality and called for the acceptance of Russia's demands of 1945 for total demilitarization.

112. The editor of *Der Ruf,* Gerhard Bednarski, had founded in 1955 the *Hannoversches Echo,* which supported neutralist-nationalist oppositionists within the BHE and Bund vertriebener Deutscher (League of Expelled Germans) and worked for a union with the DRP. Bednarski also edited for a time the DRP paper *Reichsruf.* In the spring of 1961 *Der Ruf* disappeared and was replaced by *Der Neue Ruf,* also edited by Bednarski. He became chairman of the Lower Saxon organization of the German Peace Union (Deutsche Friedens-Union, DFU) in which he represented the nationalist elements. In 1963, Bednarski was expelled from the DFU chairmanship, ostensibly on grounds of financial irregularities. In reprisal, he revealed the supposed Communist infiltration of the DFU. See *Bulletin on German Questions* (London), XV, 338/339 (August 15, 1963), 11–12.

113. In September, 1959, the Berlin Land organization of the GU decided to leave the parent organization and enter into a federalist relationship with it. Hofmann objected to the "mystical" conceptions of Hinder and Jentsch and argued for armed neutrality. He also urged the importance of being active within the framework of West German politics which includes—like it or not—political parties. For the crucial second federal congress of the GU (September 5 and 6, 1959) see *Studien von Zeitfragen, Analysen und Berichte,* VI, 13 (October 21, 1959), 218.

114. The League (Bund Neue Ordnung, BNO) was founded in March, 1958, by two former Hamburg SRP functionaries, Hans Stange and Kurt Dettmann. Ardently opposed to atomic rearmament, the BNO attempted to bring about a unified front by taking up contact with the Left-neutralist, pacifist Franconian Circle around Professsor Franz Paul Schneider, of Würzburg. See Gesellschaft zum Studium der Zeitfragen, *Analysen und Berichte,* V, 13–14 (June 16, 1958), 3–4. For Stange's *curriculum vitae* (which ends with the credo "I was a National Socialist, I am one still, and shall remain one") see (IV/10), p. 34.

115. See below, text near VI/227.

116. For Schönborn's political *curriculum vitae,* see below, VII/151. In November, 1957, Schönborn, contrary to the explicit policy of the national executive board of the German Community (DG), of which he was at that time still a functionary, urged the formation of a nationalist rally movement through collaboration and merger with other "oppositional" groups. A month later Schönborn was expelled from the DG and, together with other dissident DG officials, founded in Pforzheim the National Comradeship Circle. The hope was that the Circle might become the rallying

point of radical national socialists, especially in Germany's southwest. No such rally to Schönborn's banner took place. In February, 1959, the Kameradschaftskreis joined Hugo Jungmann's Free Socialist People's Party (Freie Sozialistische Volks–Partei, FSVP). This radical North German splinter group, led by the former SRP official and Hamburg Land chairman of the DRP, consisted initially of former SRP and DRP functionaries who had abandoned the DRP in December, 1957, because of the latter's "bourgeois" course. Specifically, they objected to the DRP's parliamentary collaboration with the FDP and BHE in Lower Saxony. Furthermore, the party's national executive disagreed with their policy of seeking to form an Arbeitsgemeinschaft der nationalen Opposition with the German Bloc (DB) and elements of Otto Strasser's DSU. See *Die Brücke,* IV, 22/23 (December, 1957), 4–11.

117. Schreiber, formerly the Hessian Land chairman of the neutralist-nationalist German Saar League (which after the recovery of the Saar by the Federal Republic was renamed People's League for Germany's Reunification), began as a functionary of Otto Strasser's German Social Union (DSU), became a member of the DRP, and in 1959 joined Jungmann and Schönborn in the Free Socialist People's Party (FSVP). Like Schönborn, Schreiber was also active in the German-Arabic Community (DArG). In 1962 Schreiber died at the age of fifty-two.

118. For the Arbeitsgemeinschaft, see Gesellschaft zum Studium von Zeitfragen, *Analysen und Berichte,* V, 8/9 (April 3, 1958), 4–5. It was formed from the reader circles of Gerhard Bednarski's *Der Ruf,* Rolf Hinder's *Gemeinschaft und Politik,* Wolf Schenke's *Neue Politik,* and Paul Schall's *Nationale Rundschau.*

119. Herbert Löbner had been the Westphalian representative of the neo–Nazi German Social Movement (Deutsche Soziale Bewegung), but he was expelled in 1956 by its chairman, Karl-Heinz Priester, for engaging in unauthorized organizational negotiations with the rival German Community (DG) and German Reich Party (DRP). Erika Löbner had been a member of the DRP. The make-up of Zusammen differed slightly in different regions. In Nuremberg, for instance, Zusammen appealed primarily to Ludendorff disciples and similarly folkish, anti-Christian religious and radically nationalist groups. In Hamburg, Zusammen consisted of the Saarbund, the League for German Unity (Bund für deutsche Einheit, BdE), the Ceres circle, and again an anti-Christian folkish group, the German Faith Fellowship (Deutschgläubige Gemeinschaft). See *Studien von Zeitfragen, Analysen und Berichte,* VII, 3/5 (February 18, 1960), 5.

120. For an example of the ease with which Right-extremists have been able to collaborate with men whom they thought to be paid Soviet agents, see Wolfgang Sarg's contemplated collaboration with Erich Teich of the FeS as reflected in a confidential letter of Natinform's deputy chief to Sarg of March 31, 1952, and Sarg's reply of April 4, 1953.

121. See *Deutscher Informationsdienst,* no. 764 (September 13, 1958), p. 102; no. 770 (October 10, 1958), pp. 1–2; no. 774 (November 1, 1958), pp. 1–4; no. 880 (May 9, 1960), pp. 3–5. *Bulletin on German Questions*

(London), X, 225 (November 17, 1958), 10–12; 227 (December 20, 1958), 16. *Feinde der Demokratie* (Lower Saxony), VII, 10 (September/October, 1958), 9–12.

122. In May, 1961, the congress formally dissolved itself.

123. On July 3, 1960, the managers of the Working Association surprised even their friends when they announced the founding of a new party, the Independent Reform Party (Unabhängige Reform-Partei) whose primary goals were the reunification of Germany (together with its neutralization), the liberation of the state "from the tyranny of incompetence," and reversal, through legal and cultural reforms, of the degeneration which had blighted the culture and legal system in Germany. Due to its close affiliation with the so-called Brotherhood Salem, which the government suppressed as a Communist-front organization, the Independent Reform Party also disappeared only four months after its establishment.

124. For details, see *Studien von Zeitfragen, Analysen und Berichte,* VII, 21/22 (*sic*) (March 21, 1961).

125. Illig's German People's Movement, Jungmann's and Schönborn's FSVP, and the All-German Working Association (Gesamtdeutsche Arbeitsgemeinschaft) of the radically nationalist former Hamburg Stahlhelm leader Walter Spohrmann belonged both to the Rally Movement and to Aktion 61. In addition, the latter (whose organizers liked to think of it as the "neutralist opposition front") attracted to its banner the Nordmark section of the nationalist German Saar League, the folkish Gemeinschaft der Freyen (Hamburg), and the Working Circle for Reunification and Neutrality (Arbeitskreis für Wiedervereinigung und Neutralität). This last organization was founded in October, 1960, by the radically nationalist former SRP official Colonel (i.R.) Max Kemmerich. In Munich the circle included Otto Strasser, General Moritz von Faber du Faur, and some of the leading supporters of *Zusammen.* In January, 1961, the Working Circle was renamed German Ring for Reunification and Neutrality (Deutscher Ring für Wiedervereinigung und Neutralität). (See *Studien von Zeitfragen, Analysen und Berichte,* VII, 21/22 [*sic*] [March 21, 1961], 5.)

126. For details on the background, the ideological demands, and organizational structure of the DFU see *Studien von Zeitfragen, Analysen und Berichte*, VIII, 1/2 (January 12, 1961).

127. Exceptions were the League for German Unity, from which Ebrecht and Nehring had resigned; von Faber du Faur's NPD; Paul Hofmann's All-German Union (GU); the Hamburg group of the German Saar League under Günther Heydt, and such personalities as Paul Schall, Gerhard Bednarski, and Walter Spohrmann, who had joined the Saar League; some friends of the Ludendorff movement; other folkish, anti-Christian, religious sects; and the radical folkish-nationalist cultural club, German Cultural Work in the European Spirit (Deutsches Kulturwerk Europäischen Geistes).

128. For more recent developments inside the DFU, see *Studien von Zeitfragen, Analysen und Berichte,* X, 5–6 (March 27, 1963) and X, 7 (April 24, 1963).

129. Two further foundings took place in preparation for the federal

election of 1961. On April 30, circles around Wolf Schenke, Hermann Schwann, a former FDP member of the Federal Diet, Colonel Bogislav von Bonin, and Bodo Manstein organized themselves into an Association for a German National Assembly (Vereinigung Deutsche Nationalversammlung, VDNV). Besides Schwann as chairman, the executive board included, among others, Joachim von Ostau (see below, XIV/66; XVI/180) and Dr. Justus Krause. Hermann Schwann's organizational efforts anticipated the possible formation of a CDU-SPD coalition after the retirement of Konrad Adenauer and the disappearance, therefore, of a parliamentary opposition. Against that eventuality Schwann sought to construct a new opposition consisting of all the forces which had hitherto failed to clear the 5 per cent hurdle, the masses of those who rejected the NATO policies of the two major parties, and of those who—in case of an economic recession—could be mobilized to support an entirely new policy which would give top priority to German reunification. For these groups, the proposals of the VDNV would become the common denominator on which consensus could be achieved. Under these circumstances, particular and mutually incompatible domestic policies could be relegated to places of lower priority where they would not disturb the nonpartisan approach to Germany's number one problem. (See *Studien von Zeitfragen, Analysen und Berichte,* X, 2–3 [February 14, 1963], 8.) In a belated attempt to form a counterweight in the federal election to the Communist-infiltrated DFU, the German Rally Movement organized in May, 1961, an Electoral Association for a Neutral Germany (Wähler Vereinigung für ein neutrales Deutschland), with the purpose of offering Land lists of candidates committed to the rapid reunification and neutralization of Germany. Unable to obtain the 2,000 signatures in each Land, the Electoral Association failed in its attempt, despite the support of Otto Strasser's organization and that of the Free Social Union. (See *ibid.*, VIII, 7 [May 18, 1961], 4. For details on the Electoral Association and polemics against the DFU from the extreme Right, see *ibid.*, VIII, 12–13 [August 17, 1961], 5–7.)

130. In 1933, Gereke was sentenced to a two-and-one-half-year jail term for misappropriation of funds in his capacity as von Hindenburg's campaign manager in the latter's successful bid for re-election to the Reich presidency. (See Niedersächsischer Landtag, Erste Ernennungsperiode *Stenographischer Bericht,* 5. Sitzung, January 9, 1947. Others speak of tax evasion and other frauds: *Der Spiegel,* IX, 33 [August 10, 1950], 8. For a third version see *Rheinischer Merkur* (Koblenz), no. 23 [June 6, 1952], p. 4.) Adenauer's explanation relied on the view that von Hindenburg's election had been effected through massive bribery of the Wirtschaftspartei and that Gereke had nobly shielded the President's son who had provided the money. (Minutes of the CDU, British Zone Committee, December 18, 1946. Quoted in Arnold J. Heidenheimer, *Adenauer and the CDU* [The Hague: Nijhoff, 1960], p. 160.) Without going into the relative merits of these various views, it may be useful to remind the reader that Hitler's seizure of power was followed by a rash of political trials in which charges of corruption were brought against political opponents on the flimsiest grounds, and sometimes on no ground at all. In 1936 Gereke was again

arrested, this time because he had whimsically affixed above the entrance to the pigsties on his farm a political placard widely used in those years in factories and bearing the inscription: "The members of this enterprise stand unanimously behind Adolf Hitler." After his release, Gereke took up contact with circles around the Right-wing, anti-Nazi Prussian Minister of Finance, Johannes Popitz, and the trade-unionist and Resistance leader, Wilhelm Leuschner. In the course of the mass arrests after July 20, 1944, Gereke was arrested for a third time. See Cornides (VI/74), p. 3891.

131. The initiative for the creation of this front organization had been Kurt Vieweg's. Vieweg was a member of the secretariat of the East Zonal Economic Commission and in July, 1950, became a member of the then newly formed SED Central Committee and of its powerful secretariat.

132. See "Gerekes 'Konserven Geschäft,'" *Der Deutsche Weg* (Hanover), II, 16 (first half of April, 1952), 5.

133. Gereke's expulsion from the CDU was effected by an Honors Court under the guidance of Adenauer's two future Ministers of the Interior, Robert Lehr and Gerhard Schröder. The nature of the procedure before the party "Court" was such that a judge presiding over a later, public trial involving Gereke was moved to call it a "farce." From a letter of Mr. J. F. G. Grosser to the author, September 10, 1961.

134. See "Der Kurs gegen Adenauer," *Der Spiegel*, IV, 33 (August 10, 1950), 9.

135. Very soon after the founding, the UBHE part of the party's name was dropped and it became known as DSP. According to the party's "Guidelines" which were provisionally adopted until the full program could be worked out, the DSP called for a "folkish renewal of Germany and of all peoples of Europe." Reunification appeared to the DSP the key to all other problems. Consequently the DSP rejected all ties to East or West and any form of remilitarization, demanding sincere readiness to achieve the reunification of Germany peacefully through negotiation between East and West. Economically, the DSP objected to "unrestrained liberalization as the cause of increasing social tensions and growing misery among the broadest layers" of the population. Cultural renewal committed the DSP to professing the "unique value of cultural and intellectual Germandom" and to the rejection of "every foreign contamination of the German essence (*Art*) through subversive [cultural] barbarism."

136. Fricke had returned in 1929, after two years in South America, and became active in the organization of the NSDAP in Lippe. Later he became SA leader in Danzig. In 1930 he joined Walter Stennes' SA rebellion and was expelled from the Nazi party. He then returned to Paraguay. For details on Fricke's South American activity, see *Die Zeit* (Montevideo), no. 91 (February, 1941), as quoted in *Kölnische Rundschau*, December 13, 1948, p. 3. Fricke's arrogant interference in the affairs of the Strasserites who had not gone into exile but stayed behind and endured years in concentration camps created enormous friction, and his quickly apparent tendencies to co-operate with unregenerate Hitler loyalists, on the one hand, and with compromised national-Bolsheviks on the other, threatened to

wreck the entire Strasser movement. The leaders in the anti-Fricke and anti-Russian faction were Waldemar Wadsack (Bad Kissingen and Munich) and Kurt Sprengel (Wildeshausen, Oldenburg). See Sprengel's letter to Otto Strasser of January 7, 1951, in *Pressedienst Information*, no. 17 (January 27, 1951), and letter of Otto Strasser of January 24, 1951, *ibid.*, no. 86 (February 14, 1951). See also *Deutsche Presse Agentur* (*dpa*), *Inf.* 92 (January 17, 1951); *Internationale Mitteilungen*, 16/51 (February 1, 1951), pp. 4–5, and 19/51 (February 22, 1951), pp. 4–5; *dpa, Inf.* 222 (February 10, 1951); 564 (April 18, 1951); *Der Informationsdienst*, no. 117 (October 2, 1951), p. 2; no. 120 (October 16, 1951), p. 3; no. 126 (November 11, 1951), pp. 1–5; no. 130 (November 23, 1951). After the first month of sounding and surveying operations on behalf of Strasser, Fricke reported his interim conclusions to the Strasser leaders in Germany: "In the course of my first round trip I have come to the conclusion that the organization of the Expellees and Victims of Injustice would probably make the most appropriate partner for us since the intellectual shapelessness (*geistige Auflockerung*), revolutionary conditions of misery, and political aimlessness of these groups would make them most receptive to our ideas." (*Deutsche Presse Agentur* [*dpa*], *Inf.* 31 [January 6, 1951], p. 2.)

137. According to the late Waldemar Wadsack, a leader of the anti-Fricke faction within the Strasser-party Deutsche Soziale Union (DSU), Gereke repeatedly claimed that the Strasser movement had gone into the DSP. This, said Wadsack, was pure bluff. The great majority refused to join what the anti-Fricke leaders insisted was "Pankow's Trojan horse." (From an interview with Wadsack, July 3, 1957.) The role and influence of former Black Front people in the DSP is controverted. Johannes F. G. Grosser (in a letter to the author, dated December 15, 1961) contends that "in reality the Strasser people never had any appreciable influence in the DSP—except for the Fricke interlude." On the other hand, Gereke's closest collaborator, his nephew Horst Schauss, had written to Grosser with reference to Peter Noeren (the representative—along with Eugen Grotz—of the Strasser forces within the DSP): "Herr Noeren is totally dedicated to the cause, and I believe one can confidently entrust him with the build-up of the organization." (Copy of copy of letter, dated March 30, 1951.) Also Olga Linke, the former DSP leader in Franconia (Nuremberg), who had left the party (along with Alfred Zitzmann and Konrad Schatz) to join the SRP, spoke of "a powerful infusion [into the DSP] of followers of Dr. Strasser and Captain Walter Stennes. . . ." ("Die Deutsche Soziale Partei, ihr Aufstieg und ihr Untergang 1951," copy of a third-class-mail document sent to the *Frankfurter Neue Presse*, and dated August 2, 1952.) According to Grosser, Stennes, who had returned to Germany after twelve years as military adviser to Chiang Kai-Shek, was "a completely solitary figure, without followers. . . . He resisted being drafted as co-chairman of the party." Also, though Grosser denied that Gereke had ever asked him, the DSP's plenipotentiary in southern Germany, to get in touch with Strasser followers, Schauss, in the previously cited letter, wrote to Grosser: "I would be especially thankful to you, if you could look a bit after [Peter Noeren]."

138. Besides Gereke and Stennes, the extended DSP executive included the chairmen of the Hesse, Lower Saxony, and Hamburg Land organizations, the publisher Johannes F. G. Grosser, the former civil servant Heinrich Siemer, and the Hamburg lawyer A. W. Rademacher. Until October, 1951, a former division chief of the Nazi Nutrition Estate, SS Major Hermann Korte, was also a member of the executive board, as was the former Nazi Gau propaganda leader for Weser-Ems, Wilhelm Assling, and Adolf Stobbe, Christian labor-union leader in Lower Saxony, who had left the CDU together with Gereke and followed him into and out of the BHE. Stobbe represented the DSP in the Lower Saxon Landtag after Gereke resigned his seat in March, 1952. In July, 1952, Stobbe left the DSP and three years later joined the SPD. (See Niedersächsischer Landtag, 2. Wahlperiode, May 6, 1951–May 5, 1955, 1.–99. Sitzung, *Tätigkeitsbericht,* pp. 40, 42, 58.) Grosser, a young idealist, seriously concerned with the spiritual future of the new Germany and horrified by Allied occupation policy as a continuation, in his eyes, of Nazi coercion, was the immediate instigator of a memorable exchange of views between Thomas Mann and Walter von Molo in which the latter sought to vindicate the moral appropriateness of "inner emigration" against Mann's grave accusations. This exchange set the stage for a protracted controversy in the first three postwar years among German intellectuals anxious to regain moral high ground after twelve years in spiritual swampland. For a record of that controversy, which also provides glimpses of Grosser's own attitude, see his edition of open letters and speeches of Mann, von Molo, Frank Thiess, Alfred Döblin, Johannes R. Becher, Wilhelm Hausenstein, Otto Flake, and others in *Die grosse Kontroverse. Ein Briefwechsel um Deutschland* (Hamburg: Nagel, [c. 1963]). After the dismal DSP experience, Grosser joined the SPD and campaigned on its ticket in the 1961 election. In 1964 he resigned from the SPD and was reported to have taken up contact with the very conservative and very Christian Abendländische Akademie (Occidental Academy).

139. The most effective of these placards—indeed, the one which evoked a response that alone made possible the founding of the DSP Land organizations in Hesse, Württemberg-Baden, and Bavaria—was a replica of the "Call for Peace" document which had been authored by Heinemann and adopted by the Wiesbaden Neutralist Conference in January, 1951. Specifically, the placard was part of the "plebiscite movement" which sought to prevent Germany's rearmament by insisting on a referendum concerning three questions: the reintroduction of compulsory military training under existing conditions, the inclusion of the two rump Germanies in hostile security alliances, and the permissibility of recruiting German citizens for military service of whatever kind. The placard concluded with a strong appeal to the disabled and the expellees: "Every billion which Germany is now spending for rearmament becomes unavailable for the pressing task of a genuinely social transformation (*Neuordnung*) in the interest of all socially weak strata (*Kreise*), especially of the expellees and those who have been damaged by the war (*Kriegsgeschädigte*)." See *Der Deutsche Weg* (Hanover), I, 2 (March 15, 1951), 3.

140. See the testimony of E. Fischer, DSP chairman of Delmenhorst, in *Der Spiegel,* V, 18 (May 2, 1951), 9: "There were generous *per diems* for the founding convention and delegates meetings, and all of it in new twenty-mark bills with the stamp B on it—that means they came from Berlin. . . ." The same observation was made by Otto Strasser's suspicious "resident commissioner," Waldemar Wadsack. It must be remembered, of course, that both Fischer and Wadsack had sharp personal axes to grind and were eager to find supporting evidence for their suspicions.

141. According to Guido Zoller in "Die gleiche Blutgruppe," *Rheinischer Merkur* (Koblenz), no. 23 (June 6, 1952), p. 4, the price was DM 1,000 per month.

142. *Der Spiegel,* V, 18 (May 2, 1951), 9. It may be remembered that the proportional representation features of the electoral law become available only to those parties which have candidates in almost every one of the electoral districts. (See above, IV/30.)

143. There is considerable agreement among those who were in the DSP leadership as to the cost of the campaign. Contrary to vastly exaggerated claims by the CDU and the BHE, campaign expenditures amounted to roughly DM 90,000 to 100,000. J. F. G. Grosser put the figure at DM 93,000. (Letter to the author, September 10, 1961.) In this connection, DSP circles have always pointed with some satisfaction to the fact that the anti-DSP propaganda of the other parties in this one election cost them approximately half a million marks.

144. The suspicions were stirred by the discovery that Gereke had precipitously left the last Landtag meeting just prior to a vote on a resolution condemning the arbitrariness and inhumanity of the East Zonal administration of justice. (In the course of a later trial, Gereke explained his sudden departure by reference to a telephone call he alleged to have received at the time of the vote. Subsequent inquiries by interested journalists disclosed that no telephone call for Gereke had been recorded at the switchboard at the crucial time.) Moreover, one of the DSP's campaign posters deepened the suscipion. It showed a map of Germany with the Zonal border along the Elbe in heavy print. Superimposed was a hand pointing to the line of separation and underneath the caption: "Away with it!" What was noticed immediately, and with utter consternation, was that the eastern outline of the German territory coincided with the Oder-Neisse line. The inference opponents of the DSP drew was that Gereke was making common cause with the veteran Communist leader, Walter Ulbricht, who had renounced in a treaty with Poland all claims to Germany's Eastern provinces. Hostile critics immediately recalled that Gereke's fateful canned-goods negotiations took place on the very day that the East German "renunciation treaty" was signed, and that Gereke had shaken Ulbricht's hand only hours after Ulbricht had set his signature to that treaty. Only much later, in the autumn of 1952, did direct testimony become available on the possible relationship between the conservative nationalist Gereke and the East German Communist regime. According to Artur von Machui's testimony (of September 12, 1952), with the outbreak of the Korean War and the

intensification of the cold war, an important shift took place in the Communist approach to propaganda. As late as August and September, 1949, the highest SED functionaries—men like Luitpold Steidle, Erwin Hoernle, Otto Grotewohl, Wilhelm Koenen, or Franz Dahlem—rejected infiltration through well-camouflaged front organizations. A few months later the SED replaced candor by deception. In this connection, von Machui heard high praise for the All German Study Circle and other activities of Gereke. Allegedly, the witness was told: "One deceitful Dr. Gereke is worth more to us than a hundred honest [men like you]!" And, again, in conversation with the high Communist officials Dahlem and Vieweg, von Machui was told: "You have come to us for reasons of your socialist beliefs; Gereke has come to us for personal reasons. It is totally immaterial which motives are better. Decisive is only who functions more effectively. And Gereke's performance is appreciably better than yours." This estimate of Gereke's effectiveness (from an East German point of view) was apparently later drastically revised. According to testimony of Fred Henrich, an associate of Grosser's, the latter surmised (on July 17, 1952) that the reason for the discontinuation of East German financial assistance to Gereke's political and journalistic ventures in mid-1952 "lay purely in the economic area. Gereke has received enormous sums from the other side, but has done nothing [of value] with them. He had not even been able to build up the party with them. That's the real reason why money has ceased to flow." (Copy of deposition, July 28, 1952. Though Henrich declared himself ready to reaffirm his testimony under oath, Grosser sought to have Henrich indicted for libel when the latter sold some of his information to the *Frankfurter Neue Presse*. The attorney-general dismissed Grosser's request.)

145. The leader of the BHE's extreme folkish-nationalist wing, Dr. Fritz Schulz, who was later to lead his friends into the SRP shortly before its suppression as a subversive Nazi party, arranged for the printing of 30,000 gummed strips of paper which in clandestine, midnight operations were pasted over every one of the DSP posters. They bore the inscription: "This placard was paid for by Moscow!" Court suits for temporary injunctions, restraining orders, and slander, which Gereke initiated and ultimately won, were much too slow to provide any relief in the period of the campaign. In this connection should also be mentioned the sensational and successful libel suit against Jürgen Hahn-Butry, the chairman of the government-subsidized anti-Communist vigilante group, People's League for Peace and Freedom. Hahn-Butry had alleged that Gereke formed the vanguard of the Eastern "bolshevizers," that he was receiving money and assistance from the Communist Party, that he had betrayed expellees and refugees to Soviet Zone authorities, and that he was, altogether, Moscow's most dangerous agent in the Federal Republic. See Hagen-Michel, *pseud.* [i.e. J. F. G. Grosser], "Politische Umtriebe," *Der Deutsche Weg* (Hanover), II, 15 (end of March, 1952), 2, and J. F. G. Grosser, "*Strafprozess gegen Bonn*," *ibid.*, II, 16 (first half of April, 1952), 1–2. For the anti-Semitism of Hahn-Butry and of his second-in-command, Eberhard Taubert, see *Feinde der Demo-*

kratie (Lower Saxony), IV, 9–10 (August-September, 1955), 55–57; *Deutscher Informationsdienst,* no. 757 (August 12, 1958). Cf. above, VI/6.

146. Niedersächsisches Amt für Landesplanung und Statistik, *Die Neuwahl zum Niedersächsischen Landtag am 6. Mai 1951,* Series F, XIV, 1 (Hanover: 1952). In not a single district did the DSP come even close to achieving a plurality, let alone a majority. It achieved a plurality in only one community out of 4,244 in Lower Saxony, and that was a village with 558 eligible voters!

147. On May 8, 1951, after the Landtag election, Gereke addressed a letter to his party workers in which he said: "I—together with my closest friends and co-workers—have the firm intention to continue with determination along the road we have started on, beyond the first parliamentary seat, and I am certain that, strengthened and confirmed by the fact that it proved impossible to kill us, we shall carry on our idea by unremitting work and make it finally decisively successful. The election in Lower Saxony was the first skirmish for our young party. . . ."

148. There was within the DSP ranks surprisingly little resistance to these extremist plans or hopes. Only the Bremen Land organization rebelled against them. When it proved intransigent, Gereke attempted to have his way over the heads of the Land officials and to this end negotiated with former SS Colonel Eberhard Hawranke, a confidant of Fricke and Stennes, on the one hand, and of the SRP and the Bruderschaft, on the other. Later, Hawranke went to jail for his part in the subversive Freikorps Deutschland. He was also second-in-command of another subversive and suppressed Nazi organization, Wolfgang Sarg's Natinform. See below, Chapter VI, Section E.

149. Testimony of J. F. G. Grosser, Frankfurt, April 12, 1952. (Copy of transcript.)

150. From the protocol of interrogation of Gereke's secretary, Lieselotte Ulrich, Hanover, August 7, 1952. (Copy of transcript.)

151. From the testimony of Artur von Machui, Frankfurt, September 12, 1952. (Copy of transcript.)

152. From the testimony of Lieselotte Ulrich. For the alleged response of Grosser to the prospect of operating his newspaper with "Eastern" funds, see the testimony of Fred Henrich, September 11, 1952. However, as there are certain inconsistencies between Henrich's unsworn statement of July 28, 1952, and his testimony under police interrogation of September 11, 1952, his reliability as a witness is open to legitimate doubt. In his own deposition Grosser declared that the capitalization of the paper involved DM 20,000, of which DM 12,000 were to be paid in installments by Horst Schauss, Gereke's nephew, and the rest by Grosser in the form of unpaid salary.

153. A closer analysis of four issues of the paper (April and May, 1952) at the height of the campaign against the then imminent Bonn Agreements and in support of the Soviet proposal for reunification of March, 1952, gives the following results: 30 per cent of the space was devoted to sharp attacks against Bonn and the West; 34 per cent to the promotion of

East-West trade and to articles favorable to the Soviet Union (many of the trade articles were, of course, also hostile to the West, frequently alleging that only Western capitalist self-interest and fear of German competition prevented trade with the iron-curtain countries); 8 per cent of the articles argued the necessity for neutrality and reunification, with frequent hostile asides against Adenauer, who was loudly suspected of treasonable Rhenish, separatist proclivities. The remaining 28 per cent were devoted to objective reportage, cinema and theater reviews, and so on. Of the paper's 35 per cent of space taken up by illustrations, 15 per cent showed Eastern developments in a flattering way, 15 per cent showed the West and Bonn in an unfavorable light, 23 per cent showed the importance or profitableness of unhampered East–West trade, and 21 per cent drove home the importance of rapid reunification. The remaining 26 per cent was employed to illustrate stories and merchandising novelties. While these four issues were representative of the paper's general orientation, their tone is somewhat more strident than that of previous issues. Herr Grosser, the editor of *Der Deutsche Weg,* hinted (in a letter to the writer of June 9, 1961) that, frankly, the growing militancy was designed to provoke the Adenauer regime into suppressing the paper and thus to veil the imminent financial bankruptcy of the venture. This is also suggested by Fred Henrich, one of the journalists of *Der Deutsche Weg,* who testified that Schauss and Grosser considered several times provoking the government into suppression of the paper. (Copy of protocol of Henrich's interrogation, Frankfurt, September 11, 1952.)

154. According to Grosser's testimony during his second interrogation (of September 17, 1952), of the edition of 25,000 papers, 3,000 were actually sold to newspaper vendors, 3,000 were sent to newspapers, organizations, and deputies, and the rest of 19,000 went to the DSP, which distributed 6,000 to its members and friends and sent 13,000 as free copies to various occupational groups.

155. From the record of Grosser's second interrogation on September 17, 1952. Cf. depositions of Mrs. Ulrich (VI/150), of the DPS's treasurer, Heinrich Siemer, August 27, 1952, and Fred Henrich, September 11, 1952.

156. From a copy of the transcript of Henrich's deposition of September 11, 1952. In his letter to the author of December 15, 1961, Grosser asserts: "I have never seen or received more twenty-mark bills, old and new, from the DSP for campaign purposes, than were current in my business as publisher and book dealer, that means, [than were current] quite generally in Frankfurt with the overprint B. Every business in West Germany, especially in Frankfurt or Hanover, had a certain percentage of such bills. That allegation with the B–bills cannot be proved."

157. From Henrich's deposition of July 17, 1952.

158. From a copy of the transcript of Meerstein's deposition of September 11, 1952.

159. From Korte's *curriculum vitae,* in his deposition, Lebbien, July 31, 1952. (Copy of transcript.)

160. *Politik und Wirtschaft,* Sondermaterial, no date, but with a "re-

ceived" stamp of August 18, 1952. The official designation which Korte is alleged to have assumed is there mistakenly given as "Reichsführer."

161. From Otto Dennstedt's interrogation protocol, Dannenberg, August 6, 1952. (Copy of transcript.)

162. According to testimony given in the course of subsequent police investigation, Dennstedt became a partner, with a capital investment of DM 8,000. Korte invested DM 20,000. Artur von Machui, a formerly Left-wing socialist agronomist, who had offered his services to the East German regime, testified that one of the Soviet Zone official Kurt Vieweg's assistants told him in October, 1951, that no expenses had been spared by Vieweg's office to replace old printing equipment with new. The cost mentioned was DM 300,000. Von Machui also alleged that Vieweg's voluble agent went into details concerning the advantages of the site at Dannenberg. Close to the Zonal border, surrounded by dense woods, the little town could be supplied with the necessary materials from the East with the least risk of detection. The reliability of this testimony, however, is not beyond question. Apart from von Machui's strong motives to "get even" with Gereke and his alleged employers and from the implausibility that a secret courier would reveal so much to a man whose hostility was known, there is directly contradictory testimony from a former editor in chief of *Wir Bauern,* who declared that the technical equipment of Landdruck, Inc., was "totally inadequate and inferior." Incidentally, von Machui turned later sharply to the Right and for some years published a journal, *Meilensteine,* together with Theodor Oberländer, the former Minister for Expellee Affairs in Adenauer's first three cabinets, who was forced to resign when his virulent Nazi past threatened to cause a major scandal.

163. "Die Ruhe zeigt unsere Stärke," *Wir Bauern* (Dannenberg), I, 25 (June 22, 1952), 1–2.

164. *Ibid.,* p. 2; cf., "Wir sind für einander bestimmt!" *Ibid.,* I, 27 (July 6, 1952), pp. 1–2.

165. See, for example, "In Konstanz wird es sich entscheiden," *ibid.,* I, 26 (June 29, 1952), 1–2, or L. Rethel, "Totengräber des Bauerntums," *ibid.,* pp. 2–3. Rethel writes, "There was a short period of flowering and freedom (*Aufatmen*) when the Reich Nutrition Estate brought honor once again to the much maligned word Farmer, bound the farmer to his soil, and protected him from the incursion of people alien to his profession (*Berufsfremde*), and when the farmer was allowed to determine his own leaders." Cf. also "Parität nur durch Marktordnung," *ibid.,* I, 29 (July 20, 1952), 1–2.

166. The two officials were Karl Schirdewan, assistant at that time to Franz Dahlem, then cadre chief of the SED, and Ernst Hansch, assistant to Kurt Vieweg, the agricultural boss of the Soviet Zone and chief of Eastern propaganda efforts among farmers, East or West. From a deposition of Artur von Machui, September 12, 1952. (Copy of transcript.)

167. See *Politik und Wirtschaft* (VI/160). The same response, we are told, greeted the disclosure that the circulation manager, a former waiter and long-term member of the Nazi Party, was embezzling funds.

168. According to testimony in the course of the police investigation, sometimes as many as 19,500 remainder copies were sold as waste paper. When a new issue of the journal was thus sold, girls were hired to tear the title sheet off the new copies, so that the wastepaper man would not notice that a "current" issue was being scrapped.

169. Korte, under police interrogation, steadfastly maintained that *Wir Bauern* was totally financed by former officials of the Nazi Ministry of Nutrition and from current income from circulation. In view of the fact that almost every one of Korte's assertions was contradicted by direct evidence and by other witnesses, this part of his testimony can also safely be viewed as pure fabrication.

170. For the entire problem of financing the Gereke ventures, DSP, *Der Deutsche Weg,* and *Wir Bauern,* the protocols of interrogation of the participants are the most useful source. Unfortunately the investigations, as far as I know, were never completed, and hence a number of interesting points were never really cleared up.

171. For our purposes it is not necessary to follow the internal frictions and skirmishes which characterized relations among the leaders of the DSP and between them and East Zonal officials. They emerge clearly from the testimony given by the principals in the course of police investigation. Nor need we try to disentangle the complex web of intrigue, machinations, and coincidence which forms the background to the never fully explained disappearance of Schauss into the East Zone and to Gereke's flight to East Berlin the following day. For Gereke's own explanation, see *Neues Deutschland* ([East] Berlin), VII (LXIII), 175 (July 27, 1952), 1, 3. Until a few years ago, Gereke was president of the East German Central Office for Breeding and Capability-Testing of Thoroughbred and Trotting Horses.

172. For this entire story, see Bodo Scheurig, *Freies Deutschland: Das Nationalkomitee und der Bund deutscher Offiziere in der Sowjetunion 1943–1945* (Munich: Nymphenburg, 1960), and Jesco von Puttkamer, *Irrtum und Schuld: Geschichte des Nationalkomitees "Freies Deutschland,"* (Neuwied: Michael, [1948]). See also Boris Meissner, *Russland, die Westmächte und Deutschland. Die Sowjetische Deutschlandpolitik 1943–1953* (Hamburg: Nölke, 1953). The best short summary is to be found in Helmut Bohn, "Die patriotische Karte in der sowjetischen Deutschlandpolitik (1)," *Ost–Probleme,* VII, 38 (September 23, 1955), 1446–1457. For a nationalist, vehemently anti-Communist view, see Peter Strassner, *Verräter: Nationalkomitee "Freies Deutschland," Keimzelle der DDR* (Munich: Schild, 1960).

173. Cited by Bohn (VI/172), p. 1450.

174. *Ibid.* Count Heinrich von Einsiedel, on the same occasion, referred to the conception of his great-grandfather, Bismarck, whose policy of a German-Russian alliance should now again be re-established.

175. SMA Order no. 35, February 26, 1948.

176. See Demokratische Gesellschaft 1952, "Links und Rechts im 'Führungsring' " (mimeographed typescript, no date), p. 2.

177. Hek Rau is the pseudonym of Heinz Erich Krause, a former

lieutenant in the Alpine troops, who began in January, 1951, the clandestine publication of a scurrilous and undisguised Nazi periodical, *Deutschland Brief*. In May, 1952, Krause was denazified and placed in Group III. On November 1, 1952, he was finally sentenced to loss of his civic rights and limitation of residence and was for five years prohibited from publishing or editing. (Letter of Hek Rau to Karl Smets, January 22, 1953.) This, however, stopped neither the publication of *Deutschland Brief* nor Krause's concealed activity on behalf of a Bewegung Reich, the loose Nazi organization which was being built up through the readership of the newsletter. See *Parlamentarisch-Politischer Pressedienst,* no. 172/51 (November 20, 1951); *Der Informationsdienst,* no. 170 (April 29, 1952); Eric A. Pechler [*sic*], "Bewegung Reich," *Das Freie Wort* (Düsseldorf), IV, 4 (January 24, 1953), "Untergrund-Bewegung Reich," *Die Wochen Zeitung* (Zurich), no. 18 (April 20, 1953). For later developments in the Bewegung Reich, especially the arrest and eventual conviction on charges of conspiracy and Nazi activities of the former Gauleiter of Westphalia South, Heinrich Vetter, and some of his chief lieutenants, see *Nürnberger Nachrichten,* November 21, 1952; *Hannoversche Presse,* May 19 and June 2, 1953; *Die Welt* (Hamburg), June 1, 1953; *Westfälische Rundschau* (Dortmund), May 22 and June 6, 1954. For the last arrests and convictions for subversive activities through the "Reich movement," see *Deutscher Informationsdienst,* no. 655 (May 25, 1957).

178. See "Befehlsausgabe? Stab oder Front?" *Deutscher Beobachter* (Hamburg), I, 2 (June 22, 1951), 2.

179. See *Deutsche Presse Agentur (dpa), Inf.* 1550 (October 20, 1951).

180. See, for example, C. Feld, "Kann man mit den Sowjets verhandeln?" *Rundbrief* (FeS), no. 7 (May, 1952), pp. 1–2.

181. *Ibid.,* no. 10 (October, 1952), pp. 1–2.

182. Report on an interview with Teich, October 29, 1952.

183. Letter of Erich Teich to a Stahlhelm leader, March 27, 1953. Note also the latter's characteristic response, in which he expressed full agreement with the stated goals, but re-emphasized "that the East must stay completely out of our domestic affairs." Confidential letter to Erich Teich, March 28, 1953.

184. The former SA Obersturmführer Münchow joined the German Party (DP) after the war and soon appeared on its extreme Right wing as a faithful paladin of Bundestag Deputy Wolfgang Hedler. Upon Hedler's expulsion, Münchow also left the DP and, with his mentor, joined the DRP. He then began to build up the blatantly Nazi youth organization Deutsche Reichsjugend. See their "Vorläufige Arbeitsplan" signed by a "Bezirksjugendführer" and their "Vorläufige Satzungen," as well as copies of Münchow's *Deutschland Ruft.* ("Arbeitsplan" and "Satzungen" are unpublished, mimeographed typescripts.) See below, text near X/132–142.

185. Münchow, according to an eyewitness account of a meeting in Flensburg, middle of October, 1951.

186. See, for example, the open letter of Hein, Baier, and Schrank to members of the Bundestag, September 26, 1951 (flier).

187. See, for example, description of such a meeting by the reporter of the *Welt am Sonntag* (Hamburg), October 28, 1951.

188. See his "Sondernummer" of the *Rundbrief*. That trouble was brewing had been evident ever since Hein published a letter to the editor of *Die Welt* (Hamburg) of December 11, 1951, accusing Communist-front organizations of misusing the FeS and even his own name for nefarious purposes of their own. In fact, he accused them of outright fraud and forgery. "The soldiers who are represented in the FeS," declared Hein, "reject Bolshevism." The FeS's answer came barely a week later in an inconspicuous notice in *Rundbrief* no. 5 announcing the resignation of Hein from his position as executive director.

At about the same time, Hein took over the Land-wide organization of the German Home Guard (Deutscher Heimatschutz), a subsidiary of the fanatical Shock Troop against Bolshevik Subversion (Stosstrupp gegen bolschewistische Zersetzung). By the spring of 1952 he had "sworn in" some three-hundred former SS leaders and other Nazis and prepared them for underground and guerrilla warfare, claiming the support of American and Federal German agencies and promising generous financial support. In July, 1952, the attorney-general of Schleswig-Holstein ordered the search of the leaders' homes and their arrest. See Schleswig-Holsteinischer Landtag, 2. Wahlperiode, *Stenographischer Bericht über die 23. Tagung, 52. Sitzung am 29. Oktober 1952 in Kiel,* pp. 167, 174.

189. Report of a discussion with Teich, October 29, 1952. As late as April, 1953, even well-informed nationalists, such as the incorrigible Nazi Regierungspräsident of Koblenz, Gerhard Mischke, refused to believe that Baier, who was known as an "impeccable National Socialist," could have any dealings with the East. (From a Stahlhelm leader's interview with Mischke, April 8, 1953.) In the middle of 1952, FeS made special efforts to maintain or establish contact with some of the more sizable Right-extremist groups and parties. To this end Jungnickel, who was collaborating with the FeS, organized a secret meeting in Filsen (on May 18, 1952) which was attended by representatives from the German Bloc and the German Community as well as by Baier, Schrank, and Adolf Scheu (of Heinemann's neutralist All-German People's Party), who acted as one of the middlemen in financing the FeS. (From a memorandum of one of the participants.) Among the other liaison men who apparently supplied the FeS with funds from Soviet—or rather, East German—sources were (according to Erich Teich) SS General Gottlob Berger, former head of the SS Main Leadership Office, and an SS Colonel Hiller. Berger had been sentenced to twenty-five years' imprisonment, but was released from Landsberg in 1952.

Incidentally, Jungnickel, who in the course of an interview on May 26, 1957, denied ever having been "close to" the FeS and merely admitted meeting with it twice, told one of his political acquaintances on September 3, 1952, that he "had separated himself from the club (FeS) but maintained regular connections and kept in touch with Schrank and Baier." Then he went on to say that just as he had come to the Essen Circle via Peace League and German Congress, so he now needed a part of the people from the Leadership Circle. Jungnickel was at that time engaged in building up the German Bloc (DB).

190. This arrangement was very largely the result of the meeting at Filsen and was engineered by Jungnickel, who had by now joined the German Bloc. See *Der Informationsdienst,* no. 198 (August 13, 1952).

191. In FeS headquarters, orders were given to hide or burn compromising documents and files. Report of a discussion with Erich Teich, January 21, 1953.

192. Memorandum of a discussion with Erich Teich, Koblenz, March 9, 1953.

193. One of the plans called for the publication of a nationalist daily newspaper with the assistance of former members of the DRP under the leadership of Herwart Miessner, who now represented the Free Democratic Party (FDP) in the Bundestag. (Report [VI/191].) Later, Teich considered trying to obtain the publishing rights of the *Deutsche Soldaten–Zeitung* (Munich), and spoke in this connection of a private source which might be interested in supplying DM 10,000 for that purpose. He also hinted vaguely at "American financial circles" as an additional source of funds. (Confidential letter of Teich to the deputy chairman of Natinform, February 14, 1953.)

194. See *Der Informationsdienst,* no. 184 (June 25, 1952), pp. 3–4.

195. See S. R., "Ein Mann namens Rudolf Steidl," *Deutsche Zeitung und Wirtschaftszeitung* (Stuttgart), no. 34 (April 28, 1954), p. 13, and cf. *Feinde der Demokratie* (Nordmark), no. 3 (December 8, 1952).

196. Von Reichenau was "introduced" to military groups as the featured speaker at one of Steidl's most elaborate conferences on July 26–27, 1952, in Munich. Of the 39 participants, 13 were of general's rank. Again the executive board of the FeS was amply represented. For details, see *Der Informationsdienst,* no. 203 (September 3, 1952), pp. 1–2.

197. *MiFo's* orientation can be gleaned, for instance, from such statements as these: "entire political parties are devoting themselves to the eulogy of national dependence on foreign powers as progress and liberation. . . . The source of German difficulties lies not on the Spree [that is, Berlin] and not always on the Rhine, but rather in Washington and Paris, and, surely, also in London. . . . There must be no German reunification at the price of hegemony of one part over the other."

198. Cf. the selections presented in *Deutscher Informationsdienst,* no. 370 (May 17, 1954), pp. 2–3.

199. *Ibid.,* no. 228 (December 3, 1952), pp. 3–4.

200. See S. R. (VI/195) and "Bürgerbräuromantik—Nationalbolschewismus unter dem Banner der nationalen Pflichterfüllung," *Christ und Welt* (Stuttgart), December 18, 1952.

201. When von Reichenau, who had appeared as sole host for the entire event, was asked who was paying for it and why, his answer was not entirely reassuring. Von Reichenau claimed that he alone was sponsoring the meeting, that he was paying for it out of his own considerable means, and

that he tendered the invitations because, after twenty years in China, he had felt the need to "be gay and have fun in the old military tradition with a group of front-line soldiers of the First and Second World Wars . . . and to exchange views on urgent problems facing Germany today." *Deutsche Presse Agentur (dpa), Inf.* 2159 (December 5, 1952).

202. Former Hitler Youth leader and Nazi propaganda leader of Berchtesgaden, Huber became after the war copublisher, with Hek Rau, of the unrestrained *Stürmer*-type *Deutschland Brief* and "charter member" of the conspiratorial Bewegung Reich. The *Deutschland Brief,* incidentally, after suppression by German authorities and years of clandestine operation, finally moved to Barcelona in 1952. There Richard Schrader-Voss edited the paper and sent it back into Germany. In the middle of 1953, the paper again appeared in Berchtesgaden, but after 1954 it returned to Spain. Despite Huber's participation at Stuttgart, Rau, in a note of January 22, 1953, to the deputy chairman of the Nazi information service Natinform, wrote: "The press reports about Stuttgart do not hit the mark. We are Rudel-people and don't have the slightest connections (*Beziehungen*) to von Reichenau. Also, Scheringer is known to me merely by name." According to the Natinform chief, Wolfgang Sarg, Hek Rau backed up this denial by suing *Der Spiegel* for having reported that Rau maintained close contact with Scheringer and the FeS.

203. Such as Hans Grimm, Maurice Bardèche, Dieter Vollmer, Alfred Rosenberg, Hans-Ulrich Rudel, General Heinz Guderian, and SS General Paul Hausser.

204. Rudel, who had left Germany in 1948, returned for the first time illegally in October, 1950. Thereafter he returned frequently, having worked out an apparently foolproof system of crossing the border without detection by unfriendly patrols. These exploits were allegedly made possible by his old French SS friends, by border guards who refused to carry out the orders to arrest him, and, above all, by highly placed friends in the Bonn bureaucracy who informed him of government plans. The outwitting of the police became a matter of intensely malicious glee and pride to this egomaniac. (See, for example, his *Zwischen Deutschland und Argentinien. Fünf Jahre in Übersee* [Göttingen: Plesse, (1954?)], pp. 153–159.) According to Wolfgang Sarg, Rudel always crossed over from France, where he also stayed between his visits to Germany. (From a discussion memorandum of January 17, 1953.) In the spring of 1953 Fritz Dorls, the former chairman of the outlawed neo-Nazi SRP, told Rudolf Diels, Göring's first Gestapo chief, that after the "outlawry of the Rightist organizations" Rudel "has gone over to the Soviets." Rudel is alleged to have said that the flag of nationalism was being held high only by the Soviets, a judgment, incidentally, with which Diels completely agreed, despite the latter's strong opposition to them. (From a confidential memorandum of a discussion with Diels on April 7, 1953.) A recent full-length feature story on Rudel (*Kölnische Rundschau,* October 21, 1962) suggested that Hitler's flying ace, after a stopover in Moscow, went on to assist in the organization of Castro's air force. Uncorroborated allegations like these must, of course, be viewed with greatest caution.

205. Details are given in a confidential report of a leadership meeting of the radical Nazi intelligence organization Natinform, January 16–19, 1953. Also cf. *Politik und Wirtschaft,* December 6, 1952, p. 2. The rumors (very likely planted) suggested that the Shanghai-Woosung army to which von Reichenau was attached as military adviser was the first to go over to the Communist side and that in the sequel von Reichenau also switched sides. Other stories sought to discredit him by maintaining that von Reichenau played the dishonorable part of a stool pigeon in the American Shanghai trials following the war. Von Reichenau also aroused suspicion in nationalist circles by his attempts to obtain information on the internal problems of some of the most important nationalist organizations. (From an unpublished confidential report of Natinform South to Natinform Headquarters, January 14, 1953, p. 2.)

206. Cf. Steidl's "confessions," "Sondernummer," *Deutsche National–Zeitung* (August, 1955), p. 2. Earlier Jurzeck had proposed that Hein take over the *Deutscher Beobachter* as the official organ of the FeS. Jurzeck's funds, which had initially come to him via the Hamburg Gesellschaft für Osthandel (GEFO), were drying up, and SED officials had refused to bail him out. This way he hoped to be able to save his paper and continue to benefit from Eastern largesse, if not directly, then indirectly. It is more than likely that the Hitler Youth Leader circle was cut off from further endowments because the SED suspected them of misusing funds for organizational purposes of their own.

207. On his frequent illegal trips to Germany, Rudel would address the circle around Hek Rau and invariably receive a hero's welcome from his Berchtesgaden fans. (His frequent visits to the Tyrolian and Bavarian Alps were necessitated by the fact that he would entrust the repair or replacement of his leg prosthesis to only one man, Master Striede in the Tyrolian skiing resort Kufstein.) See *Die Neue Zeitung* (Munich), March 5, 1952, reproduced in Hek Rau's *Deutschland Brief,* March, 1952, p. 9; Hans Habe (Bekessy), "Geier um Hitlers Adlerhorst," *Echo der Woche,* n.d., reproduced *ibid.,* March, 1952, pp. 13–15; and *Südost Kurier* (Bad Reichenhall), May 30, 1952, reproduced *ibid.,* June 1, 1952, p. 19.

208. See above, VI/97 and VI/100.

209. Brehm had been a member since 1927 of the radically folkish, Conservative Revolutionary Kameradschaftsbund (League of Comradeship), the cat's-paw of Nazism in the Sudetenland, and had worked for years on the resettlement of the so-called *Volksdeutsche.* In 1950 Brehm became executive secretary of Haussleiter's German Community (DG) and later Land secretary of the Bavarian DP. At that time Brehm also joined the FeS, where he met Rudolf Steidl. Hagen, "cultural editor" of *Das Reich,* had been the "politruk" (National Socialist Guidance Officer, NSFO) assigned to Major Remer's Berlin Guard battalion. As such he played a role in frustrating the plot of July 20. After the war, Hagen worked on the radical *Deutsche Soldaten–Zeitung.* See Helmut Steinberg, *pseud.* (*i.e.* Heinrich Härtle), "Geist und Tat: Zum 50. Geburtstag von H. W. Hagen," *Reichsruf* (Hanover), VI, 27 (May 18, 1957), 5.

210. As a defense witness for the SA before the Nuremberg Tribunal, Werner A. M. Schäfer, equipped with a remarkably selective memory, as the cross examination revealed, drew a picture of the SA and of the Oranienburg concentration camp that would have done justice to a group of choirboys and a rest home for the elderly. International Military Tribunal, *Trial of the Major War Criminals* (Nuremberg: 1947), XXI, 72–105.

211. After the war, Schall was for a time editor in chief of Albert Smagon's *Ost-West Kurier*. We later met him as editor of the nationalist-neutralist *Nationale Rundschau*. Steidl's confidant, former SS Lieutenant Colonel Hans Sperk, who had conspicuously disbursed large amounts of cash to the participants of the ill-starred "generals' meeting" in Stuttgart, became counsel of the *Deutsche National-Zeitung* (Munich). The circulation department was in the hands of former SA General Walter Nibbe, and the Düsseldorf office in those of Friedrich Karl Bornemann, Naumann's press chief and liaison to the Bruderschaft. The Hamburg office was directed by Georg Beschoner, former business manager of the Hitler Youth Leader circle's *Deutscher Beobachter* (see above, VI/72) and member of the FeS's executive board. The Lower Saxon office was supervised by Bruno Fricke (see above, VI/136) and the former SRP leader Count Wolf von Westarp.

212. Smagon died in December, 1962, at the age of sixty-five.

213. For example, *Deutsche National-Zeitung,* February 27, 1954.

214. Beschoner's dismissal in February, 1954, supposedly convinced Fricke "that the *DNZ* is largely immune to Communist infiltration." From Fricke's news service (*Freies Nachrichten Büro, fnb*) as reproduced in *Widerhall* (Munich), V, 2 (February, 1954), 21.

215. Although Hermann Schaefer denied Steidl's accusations that he was not only a good friend of the East Zonal press chief, Albert Norden, and shared many of his ideas but also received direct instructions from Norden and dutifully carried them out, he never, to my knowledge, sued Steidl for slander and libel.

216. According to Steidl's own self-serving version, pressure from the East German Socialist Unity Party for a closer hewing to lines laid down by it was transmitted to him by Werner Schäfer, who was soon joined by Hermann Schaefer. Supposedly Steidl refused to yield to the importunities and peremptoriness of the SED-Schäfer-Schaefer coalition, dismissed his editor in chief, Hermann Schaefer, and in July, 1954, closed down the *Deutsche National–Zeitung* when he saw no possibility for future collaboration with East Berlin on a basis of intellectual independence—or, more likely, when discontinuance of eastern subsidies made the closing down necessary.

217. Fritz Brehm, Walter Nibbe, Paul Stadtler (*recte* Schall), Heinz Greven (all previously of the *Deutsche National–Zeitung*), and a Munich merchant, Hans-Ulrich Steuer.

218. According to Steidl, at least: see 'Sondernummer," *Deutsche National-Zeitung,* August, 1955, p. 3.

219. There were also associated with this venture the radical Hitler Youth ideologist Gottfried Griesmayr and his friend, the veteran Kapp-

putschist and nationalist revolutionary Wilhelm Kiefer (see above, V/39–40; VI/79; and below VII/162); and Bruno Fricke, Otto Strasser's erstwhile representative in Germany (see above, VI/136), once again headed the Lower Saxon operation, as he had done for the *DNZ.* In July, 1954, Griesmayr and Kiefer assisted in the organization of a Foreign Policy Association (Gesellschaft für Aussenpolitik) whose meetings in Haigerloch (on July 31, August 1 and September 25–26, 1954) were attended by, among others, Helmut Gollwitzer, the pacifist and neutralist theologian and author of the widely known Frankfurt Manifesto; Gustav Heinemann, the former Federal Minister of Interior (see above, VI/79); Franz von Papen, the old nationalist Reich Chancellor; Hermann Rauschning; Hans Dahmen, the originator of the "Conversations from Afar" and "Place of Encounter"; Hans von Rohr, the former German National State Secretary; Walter Eckardt, the former chairman of the German Union and BHE politician; and Frank Seiboth, the Right-wing BHE and Witiko League leader. In the following months a number of FDP and BHE deputies joined the oppositionist Foreign Policy Association. Here again, however, personal and ideological differences led to the early and explosive demise of the organization in February, 1955, at a meeting in Bad Godesberg. (See *Deutscher Informationsdienst,* no. 548 [March 18, 1956], p. 3.) At that meeting von Rohr took exception to the participation on *Die Nation's* editorial board of Fritz Brehm, who in turn reminded von Rohr of his (von Rohr's) own contributions to the East-financed paper. Coming within a few days of the much-advertised officers' meeting in East Berlin, this double admission aroused the suspicion of the military participants, especially that of the Right-extremist Colonel General Kurt Student. Kiefer, whom Seiboth accused of being a French agent, also voiced his suspicions of von Rohr. (For further details on this circle and on the meeting of February, 1955, see Kugler [VI/79]. For H. J. von Rohr, see below, XIV/73.)

220. Nehring's efforts in the *Scheinwerfer* were devoted to the creation of a new, uncontaminated national socialism, to complete, so to speak, the revolution which the Nazis had begun but never carried beyond the first stage. (See Jean Pfister in *Nordsee–Zeitung* (Bremerhaven), February 29, 1949.) The *Scheinwerfer* combined a vehement hatred of all things western (and especially American) with a concern for Germany's good relations with the East. (Cf., for example, Nehring's hateful essay on Clay and McCloy, "Der alte und der neue Prokonsul." *Der Scheinwerfer,* no. 35 [1949], with his demand for a death sentence for Erich Koch, Nazi Gauleiter and Reichskommissar of the Ukraine, for squandering good will—purchased dearly with the blood of German "liberator-soldiers"—by his primitive methods of treating Ukrainians as subhuman.) Nehring's ambivalence becomes clear in the following: "Spare us the propaganda against Soviet methods in the East Zone! Here the Communist Party's otherwise unconvincing propaganda scores a point. It quite justifiably belabors the now overt English colonial system [in West Germany]. And it makes its appeal to German patriots. . . . Communism—just as it did during the war in Russia—is again stressing the national slogan. . . . We are and remain bitter enemies of the Communist Party. But that does not make us by any means Askaris of

our Western slave drivers. . . ." (*Ibid.*, p. 5.) ("Askaris" was the name given to the battalions of Russian deserters who joined the Germans and played a macabre role in the despoliation of Poland after 1943.) Cf. Ewald Hippe, ed., *Joachim Nehring—Neo-Nazismus? Der "Scheinwerfer" Prozess vor der Hauptspruchkammer München* (Munich: Hippe, 1950), a vehement protest against "the attempt to perpetuate the unholy denazification."

221. Werner Schäfer, Joachim Nehring, and Paul Schall.

222. Fritz Brehm, Heinz Greven, Hans-Ulrich Steuer. For details, see *Deutscher Informationsdienst,* no. 492 (August 10, 1955), pp. 4–5.

223. On the secret preparations, see Kugler (VI/79). See also "Aus dem Bereich des Nationalbolschewismus," *Feinde der Demokratie* (North Rhine–Westphalia), no. 4 (September 22, 1955). In 1962 Ebrecht was arrested on charges of having ordered the execution of twelve Poles in the Stutthof concentration camp in 1939. (*Bulletin on German Questions* [London], XIV, 317. [September 15, 1962], 11.) He was released again a few months later. For a reasonably complete *curriculum vitae* of Ebrecht see Christian K. Werner, *Rechts-Links* (Bad Godesberg: Hohwacht, 1963), pp. 124 ff. This crude propaganda pamphlet must, of course, be used with extreme caution.

224. See "Rundschreiben Nr. 1" of General Ebrecht, quoted in full in *Deutscher Informationsdienst,* no. 471 (May 25, 1955), p. 5. Cf. *Die Brücke*, II, 12 (December, 1955), 6.

225. Quoted in Bohn (VI/71), and in *Deutscher Informationsdienst,* no. 471 (May 25, 1955), p. 4. For a description of the meeting see *ibid.*, no. 486 (July 15, 1955), pp. 3–5. The West German participants included the incorrigible Nazi, Karl-Heinz Priester, and the author Friedrich Lenz, who later was convicted on charges of purveying literature designed to undermine the Republic's democratic institutions. (Cf. below, text near XI/59.) On the other hand, the compromised leaders of the FeS and other "front organizations" were conspicuous by their absence.

226. The chairman of the society was Major General Otto Wagener, Röhm's predecessor as chief of staff of the SA, disciple of Gottfried Feder's incompetent social-credit scheme, and later chief of the economic division of the NSDAP. In the society's leadership group were also the former pro-Nazi air-force General Kurt Student, the old nationalist (Stahlhelm) anti-Hitler General Jenö von Egan-Krieger, and the anti-Hitler General Baron von Gablentz. Furthermore, that group included the Bundestag deputy and former chairman of the FDP Land organization of Lower Saxony, Artur Stegner, who left the FDP in the wake of the Naumann revelations. On the background of von Egan-Krieger, see *Deutscher Informationsdienst,* no. 474 (June 4, 1955), pp. 1–2. On the society itself, see *ibid.*, no. 471 (May 25, 1955), and *Feinde der Demokratie* (North Rhine–Westphalia), no. 3 (July 12, 1955), p. 25.

227. For details, see *Deutscher Informationsdienst,* no. 564 (May 22, 1956), pp. 1–3, and Gesellschaft zum Studium der Zeitfragen, *Analysen und Berichte*, V, 8/9 (April 3, 1958), 7–10; VI, 8 (July 18, 1959), 8–9.

228. For the efforts of Nehring, Ebrecht, and the others behind the

MiFo to penetrate Combat SS groups, see *HIAG Informationsbrief*, no. 2 (February 6, 1957), p. 1.

229. Later Nehring and Ebrecht went to the Soviet Zone to live, but they returned in 1960 when the authorities refused to grant them asylum.

230. Journalistic disregard of this elementary fact has not infrequently brought victory to these groups in the courtroom in slander suits. In a typical case of this sort, the radical, neo-Nazi, but West-oriented *Deutsche Soldaten-Zeitung* was forced by court action to withdraw publicly the assertion that Joachim Nehring had political contacts to SED headquarters and received funds from the SED. See *Bulletin on German Questions* (London), X, 222/223 (October 20, 1958).

Chapter VII. In Search of Unity: The International of Nationalism

1. In this respect see Hitler's admission to Hermann Rauschning: "The conception of the nation has become meaningless. The conditions of the time compelled me to begin on the basis of that conception. But I realized from the first that it could only have transient validity. The 'nation' is a political expedient of democracy and Liberalism. We have to get rid of this false conception and set in its place the conception of race, which has not yet been politically used up. . . . I know perfectly well . . . that in the scientific sense there is no such thing as a race. . . . I as a politician need a conception which enables the order which has hitherto existed on historic bases to be abolished and an entirely new and anti-historic order [to be] enforced and given an intellectual basis." (Hermann Rauschning, *The Voice of Destruction* [New York: Putnam, (c. 1940)], pp. 231–233.) According to this version, Hitler had also argued, "Nations are the outward and visible forms of our history. So I have to fuse these nations into a higher order if I want to get rid of the chaos of an historic past that has become an absurdity. And for this purpose the conception of race serves me well . . ." (p. 232). Cf. Hitler's attack on the concept "Nation" in the course of a confidential speech on November 23, 1937, before leadership trainees in the Order Castle Sonthofen, in Henry Picker, ed., *Hitlers Tischgespräche im Führerhauptquartier, 1941–1942* (Bonn: Athenäum, 1951), pp. 443 ff.

2. At that time the West, too, was treated to by far the best analysis of the nature and direction of Hitler's revolutionary dynamism in foreign policy. The lesson was taught by Rauschning in his brilliant *The Revolution of Nihilism* (I/1), pp. 185–227.

3. See Hitler's postwar plans for Europe as transmitted by Goebbels in Lochner (II/1), pp. 357, 359.

4. Actually this is not entirely correct, as it overlooks the activities of Hans K. E. L. Keller and his co-workers in the so-called International Study Circle of Nationalists (Internationale Arbeitsgemeinschaft der Nationalisten, IAN) from 1934 on. At the Third International Congress of Nationalists at Oslo in July, 1936, an Academy for the Rights of the

Peoples was established under Keller's presidency, but nothing was heard from the Academy or the IAN after that. For the ideology of the IAN, see the sources summarized in *The Wiener Library Bulletin* (London), XIV, 1 (January, 1960), 8, 20. See also Paul Kluke, "Nationalsozialistische Europaideologie," *Vierteljahrshefte für Zeitgeschichte*, III, 3 (July, 1955), 240–275, and Hans-Dietrich Loock, "Zur 'Grossgermanischen Politik' des Dritten Reiches," *ibid.*, VIII, 1 (January, 1960), 37–63. Cf. George H. Stein, "The Myth of a European Army," *The Wiener Library Bulletin* (London), XIX, 2 (April, 1965), 21-22.

5. The propagandistic importance of that conception was attested to by Dr. Franz Riedweg, one of the originators of the idea of foreign SS Legions. Riedweg is a Swiss who in his early life had been strongly influenced by the pan-Europe ideals of Count Coudenhove-Kalergi. Later he turned away from them, deeply disillusioned by their "misuse" in the hands of Francophiles and liberals, such as Eduard Beneš and Aristide Briand. Riedweg now strove for a United Europe under the flag of the Conservative Revolution. Under the influence of the writings of Ernst Jünger, Edgar J. Jung, and Arthur Moeller van den Bruck, Riedweg emigrated to Germany after the creation of the Anti-Comintern, and with Himmler's and von Ribbentrop's help organized the European Liaison Office, the first administrative unit in the SS in charge of foreign "Germanic" volunteers. From an interview with Dr. Riedweg, Munich, July 4, 1957.

Compare Gerald Reitlinger, *The House Built on Sand* (London: Weidenfeld and Nicolson, 1960), pp. 354–355. Here Riedweg (whom Reitlinger mistakenly calls Fritz) is said to have been associated with the *Germanische Freiwilligen Leitstelle* and in implied opposition to a "collection of former Youth Movement enthusiasts" under Colonel Eugen Sparmann, who from 1943 on championed, not a Germanic, but an all-Europe anti-Bolshevik crusade. According to Riedweg, he himself was one of those "Youth Movement enthusiasts" who alleged having been so pained by the "Teutonic" chauvinism of his boss, Himmler, and so totally disillusioned by the latter's shortsighted policies, that he eventually requested to be relieved of his duties and joined the Waffen SS. Loock (VII/4), pp. 55–56, credits the chief of the SS Main Office, Gottlob Berger, with having conceived the idea of recruiting foreigners of "German blood" into the SS to meet the replacement needs of the SS Disposition Troops. Loock places the first discussions concerning foreign SS recruits in April, 1940. In a speech in the beginning of 1944 before generals of the army, Berger said, "The Schutzstaffel (SS) has had its sights fixed on the ultimate objective of a Germanic Reich ever since 1929, when the Reich Leader SS [i.e., Himmler] took over [the organization]. That ultimate objective was necessarily implied in the fact that the SS was an association of Nordic men." Consequently, concluded Berger, the SS had taken over the task "of constructing for the Führer the Germanic Reich." (*Ibid.*, p. 56.) Himmler thought it the task of the SS "to provide the German people, [and] the Germanic people with an elite that binds that Germanic people and that Germanic Europe and holds them together." From a speech of October 4, 1943, quoted *ibid.*, p. 63. In 1947, incidentally, Riedweg, who now lives in Munich, and a number of other Swiss Nazis who had worked for the Third Reich stood trial on charges of treason before the Swiss Federal Court in Lucerne.

6. For a brief, reliable account of the origin and internal political structure of the MSI, as well as of its development, see Mario Giovana, "New Fascists in Italy," *The Wiener Library Bulletin* (London), IX, 1–2 (January–April, 1955), 10.

7. [Club republikanischer Publizisten,] *CrP–Information,* August, 1956, p. 9. Cf. *Die Brücke,* IV, 14 (August [?], 1957), 2. The study center and journal were under the direction of Fabio Lonciari, former high Fascist official and foreign political adviser to Prince Borghese, the MSI's honorary president. The center was to supplement the work of General J. Costa, chief of the MSI's foreign organization, in establishing contact with the remnants of National Socialism and Fascism in other lands. Cf. with this Eric A. Peschler, "Braune 'Europa Akademie,'" *Die Andere Zeitung* (Hamburg), no. 28 (July 12, 1956), p. 11. Peschler also mentions MSI contacts with the National Renaissance Party, a lunatic-fringe group in the United States.

8. Amaudruz was cofounder of the Swiss People's Party and editor of its organ, *L'Appel au peuple* (Lausanne).

9. Both Albertini and Lemonnier had been close collaborators of the French Fascist leaders Jacques Doriot (Parti Populaire Français) and Marcel Déat (Rassemblement National Populaire). The young Corsican Albertini had been secretary general of Déat's party. When Marcel Déat became Minister of Labor and National Solidarity he made Albertini Director General of his cabinet. In this position Albertini remained Déat's closest collaborator until the latter joined the retreating German forces in their march eastward across the Rhine in August, 1944. Cf. Actuel Service, *Das Organisationsnetz der antidemokratischen Kräfte in der Bundesrepublik* (Copenhagen: no date), col. 5. Cf. *Deutscher Informationsdienst,* no. 46 (January 20, 1951), p. 1. Albertini later became one of Werner Naumann's Paris contacts and was, of course, on very good terms with Ernst Achenbach, Embassy Counselor in Paris during the first part of the war.

10. Following the March meeting, an important member of the MSI and leader of its so-called Left wing, Tullio Abelli, arrived in Germany to organize a representative delegation for the announced meeting which was to be camouflaged as a National Academic Congress (Fronte Universitario dell'Azione Nazionale). Abelli's negotiations centered in Hamburg in a circle around Carl Tiso, a Stahlhelm leader and friend of the Bruderschaft leader Franke-Gricksch. Here Abelli met not only Bruderschaft members but, among others, also members of the executive board of the Socialist Reich Party (SRP) (e.g., Gerhard Krüger) and such former Nazi functionaries as a Land group leader of the party's Foreign Organization (AO), E. C. Ettel. Confidential report, no date, but probably 1953.

11. *Die Europäische Nationale* (Wiesbaden), I, 14 (November, 1950), 5. According to *Deutsche Presse Agentur (dpa), Inf.* 957 (June 11, 1954), there was also present Edward A. Fleckenstein of Weehawken, New Jersey, the president of the so-called Voters' Alliance for Americans of German

Ancestry, a totally insignificant but in German nationalist circles curiously overrated group of Yorkville bigots. Others present were Pierre Péan (France), Alemán (Spain), Sir Oswald Mosley (England), Per Engdahl (Sweden), Conrad Meier-Jensen (Denmark), Erwin Vollenweider (Switzerland), Horia Sima (Rumania), Fritz Stüber (Austria), Paul van Tienen (Netherlands), Berthi (Triest), and representatives of the Norwegian Movement for Social Restitution.

12. After the break in the National Democratic Party (NDP), Priester and Dorls, of the SRP, discussed forms of collaboration. (See "Nationaldemokraten" [IV/70]. Cf. *Neuer Vorwärts* [Hanover], January 20, 1950.) They agreed to form a "working association" (*Arbeitsgemeinschaft*) until the Landtag elections in Hesse in November, 1950. After that Priester's NDP was to become the Hesse Land organization of the SRP, and Priester himself the deputy chairman of the SRP (letter of the late K.-H. Priester to the author, April 12, 1958). By July, 1950, this agreement had broken down. A conference of Right-wing groups was organized in June, 1950, by Walter Klein, that incredible agent, whose life story as a Foreign Legionnaire, Communist functionary, SS major in the SD, agent for Bonn, for the Sûreté, for Dorls, for the Soviet authorities, and possibly even for the German Office for the Protection of the Constitution, made headlines in Germany in 1952. (Interview with Priester, May 19, 1957. See *Der Spiegel,* VI, 12 [March 19, 1952].) There were represented at that conference in Neuwied (Rhine), besides the NDP: the DRP; SRP; Feitenhansl's Patriotic Union (VU); a nationalist refugee group; and Joachim von Ostau's latest organization, the recently founded Bloc of National Unification (Block der Nationalen Einigung). With the SRP representative, Gerhard Krüger, resisting a merger, no practical results could be achieved at that meeting. It did, however, lead (after Priester's break with the SRP) to an agreement in July between Priester, von Ostau, and Feitenhansl to form a National Democratic Reich Party (Nationaldemokratische Reichs-Partei, NDRP). (*Deutsche Presse Agentur* [*dpa*], *Inf.* 898 [August 2, 1950] and *Inf.* 65 [August 6, 1950]. Feitenhansl never really merged.) These efforts at a nationalist rally in no way mitigated the growing crisis within the Priester organization. (*Deutsche Presse Agentur* [*dpa*], *Inf.* 1538 [November 16, 1950], p. 2.) Priester was accused of dictatorial leadership; he countered by charging that the NDRP had been massively infiltrated by American intelligence agents as well as by agents in the pay of the East. (Interview with Priester, May 19, 1957.) The crisis led to Priester's expulsion and resignation from the NDRP (August 23, 1950). Publicly Priester explained his departure by pointing out that close identification with a particular party was hampering his work to bring "the national and democratic forces of Europe into a relationship of close collaboration." (*Frankfurter Rundschau,* August 24, 1950.) And, indeed, Priester had begun as early as July, 1949, to devote himself to the weaving of contacts with foreign folkish, Fascist, and nationalist groups. At that time he organized the Working Circle Germany of the European National (Arbeitskreis Deutschland der Europäischen

Nationale). In this he was assisted by Max Rinke and Heinz Nissel, both former members of the Nazi Party.

13. *Deutscher Informationsdienst,* no. 593 (September 15, 1956), p. 1.

14. *Deutsche Freischar,* I, 1928, p. 110, quoted in Harry Pross, *Nationale und soziale Prinzipien in der bündischen Jugend* (Doctoral dissertation, University of Heidelberg, 1949), pp. 130–131.

15. Engdahl had joined a Swedish Fascist group in his teens and later founded the extreme-Rightist party Nysvenska Rörelsen (New Swedish Movement). His newspaper, *Vägen Framåt* (*The Road Ahead*), which was edited by Yngwe Nordborg, a former Swedish Waffen SS officer who also worked for the German radio station in Königsberg during part of the war, saw in "World Jewry" the real cause of the Second World War and demanded the liquidation of Swedish Jews as punishment. Engdahl allegedly declared in his paper that "the ideological heritage of National Socialism can be suppressed neither by terror nor by violence. . . . Some day National Socialism in some new form will march again." (Quoted in Actuel Service [VII/9], col. 42.) For "neo-Nazism" in Sweden and Scandinavia in general, see Armas Sastamoinen, *Ny-nazismen* (Stockholm: Federatius, 1961). Incidentally, it was on the basis of information presented in Sastamoinen's earlier book (*Hitlers svenska förtrupper* [V/52]) that Major Ahnfeldt, who had been selected in 1956 to lead the Swedish UN contingent in the Sinai Peninsula, was forced to resign. See *The Wiener Library Bulletin* (London), XII, 5–6 (1958), 52.

16. For Per Engdahl's own corporatism and his criticism of democracy and dictatorship, see his "Demokratie—Diktatur—Korporativismus," *Nation Europa,* II, 1 (January, 1952), 21–26. Needless to say, his criticism of democracy is far more sweeping than his objection to dictatorship. It is no surprise that he has only the most unsophisticated notion of the characteristics and requisites of a modern democracy.

17. "Das Programm des italienischen Neofaschismus," *Hamburger Brief,* Sondermaterial, Anlage 1, pp. 1–2. The final communiqué of the Rome Congress contained the following revealing text: "At a time when extra-European powers are trying to enslave Europe in their own interest and to impress the last able-bodied men into the military service, the representatives of the Young Generation have come together at a Congress in Rome. . . . The plutocratic and liberal politicians who currently govern in Europe and who have been responsible for the outbreak of two world wars, have failed." (*Nation Europa,* I, 1 [January, 1951], 38.) According to Sastamoinen, the delegates at Rome resolved to take up contact with a so-called Asociacion Argentina Europa, a twenty-man committee led by Hans-Ulrich Rudel.

18. Priester and all other twenty-six German delegates, with the exception of the Bundestag deputy Fritz Rössler, alias "Dr. Franz Richter," were refused entry visas by the Swedish government. Priester charged that the denial of visas was entirely due to the combined pressure of Adenauer and André François-Poncet on the Swedish Parliament.

19. Report of the organizational committee. Rapporteur: Bengt-Olov Ljungberg, Malmö, Federal Secretary of Engdahl's party, Nysvenska Rörelsen. See also "Rechtsradikalismus in Europa" (II), *Hamburger Brief*, II, 89 (September 9, 1956). The four study commission members elected by the roughly sixty participants from France, Germany, Switzerland, Italy, Belgium, Denmark, Norway, Sweden, and the Baltic countries (*émigrés*) were Augusto de Marsanich, Maurice Bardèche, Per Engdahl, and K.-H. Priester. For an incomplete list of participants, see *Signes* (published by the French Section of the World Jewish Congress), May/June, 1956. According to *Signes,* Oswald Mosley and Otto Skorzeny were expected, but they did not arrive. De Marsanich was soon replaced by Ernesto Massi, one of the original founders of the MSI. Bardèche, formerly professor of literature at Lille, is an articulate pro-Nazi, pro-Fascist pamphleteer. In France his "fame" rests on having been made the martyr in a scandalously vindictive (successful) attempt to punish him for his antidemocratic and anti-Semitic writings. For details see the "official" eulogy in *Die Europäische Nationale* (Wiesbaden) VI, 71 (December, 1956), 5, and J. Galatier-Boissière, "Bardèche ou la verité n'est jamais bonne à dire," *Crapouillot*, no. 27 (1954), pp. 65–66. Cf. *Juna* (Pressestelle des Schweizer-Israelischen Gemeindebundes, Zurich), no. 52/2 (May 12, 1952), p. 1. In 1953, the four-man study commission established at the Malmö meeting was expanded to nine members drawn from nine countries.

20. "Die Vorschläge des Programmausschusses," *Hamburger Brief*, Sondermaterial, Anlage 4.

21. Priester founded the DSB on March 29, 1951, and presented it to a larger public at a meeting in Eschhorn near Frankfurt on May 1, 1951. With this organization Priester hoped to attract the followers of his competitors, such as Feitenhansl's Patriotic Union (VU), von Ostau's National Democratic Reich Party, the German Reich Party (DRP), Meissner's German Bloc (DB), the German Union (DU), and even the SRP outside Lower Saxony and the Ruhr area. All of these, Priester thought, were doomed to failure unless they could be rallied into one great national opposition party, presumably under his leadership!

22. *Deutschland, Ost-West Kolonie oder gleichberechtigt in einem freien Europa?* Schriftenreihe "Die Europäische Nationale," no. 1 (Wiesbaden: Europäische Nationale, 1951), pp. 1 and 2. Cf. also the aims stipulated by Priester in the course of an address at the Frankfurt meeting of his Arbeitskreis Deutschland der Europäischen Nationale, November 10, 1950 (see *Deutsche Presse Agentur* [*dpa*], *Inf.* 1516 [November 11, 1950], p. 2), and at the Bad Schwalbach meeting of the Arbeitskreis on February 10/11, 1951.

23. Priester (VII/22), p. 4. Cf. the final resolution at the Rome Congress which rejected the Strasbourg conception of a united Europe as being a thin veil for American-Jewish exploitation and which rejected equally strongly any remilitarization in the interests of extra-European powers and under foreign command. See, for example, "Hat Daladier eine

schwarze Brille?" *Die Europäische Nationale* (Wiesbaden), I, 15 (January 15, 1951), 2.

24. Priester (VII/22), p. 13. This trend of thought, freed from its mythological overtones, is typical of much of Right-extremist speculation in the years when the German state had not yet achieved equal status in the family of European nations. In those days, a demand for the integration of equal partners was merely a concealed way of demanding German equality. Moreover, the loss of sovereignty which European integration would involve for the *other* European countries would accrue directly to Germany's benefit, as the latter did not possess full sovereignty in the first place.

25. *Ibid.*, p. 14.

26. *Ibid.*, p. 10.

27. *Ibid.*, pp. 6–7.

28. *Ibid.*, p. 21.

29. *Ibid.*

30. At Malmö, Theodor Fischer, the former chairman of the Swiss Right-extremist Association of National Socialist Confederates (Verband Nationalsozialistischer Eidgenossen), tried repeatedly (but vainly) to have the congress accept his radically anti-Semitic program. The ESB's reluctance to include anti-Semitism as an official part of its program was motivated by purely tactical considerations. Though voting against Fischer's motion, Priester, for instance, saw no reason for eliminating blatant anti-Semitism from his own propaganda, as practically any 1951–1952 issue of his *Die Europäische Nationale, Rundbrief der Deutschen Sozialen Bewegung in der ESB* will show. Similarly, Bardèche delighted in anti-Jewish vulgarities which are given prominence not only in his books but especially in his newspaper *Défense de l'occident.*

31. Founded in 1949, *La Sentinelle* became the organ of the Mouvement Socialiste d'Unité Française, a Fascist organization which maintained lively contact with cognate groups in Spain, the United States, Britain, and Argentina and continued underground even after its outlawry.

32. For Amaudruz' views, see his "Von der Notwendigkeit einer Europäischen Rassenpflege," *Der Weg* (Buenos Aires), VI, 5 (May, 1952), 329–336.

33. Cf. *Die Brücke,* IV, 14 (August, 1957), 5, and Demokratische Gesellschaft 1952, "Nationalistische Neutralisten aller Länder—vereinigt Euch!" June, 1954, p. 2. See also Actuel Service (VII/9), col. 10. But see the vaguer and more moderate Zurich Program in *Der Weg* (Buenos Aires), VI, 2 (February, 1952), 107–108. In the spring of 1952 (May 9–11) another (the second) assembly of the New European Order was held in Paris to elaborate on the platform and principles of the NEO. Only four countries were represented, including, from Germany, the editor of *Widerhall,* Reinhold Kriszat. (See above, VI/94.)

34. For Schenk-Dengg, see Eric A. Peschler, "Naziverschwörung am Tegernsee," *Welt der Arbeit* (Bavarian Edition), no. 8 (February 20, 1953), and "Dunkle Wolken überm 'Lago di Bonzo,'" *ibid.*, no. 29 (July 17, 1953);

cf. also "Kulissenwechsel," [Club republikanischer Publizisten,] *CrP–Information*, September, 1956, p. 14. Schenk-Dengg, for a time director of the Tegernsee Farmers' Theater in Rottach-Egern, was the publisher of the radically nationalist *Deutsches Blatt* and the author of brochures such as, for example, *Nürnberg-Dachau-Landsberg*, in which the war-crimes trials and other occupation policies came under uncompromising attack. The second German delegate to the Paris meeting of the NEO was Walter Matthaei, the former national secretary of the SRP and leader of its youth organization Reichsjugend. In May, 1951, Matthaei had left the SRP under suspicion of having been an agent of the Federal Office for the Protection of the Constitution and having betrayed party secrets to one of the High Commissioners. (See *Florett* [Bückeburg], no date, p. 11. Cf. Otto Büsch, "Geschichte und Gestalt der SRP," in Büsch and Furth [IV/3], pp. 61, 144. This charge was reasserted in the most positive manner by Wolfgang Sarg, a former SRP functionary and head of the German section of Natinform, in a letter of September 18, 1952.) Shortly after his expulsion from the SRP, Matthaei, together with two other disaffected SRP leaders, Walter Kniggendorf and Raoul Nahrath, organized the Reichsorden. (Nahrath, incidentally, was also accused by Sarg of being an agent of the government intelligence bureau, with the specific commission to report on the German Party, one of Adenauer's coalition partners.) The Reichsorden's aims were said to be the struggle against "collectivization" and Bolshevism, the perpetuation of the notion *Reich*, the promotion of the "dienende Einordnung des Einzelnen im Sinne des sittlichen Preussentums," and the establishment of a Nation Europa. To promote the latter, Matthaei participated on January 12–13, 1952, in the founding of a short-lived German Council for the Promotion of the European Community (Deutscher Rat zur Förderung der Europäischen Gemeinschaft). Karl-Heinz Priester had organized the meeting, which was also attended by representatives from the "national-Bolshevik" Nationale Partei Deutschlands (NPD), Oskar Adler's anti-Semitic and later outlawed Bund für Wahrheit und Recht, and the Reichsjugend. From minutes of the meeting in Kassel (unpublished).

35. The last two more especially represented the European Workers Movement (Europäische Arbeiter Bewegung), which they, together with Amaudruz, had created in December, 1952. Schmid was also the leader of a nationalist youth group called Junge Garde, which maintained close contact with Richard Etzel's Youth League Eagle (Jugendbund Adler) and Matthaei's (later Nahrath's) Viking Youth (Wiking Jugend) in Germany and with Konrad Windisch's League of Patriotic Youth (Bund Heimattreuer Jugend, BHJ) in Austria. (Cf. *Feinde der Demokratie* [Lower Saxony], III, 9 [August 5, 1954], 31. For details on the youth organizations see below, Chapter X, Section E.) In 1959, Windisch was arrested on charges of neo-Nazi activity and sentenced to six months in jail. See "Neo-nazistischer Verleger in Wien verhaftet," *Frankfurter Rundschau*, January 12, 1959, and *Deutscher Informationsdienst*, no. 807/10 (April 20, 1959.)

36. Atilhan publishes in Istanbul a small anti-Semitic hate sheet, written in abominable English and entitled *The Islamic United Nations*. He is said

to have participated in every one of Hitler's annual party rallies and to have been responsible for the shooting of 151 Russian-Jewish agents in Turkey in 1934. (From a report of a Natinform meeting on January 16–19, 1953, p. 5.)

37. The DB was represented by its chairman, Karl Meissner; Ewald Gaul; the former SA Major General and Nazi Reichstag deputy, Siegfried Schug; and Schenk-Dengg.

38. Herzog was made deputy general secretary of the EVS, replacing Schenk-Dengg, who was ousted on grounds of "inadequate activity." Concerning Herzog, see letter of former SRP functionary Karl Theodor Förster to General Remer, December 5, 1952 (copy in author's possession).

39. Hedler, a "150 percent Nazi" joined the DP in 1947 and in 1949 won a seat in the Bundestag. There he was a very inconspicuous and unimportant deputy until November 25, 1949, when he addressed a meeting in Einfeld and thundered against a not exactly unfounded contention of the Socialist chief, Kurt Schumacher, that the extermination of five million Jews had dishonored the German name. Hedler objected with asperity: "I would expect a German party leader to be mindful first of all of the five to six million Germans who after 1945 were brutally killed and oppressed, or died in the course of mass expulsions from their homes." This, in the Germany of 1949, was publicly unheard of. Hedler's parliamentary immunity was promptly revoked and a criminal suit brought against him. A month later, in January, 1950, the DP federal executive committee, mindful no doubt of its new dignity as a member of the government coalition, and under considerable pressure from Adenauer, expelled Hedler from the party. (See *Bonner Mitteilungen der Bundestagsabgeordneten der Deutschen Rechts–Partei,* no. 3 [January 5, 1950]. Cf. below, XV/78.)

40. See above, VI/209, 217. One other EVS meeting (in Hanover, January, 1954) merits a footnote reference due to the fact that at least some of the invitations for it were distributed by F. C. Weiss, of Middletown, New York, and bore not only his fraternal salutation but also the comradely greetings of the National Renaissance Party (James Madole, Beacon, New York), *The American Nationalist* (Frank Britton, Englewood, California), and the Grass Roots' League (Stanley F. Morse, Charleston, South Carolina). On Weiss, cf. Arnold Forster and Benjamin R. Epstein, *Cross Currents* (New York: Doubleday, 1956), Part II, *passim.* Details on participation, resolutions, etc., are contained in an unpublished confidential report of January 29, 1954. The host of the meeting was the old Nazi party and SRP member G. Williges. Among those present were Amaudruz; Fritz Rössler (alias Dr. Franz Richter); Rudolf Karl Dinter, a member of Wolfgang Sarg's Natinform; and Hedwig Kolle, a formerly prominent Nazi women's leader (*Reichsfrauenführerin*) and SRP supporter.

41. The EVS "considère la Communauté Européenne de Défense comme un instrument pour jeter l'Europe sous la domination Américaine." Quoted in Demokratische Gesellschaft 1952 (VII/33), p. 6. With deep distrust of the West was paired venomous defamation of the Federal Republic and its Chancellor. In general, the successive meetings manifested

a clear tendency to exaggerate the growing estrangement from the "compromising tendencies" of the rival ESB and to insist, under Amaudruz' lash, on the purity of anticapitalist, anti-American, racist conceptions. The fourth congress of the National Forces of Europe was to have taken place at Lübeck (June 24–26, 1954) but was prohibited by its Lord Mayor, under pressure from the German Labor Union Federation (DGB). (See *Deutscher Informationsdienst*, no. 418 [November 3, 1954], and *Feinde der Demokratie* [Lower Saxony], III, 8 [August 5, 1954], 28–31. Cf. also *Die Brücke*, I, 15 [July/August, 1954], 1–2, and *Deutsche Presse Agentur* [*dpa*], *Inf.* 957 [June 11, 1954].) For the "extraordinary" EVS congress that took place on October 7–9, 1954, in the castle of Huizingen, near Brussels, see *Die Brücke*, I, 16 (October 30, 1954), 1–3; *Deutsche Presse Agentur* (*dpa*), *Inf.* 1529 (October 13, 1954); *Deutsche Zeitung* (Bielefeld), October 30, 1954; *Deutscher Informationsdienst*, no. 435 (January 9, 1955). Among the participants were Jean Robert Debbaudt, "leader" of the minute neo-Rexist Mouvement Social Belge (see *Deutscher Informationsdienst,* no. 449 [February 26, 1955] and no. 467 [May 10, 1955], p. 1; *Die Brücke*, II, 12 [December, 1955], 5; *Studien von Zeitfragen*, VIII, 3/4 [February 25, 1961], 16–17); J. A. Rongé and Guido Lauwers, of the rival Flemish Social Movement (see *Die Brücke*, III, 12 [October 15, 1956], 3, and IV, 16 [October, 1957], 1; *Studien von Zeitfragen*, VIII, 3/4 [February 25, 1961], 4; *Bulletin on German Questions* [London], IX, 206 [February 1, 1958]); representatives from the Flemish Bloc (Vlaams Blok) (for a detailed account of the entire nationalist movement among Flemings and Walloons, see *Studien von Zeitfragen,* VIII, 3/4 [February 25, 1961] and IX, 21/22/1961 [January 15, 1962]); Abelli and Lonciari, of the MSI; A. M. Kruit, of the Dutch section of the European Social Movement, whose leaders, Paul van Tienen and J. A. Wolthius, were sent to prison for subversive Nazi activities (see *Die Europäische Nationale* [Wiesbaden], no. 48 [September 30, 1954], and no. 49 [November 1, 1954], p. 4; cf. "Rechtsradikalismus in Europa [VII]," *Hamburger Brief,* III, 9 [November 14, 1956]); Guy Amaudruz and Hermann Roth, of the Swiss People's Party; René Binet and Maurice Achart, of the Comité National Français; W. Wiedorn, of the Austrian Freedom Rally (Freiheits-Sammlung Österreichs, FSÖ); Konrad Windisch, the leader of the Working Association of the Austrian Nationalist Youth Leagues (Arbeitsgemeinschaft Nationaler Jugendbünde Österreichs, ANJÖ) (see *Deutscher Informationsdienst*, no. 709 [December 13, 1957], p. 3, and no. 716 [January 18, 1958]; cf. *Bulletin on German Questions* [London], IX, 201 [February 18, 1958]); representatives of the Viking Youth; Vselovod Mositshkin, leader of the fanatically anti-Semitic, anti-Masonic, nationalist Russian *émigré* organization RONND (see *Deutscher Informationsdienst,* no. 426 [December 2, 1954]); and representatives of the notorious Arrow Cross, the radical Hungarian Fascist party. (For the kind of lunatic swashbuckling which is characteristic of these radical *émigré* groups, see the Hungarists' proclamation in *L'Appel au peuple* [Lausanne], no. 30 [October, 1954], quoted in Actuel Service [VII/9], col. 13. For details on Hungarian nationalist emigrant organizations, see below, VII/185. Cf. *Deutscher In-*

formationsdienst, no. 659 [June 8, 1957], pp. 1–4, and no. 676 [August 9, 1957], pp. 3–5. Cf. also "Ungarische Exil-Faschisten," *Die Andere Zeitung* [Hamburg], no. 48 [November 29, 1956], p. 1.) Meissner and Hedler (who had been invited) were conspicuous by their absence.

42. *Die Brücke*, II, 8–9 (September, 1955), 11; cf. also *Politik und Wirtschaft*, September 2, 1955; *Deutscher Informationsdienst*, no. 506 (October 4, 1955), and no. 508 (October 12, 1955).

43. There would be little purpose in describing in detail the organizational work of the ESB in the years since its founding in Malmö in 1951. In March, 1953, a meeting in Innsbruck, Austria, was attended by Priester, Bardèche, Lonciari, Conrad Meier-Jensen of the Danish Reformbevegelse, the exiled Hungarian Arrow Cross leader Arpad Henney, and the Austrian representative Oskar Hümer. In November, 1953, Per Engdahl established close links with the Spanish section under Agustín del Rio, the publisher of Primo de Rivera's works. The ESB's study commission met again in 1954 in Stuttgart and accepted Engdahl's two-volume *The Defense of the West* (*Vasterlandets förnyelse* [Malmö: Bok och Tidskrift, 1951]) as the ideological basis of the "movement." See *The Wiener Library Bulletin* (London), X, 5–6 (1956), 42.

44. See Friedrich Lenz's suggestions at the Luxemburg meeting and Wilhelm Landig's reply in *Deutscher Informationsdienst*, no. 453 (March 16, 1955), p. 4.

45. What we know of the EVS would indicate that the fears of the ESB leaders were realistic. See "Ein Urteil der politischen Justiz?" *Die Europäische Nationale* (Wiesbaden), no. 49 (November 1, 1954), p. 4, especially the subsection "Verräter am Werk," presumably referring to the activities of André M. Kruit.

46. See, for example, "Der 'Zufall' führt Regie!" *ibid.*, no. 63 (February, 1956), p. 3.

47. See the report on the meeting in *ibid.*, no. 59 (October, 1955), p. 3.

48. *Deutscher Informationsdienst,* no. 471 (May 25, 1955).

49. See Heinz Brunner, *Geblieben aber ist das Volk. Ein Schicksal, für alle geschrieben* (Graz: Stocker, [1954?]), pp. 413–420. Cf. preface to Emmanuel J. Reichenberger's *Europa in Trümmern. Das Ergebnis des Kreuzzuges der Alliierten* (4th ed.; Graz: Stocker, 1954). Eric A. Peschler even speaks of Reichenberger's United States citizenship's having been revoked because of his neo-Fascist antics at home and abroad. See "Braune 'Europa Akademie,'" *Die Andere Zeitung* (Hamburg), no. 28 (July 12, 1956), p. 11. Cf. below, XI/250.

50. "Einladung und Programm-Vorschau für die Europa Akademie in Saalfelden bei Salzburg, in der Zeit vom 13. bis 19.Juli, 1956."

51. *Die Europäische Nationale* (Wiesbaden), no. 66 (July, 1956), p. 1.

52. "Die entscheidende Stunde versäumt, . . ." *Die Europäische Nationale* (Wiesbaden), no. 71 (December, 1956), p. 4.

53. Early in 1958 Priester's newspaper, *Die Europäische Nationale* (Wiesbaden), ceased publication, because, as Priester put it, "other urgent tasks have claimed the time which is necessary for the publication of a

newspaper, particularly as the paper had achieved growing circulation." (Letter of Priester to the author, April 12, 1958.) The suspension of publication Priester considered only temporary. This was another of his many delusions. The paper was dead, and two years later, quite unexpectedly, so was he. In the half-year prior to his demise, Priester regained some notoriety and invited the attention of the police "antisubversive" squad when he called and worked for a nationalist rally which he entitled Emergency Association of Groups Faithful to the Reich (Notgemeinschaft reichstreuer Verbände). For two years after Priester's death on April 16, 1960, the DSB suspended its public activity. Its resurrection occurred at an "annual meeting" on April 1, 1962, under the aegis of Priester's former chief lieutenant, Hermann Schimmel (Cologne), the publisher of *The Road Ahead* (*Der Weg nach vorn*), the official information sheet of the DSB, after the death of *Die Europäische Nationale.* To judge from the speeches, nothing had changed in the DSB's ideology since Priester's death. In the light of the revolt of the colored world against the white man, only radical defense will save him. The whites must therefore be militarily supported everywhere, in Algiers, Katanga, or South Africa. Not one square inch must be given up. Germany's task is to become the teacher and savior of Europe, by virtue of its Prussian heritage. The division of Europe into dumping grounds for cultural trash (*Zivilisationskolonien*) and satellites must be brought to an end through an antimaterialist revolution. This rebirth cannot be effected by masses, but only by superior elites. "The white governments must be forced to bow to the demands of a [self-consciously European] elite." Liberal party democracy is a petrified and superannuated social order. It can provide no relevant answers to the challenge of Communism. Only corporatism can do that. Instead of the horizontally organized society with its class and party struggles, corporatism develops the vertical order of society in the co-operation of occupations and estates. (*Studien von Zeitfragen, Analysen und Berichte,* IX, 7 [May 17, 1962].) At the annual meeting in the summer of 1962, Raoul Nahrath was elected to the executive board of the DSB.

54. See Frédéric G. Becker, "Die Europäische Volksbewegung im Kampf mit der 'Europa-Heuchelei,' " *Europaruf* (Zurich, Munich, Salzburg) I, 8/9 (September 15, 1957), 2; cf. *Die Brücke,* II, 12 (December, 1955), 1–2.

55. Becker (VII/54).

56. For these programmatic demands, see EVB handbills entitled "Aktiv für Gesamt-Europa" (no date, but probably 1955), and "Europäer, aufgewacht!" (no date, probably also 1955); cf. Frédéric G. Becker, "Eine deutsch-französische Europa-Front muss entstehen um den Europa-Gedanken auf die rechte Bahn zu bringen!" an address before the founding party convention of the Deutsche Soziale Union (Strasser-Partei), Miltenberg (Hesse), June 17, 1956. Reprinted as "Sonderdruck," *Ziel und Weg* (Frankfurt), June, 1956.

57. Luca (alias Charles Louis Eugène Gastaut), a nephew of Marcel

Déat, organized in 1958 a self-avowed Fascist party (see *Bulletin on German Questions* [London] XI, 230 [February 2, 1959], 11), the Mouvement Populaire Français, which maintained close contacts with the outlawed Parti Nationaliste, a militant, authoritarian, and racist party. The latter, together with such organizations as the Front National Français (under Joseph Ortiz), the MP 13 (Mouvement Populaire du 13 Mai) under Robert Martel, the Mouvement Populaire pour l'Etablissement d'un Etat Corporative (under L. Lefèvre, head of the Algerian Poujadist Movement), the Mouvement Nationaliste d'Etudiants (under Pierre Lagaillarde and Jean–Jacques Susini), the Front des Combattants Nationaux (under Auguste Arnold), prepared and carried out the abortive anti-Gaullist, Fascist rebellion in Algiers on January 27, 1960. In 1961, when de Gaulle's determination to liquidate the Algerian war was translated into a practical agreement with the rebel Front de Libération Nationale (FLN), the nationalist forces of anti-Gaullist ultras formed the Secret Army Organization (OAS) under Generals Raoul Salan and Edmond Jouhaud, to prevent by force the independence of Algiers. Like the above-mentioned groups, the OAS contained a large contingent of French collaborators and former Combat SS volunteers. This state of affairs led political wits to refer to the OAS as the "OA-SS"! (See the letter of a French nationalist *colon* to N.J.Ryschkowsky, reproduced in *Studien von Zeitfragen, Informationen,* IX, 6–7 [April 11, 1962], 9.) For details on French anti-Gaullist nationalist radicalism, see *Studien von Zeitfragen, Analysen und Berichte,* VI, 16 (November 20, 1959), 17 (November 25, 1959); VII, 7/8 (March 30, 1960), 12 (June 25, 1960), 17/18 (October 13, 1960); and VIII, 10 (June 6, 1961), 7–11. Cf. also J. Plumyène and R. Lasierra, *Les fascismes français 1923–1963* (Paris: Seuil, 1963).

58. The Phalange's youth group Jeunesse Phalangiste, under Cavallier's leadership, had close connections with the Viking Youth, the Youth League Eagle, and the Austrian League of Patriotic Youth (Bund Heimattreuer Jugend), with which they joined to form a Kameradschaftsring Nationaler Jugendverbände (Comradeship Circle of Nationalist Youth Associations). See below, X/156 and nearby text.

59. See *Die Brücke,* IV, 14 (August, 1957), 7.

60. *Ibid.*

61. Contained in a handbill entitled "Aktiv für Gesamt-Europa" (no date, probably 1955).

62. See also summary of Strasser's political views in Demokratische Gesellschaft 1952, "Der Politiker Dr. Otto Strasser" (November, 1954), p. 4. In an article entitled "Das Reich muss uns doch bleiben!" Strasser demands, "European confederation, *not* integration: units, or rather entities, peoples, tribes, races (and that means boundaries, hierarchy, contours) are God-given. Only a confederation allows for this fact for which allowance must be made." Quoted in [Club republikanischer Publizisten,] *CrP-Information,* February, 1957, p. 20.

63. Interview with Waldemar Wadsack, Munich, July 3, 1957.

64. Cf. *Europa von Morgen!* (Ständedemokratischer Solidaristischer Pressedienst, Berlin), February, 1952, pp. 3–4, with Becker (VII/54).

65. The Frenchman Gaston Riou, friend and collaborator of Aristide Briand in the nineteen-twenties, was the other honorary copresident.

66. Reprinted in *Die Brücke,* II, 8–9 (September, 1955), 9–10.

67. In 1958, Tixier-Vignancour was active in the destruction of the Fourth Republic only to find himself within a year among the anti-Gaullist "ultras" around the suppressed Parti Nationaliste and the Front National Français. In 1962, he successfully defended General Salan, on trial for his life on charges of armed rebellion. Before that, Tixier-Vignancour had acted as one of the defense counsels (along with Pétain's counsel Jacques Isormi) in the trial of the rebels of the unsuccessful anti-Gaullist putsch of January, 1960. (For the development of extremist nationalism in the Fifth Republic, see above, VII/57.) In December, 1965, Tixier-Vignancour opposed Charles de Gaulle in the presidential election as the candidate of the extreme Right and gathered 5 per cent of the votes cast.

68. See *Die Europäische Nationale* (Wiesbaden), no. 66 (July, 1956), p. 9, and no. 71 (December, 1956), p. 4.

69. *Deutsche Arbeit,* devoted to the defense of German folkdom and ethnic frontier struggles, was published by Strasser's lawyer, Rudolf Aschenauer, legal counsel to the suffragan bishop of Munich. Aschenauer, a radical nationalist, had previously published *Die andere Seite* and *Der Deutsche Dienst.* Closely associated with the SRP leadership, Aschenauer was the center of early plans for the possibly camouflaged reorganization of the party after its suppression. When these plans proved unrealizable, Aschenauer, together with Remer, Dorls, and Haussleiter, considered ways of leading former SRP voters corporatively into other still-functioning, extremist parties, like Haussleiter's German Community (DG). For additional details, see below, XV/65.

70. Cecile von Goetz, "Dr. Otto Strasser, the Coming Man in Germany" (typescript, undated), p. 12.

71. During the Suez crisis, the information bulletin of the Phalange Française, *La Vague,* edited by Roland Cavallier, could still make this distinction: "The fate of the Fourth Republic may well be decided at the Suez Canal, not so, however, the fate of the real France." Quoted in *Die Brücke,* IV, 14 (August, 1957), 7.

72. To be sure, the Phalange permitted its individual members to continue their membership in the EVB, if they so desired, and Henri Roques, the secretary general of the Phalange, chose to retain his position as secretary general of the French section of the EVB.

73. See above, text at reference VII/32; also see above, VII/57.

74. In the summer of 1959 the NEO, under the chairmanship of Guy Amaudruz, organized a cultural meeting in Innsbruck, Austria, in which participated representatives of the Combat SS, the Division Mussolini, the Croat Ustashis, the Spanish Blue Division, and similar organizations from the following countries: Germany, Austria, Switzerland, Sweden, Norway, Belgium, the Netherlands, Finland, France, Italy, Greece, Spain, Portugal,

Egypt, and the Middle East. Exiles from Hungary, Rumania, and Croatia completed the group. The participants gave vent to their undying enmity to democracy and Marxism and determined to fight against all international settlements which threaten to perpetuate unjust frontiers, be they on the Oder and Western Neisse or on the Brenner Pass. (See *Bulletin on German Questions* [London], X, 265 [September 15, 1959].) Later unsubstantiated reports (as, for instance, by Rudolf Pechel in the *Deutsche Rundschau*) spoke also of a meeting in Nice in December, 1959, to plan an international anti-Semitic campaign to run through January, 1960. (*Bulletin on German Questions,* XI, 259 [April 15, 1960], p. 17.) The following April the NEO met in Lausanne. On that occasion, the then chairman of the Stahlhelm, the late Field Marshal Kesselring, while unable to attend, sent a congratulatory letter in which he expressed his sincerest wishes for the meeting's success. In October, 1960, NEO representatives from France (Cavallier), Belgium (Debbaudt), the Netherlands (van Tienen), Switzerland (Amaudruz), Italy (Arconovalto Bonacorsi, a former general of the Fascist militia, who died in 1962), and Germany (Ernst W. Ludwig) met in Paris to follow up the discussion in Spain between the former Belgian Rexist leader and Nazi collaborator, SS General Léon Degrelle, and the Hitler propagandist and Egyptian expert on anti-Semitic propaganda, Johann von Leers. The main item of the agenda was the organization of a campaign to counter the impact on world public opinion which the Eichmann trial was expected to have. In 1962 the NEO meeting in Lausanne is said to have been graced by the presence of Perón. The executive board chosen at that time consisted of Amaudruz, Giovanni Perona, of Milan, J. R. Debbaudt, of Brussels, and Jean Baumann, of Alfeld, Germany. A report on the eighth international meeting of the NEO (in April, 1965) mentioned the presence in Milan of delegates from the Barcelona branch of the Falange; Otto Karl Düpow's International Anti-Marxist Documentation Center (CIDA); All-German Working Fellowship (Gesamtdeutsche Arbeitsgemeinschaft, Hamburg, under Erich Nietsch); Restauration Nationale (Paris); and L'Avanguardia Nazionale (Rome). In addition to these, the participants included also Amaudruz, Baumann, Capotondi, and Perona. Altogether, twenty persons attended the Milan meeting. See "European New Order: Meeting in Milan," *The Wiener Library Bulletin* (London), XIX, 3 (July, 1965), 40.

75. To be quite accurate, MAC emerged in October, 1960, from a preparatory committee that called itself Action and Defense Committee of Belgians in Africa (Comité d'Action et Défense des Belgiques en Afrique, CADBA), which, in turn, had been founded in July, 1960.

76. *Studien von Zeitfragen, Analysen und Berichte,* VIII, 16–17 (November 20, 1961), 8. The chairmanship was taken by Walter Löwen, whose League of Europeans was merged with Young Europe. The executive committee consisted further of Willfried Meineke, Kurt Kohl, and Helga Jahn, all of Hanover, and Herminio Redondo, a Spaniard living in Cologne. In 1963 Löwen's German contingent again separated from Thiriart and together with other Thiriart opponents formed a Europe Front.

77. In Germany and Austria the Young Europe movement had close

ties to the nationalist League of Patriotic Youth (BHJ). In Germany the liaison man between Thiriart and the BHJ was Klaus Jahn, chairman of the Freundeskreis der nationalen Jugend. (For details on the BHJ and for some of its other international connections see below, X/181, and above, VII/35, 41, respectively.) In 1964, plans to organize a summer camp had to be abandoned when the North Rhine–Westphalian minister of the interior threatened to close it down. During the Whitsun holidays of the following year, however, Europafront, under the German leaders Wolfgang Kirschstein and Gudrun Wittig, succeeded in attracting to a camp meeting over two hundred people from Germany, France, Belgium, and Sweden. In the following year, the twenty-seven-year-old Kirschstein received a suspended sentence of five months' imprisonment for "disseminating subversive literature, continuing incitement to racial and national hatred, and promoting Nazi doctrines." The subversive literature in question was *The International Nazi Fascist* (later retitled *The Free American*), the organ of the National Renaissance Party in the United States, whose editor, Dan Burros, committed suicide in November, 1965, when the *New York Times* revealed his Jewish background. Kirschstein is the so-called chief of staff (*Stabsführer*) of an International Viking Movement which he founded, in 1963, in close association with G. Lincoln Rockwell's World Union of National Socialists. The program stresses a confederated Europe, the racial purification of the West, the restoration of greater Germany with its Austrian, Sudeten, and Danzig provinces, and, of course, eternal war against the "crime" of Communism.

78. *Studien von Zeitfragen, Analysen und Berichte,* VIII, 16–17 (November 20, 1961), 10–13. Two years after the completion of this chapter there appeared Thiriart's *Un empire de 400 millions d'hommes: l'Europe* (Brussels: Sineco, 1964). The basic message had remained the same.

79. For the complete text of the "declaration," see *Studien von Zeitfragen, Analysen und Berichte,* X, 16 (August 28, 1962), 6–8.

80. The MSI delegation consisted of the local (Venice) chairman, the attorney Giovanni Lanfré, the former minister Alberto Mellini Ponce de Leon, and Count A. Loredan.

81. The narrowness of the basis was criticized at the conference itself. Especially the MSI wanted to know why the activist French, Spanish, and Portuguese groups had not been invited. Outsiders have suggested that Mosley and Thiriart had deliberately sought to steer clear of avowed Fascist groups and of forces too closely associated with the OAS. This fastidiousness had, of course, nothing to do with ideology, but seemingly a good deal with a lively desire to stay out of the clutches of public prosecutors. In actual fact, this cautiousness was of no avail: Shortly after his return from Venice, Thiriart was arrested in Brussels and apparently charged with collaboration with the OAS and with gun running into Katanga. (See *The Wiener Library Bulletin* [London], XVI, 2 [April, 1962], 28; and 3 [July, 1962], 49.) When we said above that the absence from the conference of such organizations as Amaudruz' NEO, the EVB, or DSB was not due to ideological disagreements, we merely meant to suggest that the MAC was

hardly less radical than they. It would be wrong to assume that there were no differences of points of view among them. To Amaudruz and his NEO, even MAC's tactical antiracist position is a form of betrayal. (It will be remembered that it was Amaudruz, Binet, and their friends who split away from the ESB because of Engdahl's [also tactical] "moderation" in racist rhetoric.) To the DSB—that is, to K.-H. Priester's successor, Hermann Schimmel—it is MAC's unitarist Nation Europe that is totally unacceptable. Indeed, the DSB now rejects the entire concept Nation Europa. It insists on the maintenance and strengthening of the nations: "The demise of the nations would not create a new Nation Europe, but merely a European mash of peoples (*Völkerbrei Europa*)." The EVB also rejects the unitary European nation, but will not even accept the DSB's corporative federalism. It supports the Gaullist and Strasser thesis of a "Europe of Fatherlands," that is, really a loose confederation of sovereign nation states, a basically anti-internationalist position. See *Studien von Zeitfragen, Analysen und Berichte,* IX, 16 (August 28, 1962), 5.

82. There was also signed in Venice a relatively innocuous declaration, calling upon patriots not to waste their energies in fratricidal feuding, but rather to close ranks and face jointly the common enemy. Even this unexceptionable plea to Germans (Austrians) and Italians to bury their South Tyrolean hatchets was disavowed by the MSI, which reprimanded its delegates for having exceeded their authority.

83. See below, Chapter XII, Section B/II.

84. See below, Chapter XII, Section B/I.

85. See *Bulletin on German Questions* (London), XIV, 322 (December 1, 1962).

86. For Soucek's tales of Nazi derring-do, see "Todesurteil als Lohn für Kameradschaft," *Deutsche Soldaten–Zeitung* (Munich), no. 11 (November, 1956), p. 7.

87. Theodor Soucek, *Wir rufen Europa: Vereinigung des Abendlandes auf sozialorganischer Grundlage* (Wels, Starnberg: Welsermühl, 1956).

88. Gottfried Feder, *Der deutsche Staat* (3d ed.; Munich: Deutschvölkische Verlagsbuchhandlung, 1924). See "Geleitwort Adolf Hitlers," p. 3. Cf. Erwin Vollenweider, "Europa, hilf dir selbst," *Europaruf* (Zurich, Munich, Salzburg), I, 8/9 (September 15, 1957), 3: "[Soucek] has developed a conception in his book *We're Calling Europe* which . . . represents the catechism of a movement."

89. For a critique of "bureaucratic collectivism," see Neumann (VI/14), pp. 222–228. In more recent years, Soucek seems to have abandoned the demand for the direct control of the market through price and wage controls. See, for example, his "Droht eine Weltwirtschaftskrise?" *Europaruf* (Zurich, Munich, Salzburg), II, 5 (May 1, 1958), 1.

90. See, Friedrich Peham, "Europas Jugend zur Vereinigungsidee," *Europaruf* (Zurich, Munich, Salzburg), I, 4 (April 15, 1957), 2.

91. *Ibid.*, I, 7 (July 15, 1957), 1.

92. *Ibid.*

93. With the help of the convicted neo-Nazi author and propagandist Friedrich Lenz, an attempt was even made to organize a wide "nationalist opposition" rally around *Europaruf*. Like all similar efforts in the direction of "bloc building," this one foundered also on the rock of particularist egotism. (From an interview with Lenz, Heidelberg-Wiebling, May 13, 1957.)

94. Soucek's moderation in print was mere camouflage tactic to avoid difficulties with the law. In private conversation or closed meetings he candidly expressed his preference for dictatorship. At such a meeting in Nuremberg, Soucek said: "Dictatorship is far superior to democracy, which represents a people's stage of decline." *Stuttgarter Zeitung,* May 28, 1958.

95. See, for example, *Europaruf* (Zurich, Munich, Salzburg), I, 4 (April 15, 1957), 1; I, 5 (May 15, 1957), 7.

96. See Maurice Bardèche's article, *ibid.,* I, 7 (July 15, 1957), 7.

97. *Ibid.,* p. 4.

98. *Ibid.,* p. 3.

99. *Ibid.,* I, 10 (October 15, 1957), 1.

100. *Ibid.,* I, 7 (July 15, 1957), 7, and II, 5 (May 1, 1958), 8.

101. *Ibid.,* II, 5 (May 1, 1958), 2.

102. *Ibid.,* II, 2 (February 1, 1958), 2.

103. See, for example, *Europaruf* (Zurich, Munich, Salzburg), I, 10 (October 15, 1957); I, 12 (December 15, 1957); II, 1 (January 1, 1958). Cf. *Die Brücke* (Auslandsdienst), IV, 16 (1957), 1.

104. Greil, who more recently resigned from that position in the course of an intraorganizational controversy, gave ample space in *Europaruf* to the writings of his friend Erich Kernmayr, the former editor of the Right-radical *Deutsche Soldaten–Zeitung* and of the HIAG journal *Der Freiwillige.* The influence, in the first six issues of *Europaruf,* of the Kernmayr-Greil combination was very great. Thus, for instance, in the April, 1957, number these two alone filled almost one-third of all available space. In the later factional battle inside HIAG, Greil and Kernmayr were the leaders of those who rejected any rapprochement to the Bonn Republic and its major parties, especially the SPD. (See below, text near IX/145.)

105. *Europaruf* (Zurich, Munich, Salzburg), I, 11 (November 15, 1957), 3.

106. *Ibid.*

107. *Ibid.,* II, 1 (January 1, 1958), 1.

108. *Ibid.,* p. 3.

109. This wording is not reprinted in *Europaruf,* but is reported in *Die Brücke,* IV, 20 (1957), 2.

110. *Ibid.*

111. *Feinde der Demokratie* (Lower Saxony), VIII, 1–2 (January, 1959), 20.

112. *Europaruf* (Zurich, Munich, Salzburg), II, 12 (December, 1958), 2.

113. *Ibid.* Cf. *Bulletin on German Questions* (London), X, 226 (December 3, 1958), 12.

114. Gunnar Egmont, "Nasser Asphalt in Österreich," *Europaruf* (Zurich, Munich, Salzburg), III, 8 (August, 1959), 1–2.

115. "Verhöhnung der Verfassung," *ibid.*, IV, 6 (June, 1960), 3.

116. In 1963, Soucek, close to bankruptcy, went to Spain to find overseas employment as an "economic consultant," leaving a considerable accumulation of bad debts behind him in Austria. Within a year, reports had it that he was being deported from South Africa, where he was accused of having "founded" phantom firms.

117. Quoted from *Ziel und Weg* in [Otto Strasser,] *Dr. Otto Strasser, der unbeugsame Kämpfer für ein freies Deutschland* (Frankfurt: n.p., 1955), p. 14. Strasser had developed essentially the same ideas as long ago as 1945, in his *Deutschlands Erneuerung* (IV/115). See the relevant quotations from that work in *Afrika und Orient Informationen,* I, 8 (March, 1957), 6.

118. For an assessment of opportunities which may be available to revolutionary nationalists in the postwar world, see Erdmann Franke "Vom Sinn und Unsinn guter Einsicht," *Studien von Zeitfragen, Analysen und Berichte,* VIII, 11 (August 2, 1961), 8.

119. See *Deutscher Informationsdienst,* no. 453 (March 16, 1955), p. 3, and no. 457 (March 30, 1955), pp. 1–2.

120. All but two of the thirteen issues of Priester's *Die Europäische Nationale* which appeared between September, 1954, and December, 1955, contained long and almost fawningly favorable articles about the Arab world. The suspicion that Priester's faithful services to the Arab League, especially to Saudi Arabia, were at least partly induced by material considerations is aroused by the fact that between February, 1956, and March, 1957, fewer than half of all the issues of the paper made mention of the Near East, and the few articles included horror stories of alleged barbarities of Israeli soldiers in Gaza and elsewhere. One cannot help wondering if Priester's startling loss of zeal may not have been related to a concomitant loss in the Arabs' material appreciation. The suspicion of ties to Arab interests is strengthened by reports that call Priester "un des principaux responsables de la 'Ligue Arabe' en Europe." According to these reports, Priester's files, which had been seized in 1960 by the Frankfurt attorney-general, following the banning of Priester's planned world conference of nationalists, massively revealed the DSB chief's close collaboration with Egyptian authorities. (Union Internationale de la Résistance et de la Déportation [U.I.R.D.], Comité international pour la lutte contre le néo-nazisme, "Les arabes et le néo-nazisme," Bruxelles, April, 1965, p. 2.)

121. During the German-Israeli negotiations for restitution, Priester served as "adviser" to Moslem officials in Germany. See *Deutscher Informationsdienst,* no. 435 (January 9, 1955), p. 4.

122. See reports on the meeting of the study commission of the ESB in Luxemburg on March 5 and 6, 1955, such as *Deutsche Presse Agentur (dpa), Inf.* 443 (March 16, 1955); *Die Brücke,* II, 3 (March, 1955).

123. In April, 1962, police investigations disclosed that Jan Marais was the alias of Robert Jan Verbelen, novelist, SS spy before the war,

officer of the Belgian SS division Langemarck, and head of the Belgian Nazi Security Service. Tried *in absentia* and sentenced to death for the murder of two hundred Belgian Resistance fighters, Verbelen, who had lived in Austria since 1945 and had acquired Austrian citizenship, was arrested in Vienna. The case attracted a great deal of attention in Vienna, as it was discovered that Verbelen had applied for citizenship under his real name. The fact that the application of this war criminal was affirmatively acted upon immediately suggested to worried democrats that Nazis in official places must have covered up for Verbelen. This, in turn, raised the question, how many more mass murderers might have received the protection of the Austrian state in the past seventeen years. (See Wolfram Köhler, "Romanautor der Granaten in Kaffeehäuser warf," *Die Welt* [Hamburg], April 30, 1962. Cf. *Bulletin on German Questions* [London], XIV, 311 [June 15, 1962]; and 316 [September 1, 1962], 14.) In July, 1962, Verbelen's Austrian citizenship was revoked preparatory to extradition proceedings. For Verbelen's criminal activity during the war and for his postwar connections with the nationalist international, see "Ce 29 novembre, Verbelen, arrêté en 1962, sera jugé," *La Voix internationale de la Résistance,* VIII, 92–93 (October–November, 1965), 9. Those who had drawn worrisome inferences regarding Austria's political health from her early handling of the Verbelen case had no reason to revise their judgment when (in November, 1965) an Austrian jury acquitted Verbelen. ("A Vienne: En acquittant Verbelen un jury autrichien acquitte le Nazisme," *ibid.,* VIII, 96 [February, 1966], 5–7.) Indeed, the Verbelen case was only one of six recent trials involving war criminals which demonstrated "that it is hard to find a jury in Austria that will find Nazi mass murderers guilty." "Austrian Blocks Leniency on Nazis," *New York Times,* February 18, 1966, p. 2, col. 5.

124. Cf. Kowie Marais, "Die eurafrikanische Gemeinschaft," *Europaruf* (Zurich, Munich, Salzburg), II, 1 (January 1, 1958), 2.

125. In 1952 Leemann published in the Thomas Verlag of Zurich a "scientific" work which modestly promised an entirely new view of primary matter. In his *The Primary Matter in the Original Form* (*Der Urstoff in der Urgestalt*), Leemann, according to his publisher, "demonstrates . . . how, on the basis of the theory of primary matter there may be developed a physics of primary matter which agrees with empirical knowledge and solves problems insoluble by modern physics." That theory "resulted in a *total* quantization of the world, with accurately computable elemental units." Leemann's "physics of primary matter" is said to be "a total disconfirmation of the relativity theory." Ten years later, the Welsermühl Verlag, of Wels and Munich, brought out Leemann's massive *Original Morality in Primary Matter: The Grand Reconciliation* (*Ursitte im Urstoff: Die grosse Versöhnung*) and a slim volume entitled *The Rebirth of the Occident* (*Die Wiedergeburt des Abendlandes*). The former provides, we are told, a "revaluation of all values" which redeems us from the "Nebenordnung des Zeitgeistes" and makes it possible to grasp the "superordination of a higher totality." The Weltanschauung here presented is a "transtemporal world system" which

also includes a revaluation of ethics on the basis of a new biology of man: "We must think of man and people's community (*Volksgemeinschaft*) more biologically," and politics must be again reconciled with folkishness. To propagate Leemann's "all-encompassing world view" and to help save the occident, a Weltanschauung Primary Matter Working Fellowship (Weltanschauung Urstoff Arbeitsgemeinschaft) has been formed in Cologne under Alfred E. Manke, the co-chairman, with Richard Etzel (Memmingen), of the Deutsche Block. That association calls itself more briefly German Totality (Deutsche Ganzheit). In 1960 Leemann became contributor to the *Deutscher Beobachter,* a radically nationalist weekly owned by Elisabeth Vetter, sister of the former Gauleiter Heinrich Vetter, who was convicted in 1953 on the charge of subversive Nazi activities through the Bewegung Reich. (See above, VI/177.)

126. See, for example, I, 8/9 (September 15, 1957), 4–5. The breadth of the *Europaruf*'s editorial policy is indicated by the fact that the same paper also featured the far more moderate views on European-African understanding of Lutz Herold of Johannesburg—"Europa, Schau nach Süden!," *Europaruf* (Zurich, Munich, Salzburg), III, 10 (October, 1959), 5–6—and J. Krueger's (Capetown) scarcely enthusiastic account of South Africa's parliamentary situation, "Verwoerds starke Hand," *ibid.,* p. 8.

127. Harald Stössel, "Deutschlands General-Aufgabe: Afrika," *Bergische Wochenpost* (Wuppertal), no. 8 (February 25, 1956). For a review of Stössel's Africa "researches," see "Afrika Farblichtbilder Vorträge: 'Kornkammer Nordafrika,' " *Afrika- und Orient-Informationen,* I, 11 (June, 1957), 17. For the EURA manifesto, see *Der Deutsche Dienst,* VI (April, 1955), 6.

128. Stössel (VII/127).

129. In December, 1955, Stössel parted company with Strasser, a fact which led to the resignation of the EVB's Frédéric Becker from EURA. The break with Strasser occurred allegedly over the latter's attempt to dictate the presidency of EURA's German section, but was very likely also due to Strasser's connections with Gaullists. See *Die Brücke,* III, 3 (1956), 9. At the same time August Haussleiter and his German Community (DG) attempted to capture the Europe-Africa Union, although Stössel vigorously denied that he had any commitments to the German Community. See *Deutscher Informationsdienst,* no. 533 (January 18, 1956) and no. 558 (April 27, 1956).

130. Like so many of his ilk, Stössel worked out a totally incompetent but fantastic fiscal scheme of which he himself modestly said: "Harald Stössel was destined in the last few years to discover after more than twenty-five years of struggle the stupendous solution for an organic economic order at the core of which lies the abolition of taxes! . . . This organic economic order is not an experiment! It is simple and correct because it is based on the divine laws of nature!" *Deutscher Freiheitsorden,* I, 1 (May 1, 1957), 4.

131. For a rather complete *curriculum vitae,* see letter of Wolfgang Sarg to Main Office, South, January 1, 1953.

132. From a report of an interview with Schmidt on February 11, 1953, and of a meeting in Oldenburg in which Schmidt participated on May 2 and 3, 1953. For accounts of the scores of German-Arabic and German-African organizations, see *Die Brücke,* IV, 9 (May 1, 1957); 17 (October 1, 1957); 21 (December 1, 1957), Gesellschaft zum Studium von Zeitfragen, *Analysen und Berichte,* V, 10 (April 21, 1958); *Deutscher Informationsdienst,* no. 696 (October 22, 1957); no. 658 (June 5, 1957), pp. 1–4; *Bulletin on German Questions* (London), IX, 202 (December 5, 1957), 9–10.

133. Karl-Heinz Priester wrote to Nasser, "I beg Your Excellency to permit me to give most respectful expression to my and my comrades' unlimited respect and admiration for Your Excellency's actions in establishing, with the nationalization of the Suez Canal, Egypt's full sovereignty and unrestricted freedom. As members of the German people who have been divided by injustice and force and who are still kept under tutelage contrary to the fundamental conception of international law, we were prompted to this letter by Your Excellency's measure and by the baiting and defamation practiced in the so-called democratic West." *Die Europäische Nationale* (Wiesbaden), VI, 68 (September, 1956), 1.

134. See, for instance, Friedrich Jarschel, "Das falsche Eurafrika," *Deutsche Freiheit* (Munich), no. 6 (March 15, 1957), p. 5. Cf. also Otto Karl Düpow, "Bonner Schützenhilfe in Algerien," *ibid.,* no. 5 (March 1, 1956), p. 5.

135. Düpow's political standpoint can be gathered from his evident enthusiasm for the Italian Fascist leaders Baron Alessio Mastro della Siepe and Mussolini's nephew by marriage, the late Count Vanni Teodorani, founder of the "Legion Mussolini" and publisher of a "journal for the Fascist Revolution," *Asso di Bastoni,* and later, of the *Rivista da Roma.* Düpow called Siepe's draft of a book on a corporative *Stato Italiano del Lavoro* a "political conception which contains many valuable and original parts" and thought Count Teodorani (who was sentenced in 1959 to five years in prison and died in 1964 at the age of forty-seven) "one of the most interesting and dynamic personalities on Italy's new political stage." When *Asso di Bastoni* writes ("Crusade of the Legionnaires," February 17, 1957), "The Legion defends the holy cause of Christendom by venerating the memory of Mussolini who for twenty years fought against Bolshevism in the name of Catholicism. Forward march, then! In God's name and with the blessing of Urban II, the first Pope of the Crusades: Forward, against Moscow!," Düpow calls it a "beautiful manifestation of the patriotic and ethical spirit." See "Reiseblätter (I): Römische Impressionen," *Afrika- und Orient-Informationen,* I, 8 (March, 1957), 7–10. Incidentally, in 1958 in the *Rivista da Roma,* Teodorani bragged, "It was we who burned the Jews in ovens," a statement for which he received an eight months' prison term. The orientation of *Afror* is also partly indicated by the fact that its contributors included the late Johann (later Omar Amin) von Leers and Fritz (later Achmed) Rössler. See *Deutscher Informationsdienst,* IX, 770 (October 10, 1958), 2. The advent of Gaullism in France and the rise to prominence

of Barry Goldwater in the United States inflamed Düpow's political imagination. Dreaming of an "Atlantic Rightist Axis" in which the "presidential democracies of strong men" would replace the "anarchy" which "superliberalism" had produced everywhere and whose unified foreign policy would be Gaullistic, Düpow pinned his hopes on such "leaders" as Goldwater (U.S.A.), Charles de Gaulle or Georges Bidault (France), Juan Perón (Argentina), Otto Skorzeny (Germany), Francisco Franco (Spain), Antonio Oliveira Salazar (Portugal), Randolfo Pacciardi (Italy), Léon Degrelle (Belgium), and Adhemar de Barros (Brazil). See "Anticominform Press: 'Atlantische Rechtsachse,' " *Deutscher Informationsdienst,* XV, 1112 (October 10, 1964), 3.

136. See above, text at reference VII/99.

137. Quoted from the April issue of *Afrika- und Orient-Informationen* (*Afror*) in *Die Brücke,* IV, 9 (May, 1957), 7.

138. *Ibid.*

139. " 'Reich und Revolution' (RR)," *Deutscher Informationsdienst,* XV, 1084 (February 3, 1964), 1–2.

140. Düpow (VII/134).

141. See "Hilferufe an Otto Strasser," [Club republikanischer Publizisten,] *CrP-Information,* September, 1956. Cf. *Bulletin on German Questions* (London), IX, 178/188 (May 1, 1957).

142. See *Deutscher Informationsdienst,* VIII, 672 (July 27, 1957). The new journalistic platform was the *Nordic Culture Information* (*Nordische Kultur Information*) which later became known as *Inter-European Informations* (*Euroform*). In this venture he collaborated with such persons and organizations as the radically folkish and blatantly Nazi Konrad Windisch, leader of the Working Association of the National Youth Leagues of Austria (ANJÖ); the Committee for World Order in Cologne; the Mosleyite Karl Strauss's *Sudeten German Informations* in London; the Scottish National Party; and the Bretonic nationalist Gwan Ha Du; as well as Roger Pearson's racist Northern League for Pan-Nordic Friendship. The Northern League, with offices in Dumferline, Scotland, and Sausalito, California (and since 1962 in Amsterdam), believes in "*Heredity:* the laws of biological inheritance apply to human beings as well as to the animal and plant kingdoms. *North European Kinship:* The Keltic, Teutonic, Scandinavian, and Slav peoples of North European descent are the present day representatives of the great Indo-European family—the creators of the classic civilizations of antiquity as well as of the benefits of modern technology. *Human Progress:* Further human progress can only be sustained if the biological heritage is preserved, and a cultural decline must inevitably follow any decay in the biological heritage or falling-off of genetic quality." (From "Aims and Principles of the Northern League for Pan-Nordic Friendship.") The League, under Roger Pearson (Calcutta), Alastair Harper (Dumferline) and Peter J. Huxley-Blythe (Coventry) publishes the journals *Northern World* (later, *Folk*) and *The Northlander.* (In 1963, *Folk* had to be discontinued for economic reasons.) For the far-flung connections of

the League in Sweden, Norway, England, Denmark, the United States, Australia, Belgium, and Austria, see *Deutscher Informationsdienst,* no. 799 (March 8, 1959), pp. 2–4. In July, 1959, Pearson organized in Germany a week-long meeting of the Northern League which culminated in a demonstration at the foot of the Arminius monument in commemoration of the 1950th anniversary of the battle in the Teutoburg Forest! See Thomas Gnielka, *Falschspiel mit der Vergangenheit. Rechtsradikale Organisationen in unserer Zeit* (Frankfurt: Frankfurter Rundschau, [c. 1960]), p. 28. Associated with Huxley-Blythe is the Coventry schoolteacher Colin Jordan, who organized the anti-Semitic, anticolored National Socialist movement in Britain. In July, 1962, Jordan called an international conference to co-ordinate the "National Socialist struggle for race and nation throughout the world." Delegates were expected from most European countries, the United States, and possibly Australia and South Africa. The parley was to have taken place August 15–17, 1962, but the British government refused entrance to the delegates. "Britain Will Bar Neo-Nazis' Entry," *New York Times,* August 2, 1962, p. 2.

143. See Horst Morgenbrod's "Tätigkeitsbericht" in *Rundbrief Nr.* 3/57, reproduced in *Afrika-Orient-Information,* I, 11 (June, 1957), 4. In 1963 Düpow founded a new periodical, *Das Imperium. Nation Europa–Nation Arabien.* An inveterate spinner of international Fascist connections, a perpetual founder of Right-extremist organizations and press organs, Düpow more recently tried his luck with an "international anti-Marxist" front. In the beginning of 1963 he announced the establishment of an International Anti-Marxist Documentation Center (CIDA) with "sister organizations" in Spain and Italy. At the same time he produced a new information service, entitled *Anti-Komintern-Dienst (AKD).* After Italian socialists had prevented an international meeting featuring Perón, Skorzeny, and Düpow from convening in Rome in May, 1963, the latter continued his efforts with an enlarged version of his *AKD,* which now appeared under the title *Phalanx des Reiches,* a "journal for geopolitics, demography, and ethnology." A year later, Düpow succeeded in calling a meeting in Rome of Italian and Spanish Fascist organizations at which his information service was accepted as the official organ of CIDA, although under the altered name of *Anticominform Press.* Needless to add that Düpow's and CIDA's "anti-Marxism" is intimately linked to massive anti-Semitism.

144. This organization should not be confused with a group of the same name that was founded in Berlin in October, 1952, by the former Nazi Reichstag deputy Martin Löpelmann. Constant changes in, and expulsions from, the executive board soon condemned the Löpelmann organization to total futility. See *Politisches Archiv* (Berlin-Grunewald), BS 1/026.

145. The politically oriented organizations met separately to release a strongly worded statement in support of their solidarity with the Algerian National Liberation Front (FLN). Further, "They protested decisively against all German attempts to slander the events in Syria as Communist-inspired. . . . The vast majority of these organizations declared that they

will protest vehemently by all legal and democratic means . . . in case the German Federal Republic is preparing an anti-Arab provocation in the form of establishing diplomatic relations with Israel." (Quoted in *Die Brücke,* IV, 21 [December 1, 1957], 4.)

146. However, the precarious official position of the Delegation of the League of Arab States in Bonn did not prevent the delegates from publishing and distributing in 1959 a German translation of an unbelievably primitive anti-Semitic brochure called *Palestine's Fate.* The chief of the delegation, Fakoussa, even provided it with a foreword. (See *The Wiener Library Bulletin* [London], XIII, 1–2 [January–April, 1959], 7.) Fakoussa's earlier collaboration with the Nazis is reflected in his literary contributions to Nazi periodicals. In 1940, for instance, he published an article entitled "The Struggle in Palestine" in *Der Weltkampf,* the anti-Semitic monthly founded by Alfred Rosenberg. According to *The Wiener Library Bulletin* (London), XV, 2 (1961), 35, Fakoussa was among those to be invited to Rosenberg's abortive international anti-Jewish congress which was to meet in Cracow in the summer or autumn of 1944. On the plans for the congress and the reasons for their abandonment, see Reitlinger (VII/5), p. 254, and the references cited there. Cf. Tenenbaum (V/60), pp. 38 ff. Fakoussa was also an early contributor to the radically nationalist but West-oriented *Deutsche Soldaten–Zeitung.*

147. In actual fact, Fakoussa subsequently did just that. He also founded an organization called Friends of German-Arab Understanding (Freunde der deutsch-arabischen Verständigung). See *Deutscher Informationsdienst,* no. 837 (September 18, 1959).

148. Quoted in *Die Brücke,* IV, 9 (May, 1957), 1.

149. *Ibid.*, IV, 21 (December, 1957), 3.

150. *Ibid.*

151. Schönborn became notorious in Berlin long before he removed himself to Baden. He began by organizing an Association for the Promotion of the Veit Harlan Film *Die unsterbliche Geliebte* and soon thereafter a Working Association Nation Europe (Arbeitsgemeinschaft Nation Europa) which collaborated with the EVS. Later he tried his hand at setting up paramilitary units which closely resembled the SA. Always assured of considerable local publicity by his radicalism, Schönborn became national news in the summer of 1957 when he publicly called the President of the Federal Diet, Eugen Gerstenmaier, former member of the anti-Hitler Resistance movement, a traitor. (See "Der Prozess gegen Erwin Schönborn," *Die Deutsche Gemeinschaft* [Munich], VIII, 15 [2d September ed., 1957], 4.) This remark netted Schönborn eight months in jail. No sooner was he released than he repeated his attacks on Gerstenmaier and announced that he would fight for his rights with all the journalistic means at his disposal. In this connection, it might be mentioned that Düpow also went to jail for insulting a public official. In his case, the victim was the late Socialist chief Erich Ollenhauer, about whom he had spread anti-Semitic lies. Düpow's sentence was for five months.

152. The executive board of the new organization consisted (in addition to Schönborn) of Lieutenant Colonel Heinrich Pfeiffer, Ulrich Kirchgeorg, and M. Stüber. All were said to be members of the executive board of the FDP. (*Allgemeine Wochen-Zeitung der Juden* [Düsseldorf], February 1, 1957.)

153. Quoted in full in *Die Brücke*, IV, 17 (October 1, 1957), 8.

154. Quoted in full in [Club republikanischer Publizisten,] *CrP-Information*, December, 1956, p. 1.

155. Schüddekopf, *Linke Leute von rechts* (I/1).

156. Quoted in *Die Brücke*, IV, 17 (October 1, 1957), 8.

157. Declaration of December 13, 1956, paraphrased *ibid.*, IV, 9 (May, 1957), p. 5.

158. *Bulletin on German Questions* (London), X, 225 (November 17, 1958), 13.

159. See, for example, Jarschel (VII/134), p. 5.

160. When the complete transcripts of Adolf Eichmann's pretrial interrogation become available, much more will be learned of these shadowy, yet effective, international Nazi contacts. On September 30, 1962, the *Kölnische Rundschau* carried a lengthy account, based on the research of an anonymous newspaperman who had lived in Argentina from 1933 to 1947 and on the deposition of the self-confessed Nazi spy Angel Alcazar de Velasco, press attaché of the Spanish Embassy in London, describing the transfer in 1944 or 1945 of several hundred million pounds worth of gold and other loot from Germany through Spain to the Argentine Republic. According to the article, these enormous funds made possible the escape to Argentina of Martin Bormann and over two thousand other high-ranking or exposed Nazis.

161. *New York Times*, April 1, 1945, p. 5, cols. 6, 7; April 2, p. 12, col. 6. On February 23, 1947, the British, with support from American counterintelligence forces, mounted Operation Selection Board, which resulted in several hundred arrests. The target of this operation was a rather nebulous but evidently effective organization, mostly of former SS officers, which in addition to the maintenance and development of Nazi ideology was instrumental in replacing the badly damaged if not destroyed Hitler Youth underground railroad. (*New York Times*, February 24, 1947, p. 1.) But even this operation was unable to break up the well-organized underground escape channels. One of these was uncovered in November, 1947, by Danish authorities. The chief actor here was the former second-in-command of the German forces in Denmark, Lieutenant Colonel Günther Toepke. Toepke, after May, 1945 the chief of the German civilian labor organization in Denmark, had used his position to effect the escape to Argentina of a large number of scientists and aircraft engineers, including Professor Willi Tank. See *The Wiener Library Bulletin* (London), II, 2–3 (January–May, 1948), 10. For an account of Nazis in Argentina, see Oswald Bayer, "Neonazismo en la Argentina," *Comentario*, October–December, 1956, reproduced in *The Wiener Library Bulletin* (London), IX, 1–2 (January–April,

1957), 10. Cf. Exul foederatus, *pseud.*, "Nationale Emigration," *Nation Europa,* III, 7 (July, 1953), 45–48.

162. Kiefer's role in the Deutsche Union and in neutralist efforts to establish a broad anti-Adenauer coalition that would embrace all oppositional elements from the far Right to the far Left have already been noted. (See above, V/40; VI/79, 219.) His checkered career deserves to be recorded. In the First World War, Kiefer was a German counterintelligence agent in France and after the Armistice became an information agent for both the Weimar police and France. In 1920 he participated in the Kapp putsch. In 1922 Kiefer left the intelligence service, supposedly in protest over the murder of Rathenau and the abandonment of the Rapallo policy. As a journalist he was said to have argued for the national strengthening of Germany and for a German-Franco-Russian alliance against the Anglo-Americans, whom he ardently loathes. In 1933, Kiefer insists, he had to emigrate to escape the police. He lived in Switzerland until arrested by the Gestapo in the course of a clandestine visit across the German border. His very quick release and his subsequent enthusiasm for the Nazis suggest a considerable change of mind. After 1950 Kiefer tried hard to persuade Werner Naumann to lead the DU and thus attract the 25 percent non-voters to the nationalist banner. See *Deutscher Informationsdienst,* no. 548 (March 18, 1956).

163. From a private, confidential intelligence report. The reliability of the report could not be checked. According to Josef Lütkind in *Rheinischer Merkur* (Koblenz), April 30, 1954, Bauverd ran the news agency Agarthis for the Arab League. His earlier career was marked by the successful transmission of anti-Semitic and anti-British films from West Germany to the Near East. In this and subsequent ventures, Bauverd is said to have collaborated closely with such men as Bardèche, Binet, and Achart.

164. To what extent this organization was integrated into the Spanish operation Spider under Skorzeny, Degrelle, Eberhard von Stohrer, and others is impossible to say. Reasonably certain is only that Bishop Hudal and the Rome Association of Officers were important way stations of the underground railway carrying fugitive Nazis to safety in Egypt and Latin America in the months after Germany's defeat. Eichmann may well have been one of the many beneficiaries of Hudal's help. An enthusiastic nationalist and fanatic antiliberal, antidemocrat, and anti-Communist, Bishop Hudal sought for areas of compromise and co-operation between the Roman Church and Hitlerism on behalf of an anti-Bolshevik alliance. His efforts to build a bridge between Catholicism and biological materialism are embodied in two works, *Rom, Christentum und Deutsches Volk* (Innsbruck: Tyrolia, 1935) and *Die Grundlagen des Nationalsozialismus* (Leipzig, Vienna: Günther, 1937). Pleading for a "Christian national socialism," Hudal inveighs against the tendency of Nazi theoreticians to enlarge their political doctrine into a total Weltanschauung which would, of course, make it impossible for genuine Christians to become loyal Nazis. In these books, the Bishop accuses especially the radically folkish, anti-Christian wing of the Hitler Movement

of having retained "liberal" elements in their thinking and seeks to demonstrate that Catholicism, despite its unbreakable links to Rome, far from being incompatible with Germanism, is a necessary and glorious part of German history. In fairness to the memory of Bishop Hudal, who died in May, 1963, it is important to point out, however, that it had been he more than anyone else who in October, 1943, prevented the wholesale roundup and subsequent certain murder of the Jews of Rome. See Robert M. W. Kempner, *Eichmann und Komplizen* (Zurich: Europa, 1961), p. 341. Cf. Hilberg (II/9), pp. 428–429.

165. Later Pabst became the organizer of the paramilitary, nationalist, authoritarian, though intermittently anti-Nazi, Austrian fighting league (Heimwehr) under Rudolf Kanzler and Prince Rüdiger von Starhemberg. For Pabst's own justification of the murder of Liebknecht and Luxemburg, see his article in the Right-radical student paper *Deutscher Studenten Anzeiger* (Schwetzingen), no. 4–5, 1962.

166. On June 5 and 6, 1951, in Frankfurt, Pabst is said to have met with Lieutenant F. Karl Friedrich, a friend of the former SA and Black Front leader Walter Stennes, who now worked with the Bruderschaft, with the Conservative Revolutionary anti-Hitlerite Colonel Friedrich Wilhelm Heinz, and August Heinrichsbauer, who in the nineteen-twenty's had been instrumental in the financing of nationalist political groups and who again played that role in the formation of the German Union after the war. The following day, Pabst met with Kiefer, Gehret, and Gottfried Griesmayr of the German Union, in Stuttgart. On Stennes see *Deutscher Informationsdienst,* no. 150 (November 16, 1952). On Heinrichsbauer, see above, V/29.

167. See his own naïve and vain account of his derring-do, *Secret Missions. War Memoirs of the Most Dangerous Man in Europe,* translated from the French by Jacques Le Clercq (New York: Dutton, 1950).

168. According to A. F. X. Baron, the British Fascist who headed the National Information Bureau, Skorzeny was instrumental in channeling no less than 750,000 pounds sterling, which the Grand Mufti of Jerusalem had raised for anti-Zionist and anti-Jewish propaganda, to the various nationalist organizations around the world. (In view of the source, this intelligence must be rated as quite unreliable. From the minutes of a conference between Baron and his German colleague Wolfgang Sarg, January 16–19, 1953.) In the beginning of 1959, the Spanish government asked Skorzeny to transfer his headquarters for armaments deals from Madrid to Tangiers. It was surmised that Spain, now an "almost member" of NATO, meant this request as a gesture of friendship toward DeGaulle whose soldiers have in the past been killed by the arms supplied via Skorzeny. See *Bulletin on German Questions* (London) XI, 233 (February 16, 1959), 11. For Schacht's relationship with Skorzeny, see the former's declaration quoted in *Feinde der Demokratie* (Nordmark), no. 1 (October 14, 1952), p. 13. Lest it be thought that Skorzeny's business interests are limited to Belgium and Germany, it was reported in 1953 that he had undertaken a trip to the Belgian Congo on behalf of some American firms. See *ibid.*, no. 6 (August,

1953), p. 29. Recently Skorzeny was said to have moved part of his activities to the outskirts of Dublin.

169. Skorzeny's reputation in Egyptian government circles was apparently great. At the half-year celebration of the Naguib-Nasser revolution, in January, 1953, Skorzeny was invited to inspect the parade from a grandstand seat usually reserved for foreign dignitaries and other honored guests. The German ambassador, Günther F. R. Pawelke, was not present. See *Der Spiegel,* VII, 19 (May 13, 1953), 14.

170. See "Nach grossdeutschem Muster," *Der Spiegel*, VII, 5 (February 4, 1953), 5. Cf. Walter Z. Laqueur, *Nasser's Egypt* (London: Weidenfeld and Nicolson, [c. 1956]), *passim.* Cf. the sensationalist and unreliable tract by Irving Sedar and Harold J. Greenberg, *Behind the Egyptian Sphinx. Nasser's Strange Bedfellows: Prelude to World War III?* (Philadelphia: Chilton, [1960]), Chapters 3 and 4. Sedar and Greenberg are convinced adherents of the conspiracy–theory of world events—a theory which they paradoxically share with the Nazis and other hysterical anti-Semites. Only a little less breathless is O. John Rogge, *The Official German Report* (New York: Yoseloff, 1961), where, on the strength of Robert St. John's *The Boss* (New York: McGraw-Hill, 1960), p. 152, Voss appears as the head of the Planning Board and chief adviser to the War Ministry (p. 380).

171. General Fahrmbacher, who had been in Egypt since 1950 and began with a staff of six officers, had by 1955 a staff of 67 which, however, had by 1957 shrunk again to 20. After the arrival of Russian military equipment and military experts, the Germans became superfluous. In the beginning of 1959, Fahrmbacher returned to Germany. After 1959 there were supposedly no German officers in Nasser's service. (See *Bulletin on German Questions* [London], XI, 228/229 [January 20, 1959].) General Munzel—who edited Heinz Guderian's posthumous book on tank warfare, *Panzer—marsch! Aus dem Nachlass des Schöpfers der deutschen Panzerwaffe* ([Munich:] Schild, 1956 [c. 1955])—and most of the other officers who were in Egypt are now in the Bundeswehr. For the Syrian group under Kriebel, see the very favorable article by Wolfgang Otto, "Die geheimnisvollen 'deutschen Landsknechte im Orient,'" *Deutsche Soldaten-Zeitung* (Munich), II, 45 (November 6, 1952), 3–4. Cf. also the controversy in "Deutsche 'Berater' schüren in Kairo," *Welt am Sonntag* (Hamburg), no. 47 (November 23, 1952), and "Wer schürt eigentlich gegen wen?" *Deutsche Soldaten-Zeitung* (Munich), II, 49 (December 4, 1952), 2. Fahrmbacher—who was in charge of the army instructors—and Munzel were initially assisted by Lieutenant Colonel Böhmert, Major Mertins, Major Nülle, Colonel Bouché, and Colonel Ferchek. The naval contingent was led by Navy Captain Theodor von Mauchenheim called Bechtolsheim. See Hermann Ziock in an interview with Wilhelm Voss, *Westdeutsche Allgemeine Zeitung* (Essen), June 5, 1952, and Fahrmbacher's letter to the editor, *Frankfurter Allgemeine Zeitung*, April 3, 1963.

172. On the contrary, *Der Spiegel* reported growing discontent of the Egyptian government with some of the highest German officers, who were

accused of collaboration with the West German Embassy on intelligence matters. German rearmament and increasingly more generous military pensions (under Article 131 of the Basic Law) quite naturally diminished the enthusiasm for their Egyptian task of the self-exiled German military advisers. An ever-growing number of them packed their bags and returned home. See "Remer am Nil," *Der Spiegel*, VII, 20 (May 13, 1953). According to the *Deutsche Presse Agentur* (*dpa*) of January 12, 1957, the German Embassy in Cairo identified twenty-five officers in Nasser's employ and described their behavior during the previous years as "extremely correct."

173. In 1962 a new rumor made the rounds, according to which former SS Major Alois Brunner, one of Eichmann's special assistants, who had been living in Damascus under the alias George Fischer and had been engaged in gun running, planned to save Eichmann's life by kidnapping and holding as hostage Nahum Goldman, the president of the World Zionist Federation. See *Bulletin on German Questions* (London), XIV, 314 (August 1, 1962), 9.

174. According to St. John (VII/170), p. 153, von Leers called himself Sidi Mohamed Ali.

175. Shortly before leaving Germany in August, 1947, von Leers visited Ernst Jünger, who recorded on that occasion: "I found him unshaken in his opinions and I therefore steered the discussion away from political themes" (*Jahre der Okkupation* [Stuttgart: 1958], p. 287, quoted in Poliakov and Wulf [V/23], p. 57.) For a description of von Leers as a poor, misunderstood man who has foresworn Nazism and is doing nothing more than teaching languages to Egyptian college students, see the tale by Gerhard Frey in the *Deutsche National–Zeitung und Soldaten–Zeitung* (Munich), May 24, 1963.

176. There is little doubt that von Leers had very high qualifications for his Egyptian assignment. Few could rival his long publication list of anti-Semitic diatribes: *Fourteen Years of the Jew-Republic* (1933), *Jews are Looking at You* (1933), *History on a Racial Basis* (1934), *The Criminality of Jewry* (1937), *Blood and Race in Legislation* (1938), and twenty-two others. In Argentinian exile (1950–1956) von Leers enlarged his repertory with two brochures entitled *Traitors of the Reich* (Parts I and II) in which he presents a scurrilous account of the anti-Nazi Resistance. If the objective qualifications of the man were not enough to get him his job with Nasser, his close friendship with the notorious Hitler enthusiast, Haj Amin el-Husseini, ex-Mufti of Jerusalem, would surely have done the rest. According to R. St. John (VII/170), p. 153, the Grand Mufti publicly greeted von Leers after his arrival in Egypt and added: "We thank you for venturing to take up the battle against the power of darkness that has become incarnate in World Jewry." For a nearly complete bibliography of von Leer's major published output see *The Wiener Library Bulletin* (London), V, 3–4 (May–July, 1951), 19.

177. Again, the Eichmann interrogations should have been able to throw considerable light on von Leers's role in this regard. Until they are published,

rumor, conjecture, and imagination will continue to be very much more prominent in these matters than facts, evidence, and knowledge. (But see VII/160.) In the April, 1961, issue of *Nation Europa,* the house organ of the "nationalist international," von Leers in hurt tones of innocence denied the charge of "fanatical race-hatred and anti-Semitism." "I hate neither the Semite Arab nations nor the black, yellow, and brown races . . . but I am a consistent opponent of World Zionism as are large sections of Jewry," wrote von Leers. This is a remarkable statement for one who "demanded the physical extermination of every single Jew." See *The Wiener Library Bulletin* (London), XV, 2 (1961), 35. According to *Rheinischer Merkur* (Koblenz) (June 30, 1961), von Leers also stood behind Wilhelm Landig's *Europa Korrespondenz,* which circulates in Western Europe.

178. In the autumn of 1962 several German press reports drew attention to the presence in Egypt of yet a fourth group—the most recent addition to the German colony. This group consists of aircraft and missile specialists, hard at work, apparently, to provide Nasser with supersonic planes, rockets, and trained men. German newspapers hit upon this story in the course of following up the mysterious disappearance of Heinz Krug, chief of the Research Institute for Physics and Jet Engines and of his assistant, Wolfgang Pilz. (See *Frankfurter Rundschau,* September 15, 1962; *Kölnische Rundschau,* September 18 and 24, 1962; *Welt am Sonntag* [Hamburg], September 23, 1962; *Die Welt* [Hamburg], October 12, 1962.) Pilz reappeared at Helouan, Egypt's new aircraft and missile center. This industrial complex was said to employ more than two hundred German and Austrian scientists and other experts. By April, 1963, the presence of these German technicians in Egypt was rapidly leading to a government crisis in Israel (whose Secret Service had made attempts on the lives of several Germans). It also led to a reappraisal of German-Israeli relations and to a mounting chorus in Bonn urging the use of all legal means to curb this kind of German contribution to Egypt's war potential. (See W. Granger Blair, "Israeli Parties Ask Debate on Germans' Role in Cairo," *New York Times,* April 2, 1963, pp. 1, 8, and Gerd Wilcke, "Bonn Urged to Curb Scientists Aiding Cairo in Missile Work," *ibid.,* April 3, 1963, p. 6.) On March 31, 1963, in the British *Sunday Telegraph* (London), the frequently sensationalist and generally anti-German Sefton Delmer reported an interview with a returned aircraft technician according to whom the (Messerschmitt?) fighter project alone employed three hundred Germans. He spoke of two production units, both under Austrian experts, Hans Schönbaumsfeld and Ferdinand Brandner. The latter, a former SA colonel and a rabid Nazi, was said to have appointed the notorious Dr. Hans Eisele (see below, VII/179) to the post of unit medical officer. Erich Helmensdorfer, in the *Frankfurter Allgemeine Zeitung* of March 31, 1963, denied that Messerschmidt was in charge of Egypt's supersonic fighter production, but placed the number of German technicians on that project alone at five hundred.

179. This skepticism is warranted by the unfortunate tendency of news media to copy sensational items from other news sources without checking for accuracy. In this way pure fabrications gain currency and in the process of repeated publication take on the quality of facts. Even the same misspellings can be discovered in the identical stories reported by a number of different newspapers and information services. (For the story of Nazis in Egypt cf. *Deutscher Informationsdienst*, no. 599, October 10, 1956; *Bulletin on German Questions* [London], IX, 191 [June 20, 1957], 195 [August 21, 1957], 196/197 [September 20, 1957]; *Allgemeine Wochen–Zeitung der Juden* [Düsseldorf], July 12, 1957; [Club republikanischer Publizisten,] *CrP-Information*, July, 1957, p. 63–64; *Frankfurter Illustrierte*, August 17, 1957. See also the amusing—if not entirely persuasive—attempt to destroy the credibility of these stories by Kai Jensen [Cairo] in " 'SS-Treffpunkt Kairo'—eine dicke Ente!," *Die Brücke*, IV, 18 [October 15, 1957], 6–8.) The original sources of the news items concerning the activity of top Nazis and war criminals in the Near East appear to be the Israeli and French intelligence services—not altogether disinterested parties. In September, 1960, the former made public a list of twenty-three names (see O. John Rogge [VII/170], pp. 300 f.) which was later expanded to thirty-two, though still said to be incomplete. (See Union Internationale de la Résistance et de la Déportation, "SS et criminels de guerre au service de Nasser," [Brussels, April, 1965], and reprinted partially in *La Voix internationale de la Résistance* [Brussels], VIII, 90–91 [August–September, 1965], 16, and 92–93 [October–November, 1965], 18, 20.) According to these sources, the Egyptian secret service and political police have the benefit of the expertise of such worthies as SS General Oskar Dirlewanger, chief of the infamous penal SS brigade; SS Major Eugen Eichberger, battalion commander in the Dirlewanger-brigade; SS Colonel Leopold Gleim, chief of the Gestapo department for Jewish affairs in Poland; SS Lieutenant Colonel Bernhard Bender, Gestapo official in Poland and the Soviet Union whose knowledge of Yiddish is said to have enabled him to penetrate Jewish underground organizations; SA General Heinrich Sellmann (or Selimann?), chief of the Gestapo in Ulm; Dr. Heinrich Willermann, an SS physician who plied his craft in Dachau; SS Lieutenant Colonel Joachim Däumling (or Dämling?), Gestapo chief of Düsseldorf and later actively engaged in SS operations in Croatia; SS Major Schmalstich, Gestapo liaison officer to French collaborationists and expediter of Jewish transports from Paris to Auschwitz; SS Major Seipel, Gestapo official in Paris; and SS General Alois Moser, a war criminal who participated in the extermination of Ukrainian Jewry. A number of former Nazi officials who assisted in the organization and training of the Egyptian army were also reported in 1958 as closely associated with the then Algerian exile government. The names mentioned in this connection were an SS Colonel Baumann, who had taken a hand in the destruction of the Warsaw ghetto; Willi Berner, an SS officer at Mauthausen concentration camp; Erich Alter (or Alten?), who had been involved in the assassination of Professor Theodor Lessing in Marienbad and who later became commissioner for

Jewish affairs in Galicia; Karl Lüder (or Luder?), Hitler Youth chief of Danzig, who was involved in the murder of Otto Strasser's underground radio engineer Rudolf Formis and later assisted Wilhelm Voss in the operation of the German-occupied Skoda works in Czechoslovakia. In addition to Gestapo and SS skills, there are also other capabilities that appear to be in great demand on the Nile. Former Goebbels trainees, initially under the supervision of the late Johann von Leers, are playing—we are told—an important role in Nasser's anti-Jewish and anti-Zionist propaganda apparatus. In this connection we hear the names of Werner Witschale, Baron von Harder, Hans Appler, and Franz Buensche. But Gestapo, SS, and espionage backgrounds do not hamper access to attractive careers in the Egyptian propaganda ministry. Walter Bollmann, Nazi espionage chief in Great Britain before the war, later, as SS major, engaged in antiguerrilla and anti-Jewish operations in the Ukraine; Louis Heiden, an SS official who was transferred to the Egyptian press office during the war; Franz Bartel, an "old fighter" and Gestapo officer; Werner Birgel, an SS officer from Leipzig; Albert Thielemann, a regional SS chief in Bohemia; Erich Bunz, SA major and expert in the Jewish question; and SS Captain Wilhelm Böckler, participant in the liquidation of the Warsaw ghetto—all are reportedly engaged in anti-Jewish propaganda on behalf of Nasser. No list of former Nazi officials in the Near East would be complete without the names Eisele and Rademacher. Dr. Hanns Eisele, SS captain and medical torturer in Buchenwald, made headlines when he managed to flee to Egypt after having served a seven-year sentence for war crimes. At first employed in an Egyptian army hospital, Eisele was later reported to have become staff physician at the Helouan jet engine and rocket center (see above, VII/178). Franz Rademacher, the chief of the Foreign Office division on Jewish affairs and high up on Bonn's Nazi criminal extradition list, had been said to have been in the Syrian secret service until Syria's break with Egypt. In March, 1965, he was reported to have been arrested in Syria on charges of espionage. In a variety of news stories from the Near East the name of SS Major F. K. Wesemann keeps recurring. Wesemann, who is charged with involvement in the extermination operations in Poland and for whose extradition the British have so far vainly pleaded, is apparently still enjoying the hospitality of Nasser's Egypt. This may be the place to recall that Egypt proved an attractive haven for fugitives from justice from among the erstwhile SRP leadership. Fritz Rössler (alias Franz Richter), Otto Ernst Remer, and the Lower Saxon SRP deputy Ernst-Wilhelm Springer found new—if only temporary—employment in the lucrative field of gun running. (For Rössler and Remer, see below, XIII/78.) If we are to believe unconfirmed reports, *German* Nazis are not the only ones in Nasser's service. The Swiss Fascist Georges Oltramare (alias Charles Dieudonné), convicted in 1947 on charges of treason for having edited the collaborationist Paris daily *La France au travail,* was until his death supposedly employed by the anti-Israel propaganda division of the Egyptian Ministry of the Interior. Cairo's French propaganda broadcasts are said to be the work of Daniel Perret-

Gentil, a Swiss journalist who had been a German agent in France. A former commander of the Italian Fascist militia, Antonio Mentegazzi, is reportedly applying his experience to the build-up of an Egyptian militia. Finally, the Swedish SS volunteer Per Olaf Andersson is also thought to be engaged in the Egyptian propaganda effort. In conclusion, however, we must stress again that the reliability of reports on Nazis in Egypt is not great. It may be gauged by the fact that SS General Dirlewanger's name appears in many of these reports despite the existence of an official death certificate for Dirlewanger in the town of Altshausen (Upper Swabia), dated June 7, 1945, and in the face of the positive identification of his corpse in November, 1960, after the persistence of rumors forced the attorney-general in Regensburg to order its exhumation. (See Hellmuth Auerbach, "Die Einheit Dirlewanger," *Vierteljahrshefte für Zeitgeschichte*, X, 3 [July, 1962], 252.)

180. See above, VII/142.

181. The founding of Free Corps Germany (FD) which took place on August 17, 1951, was symbolically advanced to July 20 "as a public protest against the officers who participated in the insurrectional attempt of July 20th, 1944." The front men of the organization, which was subdivided into Freischaren bearing such names as Dönitz, Landsberg, Werl, Schlageter, Bismarck, Das Reich, were a thirty-eight-year-old former SS officer, Hermann Lamp, the twenty-nine-year-old navy noncommissioned officer Heinz Neumann, and SS Colonel Eberhard Hawranke. Behind them stood, however, the former Vienna Gauleiter and Commissioner General A. E. Frauenfeld, his friend and former Salzburg Gauleiter Gustav Adolf Scheel, the Bruderschaft's Beck-Broichsitter, and, according to Wolfgang Sarg, a man by the name of Franke who later became the leader of the Natinform sector Weser-Ems. Preparing itself to become "the bearer of the entire political life inside the German Reich," the FD saw as its immediate goals the removal of parliamentarism, the abolition of democracy, and the reintroduction of the leadership principle and of Hitler's unchangeable twenty-five-point program. Much of the membership (which was concentrated in the area around Hamburg and Bremen) came from the dissolved youth organization of the Deutsche Partei, Bund junger Deutscher, and the SRP. Frauenfeld was responsible for total schooling; the old SA leader Walter Stennes was reported to have been the FD's expert for the "political battle" as well as inspector of its paramilitary training. The FD's undisguised Nazi loyalism emerged clearly from its monthly *Mitteilungsblatt*, which specialized in bringing excerpts from the pen of the FD's patron saint, Hans-Ulrich Rudel; of the SS officers and later HIAG officials Lothar Greil and Erich Kernmayr; the French racist René Binet; the great Hitler admirer, Sven Hedin; the Danish SS collaborator Erik Laerum; Karl Dönitz; and Rudolf Hess. (See *Freikorps Deutschland Mitteilungsblatt*, nos. 3–11, March–November, 1952; also throwaways "Hans–Ulrich Rudel zu der Frage: Wo steht die deutsche Jugend heute?" and "Deutsche Männer, Deutsche Jugend!" no date.) In February, 1953, the Federal Government outlawed the FD on grounds of subversion, Nazi underground activity, and

conspiracy. In September, 1954, Lamp and Hawranke went to jail for four and two months, respectively. The indictments against Scheel, Frauenfeld, and Beck-Broichsitter were dropped for insufficient evidence. See also *Deutsche Presse Agentur* (*dpa*), *Inf.* 1187 (August 18, 1951), *Inf.* 1190 (August 20, 1951), *Inf.* 15 (January, 1952); *Hannoversche Presse,* February 15, 1952; *Frankfurter Rundschau,* February 23, 1952; *Feinde der Demokratie* (Lower Saxony), II, 1 (October–November, 1952); *Parlamentarisch-Politischer Pressedienst,* February 11, 1953, p. 1; *Die Welt* (Hamburg), February 11, 1953; *Feinde der Demokratie* (Nordmark), no. 4 (February 12, 1953), pp. 32–33; *Bremer Volkszeitung,* February 14, 1953; *Deutsche Presse Agentur* (*dpa*), *Inf.* 260 (February 16, 1953); "Das Ende des Freikorps," *Welt der Arbeit* (Nordmark edition), IV, February 20, 1953, p. 7; *Hannoversche Presse,* May 8, 1954; *Neuer Vorwärts* (Hanover), May 27, 1954.

182. But see Heinz Hoffmann's announcement, "to all Land Offices" of November 21, 1952, in which he informs all Natinform functionaries that Sarg had to be brought to the hospital with serious bleeding from the lungs, a recurrent condition, stemming supposedly from a war injury.

183. Report of a Natinform leaders' conference, October 11–12, 1952, dated October 14, 1952.

184. Report on a Natinform leaders' conference, January 16–19, 1953, dated January 19, 1953.

185. Letter of October 11, 1952. For details on the organization of the Hungarist Movement throughout the world, see letters of Szekely to Sarg of November 14, 1952, and of the former State Secretary in the Propaganda Ministry of the Szalasi government, Geza Alfoldi, to the Bavarian Minister of Culture (date omitted, but clearly in the latter part of November, 1952). For the activity of the Hungarists specifically in Bavaria, see the thirty-five-page report of Alexander Tiplt, chief of the SPD's (Bavaria) foreign affairs bureau, and Ernö Kiraly, secretary (Germany) of the Free Hungarian Trade Union. The White Book was referred to as *Denkschrift über antisemitische Hetze und neofaschistische Umtriebe durch Exilungarn in Bayern.* For a discussion of the White Book see *The Wiener Library Bulletin* (London), XIII, 3–4 (1959), 31, as well as *Welt der Arbeit* (Cologne), April 24, 1959; *Frankfurter Rundschau,* March 20, 1959; and *Stuttgarter Zeitung,* March 19, 1959.

186. Norman A. Thompson, an English engineer, supposedly inventor of the first aquaplane, and important collaborator of Baron's, characterized the work of Natinform as follows: "[It] consists in the main of three points: clarification of the racial question, the settling (*Erledigung*) of the Jewish question, and, most importantly, the treatment of the economic side." (From an interview on December 27, 1952, reported on December 28, 1952.) In actual fact, Natinform made absolutely no effort to work out an economic program.

187. Letter of October 25, 1952.

188. Letter to Main Office, South, September 18, 1952.

189. In a letter (November 16, 1952) of congratulations to General H. Bernhard Ramcke on the latter's provocative speech at Verden (see below, text at IX/119), A. F. X. Baron, "Founder and Chief of Natinform," wrote: "We hold as the result of long years of unprejudiced and careful study that it is the Allies and not Germany who are responsible for the present state of Europe and the world. It cannot be denied that Hitler . . . was the first man to warn the Gentile nations openly and fearlessly of the grave danger to their whole civilization from the plan of one of the lesser Semitic races, then culminating after 3,000 years of concealed development, to dominate the world for its own interests. . . ."

Incidentally, on December 7, 1952, Ramcke responded to this letter with greatest caution. "Unfortunately time does not permit me to concern myself at length with the contents (of the letter) or the wishes of (its) authors. . . ."

190. Letter of September 18, 1952. Cf. "Gesetze der NATINFORM" of January 20, 1953.

191. J. O. Beaty died September 9, 1961, at the age of seventy, in Barboursville, Virginia.

192. See, for instance, "Bücherliste" no. 3/52.

193. To be sure, this approval extended only to Malan's general policies, not to individual applications of that policy. In a flight of utter unreality, the Natinform leaders seriously decided that their approval must not become known to Malan lest he increase the severity of his already severe measures. See report on leaders' meeting in Oldenburg, October 11, 1952, p. 7.

194. See, for example, the leaflets "Future Jewish Plans," "21st Century Atrocities" (No. 1/11/7/49), the unbelievable "Torch Commando's!" (No. BN-72/18/3/52), "Jewish Esthers and Money," and, of course, the inevitable "Die 'Protokolle v Wyse v Sion' (Joodse Geheime Planne)." On August 13, 1961, the *Johannesburg Sunday Times*, reporting on a Nazi-type underground movement in South Africa, surmised that Rudman was its organizational head. The movement's secretary general, C. F. Vermaak, of Durban, was quoted on his group's aims, as follows: "Philosophically we strive for a state as described by Hegel—that is, the co-ordination of individual interests with the whole, and the glorification of the state. We have also borrowed much from National Socialism, as proclaimed by Adolf Hitler in *The Third Reich* (*sic*) and have adopted it to South African conditions. Above all, it is our aim to free our Fatherland—which we love fanatically—from forces that undermine our state and people. These include international capitalism, Roman Catholicism, the Jew. . . . We reject totally the democratic stateform, which we shall replace with a system based on responsible leadership and occupational representation." Quoted in *The Wiener Library Bulletin* (London), XVI, 1 (1962), 13. In 1962 the indefatigable Rudman organized a White Workers' League (Blankewerkersbond), which demanded the exclusion of Indians and Jews and an end to immigration and to the education of the Kaffirs. See *Bulletin on German Questions* (London), XIV, 318/319 (October 15, 1962), 15. For a brief account on South African nationalism,

see Brian Bunting, *The Rise of the South African Reich* ([Harmondsworth, Middlesex:] Penguin, [c. 1964]).

195. See letter "Betr.: Ergänzender Nachrichtendienst," January 20, 1953. Similarly ridiculous, but similarly characteristic for Natinform thinking, is the allegation that A. F. X. Baron kept the then Egyptian chief of government, General Naguib, informed on all preparations taken by Natinform to bring about a nationalist opposition alliance which might send at least fifty deputies into the Bundestag. Naguib was supposedly told by Baron that a nationalist victory in Germany would of course mean a radical and immediate reversal of Germany's policy toward Israel. "Baron hopes that he might get adequate funds from that source [the Egyptian government] to pay for the election campaign." From a participant's report of a conference of Natinform leaders, January 19, 1953, p. 5.

196. One observer who had ample opportunity to obtain an insight into the workings of Natinform thought that "they support each other with information, but try, on the other hand, to earn as much money through the sale of this information as is necessary to keep their heads above water. I hardly think that the various members have any political ideals but rather that money and vengefulness, possibly also a hunger for power, are the motives for their actions."

197. Chronic shortage of money sharply curtailed the efficient operation of Natinform :"I have been thinking for a long time of a meeting of all Land headquarters directors. In fact, they are supposed to take place regularly—insofar as possible. Alas, alas, Mr. A. [Armstrong] will first of all have to spew forth a few dollars. Or we'll have to win over to our side Herr Pferdmenges. After Dublin, there will also be changes in our financial situation." Letter of Sarg to his Main Office, South, December 9, 1952.

198. Confidential reports of Natinform leaders' meetings in Oldenburg, October 10–11, 1952, p. 3; January 16–19, 1953, p. 3; May 1–4, 1953, p. 6. It is, however, important to remember that a questionable character like A. F. X. Baron, the author of this allegation, could well have snatched these names out of thin air to give himself the kind of importance and respectability his pathological hunger for power and prestige required. On the face of it, it would appear more than doubtful that the two former Chiefs of the Imperial General Staff had any contact with an outfit like Natinform.

199. *Ibid.*, October 10–11, 1952, p. 3, and May 5, 1953, p. 6. Armstrong died in 1954.

200. *Ibid.*, May 5, 1953, p. 2.

201. See report of leaders' meeting of January 19, 1953.

202. See letters from Huxley-Blythe to Natinform, Main Office, South, November 10 and November 29, 1952.

203. See letters of the Main Office, South, to Ramcke, November 24, 1952, and December 4, 1952.

204. Report of leadership meeting, Oldenburg, October 10–11, 1952, n.d., p. 5.

205. *Ibid.* See also letters of Natinform Main Office, South, to Rudolf

Aschenauer, November 1, 1952, and to Ludwig Kapper (*sic*), November 1, 1952.

206. Letter of Main Office, South, to Sarg, December 17, 1952. Kapfer was very doubtful that any German general would appear at a World Aryan Congress, even if he were to speak only on behalf of and about soldiers. "Apparently you are not aware what it means to operate against Finance Capital and Jewry, a few years after millions of Jews—who, incidentally, may go to the devil—have been gassed. Here very special methods of warfare are necessary which have to be considered particularly soberly." From a report (dated December 19, 1952) of an interview with Kapfer on December 18, 1952.

207. Letter of chief of organization, Natinform, Heinz Hoffmann, to Main Office, South, Natinform, December 3, 1952; letters of Sarg to Main Office, South, December 9 and 29, 1952; H. Giess (HQ Natinform, Germany) to Main Office, South, December 30, 1952. According to Sarg, Baron felt himself cruelly betrayed by Huxley-Blythe. The latter was now accused of having pursued "wholly private goals" in organizing the Dublin rally and of having created in connection with it a political party, a journal (*National Soldiers*), and a front-fighter organization, The Legion. Control over the conference had been placed in the hands of the Legion and removed from those of Natinform. Worse yet, in building up his rival organization, Huxley-Blythe had made use of Natinform's membership files. Further investigations by Baron and Sarg were alleged to have discovered that Huxley was "a reckless adventurer with an obscure past." He once worked for the European Liberation Front and edited its journal, *Front Fighter*, in which also appeared articles by the American-born Frederick Yockey, an employee of the American Red Cross stationed in Frankfurt. While the aim of the ELF was the establishment of "authoritarian, European nationalism," Natinform accused it of East-orientation. According to Sarg, Yockey was said to have worked on the creation of a partisan (guerrilla war) organization which "would be ready to work with the Soviet occupation authorities against the Western powers." See *Natinform Informationen*, March 20, 1953, and Sarg's letter to Main Office, South, March 22, 1953. These informations accuse Yockey also of collaboration with Franke-Gricksch of the Bruderschaft.

208. Letter of January 20, 1953, p. 2.

209. A meeting in Hanover on April 29 brought together representatives of southern groups; one on the thirtieth in Oldenburg, the Lower Saxon representatives; and finally one on May 2–3, 1953, sought to call together delegates of North German organizations.

210. Kleist and Vowinckel had indicated their opposition to the meeting when the idea was first broached to them. They were against such a get-together partly on grounds of security. "The entire Federal Republic is like an ant heap that has been disturbed and, therefore, greatest care is necessary for the time being. It had been evidently planned to remove from the coming election the nationalist leaders, [and this was done] through arrests. . . .

In their opinion it is furthermore too late to achieve anything decisive in this election. . . . In no case should there be discussion of a united national front. Already twice Vowinckel had quite unsuccessfully gone through that business with friends of his. Quite apart from the danger from the police, the leaders of today's national groups would devour each other in blind egotism." (From an *aide-mémoire* of a discussion by Kleist, Vowinckel, and E. A. Schmidt on February 11, 1952.) Vowinckel suggested extending an invitation to the meeting to Professor Jakob Barion (Bonn), Count Lutz von Schwerin–Krosigk, and Helmut Damerau and A. W. Uhlig of the *Deutsche Soldaten-Zeitung*, all of whom were past masters of the art of "hewing to a line which lies between Bonn and the SS" and thereby of minimizing the danger that threatens from the Office for the Protection of the Constitution. In addition, Vowinckel and Kleist suggested the Hitler Youth lyricist Herbert Böhme and the Nazi radio commentator Hans Fritzsche, who had been acquitted at Nuremberg, but who had since been "very cautious." The former SRP leader in the Rhineland-Palatinate, Werner Körper, who—along with the former SRP chief of Baden, Karl Theodor Förster—sought unsuccessfully to create a National Rally in January, 1953 (which was promptly outlawed) and who later continued his efforts with von Thadden of the DRP, representatives of the government parties DP and FDP and some SRP people, suggested additional names for the invitation list: the former Nazi Lord Mayor of Düsseldorf, Carl Haidn; the chairman of the DG in Lower Saxony, the gynecologist Dr. Andreas Binder; and others. Discussion memorandum of February 5, 1953.

211. Report on meeting, dated May 5, 1953, pp. 1 and 6.

212. Rudel (VI/204), p. 256.

213. See Memorandum, Main Office, South, July 9, 1953.

214. See "Gesetze der NATINFORM," p. 2.

215. For all the available facts on Scholz and the ELS, especially its early history and Scholz's relations to Gaster, see the indictment brought by the then Oberstaatsanwalt Arnold Buchthal (Frankfurt) for subversive activity and conspiracy, November 28, 1956.

216. Letters of Main Office, South, to Miss Elisabeth C. Schnitzler, July 1 and 4, 1953. Miss Schnitzler, age twenty-seven, a former BdM leader whose zest for Nazism had remained undiminished since 1945, had fled to England after the war to escape denazification. There she worked closely with Baron and even more closely—if privately—with J. M. Gaster.

217. Letter of Elisabeth C. Schnitzler to Natinform Main Office, South, July 5, 1953.

218. Sarg's letters to Main Office, South, August 4 and 31, 1953. Also letter of Main Office, South, to Elisabeth C. Schnitzler, September 1, 1953. It is, of course, not beyond the range of possibility that Sarg's arrest was genuine and not simulated. We know that Sarg was at that time under constant police surveillance. But this Sarg knew better than anyone else because of his agents, a good many of whom were also working for the Federal and State intelligence agencies, the Office for the Protection of the

Constitution. Tip-offs from them had enabled him several times before to remove and hide compromising materials prior to pending police searches. Sarg had also received private warning that he might be arrested along with other officials of the Freikorps Deutschland when that organization was suppressed. (Sarg's letter to Main Office, South, of February 26, 1953.) Under these circumstances it seems unlikely that he could not have evaded arrest, had it really threatened and had he cared to.

219. Letter of Main Office, South, to Elisabeth C. Schnitzler, September 1, 1953.

220. In the first eight or ten postwar years, the Argentinian Nazi group included very prominently Dieter Vollmer and Hans-Ulrich Rudel, who have since returned to Germany where they can carry on their political and ideological work more directly.

221. This group included very prominently Professor John O. Beaty, of Southern Methodist University, who has since been called to his fathers. For the activity of these and others prior to and during the war, see John Roy Carlson, *Under Cover* (Philadelphia: Blakiston, [c. 1943]), and Rogge (VII/170).

Chapter VIII. Organized War Veterans and Rearmament

1. The full dimensions of the German catastrophe in the first post-surrender years are brilliantly exhibited in Josef Müller-Marein's *Deutschland im Jahre 1: Panorama 1946–1948* (Hamburg: Nannen, 1960).

2. For a critical review of that subject see Alfred Vagts, "Unconditional Surrender vor und nach 1945," *Vierteljahrshefte für Zeitgeschichte,* VII, 3 (July, 1959), 280–309, especially 293–305.

3. That the postwar role of Russia in Europe was not totally unanticipated by American policy makers is shown by a military strategic estimate which Harry Hopkins submitted at the Quebec Conference in August, 1943. That staff paper contained the following prediction: "Russia's post-war position in Europe will be dominant. With Germany crushed, there is no power in Europe to oppose her tremendous military forces." The policy inference drawn from this prescient assessment, however, was not the immediate build-up of anti-Russian forces in the European power vacuum, but rather the necessity of "develop(ing) and maintain(ing) the most friendly relations with Russia." See Robert E. Sherwood, *Roosevelt and Hopkins, an Intimate History* (New York: Harper, [1948]), p. 748.

4. See Hajo Holborn, "Germany's Role in the Defense of Western Europe," *Proceedings of the Academy of Political Science,* XXVI, 2 (January, 1955), 156. For a scathing indictment of the criminal folly of that decision, see the writings of Friedrich Wilhelm Foerster, as, for instance, "La position de l'Allemagne" (VI/9).

5. See Lord Ismay, *NATO: The First Five Years, 1949–1954,* [Paris?, 1954?], p. 32.

6. See Lewis J. Edinger, *West German Armament,* Documentary Research Division, Research Studies Institute, Air University [Maxwell Air Force Base, Alabama], 1955, pp. 4 ff.

7. See Gordon A. Craig, *NATO and the New German Army,* Memorandum No. 8, Center of International Studies, Princeton University, October 24, 1955, pp. 4–6. An opinion poll in October, 1950, asked a sample of German men, "Would you be prepared to become a soldier in the case of an attack on West Germany from the East?" Forty-nine per cent said no, 38 per cent said yes, and 13 per cent were undecided. (Noelle and Neumann [II/4], p. 355.) On the general trend question, "Are you for or against the participation of German troops in a West European army?" those who were against outnumbered those in favor consistently. From 1950 to 1952 the opposition accounted for 50 to 36 per cent, while those favoring a German contingent in a European army varied from 22 to 32 per cent (*ibid.,* pp. 360–361). On the question "Are you in favor of or opposed to the establishment of an independent German army," only 33 per cent "voted" pro, and 38 per cent opposed the idea of a new national army in October, 1950. By the following year the trend had been reversed; in February, 1952, only 38 per cent opposed and 46 per cent favored such an army (*ibid.,* pp. 372–373).

8. For an encyclopedic account of the great debate over remilitarization with a well-nigh exhaustive listing of all the groups involved and their arguments pro and con, see Hans Edgar Jahn, *Für und gegen den Wehrbeitrag* (Cologne: Greven, 1957). Cf. Norbert Tönnies, *Der Weg zu den Waffen: Die Geschichte der deutschen Wiederbewaffnung 1949–1957* (Cologne: Markus, 1957). An inquiry into the problem of German rearmament as discussed in the Bundestag debate of November 8, 1950, appeared as early as 1951: Christian Harwick, *Deutschland zwischen Ja und Nein: Prognose unter dem Fallbeil* (Kreuzlingen: Neptune, 1951). In the same year appeared also a symposium of military experts under the editorship of Adelbert Weinstein, *Armee ohne Pathos: Die deutsche Wiederbewaffnung im Urteil ehemaliger Soldaten* (Bonn: Köllen, 1951). In attentist fashion, the authors demanded full political and military equality as a condition of German participation in European defense.

9. See report on the hearings of a subcommittee of the House Foreign Affairs Committee which investigated whether United States pressure for German participation in European defense plans might not inadvertently bolster "neo-Nazism." Jack Raymond, "Nazi Peril Is Cited to U.S. House Unit," *New York Times,* November 24, 1951, p. 5, col. 5.

10. See Hitler's address to the General Staff, August 31, 1944, in William L. Shirer, *The Rise and Fall of the Third Reich* (New York: Simon & Schuster, 1960), p. 1087.

11. That Goebbels and Hitler themselves had few illusions, in that respect at least, emerges from their conversations as reported in Lochner (II/1), pp. 429, 435, 436, 437, 468, 477, 478. On Goebbels' anti-Bolshevik campaign as a weapon against the enemy camp, see, for instance, *ibid.,* pp. 275 and 284.

12. A particularly pure instance of the myth was offered by former Gauleiter and Commissar General Frauenfeld at an SS meeting in Hamburg in 1951. There he declared: "Germany can continue to fulfill her special historic mission of forming a bastion against the East only in the spirit of the former Waffen SS. All real German men will accept that task even if the West should once again stab us in the back in the midst of it." Quoted in *Kontakte,* December, 1951, p. 9. Cf. SS General Felix Steiner's address to his division at Schwendt on the Oderfront in March, 1945, as recalled by the Swedish SS volunteer Wiking Jerk in *Endkampf um Berlin* (Buenos Aires: Dürer, 1947), p. 77 (quoted in Reitlinger [II/36], p. 159). For a more recent example, among many, see the DRP's weekly *Reichsruf,* as excerpted in *Studien von Zeitfragen, Presse- und Buchspiegel,* VIII, 7 (July, 1961), 3. For evidence that the expectation of imminent hostilities between the erstwhile Allies even influenced the planning of Werewolf activity shortly before the unconditional surrender of May 8, 1945, see above, Chapter II, Section A. On the status of the anti-Bolshevik crusade among the Nazis' war aims, see Reitlinger (VII/5), pp. 20–25. For postwar examples of the anti-Bolshevik thesis, see Otto Bräutigam, *Überblick über die besetzten Ostgebiete während des 2. Weltkrieges* (mimeographed) (Tübingen: Institut für Besatzungsfragen, 1954); E. E. Dwinger, *General Wlassow. Eine Tragödie unserer Zeit* (Freiburg: Dikreiter, [1951]); and Jürgen Thorwald, *Wen sie verderben wollen. Bericht des grossen Verrats* (Stuttgart: Steingrüben, [1952]).

13. An important key to the entire problem of the Germans' historical self-awareness is the Institute for Contemporary History in Munich, a high-powered, government-supported research organization whose task it is to undo, through impeccably honest historical research, the propagandistic distortions which twelve years of official "double think" and the postwar years of unofficial self-justification have produced.

14. See, for example, Hans Meier-Welcker, "Die Stellung des Chefs der Heeresleitung in den Anfängen der Republik," *Vierteljahrshefte für Zeitgeschichte,* IV, 2 (April, 1956), 145–160, and Hans Herzfeld, "Zur neueren Literatur über das Heeresproblem in der deutschen Geschichte," *ibid.,* IV, 4 (October, 1956), 361–386. Herzfeld appears to suggest that only captious foreigners, such as Telford Taylor, John W. Wheeler-Bennett, and Gordon A. Craig, discover in militarism an important contributing factor in the advent of Nazism. He simply ignores such renowned German students of history and society as the late Ludwig Dehio, the late Friedrich Meinecke, and F. W. Foerster. For an excellent review article analyzing the essential conservatism of the Institute for Contemporary History, especially its approach to Germany's military tradition, see Robert L. Koehl, "*Zeitgeschichte* and the New German Conservatism," *Journal of Central European Affairs,* XX, 2 (July, 1960), 131–157.

15. Ritter, anxious to demonstrate the illegitimacy of Hitler's efforts to wrap himself in the mantle of the Prusso-German military tradition, distinguishes between "reason of state," which he approves and which supposedly characterized the "moderation" of the Prusso-German political tradi-

tion (including, incidentally, the crass conquests of Frederick II!), and "militarism," which characterized the intemperate imperialism of Hitler. Characteristically enough, Ritter labors mightily to show that this "militarism" is peculiarly un-German and seems to imply that it is really a French invention! Ritter's thesis, though presented in a large number of articles, can be best gathered in his magistral *Staatskunst und Staatsräson: Das Problem des "Militarismus" in Deutschland* (Munich: Oldenbourg, 1954). For a fair, even deferential, yet independent and critical review article of great scope and depth, see L. Dehio, "Um den deutschen Militarismus," *Historische Zeitschrift,* CLXXX (1955), 43–64.

16. Ironically enough, the myth of the army's purity was most strongly attacked, not by Nuremberg prosecution counsels, but by the German defense counsels of SS and SD defendants and their clients. See, for instance, Rudolf Aschenauer's defense of the mass murderer Ohlendorf in the Einsatzgruppen case (case 9) and Ohlendorf's own testimony, *Trials of War Criminals before the Nuernberg Military Tribunals under Control Council Law No. 10* (Nuernberg, October, 1946—April, 1949), IV, 65–71, 250–251.

17. For a brief but excellent analysis of the Weimar Reichswehr and of its sociological and ideological roots, see Wolfgang Sauer's chapter "Die Reichswehr" in Bracher (III/7), especially pp. 237–246. Particularly valuable are the carefully selected bibliographical references cited by Sauer. The present writer's analysis, however, does not employ Sauer's taxonomic scheme. Cf. the excellent work of Obermann (I/1), pp. 78 ff. "A radical enlargement of the army was not undertaken until immediately before the First World War . . . because they wanted to preserve the homogeneity of the Officers' Corps" (p. 79). ". . . the penetration of the new finance aristocracy into precisely the best regiments. This plutocratic selection did great harm to the Army. It was a sign of decadence" (p. 81).

18. For the social and ideological homogeneity of the General Staff, see General Waldemar Erfurth's excessively apologetic *Die Geschichte des deutschen Generalstabes von 1918–1945* (Göttingen: Musterschmidt, 1957), pp. 126 ff. Even the General Staff, the *sanctum sanctorum* of Prussian conservatism, had been invaded by less traditionalist South Germans. To be sure, remnants of the regimental traditions were still recognized on the verbal level, but they rapidly ceased to be operative in terms of personal commitment. The classic work on the sociology of the German Officers Corps is Karl Demeter's *Das deutsche Offizierkorps in Gesellschaft und Staat 1650–1945,* which first appeared in 1930 under a slightly different title but was recently reissued in a new and enlarged edition (Frankfurt: Bernard & Graefe, 1962). According to Demeter, the still homogeneous corps was marked by feudal (estate) elements, memories of the absolutist experience in Prussia (including absolute obedience toward the king and absolute autocracy toward the people), and nineteenth-century nationalism.

19. With the abdication of the Kaiser, the last prop to the Officers Corps' independent and exclusive status disappeared. For the Corps' main characteristic had been its direct relationship of fealty to the War Lord whose

right to rule was legitimized by tradition. This exclusive relationship had made the Corps for over a hundred years immune from the jurisdiction of civil courts, subject only to autonomous Courts of Honor.

20. Even as early as 1913 no more than 22 per cent of the Officers Corps were members of the aristocracy. See Jacques G. P. M. Benoist-Méchin, *History of the German Army since the Armistice* (Zurich; Scientia, 1939), I, 165, note 2. For the social background of the Officers Corps of the Weimar army, see Obermann (I/1), pp. 244–245.

21. That hostility to Weimar was endemic to the Officers Corps has been variously denied, especially in recent years when the rehabilitation of the officer's function, calling, and prestige had become a matter of political importance. See, for example, Hans Meier-Welcker, "Zur politischen Haltung des Reichswehr-Offizierkorps," *Wehrwissenschaftliche Rundschau,* XII, 7 (1962), 407–417.

22. For a critical summary of the military and political memoir literature see H. R. Trevor-Roper, "The Germans Reappraise the War," *Foreign Affairs,* XXXI, 2 (January, 1953), 225–237, and Sir Lewis Namier, *In the Nazi Era* (London: Macmillan, 1952), especially pp. 13–33.

23. How disruptive the presence of Nazis in the Officers Corps was felt to be by conservatives emerges clearly from the following. In a letter to Gert P. Spindler of September 19, 1951, Count Georg Dücker-Plettenberg wrote: "The differences in conceptions within the generation particularly of the last war will always impede the construction of a unity based upon the previously valid principles of decent soldierliness. This was one of the deviltries of National Socialism that it succeeded in destroying with its infiltration tactics even the loosest links among the soldiers of the generation of the last war."

24. In March, 1950, a representative sample of Germans was polled on their views of the causes of defeat in the Second World War. Thirty-three per cent attributed defeat to the overwhelming might of Germany's enemies and to Germany's relative weakness; 25 per cent saw the cause in treason and sabotage; 15 per cent blamed generally poor leadership and political mistakes; 11 per cent held Hitler personally responsible. Seven per cent found the cause of defeat in disunity among party, army, and SS; 6 per cent blamed the military leaders; 4 per cent, the Nazis. Noelle and Neumann (II/4), p. 137.

25. It is generally agreed that those who sympathized with the anti-Hitler plotters even as late as the summer of 1944 were only a small minority. Many (Allied) authors would put it even less cautiously: "My contention is," writes Henry M. Pachter, "that the 20th of July was the work of a faction rather than a national reaction against Hitler" ("The Legend of the 20th of July 1944," *Social Research,* XXIX, 1 [Spring, 1962], 110). The frankly unsympathetic William L. Shirer comes to the following conclusion: "The revolt of July 20, 1944 . . . had flickered out because almost all the men who kept this great country running, generals and civilians, and the mass of the German people, in uniform and out, were not ready for a revolution—in fact, despite their misery and the bleak prospect of defeat and foreign occupation, did not want it. National Socialism, notwithstanding the degradation it

had brought to Germany and Europe, they still accepted and indeed supported, and in Adolf Hitler they still saw the country's savior. . . . By a hypnotism that defies explanation . . . Hitler held the allegiance and trust of this remarkable people to the last." (Shirer [VIII/10], p. 1082.) For a different view, see the more scholarly—if also overly apologetic—work of Hans Rothfels, *The German Opposition to Hitler,* trans. by Lawrence Wilson (Chicago: Regnery, 1962). It is rather characteristic for the official historiography and mentality of the Bonn Republic that there is little discussion of, let alone misgivings over, the incongruous fact that a group of traditional conservative and Conservative Revolutionary aristocrats, Junkers, and upper bourgeois, whose active dislike (and sometimes violent hatred) of liberal party democracy (or any democracy) is a matter of record, should be popularly represented as *the* incarnation of anti-Nazi resistance and of the "other Germany." For a recent attack on the myth of July 20 in vindication of the importance of the democratic, socialist, and Communist resistance, see Pachter's article cited above, as well as his exchange with Hans Rothfels in *Social Research,* XXIX, 4 (Winter, 1962), 481–488. Cf. below, VIII/158. Ironically enough, General Adolf Heusinger, who in 1944 had been too much of a "nonpolitical" officer to join the military conspirators and came close to falling himself victim to the bomb plot, felt moved to issue an order of the day on July 20, 1959, in which he said, ". . . they [the men of July 20] are the noblest witnesses against the collective guilt of the German people. Their spirit and posture remain to us [shining] examples."

26. The ambivalence of German public opinion on this crucial issue is partly reflected in the results of opinion surveys of the years 1951–1952. In June, 1951, a representative sample of the population was asked, "In your opinion how are the men of July 20th to be adjudged?" While 11 per cent could not recall the events of July 20 and another 16 per cent refused to commit themselves, 30 per cent condemned the men of July 20, 40 per cent expressed their approval of them, and 3 per cent gave an ambivalent, ambiguous judgment. When in December, 1952, pollsters asked whether or not the Resistance movement should have suspended its activities for the duration of the war, only 20 per cent of the respondents thought resistance in times of war justified, 34 per cent counseled postponement, 15 per cent rejected the notion of resistance altogether, and 31 per cent were undecided. In November, 1952, 36 per cent of a representative sample thought that Germany would have very likely won the war had there not been the Resistance movement! (Noelle and Neumann [II/4], p. 138.)

27. This is not the place to assess the historiography of the plot of July 20. Yet, because of the plot's moral and ideological importance in postwar Germany, it should be stressed that the official hagiography of such traditionalist conservatives as Gerhard Ritter (*The German Resistance: Carl Goerdeler's Struggle Against Tyranny,* trans. by R. T. Clark [New York: Praeger, 1958]) and Rothfels (VIII/25) and of former Conservative Revolutionaries such as Zeller (III/10) cannot be acquitted of the charge of having fashioned a conservative mythology. The work of these historians must not be allowed to obscure the unpalatable facts that the Junker heroes

of the plot were rather late anti-Hitlerites, that their horror of Nazism was largely a function of their antiproletarian bias and of the Nazi threat to their social caste position, that their attachment to liberal and democratic values was on the whole nonexistent, that their motives were not free of opportunism, and that their approach to genuine socialist and democratic anti-Nazis from the suppressed labor and socialist movements was hesitant and suspicious. For a brief and rather harsh statement of the "de-mythologizing" point of view suggested here see Pachter (VIII/25). For a more balanced and thoughtful critique of the theoretical ambiguities and political indecision in the thought and action of Resistance leaders stemming from their conservative distrust of the masses and their view of Nazism as the ultimate consequence of democracy, see George K. Romoser, "The Politics of Uncertainty: The German Resistance Movement," *Social Research,* XXXI, 1 (Spring, 1964), 73-93. For the ethical and religious factors involved in the conservative anti-Nazi Resistance, see Mary Alice Gallin, *German Resistance to . . . Hitler* (Washington: Catholic University of America Press, 1961).

28. Cf. von Cube (II/44), p. 371.

29. Quoted by Hasso von Manteuffel, "Der Staat und wir," *Nordwest–Zeitung* (Oldenburg), August 1, 1951, p. 1.

30. See speech of the Speaker of the Bundestag, Hermann Ehlers, before the "Evangelische Akademie" quoted in *Deutsche Soldaten–Zeitung* (Munich), no. 29 (July 17, 1952), p. 5.

31. In that year also the highly nationalist Luftwaffe general Hans-Jürgen Stumpff became adviser on veterans affairs to the CDU's Land organization in Schleswig-Holstein.

32. See "Gesetz zur Regelung der Rechtsverhältnisse der unter Artikel 131 des GG fallenden Personen," May 11, 1951, in *Bundesgesetzblatt* no. 22, May 13, 1951. Cf. below, IX/56 and nearby text.

33. See, for example, H. Juergens, "Enttäuschte Hoffnungen," *Der Notweg* (Detmold), III, 11 (November, 1951), 7, and Ministerialrat Ringe, "Versorgung der Wehrmachtsangehörigen," *ibid.,* pp. 6–7.

34. That was, of course, at the time hotly denied by functionaries and members of the BvW. To them the Law of May 11, 1951, was a totally inadequate settlement, especially unfair to the noncommissioned officers of fewer than twelve years' service. They foresaw many more years of lobbying before a "fair settlement" of their claims could be achieved. Especially important, from the BvW's point of view, was the close scrutiny in the years to come of the administrative decrees which had to be issued in accordance with the Law to Article 131. For the BvW's point of view on these problems, see any of the monthly issues of *Der Notweg* (Detmold), beginning with the June issue in 1951.

35. The fact that the leadership of the DSB rested in the hands of conservative nationalists did not mean, of course, that its membership eschewed radical causes. Especially in Lower Saxony, many former officers who supported the DSB on grounds of practical, material interests also supported the frankly Nazi Socialist Reich Party which epitomized in their minds the

opposition to the "men of July 20." (Letter of Lothar Neumann to Hermann Klingspor, November 12, 1951.)

36. For the early history of this organization under the chairmanship of Sergeant Eugen Eisenschink, whose announced goal was "to represent the claims of former members of the armed forces and their dependents," see *Der Informationsdienst,* no. 61 (March 24, 1951).

37. This step the BvW had consistently refused to take, despite its willingness to make itself the spokesman, if need be, of the pension claims of the Waffen SS as well. See, e.g., Sorrel, "Soldatenverbände im Umbruch," *Der Notweg* (Detmold) III, 11 (November, 1951), 3, and F. H. Putzer (editor of the *Notweg*), "Weg zur Klärung," *ibid.,* III, 12 (December, 1951), 2. For Sorrel's fight against the authoritarian internal structure of the soldiers' organization, see also his letters to the editor of *Welt am Sonntag* (Hamburg) of November 26, 1951, January 2 and 16, 1952.

38. See *Der Informationsdienst,* no. 33 (December 4, 1950).

39. Gümbel, a member of the Nazi Party in 1923 and participant in Hitler's Munich putsch, was the recipient of the once much coveted Blood Order of the NSDAP. Some years after the organization of the BdS, Gümbel maintained friendly relations to the East-financed, radically nationalist-neutralist Leadership Circle of Former Soldiers (FeS). In fact, in 1953 he was said to have founded his own soldiers' organization which, though independent of FeS, was designed to serve as a successor organization in case the FeS should be outlawed by the government. (From a report on a discussion with FeS functionary Wilhelm Wesemeyer [Bad Godesberg], April 14, 1953.) Gümbel was also involved in efforts, in the autumn and winter of 1952, to prepare camouflaged successor organizations for the outlawed Socialist Reich Party. See below, text at XIII/33.

40. See *Der Informationsdienst,* no. 30 (November 23, 1950).

41. *Ibid.*

42. D'Alquen, it was alleged, had been "democratized"—a sardonic euphemism for "hired"—by Army Intelligence. To Willi Frischauer, D'Alquen boasted that he was "in Allied employ." Frischauer, *Himmler* (London: Odhams Press, 1953), p. 14. On D'Alquen's Werewolf activities as assistant to Hans Prützmann, see International Military Tribunal, *Trial of the Major War Criminals* (Nuremberg: 1948), XVII, 230. Cf. above, text at V/18.

43. Guderian made essentially the same conditions in an interview with the Hearst correspondent Karl von Wiegand in the spring of 1950. See *Kommentare Berichte Informationen* (*KBI*), I, 7 (August, 1950), 7–8. Von Wiegand, "an old friend of the Nazis," collaborated in 1940 with German authorities to produce "the second most successful piece of Nazi war propaganda directed at" the United States. This was a purportive interview with Hitler in which the Führer "spontaneously" sought to reassure Americans concerning his peaceful intentions and limited foreign-policy aims. See Rogge (VIII/170), pp. 233–237.

44. At the same time it should be mentioned that "usually reliable"

sources continued to report negotiations between American officials and Guderian. According to one of these, Guderian was said to have discussed tactical problems of remilitarization with U.S. High Commissioner John McCloy in three meetings following the latter's return from the United States on July 3, 1951. See *Deutsche Presse Agentur* (*dpa*), *Inf.* 109/51 (August 7, 1951).

45. Cf. above, VII/10.

46. V/67.

47. Document E 7 of an unpublished collection of prosecution documents.

48. See paragraph 12 of the British intelligence report (V/12). That memorandum, whose accuracy is not in every instance beyond question, also asserts that Naumann became the political adviser of Paul Hausser, the senior Combat SS general. The latter's early withdrawal from active participation in the organizational efforts of his own Combat SS throws some doubt on the validity of that information.

49. Such as, for example, the Nazi sculptor Arno Breker, whom Naumann's captured diary quotes as counseling against the use of discredited old-timers—even including Guderian—in the reconstruction of a massive, radical nationalist and neo-Nazi movement. See diary quotations in Wesemann (V/65).

50. As guidance officer in Major Remer's Berlin guard battalion on July 20, 1944, Hagen stiffened Remer's loyalism and thus played his dismal role in frustrating the anti-Hitler plot. (See above, VI/209.) See also Hans W. Hagen, *Zwischen Eid und Befehl. Tatzeugenbericht von den Ereignissen am 20. Juli 1944 in Berlin und "Wolfschanze"* (Munich: Türmer, [1958]).

51. How far the paper went to accommodate itself to tactical co-operation with the German government can be seen in such articles as "Lärm macht in Deutschland keinen Eindruck: Notwendige Bemerkungen zu dem neuen Feldzug gegen 'Neo-Nazismus,'" *Deutsche Soldaten-Zeitung* (Munich), no. 11 (March 13, 1952), p. 1. After pointing out that the new international position of the Federal Republic has not as yet led to a sufficiently consequential revision of the country's domestic politics, which is still being carried on in the spirit of 1945, and calling for an end to the anti-Nazi "witch hunt" in the *Lizenzpresse,* Uhlig admonishes the "radical Right": "The 'radical Right,' however, should have by now recognized who benefits from their continuing chase after an illusion of which the great mass of our people have long since been cured. The assumptions which they claim underlie their activity have disappeared with the defeat and bisection of the world. They can perform no greater service for Germany than to keep silent and thus not to disturb the process of self-scrutiny of our people. Noise no longer impresses our people, neither that produced by the radical Right nor that of the fanatics of the year 1945 who are still pounding the kettle drums." Uhlig's total "conversion" in terms of faithful support of German rearmament in NATO can be sampled in his *Atom—Angst oder Hoffnung? Die Lehren des ersten Atommanövers der Welt* (Munich: Isar, 1955).

52. Spindler's letter to the author, July 27, 1961.

53. In June, 1947, Goebel had formed his Executive Committee of Eastern Expellees and in November, 1948, unveiled the short-lived Emergency Association of Free Germans (Notgemeinschaft freier Deutscher) in collaboration with the ever-busy Joachim von Ostau and the notoriously radical Fritz Dorls. See above, IV/7, 8 and nearby text.

54. Mertens had been one of the people invited to von Ostau's widely publicized Bad Godesberg meeting of "independent Germans" mentioned above in Chapter IV, Section B.

55. The first meeting to build a co-ordinating committee which would prevent electoral competition between the growing number of expellee, refugee, and similar groups took place in Frankfurt on September 18, 1949. The fifteen-member committee represented, besides the TfD: Mattes' air-raid victims; Ott's refugees; Haussleiter's Deutsche Gemeinschaft (DG); the Emergency Associations of Bremen (Günther Enss) and Bavaria (under Waldemar Rumbaur); the Association of Free Electors of Rhineland-Palatinate (Fritz Melsheimer); the German League of Employees (under Hans Sube); the dissident, anti-Meissner German Bloc of Bavaria (under Alfred Noske); the Emergency Association of Those Damaged by the Currency Reform (Notgemeinschaft der Währungsgeschädigten), Berlin (under Oeltze von Lobenthal); and the so-called Group *Paulskirche* under Walter Eckardt and Schwannberger. (See *Hamburger Echo,* September 26, 1949; *Die Welt* [Hamburg], September 20, 1949.) Eckardt had been a high official in the Nazi Ministry of Finance and von Lobenthal had been the economic editor of Goebbels' "house organ," *Angriff.* Both were important officers of the Deutsche Union. On November 16, 1949, a peak organization was formed which brought together the various "Emergency Associations" of Bavaria, Württemberg-Baden, Bremen, and Berlin with the DG of Haussleiter, the Hessian DG under Günther Draub, and the Hamburg section of the Deutsche Block under Carl Belz. The name of the over-all organization was to be Deutsche Gemeinschaft (see *Frankfurter Allgemeine Zeitung,* November 17, 1949). In December the new party was actually launched. On its executive board were Haussleiter and Dr. Renate Malluche (representing the Bavarian DG), Mattes, Eckardt, von Lobenthal, and the former Air Force General Bruno Maass, who was the Bavarian representative of the Victims of Aerial Bombardment.

56. Mattes, he thought, was a small-bore politician of little vision and few principles. Haussleiter, in Spindler's view, was the far more intelligent but also the far more dangerous of the two. In Spindler's eyes, both were guilty of opportunism, of temporizing with existing political institutions instead of planning to sweep them away root and branch. (These views were expressed by Spindler in a letter to Draub and reported by Knothe [V/36].) Haussleiter —loath to be accused of lacking radicalism—reciprocated by accusing Spindler of aspiring to the sole leadership of the unified Deutsche Gemeinschaft. (See *Der Informationsdienst,* no. 18 [June 30, 1950].) Faced with the Landtag elections in June of 1950, Spindler and Haussleiter buried the hatchet for the sake of the larger goal, and the TfD finally merged with the DG in April, 1950. But the antagonisms would not die. At the end of May,

after having determined that the TfD was in no shape to contest the elections, Spindler resigned from the DG executive board and a month later annulled the merger. For the internal tensions and disagreements which led to the rapid break-up of the TfD merger, see the minutes of the executive board meeting of May 23, 1950, in *Informationen,* 691, June 9, 1950. The DG's side of the story is told in a mimeographed letter from the executive committee to "the members and friends of the German Community," dated July 6, 1950, and signed by Haussleiter, Draub, Mattes, and von Lobenthal.

57. See Erdmann Franke, "Am Ende des Weges: Ein pathetischer Leerlauf im Nichts," Gesellschaft zum Studium von Zeitfragen, *Analysen und Berichte,* VI, 9 (August 14, 1959), 6.

58. See Spindler's *Mitunternehmertum* (Lüneburg: Metta Kinau, Wolf & Täuber, [pref. 1951]), the programmatic essay *Der Leistungsstaat* (Düsseldorf: Komet, 1948), and the unpublished papers "Krise der menschlichen Beziehung," "Eigentum und soziale Frage," "Sozialisierung? Mitunternehmertum!" and "Dürfen uns die Flüchtlinge lästig sein?"

59. Spindler's schemes were designed to remedy the evils of our times, which he identified with the fatal polarization of Western society, brought about by liberalism and the concomitant progressive proletarization of the masses. The dragon seeds sown by the Enlightenment (the rationalist destruction of received pieties, the individualist loosening of social ties, and the pluralist subversion of social harmony) were now bearing their poisonous fruit. Man has become the cannon—and ballot-box—fodder of the bureaucratic mass state and its bureaucratic mass organizations, principally the political parties. The first order of business must, therefore, be the abolition of party parliamentarism. It must be replaced by a solidarist, corporative society along occupational estate lines, run by those who have proved their superiority by actual accomplishments: an elite of character. But real democracy remains a hollow fraud without the organic and socially just industrial organization of autonomous co-owned enterprises. This system would guarantee a healthy *economic* struggle resulting in efficiency, in lieu of the destructive *social* struggle of a liberal society which inevitably ends in the victory of Marxist principles of social organization. It would also produce identity where there is now anonymity, personal responsibility instead of bureaucratic irresponsibility; and, above all, it would reward in proportion to ability and efficiency and not—like the present system—in proportion to one's proximity to, and friendship for, those in power. See also the Tatgemeinschaft's "fundamental program," for a summary of these views. Though Spindler was frequently pleased to emphasize the novel nature of his prescriptions, there is, in fact (with one exception) nothing in them that was not in the standard repertory of German antiliberal, neoconservative ideologists. Strongly under the influence of José Ortega y Gasset, Spindler argued for the preservation of the free personality from the assaults of the masses, the state, and interest organizations. For Spindler's elitist tendencies, see *Der Leistungsstaat* (VII/58), pp. 30, 32–33, 41; for his antistatist, quasi-liberal tendencies, see p. 41; and for his defense of freedom of thought against control by political authority, see pp. 48–49.

Practicing what he preached, Spindler has made his workers and employees co-owners of his corporation. He acknowledged the workers' moral claim to their fair share of the social product which their joint labors had created, and viewed their past work as an investment equivalent in importance to that of capital, and, therefore, entitled to equivalent returns. This policy has earned Spindler the plaudits of both Leftist and Rightist critics of Erhard's neo-Manchester, oligopolistic capitalist economy. For an example of Left laudation, see Rolf Hochhut's "Der Klassenkampf ist nicht zu Ende," *Der Spiegel,* XIX, 22 (May 26, 1965), 28–44, in which Spindler is pictured as the rare humanitarian exception among the cynical malefactors of great wealth who are running the Bonn Republic for their private enrichment. On the extreme Right Spindler's policy of co-ownership received the approval of the neo-Nazi (and later outlawed) Socialist Reich Party. "In the co-ownership contract of the firm Kampf and Spindler we see one of the possible ways to solve the problem of an organic plant fellowship." (*Deutscher Ruf* [Hamburg], I, 10 [April, 1951], 5.) Similarly Karl Meissner, the Reichsführer of the radical, folkish German Bloc, told an audience in St. Goar (on November 27, 1952) that "a short while ago he had a talk with Dr. Schacht in which they covered measures for the improvement (*Gesundung*) of the German economy. Rejection of labor unions, but in their stead profit-sharing similar to that of the workers of the Spindler enterprises." (From a confidential eyewitness account of November 28, 1952.)

Two years after the completion of this chapter, Spindler published a broad–gauged analysis of contemporary industrial-managerial conditions and their future implications, along with an elaborate account of his own socio-political and organizational views and recommendations. His book, *Neue Antworten im sozialen Raum. Leitbilder für Unternehmer* (Düsseldorf, Vienna: Econ, [c. 1964]), unfortunately came to my attention too late to be integrated into the present discussion.

60. Memo of a staff meeting of *Fortschritt* and TfD officials on April 19, 1951.

61. In U.S. Department of State, Office of the High Commissioner for Germany [John J. McCloy], *Seventh Quarterly Report on Germany, April 1–June 30, 1951* (p. 68), the *Fortschritt* was considered worthy of special mention. It was there ineptly described as a "neo-Nazi" publication which "builds on petty resentments of die-hard nationalists who feel that the consequences of a lost war are a personal slight to their honor." In this connection it should be mentioned that while the paper's editorial policy was determined by Spindler in weekly and exhaustive conferences with the *Fortschritt*'s editorial board, "there appeared ever so often . . . views of the editors and of Schneyder himself that did not correspond with mine, a fact that led to disputes." (From Spindler's letter to the author, July 27, 1961, p. 8.) Examples of the disputes mentioned can be found in the minutes of Spindler's staff meeting of June 20, 1951.

62. From Spindler's letter to the author, August 28, 1962, p. 3. In the

staff meeting of October 10, 1951, Spindler said that "the *Fortschritt* should continue to serve as an important instrument to achieve the key position."

63. Cf. *Deutscher Informationsdienst,* no. 462 (April 19, 1955). See above, V/95 and nearby text.

64. Lindner had been executive secretary of the German Community (DG) in North Rhine–Westphalia after the merger of TfD with DG in April, 1950. See below, XV/20.

65. In a letter from Schneyder to the author, September 11, 1961.

66. *Aide-mémoires* of Spindler's staff meetings of June 20, 1951, p. 2, and of July 25, 1951, p. 4. In his communication to the author of January 26, 1962, Schneyder stressed the fact that he had not met Schmalz and that his contact with Heinrich Böx, a cofounder of the First Legion, was unconnected with Schneyder's editorship of the *Fortschritt.* For the First Legion, see the following note.

67. Apparently the Federal Government organized the First Legion to attract Right-extremists and nationalist officers to the Adenauer policies of resolute West-orientation and rearmament. Its three-man directory consisted of Schmalz; Böx, the former federal deputy press chief, consul in New Orleans, deputy secretary general of the Western European Union, and erstwhile friend of Adenauer; and Adolf Dedekind, the former personal secretary of DP chairman and Federal Minister Heinrich Hellwege. There is understandably very little reliable information on the First Legion. Not even the exact date of its founding is well established, as the first public announcements made in Bonn in November, 1950, occurred between four months and one year after its actual founding. In the first stages of development the names of such leading conservative or nationalist politicians as Gerhard Schröder (CDU), Kurt Georg Kiesinger (CDU), Erich Mende (FDP), and Hans-Joachim von Merkatz (DP) were consistently linked with the Legion despite repeated denials. In terms of its structure, its program, and its ideology, the Legion can be most fairly compared to Arthur Mahraun's Jungdeutscher Orden of the late twenties and early thirties. It also bore strong ideological—and even some structural—resemblance to the Deutsche Union. The language of its proclamations and programs was pungently reminiscent of the Conservative Revolution and the Nazi Party. The Legion's aim was to fight "against the disintegrating egotism of the parties, the destructive class struggle, and the corroding spirit of Marxism." (Fritz Heine in *Die Welt* (Hamburg), January 26, 1951.) We find here the old hatred of political parties as corruptors of public life and the Conservative Revolutionary demand to create a vanguard which can "advance to new forms of democracy." (See *Frankfurter Rundschau,* November 28, 1950.) According to other close observers, the First Legion was "in a way a reserve position of the CDU (based on the former conceptions of Carl Schmitt) in order to establish a '*Volksstaat*' through a coup d'état from above." (See *aide-mémoire* of a meeting of Spindler's staff, August 19, 1951, p. 3.) Schmalz put the aim of the First Legion as follows: "In the first place we want to fill the various petrified, inwardly hollowed-out party apparatuses with new ideas and new, that is to say young, blood; and in the second place,

we want to take up the fight against all radical elements, especially against Communism." (*Süddeutsche Zeitung* [Munich], no. 293, December 19, 1950.) Böx put it this way: "We want to awaken democracy from its mechanical routine and bring it to life. . . . We must get out of those corruption machines. . . . We must again put honesty and decency where hitherto only party-egotism and jobbing have prevailed." (*Ibid.*) The Legion's platform statement (the existence of which was denied for many months) declared that Germany calls for men "who put themselves selflessly at the service of the *Volksgemeinschaft*." (*Parlamentarisch-Politischer Pressedienst,* December 8, 1950.) The bylaws stated that legionnaires were "bound by the leadership to act comradely . . . to obey the leaders freely . . . even under personal sacrifice, in everything that is morally permitted and to be loyal," which "also includes maintaining silence whenever necessary." (*Ibid.*) "The Legionnaire lives in constant willing readiness to execute every task under full commitment of his person." (*Die Welt* [Hamburg], January 26, 1951 [article by Fritz Heine].) In May, 1951, the CDU Land organization of Hesse finally turned against the Legion without mincing words. (*Frankfurter Allgemeine Zeitung,* May 7, 1951.) Only four months later did the federal party follow the lead by determining publicly that the First Legion might be a threat to democracy. The Legion protested bitterly against this judgment and alleged to see in it only the reaction of a petrified party system to the political activism of the "war generation." (*Die Welt* [Hamburg], September 7, 1951.) Also see: *Neue Presse* (Coburg), November 29, 1950; *Deutsche Zeitung* (Bielefeld), December 30, 1950; *Der Informationsdienst,* no. 44 (January 10, 1951); *Die Zeit* (Hamburg), February 1, 1951; *Braunschweiger Zeitung,* March 30, 1951; *Süddeutsche Zeitung* (Munich), June 14, 1951; *Neuer Vorwärts* (Hanover), December 8, 1951.

68. Letter from Spindler to the author, August 28, 1962, pp. 1–2. "All participants saw in the meeting a beginning for the close collaboration of that circle with the officers' cadres. . . . The present circle is to remain intact." (From the minutes of the meeting of June 2 and 3, 1951, p. 4.)

69. "Through this circle with its possibility of influencing directly former soldiers, those ideas which have been so far developed are to be furthered . . . with the possibility to prepare in this way the establishment of a German contingent in the moment when it has become politically feasible." (Minutes of the meeting of June 2 and 3, 1951.)

70. The representatives of the Defense and Interior Ministries had been invited to provide the nascent opposition group with some insights into what policies the government was seriously entertaining. "Dr. Krause and Count Kielmansegg agreed to keep the circle *au courant* about developments, in closest touch with me [i.e., Spindler]." (From the minutes of the meeting of June 2 and 3, 1951.) For a recent appreciation of Count Kielmansegg, who on September 1, 1963, became General Speidel's successor as Commander of the NATO land forces in Central Europe, see *Der Spiegel,* XVII, 32 (August 7, 1963), 21–22.

71. The navy was represented by Dönitz' son-in-law, Günther Hessler, and Ramcke brought along his fellow parachutist Heinz Trettner, who in

1964 was to become General Friedrich Foertsch' successor as Inspector General of the German armed forces.

72. A few months earlier de Maizière had been a member of State Secretary Walter Hallstein's three-man team which represented Germany at the Paris Conference for the Establishment of a European Army. (U.S. Department of State [II/39], p. 8.) Promoted to the rank of general, de Maizière eventually became the Bundeswehr's chief of staff.

73. In 1958 Colonel Wilcke succeeded Count Baudissin as chief of the department "internal leadership." In the beginning of 1960 Wilcke, by now a brigadier general, was transferred to another assignment.

74. Koller's letter to Spindler, August 9, 1951.

75. Spindler's letter to Friessner, September 11, 1951. It is at least comforting to note that not everyone of the many officers to whom Spindler sent copies of this letter agreed with his point of view. General Ludwig Crüwell, the senior surviving officer of the famed Afrika Korps, wrote: "I am of the opinion that the soldiers' leagues should practice greatest reticence in party or other political questions. . . . Concerning the question of decorations I would merely call to your attention that the imperial crown can hardly be compared to the swastika." (Letter to Spindler, October 1, 1951.) General Dethleffsen wrote (September 19, 1951): "The comparison with the crown is in my opinion awry. The crown was a symbol of glory, of greatness, probity (*Sauberkeit*), decency, and of honor. The swastika, under which sign thousands of the most serious crimes were committed is none of these, and that in my opinion is decisive." (Letter to Spindler.) Major General Peter von der Groeben, highly decorated former commander of a cavalry division, had this to say (letter to Spindler of September 27, 1951): "I agree with you that the wearing of a modified war decoration, i.e., after the removal of the swastika, is impossible. Equally impossible does it appear to me to wear an order with that [insignia]. Apart from the fact that a large circle of soldiers resented the affixion of the swastika to their war decorations even during the war and that they do not wish to wear the swastika today in any form whatever, it is, in my opinion, in this question necessary to consider . . . foreign countries which would have little understanding for that." General Hasso von Manteuffel wrote (October 2, 1951, to Spindler): "I professed and profess loyalty to the democratic structure of the German state. If, beyond that, I have professed and do profess loyalty to the Federal Republic, then I have done it because I hope that this young . . . Federal Republic will one day be . . . our state. . . . I acknowledge your position in the matter of the decorations and I respect it, but cannot take a position in this connection on the matter itself, as I perceive in the formulation of your judgment an intolerance which can hardly furnish a factual basis for a productive and constructive discussion," etc. A public-opinion poll conducted in August, 1951, disclosed that only one-quarter of a random sample of the adult population agreed that if the wearing of medals is again to be allowed, the swastika should be removed from them. Forty-seven per cent objected to the issuance of "decontaminated"

medals, and 3 per cent were undecided. (Noelle and Neumann [II/4], p. 379.)

76. Jan Molitor, *pseud.* (i.e., Josef Müller-Marein), "Die Fallschirmjäger sind keine 'ohne-michler,' " *Die Zeit* (Hamburg), August 2, 1951. Cf. "Mobilizing the Fourth Reich," *The New Statesman and Nation,* XLII, 1065 (August 4, 1951), 116.

77. Arbeitsgemeinschaft Deutscher Journalisten, *Pressedienst,* August 1, 1951, p. 3.

78. *Ibid.,* pp. 3–4. A year later the embittered Ramcke sent his warm regrets to General Ernst von Reichenau for not being able to participate in the latter's neutralist Stuttgart meeting. (See above, VI/200 and nearby text.)

79. For the dissolution of the Tatgemeinschaft and the views of Spindler and his brain trust on the TfD's failure, the unpublished minutes of Spindler's staff meetings of June 27, 1951, pp. 3–4; July 4, 1951, p. 3; July 25, 1951, p. 4; and October 10, 1951, p. 2, provide important insights.

80. Letter from Spindler to the author, July 27, 1961.

81. Minutes of the staff meeting of June 20, 1951, p. 3.

82. Spindler's brain trust was there in full force. Besides Brand, who had been responsible for making the necessary arrangements, the group included the former Landrat Klaus von der Groeben, whom Spindler considered the political *primus inter pares* of his staff; another former Landrat, Emil Guilleaume, Spindler's expert on constitutional and legal questions; Rudolf von Knüpffer, the expert on expellee and refugee questions who had come to Spindler via his former partner, the expellee priest Goebel; the agrarian expert, Richard Weimert; Mr. Gernand; and the *Fortschritt*'s Erich Schneyder.

83. As Gauamtsleiter he was the personal assistant to Ernst W. Bohle, the Gauleiter of the foreign organization of the NSDAP, and later became Land group leader of German Nazis in Italy. Ehrich's own political point of view can be gathered from his *Die Auslandsorganisation der NSDAP,* Schriften der Deutschen Hochschule für Politik, II; Der organisatorische Aufbau des Dritten Reiches, no. 13 (Berlin: Junker und Dünnhaupt, 1937), especially pp. 13–14, 22 ff.

84. Ehrich had been taken along to Bonn when the DP chief, Heinrich Hellwege, became a Federal Minister in the first Adenauer cabinet. Under pressure, primarily from the labor unions, Hellwege regretfully dismissed that high Nazi official. Later, Ehrich switched to the FDP and became a high official in Lower Saxony.

85. See below, Chapter XVII, Section D.

86. See below, X/81–83 and nearby text.

87. These efforts—together, of course, with those of hundreds of others of similar bent—were eventually to bear fruit in the terrorist outbursts that brought the South Tyrolian issue before the United Nations in 1961. Lange, incidentally, was in 1959 elected chairman of the Witiko League.

88. When Hellwege assumed the Prime Ministership of Lower Saxony, Hunke was made Ministerialrat in the Social Security Ministry, replacing

the widely known Walter Auerbach of the SPD. See above, V/63, V/107; and below, text near XVII/143.

89. In a letter to the author of July 27, 1961, p. 2, Spindler had this to say: "In it [the DU] were some wise, diversely interested, and open-minded men, such as von Stauffenberg . . . Griesmayr, [Siegfried] Setgast, von Lobenthal. With this circle I was soon in touch."

90. For Griesmayr's Nazi career see above, V/39.

91. See above, VI/79, 217.

92. Brehm came to this meeting as a stand-in for Walter Becher. Becher, later chairman of the BHE parliamentary party in the Bavarian diet, was a fellow member of Brand, Lange, and Brehm in both the prewar Kameradschaftsbund and its postwar copy, the Witiko League. In the Third Reich, Becher became editor in chief of the official Nazi paper *Die Zeit* in the Sudetenland. After the war he joined Haussleiter's radical DG, came into the diet as one of its candidates, and later switched over to the BHE. From 1956 to 1959 Becher was chairman of the Witiko League, and in 1959 he cofounded a Committee for the Protection of Citizens against Defamation by the Leftist Press. (See below, XII/139, XVII/155, 156.)

93. For citation of the relevant implicating documents, see *Deutscher Informationsdienst,* no. 611 (November 27, 1956). Rahn, who had been cleared by an Essen denazification tribunal in 1949, insisted he had always been a democrat. He later became the business manager of the German branch of the Coca-Cola Bottling Corporation.

94. See "Report on the Preparatory Work in Eastern European Territories" (numbered 1039-PS, and offered in evidence as Exhibit USA-146), International Military Tribunal, *Trial of the Major War Criminals,* Proceedings, 1 December 1945–14 December 1945 (Nuremberg: 1947), III, 360. See also Riecke's own testimony before the Tribunal, *ibid.,* Proceedings, 8 April 1946–17 April 1946, XI, 589–599.

95. In 1957 Schmitt became a member of the board of directors of the Berliner Bank and in 1961, director of the giant Allgemeine Elektrizitäts Gesellschaft (AEG).

96. Mannhardt, who published one of the earliest full-dress, and cautiously approving, studies of Mussolini's Fascism (*Der Faschismus* [Munich: Beck, 1925]), wrote in 1933: "The spirit of the new epoch overwhelms the people who are ready for it as an immense life force, which strengthens them, elevates them, but also captivates them, so that they are obedient to it. . . . The exaggeration of individuality can be overcome only by hard discipline in the community. It is good that the pendulum now is also swinging far to the other side. . . . This spirit justified force and coercion in the period of transition. But there is no doubt that this spirit cannot be replaced by force and coercion . . . only those who resist must be commanded. . . . That [the new spirit] will win out, is beyond doubt. . . . Freedom of scientific inquiry . . . must not become a fetish. . . . The new epoch knows full well that there has never been absolute freedom of scholarship (*Wissenschaft*) but that it has always been tied to the prevailing spirit of the times. Thus in the future, too, scholarship will exist under [the sign of] the new

spirit of the times. We know, that this [spirit] demands special ties to the community, especially to the folk and the state. . . . Within that framework scholarship should be allowed to unfold itself. . . . It is perfectly clear that at the universities, too, parliamentarism has become barren and that there too the assured *Führer* principle must take root." *Hochschulrevolution* (Hamburg: Hanseatische Verlagsanstalt, 1933), pp. 9, 13, 17, 18, 39 and 93. Mannhardt's initial enthusiasm for the Nazis, however, soon turned into bitter disappointment. Like other folkish-nationalist gravediggers of the Weimar Republic among the upper bourgeoisie, Mannhardt had to discover that ideological proximity to the Nazis on the basis of fervid folkishness and antiliberal, antidemocratic preferences was not enough to purchase independence from the Nazi movement. Autonomous, parallel political activity, no matter how compatible with Nazism, was not tolerated. A product of the Youth Movement and the Conservative Revolution, Mannhardt returned after 1945 to his old folkish prejudices, albeit with certain qualifications. The University of Marburg refused to reappoint him to his old chair for German folkdom. For biographical sketches of Mannhardt and description of his work, as well as of his current folkish teachings, see the entirely uncritical, eulogistic Festschrift, *Weltweite Wissenschaft vom Volk, Volk-Welt-Erziehung,* edited by K. K. Klein, F. W. Riedl, R. Ursin (Vienna, Wiesbaden: Rohrer, 1958).

97. In the course of discussions on the following day, former ambassador Rahn agreed with Achenbach about the tactical usefulness of infiltrating the FDP and hollowing it out from the inside.

98. V/86.

99. Gille is one of the original founders of the BHE and in 1950 became chairman of the BHE parliamentary party in the Land diet of Schleswig-Holstein. He was furthermore chairman of the East Prussian Regional Association (Landsmannschaft Ostpreussen) and chairman of the Schleswig-Holstein organization of one of the peak associations of the expellees, Central Association of Expelled Germans (Zentralverband der vertriebenen Deutschen, ZvD).

100. See above, VIII/55.

101. Like almost all major industrialists, corporation executives, and bankers who unswervingly served Hitler in prominent positions, Hettlage had survived the fall of the Third Reich without loss of influence or prestige. On the contrary, professor of law in Mayence and professor of public finance at the University Bonn, he became also a member of the administrative council of the Research Institute for Political Economy at the University of Mayence and in 1959 even State Secretary in the Ministry of Finance.

102. Speakers for the Combat SS had even argued for the establishment of the senior SS officer, Colonel General Paul Hausser, in the president's chair of the new federation. But they were soon persuaded that such an appointment would be viewed abroad as a serious provocation and lead to great difficulties. (Letter of one of the leaders of the Oldenburg Waffen SS organization, Helmut Brahn, to Siegfried Lademacher, November 6, 1951.)

103. That this animosity was of a personal nature seemed fairly clear, but its reasons were not. Some suggested, as a possible cause of friction, the fact that Koller was not an alumnus of the 100,000-man Reichswehr and that that was an important consideration in certain army circles.

104. "Scharfe Absage an politisierende Offiziere," *Süddeutsche Zeitung* (Munich), October 4, 1951, pp. 1–2.

105. *Ibid.*

106. *Ibid.*

107. *Ibid.*

108. The fear of the "150 per cent loyalists" that their leaders might succumb to the siren calls of Bonn or Washington emerged repeatedly from their writings. Thus, for example, the crypto-Nazi SRP wrote: "It is still not clear which course the newly formed Verband deutscher Soldaten . . . will take. . . . All those who wish to appear in a favorable light in the eyes of the Bonn administration hasten to emphasize that they have come to recognize that the men of July 20 have acted from motives of moral commitment. . . . Within the former Waffen SS it has led to massive estrangement [to note] that SS General [H. O.] Gille has also started on that opportunistic road. Following the example of his precursor, [Robert] Pferdmenges' protégé, [General Hasso von] Manteuffel, he too has fallen under FDP influence and has visibly lost ground among his former comrades in arms. Particularly among former soldiers of the younger generation the question is widely discussed, whether the federation-at-all cost has not led to a watering-down of the stated aims. . . . The first pronouncement of Guderian which, one hopes, will clarify things, is being awaited with eager anticipation." *Deutsche Opposition* (Cuxhaven), September 30, 1951.

109. This writer has no evidence that Hausser's and Gille's connections to Werner Naumann were known at the time of the peak association's founding. According to the previously cited British intelligence report (V/12), par. 15, Hausser, in November, 1951, sought Naumann's approval of a press release which was designed to defend the Waffen SS against the attacks of the CDU. This release was said to have been initially worked out by Gille with the help of nationalist Lower Saxon FDP leaders. The question still remains what inferences can be legitimately drawn from these facts.

110. See *Deutsche Presse Agentur* (*dpa*), *Inf.* 1289 (September 10, 1951), p. 1. Cf. "Soldatenverband wirbt auch um 'ungediente Jugend,'" *Frankfurter Rundschau,* September 12, 1951. Bonn's—and, indeed, Washington's—tendency to identify the generally desirable policy of drawing those "who have been standing aside" into the new political order, with gaining their support for Adenauer's and America's foreign and military policies without great regard for their liberal-democratic "reformation," appeared to many sincere democrats as narrowly egotistical, shortsighted, and highly dangerous. See, for example, as representative of a large body of literature, mostly by social-democratic writers, "An den Staat heranführen," *Hannoversche Presse,* September 15, 1951.

111. See "Generaloberst a D. Friessner führt neuen Soldatenverband," *Die Welt* (Hamburg), October 9, 1951.

112. "Soldatenverband" (VIII/110).

113. *Propaganda Rundschreiben,* VI (September 18, 1951), par. 2.

114. *Ibid.*

115. *Ibid.* The CDU, which had never been quite at ease or of one mind regarding the implications of its veteran policies, now became thoroughly alarmed. The spectacle of the CDU's hesitation and uncertainty had for some time been a matter of public comment. Initially its *Deutschland–Union–Dienst,* allegedly under the guidance of Otto Lenz, the State Secretary for Internal Affairs in the Federal Chancellery, took a very favorable view of the efforts among veterans to organize themselves. Under the impact of the negative foreign reaction which greeted these efforts, the Chancellor thought it wise to slow down CDU overtures in that direction. The revised policy then appeared in an announcement of the *Christlich-Demokratischer Pressedienst,* according to which the Bonn government had decided to assume a more reserved attitude in the face of the many still unresolved questions regarding the final orientation of the veterans' organizations.

116. For a report on the contents of the press conference, see *Parlamentarisch-Politischer Pressedienst,* 3/219 (September 21, 1951).

117. "Scharfe Absage" (VIII/104).

118. Alex Schmalfuss, "Standpunkt der Soldatenbünde," *Tagesspiegel* (Berlin), October 6, 1951, p. 2.

119. It is undeniable that the large number of angry anti-Friessner tirades by veterans published in the daily press, not immediately after Friessner's press conference, but rather ten days later, after Adenauer had set the pace, is somewhat suspect: Could those whose voices self-righteously rose the shrillest have possibly been the most interested in being recommissioned in the new army? This suspicion was of course widely bruited about in ultra-Rightist circles. (See the DRP's *Propaganda Rundschreiben,* XI [December 13, 1951], par. 2.) The peculiar reticence of the Germans to speak up forcefully on matters of high political import and to take the initiative in the shaping of public opinion was noted in the course of the Friessner episode by both foreign and German observers. Thus, the highly respected journalist and author Paul Sethe had this to say: "It remains a fact that on the subject of Friessner's speech most of the public voices became audible only after the Federal Government had given the start signal. After the event, it is very difficult to find out if without Bonn's interference we would have experienced what could be called with considerable justification the revolt of public opinion. The fact remains that most of the objections to Friessner's opinion occurred after the Chancellor had shown the way. Aren't we in Germany too inert after all? Aren't we still far too ready to leave it to an official bureau to set the tone for some political development?" "Handeln wir zu langsam?" *Frankfurter Allgemeine Zeitung,* October 17, 1951.

120. *Die Neue Zeitung* (Munich), October 19, 1951.

121. In lieu of many, see the reports under the heading "Aus den Landesverbänden" in *Der Notweg* (Detmold), II, 11 (November, 1951), 4–6.

122. "Soldaten vor der Entscheidung," *Hamburger Echo,* October 20,

1951. Cf. *Die Welt* (Hamburg) for the same date, "Friessner: Den Blick vorwärts nach alter Soldatenart."

123. "Musste das sein?" *Der Notweg* (Detmold), III, 11 (November, 1951), 1–2, and "L. V. Bayern," *ibid.*, p. 6.

124. *Ibid.*, p. 1.

125. *Ibid.*, p. 2.

126. For a brief and favorable sociopolitical analysis of the Heimkehrer movement in postwar Germany, see Joachim Schilling, "Wir sind kein neuer Stahlhelm," *Die Neue Zeitung* (Munich), September 22–23, 1951. Schilling, however, forgets to mention that the Heimkehrer were not homogeneous, and that certain leaders and certain Land organizations were rather deeply implicated in radical nationalist politics.

127. *Parlamentarisch-Politischer Pressedienst*, no. 158/51, October 24, 1951.

128. See the elaborate denials by the Minister of the Interior, Robert Lehr, as reported in *IKZ*, November 27, 1951, and extensively quoted in *Der Notweg* (Detmold), III, 12 (December, 1951), 8.

129. See "Die Problematik der Soldatenbünde," *Neuer Vorwärts* (Hanover), January 11, 1952. Under these circumstances it is understandable that Spindler's radically nationalist *Fortschritt*, which had, of course, ardently defended Friessner, reported the Goslar meeting with bitter derision: "An attempt will be made to force Friessner out and to pack the executive board with men who are accustomed to dance to other people's tunes. Should this not succeed, there are plans for a competitive organization; that means the rebirth of the Reichsbanner." *Fortschritt*, November 23, 1951, quoted in *Der Notweg* (Detmold), III, 12 (December, 1951), 8. For the answer to this attack by one of the Goslar organizers, see *Parlamentarisch-Politischer Pressedienst*, December 21, 1951, item no. 6. For the allegation that all expenses were paid by the "organizers" of the meeting, consult Adolf von Thadden, *Propaganda Rundschreiben*, XI (December 13, 1951), and G. T., "Subventionierte Tradition," *Der Heimkehrer* (Göppingen), IV, 3 (March, 1953), 2. It should be kept in mind, however, that both the DRP and the Heimkehrer were profoundly hostile to Geyr von Schweppenburg and missed no opportunity to blacken his reputation. For some of the reasons underlying the Heimkehrer's hostility, see *Deutscher Informationsdienst*, no. 301 (August 28, 1953).

130. "Generaloberst a.D. Friessner tritt ab," *Die Welt* (Hamburg), December 11, 1951.

131. A year later, after the outlawry of the Sozialistische Reichs–Partei (SRP), discussions were held to devise means of keeping the hundreds of thousand SRP voters together without running the risk of being banned as a successor organization. At that time General Ramcke is said to have offered to found a United German Soldiers' Association (Gesamtdeutscher Soldatenbund) which, unlike the other veterans' organizations, would not be apolitical. Ramcke's organization would have a "very precise direction of march and activity," which he wanted to discuss with Remer and Dorls. Ramcke allegedly guaranteed to get together 500,000 men. Supposedly the

only thing that was holding back the project was the problem of camouflaging the enterprise so cleverly as to escape outlawry. Report of a conversation with Werner Körper, Land chairman (Rhineland-Palatinate) of the SRP, December 2, 1952.

132. Geyr von Schweppenburg later became Reinhard's successor as president of the Kyffhäuser League. For Reinhard's Free Corps activity, see von Oertzen (V/32), pp. 262 ff.

133. Cf. also "Organischer Aufbau," *Deutsche Soldaten–Zeitung* (Munich), II, 13 (March 27, 1952), 6, and "Einigung nun auch in Bayern," *ibid.*, p. 7. Over ten years later (at the end of 1963, to be more exact), the VdS and the Kyffhäuser League finally decided to merge.

134. In May, 1961, a new soldiers' organization was founded. Calling itself Reichsverband der Soldaten, RdS (Reich Association of Soldiers), it represented extreme Rightist attitudes among veterans. Its chairman is Colonel Walther Dahl, a prominent DRP member in Mannheim. At a meeting in Obrigheim (Palatinate), Dahl argued that the seventeen postwar years had been poisoning the German soul and called for stringent measures against the cultural and ideological subversives in press, radio, and television. Unsuccessful in its attempt to incorporate the Combat SS, which in the meantime joined the rival Association of German Soldiers (VdS), the RdS has not been able to grow beyond its initial membership of some 500. (See *Bulletin on German Questions* [London], XIII, 299 [December 20, 1961]; XIV, 311 [June 15, 1962]; and XIV, 316 [September 1, 1962], 11.) In 1963, Dahl asked Colonel Hans-Ulrich Rudel to assume the honorary presidency of the RdS.

135. For the activity, structure, and methods of such an important part of Adenauer's propaganda machinery as the Working Association of Democratic Circles (ADK), see "Arbeitsgemeinschaft demokratischer Kreise," *Rundschreiben,* no. 42 (May 6, 1953), a ten-page memorandum of the social-democratic opposition party (SPD). Cf. "Public-Relations gegen neutralnationalistische Propaganda," *Deutscher Informationsdienst,* no. 419 (November 6, 1954), pp. 3–4, and also "Militaristen wittern Morgenluft," Katholische Nachrichten Agentur (KNA), *Informationsdienst,* no. 20 (May 14, 1955), item 465, pp. 4–5. The ADK is, of course, only one of many government-subsidized groups which make CDU propaganda at taxpayer's expense. Cf. also Wolfgang Hirsch-Weber and Klaus Schütz, *Wähler und Gewählte* (Berlin: Vahlen, 1957), pp. 22–26.

136. See in this connection Wildenmann's significant study (II/5). For the questionable tendency of Adenauer and his CDU/CSU to defame the Opposition, see Uwe W. Kitzinger, *German Electoral Politics* (Oxford: Clarendon, 1960), p. 127.

137. Yet not a few foreign observers would say precisely that. Such hysterically anti-German writers as Bernard Lavergue and the men around his *L'Année Politique et Economique* have for years warned against the re-Nazification and remilitarization of Germany. For a far juster—if not entirely uncritical—assessment see Jesco von Puttkamer, "Von Zossen nach Bonn: Eine Bilanz der deutschen Wiederbewaffnung," in Hans Werner

Richter, ed., *Bestandsaufnahme: Eine deutsche Bilanz 1962* (Munich: Desch, 1962), pp. 93–105. For an excellent analysis (despite its brevity), see Wolfgang Sauer, "Militarism in the Federal Republic?" in Walter Stahl, ed., *The Politics of Postwar Germany* (New York: Praeger, 1963), pp. 249–270.

138. It remained for the Federal Diet's Personnel Screening Committee (GA), in its widely regarded interim report in December, 1957, to correct the Chancellor's delusion. Referring to former prisoners of war who had returned to Germany only after many years spent in Russian internment and work camps as war criminals (*Spätheimkehrer*) and who now thought that their past gave them a special moral claim to commissions in the new armed forces, the GA cautioned that these men had apparently failed to take into account German history since 1945: "Hatred of Communism is not in itself sufficient to grasp the meaning of our total political situation." Bundestag, "Tätigkeitsbericht des Personalgutachterausschusses für die Streitkräfte" (December 6, 1957), 3. Wahlperiode, *Drucksache* 109, p. 15.

139. The *DSZ* later called itself *Deutsche Soldaten–Zeitung und National–Zeitung* (Munich), and in the winter of 1962 was renamed *Deutsche National–Zeitung und Soldaten–Zeitung*. This change of name was presumably to draw attention to the paper's ideological blood relationship to the official organ of the pan-German and antidemocratic National Liberals in the Wilhelmian Empire. Forceful spokesman for a powerful Germany, the *DNZ* welcomed in 1963 de Gaulle's offensive to build a strong European bloc around the Bonn-Paris axis, diminish American influence in Europe, and gain freedom of action vis-à-vis the Soviet Union. In 1963 the *DNZ*'s circulation was well in excess of 70,000. (See "Deutsche National–Zeitung: Sprachrohr des Volkes," *Der Spiegel* XVII, 11 [March 13, 1963], 46–52.) By 1966, its total circulation—including some recently acquired expellee papers (see below, XVII/166)—had reached 103,000.

140. "Der Grosse Prüfstein," *Deutsche Soldaten–Zeitung* (Munich), II, 41 (October 9, 1952), 1.

141. See [Club republikanischer Publizisten,] *CrP-Information,* August, 1957, p. 73. Cf. *Feinde der Demokratie* (Lower Saxony), IV, 3 (January, 1955), 15–16, and VI, 7–8 (June–July, 1957), 28. According to the South German Radio of November 20, 1953, the monthly government subvention of the *DSZ* was DM 20,000. (From Bruno Fricke's information service [*fnb*], as reported in *Widerhall,* IV, 11/12 [November–December, 1953], 31.) According to *Der Spiegel,* the subsidy was only DM 11,000. Cf. also the scathing note in *Das Ziel,* monthly paper of the DRP, of February, 1953, p. 5, and SPD Deputy Hellmut Kalbitzer's speech: *Verhandlungen des deutschen Bundestages,* 2. Wahlperiode, *Stenographischer Bericht,* 30. Sitzung (May 21, 1954), p. 1378.

142. See *Deutsche Soldaten–Zeitung* (Munich), II, 21 (May 22, 1952), 1.

143. See the *DSZ* for August, 1957.

144. *Deutscher Informationsdienst,* no. 703 (November 13, 1957).

145. See above, VI/209.

146. For the overall orientation of the paper see Hans-Helmuth Knüt-

ter, *Geistige Grundlagen und politische Richtung der "Deutschen National–Zeitung und Soldaten–Zeitung." Dargestellt am Jg. 1961,* Sonderheft, *Für die Demokratie,* V (XIII), no. 4, 1964.

147. *The Bulletin* (Bonn), October 22, 1958, quoted in *Feinde der Demokratie* (Lower Saxony) VIII, 8 (June–July, 1959), 17. Half a year later, the Defense Ministry thought it again necessary to rebuke the *DSZ.*

148. In an open letter to the Defense Minister, the *DSZ* pointed out that actually "many soldiers of the Bundeswehr of all ranks are subscribers, readers, and buyers of the *DSZ.* We have the best of contacts to well-known officers and exchange ideas with them." *Deutsche Soldaten–Zeitung* (Munich), VIII, 11 (November, 1958). Indeed, members of the Bundeswehr, both commissioned and noncommissioned personnel, even write in the *DSZ* from time to time. Moreover, its editors appear to have access to high officers and to be invited for maneuvers, press conferences, etc.

149. Bundestag, Report of the Committee for Questions of European Security (Rapporteur: Helmut Schmidt, Hamburg), July 14, 1955, *Drucksache* 1620, Annex 1 to Bundestag (VIII/138), p. 17.

150. This interpretation is opposed by no less a person than the widely respected Wilhelm Rombach, a former Lord Mayor of Aachen and Secretary of State for Internal Affairs in North Rhine–Westphalia, who became chairman of the GA. Herr Rombach, in a communication to the author of May 17, 1962, relies for his contention that Adenauer was not opposed to the GA on a declaration of Defense Minister Theodor Blank, who said in May, 1954: "The Federal Chancellor has at no time opposed the planned institution [i.e. the GA]. Much rather, he has welcomed it." To this Rombach adds: "Also in personal discussions with me, the Federal Chancellor, whom I have known for many years, has never even remotely suggested that he did not endorse the GA. On the contrary, he has explicitly acknowledged the conscientious manner in which the GA accomplished its mission." This is perfectly true as far as it goes. Except for the extreme Right, everyone accepted the principle of a personnel screening device. Sharp disagreements, however, occurred on the question of degree of control and above all on the question whether civilian supervision was to lie in the hands of the executive or in those of an entirely independent, legislatively established commission. It is impossible to follow the legislative history of the Volunteer Act and of the GA without being impressed by the distance which separated Adenauer's conception from those of the Diet's Defense Committee and by the decisiveness of the Bundestag's victory in these matters. In a letter of July 8, 1958, to Rombach, Bundestag Deputy Helmut Schmidt (SPD), the rapporteur of the Defense Committee for the bill setting up a GA, wrote: "According to . . . Blank's conceptions, the Personnel Screening Committee was originally to be set up by the government, pursuant to its powers of [executive] reorganization. . . . This solution, however, was at that time rejected by the Defense Committee which wanted complete independence [for the GA]." Taking their inspiration from the American constitutional provision requiring Senate confirmation of major executive appointments, the Bundestag left no doubt that they saw in the GA a body

of their own creation, designed to exercise the legislature's control function with regard to military appointments. In Schmidt's words: "It follows from this history [*Entstehungsgeschichte*] that the Personnel Screening Committee fulfills its task as the representative of the Bundestag within the latter's control function ("eine im Rahmen der Kontroll-Kompetenz des Bundestages liegende Aufgabe stellvertretend für diesen wahrnimmt")." While the general notion of a screening device had occurred to Theodor Blank, the later Defense Minister, as early as December, 1952, and the CDU deputy and military expert, former Vice Admiral Hellmuth Heye, even claimed to have discussed the possibility of such a commission with the then State Secretary Otto Lenz in 1951 (see *Verhandlungen des deutschen Bundestages,* 2. Wahlperiode, *Stenographische Berichte,* 139. Sitzung [April 12, 1956], p. 7170B), the initiative for a civilian, independent board whose members would be nominated by the Diet's Defense Committee and confirmed by the Diet came from that Defense Committee. There, all parties, except for the DP, supported the bill of July 23, 1955. Before the Defense Committee (which was then still discreetly called Committee for Questions of European Security) the Adenauer government argued that the establishment of an independent screening committee would lead to a weakening of ministerial responsibility and to a concomitant weakening of the government's parliamentary responsibility. To meet these arguments, the scope of the GA's competency was limited to an absolute veto power over the Defense Ministry's nominations for high military office. The GA was not authorized to compel the executive to issue a commission, as such a power would have violated the separation-of-power doctrine. (Deputy Schmidt's letter of July 8, 1958, and cf. a letter of Deputy Fritz Erler [SPD] to the author of September 25, 1961. Deputy Erler, vice-chairman of the Bundestag Defense Committee, was one of the chief architects of the Law of July 23, 1955, and the single most influential SPD leader to effect a reversal of the earlier SPD attitude toward rearmament legislation.) For a brief, but excellent, review of the GA operations see John L. Sutton, "The Personnel Screening Committee and Parliamentary Control of the West German Armed Forces," *Journal of Central European Affairs,* XIX, 4 (January, 1960), 389–401.

151. For a list of the GA's membership, see "Soldat im demokratischen Staat," *Politische Studien,* VI, 68 (December, 1955), 35–42, or *Verhandlungen des deutschen Bundestages,* 2. Wahlperiode, *Drucksache* 1619 (July 13, 1955). The list is also reproduced in Bundestag (VIII/138), pp. 6–7.

152. For the GA's mission see par. 1 of the Law of July 23, 1955, in Bundestag (VIII/138), p. 5; and Deputy Schmidt's explication of par. 1, *ibid.,* pp. 18–19.

153. *Ibid.*

154. See, for example, "Personalgutachterausschuss am Werk," *Deutsche Soldaten–Zeitung* (Munich), V, 9 (September, 1955), 2.

155. Speier (VI/99), p. 43. Heusinger, a "nonpolitical" officer, did not join the anti-Hitler plot of 1944. Indeed, he became a victim of the attempt and was seriously injured by the explosion. Several years ago, Heusinger's promotion to the Bundeswehr's highest office was criticized not merely

because of his ambiguous position with regard to July 20, 1944, but also because of his orientation as reflected in his memoirs. For, in his *Befehl im Widerstreit: Schicksalsstunden der deutschen Armee 1923–1945* (Tübingen: Wunderlich, 1950) Heusinger typically saw the Nazi regime's major fault in Hitler's contempt for Heusinger's own expert advice and in the Nazis' interference with military efficiency and time-honored bureaucratic staff procedures. Heusinger's exploits made headlines again in December, 1961, when the Soviet government formally requested the United States to extradite the new Chairman of the NATO Permanent Military Committee on the grounds of his complicity in brutalities committed in Russia under the guise of antiguerrilla activity. Available and apparently genuine documents give substance to the charge that Heusinger at least condoned German military barbarities on Soviet soil. The American government contemptuously dismissed the Russian request as palpable and heavy-handed propaganda.

156. General Heusinger resigned from this post on March 1, 1964, and retired from active service. For a eulogy on Heusinger and his contribution to the sensitive NATO position, see Adelbert Weinstein, "Ein atlantischer General verlässt Washington," *Frankfurter Allgemeine Zeitung,* no. 51 (February 29, 1964).

157. Inside Parliament the attack against the GA and its criteria for selection was spearheaded by the nationalists in the Deutsche Partei (DP) under the leadership of Herbert Schneider (Bremerhaven). The DP's newspaper, *Deutsche Stimmen,* attacked in particular the right "to extort professions in support of the action of the resistance group of July 20." See "Personalpolitik," *Deutscher Informationsdienst,* no. 528 (December 31, 1955). Not satisfied with the determined opposition to the creation of a civilian screening committee which the DP unfolded in the Defense Committee, the DP twice sought to abolish the GA and to replace it with an Officers' Court of Honor. See the verbatim record of the debates in the Bundestag: *Verhandlungen des deutschen Bundestages, Stenographische Berichte,* 2. Wahlperiode, 139. Sitzung (April 12, 1956), pp. 7165D–7181D; and 3. Wahlperiode, 16. Sitzung (March 12, 1958), pp. 744C–748D. Cf. "Um die Ablehnungen des Gutachterausschusses," *Deutscher Informationsdienst,* no. 524 (December 12, 1955) p. 4; also "Geschäfte mit der Wiederbewaffnung?" *Feinde der Demokratie* (Lower Saxony), V, 4–5 (January–March, 1956), 53. Bundestag Deputy Fritz Erler (SPD) denies that formal profession of a "positive orientation" toward the anti-Hitler plot had ever been among the GA's criteria for political reliability. According to Erler, such a requirement would only have invited hypocrisy. Rather, the GA expected from the officer candidate a "frank presentation of [his] position to the entire problem, then and now." (Letter to the present author, September 25, 1961.) With respect, Erler's formulation appears more like a diplomatic way to stress a difference that is no difference. The GA's final *Tätigkeitsbericht* states plainly, "The Guide Lines lay a particular stress on the applicant's clear position in regard to the problem of July 20, 1944." Bundestag (VIII/138), p. 11.

158. The GA's formulation is rather ingenious. Having stressed that the

soldier's conscience must be bound by "eternal moral laws" and that the applicant must "respect the rights and the religious and political convictions of his fellow man," the Guide Lines then state that the "future soldier must acknowledge the moral decision of the men of July 20, 1944. This he will combine with respect for them and for the many other soldiers who felt duty-bound to risk their lives to the end." In the light of this formulation it is difficult to agree with Herr Rombach when he writes (in his letter of May 17, 1962) that "the GA's conception regarding the question of the 20th July 1944 was precisely stipulated (*genau festgelegt*) in our Guide Lines." (For the Guide Lines, see "Richtlinien für die Prüfung der persönlichen Eignung der Soldaten vom Oberstleutnant—einschliesslich—abwärts," Annex 3 of Bundestag (VIII/138), p. 24.) In all fairness it should at the same time be stated that, especially in recent years, official army leadership has (on ceremonial occasions) come out strongly in defense of the high moral character of the decision of the conspirators to assassinate their War Lord. In an address on July 20, 1961, the then Inspector General of the Bundeswehr, General Friedrich Foertsch, declared that the anti-Nazi resistance was in "the best German soldierly tradition" and insisted that "a state may demand our loyalty only as long as that state is guided by principles of right and justice." Even more dramatically, official efforts to anchor the plot of July 20 in the matrix of Bonn's civic ideology have taken the form of renaming five military compounds or barracks for some of the chief civilian and military conspirators (Julius Leber, Henning von Treskow, General Rommel, Count von Stauffenberg, and Alfred Delp). *The Bulletin* (Bonn), July 25, 1961, p. 5.

159. Bundestag (VIII/138), p. 12. For details see the "Richtlinien," B/III/2, *Drucksache* 109, Annex 3, p. 25. For the final executive order as published by the Federal Ministry of Defense, incorporating the GA's Guide Lines, see "Anweisungen für die Auswahl der Berufssoldaten und Soldaten auf Zeit" of May 24, 1956, and conveniently reproduced in "Zum Problem der Waffen-SS Offiziere," *Deutscher Informationsdienst,* no. 604 (October 29, 1956), pp. 1–3. The "Richtlinien" themselves had been published as early as October 13, 1955. In addition to the mishandling of SS reinstatements, considerable excitement was occasioned by a report which alleged that the Defense Ministry had refused "on principle" to give preference in personnel selection to known anti-Nazis and victims of political persecution under Hitler. (See "Neue Wehrmacht im alten Geist?" *Deutscher Informationsdienst,* no. 452 [March 14, 1955].) It was further alleged that even after the Ministry was forced to discontinue this clearly illegal practice (see the Civil Service Code and par. 4 of the Volunteer Act of 1955), there remained a startling discrepancy between the numbers of applications from former victims of Nazism and the numbers of nominations in this category submitted by the Ministry to the GA. In the light of the testimony from such men as Depuy Fritz Erler and State Secretary Rombach, these allegations appear largely unfounded. In his letter of September 25, 1961, Erler writes: "The circle of politically persecuted soldiers and officers who would have come into question for re-commissioning was not very large. There were also some cases in which there were reasons other than political why they should not

be reinstated. I had the feeling that a few members of the Defense Ministry's Personnel Division had failed to push the necessary promotion of politically persecuted soldiers, but [Defense Minister] Blank himself had simply not insisted on enough discipline. I know of no hostility on the part of Blank." Similarly, Herr Rombach cannot recollect any instance of the Defense Ministry's refusal "on principle" to commission an officer who had been victimized by the Nazis. According to him, many of the former officers in the "victim" category had no interest in returning to the military. Only a part had applied for reinstatement. Many were too old to be returned to active service, and the rest were accepted for duty with field units or in administrative positions. "May I emphasize, however," concludes Rombach, "that I never met any resistance in the Defense Ministry in regard to the recommissioning of those who had sustained losses for political reasons [under Hitler]." At the very beginning of its operation, the GA had demonstrated its sentiments in this regard by approving the few applications from "reformers" and former Resistance members which the Defense Ministry's Personnel Chief, Colonel Kurt Brandstädter, had submitted to it, in an ostentatiously quickened procedure. This demonstration of the GA's independence was widely taken to be an implied expression of displeasure over the Ministry's handling of personnel problems. Cf. "Richtlinien etc." C/6, p. 26.

160. The Defense Ministry under Blank had consistently refused to accept that part of the GA's Guide Line recommendations which called for the inclusion in the local selection boards (for applicants below the rank of colonel) of two civilians. When several cases of the recommissioning of unreconstructed SS officers became public and after Minister Blank was replaced by Franz Josef Strauss, the GA suggested to the new Defense Minister that he establish a unified examination board which would include two civilians besides the three officers and which would review all applications from former SS members, regardless of their rank. Strauss acceded to the GA's wishes in every respect. The examinations involve the same selection criteria which were established and employed by the GA. The membership of the special examination board for SS applicants (which sits in Cologne) includes several members of the GA, including its chairman, Wilhelm Rombach. According to Rombach more than 50 per cent of the relatively few nominations were rejected. Those that were affirmed represented in most cases men who joined the SS at the age of seventeen or twenty, frequently under direct or implied compulsion.

161. By September 30, 1956, of the 1,310 SS officers' applications, 33 had been approved. For noncommissioned officers the numbers were respectively 1,324 and 270, and for enlisted men 462 and 195. The 33 former SS officers represented 0.4 per cent of the 8,215 officers then on active duty. Another 28 had been taken over from the Border Patrol (*Grenzschutz*), making a total of 61, or 0.7 per cent.

162. That former officers generally clung more tenaciously to their Nazi past than enlisted men and the rest of the population was still discernible seven and eight years after the fall of the Third Reich. At that time twice as many regular and reserve officers (21 per cent) as citizens at large (11 per

cent) thought that the statement "Hitler was the greatest statesman of the century, his true greatness will be only later recognized" came closest to their own opinion. By the same token only 9 per cent of former regular army personnel thought that Hitler had been an "unscrupulous politician" as against 26 per cent of the total male population who, at least in retrospect, recognized the Führer's lack of conscience. If we add the numbers of those former professional soldiers who still thought of Hitler as the greatest statesman (29 per cent) to the number of those who agreed that Hitler had made "some mistakes, but in any case was an exemplary state leader" (15 per cent), we get a total of 44 per cent who clearly were more positively than negatively impressed by the Hitler phenomenon. Cf. Friedrich Pollock, ed., *Gruppenexperiment,* Frankfurter Beiträge zur Soziologie, no. 2 ([Frankfurt:] Europäische Verlagsanstalt, [c. 1955]), pp. 236–272.

163. See his "The New German Army," *Foreign Affairs,* XXXIV, 1 (October, 1955), 1–13. For a brief and sympathetic account of Baudissin, his conceptions, and his work, see Peter Miska, "Der unbequeme Soldat," *Frankfurter Rundschau,* June 16, 1956, p. 23. Cf. "Bürger in Uniform," *Der Spiegel,* X, 45 (November 5, 1956), 9–10. The questions what kind of an army the new Bundeswehr was to be and what its relation to the new democratic republic should be were, of course, hotly debated in the years 1952–1956. As examples of the breadth of the controversy in the earlier years, mention might be made of Ernst Buchrucker, *Die Ehre des Soldaten: Deutsches Soldatentum in europäischer Wehrmacht?* (Stollhamm: Rauschenbusch, 1953), and Werner Picht, *Wiederbewaffnung* (Pfullingen: Neske, 1954), on the side of reaction, and of Erich Dethleffsen and Karl Heinrich Helfer, *Soldatische Existenz morgen* (Bonn: Schimmelbusch, 1953) and *Der deutsche Soldat in der Armee von morgen. Wehrverfassung, Wehrsystem, Inneres Gefüge* (Munich: Isar, 1954), on the side of reform.

164. In March, 1958, under the heading "Count Baudissin's Munich Swan Song," the DSZ wrote, "There sits an enemy of genuine German soldierliness, a man who has to be removed once and for all from the Bundeswehr's 'Inner Leadership,' even if all of Social Democracy, which is that man's main support, should stand on its head." Quoted in *Feinde der Demokratie* (Lower Saxony), VIII, 8 (June–July, 1959), 18.

165. See, for example, "Blank gegen 'Diva,'" *Junge Stimme,* July 27, 1956, and "Neue Runde im Ringen um den Grafen Baudissin," *Neue Ruhr Zeitung* (Essen), August 15, 1956.

166. "Offiziere: Griff nach den Sternen," *Der Spiegel,* XVII, 52 (December 25, 1963), 40.

167. Even Adelbert Weinstein, the military editor of the *Frankfurter Allgemeine Zeitung,* a paper very close to the federal government, could write: "Superior officers who under no circumstances (*überhaupt nicht*) wished to apply the principles of the citizen in uniform or who lacked the courage of their conviction because that consideration might have impeded the rapid growth of the Army, took control in those days [when Count Baudissin sought to introduce his reforms] of many an important position." Weinstein (VIII/156).

168. The degree to which these reforms were disregarded by the over-aged company grade officers and their noncoms was widely publicized by *Der Spiegel* ("Beschwerderecht: Bauch im Dreck," *Der Spiegel,* XVIII, 6 [February 3, 1964], 23–26) when it published excerpts from the diary of a recruit, detailing the chicanery, arbitrariness, and insolence with which basic trainees were treated. "[A]pparently it had occurred to none of the recruits to defend himself against improper treatment with the aid of the relevant paragraphs of the Soldiers Law and the Defense Complaint Ordinance. . . . Even such unambiguous lectures [on the nature of illegitimate commands which tend to offend the personal dignity of the soldier] have been unable to rouse the . . . soldiers to an active defense of their noblest basic right. Colonel Karat surmized: 'They don't even notice when their human dignity has been insulted because most of them get their wisdom in that respect from obscure military penny dreadfuls (*Landserhefte*)' " (*ibid.,* p. 26). The publicity given to the problem, however, triggered an avalanche of complaints of abusive treatment (*ibid.,* no. 8 [February 17, 1964], p. 14).

169. In no Western country—except the United States in the nineteen-fifties—have the fear and hatred of Communism been so ardently fanned and become so pervasive a part of the officially approved climate of opinion. Because that seemed so natural for a divided people at the edge of the Iron Curtain, millions of whose citizens had wrought or experienced horrors in Soviet Russia, it has not been sufficiently appreciated to what extent anti-Communism has provided the bridge across which Nazis and nationalists who were left stranded in May, 1945, could reach the Bonn Republic. In the government-tolerated, unofficially promoted, amiable confusion of anti-Communism with liberal-democratic reliability, the integration of these forces into the public and economic life of the Republic was at least temporarily and conditionally effected. Cf. Gerhard Baumann, "Psychologische Rückwirkungen in der Bevölkerung der Bundesrepublik beim Aufbau einer Gesamtverteidigung," *Wehrwissenschaftliche Rundschau,* XII, 3 (1962), 123-139, but especially 133.

170. Sadly enough, the opposition to many of Baudissin's reforms has been strengthened by the attitude of certain American officers who also distrusted the Count as too radical and democratic and privately said so. Unfortunately, this was not the first time in our policy toward Germany that we placed the question of democratic reconstruction second to the practical urgency of rebuilding German strength. See Observer, *pseud.,* "Wird jetzt die 08/15 Suppe angerührt?" *Wiking–Ruf,* V, 8 (August, 1956), 12–13. For a contrary American view of the effectiveness of the Count's conceptions, see Hanson W. Baldwin, "Germany's New Army," *New York Times,* October 14, 1958. For a cautiously optimistic view of the future of Baudissin's reforms, see H. Stuckmann, "Dix jours dans la Bundeswehr," *Documents* (*Revue des questions allemandes*), XII (January–February, 1957), 36–48. For an enthusiastic endorsement of the new Bundeswehr (which, to be sure, relies almost exclusively on German government sources and charitably overlooks or downgrades countervailing evidence), see Eric Waldman, *The Goose Step is Verboten: The German Army Today* (Glencoe, Ill.: Free

Press, [c. 1964]). Unfortunately this book appeared two years after the present chapter had been concluded.

171. No less characteristic for the tug of war involving the nature of Germany's new military establishment—though almost ludicrous in its unimportance—has been the conflict over the new uniforms. Traditionalists complained over the un-German look of the new garb and charged that its universally admitted ungainliness was a purposeful attempt by "reformers" to expose the military to popular ridicule and contempt. By the middle of 1962 pressures for some modification had resulted in several concessions. The new dispensation ordered the reappearance of gold braid, flags, and similar traditional military paraphernalia. Equally important, new regiments were now to be named after famous Wehrmacht units, such as the Afrika Korps, for example. (*Frankfurter Rundschau,* June 10, 1962.) In February, 1963, the inspector general of the Bundeswehr, General Foertsch, publicly objected to the commemoration of the recent war's most staggering German defeat by broadcasting the play *Stalingrad,* by Claus Hubalek. In this objection and his admonition to all officers to counteract the impact of the play on the men under them, Foertsch was fully supported by the new Secretary of Defense, Kai-Uwe von Hassel. (*Ibid.,* February 4, 1963.) Hubalek's television play moved one official of the East Prussian Regional Association to complain publicly that "German television was infested with Jews," a remark which brought him a slander suit and disavowal by other officials of the association. (*Ibid.,* February 25, 1963.)

172. Quoted in *Feinde der Demokratie* (Lower Saxony), V, 4–5 (January–March, 1956), 52–53.

173. Cf. "Bonn kritisiert Marineoffiziere," *Hamburger Allgemeine Zeitung,* April 19, 1956, with "Abgeordnete rügen Zenker," *Die Welt* (Hamburg), April 19, 1956. The Zenker case was, of course, widely reported in the German press, as was the lively Bundestag debate. In addition to the references above, see also "Einmütigkeit im Bundestag—Raeder und Dönitz sind keine Vorbilder," *Hannoversche Presse,* April 19, 1956, and "Scharnhorst, Gneisenau," *Frankfurter Allgemeine Zeitung,* April 19, 1956.

174. Most parliamentarians, on both sides of the aisle, were prepared to grant that Zenker's previous conduct had been at least correct and were willing to see in his speech a regrettable lapse. They were prepared to believe the captain's explanation that he had been merely trying to gain for the work of naval reconstruction the support of those former naval officers whose "strong sense of tradition" had hitherto prevented them from volunteering their services. It should not be uncharitable to suggest that Zenker's own "sense of tradition" was hardly any less well developed, to say the least. Nevertheless, in the meantime Captain Zenker has been promoted to rear admiral and has become chief of Bonn's naval forces. On the nationalist and Conservative Revolutionary traditions in the German Navy of yesteryear and their postwar manifestations, see Kurt Hirsch, "Wohin segelt die Bundesmarine?" *Blätter für Deutsche und Internationale Politik,* no. 6 (June 20, 1958), pp. 425–432.

175. The "Dönitz cult" in the German Navy is another phenomenon

which has been prominently discussed in the press, especially in connection with the Dobberstein case. Lieutenant Commander Werner Dobberstein claimed he was dismissed for having dared to complain against what he calls the Dönitz cult. The Navy and the Minister of Defense denied that that was the ground for dismissal. This case also reached the public in the spring of 1956, right after the Raeder and Zenker cases. (See also "Seekrieg," *Der Spiegel,* XV, 6 [February 1, 1961], especially 39–40.) In November, 1958, a Socialist deputy's suggestion to a group of officers to the effect that two sailors who had been executed in 1917 for insurrection should be rehabilitated was greeted with expressions of outrage. When Deputy Eberhard Beermann somewhat later referred to Raeder and Dönitz as having condoned the death of six million Jews, he was interrupted with the call, "Come, come, there weren't as many as all that!" On "correcting" himself by saying, "Perhaps there were four millions," Beermann was again interrupted by a complacent "There you are." Shocked by the officers' callousness, the deputy admitted with some heat that he, for one, preferred the two executed sailors to Hitler's admirals. At this point, naval officers remonstrated, "That's the July 20 crowd. We won't let them drag the Admirals in the mud," and, together with some officers of the sister services, stalked out of the room. See the account in *Frankfurter Rundschau* of November 24, 1958. Neither the Director of the Naval College, whose officers were involved in the incident, nor the Defense Ministry in Bonn bothered to reprimand the naval officers, according to the paper. Early in 1963 a new storm arose over a speech Dönitz had made before a high-school assembly. In this address Dönitz "justified" Nazi aggression against Poland on the basis that Hitler did not expect Britain to honor its commitment to the Poles. He also tried to exonerate Hitler from culpability in ordering the invasion of Norway and ended by blaming his own imprisonment as a war criminal exclusively on Stalin. The most disturbing aspects in all this, however, were not so much Dönitz' views as the fact that the pupils responded to the ex-admiral's imbecilities with thunderous applause and that the school principal excused his approval of the invitation to Dönitz on the ground that he was "certain of the support of the citizens" of the town. Incidentally, somewhat later, under heavy pressure, the school principal committed suicide. In June, 1963, a new Dönitz incident demonstrated again the recalcitrant solidarity with Hitler's successor of Bonn's top navy men, Vice Admiral Friedrich Ruge, the then Commander of the Federal Navy, and Vice Admiral (ret.) Hellmuth Heye, the Parliamentary Representative to the Armed Forces, a prominent former CDU deputy. See *Frankfurter Allgemeine Zeitung,* June 17, 1963. Cf. "Marine Treffen: Die Luft ist raus," *Der Spiegel,* XVII, 26 (June 26, 1963), 37–39.

176. Raeder's own alibi for his continued service under Hitler is the familiar, "I was only a sailor and soldier, not a politician" (*Mein Leben,* Vol. I [*Bis zum Flottenabkommen mit England 1935*], [Tübingen: Schlichtenmayer, 1956], p. 11). Indeed, he wishes to support this notion by emphasizing that Hitler's assumption of power "caused neither shock nor friction among the rank and file of the Navy" (p. 280), that he personally felt no

qualms in swearing loyalty to his Führer, and that the blood bath of June, 1934, only confirmed his strong desire to keep the Navy out of politics. Yet on "Heroes' Day," 1939, he declared in a speech that the German nation, which had "chosen" Nazism for its creed, "follows the symbols of its rejuvenation with burning love and fanatical passion. It has experienced National Socialism, not suffered it, as so many inept critics abroad will have it! Hence, the clear and relentless fight against Bolshevism and international Jewry whose nation-destroying deeds we have fully experienced." (Quoted from *Völkischer Beobachter,* March 13, 1939, in *The Wiener Library Bulletin* [London], X, 5–6 [1956], 40.) In 1940, Raeder encouraged the armed forces to "find strength and courage in our unshakable confidence in our Führer who has given us back the faith in a free future. To follow him means to be victorious." (Quoted from *Völkischer Beobachter,* January 11, 1940, *ibid.*)

177. *Feinde der Demokratie* (Lower Saxony), V, I (October–November 1955), 47.

178. The leader of that majority was the former Admiral Günther Schubert, a prominent member of the CDU. However, Schubert's political orientation appeared to have been characterized less accurately by his CDU connections than by the fact that the conspiratorial (and later outlawed) Nazi information network Natinform considered him one of the "most important leaders" of German nationalism, along with such other worthies as Remer, Rudel, Ramcke, Hek Rau, Haussleiter, Aschenauer, Krüger, Bornemann, Johann Strunk. (See Appendix to decisions taken at the Natinform Conference of January 16–19, 1953. Copy in the author's possession.) Equally characteristic is the fact that a nationalist information agent, Eric-Uwe Müller-Schwaneck ("Eumsch"), alleged being Schubert's liaison man to France's most important ultranationalist paper, *Rivarol.* (From a report on Eumsch, August 18, 1952.)

179. See "Raeders Verzicht," *Hamburger Echo,* no. 90 (April 17, 1956).

180. See "Verzicht auf die Ehrenbürgerschaft," *Frankfurter Allgemeine Zeitung,* April 17, 1956.

181. See "Raeder Ehrenmitglied des Marinebundes," *Hannoversche Presse,* June 4, 1956.

182. Letter to the editor, *Frankfurter Allgemeine Zeitung,* October 27, 1955.

183. See "Fregattenkapitän Kretschmer: 'Raeder ist unser Kamerad,'" *Neue Ruhr Zeitung* (Essen), no. 120 (June 5, 1956), p. 2. At the time of these events (1953–1956) Kretschmer was also Chief of the Division for Military Policy of the government's propaganda organization, Working Association of Democratic Circles (ADK). That most of the postwar nationalist incidents in the armed forces involved Navy personnel, rather than the Army, can probably be explained by the far greater impact which Hitlerism had on the junior service. The old Prussian Army attitude toward the Navy had been one of contempt for the "traditionlessness" of Navy officers and for their overwhelmingly bourgeois backgrounds. The absence of ancient traditions and aristocratic ties made naval officers anxious to

prove themselves more patriotic, more nationalist, and more loyal than the aloof and powerful clique of the Army General Staff and thus made them more vulnerable to Nazi appeals. Also, excessive sensitivity to the reproach that it had been the fleet mutiny which had triggered the hated November revolution of 1918, and the Navy's traumatic experience in the Kapp putsch of 1920, had made the totally "nonpolitical" attitude a basic article of faith among Navy officers. Moreover, it is quite likely that the absence in the Navy of a relatively autonomous leadership group like the Army General Staff, and the inflexible authoritarianism of Admirals Raeder and Dönitz, also contributed to the tradition of absolute, blind obedience to superior orders, whatever their content, and to the almost total absence of even the mildest kind of anti-Hitler resistance in the German Navy. To this background was added in the postwar years the fact that the Navy's two most senior officers were still among the small handful of major war criminals in Allied custody, when practically all surviving generals had already been freed. This must have rankled the Navy men and helps to account for their extreme sensitivity on this score. For a brief account of the Navy's relation to the Third Reich, see W. Baum, "Marine, Nationalsozialismus und Widerstand," *Vierteljahrshefte für Zeitgeschichte,* XI, 1 (January, 1963), 16–18. Cf. also the apologetics of Wahrhold Drascher, "Zur Soziologie des deutschen Seeoffizierkorps," *Wehrwissenschaftliche Rundschau,* XII, 10 (October, 1962), 555–569.

184. See "Nagold: Tiefste Gangart," *Der Spiegel,* XVII, 46 (November 13, 1963), 52–59; and "Nagold: Solche Bengels," *ibid.,* 51 (December 18,

185. See above, I/11.

186. Three years earlier, Count Baudissin specifically warned against acceptance of the Legion as a viable model: "In a permanent civil war the 'unpolitical' soldier, the 'blind' citizen, will not in the long run prove an able fighter. Units of the Foreign Legion type which are held together mainly by various fears or by *esprit de corps* are reliable only under special conditions not at all like those prevailing in Europe." (VIII/163), p. 4.

187. This new office (copied from the Swedish institution of Ombudsman) and its incumbents have been highly controversial. For the debate surrounding the resignation of Vice-Admiral Heye, the second Commissioner, on November 3, 1964, see the German press on that and subsequent days and "Heye: Breitseite aus Bayern," *Der Spiegel,* XVIII, 46 (November 11, 1964), 38–39. Also "Ich will mir den Mund nicht verbieten lassen," *ibid.,* pp. 41–43. Cf. also F. Ridley, "The Parliamentary Commissioner for Military Affairs in the Federal Republic of Germany." *Political Studies,* XII, 1 (February, 1964), 1–20.

188. For a contrary view—indeed, for the view that the Bundeswehr, far from constituting a danger to democracy, has become the most important agency for the political education of large numbers of youngsters and for the inculcation of a democratic bias—see Günther Olzog, "Gefährdet die Bundeswehr die Demokratie?" *Politische Studien,* IX, 96 (April, 1958), 227–232; and Waldman (VIII/170).

189. Even in a cosmopolitan and strongly Social Democratic center like

Hamburg, a sizable minority of over one-fourth of all citizens is still incapable of viewing the potential alternation of government and opposition as something inherent in a working democracy. Rather they would construe the forming of the government by the SPD as something analogous to a change in regime. See Wolfgang Hartenstein and Günter Schubert, *Mitlaufen oder Mitbestimmen* (Frankfurt: Europäische Verlagsanstalt, [c. 1961]), 49–52.

190. A very great majority of Germans reject the notion that the right to free speech and the freedom to publish extends to the advocacy of the renunciation of Germany's eastern territories. *Ibid.*, pp. 61–63.

Chapter IX. Organized War Veterans and the Resurgence of Nationalism

1. At this writing a major work of scholarship on the history of the Stahlhelm is not yet available. Fortunately this serious gap in our knowledge of the Weimar Republic is in the process of being closed by a young German scholar, Volker Berghahn.

2. Theodor Duesterberg, *Der Stahlhelm und Hitler* (Wolfenbüttel: Wolfenbütteler Verlagsanstalt, 1949), p. 125. But cf. Heinz Brauweiler, "Der Anteil des Stahlhelm," in Curt Hotzel, ed., *Deutscher Aufstand. Die Revolution des Nachkriegs* (Stuttgart: Kohlhammer, 1934), pp. 218–227.

3. "The Stahlhelm was a product of the time of the Marxist revolution of 1918. Its creation can be understood only in the light of the conditions which prevailed in those days. . . . All over the country rioting, political arbitrariness, disorganization, and terror reigned supreme. . . . There arose in opposition, and to protect the population, militias, numerous Free Corps under brave officers. . . . At that time Capt. (i.R.) Franz Seldte . . . formed a group of old front-line soldiers to maintain the threatened peace and order in his native city Magdeburg. He gave that group the attractive name *Stahlhelm* (Steel Helmet)." Duesterberg (IX/2), pp. 7–8.

4. "The majority of the glib (*federgewandt*) heralds of the new system thought it below their dignity to go into the streets themselves to defend their political newly born with arms and clubs against the Spartacus League, and later the Communists. In distress, the call went out for the derided, old soldiers. Had these shown the same drive for self-preservation that the former [i.e., "the glib heralds of the new system"] felt, the Weimar Republic would have become the victim of a Red dictatorship before it was even born." *Ibid.*

5. At the same time it is important to remember that the Stahlhelm's monarchism was not unconditional. It would have fought against a liberal monarchy of the British type quite as strenuously as it fought against the liberal Weimar Republic. On August 9, 1925, *Der Stahlhelm* published an article, "Unser Recht auf den Staat," which demonstrates this clearly: "Even before the revolution, Germany had a constitution. We had a constitutional

monarchy which without the revolution would probably have developed into a democratic monarchy, much like England's. . . . We do not underestimate the importance of a hereditary monarchical sovereign who is independent of public opinion and the majority of interest groups. . . . But, basically, the questions of the form of state and of the colors of the flag are not decisive. . . . The decisive point and the main target of our attack is the flat and vacant democracy. . . . We front-line soldiers . . . would not have contented ourselves with the role of the taxpayer who is ruled from on high even if no revolution had taken place." Quoted in Martin (III/5), pp. 188–189. Cf. also his *Zehn Jahre Stahlhelm. Denkschrift* (Leipzig: [Fleischer], 1929).

6. Bracher, in his extraordinarily careful study, *Die Auflösung der Weimarer Republik* (III/7), thinks that the Stahlhelm's own estimate of one million members in the year 1927–1928 is an exaggeration. It certainly was, for that year. It would appear, however, that two or three years later that figure, and more, was actually achieved. Cf. the figures cited by W. M. Knight-Patterson, *pseud.* [i.e., W. Kulski], *Germany from Defeat to Conquest* (London: Allen and Unwin, 1945), p. 431.

7. That the Stahlhelm and the other radical nationalists who sought alliances with Hitler did not understand this fact was not due to any deception by the Nazis. They had consistently gone out of their way to make it crystal clear. One of the most candid—if also most brutal—clarifications of Hitler's position on "alliances" came from the pen of Joseph Goebbels. Answering a call of Conservative Revolutionaries for the merger of all nationalist opponents of the hated Weimar Republic, Goebbels wrote: "Either you believe in your state, then it is your state, its idea is your idea, then you have leased that state, that idea, and you will preach of their future with all of the effective oratory of the caller in the desert; or you do not believe in your state, then you can compromise, then you can give in to others, then you can talk around the whole thing and call for the merger of all those who believe equally little in their state. If one is in the right, then all the others are in the wrong. . . . We National Socialists are really so immodest as to believe that we and only we, all alone, are the bearers of the coming idea of the state. . . . We shall never believe in a unification, in a merger of groups which agree more or less on this or the other, rather we believe that one day the strongest will win out and that before its lock step (*Gleichschritt*) everything else will dissolve into the void of its unimportance. The problem of Germany is not unification of nationalism; but destruction of Marxism and thus fulfillment of nationalism. . . . There can be no unification. There can be only struggle until one triumphs and the others lie shattered on the ground. To the battle, then! Let us be intolerant and hard regarding everyone who does not believe, who does not think and feel as we do! But let us fight that battle among ourselves as comrades! At its end, there stands the great love." "Mitkämpfer von der Standarte," *Nationalsozialistische Briefe,* no. 23, September 1, 1926.

8. Duesterberg (IX/2), p. 14. See there also the long and fruitless exchange of letters between Hitler and Seldte-Duesterberg which gives a clear picture of the frictions between the Stahlhelm and the Nazis at a time

when the ink on the Harzburg Proclamation had not yet dried. *Ibid.*, pp. 15–33.

9. In Duesterberg's pathetically self-important and frequently less than truthful brochure in support of the thesis that the Stahlhelm was one of the most consistent and effective opponents of Hitler, and he, Duesterberg, the heroic leader of this opposition, the author writes, p. 34: "When I urged my about three million followers [Duesterberg had actually gathered not quite 2.6 million votes on the first ballot] to vote for Hindenburg, and not for Hitler, our antagonism became enmity to death. I destroyed with my appeal Hitler's cherished plan to become elected Reich President." This is nonsense. Even if every one of the Duesterberg supporters had gone over to Hitler, as the great majority of them did anyhow, Hitler would not have come close to getting the required 50 per cent of the votes cast. It was not *because* of the Stahlhelm and other nationalists that Hitler's "cherished plan" failed, but *despite* them. See Alfred Milatz, "Das Ende der Parteien im Spiegel der Wahlen 1930 bis 1933" in Erich Matthias and Rudolf Morsey, eds., *Das Ende der Parteien 1933* (Düsseldorf: Droste, 1960), pp. 763–764.

10. Duesterberg (IX/2), p. 38. Cf. for these events the description, interpretation, and purported correction by the former DNVP leader Otto Schmidt-Hannover, *Umdenken oder Anarchie* (III/36), pp. 325–330.

11. Duesterberg (IX/2), p. 48.

12. For details of the crisis within the Stahlhelm, see *ibid.*, pp. 44–63.

13. *Ibid.*, p. 63.

14. Among them were Colonel Siegfried Wagner, Major Count H. J. Blumenthal, Carl Wentzel–Teutschental, close collaborators of Carl F. Goerdeler's; Lieutenant Colonel Werner Schrader, the liaison officer between the Supreme Command of the Army and Army Intelligence and confidant of Canaris and Oster; and Baron Ferdinand von Lüninck, who was to have acted as political regional chairman after the successful coup. See Zeller (III/10), pp. 183–184, 188–189, 211, 338, 340, 386, 387.

15. Duesterberg (IX/2), pp. 81–83, 108–109, 116–117.

16. See "12-Punkte-Programm des 'Stahlhelms'" *Nordwest–Zeitung* (Oldenburg), September 3, 1951.

17. *Informationsdienst der Deutschen Partei* (Landesverband Hessen), no. 1 (March, 1952), p. 3.

18. " 'Wie beim alten Willem . . . ,' " *Hannoversche Presse,* VI, 260 (November 6, 1951), 2. Cf. *Deutsche Presse Agentur* (*dpa*), *Inf.* 1651 (November 6, 1951), p. 1.

19. " 'Wie beim alten Willem . . .' " (IX/18).

20. Quoted in "Verrat im Stahlhelm!" *Der Stahlhelm e.V.* (Landesverband Gross-Hamburg), December 17, 1953.

21. Walter Spohrmann, quoted in Volkmar Hoffmann, "Stahlhelm Rebellion um Schwarz-Rot-Gold," *Schleswig-Holsteinische Volks-Zeitung* (Kiel), LXI, 82 (April 7, 1954), 7. In a speech to the Stahlhelm leaders of the Land organization Nordmark, on September 21, 1952, Carl Simon explained Kesselring's election in terms of the Stahlhelm's campaign to effect the release of all "so-called war criminals." See *Deutsche Presse Agentur* (*dpa*), *Inf.* 1657 (September 22, 1952), p. 5.

22. The matter of radicalization was, of course, primarily a problem of tactics and had little, if anything, to do with ideology. Thus, the deputy chairman of the blatantly Nazi organization Natinform reported on January 14, 1953: "Simon writes that he agrees with the Natinform program as such, but that he objects to 'natural religions.' "

23. It is absolutely impossible for an outsider to separate truth from falsehood in this welter of accusations. Simon alluded darkly to Girgensohn's wishing to sell out the Stahlhelm, without specifying to whom the organization was to be sold out, though he presumably meant Bonn and its unconditional West–integration. He also suggested, equally vaguely, that Loske was using the Stahlhelm for purposes of private gain, in connection with some insurance contracts. Girgensohn denied that van Berg had received funds from the VFF. The only outside money came from a private firm (DM 3,000) which for purposes of camouflage made use of a liaison man, a former officer, who happened to have been a member of the VFF. Girgensohn, in turn, accused Simon of working together with an agent of the British intelligence service. (The information service in Bonn, *Politik und Wirtschaft,* appeared to be getting inside information [see the issues of May 23 and 30, 1953], but its accuracy was seriously questioned by some of the insiders. See also *Der Spiegel,* VII, 26 [June 24, 1953], 10. Cf. *Feinde der Demokratie* [Nordmark], III, 5 [June 24, 1953], 40–42; cf. also Jakob Glaser, "Im 'Stahlhelm' geht es rund . . . ," *Welt der Arbeit* [Cologne], September 25, 1953, p. 2; *Feinde der Demokratie* [North Rhine–Westphalia], no. 5 [November, 1954], p. 12.) The correspondence of some of the main actors in the struggle is also not very helpful, as they omit many of the details without which a judgment as to the actual causes of friction is impossible. (Letters of Carl Simon to Karl Smets, the leader of the Koblenz area, of June 1 and March 8, 1953; Carl Simon's letter to Field Marshal Kesselring, June 25, 1953; discussion memorandum notes of a discussion between Girgensohn and Smets.) In general, however, there is little doubt that the old enmities between the Seldte faction and the Duesterberg faction, between those who became more or less enthusiastic Nazis and those who worked in the Resistance movement, played a major role in the explosive disagreement which rocked the Stahlhelm after the war. (This is also Simon's view according to a letter to the author, July 26, 1961.) The rest must be credited to divergent positions on rearmament.

24. Simon, together with the anti-Hitler conservative-neutralist General Jenö von Egan-Krieger and the Koblenz district leader Karl Smets, formed a dissident Stahlhelm group, Traditionsgemeinschaft, which maintains local branches principally in the Rhineland, but also in Lower Saxony, Hamburg, Berlin, and Franconia, and which sees itself as the rightful heir to the Duesterberg tradition. In foreign policy the Traditions–Stahlhelm differs from the parent organization by its neutralist orientation. In domestic policy it differentiates itself by a purist notion of total national opposition, as against "opportunist" nationalism.

25. See, for instance, letter to one of the Stahlhelm leaders in the Rhineland-Palatinate of Gertrude Ossenkop, of the nationalist-reactionary Kaiserliche Reichsbewegung (Imperial Reich Movement) of May 27, 1953, in

which she complained that the Stahlhelm had so far sailed too closely to the course set out by Bonn. Cf. also the reaction of the old Nazi–loyalist, Gerhard Mischke, the former Regierungspräsident of Koblenz, who welcomed the new leadership for their expected radically nationalist, and even national-socialist, orientation. (From a confidential discussion memorandum of April 9, 1953.) Yet in foreign policy the Simon wing was probably more radical.

26. This is the title also of Kesselring's memoirs, *Soldat bis zum letzten Tag* (Bonn: Athenäum, 1953).

27. See, for instance, Miss Ossenkop's letter IX/25, in which she even speculates that the Field Marshal's apparent, and disappointing, moderation was part of the price he had to pay to the British for his release from prison.

28. Letter of the Stahlhelm official Karl Smets to Johann Szekely, Chief of Organization of the Hungarist Movement, dated December 17, 1952.

29. "Zur Klärung!" *Der Stahlhelm* (Bonn) XXI, 2 (February, 1954), 1.

30. "Generalfeldmarshall Kesselring beim Stahlhelm in München," *Der Stahlhelm* (Bonn), XXI, 1 (January, 1954), 4.

31. See, for example, the reaction of the incorrigible Nazi Wolfgang Sarg: "Moreover, the recent declaration of the Stahlhelm executive committee has offended me somewhat. In it the members are being urged to support the government parties in the election. How is one to understand that?" Letter of Sarg to the Natinform representative for southern Germany, September 18, 1952, p. 5. A very similar disappointment marks the official organ of the DRP. See "Rund um den Stahlhelm," *Das Ziel* (Hanover), II, 27 (November 21, 1953), 2.

32. Letter of Girgensohn of July 16, 1953, quoted in a letter by Walter Spohrmann of September 9, 1953.

33. *Ibid.* The political committee met on August 15, 1953.

34. By an indiscretion this letter fell into the hands of the information service *Politik und Wirtschaft,* which refused Spohrmann's request not to publicize its contents. *Ibid.*

35. See *Feinde der Demokratie* (Lower Saxony), III, 4 (January, 1954).

36. *Der Stahlhelm e.V.* (Landesverband Gross-Hamburg), "Verrat im Stahlhelm!" Hamburg, December 17, 1953 (open letter).

37. In Lower Saxony, Chairman von Rheden expelled a whole group of members who protested against the formation of a squad of uniformed bouncers and bullies. *Feinde der Demokratie* (Lower Saxony), III, 2 (October–November, 1953).

38. "Neuwahl," *Der Stahlhelm* (Bonn), XXI, 2 (February, 1954), 1.

39. *Feinde der Demokratie* (Lower Saxony), III, 9 (August 5, 1954), 40.

40. Proclamation of Kurt Rau of July 1, 1954, reproduced in *Feinde der Demokratie* (North Rhine–Westphalia), no. 1 (February 20, 1955), p. 19.

41. Bund der Frontsoldaten—Schutzkorps, "Kampfauftrag," *ibid.*, p. 14.

42. Bund der Frontsoldaten e.V., Der Chef des Stabes, "Dienstanweisung 3/54," Duisburg, October 24, 1954, reproduced in *ibid.*, p. 18.

43. Quoted in Theo Trischen, "Das fromme Märchen vom 'unpolitischen Stahlhelm,'" *Neue Ruhr Zeitung* (Essen), no. 38 (September 18, 1954), p. 1.

44. Quoted in *Allgemeine Wochen–Zeitung der Juden in Deutschland* (Düsseldorf), September 17, 1954.

45. M. Wilken, "Grundlagen unserer Stahlhelm-Arbeit: Gedanken zur Giessener Botschaft," *Der Stahlhelm* (Bonn), XXI, 5 (May, 1954), 1.

46. *Die Welt* (Hamburg), March 12, 1955, quoted in *Feinde der Demokratie* (Lower Saxony), IV, 7 (May–June, 1955), 41.

47. *Ibid.*

48. *Ibid.*, p. 44.

49. *Parlamentarisch-Politischer Pressedienst,* September 30, 1955, pp. 4–5.

50. See, for example, Franz Roth, "Fehlschüsse," *Der Stahlhelm* (Bonn), XXIII, 7 (July, 1956), 2. The loyal support of Adenauer's foreign policy was, of course, rewarded. In this connection the following minor incident is not without significance: The official organ of the CDU's youth organization, Junge Union (Young Union), criticized the wearing of uniforms at the Stahlhelm meeting in Goslar. When the Stahlhelm protested, the executive board of the Berlin CDU sent the Stahlhelm its regrets over this "political slip-up (*Entgleisung*)." See *Politik und Wirtschaft,* September 28, 1955.

51. All membership figures must be taken with great caution. In most cases they are based on rumors and guesswork. Thus in 1952 Western observers credited the Stahlhelm with 134,000 members (Hans Jaeger in *The Wiener Library Bulletin* [London], VI, 1–2 [January–April, 1952], 2). Estimates for 1958 placed membership no higher than 3,500. ("Treacherous Currents," *ibid.*, XII, 1–2 [1958], 6. This estimate derives from an article in the *Frankfurter Allgemeine Zeitung* of December 18, 1957.) Incidentally, the official organ, *Der Stahlhelm,* was forced to suspend publication in October, 1956. It resumed its operation in January, 1957, now in enlarged form, at the Schild Verlag, Munich.

52. Carl Simon sees this reason for the Stahlhelm's failure in the postwar period as decisive. In second place Simon mentions the ambiguous ideological situation that split the Stahlhelm no less than the consciousness of the entire German people. Letter from Carl Simon to the author, July 26, 1961.

53. For a typical example of the enormous literature of this genre which has appeared in Germany in the scores of radically nationalist books and journals, see Erich Kern (*recte* Kernmayr), "Die Kriegsgeneration in der Sackgasse," *Der Freiwillige,* II, 4 (April, 1957), 3–6.

54. United States, Office of the Chief Counsel for Prosecution of Axis Criminality, *Nazi Conspiracy and Aggression, Opinion and Judgment* (Washington: Government Printing Office, 1947), pp. 99–102.

55. Estimates range anywhere between 200,000 and 400,000. It is diffi-

cult to see by what arithmetic one source comes to the categorical conclusion: "There can be no doubt that at most 200,000" live today in the Federal Republic. *Feinde der Demokratie* (Lower Saxony), VIII, 10A (November, 1959), 15.

56. For details see Hans Jungkunz and Winifried Kaeppner, *Gesetz zum Artikel 131 GG* (Stuttgart: Kohlhammer, 1959).

57. See, in lieu of many others, "Erklärung des Vorstandes des Bundesverbandes der Soldaten der ehemaligen Waffen-SS zum Kollektivbegriff 'SS,'" *Der Freiwillige,* VI, 6 (June, 1961), 6–7. For a more detailed exposition of the grounds of the claims of the Combat SS, see "Um Recht und Ehre," *ibid.,* VI, 5 (May, 1961), 4–8. Cf. "Die Waffen-SS als Teil der ehemaligen Kriegswehrmacht. Eine Antwort an das Institut für Zeitgeschichte," *Wiking-Ruf,* IV, 6 (June, 1955), 13 ff; and "Die reformatorischen Leistungen der ehemaligen Waffen-SS," *ibid.,* IV, 7 (July, 1955), 10 ff.

58. See Reitlinger (II/36), p. 76.

59. *Ibid.,* p. 77.

60. In Hausser's memoirs, *Waffen-SS im Einsatz* (Göttingen: Plesse, 1952), these schools and their products are given almost as great weight as the actual war experiences of the author, who became the only SS general to lead an army corps.

61. Paul Hausser, "SS-Verfügungstruppe und Wehrmacht," *Der Freiwillige,* I, 2 (February, 1956), 4.

62. In Paul Meier-Benneckenstein, *Das Dritte Reich im Aufbau,* Vol. III (Berlin: 1939), the nature and training of the Disposition Troops is far more candidly described: "The Disposition Troops are built up according to the experiences of the Schutzstaffel [SS] based in principle on the National Socialist conceptions of selection, leadership and training [*Erziehung*]. The SS Disposition Troops . . . are an active garrisoned and armed part of the SS. The men who have been selected by the criteria of the Schutzstaffel have committed themselves to at least four years of service. *Besides their education as SS men,* these troops receive premilitary training. After completion of their obligation in the Disposition Troops, the SS men naturally return to the General SS from which they came." Quoted in Reimund Schnabel, ed., *Macht ohne Moral: Eine Dokumentation über die SS* (Frankfurt: Röderberg, 1957), p. 38. Emphasis is the present author's.

63. Reitlinger (II/36), p. 81.

64. Quoted in [Ermenhild] Neusüss–Hunkel, *Die SS* (Hanover: Norddeutsche Verlagsanstalt O. Goedel, 1956), p. 38.

65. Hausser makes a great deal of the fact that the army insisted on its right to check the budget of the Disposition Troops. Paul Hausser, "Wissenschaft oder Spekulation," *Der Freiwillige,* I, 9 (September, 1956), 4.

66. Neusüss-Hunkel (IX/64), p. 38.

67. In Hitler's order of August 17, 1938, the SS Verfügungstruppe is called "neither a part of the Wehrmacht, nor of the police. It is a standing armed unit, at my exclusive disposal." See Walther Hofer, ed., *Der Nationalsozialismus: Dokumente 1933–1945* ([Frankfurt:] Fischer Bücherei, [c. 1957]), p. 110.

68. Hausser (IX/61), p. 4.

69. See Hans-Günther Seraphim, "SS-Verfügungstruppe und Wehrmacht," *Wehrwissenschaftliche Rundschau,* V, 12 (December, 1955), pp. 573–574.

70. Neusüss-Hunkel (IX/64), p. 38. Cf. Seraphim (IX/69), pp. 569–585, and Hans Buchheim, "Die SS in der Verfassung des Dritten Reiches," *Vierteljahrshefte für Zeitgeschichte,* III, 2 (April, 1955), 127–157.

71. See Schnabel (IX/62), p. 40.

72. Hofer (IX/67), p. 111.

73. "Äusserungen des Führers über die künftige Staatstruppenpolizei," Document D-665 reproduced in Poliakov and Wulf (II/39), p. 505. Cf. Schnabel (IX/62), pp. 39–40, and Hofer (IX/67), pp. 111–112.

74. Letter of Hausser to Minister of Defense F. J. Strauss in *Der Freiwillige,* II, 5 (May, 1957), 7–8.

75. Reitlinger (II/36), p. 83. Cf. the description of Werner Best in his *Die Deutsche Polizei* (1940), quoted in Schnabel (IX/62), p. 40.

76. Hans Buchheim, *SS und Polizei im NS-Staat* [Duisdorf/Bonn: Studiengesellschaft für Zeitprobleme, c. 1964], p. 182.

77. Letter to Strauss (IX/74), p. 7.

78. Hausser overlooks the February, 1937, order of SS General Theodor Eicke to the Death's Head units, according to which prisoners were not to be abused, "much as I as a National Socialist can understand such behavior." In justification for such startling deviation from the norms of Nazi brutality, Eicke mentions the danger that the Reich Ministry of the Interior might consider the SS as incapable of treating prisoners if abuses continued. Buchheim (IX/76), p. 172. Cf. Neusüss-Hunkel (IX/64), p. 54.

79. Reitlinger (II/36), p. 126.

80. *Für die Demokratie,* I (IX), 1 (December, 1959–January, 1960). 22, entry for December 10.

81. Buchheim (IX/76), pp. 183–185.

82. Reitlinger (II/36), p. 169.

83. Neusüss-Hunkel (IX/64), p. 96.

84. See "Partial Translation of Document L-180, Prosecution Exhibit 34: Extracts from Report of *Einsatzgruppe A* covering the period from 23 June 1941 to 15 October 1941," *Trials of War Criminals before the Nuernberg Military Tribunals* (Nuernberg: October, 1946–April, 1949), IV, 165.

85. Reitlinger (II/36), p. 83.

86. "Verfügungen/Anordnungen/Bekanntgaben," 3. Band. Herausg. von der Parteikanzlei (Munich: Eher Nachf.), p. 354, reproduced in Poliakov and Wulf (II/39), p. 503. Hess's reasoning is very similar to that with which Hitler himself in 1940 justified to the military commanders the need for the Waffen SS, especially in the future: "The Greater German Reich in its final organization will not encompass within its borders exclusively those population groups which *ab initio* are friendly to the Reich. Beyond the core of the Reich it is necessary to create State Police Troops which are capable in every situation of representing and of enforcing the Reich's authority in internal affairs. This task can be accomplished only by a State Police which has

in its ranks men of the best German blood and which identifies itself unreservedly with the Weltanschauung of the Greater German Reich. Only an organization of this nature will resist corrupting influences even in critical times." "Äusserungen über die künftige Staatstruppenpolizei," quoted in Buchheim (IX/76), p. 176.

87. See examination in Nuremberg, January 7, 1946 (afternoon), of General of the Waffen SS Erich von dem Bach-Zelewski by Rosenberg's defense counsel, Alfred Thoma, reproduced in Poliakov and Wulf (II/39), p. 512.

88. Nuremberg Document PS 1919b; *IMT,* XX, 302, cited in Reitlinger (II/36), p. 196.

89. Erich Kernmayr, former officer in the Waffen SS and its literary glorifier, former editor in chief of both the *Deutsche Soldaten–Zeitung* and *Der Freiwillige* (the monthly magazine of the postwar Waffen SS organization HIAG) thinks that as many as 200,000 air-force personnel were transferred. They were humorously referred to by their new comrades as "Hermann Göring *Spende*" and enjoyed generally very low regard. (For their contributions at Oradour, see note 91 below.) Interview with Kernmayr, July 2, 1957.

90. SS General Gottlob Berger wrote on June 16, 1943, to the SS Leadership Main Office: "When an ethnic group (*Volksgruppe*) is halfway decently led, all the volunteers report, and those who do not report voluntarily, are having their houses smashed! (Such cases are said to have occurred in the last few days in the Rumanian Banat)." Doc. NO-5901 in Nuernberg Military Tribunal, Case XI (Wilhelmstrasse Case), Prosecution Document 66, p. 50, quoted in Robert Herzog, *Die Volksdeutschen in der Waffen-SS,* Studien des Instituts für Besatzungsfragen in Tübingen zu den deutschen Besetzungen im 2. Weltkrieg, no. 5 (Tübingen: May, 1955), p. 5. Herzog summarizes the German practices of "volunteer" recruitment for the Combat SS by saying: ". . . even in the case of formally flawless voluntary enlistment the use of constraint cannot be excluded in every instance."

91. Neusüss-Hunkel (IX/64), p. 107. While the Nuremberg Tribunal excluded from its condemnation "those who were drafted into membership by the state in such a way as to give them no choice in the matter," it would be unfortunate if the reader were to be left with the impression that Waffen SS men could be separated into "good" and "bad" according to whether they were drafted into the units or volunteered. There were volunteer units that fought with exemplary chivalry and fairness, and there were draftee units which committed shocking crimes. The massacre of Oradour, to mention only one example, was carried out by an SS infantry company which consisted of transferred Luftwaffe personnel and conscripted ethnic Germans from Alsace. In this connection, it should be pointed out that the Nuremberg Tribunal erred when it linked Lidice with Oradour as an example of the criminality of the Waffen SS. Lidice was razed by SD troops.

92. See the depositions of Anton Kaindl (Document D-745 b), Fritz Suhren (Document D-746 b), Max Pauly (Document D-747), and A. Harbaum (Document D-750) reproduced in Poliakov and Wulf (II/39),

pp. 507–511. Cf. Klaus C. Smitmans, "Gerechtigkeit für die Waffen-SS," *Wiking–Ruf,* no. 2 (December, 1951), p. 14. Harbaum estimated that "between March 1942 to April 1945 approximately 45,000 Combat SS men served at one time or another in the concentration camps." Cf. Heinz Wewer, "Die HIAG der Waffen-SS," *Frankfurter Hefte,* XVII (July, 1962), 450.

93. Quoted in Buchheim (IX/76), p. 137.

94. Letter (IX/74), p. 8.

95. Nothing is said, of course, about how clean *that* was, and indeed how clean it could have been in so terrible a war.

96. Reitlinger (II/36), p. 452.

97. Here, as before, we limit our discussion to *wartime* functions. We have already mentioned that to Hitler the Combat SS was at first a state police to control his internal "enemies" and that he did not doubt in 1940 that it would resume these terror functions after the war.

98. For the contrary view, see the prudishly nonpolitical apologetics of Felix Steiner, *Von Clausewitz bis Bulganin: Erkenntnisse und Lehren einer Wehrepoche* (Bielefeld: Deutsche Heimat, 1956), especially p. 238, where he demands for the armies of the future the military and leadership types which the Junker schools of the Waffen SS characteristically produced. (See, for example, p. 242.)

99. Not only the rapidly changing position of the SS within the Third Reich—especially after July 20, 1944—but also the self-image of the Waffen SS man is characterized by the fact that strong opposition to the Nazi party became widespread in Waffen SS "Resistance" circles. Their slogan was "with Adolf Hitler against the NSDAP." Incidentally, probably not much more than 10 per cent of Combat SS men belonged to the party. From an interview with Erich Kernmayr, July 2, 1957.

100. Lochner (II/1), p. 356. Similarly the decision to conscript ethnic Germans into the Combat SS rather than the Army rested on the correct belief that the political indoctrination and politization of the ethnic German would be far more intense in the Combat SS than in the Army.

101. "SS, der Soldatenfreund." Taschenjahrbuch für die Wehrmacht mit Kalendarium für 1943, Ausgabe D: Waffen-SS. Zusammengestellt: Der Reichsführer-SS . . . Adolf Sponholz Verlag, Hannover, Seiten 42–43, reproduced in Poliakov and Wulf (II/39), p. 500.

102. *Ibid.*

103. "Dich ruft die SS," SS-Hauptamt, Berlin-Wilmersdorf, Hohenzollerndamm 31 (April, 1942), reproduced in *ibid.,* p. 506.

104. Reitlinger (II/36), p. 79.

105. From a letter of a volunteer in the Sixteenth Panzer Grenadier Division, Siegfried Lademacher, to General H. O. Gille, the former Commander of the Fourth SS Panzer Corps, November 23, 1951. Emphasis mine.

106. Lademacher to Gille, January 29, 1952.

107. At the annual meeting at Rendsburg in October, 1960, Willy Schäfer, the chairman of the Schleswig-Holstein HIAG, said: "We were defamed not only by [hostile] circles, but also by former National Socialists, some of whom obviously had a bad conscience and wished to divert [atten-

tion] from themselves." "Rendsburg, ein Meilenstein," *Der Freiwillige,* V, 11 (November, 1960), 7.

108. According to one HIAG member, Heinrich von Brentano's public vituperation against the newly founded organization had the result that within a two-week period the 42 local HIAG's increased to 84 with some 10,000 members and some additional 20,000 supporters who had not yet bothered to join. From a confidential letter to Colonel Wolfgang Müller, November 25, 1951.

109. Letter of the Oldenburg HIAG official, Helmut Bruhn, to Siegfried Lademacher, September 27, 1951.

110. Letter of the Hamburg HIAG official, Harald Milde, to Siegfried Lademacher, October 20, 1951.

111. *Der Ausweg* (Hamburg), no date, but probably no. 3 (August, 1951), p. 1.

112. "Die Waffen-SS antwortet," *Wiking–Ruf,* no. 2 (December, 1951), p. 1.

113. Letter to Siegfried Lademacher, October 30, 1951.

114. *Ibid.;* emphasis mine.

115. Letter of Siegfried Lademacher to General H. O. Gille, November 23, 1951.

116. *Ibid.*

117. Basso, "Die Vergangenheit, die Zukunft und wir," *Wiking–Ruf,* no. 3 (January, 1952), p. 3.

118. Letter of Siegfried Lademacher to General H. O. Gille, January 29, 1952.

119. See, for example, the open letter of the chairman of the Hamburg HIAG, E. Wangemann, to his resigning deputy, E. A. Hintze. "Brief an einen scheidenden Kameraden," *Wiking–Ruf,* III, 10 (October, 1954), 8. Cf. Dietrich Ziemssen, " 'Wir' in Vergangenheit, Gegenwart und Zukunft," *Wiking–Ruf,* III, 6 (June, 1954), 5–6.

120. Gille's speech at Verden and the speeches of Colonel Günther Drange, representative of the League of Returnees (Bund der Heimkehrer); General Traugott Herr, representative of the VdS; and General Steiner are reproduced in full in *Wiking–Ruf,* no. 13 (November, 1952), "Sonderbeilage."

121. Emphasis in the original.

122. "Keine nazistische Verschwörung," *Weser–Kurier* (Bremen), October 27, 1952. See also in the same issue the editorial by Visurgius, *pseud.,* "Ramcke macht Wirbel." Cf. "Gehöre nicht zu euch," *Der Spiegel,* VI, 45 (November 5, 1952), 8–9, and "Die finstere Truppe," *Die Gegenwart,* VII, 168 (23) (November 8, 1952), 122–123.

123. The SS veterans at Verden were not the only ones to approve Ramcke's sentiments. When a representative sample of the population was asked to record their reactions to the first part of the quotation from Ramcke's speech reproduced above, 46 per cent admitted they liked it, while 29 per cent expressed their dislike. Another 25 per cent "didn't know." The

poll took place in November, 1952, shortly after the Verden meeting. See Noelle and Neumann (II/4), p. 276.

124. "General Steiner's speech, informed by a high sense of responsibility, again smoothed the waves of excitement which General Ramcke's last excessive remarks had created." *Wiking–Ruf,* no. 13 (November, 1952), p. 15.

125. This kind of muddled thinking only breeds further confusion. Similarly, liberal and social democrats often attack the Combat SS because of its alleged crimes and not because of its admitted, deep and convinced National Socialism. How quickly inadequately thought-out and poorly based arguments can be used against their inventors was demonstrated at the annual HIAG meeting in Rendsburg (October 23, 1960), where General Kurt Meyer, the HIAG's federal chairman, scored a clean blow against his opponents: "When a hate-filled, anti-military press always points to the fact that former members of the SS [*sic*] have taken leading positions in industry, they don't even notice that they are making themselves ridiculous. Because industry, of all places, would not call into responsible positions 'eternal freebooters' or 'sadistic criminals.' " Meyer is quite right. But the proper reason for discriminating against former members of the Waffen SS is not that they have committed sadistic crimes, but that they were, and many remained, convinced Nazis.

126. Such as, for instance, Steiner (IX/98) or Hausser (IX/60), let alone the many works of Erich Kern (Kernmayr).

127. Nonetheless the HIAG's "moderation" continued to be a matter of regret and sadness to irreconcilable, incorrigible Nazis. Thus the most "loyal" of them all, Hans-Ulrich Rudel, writes: "I am speaking there [in Frankfurt] before a circle of former Combat SS men. Their organization appears to me to be a little indifferent. However many capable and valuable men . . . may have come together here, there are nonetheless . . . many forces at work which do not even notice that they have already become the tools of American propaganda, that one is being incited against the other, that one warns against the other, and that real psychoses have broken out. The elite of yesterday is today still randomly thrown together (*bunt durcheinandergewürfelt*)." Rudel (VI/204), pp. 256–257.

128. Speech at Verden, October 26, 1952 (IX/120), pp. 2–3. Emphasis mine. For evidence marshaled to show that there is no factual basis to the claim that the Combat SS had been in reality a forerunner of NATO, see Stein (VII/4).

129. Speech at Alzey, June 20, 1953, quoted in *Wiking–Ruf,* II, 21 (July, 1953), 19.

130. *Wiking–Ruf,* IV, 2 (February, 1955), 3.

131. Michael Benestad, "Vom Bergfried aus gegen den Bolschewismus!" *Wiking–Ruf,* no. 1 (November, 1951), p. 14.

132. *Der Freiwillige,* I, 9 (September, 1956), 5.

133. Report on a speech by Willy Schäfer, HIAG chairman of Schleswig-Holstein, at a meeting at Rendsburg, October 23, 1960, in *Der Frei-*

willige, V, 11 (November, 1960), 7. At a HIAG-organized meeting of Belgian, French, and Danish Combat SS veterans at München–Gladbach in June, 1962, one of the main speakers, Karl Steinsdörfer, insisted that history "will prove that the idea of a United Europe originated with the volunteers of the Combat SS." Needless to say, Steinsdörfer also saw the Berlin Wall as "the last link in a chain that started with the SS struggle against Bolshevism." *Frankfurter Allgemeine Zeitung,* June 12, 1962.

134. A Right-wing extremist with strong neutralist orientation, Erich Teich, insisted in the course of a discussion that "Gille was being employed by [Robert] Pferdmenges, who is swimming in Adenauer's wake." Report of a discussion with Teich on March 9, 1953.

135. For details on the seamy facts of the controversy, see *Der Freiwillige,* I (September, 1956), 12–13; "Waffen-SS Hiag in der Krise," *Feinde der Demokratie* (Lower Saxony), V, 2 (November–December, 1955), 31–34; *Die Brücke,* III (August 1, 1956), 5–6; *Deutscher Informationsdienst,* no. 510 (October 18, 1955).

136. Erich Kernmayr, who writes under the nom de plume Kern, is the Austrian author of a large number of books, many of them celebrating the Combat SS or the anti-Bolshevik crusade which, Kern pretends, was the mission of the Hitler Reich. In the Nazi underground prior to the Anschluss, then member of the Vienna staff of Göring's newspaper, *Essener National-Zeitung,* later press chief of Gauleiter and Reichskommissar Joseph Bürckel, and finally a Waffen SS officer, Kernmayr was interned after the war for two and a half years and prohibited from publishing for the rest of his life. Within a few months of his release, he (as Kern) published *Der grosse Rausch: Russlandfeldzug 1941–1945* (Waiblingen: Leberecht, 1950 [c. 1948]), which was translated into six or seven languages, including Finnish and Turkish (Scribner's published it under the title *Dance of Death*). In the following year (1949) Kern wrote *Das andere Lidice;* in 1950 appeared *Das harte Leben;* that was followed by *Herz im Stacheldraht* (1951), *Die Uhr blieb stehen* (1953), *Der Dorn im Fleische* (1955), *Weisser Mann, toter Mann?* (1955), *Menschen im Netz* (1958), *Stadt ohne Gnade* (1959), *Die letzte Schlacht* (1960), *Das goldene Feld* (1961), *Von Versailles zu Adolf Hitler* (1961), *Opfergang eines Volkes* (1962), *Deutschland im Abgrund* (1963). These last three represent a trilogy on recent German history. (For additional titles and publication data, see first section of the Bibliography.)

137. In the Minden city council, permission for the giant meeting was granted by a 21 to 12 vote, the FDP and CDU voting for, the SPD against the meeting. Three BHE members abstained from voting. The Mayor explained the approval for the rally as follows: "We have here the human and political duty to help with the integration (*einbauen*) into the state of this large contingent of German persons. We want to open for them the gates into the new state."

138. One side of Meyer's war-crime trial is described by the chief prosecuting officer on that occasion, Lieutenant Colonel B. J. S. Macdonald, *The Trial of Kurt Meyer* (Toronto: Clarke, Irwin, 1954). The other side is

presented in Kurt (Panzer-) Meyer's autobiographical *Grenadiere* (Munich: Schild, 1957), pp. 358ff.

139. All quotations from Panzermeyer's speech come from the complete text reproduced in "Das war die Stunde der Hiag: 10,000 Kameraden in Minden," *Der Freiwillige,* I, 9 (September, 1956), 3–8.

140. *Ibid.,* p. 7.

141. "HIAG der Waffen-SS: 'Durchbruch nach vorn,'" *Feinde der Demokratie* (Lower Saxony), VI, 7–8 (June–July, 1957), 33.

142. This is the figure constantly used by the HIAG. It is arrived at by assuming (*a*) that all former 250,000 Waffen SS men have an equal interest in the particular demands made by HIAG, (*b*) that every one of these veterans not only will exercise the ballot but also can influence or deliver three other votes, presumably members of his family, and (*c*) that the 20,000 HIAG members are representative of the other 92 per cent. As none of these assumptions is correct, it is difficult to see why the parties were so solicitous of HIAG votes.

143. *Deutscher Aufbruch* (the official newspaper of Karl Meissner's Deutscher Block), February, 1958, quoted in *Feinde der Demokratie,* VII, 3–4 (January–February, 1958), 42. Cf. H.-U. Rudel's very similar estimate, note 127, above.

144. *Reichsruf* (official newspaper of the DRP), August 30, 1958, quoted in "Waffen-SS HiaG als politischer Stosstrupp?" *Feinde der Demokratie* (Lower Saxony), VIII, 1–2 (January, 1959), 3.

145. *Nation Europa,* no. 10 (October, 1958), quoted in *Feinde der Demokratie* (Lower Saxony), VIII, 1–2 (January, 1959), 4.

146. "Richtungskämpfe in der HIAG," *Deutscher Informationsdienst,* no. 795 (February 11, 1959), pp. 1–3.

147. "Rendsburg, ein Meilenstein" (IX/107), p. 7.

148. In the following year HIAG's official moderation led to its joining the Association of German Soldiers (VdS), an event which eleven years earlier had threatened the life of the then newborn association.

149. This, at least, is the policy of one wing of the organization, which has remained split between moderates (who wish to collaborate with all parties) and ideologues. After the sudden death of the fifty-one-year-old Kurt Meyer in January, 1962, the former SS colonel and last commander of the Viking Division, Karl Ullrich (Offenbach), became First Speaker of HIAG. Karl Cerff and Werner Bitzer were elected his deputies. Cornelius van der Horst became editor of *Der Freiwillige.* In 1965 the top HIAG post went to Rudolf Enseling, a former officer of the SS Division Das Reich. It is a significant testimony to the effectiveness of Meyer's tactics that his death produced expressions of sympathy from Chancellor Adenauer; Defense Minister Strauss; Minister Heinrich Krone; Minister-President K.–U. von Hassel (later Defense Minister); and Bundestag Deputies Erler (SPD), Eisenmann (FDP), Mende (FDP), Erwin Lange (SPD), Rasner (CDU), and the North Rhine-Westphalian FDP leader Willi Weyer. Wewer (IX/92), p. 448.

Chapter X: Postwar Youth at the Crossroads

1. In the course of a confidential discussion in February, 1953, Kurt Vowinckel, the radical-nationalist publisher, maintained that the National Opposition could not wait twenty years for a new Hitler. "Work has to be done now, but it has to be done according to plan, on the one hand through books, newspapers, etc., and on the other hand through the education and organization of German youth. That's the most important problem. With the oldsters no support can be won. At most their experience could still be used. But for the rest, it's the youth that's got to come forward." Discussion memorandum of February 12, 1953.

2. See "70,000 junge Rechtsradikale," *Für die Demokratie,* I (IX), 1 (December, 1959–January, 1960), 25–26. Cf. *Bulletin on German Questions* (London), XII, 280 (March 1, 1961), 14.

3. See Peter F. Ludemann, "Hitler schützt for Torheit nicht," *Civis,* VI, 53 (May 15, 1959), 269–273.

4. See Konrad Friesicke, "Falschspiel mit der Jugend," *deutsche jugend,* VIII, 2 (February, 1960), 85–87.

5. See *Bulletin on German Questions* (London), XII, 280 (March 1, 1961), 14.

6. "70,000 junge Rechtsradikale" (X/2), p. 26.

7. "Zur Situation der nationalen Jugendverbände," *Die Brücke,* IV, 19 (October, 1957), 1.

8. "Zur Situation der nationalen Jugendverbände," Gesellschaft zum Studium von Zeitfragen, *Analysen und Berichte,* VI, 11 (September 11, 1959), 2.

9. The Deutscher Pfadfinderbund (German Scout League) under Michael Walther Jansen (Bonn) should not be confused with its chief competitor, the Bund deutscher Pfadfinder (League of German Scouts). The latter is properly not included in any listing of nationalist youth organizations. Unlike the German Scout League, the League of German Scouts is not eager to emphasize historic ties to the radically nationalist traditions of German scoutism. The latter, a member of the Ring of German Scout Leagues (Ring der Deutschen Pfadfinderbünde), has been accorded recognition by the international bureau of scoutism in London. See *Die Brücke,* IV, 19 (October, 1957), 9.

10. "Nationalismus-Antinationalismus," *Der Pfeil,* VII, 8 (1956), 1–2.

11. Cf. also *Graue Blätter,* I, 3 (September–October, 1956), 1–2. Apologists for the folkish orientation of especially those expellees who came from areas outside the old Reich (*Volksdeutsche,* so-called) or from the ethnic frontier regions have correctly pointed out that the folkish vocabulary of these groups existed long before the Nazis and that it was, therefore, unjust to suspect them of especially lively Nazi sympathies merely because they continued to use that vocabulary. These apologists overlook the fact that a radical folk orientation was no whit more acceptable to democratic Reich Germans for being of pre-Nazi origin than if it had been a pure Nazi invention. That the intense preoccupation with folkish notions of the *Volks-*

deutsche can be readily derived from their history and the ethnic conditions under which they had for centuries lived in no way helps to make folkish conceptions politically more acceptable. To understand may be to forgive but certainly need not be to agree. For typical apologetics see Eugen Lemberg, "Der Wandel des politischen Denkens," in Lemberg and Edding (IV/7), III, 445.

12. *Die Brücke,* IV, 19 (October, 1957), 9.

13. See Appendix B.

14. The reaction inside Germany to the revelations of unbelievably inept American preparations for guerrilla warfare, with the active participation of SRP members, SS officers, and similar anti-Communist "experts," and of their connection with the BDJ, the government-supported nationalist propaganda group, camouflaged as a youth organization, as well as the reaction to the government's own evident discomfort and uneasy conscience, were as vehement as they were hostile. For weeks and months, magazines, information services, and newspapers carried commentaries, summaries, background stories, and additional sensational exposés. From the enormous amount of available secondary materials the following are the most useful: Vorstand der SPD, *Partisan gegen Bezahlung,* n.d.; *Erkenntnis und Tat,* VII, 5/6 (1956), 23–24; Hessischer Landtag, II. Wahlperiode, *Stenographischer Bericht über die 32. Sitzung* (October 8, 1952), pp. 1294–1296; *42. Sitzung,* (March 18, 1953), pp. 1709–1726; Federal Republic of Germany, Bundestag, *Stenographischer Bericht,* 235. *Sitzung* (October 23, 1952), pp. 10799–10834; Schleswig-Holsteinischer Landtag, 2. Wahlperiode, *Stenographischer Bericht über die 23. Tagung, 52. Sitzung* (October 29, 1952), pp. 153–216; *Feinde der Demokratie* (Nordmark), no. 2 (November 15, 1952), pp. 1–23. The report of the subcommittee of the Bundestag Committee for the Protection of the Constitution is reproduced in *Neuer Vorwärts* (Hanover), no. 31 (July 31, 1953), p. 1. The more than surprising decision of the Third Criminal Senate of the Federal Court to discontinue the case against the five BDJ leaders (a decision which the Attorney-General had requested!) can be found in Paul Lüth's *Vertrauliche Briefe der Gesellschaft zum Studium von Zeitfragen,* V, 20 (July 16, 1957). (Paul Lüth had been chairman of the BDJ and was thought to have been deeply involved in the so-called Technical Service, the guerrilla training outfit.) See also Lüth's "Für jedes Wort stehe ich gerade," *Die Zeit* (Hamburg), no. 52 (December 25, 1952), p. 2. A good summary can be found in "Bürger und Partisanen: Die Enthüllungen über den 'Technischen Dienst des BDJ,' " *Die Gegenwart,* November 8, 1952, pp. 727–731. See above, text near VI/46.

15. See "Zweimal Jugendring," *Die Andere Zeitung* (Hamburg), no. 29 (November 24, 1955), p. 3.

16. Of course, one must also keep in mind that the Federal Government provides considerable funds through the Federal Youth Plan and the Federal Youth Ring for political education in non-political youth organizations. How effective that is, and how many youngsters are regularly exposed to these educational efforts, is difficult to estimate.

17. See Helmut Schelsky, ed., *Arbeitslosigkeit und Berufsnot der Jugend*

(Cologne: 1952), referred to in his *Die skeptische Generation, eine Soziologie der deutschen Jugend* (Düsseldorf: Diederichs, 1957), p. 439.

18. DIVO, *Basic Orientation and Political Thinking of West German Youth and their Leaders, 1956, Report on a Nationwide Survey* (mimeographed), 1956, p. 36.

19. Three things should be noted here. In the first place, the two questions concerning the single national party and the national leader only appear to be parallel, but in fact are not. The clause "as before" in the latter introduces a new and entirely unweighed factor into the situation. Secondly, if one were to assume that those who approved a single national party would also be more inclined than the others to approve a strong-arm national leader (an assumption for which the DIVO study presents no independent evidence), some explanation is needed to account for the 50 per cent loss in "totalitarian orientation" between the first and the second question. Finally, it is well to note that both questions introduce a perfectly gratuitous element by including in the posed question reference to "the interests of all classes of our people" and to "the welfare of all." As we do not know the status of these conceptions within the attitudinal structure of the individual respondents, we are dealing here with an additional unknown which may well have influenced the results decisively.

20. Incidentally, in view of the eight-percentage-point difference in "authoritarianism," it is difficult to see what DIVO meant when it said that "the results [to the last question] are similar to those observed to the query on strong-arm leadership."

21. An obvious factor, the Chancellor's prestige, was, however, statistically found to have not been really decisive in this context. DIVO (X/18), p. 41, especially Table 36.

22. *Ibid.*, pp. 48–49.

23. Schelsky, *Die skeptische Generation* (X/17), pp. 439–440.

24. It is in this connection not crucial, but nonetheless interesting, that further interviews with representative panels of those who had been asked about their views of Hitler demonstrated the weakness of formal opinion polling, especially in areas so fraught with emotional inhibitions and counter pressures as is the question of Nazism in present-day Germany. Whereas, for instance, only 19 per cent of the female respondents admitted in the course of the formal poll that they still liked Hitler, answers in the course of lengthy and freely conducted interviews indicated that actually about 25 per cent of young girls secretly nursed an admiration for the "lonely man on the Obersalzberg." Even more startling is the shift in the percentage of girls who spontaneously had answered the formal poll question rejecting Hitler. Initially there were 43 per cent of them. This seemingly large number of "Hitler detractors" melted away in the course of further interviewing to a mere 21 per cent, while the percentage of those who gave ambiguous answers rose steeply from 8 per cent to 23 per cent. These results are not surprising when the social pressures against public declarations of Nazi support are taken into account, but they demonstrate nicely the questionable reliability of the much-used, straightforward "opinion poll."

25. Schelsky, *Die skeptische Generation* (X/17), pp. 443–444.

26. The polls, for instance, tell us that no more than a quarter of all those who pretended to see in Hitlerism more good than bad were willing to agree to the cardinal principle of authoritarianism, namely, the importance of a strong, national leader, or that almost 70 per cent of those who favored a strong-arm national leader felt that final decisions should lie with the Bundestag. Again the EMNID investigations from the years 1953–1955 furnish further and equally startling "results." In 1953, youngsters between the ages of fifteen and twenty-four were asked, "How do you feel about the following proposition, or rather, do you agree with it or not: Instead of everyone interesting himself in the politics of his country and feeling himself coresponsible for it, it would be better to leave that to the man who has the political power in his hands." Of all respondents, 37 per cent agreed (by 1955 that figure had gone up to 41 per cent). Yet, when the results of a direct question concerning the respondents' attitude toward the Bonn Republic was correlated with the results from the "clearly authoritarian" question, it turned out that of the supporters of the postwar, liberal-democratic, anti-Nazi, Allied-supported, bourgeois-capitalist regime, 36 per cent agreed with the "authoritarian" question, whereas those who indicated clear hostility to the postwar developments were hardly more "authoritarian" (38 per cent). See *ibid.*, pp. 447, 448.

27. This is also the conclusion reached by H. Kluth in his chapter "Das Verhältnis der arbeitslosen Jugendlichen zum Staat und zur Politik," in Schelsky, *Arbeitslosigkeit* (X/17), and, following him, by Schelsky, *Die skeptische Generation* (X/17), pp. 445–446.

28. The EMNID study of 1955 indicated that 62 per cent of the youthful respondents were politically uninterested (in 1954, 57 per cent fell into that category) and that only 39 per cent would decisively defend the Bonn Republic in an argument, while 19 per cent opposed it (in varying degrees of intensity) and 42 per cent had either a noncommittally neutral or, at best, a "lukewarm" orientation toward the German Federal Republic. (Rolf Fröhner *et al., Wie stark sind die Halbstarken? Beruf und Berufsnot, politische, kulturelle und seelische Probleme der deutschen Jugend im Bundesgebiet und Westberlin* [Bielefeld: Maria von Stackelberg, 1956], pp. 113–117, 121–122, 294–300, 314–315.) In the same poll, 54 per cent of the youngsters in 1955 (but only 47 per cent in 1953) thought that young people should not criticize, but follow orders (*ibid.*, pp. 117–118, 301–302). Analogously, the percentage of those who thought that political power must be shared by all and not left exclusively in the hands of leaders had also slightly decreased between 1953 and 1955. Still, in 1955, 55 per cent felt themselves coresponsible for political decisions (*ibid.*, pp. 118, 303–304). As to Hitlerism, that had by 1955 become to the children a matter of the dim historical past, of no direct relevance to them: 43 per cent of the youngsters had no opinion on Nazism or Hitler (*ibid.*, pp. 119–121, 305–310). Cf. F. Mouricou, "La Jeunesse allemande de l'ouest," *Allemagne d'Aujourd'hui,* July–October, 1957, pp. 180–194.

29. DIVO (X/18), p. 51.

30. In July, 1952, a public-opinion survey attempted to sound out popular attitudes toward Hitler with a series of four statements among which the respondents had to select the one that expressed most nearly their own feelings in the matter: "While Hitler accomplished a number of good things, his fatal deeds and characteristics outweighted them by far"—40 per cent; "Hitler was an unconscionable politician who is responsible for much horror"—28 per cent; "While Hitler made some mistakes, he was at any rate a first-class chief of state (*Staatsführer*)"—22 per cent; "Hitler was one of the greatest statesmen of this century; his real greatness will be recognized only in the future"—10 per cent. Noelle and Neumann (II/4), p. 136. Four years earlier, in October, 1948, a very small sample of respondents was asked whether there was anything they disliked about National Socialism, and 99 per cent answered "Yes." *Ibid.*, p. 134.

31. Cf. Schelsky, *Die skeptische Generation* (X/17), pp. 458–459.

32. Cf.—with the explanatory scheme offered here—the suggestions made by H. Schreiber and K. H. Wocker in *Stuttgarter Zeitung*, March 10 and 11, 1960. The authors in this article series distinguish between organized, contaminated, and "disposed" youths.

33. J. Habermas, L. von Friedeburg, C. Oehler, and F. Weltz, *Student und Politik* (Neuwied: Luchterhand, 1961).

34. *Ibid.*, pp. 147–149.

35. Among students, the intellectual elite and Germany's future leaders, Habermas and his research colleagues found 30 per cent "genuine democrats," 39 per cent "formal democrats," and 9 per cent "indifferents," in addition to the 22 per cent "authoritarians" mentioned above. But of the "genuine democrats" only 57 per cent can be counted among the politically engaged citizens, ready to take the initiative in the defense of the democratic order. Another 31 per cent can be considered no more than "fellow travelers" who will follow the lead of others under favorable circumstances. Another 12 per cent are either unpoltical or "irrationally distant" from all political affairs. (*Ibid.*, p. 148). But even the 38 per cent "engaged citizens" (of whom not quite half can be considered genuine democrats) include really two categories, namely, the truly "engaged," "involved," or "committed" activists (which type of "disposition" Habermas found in only 9 per cent of the entire sample), and the "thoughtful citizen" type which accounts for 29 per cent of all respondents. *Ibid.*, p. 74.

36. Schelsky, *Die skeptische Generation* (X/17), p. 540.

37. For a large number of typical responses of German boys and girls regarding their own view of the state and the fatherland, see Wilhelm Roessler, *Jugend im Erziehungsfeld* (Düsseldorf: Schwann, 1957), pp. 372–383. The following appears to be a typical "opinion": "The state itself is an abstraction. One could say it is an administrative framework which encompasses the body politic (*Volkskörper*) in order to maintain a meaningful order. This order, the state, imposes on the citizen duties and [acknowledges] rights. Thus, since the citizen has duties, the state has also tasks." *Ibid.*, p. 379. Cf. also the brilliant introductory section in Habermas *et al.* (X/33),

pp. 13–56. See also Toni Thurnreiter, "Jugendfremde Politik," *Hessische Jugend,* no. 6/7 (1958), pp. 2–3.

38. Schelsky, *Die skeptische Generation* (X/17), p. 454. Cf. F. Zimmermann, "Jugend und Politik," *Freiheit und Verantwortung,* no. 79 (1956).

39. A small sample of 370 noncollege youths in southwest Germany yielded in December, 1947, the following answers as to their political interests: 2 per cent admitted to an intense interest in politics; 25 per cent, to at least some interest. To 43 per cent politics was of little concern; to another 23 per cent, of no interest whatever; and to 6 per cent politics was downright disagreeable. Noelle and Neumann (II/4), p. 127.

40. Walter Jaide, *Eine neue Generation. Eine Untersuchung über Werthaltungen und Leitbilder der Jugendlichen* (2d ed.; Munich: Juventa, 1963 [c. 1961]).

41. *Ibid.,* pp. 23–45.

42. *Ibid.,* p. 104.

43. *Ibid.,* p. 111.

44. The unique quality of the rebellion of youth has fascinated scholars and publicists for decades. As a consequence, the literature on this movement is immense, comprising at a recent count 3,583 books, booklets, dissertations, and the like. I have found useful, in addition to the sources cited in the text, Hans Blüher's classic, if eccentric and often scurrilous, two-volume *Wandervogel. Geschichte einer Jugendbewegung* (4th ed.; Berlin: Weise, 1919) and his sensational *Die deutsche Wandervogelbewegung als erotisches Phänomen* (Berlin: Weise, 1912). Also his brief *Karl Fischers Tat und Untergang: Zur Geschichte der deutschen Jugendbewegung* (Bad Godesberg: Voggenreiter, 1952) is worth perusing. Very useful, too, are Günther Ehrenthal, *Die deutschen Jugendbünde* (Berlin: Zentralverlag, 1929); Fritz Borinski and Werner Milch, *Jugendbewegung: The Story of German Youth, 1896–1933,* German Educational Reconstruction, no. 3–4 ([London: German Educational Reconstruction, (pref. 1945)]); Karl O. Paetel, *Das Bild vom Menschen in der deutschen Jugendführung* (Bad Godesberg: Voggenreiter, 1954); and the unpublished doctoral dissertations by Pross, (VII/14); Ernst M. Jovy, *Deutsche Jugend und Nationalsozialismus: Versuch einer Klärung ihrer Zusammenhänge und Gegensätze* (Cologne, 1953); and Mario Domandi, *The German Youth Movement* (Columbia University, 1960). For brief summaries it may be convenient to consult Franz Strebin, "Autorität und Freiheit," *Aus Politik und Zeitgeschichte* (Supplement of *Das Parlament*), January 13, 1960; Hermann Mau, "Die deutsche Jugendbewegung," *Zeitschrift für Religion und Geistesgeschichte,* I (1948), 135–149; and Pross (II/7), pp. 104–128. In 1964 Harry Pross published his studies of the Youth Movement in *Jugend-Eros-Politik. Die Geschichte der deutschen Jugendverbände* (Bern, Munich, Vienna: Scherz, 1964).

45. Ludwig Gurlitt, as quoted in Else Frobenius, *Mit uns zieht die neue Zeit: Eine Geschichte der Deutschen Jugendbewegung* (Berlin: 1927), p. 27 and requoted in Roessler (X/37), pp. 183–184.

46. The Youth Movement also had a Left wing at one time or another.

We are not concerned with it here. For a sympathetic account of that aspect, see Laqueur (I/1), pp. 94–104, 111–120, 123–127. Cf. also Karl O. Paetel, *Jugendbewegung und Politik* (Bad Godesberg: Voggenreiter, 1961), pp. 34–38. This book appeared in 1963 under the new title of *Jugend in der Entscheidung 1913, 1933, 1945,* in a second, greatly enlarged edition which includes the political development of the Youth Movement after 1945. Unfortunately the new edition came to my attention only long after the present chapter had been concluded.

47. In this brew of romantic pathos, sentimentality, and submergence of the self in the "organic" group, a murky conception of the leader-follower relationship was an essential ingredient. The high priest of *jugendbewegt* youth, the poet Stefan George, had put the romantic vision of leadership into words which characterize the entire movement better than could pages of exposition: "Be he your leader who demands much and with rigor, who yet possesses—though outwardly with clear, calm eyes—within himself the true fire without artificiality, who makes you tremble with his burgeoning life, who liberates you from the fear of the gloom, who by his love elevates you to be a man (*Mensch*), whose diction and bearing have something free, candid, and noble." Quoted in *Wandervogel, Monatsschrift für deutsches Jugendwandern,* Part I (1919), p. 244, and re-quoted in Roessler (X/37), p. 291. We could go on quoting indefinitely. Two more examples will give the Anglo-Saxon reader an inkling of a mental orientation which is so alien—indeed, so repulsive—to him. It is here that we get a glimpse of one aspect of the pathology of German political life in the first half of the twentieth century: "Out of the fraternal groups (*Bünde*) must arise a towering leader and king, otherwise the Wandervogel has lost its *raison d'être.* But such a king will not be found in every province (*Gau*). In those provinces supreme power must not lie in the hands of the masses but only in those of the provincial nobility (*Gauadel*). Then we will have an aristocracy (rule of the nobles). There is no one, we hope, who will maintain that there is a province without such higher, superior, noble men; and if there is one, that province would merit annihilation. The aristocrats [noble men] recognize each other and join together; they are not elected by the people. Aristocracy requires of us loyalty, courage, and chivalry, and forms us into a true youth movement." *Wandervogel,* 1920, p. 66, quoted *ibid.,* p. 192. The longing for the leader is given even clearer expression in the following: "The call for the leader sounds shrilly (*gellen*) through the ranks. I am certain our rebellion will find leaders and that they will find us. Woe unto them that have deceived us. The flame of longing for the Führer is burning. When the Führer comes with his proud race (*Geschlecht*), light and fulfillment will take possession (*einziehen*) of the Wandervogel." *Wandervogel,* 1920, p. 158, quoted *ibid.* At the same time it should be pointed out that the Youth Movement between roughly 1897 and 1923, in the form of Wandervogel and Freideutschtum, developed also a wing which showed republican tendencies and rejected nationalist-chauvinist excesses. Gustav Wyneken, in particular, sharply took issue with the irrationalism of the "folkish" wing of the movement. Besides the Wyneken group, the Academic Freischar and parts of the Young Wander-

vogel—that is, some of the most important elements of Freideutschtum—manifested similarly antifolkish, antichauvinist tendencies. For a warmly appreciative appraisal of Wyneken, see Laqueur (I/1), *passim.*

48. Prior to 1914 the Youth Movement had been largely oriented toward self-improvement. After 1923, the *bündisch* movement was primarily an attempt to reform society. In a very confused way, it became a political protest and "a romantic attempt to cope with realities." The *Lebendsbund* now became characteristic of the new forms of relationship which the *Bünde* sought to realize. The emphasis, in contradistinction to the old Wandervogel, was now on greater group integration, cohesion and formality, rigor and soldierliness. The colorful and highly individualistic hiking fashions of the Wandervogel now gave way to a uniform, the former so-called "nest evenings" were now called "service," the loose roving aggregations of the Wandervogel now became more highly organized, hierarchically structured, centrally administered groups. See H. Dähnhardt and Giselher Wirsing, "Die bündische Jugend," in Hertha Siemering, ed., *Die deutschen Jugendverbände* (Berlin: Heymann, 1931), pp. 61–63. See also Paetel (X/46), p. 90, and Laqueur (I/1), pp. 129, 134. Without a doubt the best and most richly documented account of the specifically *bündisch* parts of the Youth Movement is Felix Raabe's *Die bündische Jugend: Ein Beitrag zur Geschichte der Weimarer Republik* (Stuttgart: Brentano, 1961). In this connection it would be well to recall, however, that the *bündisch* form was not the only manifestation of the Youth Movement after 1923. Around 1929 a reaction to *bündisch* forms took place which is usually referred to as the "autonomous" Youth Movement, or *Jungenschaft* movement. It was partly an attempt to recapture the style and forms of the prewar Youth Movement in its more nonfolkish aspects, partly a somewhat eccentric radicalization of *bündisch* values and forms. Unlike the nationalist *Bünde,* the "autonomous" organizations were able to recruit some of their members even from the working class. These groups tended to be strongly anti-Nazi. See Arno Klönne, *Hitlerjugend* (Hanover: Norddeutsche Verlagsanstalt O. Goedel, 1956), pp. 48–49 and Laqueur (I/1), Chapter XVII. In Walter Flex's celebrated *Der Wanderer zwischen beiden Welten* (Munich: Beck, [1938?]), the universe of sentiment and ideology which had characterized the original Youth Movement was given its definitive shape. For an excellent and sympathetic treatment of the *political* ideology growing out of the conceptual world of *bündisch* youth, see Hornung (IV/111), *passim.* Note also Hornung's very useful bibliography.

49. See Roessler (X/37), p. 230.

50. *Ibid.* The Youth Movement, or more properly, the *bündisch* movement of the nineteen twenties, consisted really of three strands which differed with regard to their genealogical roots. One strand derived from the folkish, anti-Semitic, nationalist Wandervogel and consisted of such groups as Jungdeutscher Bund (Young German League), Wandervogel-Völkischer Bund (Wandervogel-Folkish League), Deutsch-Akademische Gildenschaft (German Academic Guild Association), Adler und Falken (Eagles and Falcons), Geusen, etc. The other strand of *bündisch* youth resulted from the marriage

of scoutism and the Youth Movement. The most important of the Scoutist-*bündisch* organizations was the Bund deutscher Neupfadfinder (League of German Neo-Scouts), which joined in 1925 the League of German Ring Scouts (Bund der deutschen Ringpfadfinder) and became in the following year the Greater German Scout League (Grossdeutscher Pfadfinder-Bund). The latter merged in April, 1926, with the Altwandervogel and the Wandervogel into a League of Wandervögel and Scouts, which in turn merged late in 1926 with the Köngener and other *Bünde* to form the Deutsche Freischar, the most important and least nationalist *Bund* down to 1933. The Deutsche Freischar was the only one of these *Bünde* which included elements of the former Left Youth Movement, some of whose members belonged to the Social Democratic Party and the German Democratic Party, two of the three pillars of the Weimar Republic. Alongside the League of German Neo-Scouts, and later the Deutsche Freischar, there were the Deutscher Pfadfinderbund (German Scout League), Bund deutscher Reichspfadfinder (League of German Reich Scouts), Jungnationaler Bund (Young National League), and Grossdeutscher Jugendbund (Greater German Youth League). The last two merged in 1930 (including for a few months the Deutsche Freischar) to form the Freischar junger Nation, under Vice-Admiral Adolf L. von Trotha, the leader of the Greater German Youth League. The third strand, numerically the weakest, consisted of the so-called national–revolutionary *Bünde*. Among them the most important were Hans Ebeling's Jungnationaler Bund–Deutsche Jungenschaft, the Hoven brothers' Freischar Schill, Wikinger Jugendkorps, Jungpreussischer Bund, and Pfadfinderschaft Westmark. These youth groups were, of course, in close touch with the national–revolutionary adult groups of the Conservative Revolution and, along with the latter, found themselves at times going part of the way with the Communist Party. This was the only part of the nationalist *bündisch* youth which organized an underground resistance movement against Hitler after 1933. At that time, the national–revolutionary groups began to collaborate closely with the "autonomous" youth leagues. See Arno Klönne, *Gegen den Strom: Bericht über den Jugendwiderstand im Dritten Reich* (2d ed.; Hanover, Frankfurt: Norddeutsche Verlagsanstalt O. Goedel, 1960), pp. 49–51, 93–95, and Paetel (X/46), pp. 40–68, 90, 146 ff. See also Hans Ebeling, "Unvergessen: Theo Hespers. Katholische und freie Jugendbewegung im Widerstand gegen das NS-System," *Graue Blätter,* I, 1 (May, 1956), 12–14. Of course, in the non-*bündisch* parts of the Youth Movement, especially among "autonomous," confessional, and political youth groups, "there was resistance against the Hitler regime . . . from the very first! And along a considerable front, at that." Klönne, *Gegen den Strom,* p. 25. In the light of existing evidence which Klönne marshals expertly, it is difficult to understand Laqueur's condescending comment that the anti-Nazi resistance record of the national-Bolshevist *Bünde* "is certainly no worse, on the whole, than that of the neutral *Bünde*" ([I/1], p. 187). This comment is, however, in line with Laqueur's peculiar fondness for the Deutsche Freischar and his reluctance to see in the *bündisch* movement the fatal trail blazer for Nazism among middle-class youth. An even less persuasive attempt at demonstrating the inadmissibility of counting the *bündisch* youth among the gravediggers of the Republic and pathbreakers for Hitler is made by Raabe (X/48). In the name of subtler distinctions than have often been made, Raabe elaborately seeks to prove the basically democratic, anti-Nazi orientation of the *Bünde*. While even he cannot deny the almost universal condemnation of the Weimar Republic among *bündisch* youth and its intense antiparliamentary, antipolitical affects, Raabe clings nevertheless to his very positive assessment of a fatal movement. This he can only do by including in the term *bündisch* religious youth groups (such as Quickborn, Kreuzfahrer, Neudeutscher Bund, Christdeutscher Bund, Bund deutscher Jugendvereine, Neuwerkbewegung), which were not narrowly *bündisch,* and by selecting almost all of his examples of democratic, tolerant, antinationalist, and antimilitarist attitudes from them. In addition, Raabe vastly exaggerates the impact and importance of those parts of the *bündische* Youth Movement (in the narrower sense) which were moderate, willing to support a parliamentary party-democracy, tolerant toward Jews, and antinationalist. To deny that there were such groups would be to fly in the face of plain facts. To argue that they were somehow significant, let alone representative of the *bündisch* youth, would be equally mistaken. In this perspective even an anti-Republican authoritarian like Mahraun could be viewed as essentially democratic because he fled into a temporary, uneasy alliance with genuine democrats. A similar ambivalence mars the most sophisticated account of the Youth Movement in the English language. Laqueur (I/1) effectively presents the overwhelming evidence of the Rightist *Bünde*'s contempt for liberalism, democracy, parliamentarism, and the politics of compromise, their chiliastic romanticism, anti-Semitism, intolerance, pan-Germanism, and radical nationalism. He admits the close contact between some *Bund* leaders and leaders of the Hitler Youth and the widespread sympathy among the *Bünde* for the principles of National Socialism. He mentions the deceptive use by the Hitler Youth of many of the trappings and much of the rhetoric of the *Bünde.* Despite all this, Laqueur concludes that the "sins [of the Youth Movement] were those of omission rather than commission" ([I/1], p. 197) and weakly suggests that "it did less than it could have done to develop an ethos of individual political responsibility" (*ibid.*). This is a massive understatement in view of the *Bünde*'s radical political irresponsibility, their contempt for political individualism, their characteristic exultation of group identity, comradeship, and charismatic leadership. Again, Laqueur admits that "what [the *Bünde*] resented was not so much the principles or the aims of the new [Nazi] government, but simply that their own *Bünde* were doomed to disappear. . . . Had the new marching columns been less vulgarly ostentatious and better drilled; above all, had they taken the *Bünde* into their ranks, and acknowledged their merits and their prior claim to be builders of the German future, perhaps no such resentment would have been expressed" (p. 203). Yet, despite all these admissions, Laqueur clings to the comfortable delusions that "in the last analysis the fatal weakness was moral relativism and indifference" (p. 206) and that because of the *Bünde*'s elitist fastidiousness and contempt for politics it is "incorrect to classify the Youth Movement . . .

among the 'precursors of National Socialism' " (p. 234). It is equally difficult to follow Laqueur when he opines that the Youth Movement "showed signs of great promise, perhaps of universal significance" (p. 236). Had it really been of universal significance, it could have led only to universal catastrophe. Similar difficulties mar the pamphlet by Borinski and Milch (X/44).

51. Klönne sees the *bündisch* youth as pathbreakers for National Socialism among the bourgeoisie. With its folkish ideology, its conception of *Bund und Reich,* "Leader and followers," "folkish elite," sword dances, and banners bearing old Germanic runes, with its mobilization of the Germans living in other lands (*Volkstumsarbeit*) by awakening or strengthening their nationalist (or ethnic) consciousness, and with its labor service, *bündisch* youth effectively played into Hitler's hands. The latter, of course, promptly misused the idealism of the *Bündische,* no less than their willingness to collaborate. See Arno Klönne, "Wir sind wieder völkisch," *Freie Presse* (Bielefeld), July 4, 1955.

52. Raabe (X/48), pp. 130–132, even denies that the Youth Movement, or rather its *bündisch* elements, was a part of the Conservative Revolution. Indeed, he rejects the term "Conservative Revolution" as misleading. For a similar attempt to exonerate the Youth Movement of any blame for the demise of Weimar and the advent of Hitler, see Jovy (X/44). This attempt, much like Raabe's, involves a remarkable blindness toward the ravages caused by political conservatism in the Weimar Republic. The last-minute rescue attempts of authoritarian dreamers like Mahraun, of nationalists like the reactionary Max Habermann, Count Kuno von Westarp, Otto Hoetzsch, and the others of the Conservative People's Party (Konservative Volks-Partei, KVP), are seen as acts of political heroism without considering the contributions of these men to the destruction of a liberal-democratic republic.

53. Klönne puts it this way: *Bündisch* youth provided Nazism with break-through areas even where it viewed the Nazi Party with considerable skepticism. It performed the service of a "fifth column" by virtue of its *bündisch* structure and ideology, of the identification of *bündisch* youth with folkish tendencies, of its conceptions of "leading and following" and the "Third Reich," of its substantial antirationalism and political naturalism (racial materialism), of its rejection of Weimar and its propagation of chauvinistic pan-Germanism. Drunk with nationalist pathos, possessed by nationalist fervor and militarism and by a romantic leadership mythology, the *bündisch* youth, at first an unwitting accomplice of Hitler's, later became a ready passenger on the Nazi band wagon once it began to roll. "A large part of the methods and teaching aids (*Gestaltungsmittel*) of Nazi youth work, of the group formations and organizational structure of the Hitler Youth had its origin in the *bündisch* [experience]" (Klönne [X/48], p. 52). Similarly, most of the large-scale programs of the Hitler Youth (for example, "Rural Service," "Folkdom Support" [*Volkstumsarbeit*], "Eastern Mission" [*Osteinsatz*], and "Labor Service" [*Arbeitsdienst*]) were brazen plagiarisms. Cf. Paetel (X/46), pp. 123 ff, and Laqueur (I/1), pp. 109–110.

54. This was particularly evident in the Jungvolk, that is, that part of

the Hitler Youth organization (in the wider sense) which accommodated boys in the ages from ten through thirteen. See Klönne (X/48), pp. 71–73, 91, and Klönne (X/50), pp. 23–24, 47–50.

55. In this respect the work of Roessler (X/37), especially pp. 231–243, is refreshing. He is unwilling to distort the historical picture for the sake of political pieties which in areas outside of scholarship may well be of primary importance. Similarly Klönne ([X/48], pp. 52–55), one of the foremost German students of the Youth Movement, refused to be misled into the ex post facto invention of anti-Hitler "resistance" and "opposition" by the great majority of the *bündisch* youth. Naturally the situation among the "autonomous" groups and political or "confessional" youth organizations was totally different. Here opposition from a standpoint of consistent anti-Nazism was possible (*ibid.*, pp. 87–97). Cf. Klönne (X/50), Chs. III, IV, V. The modified anti-Hitler resistance among certain Right- and Left-wing youths has recently also been the subject of Olaf Kén, *Der halbe Partisan* (Kreuzweingarten/Rhld.: Zeitbiographischer Verlag, 1964).

56. Quoted in Roessler (X/37), p. 232. Arnold Littmann, former member of the Altwandervogel and Deutsche Freischar and chronicler of the history and nature of the *bündisch* youth, gushed unashamedly: "Jubilant over the good fortune of the national unification which Adolf Hitler has brought about . . . we are still incapable of comprehending the historic importance (*Tragweite*) of this secular event. The year 1933 brought after all not only the fulfillment of the dreams of the National Socialist comrades. . . . The thundering symphony of the German revolution (*Erhebung*) has still another overture to which had rallied the entire youth, from 1900 to 1933. . . . The Führer walks among them, the grand blaze of the National Revolution is being lighted, and on January 30, 1933, the entire young generation lines up in closed ranks for the torchlight parade which comes to a close with the song of the dead Sturmführer Horst Wessel, youth's introductory movement to the symphony of the entire people, now opening with thundering chords." "Die bündische Jugend von 1925–1933," in Vesper (I/10), p. 187.

57. In this connection it is not uninstructive to note that Admiral von Trotha's enthusiasm for "this *Führertum*" even survived the serious controversy with Baldur von Schirach, the supreme Hitler Youth leader, whose insatiable appetite for monopolistic control over *all* youth von Trotha at first resisted. The Greater German Youth League, a last-minute union of youth organizations with pan-German tendencies which von Trotha headed, was banned, and its members were incorporated into the Hitler Youth, before the year of the "seizure of power" had run its course. On this incident see von Schirach's testimony at Nuremberg, May 23, 1946 (afternoon session). International Military Tribunal, *Trial of the Major War Criminals* (Nuremberg: 1948), XIV, 374. In von Trotha's honor, however, be it recorded that he did not join the Nazi Party; he merely gratefully accepted the honorary Presidency of the Navy's Hitler Youth. As to the reasons why *bündisch* youth was, on the whole, so readily and smoothly integrated into the Hitler movement, even former Youth Movement enthusiasts who proved their

opposition to Nazism by self-exile or in dangerous underground missions are still reluctant to admit the frequently close ideological family resemblance between the two movements. Thus Hans Ebeling argues that the Youth Movement was tripped up by its traditional "total neutrality towards all parties," including the Nazis (*The German Youth Movement: Its Past and Future* [London: New Europe, 1945]) and Paetel insists that its naïveté and opportunism were to blame ([X/46], pp. 116, 120–140).

58. Before the *Feldherrnhalle* in Munich three thousand nationalist revolutionaries, led by Adolf Hitler and General Erich Ludendorff, were scattered by the first hail of bullets from some hundred policemen. The date was November 9, 1923.

59. Baldur von Schirach, *Revolution der Erziehung* (1939), pp. 27–31, quoted in Roessler (X/37), p. 235. Cf. also von Schirach's appreciation of Houston Stewart Chamberlain, one of the most important inspirers of the revolt against reason, reproduced *ibid.*, p. 494.

60. Von Schirach was the leader of that faction of Nazis who had most vehemently condemned the Youth Movement as "antifolkish," antinational-socialist and opposed to the construction of the Third Reich and who had most loudly called for the total extirpation of the *Bünde* as dangerous, potentially anarchic and subversive social forms. The other school of thought among Nazi Youth Leaders saw in the Hitler movement and the Third Reich the fulfillment of Youth Movement ideas.

61. International Military Tribunal (X/57), p. 365.

62. *Ibid.*, p. 462. Incidentally, von Schirach's self-contradiction when he said the Wandervogel songs "did not have anything to do with our time" remained apparently unnoticed by both defense and prosecution.

63. Hans Blüher, *Werke und Tage* (Munich: 1953), p. 169, quoted in Roessler (X/37), p. 495. That Blüher's early enthusiasm for the Nazis was at least partly a function of his radical, racist anti-Semitism need not be doubted.

64. Hans Friedrich Blunck, "Vom Wandervogel zur SA," in Vesper (I/10), pp. 1–7.

65. Littmann (X/56), pp. 124, 159, 186.

66. Quoted in Paetel (X/46), pp. 126–127. For other examples of undignified, nauseating flattery of the man who destroyed all Youth Leagues in a matter of months, see Raabe (X/48), pp. 164–174. But compare the carefully stated, yet unmistakable, critique of the totalitarian claims of the Hitler Youth in Udo Smidt, "Sinn und Sendung evangelischer Jugendführung," in Vesper (I/10), pp. 345–359, and Josepha Fischer, "Jugendverbände und Jugendbewegung in der Geschichte der katholischen Jugendführung," *ibid.*, pp. 360–375.

67. A description of the "Rural Year's" emotional and pedagogic meaning testifies to the almost unadulterated Youth Movement orientation which underlay it. "The task was clear: to form vital relatedness to the world through the great experienced event (*Erlebnis*), to lead to a primary experience and comprehension of homeland and folk through outing, and beholding (*Schauen*), to shape from the essence of things, and not to communicate

intellectual, rational theses. It was not the romanticism of a short school vacation which can make life in the country appear idyllic; it was the exalted law of the daily round, of the succession of seasons, and the apprehension of superhuman forces in tempest, rain, storm, and the starry sky. . . . Cross-country sports, hiking trips, and tent encampments, night marches, and evenings around the campfire with songs, musical instruments, reading aloud, storytelling, celebrating the nation, village feasts, experienced a hundredfold and absorbed with every fiber—these are stored-up vital forces which will transform themselves into the accomplishments and the attitudes of tomorrow's men and women. The great trek was the high point of the Rural Year: comradeship became even more important, as did the file leader, the marching unit with the flag and the drummer at its head. . . . Thereby the Rural Year Youth became a shock troop which formed, without ado, the ranks of the fighters for folkdom and homeland." W. Fritsche, "Das deutsche Landjahr," *Internationale Zeitschrift für Erziehung* (1935), pp. 17 ff, quoted in Roessler (X/37), p. 236.

68. A most valuable and moving human document testifying to the irresistible lure of Nazi idealism is Melita Maschmann's autobiography, *Fazit. Kein Rechtfertigungsversuch* (Stuttgart: Deutsche Verlags–Anstalt, 1963).

69. Inge Scholl, *Die weisse Rose* (Frankfurt: 1952), pp. 10–11, quoted in Roessler (X/37), p. 239. Hans Scholl, an enthusiastic Hitler Youth leader at first, eventually became disillusioned and joined an illegal Jungenschaft group. See the account of the part of the anti-Nazi Resistance "movement" involving the Scholls in Donohoe (IV/71), Chapter IV.

70. *Jugend unterm Schicksal,* 1950, p. 63, quoted in Roessler (X/37), p. 243.

71. There are also *Bünde* which are distinctly non-nationalist and not hostile to the liberal-democratic republic. But these are, of course, disregarded in our discussion.

72. The Thule Orden calls itself "a young, *bündisch* fellowship of life, with the intent to build within itself a natural nobility in loyalty, truthfulness, purity, and freedom, with firm ties to folkdom and God." *Schwarzer Reiter,* no. 5 (Brachet [June], 1951), published (as an internal round letter) by Hellmut Ortlepp, the leader of the Order.

73. Hellmut Ortlepp, "Deutschland," *Schwarzer Reiter,* no. 6 (Gilbert [October], 1951), p. 2.

74. See below, XI/132–155, and nearby text.

75. *Bauhütten* were the powerful medieval guilds of stonecutters and builders which emerged at the end of the twelfth and the beginning of the thirteenth centuries. Possessed of their own judicial system, and as the repositories of the craft secrets of the medieval builder's art, they became with their secret rituals, symbols, and their three degrees of understanding and education the precursors of the Freemasons. See also below, XI/585–589, and nearby text.

76. See below, XI/594–605, and nearby text.

77. See below, XI/570–572, and nearby text.

78. The battle of the so-called *Grenzlanddeutschtum* (the Germandom

at the ethnic frontiers) has been the subject of innumerable learned, propagandistic, and fictionalized accounts. In fact, it is the stock in trade of an entire genre of folkish literature. As an interesting and typical autobiographical account of a *Grenzlanddeutscher* (border-area German)—in this case an Austrian on the Slavonian frontier in Carinthia—and the natural stages by which he moved from the folkish Youth Movement into the Nazi movement, see Brunner (VII/49). See below Chapter XI, Section B/V/b.

79. The Weser development was the work of Werner Ahlendorf (called Aquilla), whom Höller had met at a delegates' conference of the Deutsche Rechts–Partei (DRP) and who now became the Führer of the Jugendbund Junge Adler.

80. Some of the participating groups continued to function under different labels, and some joined other groups, even nonpolitical and nonfolkish groups, such as the Jungenschaft and the reconstituted Freischar. The rest regrouped itself under a new name, Der Horst (The Eyrie). Der Horst was kept together by the Gauführer of Lower Saxony, Gerhard Nickol, of Nienburg, under whose leadership the *bündisch* elements were strongly fostered. Nickol, an active member of the DRP, drowned in a boating accident in May, 1952. See *Das Ziel* (Hanover), I, 2 (July, 1952), 4.

81. See above, VII/86, 87. On the Eagles and Falcons, see H. Lemme, "Adler und Falken, Bund deutscher Jugendwanderer e.V." in Siemering (X/48), pp. 88–89.

82. The North Rhine–Westphalian Young Eagles had been founded by two of the participants in the South Tyrolian "Folkdom rescue operation," Heinz Ostrowski and Gerd Strunck. The former federal leader of the Lower Saxon Junge Adler, Willi Langbein (named Kostja) remained in the merged organization as Lower Saxon Gau leader until November, 1952, when he left under the suspicion of homosexuality.

83. Subsequently, Lange organized a new youth group under the label Junge Adler 1947.

84. While the Young Eagles should still be counted in the nationalist wing of the Youth Movement and in fact see themselves as belonging to that wing, the moderation under the leadership of Günther Gustavson, and later J. Schulz-Thomale, has led to their acceptance in the Youth Rings of various cities and counties. See "Zur Situation der nationalen Jugendverbände," *Die Brücke,* IV, 19 (October, 1957), 8. Cf. Siegfried Schmidt, "Überblick über die äussere Entwicklung der nationalen Jugendverbände," *Erkenntnis und Tat,* VII, 5/6 (May–June, 1956), 18–19. Schulz-Thomale, former member of the Hitler Youth and SS, joined in the postwar years the German Union (DU) and later the circle of former Nazis around the ultranationalist executive secretary of the Lower Saxon FDP, Horst Huisgen. See *Feinde der Demokratie* (Lower Saxony), II, 8 (May–June, 1953).

85. This grouping should not be confused with the Ring bündischer Jugend (Ring of *bündisch* Youth), which was founded much later (May 14, 1958).

86. The Fahrende Gesellen are the postwar edition of the wandering youth of the radical German National Association of Commercial Employees

(Deutschnationaler Handlungsgehilfen Verband) whose quondam leader, Franz Stöhr, had been one of the earliest German National converts to Hitler. For a short account of the original organization and its ideology and objectives, see H. Schumacher, "Die Fahrenden Gesellen e.V.," in Siemering (X/48), pp. 85–87. Its close relationship to an adult organization placed the Fahrende Gesellen of the nineteen twenties at the periphery of the "real" *Bünde*.

87. The Jungenschaft im Bund is partly an offshoot from the radicalized Gefährtenschaft (Wayfarers' Fellowship), and was founded in 1954 by Henning Meinke, of Hamburg. Meinke's strongly *bündisch* orientation even before his secession emerges clearly from his "Aufgaben der deutschen Jugend," *Der Widerhall,* II, 10 (end of January, 1952), 7–9.

88. Such as the Deutsche Jungenschaft (German Boys' Fellowship), the Freischar (Volunteer Corps), the Wandervogel (the Rovers), the Neue Deutsche Jungenschaft (New German Fellowship of Boys), and the Deutscher Wanderbund (German Roving League). The Jungenschaft was the first *Bund* to be reorganized after the war. It made its first appearance in Stuttgart and Cologne in the autumn of 1945.

89. The Deutsche Jungenschaft and the Wandervogel.

90. Arno Klönne, "Im alten Geist—ungebrochen weiter!" *Solidarität,* VI, 5 (May, 1956), 80.

91. The Wandervogel deutscher Bund was the product of a secession in January, 1930, from the Bund der Wandervögel und Kronacher, which itself had been the product of a merger in 1928 of the Bund der Wandervögel, e.V., and the Kronacher Bund der Alten Wandervögel. When that merger took place, the Bund der Wandervögel itself was only one year old, for it had emerged in 1927 from a fusion of the Wandervogel–Völkischer Bund and the Deutsche Wandervogel Gemeinschaft and three other splinter Wandervögel groups. The radically anti-Semitic program of the Wandervogel deutscher Bund was a natural consequence of the fact that most of its members had come from the Wandervogel–Völkischer Bund. For the complex interrelationships of these various groups and their ideological or doctrinal positions, see Siemering (X/48), pp. 64–65, 92–93.

92. It is similarly characteristic of the ambiguous position of the German Roving League that its journal, *Der Nordpfeil,* opens its pages to critical comments regarding the relevance of folkish radicalism to the realities of postwar Germany. In a contribution by Erwin Friz we find the following sober critique "from the inside": "We can serve our people's future only if we determinedly shed all the pseudo values which have been burned to cinders in the inner and outer crises (*Not*) of the 'twilight of the gods' that lies behind us. Every attempt to revive them at all cost (*krampfhaft*) can only spread new poison. Never again must we revive overweaning nationalist estimation of ourselves, racial romanticism, blind militarism, . . . every narrowing, exaggerated exaltation of the folk (*Volkstümelei*), and overweaning estimation of a 'genuine,' 'German' way of life, of mores, poetry, etc., and the unrealistic (*lebensfremd*), presumptuous withdrawal from the life and events of our times." Quoted in *Graue Blätter,* I, 3 (September–October, 1956), 17.

93. See above, VI/94, VII/33. Cf. Arno Klönne, "Mit dem Rücken zur Wand," *Graue Blätter,* I, 1 (May, 1956), 7.

94. From a fund-raising letter of K. H. Heubaum to the *Widerhall's* readers, June 30, 1953. For Heubaum, see above, VI/94.

95. In a book review of Heinz Guderian's *Erinnerungen eines Soldaten* (Heidelberg; Vowinckel, 1951), the Nazi general is accused of an inadequately loyal attitude in connection with the plot of July 20, 1944: Guderian, to be sure, refused to have anything to do with the plot, but "Why? Not perhaps because of a spontaneous inner indignation at this suggestion to participate in the removal of a man who alone had been responsible for creating—out of a totally degenerate (*verwahrlost*) heap in 1918—a folk and a Reich the like of which had never been seen before in history." *Der Widerhall,* II, 10 (end of January, 1952), 15. Cf. the brutal—if shallow—nihilism in Henning Meinke, "Wir sind noch zu moralisch," *ibid.,* II, 11 (end of February, 1952), 1–5, although the editor disclaims in this specific instance any responsibility for the views of his author.

96. See, for example, R. A. (Rudolf Aschenauer?), "Die Windfahne," *ibid.,* III, 3 (September, 1952), 11–12, and Colin Ross, "Die Vereinigten Staaten und Sowjetrussland als wesensverwandte Herrschaftsformen" (from *Die Welt auf der Waage,* 1941), *ibid.,* pp. 12–13. One of the contributors to *Widerhall* is criticized for his radical individualism and for a trend of thought which might lead to a pollyannish disregard of the dangers facing national Germany from both democracy and Bolshevism. But nothing in the criticism suggests any disagreement with the following views of the original author: "Bolshevism is the enemy par excellence. However, Western freedom is no less so. And above all, Western decadence–democracy. Those people nauseate us to the depth of our soul. So nauseating, that we do not even bother to conceal our dislike and contempt, let alone to offer supportive arguments. We simply don't like them. We don't do anything to them. We just let them die out. They are withering from lack of substance." Hinnerk Mende, "Ein Brief aus Köln," *ibid.* III, 1 (July, 1952), 18–19. Cf. also "Ihr, unsere Opfer," *ibid.,* IV, 11/12 (November–December, 1953), 1–6.

97. See, for example, Gisl, "Rasse und Wurzelgrund," *ibid.,* III, 3 (September, 1952), 18–21. "Ein Gespräch über den Kanal hinweg," *ibid.,* II, 12 (March, 1952), 6–9. Also "Führertum in der Sackgasse" and "Quantität und Qualität," *ibid.,* II, 14 (May, 1952), 9–12 and 13–14. Despite disingenuous disclaimers, the massive anti-Semitism of the *Widerhall* is palpable, so patent, in fact, that the periodical was eventually suppressed by court injunction. See, for example, the entire issue of August, 1952 (III, 2). Cf. "Die Engländer haben diese Tatsache gewusst" and "Andere Aktion 'Frieden mit Israel,' " *ibid.,* III, 3 (September, 1952), 7–9; cf. also Drowe, "Der Hecht im Karpfenteich," *ibid.,* III, 4 (October, 1952), 10–12, and W. Wittkemper, "Das grosse Spiel beginnt. . . . Augen auf!" *ibid.,* pp. 13–15. See also the entire issue of July, 1953 (IV, 7), and K. Heide's review of Edmund Herbert's *Wir sprechen Hitler frei, ibid.,* IV, 11/12 (November–December, 1953), 30–31, as well as his review of Hans Fritzsche's *Das Schwert auf der Waage, ibid.,* V, 2 (February, 1954), 17–18.

98. See, for example, Wulf Sörensen, "Die Stimme der Ahnen," *ibid.*, IV, 7 (July, 1953), 8–12, or Gisl, "Was wäre denn Weihnachten. . . . ," *ibid.*, V, 1, (January, 1954), 2–5, and De Baas's letter, as that of Norman, *ibid.*, IV, 7 (July, 1953), 12–17. Cf. N.N.'s letter to the editor, *ibid.*, V, 2 (February, 1954), 11–13.

99. See F. W. Fabricius' history of "Der Deutsche Pfadfinderbund" in Siemering (X/48), pp. 45–47.

100. Initially little more than a "reservoir for premilitary training," the original DPB, it is true, turned toward *bündisch* forms only reluctantly and belatedly, after a number of internal rebellions and secessions had fatally weakened it. See Paetel (X/46), pp. 62–65, 90.

101. Suleck had previously organized and led the Deutsche Pfadfinderschaft (German Scoutism) and merged with other small splinter groups to form in the summer of 1952 the Pfadfinderschaft Nation Europa, whose leader he subsequently became. (From a letter of Suleck's to the Deputy Chairman of Natinform, August 20, 1952.) The honorary chairmanship of the Nation Europe Scouts was tendered the self-exiled Nazi hero H.-U. Rudel. Suleck himself was later convicted on charges of fraud. (See [Club republikanischer Publizisten,] *CrP-Information,* October, 1956, p. 28.)

102. This was the organization which Beck-Broichsitter formed after his split from Franke-Gricksch. It consisted largely of those parts of the original Bruderschaft which had constituted the "Beck-Broichsitter faction." See above, Chapter V, Section B; and Chapter VI, Section C.

103. Letter of August 20, 1952, quoted in a confidential report of August 26, 1952. Suleck's efforts, prior to his fusion with the DPB 1911, to form some kind of joint organization with such suspect groups as Walter Matthaei's Reichsjugend (Reich Youth) and the Bund Deutscher Jugend (League of German Youth) were watched with some apprehension in radically Nazi circles. Both the Reichsjugend and the BDJ were widely known to have contact with government agencies, and anyone working with them had to be prepared to incur the fatal reputation of being in the pay of the federal government. (Letter of Natinform chief, Wolfgang Sarg, to his deputy, September 19, 1952, p. 2. Cf. memorandum on a secret Natinform staff meeting of October 11 and 12, 1952, p. 6, and letter of Sarg to his deputy, February 25, 1953. For the deputy's firsthand impressions of Suleck, see his interview memorandum of May 14, 1953, in the possession of the author.) Suleck himself stressed, of course, the fact that he was the victim of constant harassment by the government's intelligence agency, rather than being the latter's cat's-paw. (From Suleck's interview with the deputy chairman of Natinform, May 13, 1953.)

104. See *Die Brücke,* IV, 19 (October, 1957), 9. The *Junger Beobachter* became an outlet for the writings and organizational notices of the radically nationalist and patriotic-militarist sector of non-*bündisch* youth groups, such as, for example, Reichsjugendkorps Scharnhorst, Jugendbund Adler (not to be confused with the Junge Adler, which had become *bündisch*), Jungdeutschlandbund, Jungsturm e.V., Bismarck-Jugend, Reichsjugend. Klönne (X/93), p. 6, reports a number of sentiments which amply characterize the

Junger Beobachter: "Those people who demonstrated against the Stahlhelm, that pack of 'Falcons' [i.e., Socialist youths], trade-unionists, and Communists . . . should have been chased across the Zonal border." Or, the Nazi phrase "hard as Krupp steel" is said "to have retained its full validity even today"; and "after an incomparably heroic struggle, the Reich collapsed in 1945, under an overwhelming superiority of might"; "our fatherland needs rugged (*kernig*), hard youths—it will depend on the German boys whether or not Germany will assume her rightful place among the peoples"; "and even though God had not granted us victory, our soldiers' blood did not flow in vain," etc.

105. See Klönne (X/51). The same essay appeared as "Nichts vergessen—nichts dazugelernt," *Die Andere Zeitung* (Hamburg), no. 4 (June 2, 1955), p. 13. To my knowledge, the federal government never directly denied the allegations of subsidy made by Suleck himself. A news service, very friendly to the government, was permitted to say that "these assertions [of support] will not bear scrutiny." (*Deutscher Informationsdienst,* no. 586 [August 17, 1956], p. 3.) This persuaded no one.

106. The Suleck faction resumed independent existence under the label under which they had at first come into the DPB 1911, namely, Scoutism Nation Europe. A tiny group remained behind under the label DPB 1911, but it lost whatever significance the organization ever had. In the fall of 1956, the Association of German Book Dealers (Börsenverein des Deutschen Buchhandels) accused Suleck, proprietor of the publishing firm Verlag Jugend und Sport, in Assmannshausen, of fraudulent business practices. Subsequently these charges were substantiated. (See above, X/101.)

107. *Die Deutsche Presse 1961, Zeitungen und Zeitschriften* (Berlin: Duncker & Humblot, 1961), pp. 433–434.

108. See, for example, N. J. Ryschkowsky in *Die Brücke,* IV, 19 (October, 1957), 9.

109. From December, 1949, until 1951 the Jungdeutsche Freischar was led by Eberhard Lebrecht, of Darmstadt; from 1951 until autumn, 1952, by Hansl Späth, of Munich; from November, 1952, until June, 1953, by Karl Lehmann, of Nuremberg; and from July, 1953, on by Karl Wenck, of the same city. See Schmidt (X/84), pp. 18–23.

110. The Deutsche Jugend was founded in September, 1951, by Alfons Höller, the original leader of the Young Eagles in 1947–1948. Its guiding principles were published in the form of an "Appeal to German Youth." Opponents characterized these principles as "only slightly modified phrases from the Hitler period." Among other things, Höller said: "We have lined up not with the West against the East, nor with the East against the West. Our service and our sacrifices are for the Reich of the German and European community of fate." See *Der Informationsdienst,* no. 229 (December 7, 1952). For Höller's later exploits, see below, X/143 and 213.

111. The Young Gray Front was meant to become the youth group of a nationalist veterans' organization, called Gray Front, which August Haussleiter, of the radical Deutsche Gemeinschaft (DG) (German Community), had hopes of putting on its feet. These plans miscarried, and the DG's own

youth group, the so-called Junge Deutsche Gemeinschaft (Young German Community) was partly merged with the Young Gray Front, which also received some influx from an insignificant Augsburg group calling itself Schwalben (Swallows).

112. In this founding participated some groups of the radically nationalist Deutsche Reichsjugend of Herbert Münchow and of the Jugendkorps Scharnhorst, the youth organization of the Stahlhelm. The Deutsche Jungsturm was led first by Lothar Hartmann, then by Karl Lehmann (who had earlier led the Jungdeutsche Freischar), then by Alfred Zitzmann, followed by Wilhelm Preis, and after the latter's removal from office and expulsion, again by Zitzmann. Preis, on leaving the Jungsturm, formed a *bündisch* group which he called Deutsch-Wandervogel.

113. The renaming occurred only after the brusque rejection of Leger's bid to merge with a group of identical name, headed by Karl Klauka and Theodor Thöne. These men had revived the old Jungsturm, one of the oldest nationalist (non-*bündisch*) superpatriotic youth organizations, which had first been founded in 1897 under the label Blau-Weiss-Blau Union and in 1913 was renamed Jungsturm. Mindful of the watchful eyes and ears of Bonn's Federal Office for the Protection of the Constitution, Thöne went out of his way to allay fears that his Deutscher Jungsturm might pursue Right-radical and militarist goals. Still, at the founding meeting he declared "that most of the youth organizations in the federal territory lack a clear patriotic profession of their Germandom. The Jungsturm will now fill this vacuum in the education of youth. . . . It is well known that it won't be easy to bring the Jungsturm's ideas to the young generation, because the propaganda which started immediately after the war, the defamation, and disrespect, have permitted patriotic sentiment to cool." (Quoted in [Club republikanischer Publizisten,] *CrP-Information,* September, 1956, p. 17. For the early history and objectives of the original Deutsches Jugendkorps "Der Jungsturm," see Captain L. von Münchow's article in Siemering [X/48], pp. 31–33.) Leger, too, chose the name of his new group, Deutscher Jugendsturm, to point up this genealogy. He meant to underline the parallel to 1920 when the radically folkish elements of the original Jungsturm under the direction of Generals Ludendorff, Lettow-Vorbeck, and Ritter von Epp (three of the most determined gravediggers of the Weimar Republic) seceded to form a folkish group which they called Deutscher Jugendsturm. In the autumn of 1954, the new Deutscher Jugendsturm formed an Arbeitsgemeinschaft Volksbewusster Jugendbünde (Working Association of Folk-conscious Youth Leagues) with the rest of The Goths and a so-called Deutsche Jungkameradschaft, yet another offshoot from the Jugendkorps Scharnhorst.

114. The secessionists were led by Franz Links and enjoyed the support of the anti-Christian Ludendorff veterans' organization, Reich Flag—League of Folkish Front Fighters (Reichsflagge—Bund völkischer Frontkämpfer).

115. The original Deutsch-Wandervogel had been founded by folkish oppositionists from inside the Wandervogel deutscher Bund, in conjunction with the Germanische Glaubensbewegung, a folkish-paganist religious move-

ment. The postwar reincarnation of the Deutsch-Wandervogel was similarly constituted mostly of members of anti-Christian, Teutonic religious groups. It was joined by a Nordischer Mädelbund (Nordic Girls' League), a *bündisch*-folkish league, by the Deutsche Mädelbund (German Girls' League), a folkish, non-*bündisch* group which had emerged from the Jungsturm in April, 1954, under the leadership of Mrs. Ursula Links, and which now returned to the Jugendsturm under the leadership of Mrs. Auguste Zitzmann, the wife of the latter's leader.

116. Zitzmann shared the leadership with Gustav Achenbach, of Ulm, who operates under the *nom de guerre* "Hildebrandt." A member of Haussleiter's German Community (DG), the sixty-five-year-old Achenbach has been an active "communicant" of the anti-Semitic, anti-Christian *deutschgläubig* movement. Later, Achenbach was replaced by Winfried Glass, of Aschaffenburg.

117. Zitzmann deserted the DSP in August, 1951, because he had found out that Gereke had been involved in the plot of July 20—in short, was a "traitor" in his eyes. In terms of youth associations, Zitzmann came from the Deutsche Reichsjugend, Jungdeutsche Freischar, Pfadfinderschaft Nation Europa, Junge Graue Front, Die Goten, and finally Deutscher Jungsturm. See Peter F. Ludemann, "Schwarz-weiss-rot mit Schulterklappen," *Civis,* VI, 59 (November 15, 1959), pp. 94–96.

118. The Deutschgläubige Gemeinschaft, the Germanische Glaubensbewegung, and Herbert Böhme's Deutsches Kulturwerk Europäischen Geistes.

119. Such as Nordische Glaubensgemeinschaften (Nordic Fellowships of Faith) in Austria and Thiodingen in Sweden. This grouping is called Artgemeinschaft and is under the direction of Alfred Conn, of Hamburg. Conn, who also heads up the Deutschgläubige Gemeinschaft, declared Zitzmann's Deutsch-Wandervogel to be its youth organization, much to the embarrassment of Zitzmann, who insists that his organization is religiously neutral and not anti-Semitic.

120. From a letter of Alfred Zitzmann to N. J. Ryschkowsky, published by the latter in "Deutsch-Wandervogel," Gesellschaft zum Studium von Zeitfragen, *Analysen und Berichte,* VI, 11 (September 11, 1959), 12.

121. *Ibid.,* p. 13.

122. Quoted from Zitzmann's paper *Sturmruf* in Ludemann (X/3), p. 270.

123. "Leitbrief" of the *Deutsch-Wandervogel,* no. 1, 1958, quoted in Ryschkowsky (X/120).

124. Quoted from the *Sturmruf,* the journal of the Deutsch-Wandervogel, *ibid.,* pp. 13–14.

125. Ludemann (X/117), p. 94.

126. See Eberhard Stammler, "Die politische Bildung und das Hakenkreuz," *deutsche jugend,* VIII, 2 (February, 1960), 64.

127. For a perfectly good example of the distinctions which *bündisch*-folkish leaders like to draw, see Siegfried Schmidt, "Die nationalen und

völkischen Jugendverbände," *Erkenntnis und Tat,* VII, 5/6 (May–June, 1956), 15, 17.

128. *Ibid.*

129. *Ibid.,* p. 17.

130. *Ibid.*

131. *Ibid.,* p. 18.

132. Walter Schudnagis, "Reichsjugend und Herbert Münchow," unpublished manuscript in possession of the author. For a description of a very similar ceremony, see *Feinde der Demokratie* (Nordmark), no. 5 (June 24, 1953), pp. 4–5.

133. From a letter of Walter Schudnagis to Rüdiger Proske, April 22, 1952.

134. See "Das Vorleben des Herrn Münchow," *Flensburger Tageblatt,* March 1, 1950.

135. See above, VI/184, and nearby text.

136. The preamble to the DRJ's bylaws asserts that the DRJ wishes "to disassociate itself from the twisted views of German boys and girls which ultimately are the result of the inflexible systems imposed, after the catastrophe of 1945, by the fateful educational pressures on both sides of the Iron Curtain." See *Politisches Archiv* (Berlin–Grunewald), WRS lt/036.

137. Speaking of businessmen whom he suspected of supporting financially the Communist Free German Youth (Freie Deutsche Jugend, FDJ), Münchow evoked memories of the political murders of the nineteen-twenties. "The German Reich Youth will remember these people most distinctly and will, at the appropriate time, call these traitors to account." "An die deutsche Jugend," mimeographed appeal "To the German Youth" by Münchow, n.d.

138. See Münchow's "Offener Brief an den Oberbürgermeister der Stadt Flensburg, Herrn Fritz Drews," February 18, 1951.

139. "Warum Jugendgruppen?" mimeographed handbill signed by the DRJ's District Youth Leader Wilhelm Schneekloth, n.d.

140. *Ibid.*

141. "An die deutsche Jugend" (X/137).

142. Münchow, however, refused to recognize the legality of his demotion and continued to lead a group of deluded youngsters under the original label of German Reich Youth. This lasted until 1958, when he began a sentence of four and a half years for a second conviction for molesting minors. (*Frankfurter Allgemeine Zeitung,* March 10, 1958.) The Attorney-General, incidentally, ordered an investigation of Wegener on suspicion of "conspiracy, continuation of an outlawed organization, endangering the democratic basic order and reintroducing the Nazi spirit." (*Politisches Archiv,* WRS lt/036.) In the beginning of 1956 Wegener was finally tried and convicted. Not long before that trial, he had been in jail for three months on a larceny charge. The second conviction resulted in a five-months sentence. See "Die H-J Fahnen hoch . . . ," *Jugendecho,* May 1, 1956, as reproduced in [Club republikanischer Publizisten,] *CrP-Information,* September, 1956, p. 16.

143. See above, X/110; and below, X/213. The spirit pervading Höller's Reich Youth might best be conveyed in the form of a quotation from a speech by Major Rudolf Krüger, DRP leader of North Rhine–Westphalia, at a "German Evening" organized by Höller's group in Duisburg: "Our Reich is the ordering power in Europe. We do not fear a United States of Europe, but we don't wish to be ruled by the Jew Mendès-France. . . . After World War I the Judas penny contaminated (*durchseucht*) the German peasantry and only a sound agricultural policy was able to bring relief. . . . Since time immemorial German leaders have saved Europe from the East! . . . History will one day show that a leader of this Reich already had the East by the throat before Stalingrad when our enemies stabbed him in the back." The Reich Youth, in brown shirts, neckerchiefs, shoulder straps, and Sam Brown belts, applauded heartily. (For report, see *Neuer Vorwärts* [Köln], October 22, 1954.) These and similar public pronouncements led eventually to an investigation by the Land Attorney-General's office of Höller's Reich Youth. In February, 1957, it was promptly suppressed by the Land Ministry of Interior of North Rhine–Westphalia, and Höller himself was placed under arrest. ("Ein Reichsjugendführer verhaftet," *Frankfurter Allgemeine Zeitung,* June 26, 1957. Cf. "Rechtsradikale 'Reichsjugend' aufgelöst," *Internationaler Jugend Presse Dienst* [*ijpd*], VII, 237 [1957], 2.) Later, Höller was convicted on charges of subversion and given a prison term.

144. See Büsch and Furth (IV/3), pp. 142–144.

145. See above, VII/34.

146. The JBA must not be confused with the distinctly *bündisch* Young Eagles.

147. Friedrich Grimm, "Die Krankheit unserer Zeit," *Der Adlerführer,* VI, 4 (1957), 1–2.

148. *Ibid.,* p. 3.

149. See, for example, "Gedanken über Südtirol" and Konrad Windisch, "Wo bleiben die Taten? Einmal muss das Recht wieder Recht werden," *ibid.,* pp. 4–7.

150. *Ibid.,* pp. 5–6.

151. *Ibid.,* pp. 9 and 11.

152. "Kampfspruch," *Unsere Arbeit,* V, 4 (1957), 1.

153. "Wer jetzig Zeiten leben will," *ibid.*

154. Normally no more than three or four pages of the roughly thirteen pages of the periodical are devoted to announcements and reports of the various groups.

155. *Ibid.,* p. 8.

156. A contract of collaboration was drawn up which stipulated (1) exchange of publications and membership lists, (2) mutual invitations to camping and other events, (3) joint leadership meetings at least once every year. See *Die Brücke,* I (July–August, 1954). Cf. also "Abkommen zwischen den Jugendverbänden 'Jugendbund Adler,' 'Wikingjugend' und 'Bund heimattreuer Jugend,' Wien," *Unsere Arbeit,* III, 2 (1955).

157. Nahrath was one of the leaders of the palace revolt against what the rebels called the dictatorial attitudes, the arbitrariness, the near fraudu-

lence, the extravagance, and dishonorableness of the SRP leadership trio, Dorls, Remer, and August Finke, the chairman of the Lower Saxon organization. Nahrath had been district chairman, chief speaker, and member of the Land executive committee of the SRP. Together with Walter Matthaei, Walter Kniggendorf (alias Bergmann, see above, VII/34) and other former functionaries who seceded from the SRP, Nahrath founded a Reichsorden. Apart from personal conflicts, the most important reason for the revolt and the subsequent founding of the Reichsorden was the rebels' unwillingness to accept the radical "ohne mich" neutralism which the party leadership had decreed. In opposition to the SRP's inflexible refusal to side with the West in the sharpening contest with the Soviet Union, the Reich Order declared "war on Communism" and committed itself to "participation in all actions against Bolshevism and its front organizations, even when the organizer (of the action) belongs to a different ideological camp." See *Florett,* Sonderausgabe, n.d., p. 1. "The neutralisation of Central Europe in the camouflage of the Tauroggen myth must be rejected as a fatal fiction. To fight against this thesis in the nationalist and 'ohne mich' camp is the main task of the Reich Order. . . . The Reich Order has no party status. It is going the way of the elite, and co-operates in the formation of an anti-Bolshevik fighting bloc." From "Ziel und Weg des 'Reichsordens,' " reproduced in full in *Der Informationsdienst,* no. 186 (July 1, 1952), p. 5. Nahrath's itemized bill of charges against August Finke is contained in his open letter to Finke, entitled 'In Kameradschaftlicher Verbundenheit . . . ?" which Nahrath made public in July, 1952. In 1962 Nahrath joined the executive board of the Deutsche Soziale Bewegung.

158. The Vikings were led by Ernst W. Ludwig, and Reich Youth was under Helmut Herrmann. The latter had previously constituted themselves as Völkische Reichsjugend (Folkish Reich Youth). In addition, the Junge Nation (Young Nation) joined the new Jungdeutschlandbund, and its leader, E. Nachtsheim, became the League's federal leader in lieu of Fritz Striewe.

159. The invitations were tendered by Striewe, who had been removed from the leadership of Young Germany League; Hinterleitner, who had been forced to lay down the leadership of the Vikings after he had captured that position by accusing Matthaei of homosexuality; Ernst Ludwig, who had only recently led a strong contingent of dissident Vikings into the Young Germany League; and Horst Nolte, one of the founders and deputy leader of the militarist-patriotic Deutsche Jungkameradschaft (German Young Comradeship), which emerged in 1953 from a group of dissidents (mostly former members of the neo-Nazi SRP) who had left the Jugendkorps Scharnhorst (Youth Corps Scharnhorst), the youth organization of the Stahlhelm. It may not be unfair to infer the nature of this group's orientation from the fact that its uniforms and flags sport the victory rune, the symbol of the Hitler Youth–Jungvolk. That orientation becomes clear also from the German Young Comradeship's stated purpose "to give to German Youth again what is today being consciously suppressed: love for homeland, love for people and fatherland, respect for Germany's great historical past, which slumbers deep in the heart of every genuine German boy." Quoted in [Club republi-

kanischer Publizisten,] *CrP-Information,* September, 1956, p. 17. The SRP background of many or most of the group's members was established in the course of a police search of its central offices. (*Ibid.*) In the meantime, Nolte had again split with Max Höper, the leader of the Deutsche Jungkameradschaft, and in December, 1954, joined Alfons Höller, who was now running a Deutsche Reichsjugend (German Reich Youth), the remnants after various secessions of Münchow's original Reich Youth. Höller was subsequently charged with having contrived the revival of the youth organization of the outlawed SRP and—as mentioned above—was sent to jail for subversive activities. (See above, X/143.)

160. Richard Etzel represented the Youth League Eagle; Nahrath, *père* and *fils,* the Viking Youth; Münchow, Wegener, and Höller represented the various Reich Youth splinters which they led; Will Mayer and Walter Vogel came on behalf of Strasser's Bund für Deutschlands Erneuerung (League for Germany's Renewal); Theodor Thöne represented the Hanover branch of Klauka's Jungsturm e.V. Also participating in the meeting were the Munich group of Nationalist Students, the Youth Corps Scharnhorst, the German Scout League 1911, Alfred Zitzmann's section of the Deutscher Jugendsturm, the splinter Gau Ferdinand von Schill (Paul Rohkst, Bonn), and the so-called Stamm Hohenstaufen, Nachtsheim's Jungdeutschlandbund, and Deutsche Jungkameradschaft. Finally there were also at the Cologne meeting delegates from the so-called Jugendsozialwerk—Hessen (Youth Social Work—Hesse), the Jugendverbindungsstelle Aachen (Youth Liaison Center Aachen), the youth committee of the German Reich Party, Herbert Böhme's Deutsches Kulturwerk Europäischen Geistes, the Flemish Social Movement of Belgium, and the Austrian League of Patriotic Youth, which had been reorganized into an Arbeitsgemeinschaft Nationaler Jugendbünde Österreichs (ANJÖ) (Working Association of Austrian National Youth Leagues). See *Deutscher Informationsdienst,* no. 445 (February 12, 1955), pp. 1–2, and no. 457 (March 30, 1955), pp. 3–4; C. C. Kaiser, "Der junge teutsche Reigen," *deutsche jugend,* IV, 5 (May, 1956), pp. 207–212; Ludemann (X/3), pp. 269–273; *Ja und Nein,* III, 4 (April, 1960).

161. According to a report appearing in the *Deutscher Informationsdienst,* no. 445 (February 12, 1955), pp. 1–2, the mutual hostilities between Nahrath of the Viking Youth, Thöne of the Jungsturm Hannover, and Will Mayer and Vogel of Strasser's League for Germany's Renewal led to the disruption of the proceedings after the first day. Only the "good offices" of N. J. Ryschkowsky, the publisher then of *Die Brücke,* enabled a resumption of the negotiations on the second day of the scheduled two-day meeting.

162. They were the German Young Comradeship, the various Reich Youth splinters, the Jungdeutschlandbund, the small groups of the Stamm Hohenstaufen and Gau Ferdinand von Schill.

163. See "Wir folgen der Fahne . . . ," *Informationen der Naturfreunde Jugend,* November 10, 1955.

164. See above, VII/35. KNJ's international contacts also included cognate groups in the Netherlands and Belgium, the British Nazi Colin Jordan, the French radical anti-Semite Roland Cavallier (coeditor of *l'Europe*

Réelle, the journal of the Belgian Social Movement), and Spanish, Portuguese, Icelandic, Brazilian, and Argentinian radicals.

165. Available evidence suggests that most of the groups which had joined the KNJ at the meeting of February, 1955, resumed their independence in the following year or two. On the other hand new organizations joined it. The League of National Students (BNS) (Klausdieter Ludwig) became a member of the KNJ, as did the Young German Community and a splinter of Zitzmann's Deutsch-Wandervogel under Siegrim Hammerbacher, of Lindau in Swabia (see Zitzmann's reply in Ludemann [X/117]), the Kameradschaft Deutscher Jungen (Comradeship of German Boys) under Hans Uwe Walter, and the Bund Heimattreuer Jugend Franken (League of Patriotic Youth Franconia). Subsequently Walter's Comradeship of German Boys dissolved itself and the Young German Community was forced by the autocratic chairman of its parent organization, August Haussleiter, to withdraw from the KNJ. The Comradeship of German Boys (KDJ) was first founded illegally in 1953 in an internment camp of the Soviet Zone. H. U. Walter, its *spiritus rector,* belonged to the younger group of Hitler Youth leaders, became a Communist, turned against Communism, and was eventually interned on charges of anti-Communist activity. Upon his release, Walter came to West Germany and promptly organized the Comradeship. Militantly nationalist, and now fanatically anti-Communist, the KDJ stoked radical irredentism and accused all antinationalists of being willing or unwilling tools of Bolshevism. (See Gesellschaft zum Studium von Zeitfragen, *Analysen und Berichte,* VI, 11 [September 11, 1959], 3–4.) In 1958 the Schiller Youth joined the KNJ. This group had emerged from the celebrations in 1955 of the 150th anniversary of Friedrich Schiller's death which were organized by the folkish SA poet Herbert Böhme. For these festivities, Böhme succeeded in mobilizing not only folkish and nationalist-extremist groups but also traditionalist-conservative nationalists, such as the refurbished, but hardly reformed, association of fraternities Coburger Convent and Deutsche Burschenschaften and nationalistic elements in the youth groups of some of the *Landsmannschaften.* (Especially the Sudeten German Youth is still quite considerably under the influence of nationalist leaders. See, for example, "Sudetendeutsche Jugend einst und jetzt," *Sudetendeutsche Jugend,* no. 9, 1956.) The organizational upshot of the Schiller memorial was a Schillerbund Deutschland under the chairmanship of Hans Seidenfaden, folkish-nationalist son of the minor Nazi poet Theodor Seidenfaden. The youthful contingent of the Schillerbund called itself Schiller League of German Youth (Schiller Bund der deutschen Jugend) and, like its progenitors, was characterized by a marked preference for folkish mumbo-jumbo and the requisite penchant for a form of Teutonic Christianity, from which have been extirpated the contaminating and corrupting elements of Judaism that were thought to infect the very core of the more traditional varieties of Christianity. (See Eric A. Peschler, "Hinter den Kulissen der bündischen Jugend," *deutsche jugend,* IV, 6 (June, 1956), 277–278.) These efforts, however, led nowhere. From the ruins of the Schiller League of German Youth emerged a folkish-nationalist book club, Junge Buchkameradschaft (Young Book Comradeship)

under Otto Mahler, of Heidelberg, as well as the Schillerjugend mentioned above. Within a few years it, too, had ceased to exist.

166. Hessler once headed Haussleiter's Young German Community, later seceded from it, and in 1957 founded the Jungdeutsche Freischar.

167. From *Der Adlerführer,* Sondernummer 1/59, quoted in Gesellschaft zum Studium von Zeitfragen, *Analysen und Berichte,* VI, 11 (September 11, 1959), 5.

168. For details on the organizational structure, size, personnel, and ideological orientation of the NPD see a confidential report of Fritz Zietlow, n.d., but probably April 1952; *Der Informationsdienst,* no. 184 (June 25, 1952); Report of V. Wilmsdorff to editor of the *Welt am Sonntag* (Hamburg), June 26, 1952; *Lokale Hessissche Nachrichten,* October 11, 1952; *Feinde der Demokratie* (Lower Saxony), II, 6 (March–April, 1953), and III, 8 (May–June, 1954); *Der Informationsdienst,* no. 218, (October 29, 1952), pp. 1–3; *Die Brücke,* II, 12 (December, 1955), 3–5; Gesellschaft zum Studium von Zeitfragen, *Analysen und Berichte,* V, 8/9 (April 3, 1958), 6. From June, 1951, on the monthly *Freiheitsbriefe* and *Der Freiheitsbote* are the best source for a continuous account of the NPD's political orientation and policy demands. The latter ceased publication in 1961.

169. Reproduced in Gesellschaft zum Studium von Zeitfragen, *Analysen und Berichte,* VI, 12 (September 15, 1959), 1.

170. Unconfirmed reports, however, maintain that the Hamburg groups of these two organizations seceded to join the Young German Movement. The Viking splinter was led by Uwe Siebrands, and the Deutsch-Wandervogel splinter by Kurt Voss. See *Bulletin on German Questions* (London), VI, 246 (October 1, 1959). It would also appear that Karl Lehmann led his Nuremberg local of the Deutsch-Wandervogel into the Young German Movement. The other four participants were the Jungdeutsche Freischar under Günther Hessler, the Nationale Jugend Deutschlands—Berlin (National Youth of Germany—Berlin) under Peter Bernau, the Deutschsozialistische Jungsturm under the former Strasser man Werner Diehl (and later under Karl-Heinz Nill), and the Schiller Youth under Hans-Ulf Siebrands, of Herne. (Nill, incidentally, is said to be closely connected with the anti-Semitic, anti-Masonic, anti-Catholic, and anti-Christian Ludendorff League for God Cognition [L] [Bund für Gotterkenntnis (L)]. See Gesellschaft zum Studium von Zeitfragen, *Analysen und Berichte,* VI, 12 [September 15, 1959], 2.) The initial invitation had, in fact, been issued in the name of the National Youth Fellowship, the Jungdeutsche Freischar, and the Deutschsozialistische Jungsturm. In 1962 the Siebrands brothers, Hans-Ulf and Uwe, were sentenced to three months' imprisonment for subversive activities.

171. For Schönborn, see above, VI/116 and VII/151. See Gnielka (VII/142), p. 10. This essay, originally published under the title "Das deutsche Volk muss wieder auf Vordermann gebracht werden," *Frankfurter Rundschau,* June 22, 1959, must be used with caution. Excessively sensationalist, its facts are not always entirely reliable.

172. Gnielka (VII/142), p. 12.

173. *Ibid.,* p. 11. On January 2, 1960, Peter Bernau was to earn new

laurels. On that cold winter evening he and his minions marched out to a Berlin park for a Teutonic solstice celebration, swastika flag unfurled, and lustily intoning the songs which they had carefully rehearsed in their "home evenings." The police intervened, and a widely reported "incident" resulted. The weeks subsequently spent in prison seemed a small price to pay for the greater glory of the coming Reich. (See also below, text at X/327.)

174. Gesellschaft zum Studium von Zeitfragen, *Analysen und Berichte,* VI, 12 (September 15, 1959), 3.

175. Quoted *ibid.,* p. 4.

176. Quoted *ibid.,* p. 3.

177. From a letter of Hans Schulz of April 26, 1959, quoted *ibid.,* p. 4.

178. Although Horst Nolte seceded from the KNJ with his handful of followers to merge into the Young German Movement (Jungdeutsche Bewegung, JDB), its largest group, the Schiller Youth, reconsidered and finally refused to dissolve itself and merge into the JDB.

179. For Windisch's connections with the Fascist International, see above, VII/35, VII/41. In the summer of 1963, the Comradeship Circle of National Youth Associations (KNJ), now reduced to a corporate membership of three youth groups, changed its name to Comradeship Circle of National Youth. Its chairmanship went to Herbert G. Welsch and the deputy chairmanship to Wilfried Walter. (Cf. below, X/187.)

180. See *Deutscher Informationsdienst,* no. 807 (April 20, 1959).

181. In 1961 the leadership of the BHJ was taken over by Horst Löffler, the editor of *Der Trommler.* The previous chairman, Hans Hübner, became vice-chairman. Subsequently Dieter Hoehne (Bad Homburg) and H. Möring (Bremen) took over the chairmanship and vice-chairmanship, respectively. Not quite a year later, in February, 1962, the Federal Ministry of the Interior withdrew from the BHJ its official classification as a club primarily concerned with youth work. This automatically prohibited the BHJ from wearing a uniform. At that time the BHJ also developed closer ties with the newly founded Young Europe movement of international fascism. (See above, VII/77.) The BHJ leader of Kassel, Reinhard Schimmelpfeng, became youth leader of the German branch of Young Europe, and a former Austrian BHJ leader, Fred Borth, who in 1954 had formed his own group (Legion Europe) after leaving the BHJ, merged with the Austrian Young Europe movement. For the financial support of the BHJ and the Wiking Jugend, a Freundeskreis der Nationalen Jugend was organized in 1962. As its available funds grew, the Friends of Nationalist Youth made plans to extend their largess to other youth groups and to promote in them more vigorous ideological training. See *Studien von Zeitfragen, Analysen, Berichte, Informationen zum nationalen Nonkonformismus,* XI, 2 (February 12, 1964), 6.

182. *Der Trommler,* no. 26 (1958), quoted in Gesellschaft zum Studium von Zeitfragen, *Analysen und Berichte,* VI, 11 (September 11, 1959), 8–9. For additional excerpts see [Club republikanischer Publizisten,] *CrP-Information,* September, 1957, pp. 89–90.

183. From a handbill of the ANJÖ quoted in Gesellschaft zum Studium von Zeitfragen, *Analysen und Berichte,* VI, 11 (September 11, 1959), 10.

184. See below, Chapter XII, Section B/I.

185. *Kölnische Rundschau,* July 18, 1962.

186. Gesellschaft zum Studium von Zeitfragen, *Analysen und Berichte,* VI, 11 (September 11, 1959), 14–15.

187. *Ibid.,* pp. 15–16. The propaganda work of the radically nationalist, non-*bündisch* youth groups has more recently been journalistically supported by a Munich Propaganda Center for Nationalist Youth (Schriftenzentrale der Nationalen Jugend), under the guidance of Wilfried Walter. In handbills and brochures the Center calls for radical solutions to Germany's "Eastern problem," indulges in justifications of Germany's recent past, fulminates against the Western Allies, and glorifies Nazi Germany's war experiences. The Center maintains close contact with the Committee for the Restoration of Historical Truth (Komitée zur Wiederherstellung der geschichtlichen Wahrheit) (see below, XII/131–134, and nearby text), claims the support of the provincial expellee organizations (Landsmannschaften) of Sudeten Germans, Silesians, and Pomeranians, of such publishing firms as Schild Verlag and Friesen Verlag, and receives publicistic support from *Deutscher Studenten-Anzeiger, Adlerführer, Nation Europa,* and others. See "Call for Another Anschluss," *The Wiener Library Bulletin* (London), XVIII, 1 (January, 1964), 2.

188. "Arbeitsordnung und grundsätzliche Bestimmungen" of the Deutsche Jugend im VdS, Landesmark Niedersachsen (mimeographed, n.d.), p. 1.

189. *Die Brücke,* IV, 19 (October, 1957), 4. But cf. the bylaws of the Lower Saxon Land organization of the Youth League Kyffhäuser (October 10, 1955), paragraph 2, where all reference to "rigor" has been omitted. Instead, part of its goals is said to be "voluntary submission (*Einordnung*) to the community of youth on the basis of comradeship, truthfulness, courage, determination, inner and external cleanness, chivalry and loyalty. Fight against filth and trash."

190. See *Die Junge Front* (*Bundesbrief des Deutschen Jugendbundes Kyffhäuser im Kyffhäuserbund e.V.*), I, (September–October, 1956), 16. Cf. "Scharnhorst Jugend," in *Der Stahlhelm,* XXIII, 7 (July, 1956), 5.

191. See Unabhängige Vaterländische Jugendverbände der Bundesrepublik Deutschland, "Einladung," October 10, 1956.

192. Cf. J. Eppe, "Generalangriff der Bundeswehr auf die deutschen Jugendverbände?" *Solidarität,* December 11, 1958, pp. 187–189.

193. See "Augen Rechts" in *Berliner Allgemeine,* February 1, 1957, as reproduced in [Club republikanischer Publizisten,] *CrP-Information,* March, 1957, pp. 31–32.

194. Quoted in "Nach Ostland wollen wir reiten!" [Club republikanischer Publizisten,] *CrP-Information,* November, 1956, p. 41.

195. *Ibid.* and "Augen Rechts!" (X/193).

196. Only in April, 1955, did the Scharnhorst Youth officially become a national organization on the federal level. See *Feinde der Demokratie* (Lower Saxony), IV, 5 (March–April, 1955), 31.

197. In view of the Scharnhorst Youth's blood relationship to the Stahlhelm, its ideological orientation need not be described at length. Suffice it to refer briefly to the goals of the organization as prescribed by its federal leader, Walter Girgensohn. (*Der Stahlhelm,* XXIII, 1 (January, 1956), quoted in *Feinde der Demokratie* [Lower Saxony], V, 4/5 [January–March, 1956], 52): "We derive our strength from the military virtues, we fortify mind and body through genuine, decent comradeship, which strengthens the weak, provides the hesitant with drive to develop, and suppresses egotism. We want to direct the young German to his obligation to commit himself to Western culture and civilization. We juxtapose to licentiousness, genuine inner and outer freedom which finds its due measure in the community of state and nation." For the development of the Scharnhorst organization after World War I, see Captain (i.R.) Werner's essay in Siemering (X/48), pp. 36–38.

198. For a short description of the objectives of the pre-Hitler edition of the Kyffhäuser Youth, see *ibid.,* p. 33. In 1930 it had some 65,000 members.

199. Among the groups which merged with the Kyffhäuser Youth were Karl Klauka's so-called Deutscher Jungsturm e.V. (see above, X/113); the Jungdeutschlandbund (see above, X/158); the Deutsche Jungkameradschaft under Max Höper (the product of a sizable defection from the Jugendkorps Scharnhorst in 1953; see above, X/159); the Lübeck Youth Corps 1912 (Lübecker Jugendkorps 1912); a group known as Deutsche Pfadfinderschaft (German Scoutism); a splinter group under the label Wikinger (Vikings) (which must not be confused with the nationalist-ideological Viking Youth under Raoul Nahrath); Ebbo Beneke's League of German Boys (Bund deutscher Jungen had also been formed by a fraction of Scharnhorst Youth which defected to the Deutscher Jungsturm in 1953, only to secede again as an independent group in the following year); and a group of the monarchist-reactionary Alt-Wandervogel (which had nothing whatever to do with the key group of identical name in the early Youth Movement). See W.L.R., "Rechts um!" *deutsche jugend,* no. 1 (January, 1956), 38–39, and *Die Brücke,* IV, 19 (October, 1956), p. 4.

200. Since 1962 the DJVdS has called itself Deutscher Jugendbund Steuben.

201. The Bismarck Youth was no doubt meant to continue the traditions of the youth organization of the reactionary, monarchist German National People's Party (DNVP) of Weimar days. The youth group was established in the autumn of 1922. In January, 1929, the organization's name was changed from Bismarck Youth to Bismarck League. It claimed roughly 40,000 members. See Siemering (X/48), pp. 255–258.

202. A few months later, the Working Fellowship once again published a resolution to the effect that it "considers it incompatible with basic democratic principles that only a part of the youth organizations . . . which acknowledge the Basic Law is being supported by the funds of the Federal Youth Plan. . . . We, therefore, demand a revision of the Federal Youth

Plan." Again, the associated youth groups decided to move jointly to crash the membership of the Youth Ring and thus become eligible for federal subsidies. The resolution is quoted in *Die Brücke,* IV, 19 (October, 1957), 6.

203. According to the Naval Youth leader, Georg Hartmann, the Naval League "sees a positive attitude toward democracy as its most important educational means (*sic*) . . . especially through its espousal of German naval ideals (*Seegedanken*). . . . Premilitary training is being decisively rejected. . . . There are no contacts with Right-radical groups or veterans' associations. . . . A Third Reich tradition does not exist in the Naval League." "Was die Marinejugend will," *Junge Stimme,* no. 15 (August 9, 1958). Hartmann's assurances should be taken with a grain or two of salt. (Cf. also "Marinejugend," *Informationsdienst des Landesjugendringes Niedersachsen,* no. 62 [1956–1957], p. 5.) At the same time the Naval League's eagerness for a reputation of democratic respectability is beyond doubt.

204. Walter Girgensohn, "Pharisäer!" *Der Stahlhelm* (Bonn), XXIII, 7 (July, 1956), 5.

205. "Die Treue ist das Mark der Ehre!" *ibid.*

206. "The army—used to victory, victoriously deployed on enemy soil—protected Germany until the day when it had to agree to a truce, after having been left in the lurch by the home front." From *Der Scharnhorst Junge,* March, 1957, quoted in *Die Brücke,* IV, 19 (October, 1957), 5. Cf. also the description of a tent encampment in "Zeltlager Landau/Pfalz," *Der Stahlhelm* (Bonn), XXIII, 7 (July, 1956).

207. See, for example, *Jugendbrief,* 11/56 (November 15, 1956) and 12/56 (December 15, 1956), of the Land organization of Lower Saxony under Herbert Ackermann. See especially the annex to *Jugendbrief* 12/56, pp. 5–6, entitled *"Lagerordnung," "Zeltordnung,"* and *"Wachordnung."*

208. *Jugendbrief,* 12/56 (December 15, 1956), p. 1.

209. "Führerschulung beim Kyffhäuser-Bund," [Club republikanischer Publizisten,] *CrP-Information,* February, 1957, p. 16.

210. Quoted in Arno Klönne, "Jugendarbeit 'rechtsaussen,' " *Politische Studien,* IX, 101 (September, 1958).

211. See "Einige Arbeitshinweise für die Winterarbeit," *Die Junge Front,* I, 1 (September–October, 1956), 18.

212. See above, X/110, 143.

213. According to Gesellschaft zum Studium von Zeitfragen, *Analysen und Berichte,* VI, 12 (September 15, 1959), Höller was supposedly removed from that post after only a few months because of serious policy disagreements. A few years later, the irrepressible Höller pulled a new youth group out of the hat. The name of the group, Bund Deutscher Jugend (BDJ) (League of German Youth), was presumably chosen to conjure up memories of the government-subsidized, anti-Communist sham "youth group" whose antics and embarrassing connections with the secret, American-trained guerrilla war outfits led to its disbandment in 1953. (See above, X/14, and nearby text.) Höller's new BDJ loudly proclaims loyalty to the Basic Law and professes political neutrality. This does not hinder it from seeing in "eternal loyalty to Nation and Reich its supreme law." Before forming the BDJ,

Höller—on being expelled from the DJB Kyffhäuser—took his North Rhine-Westphalian organization with him and attached it to the Bund Vaterländischer Jugend. See above, X/185 and nearby text.

214. Cf. Schmidt (X/84), p. 23.

215. See above, Section C.

216. There are, furthermore, literally hundreds of articles and dozens of books and monographs on the problem of the relationship of German youth to the democratic state, on the nature of civic education (*politische Bildung*) and of the study in public schools of contemporary history and its effect on the political orientation of the future citizen. Under the circumstances the interested reader is best advised to consult the absolutely indispensable *Archiv-Bericht,* the bimonthly annotated bibliography of the Deutsches Jugendinstitut (formerly Deutsches Jugendarchiv), Munich 23, Leopoldstrasse 5. The vast holdings of this unique, and uniquely useful, specialist reference library dealing with every facet of youth are available to foreign investigators on loan or in the form of photostats at very modest rates. From June, 1964, on, the *Archiv-Bericht* has appeared in the modified and enlarged form of *Dokumentationen zur Jugendforschung und Jugendarbeit.*

217. Some of the most inept errors in this respect are committed by foreign observers who evidently know little about postwar Germany. A good—because relatively recent—example of this type of error is supplied by Benjamin Fine, the otherwise highly competent former education editor of *The New York Times.* (*German Schools on Trial* [published and distributed by the German Information Center, New York].) In a number of superficial and self-contradictory articles summarizing his impressions of the German educational scene, Fine comes to ecstatic conclusions regarding the profundity of democratic thinking and antiauthoritarian feeling of the present grammar- and high-school generations. In reliance on a questionnaire survey, Fine concludes that "today German youth are virtually unanimous in thinking Hitler their country's greatest evil." (Strangely enough, he comes close to reporting the reason for this state of affairs without even suspecting it: "More than fifty percent listed as his greatest harm the fact that he [i.e., Hitler] brought Germany into war, and destroyed Germany's reputation throughout the world," p. 4.) Fine goes on naïvely, "Among all the interviews I had with students and the 1500 written questionnaires, not a single answer indicated a favorable opinion of Hitler" (p. 4). The complete unanimity, apart from the fact that it is totally contradicted (as we have already noted) by any number of other polls and interviews, should have aroused Fine's suspicion. That it did not can be explained by his "will to believe." But only his inexperience in the field of German postwar nationalism can account for Fine's inability to see that the "answers" he received were, in any case, entirely irrelevant to what is really significant. The children's alleged "opinion of Hitler" bears, as we know, little relation to their orientation toward alternatives to liberal-democratic social, political, and cultural values. How amateurish Mr. Fine's "research" was emerges amusingly from his attempt to get at this orientation. Twenty-five hundred

boys and girls were subjected to these "questions": "Do you want to continue to live in a democracy? What are the advantages and disadvantages of your government? Would you want to change either to a monarchy or to a dictatorship?" The result: "Ninety-five percent of the students . . . said they preferred a democracy to any form of government" (p. 6). In the light of our previous discussion, the reader will have no difficulty in recognizing the reasons for the inadmissibility of this kind of question in the German context and the consequent meaninglessness of the so-called "answers." (See above, Section C.) Nothing further need be added here. If it is surprising that so excellent a journalist as Benjamin Fine could not himself discover the inadequacy of his procedure, it is even more disconcerting that he did nothing to reconcile the self-contradiction in his report. Thus he writes: "Until now the ugly truth was soft-pedaled" (p. 1); "the emphasis in the schools is not on the evils of the past" (p. 4); "the [television] station [presenting a series of programs on the Nazi period] gets a heavy influx of mail. It is almost equally divided among those who say 'let's not poke into the past' and those who say 'it is good to know more about what happened under Hitler' " (p. 5); "schools are now taking a more active part in training their youth for democracy. . . . But much remains to be done . . ." (p. 6). "In most cases nothing is said officially, at any rate about modern history, until the eighth grade" (p. 8), ". . . as a result too often the 1933–1945 period gets less than one week of study" (*ibid.*). "But many of the old teachers, particularly those who taught under Hitler or had been members of the Nazi Party, find the adjustment hard. . . . It is estimated that 50 percent of the teachers in Germany today taught under the Hitler regime. They swore allegiance to him, hailed his name in classrooms and taught the approved Nazi doctrines. . . . Of course some teachers who sang Hitler's praises take the easy way out: they steer clear of discussing 20th century politics" (p. 16). "An analysis of the most popular textbooks shows that many are evasive. Sometimes they give half-truths and fragmentary information" (p. 20); "a vast amount of misinformation exists among the German students concerning the recent past. Although Hitler is only 16 years dead, it might as well be in the crusade age as far as many students are concerned. . . . They were particularly vague about the Jewish question" (p. 20). ". . . Dr. Walter Stahl . . . sums up the problem this way: 'One of the weakest points in the structure of German democracy is that of the political education and training of the youth of the country' " (p. 19). The university student "is not educated for life. He is, in large measure, politically naive, not interested in politics, nor in the everyday problems of living in a democracy. Surveys found that 50 percent were indifferent to national or international problems" (p. 22).

One might have thought that a careful rereading of what he himself had written might have given Fine pause in naïvely falling into the questionnaire trap and might have prevented him from the following totally incongruous and, hence, thoroughly discredited "summary": "With the exception of a small unimportant fringe of neo-Nazis, the overwhelming majority of German youth believes in democracy of the Federal Republic. . . . They may not understand all the subtleties of democracy, but they do know that Nazism means concentration camps" (p. 23). Of whatever service Fine's articles might have been to the German Embassy and its Information Service in New York, they did not serve to enlighten the intelligent newspaper-reading public. A good survey of the *real* situation can be found in *Politische Studien,* XIV (May–June, 1963). Early in May, 1959, a widely seen Hesse television program ("Eyes on our Youth") created a sensation when it presented the answers of grammar- and senior high-school students to the question with what they associated the name Hitler or the words National Socialism. To the consternation of many, the overwhelming majority associated Hitlerism with the abolition of unemployment, the reduction of the crime rate, the restoration of discipline, with rearmament and Germany's achievements as a world power, with *Autobahnen,* government-subsidized vacations, increased national prestige, and with economic prosperity. Not a single pupil alluded to genocide, international aggressions, or the enslavement of mind and body. Identical responses had been reported half a year earlier in the course of an investigation of a number of Munich schools. (See *Süddeutsche Zeitung* [Munich], July 26/27, 1958.) In addition to the works previously cited (see above, X/17, 18, 26, 33, 37, 40), see also, for instance, Helmut von Bracken, "Die deutsche Jugend von 1953 im Spiegel der Meinungsforschung," *deutsche jugend,* II, 4 (April, 1954), 155–163; M. F., "Die Argumente der starken Hand," *ibid.,* II, 5 (May, 1954), 227–228; Carl Christian Kaiser, "Politische Meinungen der westdeutschen Jugend," *ibid.,* V, 8 (August, 1957), 367–376; and "Zur politischen Grundhaltung der westdeutschen Jugend," *ibid.,* VI, 1 (January, 1958), 21–27; Ute Bernhard, "Wie Jugendliche die Juden sehen," *ibid.,* VIII, 2 (February, 1960), 69–73; " 'Einiges war aber doch gut': Oberschüler diskutieren über den Nationalsozialismus," *Junge Stimme,* no. 7 (1958).

218. Indeed, field work in the highly sophisticated and liberal cosmopolis of Hamburg revealed that well over a third of the population rejects the thorough discussion of Nazism in the schools and that only a bare third of the respondents not only supported the idea of the broadest possible treatment in the schools of the Nazi period but also gave evidence of having "liberated itself from the relics of National Socialism." Wolfgang Hartenstein and Günter Schubert (VIII/189), pp. 80–85.

219. This problem of the "missing fathers" is dramatically analyzed in the brilliant—if bitter—first novel *Anfrage* of the young German author Christian Geissler. Translated into English, it appeared under the title, *The Sins of the Fathers* (New York: Random House, 1962).

220. At the time of this writing the Stuttgart students, in the words of the *New York Times* report, "will not be able to take a critical look at their teachers. Their school refused participation in the contest on the grounds that taking part in it was merely recommended and not an order." "German Teachers Irked by Contest," *New York Times,* August 15, 1965, p. 24, cols. 1–2.

221. For a brief review of German historiography, see Adolf Grote,

"Die beschönigte Katastrophe: Lage und Praxis der gegenwärtigen deutschen Geschichtsrevision," *Deutsche Rundschau,* LXXXII, 1 (January, 1956), 21–26.

222. Indeed, the Land government of Baden-Württemberg, for instance, admitted in connection with the essay contest mentioned above "that the neglect of civic education at many public schools had prompted it to include the subject in this year's contest," as did the "too frequent" complaints about the students' lack of interest in their own student councils. "German Teachers Irked by Contest" (X/220).

223. To these positive forces should be added those who are engaged in the political education of unorganized youth. The German Federal Government disburses annually five million marks for that purpose. These funds are distributed to the various confessional adult education centers (such as, for instance, the Evangelical Academies and the Catholic-Social Educational Institutes [Katholisch-Soziales Bildungswerk]), the nondenominational Adult Education Colleges (Volkshochschulen), the Working Fellowship Work and Life (Arbeitsgemeinschaft Arbeit und Leben), which has close ties to labor unions, and five so-called East-West Institutes (Ost-West Institut) that combine research with anti-Communist training. Probably more than a hundred thousand people annually receive some political education through these efforts. How many of them become mired in the aridity of mere anti-Communism is, of course, difficult to say. Unfortunately, in the climate of postwar Germany, with its facile and politically inspired identification of democracy with anti-Communism, one is constrained to assume that a considerable portion of political education ends by being psychological warfare indoctrination.

224. "They [the students of the late nineteenth century] took over the political and social ideas of the various shades of bourgeoisie, especially those of a conservative, feudal bourgeoisie which adorned itself with the prestige of a classical education (*Bildungshumanismus*) in the sense of cultural aristocratism (*geistesaristokratisch*)." Habermas (X/33), p. 203. Cf. also Knoll (V/43), pp. 120–123, 170–177, 195–230.

225. Wolfgang Abendroth, "Zur Funktion der Gewerkschaften in der westdeutschen Demokratie," *Gewerkschaftliche Monatshefte,* III, 11 (November, 1952), 646–648.

226. For the German postwar student's conception of the role and function of the university and higher education, see Institut für Sozialforschung, "Universität und Gesellschaft (Studentenbefragung)" (Frankfurt, 1956), research report in the archives of the Institute, cited in Habermas (X/33), pp. 258–259. The earlier study disclosed a remarkable discrepancy between the motives for attending the university (over 40 per cent of the students saw their studies merely as means to the very practical end of making a good living) and the students' refusal to see in their studies merely the necessary professional training (66 per cent insisted that their studies meant more than mere professional training). To Habermas this discrepancy "confirms the conjecture that the respondents hardly take seriously any

longer those [studies] which are being carried on at the university as general liberal arts education (*Allgemeinbildung*)." *Ibid.*, p. 259.

227. This is, of course, not to deny the trend toward a reduction in the degree to which higher education is a social privilege. On this point see Helmut Plessner, "Über Elite und Elitebildung," *Gewerkschaftliche Monatshefte,* VI, 10 (October, 1955), 602 ff., and Dietrich Goldschmidt, "Elitebildung in der industriellen Gesellschaft," *Die Neue Gesellschaft,* V, 1 (January–February, 1958), pp. 34 ff. Still, twelve years after the end of World War II, only 5 per cent of all students in Germany came from the lower classes, which represent 52 per cent of the German population. See Ralf Dahrendorf, *Gesellschaft und Freiheit: Zur soziologischen Analyse der Gegenwart* (Munich: Piper, 1962), p. 185. Cf. the figures in Morris Janowitz, "Soziale Schichtung und Mobilität in Westdeutschland," *Kölner Zeitschrift für Soziologie und Sozialpsychologie,* X, 1 (1958), 20, Table 10. (This article appeared as "Social Stratification and Mobility in West Germany," *American Journal of Sociology,* LXIV, 1 [July, 1958], 6–25.) In November, 1964, the Bavarian Statistische Landesamt published figures indicating that "the social background of the students [in Bavarian universities] has hardly changed in the last years." Fully a third stem from civil service families, slightly over 25 per cent of all students come from families of white collar employees. More than a third of the students come from university-trained families. Over 30 per cent come from professional, commercial and business families. Worker and farm families are represented by a mere 10 per cent of the student body. See "Wer in Bayern studiert," *Süddeutsche Zeitung* (Munich), no. 273, November 13, 1964, p. 13.

228. This percentage gains added significance in the light of the fact that roughly 2 per cent of all students are *politically* organized. See Friedrich Thomas' " 'Bruder Studium' meidet die Politik," *Christ und Welt* (Stuttgart), no. 14 (March 31, 1960). According to Habermas (X/33), p. 289, 5 to 7 per cent are politically organized. Although Habermas included in his interview schedule a question concerning membership in student corporations, he does not report on the numbers involved.

229. As early as 1953 the student corporations were "again at least as strong as they were at the time of their dissolution. Despite rejection by the academic authorities, regardless of the criticisms of many students and the doubts of the broader public, they have returned in their old form." Ulrich Gembardt, "Gespräch ohne Partner?" *Deutsche Universitäts–Zeitung,* VIII, 2 (January 26, 1953).

230. See Paul Ssymank, "Geschichtlicher Überlick über deutsches Hochschulwesen und deutsches Studententum," in Michael Doeberl *et al.*, eds., *Das akademische Deutschland* (Berlin: Weller, 1931), II, 21. The best —though uncritical—source on the Corps is still Wilhelm Fabricius, *Die deutschen Corps* (2d ed.; Frankfurt: Deutsche Corpszeitung, 1926).

231. The best source of materials on the Burschenschaften is still Hermann Haupt, ed., *Quellen und Darstellungen zur Geschichte der deutschen Burschenschaft und der deutschen Einheitsbewegung,* 17 vols. (Heidelberg:

Winter, 1910–1940). Within this enormous collection, the best histories of the remarkable movement are Georg Heer's rather nationalist *Geschichte der deutschen Burschenschaft* and Hermann Haupt's and Paul Wentzcke's *Hundert Jahre deutscher Burschenschaft.* Heer's four-volume work represents Volumes VI, X, XI, and XVI (1919–1939) of the *Quellen und Darstellungen,* and the latter is Volume VII (1921). A short English account of the early years of the Burschenschaften can be conveniently found in Krieger (I/1), 261–272. For a brief review of the entire development see Pross (II/7), pp. 39–80.

232. For a good example see the writings of Wolfgang Menzel, or their analysis in Robert A. Kann, "Wolfgang Menzel: Pioneer of Integral Nationalism," *Journal of the History of Ideas,* VI, 2 (April, 1945), 213–230.

233. Pinson (VI/10), p. 63.

234. Peter Viereck, borrowing from the democratic firebrand, Karl Follen, aptly called Jahn "The First Storm Trooper." See his *Metapolitics* (I/1), Chapter IV.

235. Sell (I/1), p. 89.

236. *Ibid.* Sell's over-all assessment, quite understandable in one who has witnessed the enormities of Hitler's racist Teutomania, appears nonetheless somewhat harsh: "As much or as little as the Hitler Youth of the twentieth century participated in the excesses of National Socialism, that great or that small was the part the Burschenschaft played in the activities of the fanatics in their midst. . . . From idealistic romantic enthusiasm, from nationalist megalomania, muscular terror, anti-Semitic brutalities, and the boorishness of the book burning at the Wartburg, the Burschenschaft drifted into murder." *Ibid.,* p. 90. In 1827, under the impact of the growing liberal wing, a congress of Burschenschaft delegates in Bamberg abrogated the "Christian character" of the organization and opened the membership to Jews. But the organized political anti-Semitism of the eighteen-seventies and eighties led in 1896 to the expulsion of Jews from the Burschenschaften. See Ssymank (X/230), pp. 28, 36.

237. In addition to Corps and Burschenschaften, two other forms of corporation require mention, the Landsmannschaften (or Regional Associations) and the Catholic Corporations. The former (not to be confused with their sixteenth-century namesake) were organized after 1830 and in general copied the rituals and forms of the older corporations with regard to dueling and the wearing of "color." Eventually they joined the Turnerschaften (Gymnastic Clubs) in a unified organization called the Coburger Convent (CC). The Catholic Corporations appeared first in the middle of the nineteenth century and have occupied a rather special position ever since. Although many of them carry a ceremonial saber on festive occasions, they reject the duel as a matter of principle. As to the wearing of "color," some of the largest Catholic groups do it, while other equally powerful organizations reject it. Finally, mention must also be made (for the sake of completeness) of a large number of smaller associations with more or less marked corporative character. In 1951 many of them joined the nonconfessional student corporations in the so-called Convent deutscher Korporationsver-

bände (CDK). To the CDK belong, in addition to the Corps (Kösener Senioren Convents-Verband, KSCV), the Deutsche Burschenschaften (DB), and the Coburger Convent (CC), the following: Akademischer Turnerbund (ATB), Deutsche Sängerschaft (DS), Miltenberger Ring (MR), Sonderhäuser Verband (SV), Wingolfbund (WB), Verband der Vereine deutscher Studenten (VVDSt). See *Deutsche Presse Agentur, (dpa) Inf.* 913 (June 13, 1955). Cf. Dieter Grossherr, "Die Korporationen und die Demokratie," *Die Neue Gesellschaft,* III, 6 (November–December, 1956), 442–455.

238. For a short account of the relationship of the folkish student associations to National Socialism, see Hans Heigert, "Der Selbstmord der deutschen Studentenschaft," *Frankfurter Allgemeine Zeitung,* no. 80 (April 5, 1958).

239. *Burschenschaftliche Blätter,* no. 3 (1954), quoted in Grossherr (X/237), p. 447. Paul Ssymank wrote in 1930: "For German students November 9, 1918, was the end of their old history. . . . Therefore, they could not agree in their hearts to the political change, but stood in sharpest opposition to the newly established authorities" ([X/230], p. 42).

240. Ernst Röhm, *Geschichte eines Hochverräters* (7th ed.; Munich: 1934), p. 264 quoted in Waite (I/1), p. 209.

241. *Ibid.,* p. 242, quoting E. J. Gumbel, *Verschwörer: Beiträge zur Geschichte und Soziologie der deutschen nationalistischen Geheimbünde seit 1918* (Vienna: 1924), p. 109, and Carsten Curator, *Putsche, Staat und Wir!* (Karlsruhe: 1931), p. 43.

242. Cf. George H. Danton, *Germany Ten Years After* (Boston: Houghton Mifflin, 1928), p. 172, and Werner Richter, *Re-Educating Germany* (Chicago: University of Chicago Press, 1945), pp. 70, 71. See also Fischer-Baling (I/1), pp. 186–187. Golo Mann described the political orientation of the German professor as follows: "The professor, employed by the state for a specific task, acknowledged authority—Luther's *Obrigkeit.* He'd have nothing to do with politics, said once a very notable professor of philosophy in my presence.—But would you not try to help if the house were afire?—No, answered he thoughtfully, if the house were burning, he'd call the fire department. To fight fires, to overcome a political or economic crisis, that was for him a trade that had to be learned. He, the professor, had not learned it, he had learned much more, to philosophize. . . . But if a professor did mix into politics, then it was the most natural thing in the world that in doing so he would represent the interests of the state and support it through historical arguments such as the notion of the German mission of Prussia, if he taught at a Prussian university." *Die deutschen Intellektuellen. Texte und Zeichen,* no. 4 (Berlin and Neuwied: 1955), p. 488, quoted in Schonauer (I/1), p. 165. The effect of the universities as breeding grounds of radical nationalists, or at least as key career channels for Right-wing youth, was statistically demonstrated in a brilliant piece of research in 1950. That survey found that academicians were far more pro-Nazi and anti-Western than the rest of the population and that their nationalism was exceeded only by that of peasants and of veterans with more than six years' service. Pollock (VIII/162), pp. 236–272.

243. Richter (X/242), p. 69.

244. *Ibid.*, pp. 72–75. Cf. Edward Y. Hartshorne, Jr., *The German Universities and National Socialism* (London: Allen & Unwin, 1937), pp. 43–44.

245. Danton (X/242), p. 205.

246. See Bracher (III/7), pp. 146–149. Cf. Eduard Spranger, *Mein Konflikt mit der Hitler-Regierung 1933,* written in 1945 but printed as manuscript in March, 1955. Excerpts in Poliakov and Wulf (V/23), pp. 89–94.

247. Quoted in Hartshorne (X/244), p. 46.

248. *Ibid.*, p. 55. Cf. also the infamous "enlightenment operation" organized by the Deutsche Studentenschaft from April 12 to May 10, 1933, under the motto "Against the un-German spirit." The orientation of the "operation" emerges clearly from the "Twelve Theses of the Studentenschaft," which were given maximum publicity. See *Deutsche Kultur-Wacht,* no. 9 (1933), p. 15, as reproduced in Poliakov and Wulf (V/23), pp. 117–118.

249. *Ibid.*, quoted from *The Times* (London) of April 26, 1933.

250. *Ibid.*

251. Danton, a great Germanophile, adds a highly personal observation. "It was my impression that the faces of the students in the fraternity were by no means those of fine, clear-cut young men. . . . I have seldom seen in a group of university students anywhere a less aristocratic or even a less intellectual group of young men" ([XI/242], p. 234). For a description of the "book burning," see *Neuköllner Tageblatt,* no. 111 (May 12, 1933) as reproduced in Poliakov and Wulf (V/23), pp. 119–122. "At 9:30 p.m.—accompanied by a large crowd—the marching column in which were united large numbers of uniformed students [SA], officers (*Chargierte*) of the corporations, color-wearing students, and nonfraternity students, arrived in front of the Student Union. In Oranienburg Street an additional large crowd had gathered to witness the great march. . . . At 11 o'clock the vanguard of the column, in brown shirt or wearing color . . . arrived at the Opera Square. They marched onto the broad square and threw their torches into the pyre which had been erected in its center. . . . At 11:20 p.m.—accompanied by the exultation of the crowd—the first of more than 20,000 books which are burning today on this pyre as a symbolic act, was thrown into the flames" (*ibid.,* p. 120). Cf. Wulf (III/13), pp. 41–59.

252. Richter (X/242), p. 78.

253. In actual fact, here, as in many other areas of German society, the totalitarian objectives of the Nazi movement far exceeded its actual accomplishments. By 1938, at the latest, the corporations had informally (and illegally) re-established themselves behind the unitarian façade of the National Socialist German Student League. See *Der Convent,* no. 6 (1954), quoted in Grossherr (X/237), p. 450.

254. After completion of this chapter there appeared Lutz E. Finke's hard-hitting indictment *Gestatte mir Hochachtungsschluck: Bundesdeutschlands korporierte Elite* (Hamburg: Rütten & Loening, [c. 1963]). Finke's analysis and judgments agree in general closely with those presented here. The only important divergence consists in Finke's unwillingness to recognize (1)

that the views of the old grads and of the house organs under their editorship do not in every detail reflect the thinking of the active fraternity membership and (2) that the restoration of the reactionary-nationalist corporations has been unable to prevent some changes (though not basic ones) in the operation and outlook of even the most petrified fraternity.

255. At times, candor suggests another reason for the "nonpolitical" attitude of the "corporated" students: "The Burschenschaft cannot as yet tie itself down politically because there does not as yet exist a party as far to the Right as the Burschenschaft wishes it." Quoted in Kurt Hirsch, "Studentenverbindungen und ihre politische Bedeutung," *Textil-Bekleidung,* Organ der Gwerkschaft Textil Bekleidung (Düsseldorf), no. 10 (May 15, 1957), p. 3. As Habermas *et al.* have not related their findings to the special category of "corporated" students, it is impossible to say to what extent and in what specific way the "nonpolitical" attitudes which we find so characteristic of the "political thought" of the fraternities are related to Habermas' nonpolitical type which represents 13 per cent of the student body, or rather with the disposition of the "irrationally dissociated" type (Habermas [X/33], pp. 75–98). It is, of course, perfectly clear that the "nonpolitical" pathos affected by the present-day corporation is a direct offspring of that "unpolitical" stance which the young Thomas Mann celebrated (in his *Betrachtungen eines Unpolitischen*) and which, since the days of Nietzsche and Stefan George, has reflected the total surrender of the upper bourgeoisie to the pan-Germanist authoritarianism of the late nineteenth and early twentieth centuries.

256. *Burschenschaftliche Blätter,* no. 6 (June, 1954), quoted in Grossherr (X/237), p. 446. The rejection of dueling was merely tactical, a condition to be endured only as long as the almost unanimous opposition of the rectors persisted. In the case of the Burschenschaft the so-called "rejection" of dueling was coupled in its official journal with a sentiment such as this: "Consequently, all attempts to extirpate the duel in European countries are senseless and vain; because it is the most uninhibited expression of the Western moral sense." *Burschenschaftliche Blätter,* LXVII, 8/9 (August–September, 1952), 292. On the "traditional concept" of Burschenschaft "honor," see Fritz Gruenagel, "Vom Schwund des Ehrbegriffes," *ibid.,* pp. 266–273. According to Gruenagel the "honor of the individual is threatened with being oppressed by the stupidity of the masses," a result of the "infection" of "collectivist thinking" which is a degenerative process originating possibly in Asia! Gruenagel sees the chief disease carrier in the labor union!

257. *CC-Blätter,* no. 7 (1952), quoted in Grossherr (X/237), p. 446.

258. Erich Kitzing, "Um die Studentin," *Burschenschaftliche Blätter,* LXVII, 7 (July, 1952), 232.

259. *CC-Blätter,* no. 2 (1952), quoted in Grossherr (X/237), p. 446.

260. Kitzing (X/258), p. 232.

261. Heinz Amberger, "Wir und Europa," *Burschenschaftliche Blätter,* LXVII, 6 (June, 1952), 173. Cf. also "Der 'Westen' und die deutsche Freiheit," *ibid.,* LXVII, 8/9 (August–September, 1952), 291.

262. Amberger (X/261), p. 175.

263. The reactivation of folkish concerns was decided in the Deutsche

Burschenschaft as early as the Burschentag of 1952. See *Burschenschaftliche Blätter,* LXVII, 6 (June, 1952), 198, and 7 (July, 1952), 224, 226, 236.

264. *Burschenschaftliche Blätter,* no. 2 (1955), quoted in Grossherr (X/237), p. 452.

265. From a speech of Dr. Wirth, the guest speaker at the original Hambach meeting on May 27, 1832, approvingly quoted (with emphasis) in "Der 'Westen' und die deutsche Freiheit" (X/261), p. 291.

266. *CC-Blätter,* no. 2 (1953–54), quoted in Grossherr (X/237), p. 446.

267. *Burschenschaftliche Blätter,* no. 8 (1953), quoted in Hirsch (X/255), p. 3. Cf. also Grossherr (X/237), p. 455.

268. *Burschenschaftliche Blätter,* no. 8 (1953), quoted *ibid.,* p. 447.

269. *Burschenschaftliche Blätter,* no. 3 (1955), quoted *ibid.*

270. *CC-Blätter,* no. 5 (1954), quoted *ibid.*

271. Quoted from the *Burschenschaftliche Blätter* in Hirsch (X/255), p. 3.

272. *Burschenschaftliche Blätter,* no. 9 (1954), quoted in Grossherr (X/237), p. 447.

273. *Burschenschaftliche Blätter,* no. 1 (1953), quoted *ibid.,* p. 451.

274. *Burschenschaftliche Blätter,* no. 2 (1955), quoted *ibid.,* p. 452.

275. *Burschenschaftliche Blätter,* quoted in Hirsch (X/255), p. 3.

276. See, for instance, Hohlbaum's "Deutsche Burschenschaft von Heute," in which contempt for the democratic, industrialized society is coupled with romantic longing for the "German spirit of yore."

> Alas, in the whirr of the machines
> We are merely restless cogs,
> Burden-suffering worker bees,
> Bent low by yoke on the path of life.
> Happiness of the herd and misery of the herd
> Cut down to size the largest soul;
> We may nevermore be the active hammer,
> But must evermore remain the anvil. . . .
>
> . . . .
>
> Night of dreamers, night of the fathers,
> Which points to the old sky,
> Look, we too are again worshippers
> Of the German spirit of yore!

—*Burschenschaftliche Blätter,* LXVII, 5 (May, 1952), 129–131.

277. Cf. H. Schlömer, "Denkt die Burschenschaft noch völkisch?" *Civis,* II, 14 (1956), 128–129.

278. Cf. Erich Weniger, "Das Korporationswesen als soziologisches Problem," *Die Sammlung,* VII, 2 (February, 1952), 125–131.

279. See Eric A. Peschler, "Studentische Verbindungen Anno 1951," *Die Neue Zeitung* (Munich), VII, 189 (August 14, 1951), 6; 190 (August 15, 1951), 8; and 195 (August 21, 1951), 6.

280. Cf. Clara Menck, "Neue Burschenherrlichkeit? Die westdeutsche

Nachkriegsuniversität und ihre Hörer," *Wort und Wahrheit,* IX, 2 (February, 1954), 117–125.

281. At the University of Frankfurt, roughly 80 per cent of the student body come from families of high- or middle-range officials, free professionals, and the self-employed. Only approximately 5 per cent come from working-class families, and 1 to 2 per cent from farm families. Habermas (X/33), p. 288.

282. Defenders of color-wearing fraternities have consistently maintained that the postwar corporations—in contradistinction to their predecessors—were not class institutions. Of the membership in 1953, it was claimed that 60 per cent had to hold part-time jobs to eke out inadequate allowances. See, for example, Wilhelm Lütkemann, chairman of the alumni of the nondueling corporation Wingolfbund, "Wiedergewinnung der Solidarität," *Deutsche Universitäts-Zeitung,* VIII, 22 (November, 1953), 10.

283. *Deutsche Korpszeitung,* quoted in Hirsch (X/255).

284. *Burschenschaftliche Blätter,* no. 9 (1955), quoted in Grossherr (X/237), p. 454.

285. *Burschenschaftliche Blätter,* no. 5 (1954), quoted *ibid.*

286. *Akademische Monatsblätter—Zeitschrift des Kartellverbandes der katholischen deutschen Studentenvereine,* no. 1 (1954), quoted *ibid.*

287. *CC-Blätter,* no. 1/2 (1955), quoted *ibid.*, p. 455.

288. "Entscheidung im Bonner Farbenstreit," *Burschenschaftliche Blätter,* LXVII, 5 (May, 1952), 169.

289. This is not to deny the essential correctness of Habermas' observation ([X/33], pp. 165–166) that the old, traditional, academic bourgeoisie, the intelligentsia of lawyers, physicians, teachers, professors, and high officials, has been after 1945 unable either to maintain itself as a clearly defined social estate or to retain in *unmodified* form its class (or stratum) consciousness. Its former proud self-assurance has become mixed with certain defensive affects in the face of more rapid social mobility and the consequent changes in the functions of the academic professions and the relative loss of status of the academic bourgeoisie. Indeed, Habermas stipulates the existence of a specific, autochthonous social image which reflects these changes and which he calls "the image of the descending academic middle class." Yet Abendroth (X/225), p. 646, writes: "When the concretely existing stratum of the bearers of that unity of bench, bar, bureaucracy, and higher education (whose tradition originated in the monarchist *Obrigkeitsstaat* and, because of its enmity against Weimar and its adaptation to the Third Reich, has remained fundamentally unchanged) negotiates with the holders of economic power about the latter's—frequently diverging—special interests, [that stratum] thinks of itself as representing the General Interest, thus fulfilling the obligation which its position in the state imposes on it: However, this General Interest is only a sham. In reality [that stratum defends] a restorative scheme (*Ordnungsbild*) for the maintenance of social privileges which is directed against the democratization of society and against the extension of the principle of equality to the members of society." For the

remarkable social continuity in the formation of these elites, see Ossip K. Flechtheim, "Parteien und Organisationen in der Bundesrepublik," *Gewerkschaftliche Monatshefte,* VIII, 5 (May, 1957), 263. Cf. John H. Herz, "German Officialdom Revisited," *World Politics,* VII, 1 (October, 1954), 63–83. See also Herz's "Political Views of the West German Civil Service," in Hans Speier and W. Phillips Davison, eds., *West German Leadership and Foreign Policy* (Evanston, Ill.: Row, Peterson, [1957]), pp. 96–135; Kurt Nemitz, "Das Regime der Mitläufer; Soziologische Notizen zur Renazifizierung," *Die Neue Gesellschaft,* II, 3 (May–June, 1955), 39–45; and Edinger (II/9).

290. In 1961, fully 16 per cent (or 81 men) of the members of the German Bundestag were corporation alumni, or over half of all deputies who had a university degree.

291. *New York Times,* May 7, 1961, p. 24, col. 1.

292. "Korporationsverbände werden erstmals aus dem Bundesjugendplan gefördert," *Informationen aus der Studentenschaft,* no. 2 (February, 1961), pp. 4–5.

293. For much of the following, see the investigations of Walter Gong reported in "Couleurstudenten 1961," in *Die Zeit* (Hamburg), no. 22 (June 2, 1961), p. 7; no. 23 (June 8, 1961), p. 6; and no. 24 (June 16, 1961), p. 8.

294. See "Schmisse und Farben," *Junge Stimme,* no. 15 (1960), p. 5.

295. In Habermas' investigation of the present-day university student's social perspective, parts of this elite orientation to intellectual pursuits and the class which embodies them appear in two quite specific clusters of attitudes and social perceptions which Habermas denotes respectively as "the social image of spiritual values (*innere Werte*)" and "the social image of an intellectual elite" ([X/33], pp. 171–186). The former is evident in 10 per cent of the student body, and the latter, in 23 per cent. "The social image of an intellectual elite" was found to be the single most widely held conception among students.

296. Quoted in Danton (X/242), pp. 220–221.

297. *Ibid.,* p. 221.

298. Weniger suggests that the fraternities of the postwar period have, if anything, increased in importance as employment channels. This, he argues, is largely due to the fact that the postwar universities have opened their doors (to a greater extent than ever before) to students of merely average intelligence who could not make their way without "pull." (X/278), pp. 129–130.

299. Gong (X/293), no. 23, p. 6.

300. On the early postwar student's financial situation, see Rudolf Herlt, "Wer finanziert das Studium?" *Deutsche Universitäts-Zeitung,* VII, 13 (July 4, 1952), 14–16.

301. This is well brought out in "Die studentischen Korporationen," *Feinde der Demokratie* (Lower Saxony), III, 4 (January, 1954).

302. As we have noticed above, X/227, the postwar German rate of social mobility as reflected in university attendance by working class people is not high. Still, to members of the traditional elites the threat to their

monopoly position from previously unqualified classes appears very great indeed.

303. In this connection a word or two about the changed pattern of fraternity recruitment is important. Contrary to the "rushing" practices in pre-Nazi days, little, if any, recruiting is nowadays done by the actives themselves. That lies now almost exclusively in the hands of the "old grads." In many instances the pledge prospect has actually no choice at all. His father may be an old, faithful Corps alumnus or Burschenschafter, and as long as the son can remember, it was simply assumed that he would go to a university and would join his father's fraternity. In many other cases, where the father is dead, or possibly had not belonged to a corporation when he was at college, the freshman arrives with a recommendation from some fraternity alumnus (not infrequently, a respected high-school teacher) who has judged the young man to be appropriate corporation material and has been able to persuade him of the value of membership. For the relationship between academic background and nationalist and Right-extremist sentiments, see above, X/242. After the completion of this chapter this author found a very similar analysis in Hans Heinz Holz' excellent—if somewhat exaggerated—"Die verschleierte Klassengesellschaft," in Horst Krüger, ed., *Was ist heute links? Thesen und Theorien zu einer politischen Position* (Munich: List, [c. 1963]), pp. 69–84, esp. pp. 72–74.

304. Indeed, among the German student body as a whole, no more than 10 per cent appear to orient themselves by social conceptions which reflect, without major modifications, nineteenth- and early twentieth-century ideological positions. Habermas divides these "autochthonous" ideological models into an "upper class model" (4 per cent), a "lower class model" (1 per cent), and a "model of the descending academic middle class" (5 per cent). See Habermas (X/33), pp. 160–171. At the same time it would be unrealistic to anticipate that "adjusted" behavior, and even "adjusted" belief systems, would be maintained under radically changed circumstances. Political reliability is not likely to result from more or less opportunistic "adaptation" or "adjustment."

305. For details of the struggle between corporations and university administration in regard to the prohibition of dueling, see Volker R. Berghahn, "Die Entwicklung der Mensur im Nachkriegsdeutschland," *Deutsche Universitäts-Zeitung,* XIX, 1 (January, 1964), 12–18. For a defense of dueling, see the lengthy interview with the chairman of an interfraternity committee at the Institute of Technology in Darmstadt, "Von Mensuren hört man nichts," *Der Spiegel,* XI, 32 (August 7, 1957), 22–29. More recently, university administrators have authorized lecturers at Heidelberg University to exclude from their classrooms students with bandaged facial gashes, if they can clearly prove that the wound had been received in a duel. See "Heidelberg Sets Truce on Dueling," *New York Times,* December 7, 1961, p. 34, col. 3.

306. Amusingly enough, there existed for a while a possibility that dueling, that "ultimate test of manhood" which neither Allied prohibition nor the ukase of august university rectors could stop, might be consigned to

oblivion by nothing more romantic than a decision of the German health insurance companies that they will not pay for the treatment of dueling gashes. (See "German Insurers Bar Duel Claims," *New York Times,* May 7, 1961, p. 24, col. 1.) Continued and rising practice of fraternity dueling since 1961 has indicated, however, that the threat of the health insurance companies was not effective in discouraging bloodletting.

307. This should, of course, not be taken to mean that the political literacy and realism of the "average" fraternity man is very high. In fact, both his political interest and sophistication are on the whole dangerously low. To the extent that corporated students tend to exhibit authoritarian political potential, it is very likely that "irrationally dissociated" disposition types, to use Habermas' categories, are represented in color-wearing fraternities in considerably greater numbers than in the student body as a whole, where they account for 11 per cent. A characteristic feature of that type is that he will conceal his political antipathies against the prevailing state of affairs behind an elaborate façade of political apathy.

308. See above, X/33–35 and nearby text; X/226, 228, 255, 281, 289.

309. The research design called for an open-ended, extensive interview of 171 students (which was administered in the summer semester of 1957) and a supplementary questionnaire interview of 550 students (which took place in February and March, 1959) for control purposes. See Habermas (X/33), Annex II, pp. 279–315. A question concerning fraternity membership occurred only in the supplementary interview and was not discussed in the published research report.

310. Cf. Karl Martin Bolte, *Sozialer Aufstieg und Abstieg. Eine Untersuchung über Berufsprestige und Berufsmobilität* (Stuttgart: Enke, 1959), pp. 171–202, 205. Janowitz (X/227), p. 21, comes to the conclusion that "university education represents for the sons of manual laborers no realistic possibility." "As the chance to be educated is very class-bound, the preconditions in Germany for mobility based on personal achievement . . . are not yet fulfilled" (p. 22).

311. Habermas (X/33), Table 23, p. 235.

312. The following account, with minor exceptions, is based on the work of Volker R. Berghahn. I am most grateful to Mr. Berghahn for his generous permission to use his material. It goes without saying that for the selection of the material and the emphases of interpretation, the present writer bears exclusive responsibility. After completion of this chapter, Berghahn's study was published as "Right Wing Radicalism in West Germany's Younger Generation," *Journal of Central European Affairs,* XXII, 3 (October, 1962), 317-336.

313. This 1956 group must not be confused with a National Student League which formed itself at Munich and whose request for a license was rejected by the University of Munich as early as 1954. See "aus dem hohlen bauch geholt," *Colloquium,* XI, 6 (June, 1957).

314. See below, Chapter XII, Section B/I.

315. See "Polemik um 'nationale Studenten,'" [Club republikanischer Publizisten,] *CrP-Information,* March, 1957, p. 28.

316. *Satzung des Bundes Nationaler Studenten* (BNS), Preamble.

317. BNS leaflet, n.d.

318. "Polemik um 'nationale Studenten," (X/315).

319. Cf. above, VII/210 and nearby text; and below, XI/156–173 and XI/86–95 and nearby text.

320. See above, IX/136 and nearby text.

321. See above, III/56 and nearby text; IV/18; and below, XIV/76, and XVII/75 and nearby text.

322. See above, X/156; X/165 and nearby text.

323. See above, X/173.

324. Through its association in the KNJ, the BNS also participated in the international youth meetings organized by the radical-nationalist groups of Austria.

325. See below, Chapter XII, Section B/II.

326. *Student im Volk,* no. 3 (February, 1959), p. 2.

327. See above, X/173.

328. In 1963 the paper was said to have had a circulation of 12,000, and by the beginning of 1965, over 20,000.

329. See below, XI/539–551.

330. Thus the DSA reprinted Herbert Cysarz' programmatic speech at the GfP's annual meeting of 1962. Cf. below, text at XII/151–153.

331. More recently the *DSA* has been published, on a bimonthly basis, by Peter Dehoust of Schwetzingen. It now boasts five local editions in Marburg, Giessen, Hanover, Hamburg, and Kiel. (*Bulletin on German Questions* [London], XVIII, 407/408 [June, 1966], 12.)

332. In July, 1963, six political university groups founded a so-called Free Democratic Student League (Freier Demokratischer Studentenbund, FDS), which was meant as an extreme Right opposition group to the clearly Left–liberal Liberal Student League of Germany (Liberaler Studentenbund Deutschlands, LSD) of the FDP. Among the FDS's founders were former members of the BNS, and the founding itself was given benevolent publicity in the *Deutscher Studenten–Anzeiger.* ("Suchende Söhne," *Der Spiegel,* XVII, 29 [July 17, 1963], 30–31.) In December, 1963, the FDS changed its name to Free–German Student League (Freiheitlich–Deutscher Studentenbund).

Chapter XI: The Ideas and Literature of Nationalism (I)

1. In the course of a discussion in February, 1953, in which participated Peter Kleist, a former high Nazi official, and his publisher, Kurt Vowinckel, and which canvassed the political possibilities open to the National Opposition to prevent the acceptance in Germany of the EDC treaty, Kleist and Vowinckel agreed that the National Opposition no longer had such a possibility. Instead, they argued, nationalists "through the distribution of books, newspapers, journals, etc. must enlighten the German people about the

advantages of National Socialism in order that they may recognize that the Nazis could not have been as bad as they are today generally depicted. That has to be constantly drummed into their heads." From a confidential report of the discussion of February 11, 1953, at Heidelberg.

2. On the political and social thought of the Conservative Revolution and on its relationship to Nazism, see Sontheimer (I/1).

3. Another difficulty in using the ideological platform of Christian conservative nationalism as a springboard from which to launch a postwar opposition movement was its proximity in most respects to the ideological position of the non- and antinationalist, universalist, Catholic conservatives whose theoretical models derive partly from the romanticism of Hardenberg-Novalis' *sacrum imperium,* partly from the pan-German federalism of Konstantin Frantz, partly from the Catholic social thought of Pope Pius XI, and from the political philosophy of the nineteenth-century Spanish thinker Juan Donoso Cortés.

4. Such works of the National Opposition as do pretend to serious analysis are either historical in approach or philosophical. A good example of the latter genre is Edmund Marhefka's *Die Herren dieser Welt und das Problem der Macht* (Berlin: Maximilian, 1962), which a friendly reviewer compared to Montesquieu's *L'Esprit des Lois!* Marhefka's political theory sees family, society, nation, and state as "energieverbundene Spannungsbereiche" whose requisites for maintenance are "by nature" identical with those of physical atoms! See *Studien von Zeitfragen, Presse- und Buchspiegel,* no. 8–9 (September 29, 1962), p. 9.

5. The absence after World War II of the chiliastic visions of earlier generations of Romantics who dreamed of reconciling ancient contradictions, of solving age-old dilemmas in one supreme moment of millennial fulfillment, is often regretted, even though it also implies the absence of political Messianism and revolutionism. Thus, in the words of Wolfgang Cordan: "Blessed time of our juvenile foolishness: Free *Schulgemeinden,* Wandervogel, the fascination of Communism, nudism, human rights, surrealism—a mad whirl of contradictions, but what a rebellion, what a rebellion! And today? One asks oneself if there is such a thing as youth in a sense other than the purely biological. Where are their programs, where are their ways of life (*Lebensformen*), where their bravado? They don't exist. If they have a passion then it is that of landing as quickly as possible in a 'secure position.' To whom ought one then to address onself? And when all governments are again staffed with people who once before have done everything wrong, when politics is [again] nothing but a muddling through with inappropriate means, then creative persons simply throw up the sponge (*geht der Atem aus*). The *revenants* govern, youth has slipped into Philistinism or into its negative variation—gangsterism. What is there left to be expressed? Necessarily, therefore, we live in a period of depressionism instead of expressionism." *Klaus Mann zum Gedächtnis,* 1950, p. 28, quoted in Roessler (X/37), p. 261.

6. Hans-Helmuth Knütter, *Ideologien des Rechtsradikalismus im Nachkriegsdeutschland. Eine Studie über die Nachwirkungen des Nationalsozialismus,* Bonner Historische Forschungen, Vol. 19 (Bonn: Röhrscheid, 1961).

A much less comprehensive and insightful attempt at an identification and typology of the ideology of "neo-Nazism" is Enno de Vries, *pseud., Neo-Nazismus in der Bundesrepublik* (Hamburg: 1956). This study is mimeographed. Knütter's work suffers from his relative neglect of the positive, programmatic, political, social, and economic suggestions of the National Opposition. Characteristically, Knütter gives to them roughly ten pages while he discusses in 140 pages the many justifications and apologies of the Hitler regime and its various policies. This unbalance is due to the fact that Knütter devoted himself almost exclusively to the analysis of the more permanent literary products of the extreme Right and largely ignored the avalanche of proclamations, programs, "guide lines," statements of principle, and appeals that the Right-radical groups, parties, working circles, and associations have poured forth in the past twenty years. The lack of balance in Knütter's account is partly due also to his having paid only inadequate attention to the writings of conservative nationalists. Their tradition is richer in symbolic and ideological materials than that of national socialism and has made possible a somewhat more comprehensive ideological reformulation of their ideas.

7. More than two years after the completion of this chapter, an account of nationalist literature appeared in Germany, Heinz Brüdigam's *Der Schoss ist fruchtfar noch . . .* (Frankfurt: Röderberg, [1964]). Unfortunately I have been unable to obtain that book.

8. Jenke (V/85).

9. Hans Friessner, *Verratene Schlachten* (Hamburg: Holsten, [1956]).

10. Guderian (X/95) and (VII/171); and Malte Plettenberg's *Guderian: Hintergründe des deutschen Schicksals von 1918–1945* (Düsseldorf: abz, 1950).

11. Raeder (VIII/176).

12. H. Bernhard Ramcke, *Fallschirmjäger—damals und danach* (Frankfurt: Lorch, 1951).

13. Lothar Rendulic, *Gekämpft, gesiegt, geschlagen* (Wels, Heidelberg: Welsermühl, 1952).

14. Hausser (IX/60).

15. Kesselring (IX/26).

16. Erich von Manstein, *Verlorene Siege,* Vol. II (Bonn: Athenäum, 1955), and *Aus einem Soldatenleben 1887–1939,* Vol. I (Bonn: Athenäum, 1959).

17. Siegfried Westphal, *Heer in Fesseln. Aus den Papieren des Stabschefs von Rommel, Kesselring und Rundstedt* (Bonn: Athenäum, 1950).

18. Nuremberg Document PS-4064, reproduced in Poliakov and Wulf (II/39), pp. 451–453.

19. See *The Wiener Library Bulletin* (London) V, 1–2 (January–March, 1951), 2.

20. The memoirs of the Austrian General Valentin Feurstein, *Irrwege der Pflicht 1938–1945* (Munich, Wels: Welsermühl, 1964), appeared too late to be included in our account.

21. Joachim von Ribbentrop, *Zwischen London und Moskau: Erinnerungen und letzte Aufzeichnungen* (Leoni: Druffel, 1953).

22. Paul Schmidt, *Statist auf diplomatischer Bühne, 1923–1945* (Bonn: Athenäum, 1949).

23. Von Ribbentrop (XI/21), p. 50.

24. Konstantin Hierl, *Gedanken hinter Stacheldraht* (1953) and *Im Dienst für Deutschland, 1918–1945* (1954) both published in Heidelberg, Kurt Vowinckel Verlag.

25. Wilfred von Oven, *Mit Goebbels bis zum Ende* (2 vols.; Buenos Aires: Dürer, 1949).

26. Alfred Rosenberg, *Letzte Aufzeichnungen. Ideale und Idole der nationalsozialistischen Revolution* (Göttingen: Plesse, 1955).

27. Prinz Friedrich Christian zu Schaumburg-Lippe, *Zwischen Krone und Kerker* (Wiesbaden: Limes, 1952).

28. Karl Wahl, *". . . es ist das deutsche Herz." Erlebnisse und Erkenntnisse eines ehemaligen Gauleiters* (Augsburg: Wahl, 1954).

29. Hermann Schild, ed., *Mit offenem Visier. Aus den Lebenserinnerungen eines deutschen Rechtsanwalts, Professor Dr. Friedrich Grimm* (Leoni: Druffel, [1961]).

30. Hanna Reitsch, *Fliegen—mein Leben* (Stuttgart: Deutsche Verlags–Anstalt, [1951]).

31. Hans-Ulrich Rudel, *Trotzdem,* preface by the author's parents (Waiblingen/Württemberg: Leberecht, [pref. September, 1950]); *Aus Krieg und Frieden. Aus den Jahren 1945–1952* (Göttingen: Plesse, 1953); *Zwischen Deutschland und Argentinien* (VI/204); *Von den Stukas zu den Anden. Am höchsten Vulkan der Erde* (Leoni: Druffel, 1956).

32. Otto Strasser, *Hitler und Ich* (Konstanz: Asmus, 1948); *Dr. Otto Strasser, der unbeugsame Kämpfer für ein freies Deutschland* (Frankfurt: n.p., 1955); and *Exil* (IV/108).

33. Ilse Hess, *Gefangener des Friedens: Neue Briefe aus Spandau, 1952–1955* (Leoni: Druffel, 1956).

34. Hans Werner Richter, "Strafanzeige . . . warum?" *Die Kultur* (Munich), May, 1956, p. 5. See the mimeographed announcement of the Druffel Verlag, "Warum die Hess Briefe und die Ribbentrop-Memoiren beschlagnahmt wurden"; *Parlamentarisch–Politischer Pressedienst* (ppp) 69/57 (June 26, 1957); "Bücher von Rudolf Hess bleiben beschlagnahmt," *Die Welt* (Hamburg), May 4, 1957; Wilhelm Maschner, " 'Alter Feind, was nun?' " *ibid.,* May 7, 1957; "Verleumdungsaktion des 'Grünwalder Kreises' gescheitert," *Reichsruf* (Hanover), VI, 19 (May 11, 1957); *Feinde der Demokratie* (Lower Saxony), VI, 5–6 (April–May, 1957), 42–43; *Deutscher Informationsdienst,* no. 709 (December 13, 1957); and *Druffel-Mitteilungen* (Autumn, 1956), pp. 1–3.

35. The "democratic" component of National Socialism was an important element of Nazi ideology. In the words of a Nazi ideologist, "German and parliamentary democracy differ (1) [because] in German democracy the best and bravest always leads, [while] in parliamentary democracy a majority governs which necessarily (*von Natur aus*) rejects every great leadership personality; (2) in German democracy authority dominates those below and accountability [is owed] to those above. Every leader can be held

responsible. In parliamentary democracy no responsibility exists because of the immunity and anonymity of the parliamentarians." Griesmayr, *Unser Glaube* (V/39). Cf. Erwin Noack and G. A. Walz, *Deutsche Demokratie* (Berlin: Deutscher Rechtsverlag, 1938).

36. See below, XII/26.

37. Quoted in *The Wiener Library Bulletin* (London) VII, 1–2 (January–April, 1953), 2.

38. *Frankfurter Rundschau,* August 26, 1957. In the summer of 1963 the prince switched over to Haussleiter's German Community (DG). At that time began also a serialization of a new book by Friedrich Christian in the pages of the extreme-Rightist *German National News.* The book, entitled *Dr. G. Ein Porträt des Propagandaministers,* was simultaneously published by the Limes Verlag of Wiesbaden. In an interview with the editor of the *German National News,* Prince zu Schaumburg insisted that for him "the past is irretrievably ended" and that he could not have written the new book if he "still felt [himself] bound by [his] former obligations toward the national socialist revolution." At the same time he pointed out that he would never "disavow" (*leugnen*) the "national socialist idea." (*Studien von Zeitfragen, Analysen, Berichte, Informationen zum nationalen Nonkonformismus,* X, 2 [August 15, 1963], 7.) The prince's new book came to my attention too late to be considered here.

39. Schild (XI/29), p. 123.

40. *Das Deutsche Führerlexikon 1934/1935* (Berlin: Stollberg, [c. 1934]), Part II, p. 30.

41. Schild (XI/29), pp. 123, 242.

42. In the present category belong also the memoirs of the nationalist playwright and Nazi official Sigmund Graff, who presents his former activities in the Stahlhelm and, later, in the Nazi machinery for the control of theatrical art as inadvertent manifestations of a profoundly nonpolitical personality. Entitled *Von S.M. zu N.S. Erinnerungen eines Bühnenautors (1900 bis 1945)* (Munich, Wels: Welsermühl, [c. 1963]), Graff's memoirs unfortunately came to my attention too late to receive more than a scanning.

43. August Kubizek, *Adolf Hitler, mein Jugendfreund* (Graz: Stocker, 1953).

44. Erich Kempka, *Ich habe Hitler verbrannt* (Munich: Kyrburg, [1950]). According to the *New York Times* of February 22, 1964, Soviet Marshal Chuikov, in an autobiographical essay, contradicts Kempka's story and maintains that his soldiers found Hitler's still smoldering body wrapped in a blanket on May 2, 1945, two days after the presumed double suicide and the burning of the corpses and disposal of the ashes, as described by Kempka and others.

45. Hans Baur, *Ich flog Mächtige der Erde* (Kempten im Allgäu: Pröpster, 1956).

46. Annelies von Ribbentrop, *"Verschwörung gegen den Frieden." Studien zur Vorgeschichte des zweiten Weltkrieges* (Leoni: Druffel, 1962).

47. Henriette von Schirach, *Der Preis der Herrlichkeit,* with a preface by Hans Carossa (Wiesbaden: Limes, 1956).

48. G. W. Opitz, "Zwischen Skepsis und Hoffnung," *Studien von Zeitfragen, Presse- und Buchspiegel,* X, 1 (January 31, 1963), 2.

49. This view has recently obtained additional support in the work of Keith Eubank, *Munich* (Norman, Okla.: University of Oklahoma Press, [1963]).

50. For the "Grossraum" policy of Nazi Germany and its relation to a German "Monroe Doctrine," see Lothar Gruchmann, *Nationalsozialistische Grossraumordnung: Die Konstruktion einer "deutschen Monroe-Doktrin"* (Stuttgart: Deutsche Verlags–Anstalt, 1962).

51. Gerda-Luise Dietl and Kurt Herrmann, eds., *General [Eduard] Dietl: Das Leben eines Soldaten,* rev. by Max Dingler (Munich: Münchner Buchverlag, [1951]).

52. Rudolf Nowotny, ed. *Walter Nowotny: "Tiger vom Wolchowstroj" —"Fliegerwunder aus Österreich." Berichte aus dem Leben meines Bruders* (Leoni: Druffel, 1957).

53. W. von Asenbach, *pseud., Adolf Hitler, sein Kampf gegen die Minusseele. Eine politisch-philosophische Studie aus der Alltagsperspektive* (Buenos Aires: Editorial Prometheus, n.d.).

54. *Ibid.,* p. 14.

55. *Ibid.,* pp. 19–20.

56. *Ibid.,* p. 27.

57. *Ibid.,* p. 44.

58. *Ibid.,* p. 49.

59. *Ibid.,* pp. 184–185. Another Hitler biography by Hans Severus Ziegler, entitled *Adolf Hitler aus dem Erleben dargestellt* (Göttingen: Schütz, 1964), appeared too late to be included here. Ziegler, one of the key Nazi "cultural managers," was the co-organizer of the notorious propaganda exhibit "Corrupt Music" and one of the most vicious anti-Semitic apologists for suppression, censorship, inquisition, and boycott in the cultural areas. Arguing that "National Socialism makes a claim to totality in *all* fields of German life and will never relinquish it," Ziegler warned that "he who thinks that the superindividualism of the liberal past which has been eliminated from every aspect of the people's life, may persist in the fields of art, has no notion of the task and scope of National Socialism. He who thinks that politics has nothing to do with art . . . has no idea of National Socialism" (*Entartete Musik. Eine Abrechnung* [Düsseldorf: Völkischer Verlag, n.d.], pp. 3, 5). His exhibit "Corrupt Music" Ziegler called "a replica of a real Witches' Sabbath and of the most frivolous intellectual-artistic cultural Bolshevism, a representation of the triumph of subhumanity, of arrogant Jewish insolence, and of complete mental cretinization" (*ibid.,* p. 16). These epithets he applied to the person and works of Arnold Schönberg, Anton von Webern, Otto Klemperer, Paul Hindemith, Kurt Weill, Leo Fall, Oskar Strauss, and many others. (Cf. also Ziegler's *Praktische Kulturarbeit im Dritten Reich: Anregungen und Richtlinien für die künftige Volkserziehung,* Nationalsozialistische Bibliothek, no. 22 [3d impr. ed.; Munich: Zentralverlag der NSDAP, 1934], in which he calls for ever more repressive laws to cover all human activity from marriage and procreation to publishing

and composing.) As one of the earliest followers of Hitler, Ziegler, close collaborator of Fritz Sauckel and deputy Gauleiter of Thuringia, had been "active [since 1923] without interruption as politician, speaker, organizer, and journalist for the all-folkish cause" and was said to have "vindicated the basic propositions of a folkish culture with clear vision, undeviating firmness, and ever with equal tirelessness" (Fritz Fink, in his introductory panegyric in Ziegler's *Wende und Weg. Kulturpolitische Reden und Aufsätze* [Weimar: Fink, 1937], pp. v–vi). What this "vindication" amounts to appears in all of Ziegler's essays and speeches. Thus he writes: "This Nordic-racially determined Germandom has [such] unheard-of powers of shaping culture and creating art, as no other people in the whole wide world: That is not arrogance, but a . . . scientific fact. The highest scientifically incontrovertible example of this fact is the person of Adolf Hitler himself. . . . Hitler's character is the ideal German character. . . . Hitler's disposition [*Gesinnungen*] is the most ideal German disposition" (*ibid.*, pp. 4–5).

60. Friedrich Lenz, *Der ekle Wurm der deutschen Zwietracht. Politische Probleme rund um den 20. Juli 1944* (2d ed.; Heidelberg: Lenz, [1953]).

61. Lenz, *Zauber um Dr. Schacht* (Heidelberg: Lenz, 1954).

62. Lenz, *Stalingrad, der "verlorene" Sieg* (Heidelberg: Lenz, 1956).

63. Karl Bartz, *Die Tragödie der deutschen Abwehr* (Salzburg: Pilgram, 1955).

64. *Ibid.*, p. 9.

65. "I have limited myself to the illumination and interpretation of historical facts, without prejudice, committed only to Ranke's injunction to represent the course of history as it actually was" (p. 7) and "I have done everything . . . to come as close to truth as possible, to find it, and not to mitigate it through any partisanship" (p. 8).

66. Canaris, the traitor, is also the subject of a pamphlet, *Canaris zwischen den Fronten* by Heinz Kiel (Bremerhaven: Hermann, 1950). For an excellent brief account of Canaris and the extent of anti-Hitler activity in the Office of Intelligence, see Gert Buchheit, *Soldatentum und Rebellion: Die Tragödie der deutschen Wehrmacht* (Rastatt: Grote, 1961), pp. 222–260. Buchheit is most anxious to reject as a groundless and vicious defamation the legend that Canaris ever betrayed his country (*Landesverrat*) (pp. 234–235, 254).

67. A circle of former security officers and friends of Admiral Canaris (under Colonel [ret.] Behrens) determined to investigate Bartz's allegations in conjunction with the researches of the Munich Institute for Contemporary History under Helmut Krausnick. The latter declared that never had the high demands of impartial scholarship been appealed to with less justification than in Bartz's book. To Krausnick the "decisive objection to this book remains the fact that it totally ignores the historical background, against which the tragedy of the Counter-Intelligence Office and of the truly national and deeply moral German officer unfolded." *Deutscher Informationsdienst*, no. 575 (September 14, 1956), p. 4. See also *ibid.*, no. 611 (November 27, 1956), and *SPD Pressedienst* P/XI/96 (April 25, 1956), pp. 5–6. For a comprehensive critique of Bartz's book see "Vorgeschichte, Aufstieg, und

Ende des deutschen militärischen Geheimen Melde-, Sabotage-, und Abwehrdienstes der Abwehrabteilung, später Amt Ausland/Abwehr im OKW" by Will Grosse (manuscript), important excerpts of which appear in Buchheit (XI/66), pp. 481–483.

68. In this connection see Erich Kernmayr's latest book, *Verrat an Deutschland: Spione und Saboteure gegen das eigene Vaterland* (Göttingen: Schütz, 1963). Unfortunately it arrived too late to receive critical assessment here. Kernmayr appears to convict of treason everyone who ever tried to rid Germany of Nazism.

69. Remer (IV/23).

70. Hagen (VIII/50).

71. Hans-Ulrich Rudel, *Dolchstoss oder Legende?* (very likely Buenos Aires: n.p., n.d. [1951?]).

72. *Ibid.*, pp. 41–42.

73. Hugo C. Backhaus, *pseud.* [i.e., Herbert Grabert], *Wehrkraft im Zwiespalt. Zur Psychologie des Besiegten* ([Göttingen:] Göttinger Verlagsanstalt, [c. 1952]).

74. *Ibid.*, p. 88.

75. Niedersächsischer Landtag, Dritte Wahlperiode, *Landtagsdrucksache Nr. 177*, "Bericht des 6. Parlamentarischen Untersuchungsausschusses des Niedersächsischen Landtages, betreffend die Vorgänge, die zur Berufung des Abg. Schlüter zum Niedersächsischen Kultusminister am 26. Mai 1955 führten" (Hanover: February 4, 1956; distributed February 6, 1956), p. 666. In this connection it is depressing, although not surprising, to note that this book received high praise from the press of the bourgeois Right. The *BHE-Ruf* thought it "excellent"; the organ of the Bavarian FDP (*Freie Presse*) compared Grabert with Ortega y Gasset; the newspapers of the North Rhine–Westphalian FDP (Siegfried Zoglmann's *Die Deutsche Zukunft*) and of the Lower Saxon FDP (*Sprachrohr*) called it sober, conscientious, and altogether a cause for rejoicing. Indeed, one of these FDP Land organizations sent sixty copies of the book to the members of its political committee with the remark that it was basic reading for the FDP! (See "Vor einem Verfahren gegen Schlüter," *Reichsruf* [Hanover], VI, 6 [February 9, 1957], 3.)

76. Backhaus (XI/73), p. 69.

77. *Ibid.*, p. 83.

78. *Ibid.*, p. 84.

79. Rudolf Berg, *pseud.* [i.e., Dietrich Klagges], *Angeklagter oder Ankläger?* ([Göttingen:] Göttinger Verlagsanstalt, [1954]).

80. On the political conditions in Brunswick in the crucial years 1930–1933 and on Klagges during those years, see Ernst-August Roloff, *Bürgertum und Nationalsozialismus 1930–1933. Braunschweigs Weg ins Dritte Reich* (Hanover: Literatur und Zeitgeschehen, 1961). Incidentally, Klagges was released from prison after serving a third of his fifteen-year sentence.

81. *Ibid.*, pp. 72–79.

82. Edmund Herbert, *pseud.* [i.e., Edmund Gleede and Mathias Kluchen], *Wir sprechen Hitler frei* (Lüneburg: Arbeitsgemeinschaft 33, [1953]).

83. *Ibid.*, pp. 27–29.
84. *Ibid.*, p. 42.
85. *Ibid.*, p. 43.
86. Helmut L. Sündermann, *Alter Feind—was nun? Wiederbegegnung mit England und Engländern* (Leoni: Druffel, 1956).
87. These friends are members of the Link, a prewar Anglo-German friendship group which busily broadcast Nazi and anti-Semitic propaganda.
88. Hans Buchheim, *Das Dritte Reich: Grundlagen und politische Entwicklung* (Munich: Koesel, 1958).
89. Helmut L. Sündermann, *Das Dritte Reich. Eine Richtigstellung in Umrissen* (Leoni: Druffel, 1959).
90. *Ibid.*, p. 16.
91. *Ibid.*, p. 15.
92. *Ibid.*, p. 25.
93. *Ibid.*, pp. 80 ff.
94. *Ibid.*, pp. 65–67.
95. *Ibid.*, p. 83. For a detailed critique of this book see Heinrich Bodensieck, "Nationalsozialismus in revisionistischer Sicht," *Aus Politik und Zeitgeschichte* (Supplement to *Das Parlament*) B 13/61 (March 29, 1961), pp. 175–180.
96. Julius Lippert, *Lächle . . . und verbirg die Tränen* (Leoni: Druffel, [1955]).
97. Quoted in *Die Kultur* (Munich), May, 1955.
98. Lippert (XI/96), p. 29.
99. *Ibid.*, pp. 220–221.
100. Prinz Friedrich Christian zu Schaumburg-Lippe, *Souveräne Menschen. Kleine Lebensregeln—grossgeschrieben* (Leoni: Druffel, [1954]).
101. Konstantin Hierl, *Schuld oder Schicksal: Studie über Entstehung und Ausgang des zweiten Weltkrieges* (Heidelberg: Vowinckel, 1954).
102. Edwin Hennig, *Zeitgeschichtliche Aufdeckungen. Ein Beitrag zur Erforschung der jüngsten Vergangenheit* (Munich: Türmer, [1964]).
103. Hennig, *Ganzheit und Einzelwesen im Lichte des Entwicklungsgedankens* (Tübingen: Heine, 1935), p. 5.
104. For a description of the aims of the German Faith Movement see Wilhelm Schloz, *Kampf und Ziel der Deutschen Glaubensbewegung,* Durchbruch-Schriftenreihe, no. 1 (Stuttgart: Durchbruch-Verlag Bühler, n.d. [1937]). There Schloz characterizes the Movement as "a radically anti-Christian fighting fellowship with the only goal to become German, German through and through—also in the faith" (p. 12). Cf. below, XII/59.
105. Hennig, *Das naturwissenschaftliche Weltbild der Gegenwart.* Durchbruch-Schriftenreihe, no. 6 (Stuttgart: Durchbruch-Verlag Bühler, [pref. 1937]), pp. 39–40.
106. Bruno Brehm, *Schatten der Macht. Ein Buch vom Gift der Welt* (Graz: Stocker, [1949]).
107. Brehm, *Am Rande des Abgrunds: Von Lenin bis Truman* (Graz: Stocker, [1950]). This book constitutes a greatly expanded version of the fourth part of *Schatten der Macht.* Initially, when a third edition of *Shadow*

of Power became necessary, Brehm thought of expanding it into a two-volume work under its original title. Thus in 1950 the first volume appeared with the subtitle *From the Pharaohs to the Last Czar,* and the second volume was to bring the record of man's cruelty to man up to date under the subtitle *From Lenin to Truman.* When it was published, however, it appeared as an independent work under a new title: *At the Brink of the Abyss. From Lenin to Truman.*

108. The classic use of this technique is demonstrated in Gerhard Ludwig's *Mass Murder in World History* (*Massenmord im Weltgeschehen. Bilanz zweier Jahrtausende* [Stuttgart: Vorwerk, 1951]). Cf. below, text at XI/261.

109. Bruno Brehm, *Das zwölfjährige Reich.* (1) *Der Trommler* (1960), (2) *Der böhmische Gefreite* (1960), (3) *Wehe den Besiegten allen* (1961) (Graz: Stocker [later, Styria], 1960–1961).

110. Edwin Erich Dwinger, *Wenn die Dämme brechen. . . .* (Frankfurt-Überlingen: Dikreiter, 1950).

111. Dwinger, SS Captain and laureate of Nazi literary prizes, whose Weltanschauung his SS supervisors found "firm and immaculate," performed for awhile Himmler's errands in occupied Russia. See Wulf (III/13), pp. 268, 309, 371 ff.

112. Dwinger (XI/110), p. 597.

113. *Ibid.,* p. 605.

114. Joachim Fernau, *Deutschland, Deutschland über alles. . . . Von Arminius bis Adenauer* (Oldenburg: Stalling, 1952).

115. Cf. the primitive history for children by Arthur Ehrhardt (the editor of the Right-extremist *Nation Europa*), *Der Junker und der deutsche Traum: Die Wiedergründung des Reiches durch Otto von Bismarck* (Leoni: Druffel, 1959).

116. Fernau (XI/114), p. 101.

117. Cf. the review of Heinrich Schmidt, "Eine deutsche Geschichte," *Deutsche Universitäts-Zeitung,* VIII, 7 (April 7, 1953), 13.

118. Erich Kern, *pseud.* [i.e., Erich K. Kernmayr], *Von Versailles zu Adolf Hitler: Der schreckliche Frieden in Deutschland* (Göttingen: Schütz, 1961).

119. Helmut Herda, *Die Schuld der Anderen* (Augsburg: Kraft [1953]).

120. Heinrich Härtle, *Kriegsschuldlüge und Friedensvertrag* (Hanover: Reichsruf, 1959).

121. Fritz Hesse, *Das Spiel um Deutschland* (Munich: List, 1953).

122. In 1964 appeared Udo Walendy's *Wahrheit für Deutschland: Die Schuldfrage des zweiten Weltkrieges* (Vlotho/Weser: Volkstum und Zeitgeschichtsforschung, 1964) (*Truth for Germany: The Question of Guilt for the Second World War*). Walendy, a young German historian who received all of his training after the war, published the book himself, under the supervision of the late Hans Grimm's Klosterhaus Verlag. Unfortunately this revisionist work, which claims to be methodologically respectable and accurate, came out too late to be critically considered here. Similarly, Willy Glasebock's *Was Germany Alone Responsible for the Second World War?* (*War Deutschland am 2. Weltkrieg allein schuld?* [Niederpleis/Siegburg:]

Ring, [1963]) came to the author's attention too late to be more closely scrutinized. A preface by Berthold Rubin, a professor of Byzantine History at the University of Cologne and permanent contributor to Gerhard Frey's Right-extremist *German National News—German Soldiers' News* (where Glasebock's book had first appeared in 119 installments) quite properly places this revisionist work in the line of David Hoggan, C. C. Tansill, Harry Elmer Barnes, Freda Utley, Russell Grenfell, F. J. P. Veale, and A. J. P. Taylor. For a review and critique of the book, see *Bulletin on German Questions* (London), XV, 348/349 (January 25, 1964), 19–20. There Glasebock's work is called "only a tame descendant of Hoggan's book. . . . Glasebock is much more scientific, but has uncritically accepted what the nationalists had taught for decades." Cf. also *The Wiener Library Bulletin* (London), XVIII, 2 (April 1964), 16.

123. See Knütter (XI/6), pp. 100–132.

124. Ernst von Salomon, *Der Fragebogen* (Hamburg: Rowohlt, 1951).

125. Erich Kern, *pseud.* [i.e., Erich K. Kernmayr], *Opfergang eines Volkes. Der totale Krieg.* (Göttingen: Schütz, 1962). The third volume of the trilogy, *Germany in the Abyss* (*Deutschland im Abgrund*) (Göttingen: Schütz, [c. 1963]), was published too late to be included in our survey.

126. Robert Ernst, *Rechenschaftsbericht eines Elsässers* (2d ed.; Berlin: Bernard & Graefe, [1954]).

127. Brigitte Pohl, *Fastnacht der Dämonen. Erlebnisse einer Wienerin* (Leoni: Druffel, [1963]).

128. See, for example, *ibid.*, pp. 207–208.

129. *Ibid.*, p. 36.

130. Hans Grimm, *Volk ohne Raum* (Lippoldsberg: Klosterhaus, [1956]).

131. Social imperialism has characterized much of German antiliberal and antidemocratic thought since the founding of the Reich in 1871. It is the necessary consequence of what is known as "German socialism." In violent opposition to Marx's international socialism, national or "German" socialism sees the key to social improvement, not in class war and social revolution, but in the free subordination of the partial, egotistic interests of capital and labor to the higher interests of the *Volksgemeinschaft*. Since a system which gives absolute priority to social harmony and national unity cannot provide internal reforms at the expense of one or the other of the parties to a social conflict, these internal social antagonisms have to be "resolved" by turning them toward a common enemy outside the *Volksgemeinschaft*. For the most brilliant presentation of the thesis of social and racial imperialism as the key to an understanding of the phenomenon of Nazism, see Neumann (VI/14), pp. 98–129, 184–218. The German tradition of social imperialism in its corporatist guise is traced in Ralph H. Bowen's *German Theories of the Corporative State* (New York: Whittlesey House, 1947). A generalized account of social imperialism can be found in Bernard Semmel, *Imperialism and Social Reform: English Social-Imperial Thought 1895–1914* (Cambridge, Mass.: Harvard University Press, 1960), pp. 13–28. Despite the dates in the subtitle of Semmel's book, it includes

an account of the ideological development of the British Fascist leader Sir Oswald Mosley in the nineteen-thirties which presents suggestive parallels to the social-imperialist movement in Germany.

132. Hans Grimm, *Die Erzbischofschrift: Antwort eines Deutschen* (Göttingen: Plesse, 1950). (*Answer of a German: An Open Letter to the Archbishop of Canterbury,* trans. by Lynton Hudson [Dublin: Euphorion, 1952]).

133. Grimm, *Warum—woher—aber wohin? Vor, unter und nach der geschichtlichen Erscheinung Hitler* (Lippoldsberg: Klosterhaus, 1954).

134. Thus, it is typical that a letter to the editor of the *Frankfurter Allgemeine Zeitung* of November 17, 1955, objecting to a previous and negative appreciation of one of Grimm's public lectures, should stress Grimm's exemplary honesty: "He has not been afraid of anything or anybody, and has always only tried to profess courageously and unafraid what he has recognized as true; much to his disadvantage in the Third Reich, as far as I know." Yet Nazi theorists had no great difficulty in demonstrating the congruity between Grimm's and Hitler's ideas in four important areas. See Edgar Kirsch, *Hans Grimm als Wegbereiter nordischer Gedankenschau* (Ph.D. dissertation, University of Leipzig, 1937), p. 49, cited in Wulf (III/13), pp. 294–295.

135. "At the Chicago World's Fair, under the motto 'Seven German World Wonders,' a book will be placed beside the top achievements of German technology: Hans Grimm's gripping novel, *People Without Living Space*. In thus honoring the German book, the German Reich unambiguously manifests its will to promote powerfully the life of the spirit, poetic and artistic creativity." *Die Neue Literatur,* XXXIV, 9 (September, 1933), 544.

136. See the discussion of the literary criticism of Heinz Kindermann, Franz Koch, Hellmuth Langenbucher, Walther Linden, Josef Nadler, Paul Fechter, and others—the "official" literary critics of the Third Reich—in Henry G. Atkins, *German Literature through Nazi Eyes* (London: Methuen, [1941]), especially pp. 84 ff.

137. *Ibid.,* p. 85.

138. Grimm (XI/132), p. 163.

139. *Ibid.,* pp. 86–87. In the early thirties, Grimm, the "conservative reactionary," "reproached National Socialism with favoring proletarians and thus becoming Bolshevik. [In] his 1932 speech [entitled] 'On Bourgeois Honor and Bourgeois Necessity,' [Grimm] turns sharply against the anti-bourgeois attitude of National Socialism which in Grimm's eyes amounts to [embracing] the Bolshevik 'pariah-ideal'." Walther Linden, "Entwicklungsstufen scheidender Bürgerlichkeit. Thomas Mann, Hans Grimm und der neue Heroismus," *Zeitschrift für Deutschkunde,* no. 1 (1933), p. 358, cited in Geissler (I/11), p. 147.

140. Grimm (XI/132), p. 136. At times, Grimm pretends to shed his nationalist neurosis and speaks of "my European creed." To substantiate that, he starts, as always, with his childhood, and for the first time mentions

his mother: "Part of my youth was also the beloved Austrian mother, with her Suabian, Alsatian, warm Viennese blood, and part of it was also the splendid vacations on my grandmother's estate in Austria, in that ancient federal state which one day will be a European model and which was torn asunder by the political aberration of 1918." *Erkenntnisse und Bekenntnisse* (2d ed.; [Göttingen:] Göttinger Verlagsanstalt, [1956]), p. 9. But all this is hypocrisy and dishonesty. The Austrian folkish-nationalist Heinz Brunner relates a conversation in which Grimm said: "I reject Hitler as a person, above all the Austrian in him. . . . In myself, too, I hate the Austrian, the soft, sentimental." Brunner is offended and cleverly toasts Grimm's mother, " 'I beg you to drink to the health of your honored mother who is an Austrian.' The guests looked up, frightened. Mrs. Grimm and her daughter glanced anxiously at the father. . . . Grimm is disarmed in the face of this gambit; he can't find an answer. He cannot speak against his own mother. So he slowly raises his glass. . . . The sound that fills the room is somewhat brittle." Brunner (VII/49), pp. 396–397.

141. Grimm (XI/132). For a brief review of published reactions to Grimm's book, and for a typical assessment of the work by a radical nationalist, see Rudolf Aschenauer, "Hans Grimms 'Antwort eines Deutschen' im Kreuzfeuer der Kritik," *Die andere Seite, Informationsdienst,* no. 7 (November, 1950), pp. 7–8.

142. Grimm (XI/133), pp. 7–8.

143. *Ibid.,* p. 468.

144. *Ibid.,* p. 145.

145. Eric A. Peschler, "Warum—woher—aber wohin?" *Mannheimer Morgen,* no. 292 (December 15, 1954), p. 8.

146. Grimm (XI/133), p. 147.

147. *Ibid.,* p. 161.

148. *Ibid.,* p. 162.

149. *Ibid.,* p. 145.

150. *Ibid.,* p. 198.

151. *Ibid.,* p. 290.

152. *Ibid.*

153. *Ibid.,* p. 198.

154. *Ibid.,* p. 294.

155. *Ibid.,* p. 178. On page 160, Grimm identified the men responsible for causing "disappointments and growing disinclinations" as "an intermediary layer which—though [consisting] in most cases [of] only recent followers—might well have thought of itself as National Socialist, but which had only learned to imitate how one cleared one's throat or spat or pounded one's chest in a National Socialist manner and which exploited the boom of the Leader State with conviction and impertinence."

156. Peter Kleist, *Auch Du warst dabei. Ein Buch des Ägernisses und der Hoffnung* (Heidelberg: Vowinckel, 1952).

157. Kleist, *Zwischen Hitler und Stalin. 1939–1945* (Bonn: Athenäum, 1950).

158. Kleist (XI/156), pp. 10–11.
159. Hans Buchheim, "Zu Kleists 'Auch Du warst dabei,'" *Vierteljahrshefte für Zeitgeschichte,* II, 2 (April, 1954), 181–182.
160. Kleist (XI/157), p. 67, quoted also in Buchheim (XI/159), p. 179.
161. Kleist (XI/156), p. 248.
162. Kleist (XI/157), p. 81, quoted in Buchheim (XI/159), p. 179.
163. Kleist (XI/156), p. 252.
164. *Ibid.,* p. 329.
165. See Albert Wucher, *Eichmanns gab es viele* (Munich, Zurich: Droemersche Verlagsanstalt Th. Knaur Nachf., 1961), pp. 77–88.
166. Kleist (XI/156), p. 327.
167. SS Brigadier General Franz Stahlecker's mobile killing unit alone was able to report proudly, as early as January 31, 1942, that "the goal [of the most complete possible removal of Jews] has . . . been essentially achieved through the execution of 229,052 Jews until now." Wucher (XI/165), p. 87.
168. Kleist (XI/156), p. 231.
169. *Ibid.,* p. 95.
170. *Ibid.,* pp. 353–354.
171. Buchheim (XI/159), p. 191.
172. Confidential report of a discussion between Kleist, his publisher, Kurt Vowinckel, and the free-lance intelligence agent E. A. Schmidt, in Heidelberg, February 11, 1953.
173. *Ibid.*
174. Hugo C. Backhaus, *pseud.* [i.e., Herbert Grabert], *Volk ohne Führung* ([Göttingen:] Göttinger Verlagsanstalt, [1955]).
175. *Ibid.,* p. 16.
176. *Ibid.,* p. 35.
177. *Ibid.,* p. 41.
178. *Ibid.,* pp. 157–168.
179. *Ibid.,* p. 192.
180. *Ibid.,* p. 205.
181. *Ibid.,* pp. 233–234.
182. "Das Ende eines Skandals: Der Bericht des 6. Parlamentarischen Untersuchungsausschusses," *Du und Dein Landtag, Parlamentsberichte der SPD Fraktion im Niedersächsischen Landtag,* no. 22 (February, 1956), p. 29.
183. The court sentenced Grabert to a nine months' suspended jail term and fined his publisher, Schlüter, DM 1,200 in lieu of two months' imprisonment. Moreover, the court impounded the unsold copies of the subversive book and ordered the 3,600 sold copies to be confiscated. The delay in bringing the matter before a court was largely due to the hesitancy of the Lower Saxon diet to suspend the parliamentary immunity of Schlüter, who at that time was an independent deputy. The diet was unable to come to a decision in 1957 and turned the problem over to its Committee for Legal and Constitutional Questions. Rightly jealous of the parliamentarian's

right to immunity from prosecution for all but the most serious charges, the committee was able to return with a report only after long-drawn-out discussions and debate. Finally in April, 1958, a committee report in favor of suspension was passed by the House. (See *Feinde der Demokratie* [Lower Saxony], VII, 6–7 [May–June, 1958], 33–34.) Incidentally, in the course of Schlüter's trial, the defendant was said to have used as a part of his defense the fact that a large order for the book was placed by Minister Oberländer's Ministry for Expellees, Refugees and War-damaged Persons and that another order came in from a Land organization of one of the Lower Saxon governing coalition parties (which meant either DP–CDU or FDP–BHE) with the note, "We would like to use this book for our training meetings (*Schulungstagungen*)"! (See "Vor einem Verfahren gegen Schlüter" [XI/75], p. 3.) Grabert is the man of whom the American historian David L. Hoggan (see below, XI/670–674 and nearby text) has written: "Equally wide of the truth is the assertion that Grabert has published many 'neo-Nazi' books and articles since the Second World War. Quite to the contrary, the theme of Grabert's political writings since the war has been a plea for greater academic and political freedom in Germany, and [a plea that] the Adenauer government develop a more mature, independent, responsible and dignified political program." Letter to the editor of the *American Historical Review,* LXVIII, 3 (April, 1963), 914.

184. Kleist (XI/156), p. 326.

185. *Dokumente zum 2. Weltkrieg: Alliierte Kriegsverbrechen und Verbrechen gegen die Menschlichkeit* (Buenos Aires: Dürer, 1954).

186. Rudolf Aschenauer, *Landsberg: Ein dokumentarischer Bericht von deutscher Seite* (Munich: Arbeitsgemeinschaft für Recht und Wirtschaft, 1951).

187. Aschenauer, *Zur Frage einer Revision der Kriegsverbrecherprozesse* (Nuremberg: [Aschenauer], September 1, 1949).

188. Karl Siegert, *Represalie, Requisition und höherer Befehl: Ein Beitrag zur Rechtfertigung der Kriegsverurteilten* ([Göttingen:] Göttinger Verlagsanstalt, [1953]).

189. This folkish-anti-Semitic law professor wrote in 1937: "Our legal institutions (*Rechtsleben*) are dominated neither by the intellect (*Geist*), the idea, nor by reason (*Vernunft*) in itself. Rather the starting point and at the same time the goal of the law is the blood as indestructible unity of body and spirit, body and soul. Therefore, we reject a one-sided biological conception quite as much as a one-sided psychological one, and profess the unity of racial body and racial soul. . . . The position of the law can be further explicated by considering briefly the incursion of racially alien Jewish thought into our law. For the European spirit and body form an inseparable unity. . . . In contradistinction, the Near Eastern spirit, which is particularly strong in Jewry, seeks to destroy all other values and to become 'pure spirit.' " From A. Schürmann, ed., *Volk- und Hochschule im Umbruch* (Oldenburg: Stalling, 1937), pp. 119–121, quoted in Poliakov und Wulf (V/23), p. 111.

190. Lothar Greil, *Die Wahrheit über Malmédy* (Munich: Schild, 1958).

191. Greil, *Die Lüge von Marzobotto* (Munich: Schild, 1959).

192. Lothar Rendulic, *Glasenbach-Nürnberg-Landsberg. Ein Soldatenschicksal nach dem Krieg* (Graz: Stocker, 1953).

193. Joseph Hiess, *Glasenbach: Buch einer Gefangenschaft* (2d ed.; Wels: Welsermühl, [1956]). This came out in the following year as the fifth volume of Hiess' autobiography (*Der Lebensbogen*) under the title *Wir kamen aus Glasenbach: Buch einer Heimkehr* (Wels, Munich: Welsermühl, [1957]). Hiess, an Austrian folkish fighter, was honored in 1944 by his Nazi friends in the Folk League for Germandom Abroad (VDA) with a *Festschrift* which proclaimed Hiess "prophet and pathbreaker of a greater Germany. Party Comrade Josef (*sic*) Hiess for twenty years in uninterrupted action [*Einsatz*] as speaker and author." *Dienstanweisungen und Mitteilungen des VDA-Gauverbandes Oberdonau,* Sonderbeilage (Linz: [1944]).

194. K. W. Hammerstein, *pseud.* [i.e., Kurt Wentzel], *Landsberg: Henker des Rechts* (Wuppertal: Abendland, 1952).

195. Friedrich Oscar, *Über Galgen wächst kein Gras: Die fragwürdige Kulisse der Kriegsverbrecherprozesse im Spiegel unbekannter Dokumente* (Brunswick: Erasmus, [1950]).

196. Erich Kern, *pseud.* [i.e., Erich K. Kernmayr], *Der Tag des Gerichts* (Munich: Türmer, [1961]).

197. Hildegard Springer, *pseud.* [i.e., Hildegard Fritzsche], ed. *Das Schwert auf der Waage: Hans Fritzsche über Nürnberg* (Heidelberg: Vowinckel, 1953). Fritzsche's response to the accusations of the prosecution at Nuremberg was published in the form of a short book entitled *Es sprach Hans Fritzsche* (Nuremberg: Thiele, [1949]). It had first come out in Switzerland under the title of *Hier spricht Hans Fritzsche* (Zurich: Interverlag, 1948).

198. Hermann Eich, *Die unheimlichen Deutschen* (Düsseldorf: Econ, 1963). (*The Unloved Germans,* trans. by Michael Glenny [New York: Stein and Day, (c. 1965)].)

199. Josef Nowak, *Mensch auf den Acker gesät. Kriegsgefangen in der Heimat* (Hanover: Sponholtz, 1956).

200. Mention might also be made of a more sober book that deals with the same experience; namely, the weeks in the open prisoner-of-war compounds on the Rhine. The accusations are implicit, but all the more effective. The book is Fritz vom Hellweg's *Rheinwiesen 1945* (Wuppertal-Vohwinkel: Huth, 1951).

201. Heinrich Zerkaulen, *Zwischen Nacht und Tag: Erlebnisse aus dem Camp 94* (Munich: Mühlberger, 1951).

202. Helmut Mildenberger, *Heimweh hinter Stacheldraht* (Buenos Aires: Dürer, 1951).

203. From the publisher's blurb.

204. Heribert Schwarzbauer, *Menschen ohne Angesicht* (Graz, Vienna, Stuttgart: Stocker, 1950).

205. Assi Hahn, *Ich spreche die Wahrheit* (Esslingen: Bechtle, 1951).

206. Quoted in Eric A. Peschler, "Der Fall Kurt Ziesel," *Die Andere*

Zeitung (Hamburg), no. 21 (September 29, 1955), p. 6. Ziesel's review article on Euringer had appeared in Giselher Wirsing's *Münchener Neueste Nachrichten,* one of the top Nazi papers. As an enthusiastic soldier in "the battle-fellowship of Adolf Hitler's brown army," Euringer, the "poet," wrote: "National Socialist poetry, above all its [inner structure] (*Gesetz*), cannot be demonstrated by the individual [poet], but rather by National Socialism itself. I do not hesitate to say, that I expect the required poetry above *all* from the Party. The Party is the body of the National Socialist spirit, and in the National Socialist body resides after all the National Socialist spirit which demonstrates its typical poetry. This does not mean that National Socialist poetry has to be 'Party poetry'; after all, for the National Socialist the Party is not 'party,' but the yeast of life. [The Party] is the eternally living (*wirkend*) Germany of this day and age and of its future. It is not only the State of the Third Reich, but [also] the folk in its embodiment, and [the Party] *is* the emerging Reich." "Gibt es nationalsozialistische Dichtung?" *Wille und Macht,* August 15, 1935, pp. 13–14, cited in Wulf (III/13), p. 318.

207. Richard Euringer, *Die Sargbreite Leben: Wir sind Internierte* ([Hamm:] Grote, [c. 1952]).

208. *Ibid.,* p. 260.

209. *Ibid.,* p. 261.

210. Karl Vogel, *M–AA 509: Elf Monate Kommandant eines Internierungslagers* (Memmingen: Vogel, 1951).

211. Edwin Erich Dwinger, *Die Verlorenen Söhne: Eine Odyssee unserer Zeit* (Salzburg: Pilgram, 1956).

212. It is perhaps symptomatic of the German political climate that the reviewer of the conservative weekly *Christ und Welt* (Stuttgart, April 25, 1957) gave credit to Dwinger for "trying to repair the gross injustices inflicted on those on our side who sought to resist Bolshevism."

213. Sigmund Graff, *Goethe vor der Spruchkammer oder Der Herr Geheimrat verteidigt sich* (Göttingen: Plesse, 1951). For Graff's latest book, see above, XI/42.

214. In a letter to the Rector of the University of Munich of October 19, 1944, Koellreutter wrote: "My folkish orientation that emerges from my writings proves that any kind of philo-Semitism has been always alien to me." Quoted in Poliakov and Wulf (V/23), p. 300.

215. Such as *The National Rule of Law State* (*Der nationale Rechtsstaat. Zum Wandel der deutschen Staatsidee,* Recht und Staat in Geschichte und Gegenwart, no. 89 [Tübingen: Mohr (Siebeck), 1932]), *The Meaning and Nature of the National Revolution* (*Vom Sinn und Wesen der nationalen Revolution* [Tübingen: Mohr, 1933]), *The German Leader State* (*Der deutsche Führerstaat* [Tübingen: Mohr, 1934]).

216. See, for example, Koellreutter's criticism of the Nazi jurist Roland Freisler's definition of *Rechtsstaat* as the "organized activation of the concentrated charge of folkish power for the protection of the people's way of life." This cynical bit of verbal legerdemain Koellreutter denounced as "dangerously one-sided" and warned that "if [the nationalist *Rechtsstaat*]

wishes to remain a *Rechtsstaat* it will have to protect carefully the position and independence of the judicial organs. The independence of the judicial position distinguishes the German judge from the Bolshevik judge and is an essential characteristic of the *Rechtsstaat*." (Koellreutter, *Der nationale Rechtsstaat* [XI/215], p. 27.) Not surprisingly, ten years later, it was to be Roland Freisler as much or more than anyone else who replaced even the last remnants of the rule of law by a naked system of judicial terror.

217. Gau Leader's Office, Munich, April 22, 1943, quoted in Poliakov and Wulf (V/23), p. 330.

218. Otto Koellreutter, *Die Entnazifizierung—eine Sünde wider Recht und Ehre* (Landau: Vollmer, [1954]).

219. Koellreutter, *Über Schuld und Aufgabe der geistigen Führungsschicht im deutschen politischen Leben der Gegenwart* ([Göttingen:] Göttinger Verlagsanstalt, [c. 1955]).

220. Koellreutter, *Das Wesen der Spruchkammern und der durch sie durchgeführten Entnazifizierung* ([Göttingen:] Göttinger Verlagsanstalt, [c. 1954]).

221. In 1934 Grimm published *Hitler's German Mission,* in which he wrote: "He who has observed Adolf Hitler from close range, who has stood under the spell of his captivating speech, cannot fail to become aware that this man has a mission, which fills him, in which he believes, in which all his followers believe with a strength that moves mountains. The essential element in this awareness, however, is that the mission which was given to Adolf Hitler, that the historic mission which elevates him above all other members of our race (*Volksgenossen*), is a German mission, a mission which concerns us all, which we cannot escape, whatever view we may individually take of the movement and its goals, a mission which is guided by an enormous ultimate idea to which everything that is small and inconsequential must yield. That idea is one Racial People, one Reich, one Leader; overcoming of German particularism in every form; a German people, the Reich of the Germans; the realization of the centuries-old longing; that is Hitler's German mission." Quoted in Poliakov and Wulf (V/23), p. 53.

222. "The Devil's Advocate," *The Wiener Library Bulletin* (London), VIII, 1–2 (January–April, 1954), 18. After the Second World War, however, Grimm wrote: "It can hardly be prevented that the supporters of the political murderer, if he acted out of conviction, will acknowledge him and will honor his sacrifice, if he has risked his life in the performance of the deed. The acknowledgment of the person of the perpetrator, however, must not mean approval, let alone glorification, of the deed as such, i.e., of the political murder. No state founded on law can permit political murder. In any case, political murder and hero worship are sensitive topics." *Politische Justiz, die Krankheit unserer Zeit* (Bonn: Verlag Bonner Universitäts-druckerei Gebr. Scheur, 1953), p. 111.

223. Grimm had been released as a prisoner of war in July, 1946, but was again arrested in August, 1947, and kept in various internment camps and prisons for sixteen months. See Schild (XI/29), pp. 240–273.

224. Grimm (V/85).

225. Grimm (XI/222). To what extent Grimm speaks *pro domo* and the degree of credence he deserves can be more adequately gauged by reading such works as E. J. Gumbel's *Vom Fememord zur Reichskanzlei* (Heidelberg: Schneider, 1962) and F. S. Grosshut's *Staatsnot, Recht und Gewalt* (Nuremberg: Glock & Lutz, [c. 1962]). Grimm's own accounts often have the ring of pure fantasy.

226. See, for instance, Grimm's report of two conversations with unnamed persons (XI/222), pp. 116, 147–148. In the course of a critique of the finding of the Permanent International Court of Justice in favor of the League of Nations and against the Free State of Danzig for its enactment of retroactive legislation on the Hitler model, Grimm, who represented Danzig's cause, alleges that the Court's Secretary General told him prior to the hearing: "But do you really think you will convince them? After all, this is a political case! Since the recall of Professor Schücking, Germany is no longer represented on the panel of judges. Hence you can count only on Italy and Japan. The others will vote with England and France. You can imagine what the decision will be like." An even more unlikely conversation is related in which his interlocutor is said to be "an important representative of the Opponent's side," who introduced himself to Grimm as a university professor. Grimm was pointing out that he "condemned injustice wherever I encounter it, but especially when our side perpetrates it," but then proceeded to go into great detail about the atrocity mongering which has traditionally accompanied Western warfare against Germany and ended by suggesting that the recent (May, 1945) figures of millions of murders in concentration camps were mere propaganda. "At this point my visitor blurted out: 'I see that I am facing an expert. Now I want to tell you who I am. I am not a university professor. I work at the central office of which you spoke. For months I have been carrying on what you have correctly described as atrocity propaganda—and with it we won total victory.' " When Grimm interrupted with " 'I know, but now you have to stop it,' " the mysterious visitor retorted: " 'No, now we are really starting! We shall continue the horror propaganda, we shall increase it, until no one will be willing to hear a kind word about the Germans, until the sympathy that you might have enjoyed in other countries has been destroyed, and until the Germans themselves will become so confused that they will no longer know what they are doing!' " For a slightly different version of the same incident, see Grimm's posthumous autobiography (Schild [XI/29]), pp. 248–249.

227. Grimm (XI/222), pp. 2–3. In 1961, Herbert Grabert, together with other friends of Friedrich Grimm, published a memorial brochure in his honor entitled *Friedrich Grimm: Ein Leben für das Recht. Tatsachen und Dokumente zur Erinnerung an das Wirken eines grossen Anwalts und Patrioten* (Tübingen: Deutsche Hochschullehrer–Zeitung, 1961).

228. Grimm (XI/222), pp. 140–141.

229. *Ibid.*, p. 98.

230. Grimm, *Generalamnestie als völkerrechtliches Postulat* (Cologne, Opladen: Westdeutscher Verlag, 1951).

231. Grimm, *Nun aber Schluss mit Rache und Vergeltung: Eine ernste*

Betrachtung zehn Jahre nach dem Zusammenbruch ([Göttingen:] Göttinger Verlagsanstalt, [1955]).

232. Herwart Miessner, *Um die Sicherung des Berufsbeamtentum* ([Göttingen:] Göttinger Verlagsanstalt, [1953]).

233. Brehm (XI/107).

234. *Ibid.*, p. 16.

235. *Ibid.*, p. 17.

236. Brehm (XI/106).

237. See, for example, his Chapters 11 ("Lidice"), 12 ("The Greatness of the Jews in Adversity"), and 14 ("KZ Maidanek").

238. For a balanced judgment on the extent and seriousness of the brutalities incident upon the transfer of German populations from the Sudetenland, Poland, and Southeastern Europe, see Schechtman (II/3).

239. Brehm (XI/107), p. 401.

240. *Ibid.*, pp. 403–404.

241. *Ibid.*, p. 375.

242. *Ibid.*, p. 383.

243. *Ibid.*, p. 410.

244. *Ibid.*, pp. 642–643.

245. Reichenberger (VII/49).

246. *Ibid.*, p. 15.

247. *Ibid.*, p. 12.

248. *Ibid.*, p. 19.

249. *Ibid.*, p. 18.

250. In 1955 there appeared a volume of reminiscences which Reichenberger called *Wider Willkür und Machtrausch: Erkenntnisse und Bekenntnisse aus zwei Kontinenten* (Graz: Stocker, 1955) (*Against Arbitrariness and Power Delirium: Insights and Professions of Faith from Two Continents*). Neither the insights nor the professions were new; they merely reinforced impressions imparted by Reichenberger's earlier works. They underline his massive Anglophobia and his deep resentment of the United States. In the course of two postwar trips to Germany, Reichenberger chose large mass meetings to assail American foreign policy, especially as it related to the expellee problem. The United States Department of State thought that "his embittered nationalism served to cause disquiet among the refugees, to awaken irredentist sentiments, and to contribute to radicalism among them": it promptly withdrew Reichenberger's passport. Reichenberger, "Wachet auf und wecket einander!" *Der Weg* (Buenos Aires), VI, 5 (1952), 357. Cf. above, VII/49.

251. Erich Kern, *pseud.* [i.e., Erich K. Kernmayr], *Das andere Lidice: Die Tragödie der Sudetendeutschen* (Wels: Welsermühl, [1950]; [Klagenfurt:] Kaiser, [1950]).

252. Kern, *Stadt ohne Gnade. Ein Roman um Berlin* (Wels: Welsermühl, 1959).

253. Olga von Barényi, *pseud.* [i.e., Olga Gerstberger], *Prager Totentanz* (Munich: Schild, 1959).

254. Gero Wecker, *Die Letzten von Prag* (Freiburg i. Br.: Dikreiter, [1953, c. 1952]).

255. Günter Fraschka, *Prag, die blutige Stadt. Der Aufstand vom 5. Mai 1945* (Rastatt/Baden: Pabel, 1960).

256. Raymond de Geouffre de la Pradelle, Jean de Pange, *et al., Verjagt–beraubt–erschlagen. Die Austreibung aus den alten deutschen Grenzmarken. Schicksal und Völkerrecht* (Wiesbaden: Priester, [c. 1961]). It is interesting to note that the book is introduced by a professor, Bolko Freiherr von Richthofen, who not only sees this symposium as "a contribution to a real overcoming of the past in the service of international reconciliation and of the future" but thinks that this laudable purpose is being served "by the other publications of the firm of Karl-Heinz Priester" (*ibid.*, p. 7). Priester, it will be recalled, publishes the polemics of Maurice Bardèche, Paul Rassinier, and F. J. P. Veale, as well as the revisionist writings of Harry Elmer Barnes and of the French group of René d'Argile, Pierre-Antoine Cousteau, J. Ploncard d'Assac, and others.

257. Inge Merten, "Mitten aus dem Geschehen. Tagebuchblätter," *ibid.*, pp. 175–271.

258. Weeks after Germany's unconditional surrender, Miss Merten was still certain that the war was continuing, that it would ultimately be won by the Germans, and that the Americans would join the Third Reich in an anti-Bolshevik crusade.

259. Max Walter Clauss, *Der Weg nach Jalta: Präsident Roosevelts Verantwortung* (Heidelberg: Vowinckel, 1952).

260. Helmut Sündermann, *Potsdam 1945. Ein kritischer Bericht* (Leoni: Druffel, 1962).

261. Ludwig (XI/108).

262. Hermann Lutz, *"Verbrecher-Volk" im Herzen Europas?* (Tübingen: Schlichtenmayer, 1959).

263. Wilhelm Schilling, *Über die Verantwortung für die Demontage deutscher Wissenschaft* ([Göttingen:] Göttinger Verlagsanstalt, [1953]).

264. Herbert Grabert, *Hochschullehrer klagen an: Von der Demontage deutscher Wissenschaft* (2d enl. ed.; [Göttingen:] Göttinger Verlagsanstalt, [1953, c. 1952]).

265. Such as, for instance, *The Protestant Mission of the German People* (*Der protestantische Auftrag des deutschen Volkes* [Stuttgart: Gutbrod, 1936]), *Crisis and Task of the Folkish Faith* (*Krise und Aufgabe des völkischen Glaubens* [Berlin: Nordischer Verlag, 1937]), and *The Folkish Task of the Science of Religion* (*Die völkische Aufgabe der Religionswissenschaft* [Stuttgart, Berlin: Truckenmüller, 1938]). In 1935 Grabert edited the third edition of Hauer's introductory brochure entitled *What is the Aim of the German Faith Movement?* (*Was will die Deutsche Glaubensbewegung?* [Stuttgart: Gutbrod, 1935]). Cf. below, XII/59.

266. Grabert, *Die völkische Aufgabe* (XI/265), p. 58.

267. Quoted in J. Lesser, "Loss to Learning?" *The Wiener Library Bulletin* (London), VIII, 1–2 (January–April, 1954), 8. These views doubtlessly

stood Grabert in good stead during his four-year activity in Alfred Rosenberg's East Ministry.

268. Grabert, *Die völkische Aufgabe* (XI/265), p. 59. Under the circumstances it is amusing to see the American historian David L. Hoggan describe Grabert as "a devout Lutheran" who "has been one of the most prolific authors of pro-Christian books and articles in Germany since 1928." Letter to the editor of the *American Historical Review*, LXVIII, 3 (April, 1963), 914.

269. In 1953 in Tübingen, Grabert began to publish the *Deutsche Hochschullehrer-Zeitung* as the usually quarterly organ of the Association of Dismissed University Teachers.

270. See in this connection Grabert's highly characteristic comparison between the breaches of university autonomy in 1933 and 1945. Grabert (XI/264), pp. 34–35.

271. Despite the protests of the Rector's Conference against Grabert's accusation that five thousand university teachers had been dismissed for political reasons, neither the second nor third enlarged edition of the book (which came out within a year of the initial publication) was corrected in that respect.

272. *Ibid.*, pp. 19–20.

273. Cf. *ibid.*, pp. 34–35.

274. Grabert, *Die völkische Aufgabe* (XI/265), pp. 58–59.

275. Grabert (XI/264), pp. 15–16.

276. *Ibid.*, p. 72.

277. Thus the postwar description of the Third Reich as "twelve horrible years of corruption (*Verderben*)" Grabert rejects as "a propagandistic value judgment which first has to pass the muster of a historical investigation." (*Ibid.*, p. 52.)

278. Thomas Mann, "Gedanken im Krieg," in his *Friedrich und die grosse Koalition*, Sammlung von Schriften zur Zeitgeschichte, Vol. 5 (Berlin: Fischer, 1915), pp. 12–15.

279. Quoted in Mohler (I/1), p. 178.

280. Some of Germany's best authors belong to this group. We might mention Hans Werner Richter (*Die Geschlagenen; Sie fielen aus Gottes Hand*), Gert Ledig (*Die Stalinorgel; Die Vergeltung; Mein General*), Karl Ludwig Opitz (*Der Barras*), B. Müller (*Hinter Gottes Rücken*), Gerhard Krämer (*Wir werden weiter marschieren*), Heinrich Böll (*Wo warst Du Adam?; Wanderer kommst Du nach Spa*), Bruno E. Werner (*Die Galeere*), Erich Maria Remarque (*Zeit zu leben, Zeit zu sterben*), Wolfgang Ott (*Haie und kleine Fische*), Hans W. Pump (*Vor dem grossen Schnee*), Albrecht Goes (*Unruhige Nacht*), Hans Erich Nossack (*Interview mit dem Tode*), Erich Weinert (*Memento Stalingrad*).

281. For a short but good review article of German war novels, see Rolf Rostocker, "La Condemnation de la guerre dans le roman," *Documents* (*Revue des questions allemandes*), XII (May–June, 1957), 521–527.

282. Kern (IX/136).

283. From an interview with Erich K. Kernmayr, Munich, July 2, 1957.

284. Erich Kern, *pseud.* [i.e., Erich K. Kernmayr], *Die Uhr blieb stehen* (Wels: Welsermühl, 1952).

285. Kern, *Buch der Tapferkeit* (Leoni: Druffel, [1953]).

286. *Ibid.,* p. 5. The deeds of valor celebrated by Kern are all German with one exception, and all martial, again with one exception. The only non-German hero described is the French flying ace Pierre Clostermann whose chivalry vis-à-vis his German opponent, Walter Nowotny, is warmly praised (pp. 179–184). The only non-soldier among Kern's heroes is the woman flyer and dedicated Nazi Hanna Reitsch (pp. 185–191).

287. Hans-Ulrich Rudel, *Trotzdem* (XI/31).

288. Rudel, *Aus Krieg und Frieden* (XI/31).

289. Paul C. Ettighofer, *44 Tage und Nächte: Der Westfeldzug 1940* (Stuttgart: Veritas, 1953).

290. This is the title of the English translation (by A. and E. Wilson. London: Kimber, [c. 1957]). The German title is *Der Ruf der äussersten Grenze: Tagebuch eines Frontsoldaten* (Tübingen: Schlichtenmayer, 1953).

291. Parzival Kemmerich, *Im Vorfeld von Stalingrad. Tagebuchblätter* (Munich: Türmer, [1964]).

292. *Ibid.,* pp. 108–109.

293. Günter Fraschka, . . . *mit Schwertern und Brillianten. Aus dem Leben der 27 Träger der höchsten deutschen Tapferkeitsauszeichnung* (Rastatt/Baden: Pabel, 1958).

294. Fraschka, *Gnade für Paris: Frankreichs Hauptstadt zwischen den Fronten* (Rastatt/Baden: Pabel, 1959).

295. Fraschka, *Fertigmachen zum Erschiessen: Zwischen Willkür und Gewissen. 8 Kriegsgerichtsfälle* (Rastatt/Baden: Pabel, 1959).

296. Fraschka, *Das letzte Aufgebot: Vom Sterben der deutschen Jugend* (Rastatt/Baden: Pabel, 1960).

297. Fraschka, *Aufstand in Warschau: General Bor kämpft für die Freiheit seines Volkes. 1. August 1944* (Rastatt/Baden: Pabel, 1960).

298. Fraschka (XI/255).

299. Fraschka, *20. Juli 1944. Ein Bericht* ([Rastatt/Baden:] Pabel, [c. 1961]).

300. These authors include Hermann Frank (*Landser, Karst und Skipetaren: Bandenkämpfe in Albanien,* [1957]), Adolf von Ernsthausen (*Wende im Kaukasus* [1958] and *Die Wölfe der Lika* [1959], dealing with the Nazi war against Tito), Erich von Stering (*Jeder war ein Stück von uns* [1959], an account of the exploits of a line unit in the Balkans, and *Wir tragen die Fahne. Panzerjagd in Süddeutschland 1945* [1961]), Ingo Petersson, *pseud.* [i.e., F. E. Porsch] (*Ein sonderlicher Haufen: Die Saga vom Sturmbatallion 500* [1959]), Werner Jester (*Im Todessturm von Budapest 1945* [1960]) and Karl-Heinz Lotze (. . . *und es saust der Frack. Luftjagd über die Normandie und in der Reichsverteidigung 1944/45* [1961]).

301. Alkmar von Hove, *Achtung Fallschirmjäger: Eine Idee bricht sich Bahn* (Leoni: Druffel, [c. 1954]). Together with Generals Kurt Student and Hermann Bernhard Ramcke, von Hove edited the monthly *Der deutsche Fallschirmjäger,* which first appeared in December, 1951, and by the middle of 1953 had a circulation in excess of 15,000.

302. Walter Hawemann, *Achtung, Partisanen! Der Kampf hinter der Ostfront* (Hanover: Sponholtz, [c. 1953]).

303. Richard Hasemann, *Südrand Armjansk* (Pfullingen: Neske, 1952); *Nasses Brot* (Pfullingen: Neske, 1952).

304. Herbert Bruder, *Ich komme wieder. Ein deutscher Soldat erzählt* (Leoni: Druffel, [c. 1958]).

305. Hanns Möller-Witten, *Männer und Taten: Ritterkreuzträger erzählen* (Munich: Lehmann, 1958).

306. See G. Halberstadt, "Schutz vor Schund," *deutsche jugend,* VIII, 3 (March, 1960), 117–123, and L. Weinsheimer, "Diskussion über Kriegsbücher," *Aufwärts* (Giessen), no. 1 (1960), p. 4.

307. Hausser (IX/60). A court decree later ordered the book permanently withdrawn.

308. Kern (XI/252).

309. Heinz G. Konsalik, *pseud.* [i.e., Heinz A. M. Günther], *Sie fielen vom Himmel: Roman einer Generation* (Darmstadt: Schneekluth, [1958]).

310. Petersson (XI/300).

311. Hans Gustl Kernmayr, *Wir waren keine Banditen* (Düsseldorf: Bourg, 1952). This author, incidentally, ecstatically celebrated Hitler's "liberation" of Austria in 1938 in a book entitled *A People Returns Home* (*Ein Volk kehrt heim. Österreichs Kampf und Befreiung* (Berlin: Deutscher Verlag, [c. 1938]).

312. Kernmayr, *Wir waren keine Banditen* (XI/311), pp. 7–8.

313. *Ibid.,* pp. 269–270.

314. W. Moengal, *pseud., Mögen wir auch untergehen* (Vienna: Europäischer Verlag, 1962).

315. Hermann Wartenberg, *Spähtrupp* (Göttingen: Plesse, 1955).

316. Wartenberg, *Die Front geht mitten durchs Herz* (Bielefeld: Uhlenburg [c. 1953]).

317. Heinrich Eisen, *Die verlorene Kompanie* (Freiburg: Dikreiter, 1953).

318. Eisen, *Bahnhof Russkinaja meldet sich nicht* (Darmstadt: Röhrig, 1955).

319. Eisen, *Der Schienenwolf* (Darmstadt: Röhrig, 1956).

320. Hans Dietrich Röhrs, *Mit Arztbesteck und Sturmgewehr. Zwischen Tatra und Teiss 1944/45* (Neckargemünd: Vowinckel, 1961).

321. Cited in Jürgen Willbrand, *Kommt Hitler wieder? Rechtsradikalismus in Deutschland* (Donauwörth: Auer-Cassianeum, [1964?]), p. 106.

322. Kurt Assmann, *Deutsche Schicksalsjahre—Historische Bilder aus dem 2. Weltkrieg und seiner Vorgeschichte* (Wiesbaden: Eberhard Brockhaus, 1950).

323. *Ibid.,* p. 163.

324. *Ibid.*, p. 57.
325. *Ibid.*, p. 540.
326. *Ibid.*, p. 17.
327. *Bilanz des zweiten Weltkrieges: Erkenntnisse und Verpflichtungen für die Zukunft* (Oldenburg: Stalling, [c. 1953]).
328. The Clemency Board later reduced the sentence to time served.
329. *Bilanz* (XI/327), pp. 20-21.
330. *Ibid.*, p. 374.
331. *Ibid.*, p. 423.
332. *Ibid.*, p. 426.
333. Erfurth (VIII/18).
334. *Ibid.*, p. 325. Incidentally, Erfurth also wrote a history of the Finnish war, in which he was personally engaged: *Der finnische Krieg 1941–1944* (Wiesbaden: Limes, 1950).
335. Werner Beumelburg died in Würzburg in March, 1963, at the age of sixty-four.
336. Werner Beumelburg, *Jahre ohne Gnade: Chronik des zweiten Weltkrieges* (Oldenburg: Stalling, [c. 1952]).
337. Karlheinrich Rieker, *Ein Mann verliert einen Weltkrieg. Die entscheidenden Monate des deutsch-russischen Krieges 1942–1943* (Frankfurt: Fridericus, [c. 1955]).
338. Quoted in *Feinde der Demokratie* (Lower Saxony), V, 1 (October–November, 1955), 22.
339. Erich Kern, *pseud.* [i.e., Erich K. Kernmayr], *Die letzte Schlacht. Ungarn 1944–45* (Göttingen: Schütz, [c. 1960]).
340. Hans Rumpf, *Das war der Bombenkrieg* (Oldenburg: Stalling, 1961).
341. Hermann Boehm, *Norwegen zwischen England und Deutschland* (Lippoldsberg: Klosterhaus, 1956).
342. Albert Kesselring, *Gedanken zum zweiten Weltkrieg* (Bonn: Athenäum, 1955).
343. Günther Hecht, *General Wlassow* (Limburg/Lahn: Zeitbiographischer Verlag, 1961).
344. Dwinger (VIII/12).
345. Steiner (IX/98).
346. In the preface to the 1933 edition of Hans F. K. Günther's *Racial Elements in German History* (which had first appeared in 1922), Messrs. J. F. Lehmann said this: "When we brought out the first edition in 1922, Race Science was nearly unknown in Germany; today Race Science and Racial Hygiene have become school subjects. Author and publisher look back upon this development with satisfaction. In such books the real calling of the publisher is being fulfilled, [namely] to be protector and promoter of the German spirit." Besides publishing Günther, the dean of Nazi race theorists, Messrs. Lehmann also put out the racist works of such worthies as Otto Siegfried Reuter, Ludwig Schemann, Friedrich Burgdörfer, Gustav Sondermann, Hermann Wirth, and Ludwig Ferdinand Clauss.

347. Rudolf Lusar, *Die deutschen Waffen und Geheimwaffen des zweiten Weltkrieges und ihre Weiterentwicklung* (Munich: Lehmann, 1956).

348. Bernhard von Lossberg, *Im Wehrmachtsführungsstab* (Hamburg: Nölke, 1949). Helmut Greiner, *Die oberste Wehrmachtsführung 1939–1945* (Wiesbaden: Limes, 1952). Hermann Teske, *Der silberne Spiegel: Generalstabsdienst unter der Lupe* (Heidelberg: Vowinckel, 1952).

349. Walter Dornberger, *V-2: der Schuss ins Weltall. Geschichte einer grossen Erfindung* (Esslingen: Bechtle, [c. 1958]). Despite its appearance in the catalogues of nationalist book dealers, Dornberger's work is in places highly critical of the Nazi leadership.

350. Josef Priller, *Geschichte eines Jagdgeschwaders* (Heidelberg: Vowinckel, 1956).

351. H. D. Herhudt von Rohden, *Die Luftwaffe ringt um Stalingrad* (Wiesbaden: Limes, 1950).

352. Werner Baumbach, *Zu spät? Aufstieg und Untergang der deutschen Luftwaffe* (2d ed.; Munich: Pflaum, [1949]).

353. Karl Bartz, *Als der Himmel brannte: Der Weg der deutschen Luftwaffe* (Hanover: Sponholtz, 1955).

354. Harald Busch, *So war der U-Boot Krieg* (Bielefeld: Deutsche Heimat, 1952).

355. Wolfgang Frank, *Die Wölfe und der Admiral. Triumph und Tragik der U-Boote* (Oldenburg: Stalling, 1953).

356. Heinz Schaeffer, *U-977: 66 Tage unter Wasser* (Wiesbaden: Limes, 1950).

357. Fritz Otto Busch, *Das Geheimnis der "Bismarck"* (Hanover: Sponholtz, [1950]). For Busch's activity as a leading member of the Nazified German delegation to the international PEN Club meeting at Dubrovnic in May, 1933, see Wulf (III/13), pp. 60–80.

358. F. O. Busch, *Tragödie am Nordkap: Der Untergang des Schlachtschiffes "Scharnhorst"* (Hanover: Sponholtz, [1952]).

359. Cajus Bekker, *pseud.* [i.e., Hans–Dieter Berenbrok], *Kampf und Untergang der Kriegsmarine* (Hanover: Sponholtz, [c. 1956]).

360. Bekker, *. . . und liebten doch das Leben. Die erregenden Abenteuer deutscher Torpedoreiter, Froschmänner und Sprengbootpiloten* (Hanover: Sponholtz, [c. 1956]).

361. Wolfgang Frank and Bernhard Rogge, *Schiff 16: Die Kaperfahrt des schweren Hilfskreuzers Atlantis in den sieben Weltmeeren* (Oldenburg: Stalling, 1955).

362. Bekker, *Die versunkene Flotte: Deutsche Schlachtschiffe und Kreuzer 1925–1945* (Oldenburg: Stalling, [1961]). Bekker's more recent books, *Augen durch Nacht und Nebel. Die Radar-Story* (2d imp. ed.; [Oldenburg, Hamburg:] Stalling, [1964]), which had first been published under the title *Radar-Duell in Dunkel,* and *Flucht übers Meer. Ostsee-deutsches Schicksal 1945* (2d rev. enl. ed.; [Oldenburg, Hamburg:] Stalling, [1964]), which in the first edition was entitled *Ostsee-deutsches Schicksal 1944/45,* came to my attention too late to be included here.

363. Jan Mayen, *Alarm—Schnellboote! Zwischen Kanal und Kauka-*

suskiiste: ein Tatsachenbericht vom Einsatz der kleinen Boote (Oldenburg: Stalling, [c. 1961]).

364. Hausser (IX/60).

365. The French condemned Lammerding to death *in absentia*. German authorities could not locate him, despite the fact that the *Sozialdemokratische Pressedienst* of February 6, 1953, claimed that he had again surfaced and was, like many other Nazi greats, filling an important post in the Ruhr industry.

366. Hilberg (II/9), pp. 216, 451.

367. Ernst Günther Krätschmer, *Die Ritterkreuzträger der Waffen-SS* (Göttingen: Plesse, [c. 1957]).

368. *Waffen-SS im Bild* (2d ed.; Göttingen: Plesse, [c. 1957]).

369. Mention should also be made here of yet another book by the prolific Erich Kernmayr, which, however, came to my attention too late for closer scrutiny: *General von Panwitz und seine Kosaken* (Neckargemünd: Vowinckel, [1963]).

370. Felix Steiner, *Die Freiwilligen: Idee und Opfergang* (Göttingen: Plesse, [1958]). Steiner's later *laudatio* on the Combat SS men whom he had once led is entitled *Die Armee der Geächteten* (Göttingen: Plesse, [c. 1963]) (*The Army of the Ostracized*).

371. Cited by Wolfgang Kubala, "Mit Lastwagen voller SS Bücher geflüchtet," *Süddeutsche Zeitung* (Munich), no. 106 (May 4, 1965), p. 5.

372. *Ibid.*, July 27, 1963.

373. Otto Skorzeny, *Wir kämpften—wir verloren* (Niederpleis/Siegburg: Ring, 1963) and *Lebe gefährlich* (Niederpleis/Siegburg: Ring, 1963).

374. Hans Domizlaff, *Es geht um Deutschland* (Hamburg: Dulk, 1952). This book is in many of its aspects similar to Herbert Grabert's *People without Leadership* (see above, XI/76). If the two books are not discussed within the same category, it is because Domizlaff views Hitler as a Jacobin and has no interest in heroizing him. In point of authoritarianism and antidemocratic elitism, Grabert and Domizlaff agree completely. And in point of counter-indictment, Domizlaff is hardly less aggressive than the resentment-laden Grabert: "However long the register of human sins of the German people might be . . . no one can deny that the victors' acts of terror during the war, and the acts of revenge after the collapse, with their destruction of innocent women and children, merit in no way the primacy in point of noble humanitarianism. Even the gruesome National Socialist murder of five million Jews which can be explained only [as] . . . insanity, has been fully counterweighed, eye for eye, tooth for tooth, and number for number, by the blood sacrifice of innocent . . . people." Domizlaff (XI/374), p. 75.

375. From an unpublished manuscript by Kurt Hirsch, "Rechtsradikale Literatur in der Bundesrepublik," n.d.

376. Domizlaff (XI/374), p. 35.

377. *Ibid.*, p. 65.

378. *Ibid.*, p. 67.

379. *Ibid.*, p. 38. Cf. also pp. 69–70.

380. *Ibid.*, pp. 29–31.

381. *Ibid.*, p. 119.

382. *Ibid.*, pp. 283–284.

383. Hans-Ulrich Rudel, *Es geht um das Reich* (Buenos Aires: Dürer, [1952]).

384. Gerhard Krüger, *Das unzerstörbare Reich* (Hamburg: Gutenberg, [c. 1952]).

385. Hans B. Schwabe, *Deutschland in seiner tiefen Erniedrigung: Das deutsche Reich—eine europäische Wirklichkeit* (Lindau: Palm Schriften, [1961]).

386. *Ibid.*, pp. 49–50.

387. *Ibid.*, p. 51.

388. *Ibid.*, pp. 53–54.

389. Bert Waser, *Demokratische Wahrheiten. Betrachtungen eines simplen Zeitgenossen* (Lindau: Palm Schriften, [1964]).

390. *Ibid.*, pp. 32–39.

391. *Ibid.*, p. 34.

392. Berg (XI/79), p. 74.

393. Dietrich Klagges, *Die Lage des Nationalismus* (Bad Harzburg: [Klagges,] 1962).

394. Grimm (XI/140).

395. *Ibid.*, p. 135.

396. *Ibid.*, p. 156.

397. *Ibid.*, pp. 158–159.

398. *Ibid.*, p. 190.

399. Herbert Schweiger, *Wahre Dein Antlitz. Lebensgesetz, Politik und die Zukunft des deutschen Volkes* (Munich: Türmer, [1963]).

400. *Ibid.*, pp. 42, 44.

401. *Ibid.*, p. 52.

402. *Ibid.*, p. 53.

403. Heinz Guderian, *So geht es nicht! Überlegungen zur Wiederbewaffnung* (Heidelberg: Vowinckel, 1951).

404. Hans-Ulrich Rudel, *Wir Frontsoldaten zur Wiederaufrüstung* (n.p., n.d.).

405. Erich Kern, *pseud.* [i.e., Erich K. Kernmayr], *Das grosse Kesseltreiben: Bleibt der deutsche Soldat vogelfrei?* (2d enl. ed.; Göttingen: Plesse, [c. 1960]).

406. Hans W. Hagen, *Durchbruch zur neuen Mitte. Drei Studien zur Überwindung der Kulturkrise* (Munich: Türmer, [1957]).

407. Richard W. Eichler, *Könner, Künstler, Scharlatane* (2nd enl. ed.; Munich: Lehmann, [c. 1960]).

408. *Ibid.*, p. 214. Having come upon a successful formula, Eichler has continued his virulent attacks on modern art. His more recent *Der gesteuerte Kunstverfall. Ein Prozess mit 129 Bildbeweisen* (Munich: Lehmann, [1965]) unfortunately appeared too late to be included here.

409. Griesmayr, *Der politische Weg* (V/39).

410. Griesmayr, *Ist Wiedervereinigung überhaupt noch möglich?* (Stuttgart: Fink, 1962).

411. Backhaus (XI/73), pp. 98–102.

412. Olga von Barényi, *pseud.* [i.e., Olga Gerstberger], *Der tote Briefkasten* (Munich: Schild, 1960).

413. Erich Kern, *pseud.* [i.e., Erich K. Kernmayr], *Menschen im Netz* (Wels: Welsermühl, 1958).

414. Merely for the sake of completeness we mention a scurrilous campaign brochure which, under the title *Our Chancellor Ollenhauer and his Palladins* (*Unser Kanzler Ollenhauer und seine Palladine*), unfairly attacked the 1957 Socialist candidate for the chancellorship. The pamphlet was written and published by the fanatical Friedrich Lenz of Heidelberg. It appeared at the same time in a Cairo publishing firm under the pseudonym Fritz Büttner.

415. Hans Venatier, *Der Major und die Stiere* (Düsseldorf: Bourg, [c. 1953]).

416. Cf. "Leiche im Auto," *Der Spiegel,* XI, 4 (January 23, 1957), 46.

417. Venatier, *Der Boss und seine Narren* (Düsseldorf: Muth, [c. 1956]).

418. *Ibid.,* p. 187.

419. *Ibid.,* p. 247.

420. Erich Kern, *pseud.* [i.e., Erich K. Kernmayr], *Das harte Leben* (*Auszüge aus einem Tagebuch 1947 bis 1950*) (Wels: Welsermühl, [c. 1950]).

421. Kern, *Der Dorn im Fleische. Roman der Fremdenlegion* (Wels: Welsermühl, [1955]).

422. *Feinde der Demokratie* (Lower Saxony) VII, 6–7 (May–June, 1958), 30. For Ziesel's poisonous Nazi activity, see Walter Wenzel, "Schluss mit der Ziesel-Reklame," *Die Andere Zeitung* (Hamburg), no. 21 (September 29, 1955), p. 6.

423. *Feinde der Demokratie* (XI/422).

424. For the objectives, organization, meetings, and legal involvements of the Grünwalder Kreis, it is best to consult *Die Kultur* (Munich), one of whose editors, Hans Werner Richter, was also the chairman of the Grünwald Circle. Two pages of each issue of *Die Kultur,* from February, 1956, on, were reserved to the Circle. For the controversies and lawsuits, especially against *Deutsche Soldaten–Zeitung* (Munich) for its scurrilous attack "Grünwalder Kreis ohne Maske" (June issue, 1956), which was said to be the work of Erich Kernmayr, see Paul Schallück, " 'Grünwalder Kreis ohne Maske,' " *Die Europäische Zeitung* (Bonn), IV, 8/9 (August 25, 1956), 13; Gerd Hover, "Verschwörung gegen die Freiheit," *Nation Europa,* VI, 9 (September, 1956), 67–72. Cf. also D. G. (Dieter Grossherr?) "Bündnis deutscher Republikaner," *Colloquium,* X, 11 (November, 1956), and "Nazismus in der Zange des Intellekts," *ibid.,* X, 12 (December, 1956).

425. Kurt Ziesel, *Das verlorene Gewissen: Hinter den Kulissen der Presse, der Literatur und ihrer Machtträger von heute* (Munich: Lehmann, [c. 1958]).

426. As to the "revelations" of this German Westbrook Pegler, quite a number of them were challenged and brought Ziesel into conflict with the

law. At a public meeting in Hamburg (for Ziesel had become a much-sought-after lecturer before Right-extremist groups) which, characteristically, had been organized by Otto Reuter, a dealer in Nazi and ultranationalist literature, one of the victims of Ziesel's smear campaign accused him publicly of gross "errors." Erich Lüth, the press chief of the Social Democratic City-State government, leading force behind the German Association of Christians and Jews, organizer of "Peace with Israel" actions and of Anne Frank memorial meetings at the Bergen-Belsen concentration camp, frankly told Ziesel: "If all the references in the book *The Lost Conscience* are based on so erroneous a foundation as the attack against me, then the entire book is not worth a red penny." Erich Lüth, "Die Beschmutzung des freien Wortes," (mimeographed brochure), May 2, 1958.

427. Ziesel (XI/425), p. 14.

428. *Ibid.*, p. 65.

429. Ziesel, "Kurt Ziesels Antwort an Jan A. van der Made," *Nation Europa,* VIII, 5 (May, 1958), 66.

430. "Ziesel—oder: Die verlorenen Massstäbe," *Feinde der Demokratie* (Lower Saxony) VII, 6–7 (May–June, 1958), 30–33.

431. Ziesel (XI/425), pp. 16–17.

432. Ziesel, *Die Geister scheiden sich: Die interessantesten Leserbriefe und wesentlichsten Pressestimmen* (Munich: Lehmann, [1959]).

433. Ziesel, *Die verratene Demokratie* (Munich: Lehmann, 1960). At this point might also be included Zdenko von Kraft, *Verwirrung oder Verfall? Ein Buch vom Ungeist der Zeit* (Graz, Stuttgart: Stocker, 1964). Unfortunately it came to the author's attention too late to be discussed here.

434. Ziesel, *Dankt das Abendland ab? Ein Vortrag der in Wien nicht stattfinden durfte,* Eckartschriften, no. 11 (Vienna: [Österreichische Landsmannschaft,] June, 1963).

435. Ziesel, *Die Pressefreiheit in der Demokratie: Eine kritische Untersuchung* (Munich: Lehmann, [1962]).

436. See, for instance, I. B. (Inge Bethge?), "Politischer Schriftsteller oder Advokat?" *Studien von Zeitfragen, Presse- und Buchspiegel,* VIII, 8–9 (August–September, 1961), 2–3. In the same information service I. B. had previously very favorably reviewed all the other Ziesel publications.

437. Ziesel, *Der rote Rufmord. Eine Dokumentation zum kalten Krieg* ([Tübingen: Schlichtenmayer, 1961]).

438. Ziesel's latest polemic against "left totalitarianism," pornography, and the destruction of the German language, which to that unbalanced author appear as necessarily related and as characteristic of contemporary literature, arrived too late to be critically analyzed. (*Die Literaturfabrik* [(Vienna, Cologne:) Wancura, (c, 1963)].) So did Ziesel's interpretation of the *Spiegel* affair, *Der deutsche Selbstmord. Diktatur der Meinungsmacher* ([Velbert-Kettwig:] blick + bild Verlag für politische Bildung, [1963]).

439. Victor Silling, *pseud.* [i.e., Artur von Machui], *Die Hintergründe des Falles Oberländer* (Gross Denkte/Wolfenbüttel: Grenzland, Rock, [c. 1960]).

440. Hermann Raschofer, *Der Fall Oberländer. Eine vergleichende*

Rechtsanalyse des Verfahren in Pankow und Bonn (Tübingen: Schlichtenmayer, 1962).

441. From a deposition (Frankfurt, September 12, 1952) von Machui made in the course of police investigations following the "flight" to East Berlin of former Lower Saxon Minister of Agriculture Günther Gereke. See above, VI/162, 171.

442. Rudolf Diels, *Der Fall Otto John: Hintergründe und Lehren* ([Göttingen:] Göttinger Verlagsanstalt, [1954]).

443. From a confidential report of discussions with Diels at Berghausen, Rhineland-Palatinate, April 7 and May 13, 1953. Much information about Otto John appeared also to have come from his sister, who was married to a local acquaintance of Diels.

444. Diels (who, incidentally, was a constant contributor, under a variety of pseudonyms, to the DRP's weekly organ *Reichsruf*), was killed in a hunting accident in November, 1957. For a eulogy on Diels the "humanitarian," see Harry Wilde, "Rudolf Diels—Porträt eines verkannten Mannes," *Politische Studien,* IX, 99 (July, 1958), 475–481.

445. *Die grosse Hetze* (III/56). For Schmidt-Hannover see also III/36. For a discussion of the Schlüter case, see Chapter XVII, Section C.

446. Friedrich Grimm's *Lawlessness under the Rule of Law* (see above, XI/224 and nearby text), might, of course, well have come under the present category.

447. Naumann (V/I).

448. See above, V/64.

449. Gerd Hover, *Der Fall Schmeisser ohne Schminke* (Oberammergau: Roeder, 1956).

450. Eric A. Peschler, "Grünwalder Kreis und halbamtliche Verleumdung," *Die Andere Zeitung* (Hamburg), no. 20 (May 16, 1957), p. 11. F. V. Risse operated a small publishing establishment in which he produced a number of brochures with such titles as *The Policy of Conquest of the Kremlin Power Holders* and *This Is How Moscow Subverts the West.* To intensify the effectiveness of his propaganda, Risse formed an International Democratic Fighting League (Internationale Demokratische Kampfliga, INDEKAL). While claiming for this organization loyalty to Western constitutionalism and freedom, Risse "disavows (*abrücken*) the old-fashioned strait-jacketing of the intellect (*Geist*) through party politics." *So zersetzt Moskau den Westen* ([Munich:] Internationale Demokratische Kampfliga, [1954]), p. 63. What kind of "anti-Communism" is here involved becomes plain when one notices that Risse attacks the Waffen SS trials, Nuremberg trials, SD trials, war-crimes trials, and collaborationist trials, as well as administrative extradition decisions, as essentially playing Moscow's game. The same spirit pervaded the biweekly journal *Alarm—im Dienste der Wahrheit und Aufklärung* which he produced in 1955 (together with Lothar Greil).

451. Helmut Sündermann, *Das Erbe des falschen Propheten. Moskaus Kampf um Deutschland von Lenin bis heute—und morgen?* (Leoni:Druffel, 1957).

452. Sündermann, *Die Pioniere und die Ahnungslosen. Skizzen amerikanischer Vergangenheit und Gegenwart* (Leoni: Druffel, [1960]).

453. Peter Kleist, *Chruschtschow 50 km vor Hamburg* (Göttingen: Plesse, [c. 1959]).

454. Kleist, *Deutschland, Europa und der Ost-West-Konflikt* (Hanover: National, 1961).

455. Priester (VII/22).

456. Otto Strasser, *Deutschland und der 3. Weltkrieg* (Munich: Deutsche Freiheit, 1961).

457. Gottfried Griesmayr, *Bolschewistische Weltrevolution—Gespenst oder Wirklichkeit?* (Stuttgart: Fink, 1962). (Republished in 1964 as *Weltrevolution und deutsche Frage.*)

458. Lothar Rendulic, *Weder Krieg noch Frieden. Eine Frage an die Macht* (Wels, Munich: Welsermühl, 1961).

459. Felix Steiner, *Die Wehridee des Abendlandes* (Frankfurt: Parma, 1951).

460. Heinz Guderian, *Kann Westeuropa verteidigt werden?* (Göttingen: Plesse, [1950]).

461. Soucek (VII/87).

462. E. J. Reichenberger, *Rettung Europas?* (Munich: Tribunal, 1960).

463. August Winnig, *Europa—Gedanken eines Deutschen* (Berlin: Eckart, 1952).

464. Heinrich Sanden, *pseud.* [i.e., Helmut L. Sündermann], *Europa ohne Phrase* (Leoni: Druffel, 1953).

465. Kurt Borries, *Deutschland im Kreise der europäischen Mächte* (Stuttgart: Silberburg, 1962).

466. Anton Zischka, *Asien. Hoffnung einer neuen Welt* (Oldenburg: Stalling, 1950).

467. Zischka, *Afrika—Europas Gemeinschaftsaufgabe Nr. 1* (Oldenburg: Stalling, 1951).

468. Zischka, *Welt in Angst und Hoffnung* (Oldenburg: Stalling, 1955).

469. Zischka, *Frieden in einer reicheren Welt* (Oldenburg: Stalling, 1956). In 1940 Zischka made his contribution to war propaganda with an elaborate demonstration of Britain's perfidy entitled *Englands Bündnisse. Sechs Jahrhunderte britische Kriege mit fremden Waffen* (Leipzig: Goldmann, 1940).

470. Wahrhold Drascher, *Schuld der Weissen?* (Tübingen: Schlichtenmayer, 1960).

471. Drascher, *Die Vorherrschaft der weissen Rasse* (Stuttgart: Deutsche Verlags-Anstalt, 1936).

472. Quoted in "The 'Hand of Paternalism,'" *The Wiener Library Bulletin* (London), XV, 3 (1961), 48.

473. Drascher (XI/470), pp. 158–159.

474. *Ibid.*, pp. 139–140.

475. Erich Kern, *pseud.* [i.e., Erich K. Kernmayr], *Algerien in Flammen: Ein Volk kämpft um seine Freiheit* (2d. imp. ed.; Göttingen: Plesse, [1958]).

476. Erich Kern, *pseud.* [i.e., Erich K. Kernmayr], *Weisser Mann, toter Mann? Ostasien im Umbruch—Ein Augenzeugenbericht* (Starnberg, Wels: Welsermühl, [1955]).

477. Heinrich Georg Stahmer, *Japans Niederlage—Asiens Sieg. Aufstieg eines grösseren Ostasien* (Bielefeld: Deutsche Heimat, 1952).

478. Hermann Karge, *Mensch und Volk: Eine naturphilosophische Betrachtung* (Uelzen [Hanover]: Klatte, 1953).

479. *Ibid.*, pp. 126, 135, 168.

480. *Ibid.*, p. 66.

481. *Ibid.*, p. 139.

482. *Ibid.*, p. 85.

483. *Ibid.*, pp. 135–136.

484. *Ibid.*, pp. 190–191.

485. *Ibid.*, pp. 106–107, 141.

486. *Ibid.*, p. 138.

487. *Ibid.*, p. 169.

488. *Ibid.*, p. 172.

489. *Ibid.*

490. Dieter Vollmer, *Vom Wesenhaften* (Göttingen: Plesse, 1955).

491. *Ibid.*, pp. 52–60.

492. *Ibid.*, pp. 65–66.

493. *Ibid.*, pp. 76–77.

494. Herbert Böhme, *Bekenntnisse eines freien Mannes* (Munich: Türmer, 1960).

495. Brunner (VII/49).

496. *Ibid.*, p. 319.

497. *Ibid.*, p. 417. Still, the entire book is more than a lament for Brunner's lost homeland. It is largely an impertinent rehabilitation of the Third Reich and, in spots, an even more insolent denial of its enormities. Thus the author writes, "In Gmunden [Brunner] made his first acquaintance with a former concentration camp inmate, who had sat behind barbed wire since 1935. . . . Why had he been there? As often as that unfortunate spoke of it, he gave another reason. The man's origin—in darkness; his profession—in darkness. Even his name became a secret. Doubtless there were thousands (*sic*) of people whom the National Socialist state had unjustly put behind lock and key; this one was a pathological liar. . . . Inwardly destroyed, hollowed out, burned out, he resembled an insane person who thirstily grasped for life, drank, whored, as though he wanted to make up in months what he had missed in years" (p. 336).

498. The fictionalized account of the dissolution of the Habsburg empire consists of *Apis und Este* (1931), *Das war das Ende* (1932), and *Weder Kaiser noch König* (1933). All were published by Piper's, of Munich. In 1951, the same publisher reissued them in a one-volume edition, under the title *Die Throne stürzen.*

499. *Die Neue Literatur,* XL, 6 (June, 1939), 320.

500. Bruno Brehm, *Heimat in Böhmen* (Salzburg: Pilgram, [1951]).

501. For a brief history of the Free Corps and its role as a terror

organization and instrument of Hitler's policy to force the complete destruction of the Czechoslovak state, see Martin Broszat, "Das sudetendeutsche Freikorps," *Vierteljahrshefte für Zeitgeschichte,* IX, 1 (January, 1961), 30–49.

502. Ernst Frank, *Leidenschaftliches Egerland* (5th ed.; Frankfurt: Heimreiter, 1954).

503. Frank, *Heimat ohne Vaterland* (Frankfurt: Heimreiter, [c. 1958]).

504. Günther Berka, *Gibt es eine österreichische Nation?* Eckartschriften, no. 7 (Vienna: [Österreichische Landsmannschaft], 1961).

505. Heinrich Dauthage, *pseud., Brennendes Land—Land am Brenner* (Vienna: Typographische Anstalt, 1961).

506. Franz Burri, *Deutsches Südtirol. Selbstbestimmung—Autonomie —Rückgliederung* (Lindau: Palm Schriften, [1961]).

507. Wolfgang von Welsperg, *pseud.* [i.e., Manfred von Ribbentrop], *Süd Tirol: Kampf für Recht und Volkstum* (2d ed.; Hamburg: Hutten, 1962 [c. 1959]). A more recent, and far shorter, book on South Tyrol, Franz Huter's *Südtirol. Tausendjährige Heimat* (3d rev. ed.; Innsbruck, Vienna, Munich: Tyrolia, [1964]), was brought to my attention too late to be included here.

508. Viktor Miltschinsky, *Kärnten wehrt sich,* Eckartschriften, no. 9 (Vienna: [Österreichische Landsmannschaft], 1962).

509. Paul Anton Keller, *Väterheimat zwischen Drau und Sann. Ein Buch der Erinnerung* (Vienna: Wancura, [1956]).

510. Hubert Koch, *Der Väter Land. Deutsche Heimat zwischen Weichsel und Memel* (Leer: Rautenberg & Möckel, 1953).

511. F. H. Falkenbach, *pseud.* [i.e., Friedrich Heiss], ed., *Mitten durch unser Herz* (Munich: Andermann, 1956).

512. Sepp Frisch, *Die Saar bleibt deutsch. Zur Heimkehr der Saar. Ein Rückblick 1680–1955* (Leoni: Druffel, 1956).

513. Ernst Siegfried Hansen, *Kurier der Heimat. Das Spiel um Schleswig zwischen Kapitulation und Programm Nord* (Bielefeld: Deutsche Heimat, [c. 1955]).

514. Hansen, *Disteln am Weg: Von der Besetzung Dänemarks bis zu den Bonner Erklärungen* (Bielefeld: Deutsche Heimat, [c. 1957]).

515. Johannes Schmidt, *Von Wodder nach Kopenhagen, von Deutschland nach Europa. Mein politischer Werdegang* (Flensburg: Wolff, [c. 1951]).

516. *Der Weg* (Buenos Aires), VI, 6 (1952), 439.

517. [Wilhelm] Harun-el-Raschid Bey, *Aus Orient und Occident: Ein Mosaik aus buntem Erleben* (Bielefeld: Deutsche Heimat, 1954).

518. Hans F. K. Günther, *Gattenwahl zum ehelichen Glück und erblicher Ertüchtigung* (3d rev. ed.; Munich: Lehmann, 1951).

519. Ministerial Counselor Hagen of Bonn writing in the July, 1952, issue of *Der öffentliche Gesundheitsdienst* and quoted in Hirsch (XI/375), p. 2. In March, 1952, in an open letter to the Bavarian Parliament and the Market Association of German Publishers, a group of authors, professors, and publishers demanded the immediate retraction of the Günther book,

through legal action, if need be. Furthermore, they asked that the Land Association of Bavarian Book Sellers expel Messrs. J. F. Lehmann from membership "as an unambiguously neo-Nazi publisher." See *Die Neue Zeitung* (Munich), March 22/23, 1952. For a recent study of H. F. K. Günther, see James A. Gregor, "Nordicism Revisited," *Phylon,* XXII (1961), 351–360.

520. Günther, *Formen und Urgeschichte der Ehe* (3d rev. ed.; Göttingen: Musterschmidt, 1951). In rebuttal to a scathing critique of the book in *Welt am Sonntag* (J. Hennemann, "Doch wieder Rasse-Günther?" no. 44 [November 4, 1951]), Musterschmidt attempted to argue that this book was not racist but ethnological in nature, that Günther began writing long before the formation of the NSDAP and therefore could not be called specifically a Nazi scientist, and, above all, that after 1933 the NSDAP misused, and later attacked, the "scientific research results" of Günther. The publisher also contended that Günther soon fell into disgrace with the party, being considered "old-fashioned." (Letter of November 13, 1951.) Oddly enough a Göttingen professor of anatomy, Gerhard Heberer, also attempted to defend Günther as a "scientist." (Letter of November 13, 1951.) Heberer repeated the argument of Günther's allegedly bad rapport with the Nazis and pointed out that, in any case, Günther's books had been scrutinized by a denazification tribunal and had been found unobjectionable. In response to these arguments, the editor of *Welt am Sonntag* had no difficulty in demonstrating that Günther had been the foremost popularizer of a thoroughly unscientific, and hence all the more political, racism which culminated in the demand for world domination by the Nordic race. His great impact on Hitler and the NSDAP was, according to the editor, beyond question. Such estrangement as there was between the party and Günther was due, not to any disagreement on the question of racism, but rather to the internecine battles between Rosenberg and Himmler that brought constant turmoil to the Nazi ideological front. So little can it be said that Günther was generally *persona non grata* with the Nazis that, as late as July, 1944, his was to have been the honor of addressing a planned (but never held) highest-level international anti-Semitic congress in Cracow. Günther intended to read a paper entitled "The Invasion of the Jews into the Cultural Life of the Nations." (Weinreich [V/23], p. 232.) As to Heberer's recommendation of Günther, it came from a man who himself enjoyed great prestige in the Third Reich and who contributed after the war to *Der Weg* of Buenos Aires, the most unrestrained Nazi journal then extant. (See e.g. his "Woher kommen wir?" *Der Weg,* VI, 7 [July, 1952], 466–471.) Heberer's symposium *The Evolution of Organisms* (Jena: Fischer, 1943) received the highest praise of Walter Gross, head of the Racial Policy Office of the NSDAP (Rassenpolitisches Amt). (Weinreich [V/23], p. 175, note 385.) Incidentally, it was reissued in a second edition in 1954 under the imprint of Gustav Fischer, now of Stuttgart. For the importance of the former SS major Heberer as one of the most *engagé* Nazi race theorists, see Karl Saller, *Die Rassenlehre des Nationalsozialismus in Wissenschaft und Propaganda* (Darmstadt: Progress, [c. 1961]), pp. 57–58.

521. *Die Neue Literatur,* XXXVI, 10 (October, 1935), 630.

522. *Völkischer Beobachter,* February 16, 1941, quoted in *The Wiener Library Bulletin* (London), VI, 1–2 (January–April, 1952), 3.

523. Günther (XI/518), p. 16, quoted by Dr. Kurth (Göttingen) in a letter to the editor of *Welt am Sonntag* (Hamburg), November 13, 1951.

524. Günther (XI/518), pp. 146–147, quoted *ibid.* Cf. Adolf Volbracht, "Dokumentation zum roten und braunen Faschismus," *Kontakte,* January, 1952, p. 9.

525. Günther, *Frömmigkeit nordischer Artung. Ein Querschnitt durch das Indogermanentum von Benares bis Reykjavik* (6th ed.; Pähl: Von Bebenburg, 1963).

526. Quoted by M. K., "Wörterbuch der Völkerkunde," *Die Mahnung,* IV, 10 (May 15, 1957).

527. *Ibid.*

528. Richard Beitl, *Wörterbuch der deutschen Volkskunde* (Stuttgart: Kröner, 1956).

529. Quoted in [Club republikanischer Publizisten,] *CrP–Information,* January, 1957, p. 5.

530. All quotations from *ibid.*

531. Hermann Wirth, *Was ist deutsch?* (Vienna: Editio Totius Mundi, 1956).

532. Strassner (VI/172). A second edition of this work appeared in 1963 in the Ring-Verlag Cramer in Niederpleis/Siegburg.

533. Peter Kleist, *Die europäische Tragödie* (Göttingen: Schütz, [c. 1961]).

534. Stefan Yowev, *pseud., Bricht der Weltkommunismus zusammen?* (Tübingen: Schlichtenmayer, 1961).

535. Yowev supports his contention that the Communist camp is in serious difficulties in a book entitled *Die kommunistische Weltbewegung in der Krise* (Duisdorf/Bonn: Studiengesellschaft für Zeitprobleme, n.d.). Here he analyzes in detail the Twenty-second Party Congress of the CPSU and the subsequent debates within the Communist parties of the Eastern bloc states.

536. Polonius, *pseud., Keine Angst vor Sowjetrussland* (Heidelberg: Vowinckel, 1951).

537. If we do not include here William S. Schlamm's very similar *Die Grenzen des Wunders* ([Zurich:] Europa, [1959]) (*Germany and the East-West Crisis. The Decisive Challenge to American Policy* [New York: McKay, (1959)]) or Bernhard Martell's *Aufstand des Abendlandes. Eine politische Provokation* (Schweinfurt: neues forum, [1961]), both of which argue for offensive psychological and economic warfare against the Soviet Union even at the risk of atomic war, it is because they call for continued and ever closer co-operation with the United States and thus are acceptable neither to the Gaullist nor to the neutralist nationalists.

538. Günther Wick, *Wandlungen des Marxismus* (Lindau: Palm Schriften, [1963]).

539. Helmut Steinberg, *pseud.* [i.e., Heinrich Härtle], *Marxismus–Leninismus–Stalinismus. Der geistige Angriff des Ostens* (Hamburg: Holsten, 1955).

540. Heinrich Härtle, *Nietzsche und der Nationalsozialismus* (Munich: Eher, 1937).

541. *Ibid.*, p. 5.

542. *Ibid.*, p. 38.

543. *Ibid.*, p. 45.

544. *Ibid.*, pp. 63–64.

545. *Ibid.*, p. 114.

546. *Ibid.*, p. 163.

547. *Ibid.*, p. 164.

548. *Ibid.*

549. Weinreich (V/23), p. 232.

550. Härtle (XI/540), p. 130.

551. *Ibid.*, p. 86.

552. For the background history of Roeder and the Widar Verlag, see "Der falsche Fünfzehner," *Der Spiegel,* X, 33 (August 15, 1956), 11–14.

553. Guido Roeder, *Im Morgenrot der Weltrevolution* (2d ed.; Oberammergau: Widar, 1955).

554. Dietrich von Kuenheim, ed., *Sovjet-Agenten überall* (Oberammergau: Widar, 1955). On the authorship of this screed, see "Der falsche Fünfzehner" (XI/552), p. 14.

555. Oddly enough, the astrologer Roeder, who practiced the occult arts and whose publishing firm was closed down by the Nazis for its evidently insane extremism, himself ended up in Dachau for having given vent to his dislike of the Nazis by calling Hitler the offspring of Eastern Jews.

556. Other writings of Hover's, such as his attack on the Grünwalder Kreis in the pages of *Nation Europa* (Hover [XI/424]), only deepen that impression.

557. Gerd Hover, *Von Liebknecht über Hitler zum Warschauer Pakt* (Oberammergau: Widar, n.d.).

558. Hover, *Von der Reichswehr zum ersten Bundeswehr "Deserteur"* (Oberammergau: Widar, n.d.).

559. A very similar spirit breathes through the prison notes of the Luftwaffe Judge Advocate General Manfred Roeder, which (edited by his daughter) were published by the SRP publisher Hans Siep under the title *The Red Band* (*Die rote Kapelle*).

560. Friedrich Nieland, *Wieviele Welt- (Geld-) Kriege müssen die Völker noch verlieren? Offener Brief an alle Bundesminister und Parlamentarier* (Hamburg–Wellingsbüttel; n.p., 1957).

561. See the open letter to the Presidents of the District and Supreme Courts in *Hamburger Morgenpost,* January 10, 1959, *Frankfurter Allgemeine Zeitung,* January 10, 1959, *Die Welt* (Hamburg), January 10, 1959, *Hamburger Abendblatt,* January 10/11, 1959, *Hamburger Echo,* January 10, 1959, *Bild Zeitung* (Hamburg Edition) January 10, 1959.

562. From a confidential report of a Natinform conference, Oldenburg, January 16–19, 1953.

563. Ernst Jaeckel, *Dämon Gold* (Düsseldorf: Strunk, [1952]).

564. Lothar Kahn, "The Swastika in German Novels," *The Wiener Library Bulletin* (London), XIV, 2 (1960), 29.

565. For a pre-Nazi, but distinctly friendly, assessment of the literary movement represented by these authors, see Paul Kluckhohn, "Die Konservative Revolution in der Dichtung der Gegenwart," *Zeitschrift für deutsche Bildung,* IX, 4 (1933), 177–190. In that review article, Kluckhohn considers the works of Stefan George, Paul Ernst, Otto Gmelin, Wilhelm Schäfer, Ernst Bertram, E. G. Kolbenheyer, Hermann Stehr, Otto Stössl, H. F. Blunck, Hans Grimm, Heinz Steguweit, E. E. Dwinger, F. Schnack, Hanns Johst, F. A. Schmid-Noerr, Will Vesper, Friedrich Griese, Benno von Mechow; the Austrians Paula Grogger, K. H. Waggerl, R. Billinger, and Julius Zerzer; Wilhelm von Scholz, Paul Alverdes, Emil Strauss; the Swiss anthroposophist Albert Steffen; Georg von der Vring, Hermann Claudius; also some of the writings of Walter von Molo, Ernst Lissauer, Ina Seidel, Kasimir Edschmid, Ernst Wiechert, Hans Carossa, and the religiously toned works of Hugo von Hofmannsthal, R. A. Schröder, R. von Schaukal, Rudolf Paulsen, Karl Wagenfeld, Max Mell, J. Kneip, K. B. Heinrich, F. J. Weinrich, Ruth Schaumann, Gertrud von Le Fort, Gustav Schüler, Karl Röttger. For the thirty-six members of the German Academy of Poetry in 1934, see *Das Deutsche Führerlexikon 1934/1935* (XI/40), Part II, pp. 127–128. See also Wulf (III/13), pp. 23–35.

566. In this connection see the totally unconvincing apologetics of Hans Grimm (XI/133), pp. 162–166.

567. For a brief review of Nazi literary policies prior to the war, see Walter A. Berendsohn, *Die humanistische Front: Einführung in die deutsche Emigranten-Literatur,* Part I (von 1933 bis zum Kriegsausbruch 1939) (Zurich: Europa, [c. 1946], pp. 9–50. Of course, the standard work in this field is still Dietrich Strothmann's encyclopedic *Nationalsozialistische Literaturpolitik. Ein Beitrag zur Publizistik im Dritten Reich* (2d impr. enl. ed.; Bonn: Bouvier, 1963 [c. 1960]).

568. Werner Beumelburg, *Nur Gast auf dunkler Erde* (Oldenburg: Stalling, 1951).

569. Beumelburg, *Hundert Jahre sind wie ein Tag* (Oldenburg: Oldenburger Verlag. [1950]).

570. In 1942, Blunck, "the most effective" representative of "Nordic-Germanic" culture, wrote this paean to his Führer:

> We know that you, Führer, have taken
> Painfully upon yourself our longing and all the hopes,
> And, though the greatest had left it unfulfilled,
> You have completed the folk from which you sprang.
> And now we stand before you, overwhelmed,
> And hardly find apt words of gratitude.
> Too great is our happiness. From every home
> Greets you today the Germany which you bore—which bore you.

Wulf (III/13), pp. 290, 357. Cf. also p. 264. At the end of 1963 a seemingly redundant Society of Friends of the Works of H. F. Blunck, dedicated to their promotion, was founded in Bad Segeberg. (*Bulletin on German Questions* [London], XV, 347 [December 30, 1963], 9.)

571. H. F. Blunck, *Unwegsame Zeiten* (Mannheim: Kessler, 1952). This is Volume 2 of his *Lebensbericht,* the first volume of which, entitled *Licht auf den Zügeln,* appeared in 1953, also at Kessler's of Mannheim.

572. Blunck had early recognized the artistic pretensions of the top Nazi leaders, fully half of whom were frustrated—if inferior—artists, and had given official voice to the importance of their "aesthetics" for the Nazi regime in his essay on *Kultur* policy in the symposium *Germany Speaks.* Peter Viereck, who in his *Metapolitics* (I/1) makes much of the "armed bohemia" or "Greenwich Village warriors" aspect of the Nazi revolution, fully exploits Blunck's apologia. (*Ibid.,* pp. 154–156.) Cf. Wulf (III/13), p. 169.

573. See *Cellesche Zeitung,* December 7, 1955.

574. Peter Dörfler, *Apollonia Trilogie. Roman eines Geschlechts. (I) Die Lampe der törichten Jungfrau. (II) Apollonias Sommer. (III) Um das kommende Geschlecht* (Hamm: Grote, 1952). Dörfler's *Die Wessobrunner* and his postwar story *Das Osterlamm* appeared in the Catholic-conservative publishing house of Schnell and Steiner in Munich.

575. *Der Weg* (Buenos Aires) VI, 8 (1952), 582.

576. The degree to which the Nazis exploited Ernst becomes clear from the fulsome obituaries upon his death, some twelve weeks after Hitler's accession to power. (One of the most offensive of these is Will Vesper's eulogy, "Paul Ernst," in *Die Neue Literatur,* XXXIV, 6 [June, 1933], 313.) Almost every issue of *Die Neue Literatur* in the first two years after Ernst's death contained a photograph of the author and an uncritical appreciation. The Hitler Youth organized special Paul Ernst memorial evenings, and Ernst readings and lectures became important parts of Nazi culture. Indeed, as early as 1923, Ernst, who had difficulty finding a publisher for his massive epic, "The Emperor Book," turned to Dietrich Eckart to inquire if the Nazi movement might not wish to publish his work. (See *Die Neue Literatur,* XXXVI, 8 [August, 1935], 451, 504.) Under these circumstances it is pure myth making to see Ernst's relations to all radically antiliberal, antidemocratic movements in terms such as those suggested by Wolfgang Heilmann when he writes: "At that time—1933—[Ernst's] conservative ties to folkish, but also supranational, orders were being misused from time to time (*vereinzelt*) for political purposes, in the mistaken identification of 'conservative' and 'nationalist.'" (Historische Kommission bei der Bayerischen Akademie der Wissenschaften, ed., *Neue Deutsche Biographie* [Berlin: Duncker & Humblot, 1959], IV, 630.)

577. See, for instance, Paul Ernst's elephantine, six-volume epic, *Das Kaiserbuch,* which sought, by its glorification of the medieval German emperors, to demonstrate the best features of the German people and to reawaken the myth of its "historic mission," of the *sacrum imperium.* At the same time Ernst contributed also more directly to the political orientation of the Conservative Revolution in the Weimar years, especially with his *The Collapse of German Idealism* (*Der Zusammenbruch des deutschen Idealismus* [Munich: Müller, 1918]) and *The Collapse of Marxism* (*Der Zusammenbruch des Marxismus* [Munich: Müller, 1919]).

578. In a widely publicized speech in Berlin in the early nineteen-twenties, Wilhelm Schäfer, for one, sought to draw an unmistakable line between himself and the radically racist anti-Semites and National Socialists. See "Die deutsche Judenfrage. Ein Rede in Berlin," in his *Der deutsche Gott. Fünf Briefe an mein Volk* (Munich: Müller, 1923), especially pp. 245–246, 263–264.

579. Even before 1933, Albert Langen–Georg Müller published authors like Paul Ernst, E. G. Kolbenheyer, H. F. Blunck, Hermann Claudius, Hans Grimm, Wilhelm Schäfer, and Ernst Jünger. For an appreciation of Griese's "art" in the Third Reich, see Hellmuth Langenbucher's essay, partly quoted in Wulf (III/13), p. 308. Cf. Geissler (I/11), pp. 131–134.

580. *Deutsche Soldaten–Zeitung* (Munich), VI, 11 (November, 1956), 2.

581. Cited in Wulf (III/13), p. 319.

582. A case, though a weak one, can be made out for the blood relationship between the expressionism of the post-World War I period and the "New Nationalism" of the later twenties, which became the "official" art form of the Third Reich. For an attempt to trace these lines of similarity, see Richard Samuel and R. Hinton Thomas, *Expressionism in German Life, Literature, and the Theatre (1910–1924)* (Cambridge: Heffer, 1939), pp. 177–186.

583. Hanns Johst, *Gesegnete Vergänglichkeit* (Frankfurt: Pandion, [c. 1955]).

584. Ernst Frank, "Der Lebens- und Schaffensweg E. G. Kolbenheyers," *Der Bauhütten Brief,* II, 2 (1956), 12.

585. Kolbenheyer's philosophy, says one of his disciples, will appeal to those only "who do not only cling to the rationalism of the word, but also to what in the past one had called the light of nature—those, in short, who grasp the processes of nature intuitively. . . . For them the most precious things lie not only in the logical but also in the emotional apprehension of the Essential in Nature." Manfred Ruttner, "Was bedeutet uns Kolbenheyer?" *Ibid.,* II, 3 (1956), 6.

586. From Kolbenheyer's *Die Philosophie der Bauhütte* (Vienna: Neff, 1952), quoted in [Club republikanischer Publizisten,] *CrP–Information,* August, 1956.

587. Erwin Guido Kolbenheyer, *Die Bauhütte. Grundzüge einer Metaphysik der Gegenwart* (Munich: Langen-Müller, 1940). For an explanation of the word *Bauhütte,* see above, X/74. Cf. [Rudolf Aschenauer?] "Die Bauhütten-Philosophie Kolbenheyers in der Krise unserer Zeit," *Die andere Seite,* III, 3 (July, 1952), 6–9.

588. Seven years earlier, a so-called Bochum Circle appealed for funds for Kolbenheyer. Characteristically, the appeal was made through the monthly *Der Weg* (Buenos Aires), which remained for years the most radical Nazi journal extant. The leading members of the Bochum Circle, besides Kolbenheyer, were Dr. Marquardt, Dr. Niemann, and W. A. Reuter. Despite these efforts, Kolbenheyer's literary chef d'oeuvre, the massive

Paracelsus trilogy, was not republished until 1964, when it appeared under the imprint of J. F. Lehmann (Munich).

589. Kolbenheyer, *Menschen und Götter* (Darmstadt: Wittich [for the Kolbenheyer Association], 1956).

590. For Agnes Miegel's hysterical adulation of Hitler, see her poem, "To the Führer," on Hitler's birthday, April 20, 1940, in *Die Neue Literatur,* XLI, 4 (April, 1940), 81.

591. *Die Neue Literatur,* XXXV, 9 (September, 1934), 599 (quoted also in Schonauer [I/1], pp. 51–52). The typically Teutomanic arrogance which characterizes this passage also emerges from a message which Baron Münchhausen composed on behalf of the Senate of the Prussian Academy of Arts and had published by the press. Shocked by the tendency of the Nazi press to judge works of art by the political soundness of the artist rather than by the artistic quality of his work, von Münchhausen warned against jeopardizing "the reputation of German [critical] judgment which for a century and a half has been the final judgment in literary questions, including those of foreign nations." The message is reproduced in Grimm (XI/133), pp. 163–165.

592. Börries Freiherr von Münchhausen, *Das Baladenbuch* and *Das Liederbuch,* both published by the Deutsche Verlags–Anstalt in Stuttgart, 1955–1956.

593. Wilhelm Schäfer, *Die dreizehn Bücher der deutschen Seele* (Munich: Müller, 1925 [c. 1922]). Along with "Winkelmann's End," the Sudeten German Adam Kraft Verlag of Augsburg also reissued Schäfer's short stories, *The Necklace of a Queen, The Baden Cure,* and *A Man Named Schmitz.* For Oskar Loerke's estimate of Schäfer as a "hollow, nasty rowdy," "a screaming, black Alberich . . . with his tendency to hysterical rages," see Wulf (III/13) p. 34.

594. Quoted in Hirsch (XI/375), p. 14.

595. Quoted in Will Vesper, "Unsere Meinung," *Die Neue Literatur,* XXXIV, 4 (April, 1933), 230.

596. *Frankfurter Zeitung,* May 11, 1933, quoted in Hirsch (XI/375), p. 14.

597. "When a German girl has sexual relations with a Jew," wrote Vesper, "both will be quite properly convicted [on the charge] of defilement of race (*Rassenschande*). When a German author and a German book dealer enter into relations with Jewish publishers—is that not a worse and more dangerous [act of] defilement of race?" *Die Neue Literatur,* XXXVIII, 2 (February, 1937), 103–104.

598. *Ibid.,* XL, 5 (May, 1939), 225–226; XLI, 9 (September, 1940), 201. Cf. also "Dem Führer Dank!" *ibid.,* XXXIX, 4 (April, 1938), 217.

599. Will Vesper, *Das harte Geschlecht* (Graz, Göttingen: Stocker, 1952).

600. *Ibid.,* pp. 5–6.

601. *Die Neue Literatur,* XXXVIII, 10 (October, 1937), 528.

602. Alfred Weber, "Im Schatten der braunen Utopie" (typescript, 1952), p. 71.

603. *Die Neue Literatur,* XXXVIII, 10 (October, 1937), 527–528.

604. Vesper, *Die Ernte. Unvergängliches Gedicht aus 8 Jahrhunderten deutscher Lyrik* (Burg Stettenfels/Heilbronn: Hünenburg, [c. 1958]).

605. Vesper, *Seltsame Flöte: Hundert Geschichten aus verzauberter Welt* (Burg Stettenfels/Heilbronn: Hünenburg, [1958]).

606. Mostly by the Dikreiter Verlag, Freiburg.

607. Here we might also mention *It Happened in the Year 1965* (*Es geschah im Jahre 1965* [Salzburg: Pilgram, 1957], a postatomic-war novel which gives Dwinger an opportunity to exercise his anti-Bolshevism, his somewhat more subdued anti-Americanism, and his unchastened German nationalism.

608. Cf. Harry Pross, *Literatur und Politik* (Olten, Freiburg i. Br.: Walter, [1963]), p. 125.

609. Quoted by Eric A. Peschler, "Schmutziger Lorbeer," *Welt der Arbeit* (Bavarian edition), July 13, 1956.

610. Thus, for instance, Steguweit is represented in the so-called Kleine Westfälische Reihe of which its publisher, Deutscher Heimat Verlag, of Bielefeld, says, "Also, and in particular, school children are to be addressed [by this edition]."

611. Georg Dammers, "Gefährlich missbrauchte Freiheit," *Kontakte,* June, 1953, p. 14.

612. Anton Dörfler's political background is sufficiently characterized by a poem he composed while German units were occupying Austria in March, 1938:

> Magnificent joy: To be fruit of the tree.
> More magnificent yet: To die for it.
> Germany! Sparklingly flows thy name,
> In the mind's eye, like blood.
>
> Deep like creation is death for us now,
> Rooting in one: Fatherland, Germany!
> Rise then, oh eagle, spread your wings
> Mightily over the Danube!
>
> —"Ruf aus der Ostmark," *Die Neue Literatur,* XXXIX, 12 (December, 1938), 665.

613. Werner Klose, *Generation im Gleichschritt* ([Oldenburg:] Stalling, [1964]), p. 154, quoting a Nazi Party critic.

614. Hoettl, alias Walter Hagen, was arrested by the Americans in 1953 in connection with Communist espionage.

615. *Deutscher Informationsdienst,* July 25, 1956, quoting from "Der Dichter und die Wiedervereinigung," *Publikation* (Detmold), March, 1956. Pleyer's spirit emerges from an announcement on the birth of his first son which he sent to his friend Vesper. Announcing that his child was born on September 29, 1938, "the Sudeten Germans' day of salvation," he writes:

"Now everything is very, very, very good and I am glad that in a kind of religious fanaticism I remained here even during the dirtiest weather. Even on the day the Germans marched in, they [the Czechs] were still looking for me, but didn't find me. *HEIL HITLER!!!*" Replica of the announcement in *Die Neue Literatur,* XXXIX, 11 (November, 1938), 565 (attached).

616. See, for instance, the remarks in a letter to the editor of *Die Zeit* (Hamburg), August 9, 1956, by Theo Basenhausen.

617. J. W., "Dürfen wir vergessen?" *Norddeutsche Zeitung* (Hanover), July 30, 1956.

618. *Nobis* (Mainz), no. 1 (1953), quoted in *The Wiener Library Bulletin* (London), VII, 5–6 (September–December, 1953), 30.

619. Quoted in Schonauer (I/1), pp. 121–122.

620. Of course, Möller may also be remembered for his scandalous propaganda play of 1934, *Rothschild Wins at Waterloo,* where he "vindicates," by fake history, his preferred obsession, namely, that all wars are caused by, and conducted for the profit of, supranational Jewish finance circles. Möller also has the dubious honor of being the author of *Der Führer* (Munich: Eher, [c. 1938], a short Hitler biography, evidently for the Hitler Youth. Here sycophantic flattery and ruthless falsification of history reach breath-taking proportions. This is how Möller sees the Nazi mass murders ordered by Hitler in June, 1934: "That was the face of the ruler and the judge, turned white as a sheet in the passion of wrath, stony in the rigor of his office. That was the exalted hero whom Dante had once conceived and described in his *De necessitate monarchiae.* That was the sacred monarchy of the Reich itself which exercises the *sacratissimum ministerium* in the name of the German People, the High Judge over the outrage against the spirit, the order and peace of the world. . . . That was the bold genius, who rose above all the petty and human doubts of the 'poor mortal,' in order to maintain the lives of the mortally threatened Germans, [and] who returned to the nations their hopelessly destroyed order and who regained for the world her betrayed peace" (*ibid.,* pp. 157–158). So gross was the bad taste of Möller's screed that even Rosenberg sought to have it withdrawn from circulation and revised. See Wulf (III/13), pp. 206–211.

621. In 1963 the Holsten Verlag, of Hamburg, brought out Möller's novel *Chicago or The Man Who Stepped on the Bread* (*Chicago oder Der Mann der auf das Brot trat*). It came to my attention too late to receive critical consideration here.

622. Karl August Kutzbach, *Autorenlexikon des zwanzigsten Jahrhunderts* (Bonn: Bouvier), quoted in "Fröhliche Urständ!" *Deutsche Rundschau,* LXXVIII, 9 (September, 1952), 969.

623. See Schumann's autobiographical sketch in Wulf (III/13), pp. 376–377.

624. "Fröhliche Urständ!" (XI/622).

625. Quoted in Schonauer (I/1), p. 113. Cf. Schumann's "Sons of the Fighters" and "Promise to the Führer" reproduced in Wulf (III/13), pp. 305, 365.

626. Some of Schumann's poetry would indicate that he himself became

aware of the inner hollowness of Hitlerism as early as 1941. Nonetheless, he continued as SS captain to support the regime and to "represent" it as its inspired troubadour until 1945. See his "Lieder der Umkehr," reproduced in *Der Ruf* (Munich), I, 2 (September 1, 1945), 12.

627. Quoted in Wulf (III/13), p. 272. Cf. Strothmann (XI/567), pp. 39–40, p. 328, n.261.

628. Atkins (XI/136), pp. 16–17. In addition to editing *Contemporary Folkish Poetry,* Langenbucher set quasi-official standards for aesthetic and literary orthodoxy along Nazi lines with such titles as *National Socialist Poetry* (*Nationalsozialistische Dichtung*) and *Poetry of the Young Crew* (*Dichtung der jungen Mannschaft*).

629. Hellmuth Langenbucher, ed., *Ins Herz hinein. Ein Hand- und Lesebuch für Feier und Besinnung in Schule und Haus.* Volume 1: *Geleit durch das Jahr, Tage und Wochen* (Bad Reichenhall: Neue Schule, Leitner, [c. 1957]).

630. *Bulletin on German Questions* (London), IX, 192 (July 4, 1957).

631. While this anthology quotes Blunck twenty-six times, Will Vesper and Hermann Claudius fifteen times each, and Frederick the Great even twenty-four times, Langenbucher was unable to find anything worth quoting in Thomas Mann, Heinrich Mann, Bert Brecht, Robert Musil, or Joseph Roth and discovered only one quotable passage each in the works of Heinrich Heine, Franz Werfel, Erich Kästner, Alfred Mombert, Romain Rolland, or Theodor Heuss.

632. Hermann Pongs, *Im Umbruch der Zeit: Das Romanschaffen der Gegenwart* ([Göttingen:] Göttinger Verlagsanstalt, [1954]). In 1963 appeared the 4th edition under the new title *Romanschaffen im Umbruch der Zeit. Eine Chronik von 1952 bis 1962* (4th rev. enl. ed.; [Tübingen:] Deutsche Hochschullehrer–Zeitung, 1963).

633. See letter to State Commissioner Hans Hinkel of July 29, 1933, reproduced in Wulf (III/13), p. 234. Cf. Strothmann (XI/567), p. 328, n.261.

634. Cited in Wulf (III/13), p. 322. Cf. Strothmann (XI/567), pp. 332–333.

635. Fechter's history was republished, together with the rest of his voluminous work, by C. Bertelsmann, of Gütersloh, and Nadler first came out—accompanied by much protest—at the Oesterreichischer Verlag für Belletristik und Wissenschaft, in Linz, and three years later, in 1951, at the Johann Günther Verlag, Vienna.

636. From this viewpoint it is difficult to understand why, for instance, the State Examining Commission for the students' libraries of the Higher Teachers' Seminaries of Bavaria (the only Land to have such a commission) should officially approve works by H. F. Blunck, Paul Alverdes, the racist Hjalmar Kutzleb, the Ludendorff enthusiast Wilhelm Matthiessen, Karl Springenschmid, SS Captain and Hitler Youth Leader Fritz Helke, Hans Baumann, and the race theorist Ludwig F. Clauss. See *Das Feuilleton des Sozialdemokratischen Pressedienstes,* F/XI/94 (May 17, 1956), pp. 1–2.

637. Grabert (XI/264).

638. In line of this duty, in 1939 Plassmann published a fulsome justification of the Anschluss and the dismemberment of Czechoslovakia under the title *German Land Returns Home: The Eastern March and Sudetenland as Germanic Ethnic Soil.* (*Deutsches Land kehrt heim. Ostmark und Sudetenland als germanischer Volksboden* [Berlin: Ahnenerbe, 1939].)

639. Josef O. Plassmann, *Princeps und Populus: Die Gefolgschaft im ottonischen Staatsaufbau nach den sächsischen Geschichtsschreibern des 10. Jahrhunderts* ([Göttingen:] Göttinger Verlagsanstalt, [1954]).

640. Meyer had also held appointments as staff member of the SS Race and Settlement Main Office (Rasse- und Siedlungshauptamt, RuSHA) and as Department Chief in the Reich Commissariat for the Strengthening of German Folkdom (Reichskommissariat für die Festigung deutschen Volkstums).

641. Konrad Meyer, *Nahrungsraum und Übervölkerung: Ein Weltproblem der Gegenwart* ([Göttingen:] Göttinger Verlagsanstalt, [1953]).

642. In the course of an Institute conference on the Jews in July, 1938, Burgdörfer demonstrated on the basis of statistical materials that Jewry was unmistakably parasitical in character. The Jews in Germany were a "definitely urbanized, highly over-aged, unusually child-poor population group, of totally one-sided . . . economic and social structure." Poliakov and Wulf (V/23), pp. 387, 390. Burgdörfer was also coauthor of *Genetics, Racial Hygiene, Population Policy: Vital Questions for the German People* (Heinz Woltereck, ed., *Erbkunde, Rassenpflege, Bevölkerungspolitik: Schicksalsfragen des deutschen Volkes* [Leipzig: Quelle & Meyer, 1935]).

643. Friedrich Burgdörfer, *Bevölkerungsdynamik und Bevölkerungsbilanz* (Munich: Lehmann, 1951). Incidentally, Burgdörfer's publisher, a former specialist in racism, has also brought out a new booklet by the folkish physician Gustav Sondermann, who in 1924 wrote the widely circulated *The Meaning of the Folkish Mission* (*Der Sinn der völkischen Sendung*). Probably wiser, as well as older, Sondermann is now concerned with less revolutionary notions, for his new brochure is a compilation of the worries of German physicians, entitled, *Physician—Health Insurance—National Health* (*Arzt—Kasse—Volksgesundheit.* [Munich: Lehmann, 1952]).

644. Karl-Heinz Pfeffer, *Handwörterbuch der Politik* (Darmstadt: Leske, 1956).

645. Pfeffer, *Die deutsche Schule der Soziologie* (Leipzig: Quelle & Meyer, 1939), p. 3.

646. Pfeffer, *Das Judentum im osteuropäischen Raum* (Essen: Essener Verlagsanstalt, 1938).

647. Philip Leibrecht in *Die Neue Literatur,* XL, 9 (September, 1939), 451.

648. Pfeffer, *Der englische Krieg ist auch ein jüdischer Krieg* (Munich: Eher, 1943). Three years earlier Pfeffer had published *England: Vormacht der bürgerlichen Welt* (Hamburg: Hanseatische Verlagsanstalt, 1940), in which he sought to demonstrate that England's "bourgeois-capitalist spirit" was facing its doom in the struggle against the "young peoples" and "the forces of the National Socialist–Fascist Twentieth Century." In the same year

Pfeffer produced a brochure on *The Concept and Essence of Plutocracy* (*Begriff und Wesen der Plutokratie* [Berlin: Junker & Dünnhaupt, 1940]).

649. To Hannah Arendt (*The Origins of Totalitarianism* [New York: Harcourt, Brace, 1951], p. 332), Neesse and his colleague Reinhard Hoehn, whose stars rose after the fall from grace of the brilliant political theorist and early Nazi sympathizer, Carl Schmitt, were prime evidence for the following generalization: "Totalitarianism in power invariably replaces all first-rate talents, regardless of their sympathies, with those crackpots and fools whose lack of intelligence and creativity is still the best guarantee of their loyalty."

650. Gottfried Neesse, *Staatsdienst und Staatsschicksal* (Hamburg: Holsten, 1957). For excerpts from Neesse's Nazi works, see Poliakov and Wulf (V/23), pp. 60–61, and University of Colorado, Department of Philosophy, eds., *Readings on Fascism and National Socialism* (Denver: Swallow, n.d.), pp. 65–67, 77, 78, 79, 82–83, 89.

651. Neesse (XI/650), p. 115.

652. *Ibid.*, p. 12.

653. *Ibid.*, p. 19.

654. Marc Augier, *Götterdämmerung: Europa 1945* (Leoni: Druffel, 1956).

655. Maurice Bardèche, *Die Politik der Zerstörung: Nürnberg oder Europa* (Göttingen: Plesse, 1951).

656. Bardèche, *Der Weg nach vorn* (Göttingen: Plesse, [1951?]).

657. Bardèche, *Nürnberg oder die Falschmünzer* (Wiesbaden: Priester, 1957).

658. René d'Argile, Jacques Ploncard d'Assac, *et al.*, eds., *Das Geheimnis um die Ursachen des 2. Weltkrieges* (Wiesbaden: Priester, 1958).

659. Léon Degrelle, *Die verlorene Legion* (Göttingen: Plesse, 1952).

660. Emilio Esteban-Infantes, *Blaue Division. Spaniens Freiwillige an der Ostfront,* trans. by Werner Haupt (Leoni: Druffel, [1958]).

661. Jerk (VIII/12). The Swedish original bore the title *Ragnaroek* (*Twilight of the Gods*).

662. Willem Sluyse, *Die Jünger und die Dirnen* (Buenos Aires: Dürer, [1954]).

663. Oswald Mosley, *The Alternative* (Ramsbury [Wilts.]: Mosley Publications, 1947).

664. Mosley, *Ich glaube an Europa. Ein Weg aus der Krise. Eine Einführung in das europäische Denken,* trans. by Heinrich Härtle (Lippoldsberg: Klosterhaus, [c. 1962]). (*Europe—Faith and Plan: A Way Out from the Coming Crisis and an Introduction to Thinking as a European* [London: Euphorion, 1958].) In this programmatic book, Mosley calls for the creation of a unified European state in some kind of economic union with Africa. Moreover, he insists that the future order must be built upon a peaceful arrangement with the Soviet Union and pleads for the replacement of capitalism by what he calls "European socialism," which means a modicum of planning without major state compulsion.

665. Severin Reinhard, *pseud.* [i.e., René Sonderegger], *Spanischer Sommer* (Affoltern a. Albis [Switz.]: Aehren, [c. 1948]; Buenos Aires:

Dürer, 1952). Initially an ardent anti-Nazi, Sonderegger became an equally fervent admirer of Hitler. His literary glorifications of his hero were suppressed by the Swiss government in 1940–1941. Sonderegger is said to have moved permanently to Spain in 1953.

666. See *The Wiener Library Bulletin* (London), III, 3–6 (September–November, 1949), 38, and VI, 1–2 (January–April, 1952), 6. Sonderegger's elaborate historical frauds designed to show the involvement of one "Sidney Warburg" and his wide-flung Jewish business associates in the financial support of the Nazi movement have been revealed by Hermann Lutz, *German-French Unity: Basis for European Peace* (Chicago: Regnery, 1957), pp. 189–199. (*"Verbrecher Volk" im Herzen Europas?* [XI/262].)

667. Austin J. App, *History's Most Terrifying Peace* (San Antonio: Boniface Press, 1946). In 1950 it was translated by E. J. Reichenberger as *Der erschreckendste Friede der Geschichte* (Salzburg: Hellbrunn, 1950).

668. See also the discussion of American efforts on behalf of German expellees in Karl O. Kurth, "In der Sicht des Auslandes," in Lemberg and Edding (IV/7), III, 513–530.

669. Lutz (XI/262).

670. David L. Hoggan, *Der erzwungene Krieg. Die Ursachen und Urheber des 2. Weltkrieges,* trans. by M. E. Narjes and H. Grabert (4th ed.; [Tübingen:] Deutsche Hochschullehrer–Zeitung, 1963 [c. 1961]).

671. At the time of this writing Hoggan had not yet found an American publisher for his controversial book, though Devin-Adair was said to be giving the manuscript some consideration.

672. Hoggan's Harvard doctoral dissertation of 1948, entitled *The Breakdown of German-Polish Relations in 1939: The Conflict between the German New Order and the Polish Idea of Central Eastern Europe,* already evinces a pronounced anti-Polish and anti-British bias.

673. [Hermann Graml,] *David L. Hoggan und die Dokumente,* Sonderdruck, Vierteljahrshefte für Zeitgeschichte (Stuttgart: Deutsche Verlags-Anstalt, n.d. [1963]), pp. 1, 2. Gotthard Jasper in his review in *Vierteljahrshefte für Zeitgeschichte* (X, 3 [July, 1962]) stated: "Hoggan's work can be accorded the rank of a scholarly performance neither [with respect] to his historical conceptualization, nor [with respect] to his evaluation, and least of all [with respect] to his handling of sources and secondary literature" (p. 338). Cf. Lutz Niethammer, "Hoggan auf Deutschlandfahrt," *Der Monat,* XVI, 190 (July, 1964), 81–90. Also see book review by Gerhard L. Weinberg in the *American Historical Review,* LXVIII, 1 (October, 1962), 104. This review and Hoggan's and Harry Elmer Barnes' rebuttals to it (*ibid.,* 3 [April, 1963], 914–917), not only brought a supplementary confirmation of the critical position initially taken by Weinberg (*ibid.,* 917–918) but also further responses by Hoggan (*ibid.,* LXIX, 1 [October, 1963], 303) and Barnes (*ibid.,* 304), and an additional contretemps between William L. Langer (*ibid.,* 304–305) and Barnes (*ibid.,* 306–307). In 1964, Hoggan, whose first book achieved five editions in the first two years after publication and appeared for some time on the best-seller list, followed up with *France's Resistance Against the Second World War* (*Frankreichs Widerstand gegen*

den 2. Weltkrieg. Die französische Aussenpolitik von 1934–1939 [Tübingen: Deutsche Hochschulleher–Zeitung, 1964]), in which he "proved" that only British wiles and trickery brought France into the war against Nazi Germany. In the beginning of 1964, Hoggan made international news (see "Germans Debate Brief for Hitler," *New York Times,* May 3, 1964) when the Society for the Promotion of Historical Research (see below, XII/133-134 and nearby text) awarded Hoggan the DM 10,000 Leopold von Ranke Prize, the similarly nationalist Society for Free Journalism (see below, XII/144 and nearby text) foisted its DM 5,000 Ulrich von Hutten Prize on the American, Herbert Böhme's German Cultural Work in the European Spirit (see below, Chapter XII, Section B/I) prepared to bestow a candelabra on him, and even the archconservative Rhine-Ruhr Club invited Hoggan to its premises. Official pressures forced the cancellation of this latter invitation, and the other festivities had to be considerably modified. For a detailed discussion of Hoggan's first book, the circumstances surrounding its publication, and the "triumphal" tour of its author through the Right-extremist regions of the German political landscape, as well as for a most revealing interview with Hoggan, see also "Hoggan: Einfach schön," *Der Spiegel,* XVIII, 20 (May 13, 1964), 28–35, and "War Hitler ein Friedensfreund?" *ibid.,* pp. 36–48. The same issue of *Der Spiegel* also reproduced (on p. 44) parts of Graml's devastating documentation which we mentioned above. Incidentally, it was also reprinted in its entirety in *Geschichte in Wissenschaft und Unterricht,* XIV, 8 (August, 1963).

674. From an interview with Hermann Graml, Munich, November 25, 1964.

675. Harry Elmer Barnes, ed., *Perpetual War for Perpetual Peace. A Critical Examination of the Foreign Policy of Franklin Delano Roosevelt and Its Aftermath,* with the collaboration of William Henry Chamberlin, Percy L. Greaves, Jr., George A. Lundberg, George Morgenstern, William L. Neumann, Frederic R. Sanborn, and Charles C. Tansill (Caldwell, Idaho: Caxton, 1953). (Barnes, ed., *Entlarvte Heuchelei.* [*Ewig Krieg um ewigen Frieden.*] *Revision der amerikanischen Geschichtsschreibung. Kritische Untersuchung der amerikanischen Aussenpolitik seit Franklin Delano Roosevelt,* in collaboration with W. H. Chamberlin, W. N. Neumann, F. R. Sanborn, and C. C. Tansill, with a preface by Herbert Grabert; trans. by Marie Adelheid Princess Reuss zur Lippe [Wiesbaden: Priester, 1961].) The symposium presents the familiar charges that Roosevelt had provoked Pearl Harbor and tricked the American people into a war they did not want and that was not in the best interests of the United States. Barnes' introductory chapter has been rewritten for the German edition. It constitutes the ancient revisionist lament against the historical falsifications perpetrated by the "court" historians of both postwar periods and seeks to demonstrate the unscrupulous lengths to which the "party line" historians and their helpers in academic chairs and editorial offices are willing to go to deny to revisionists access to the supposedly free and open market place of ideas.

676. Peter H. Nicoll, *Englands Krieg gegen Deutschland. Die Ursachen, Methoden und Folgen des zweiten Weltkriegs* (Tübingen: Deutsche Hoch-

schullehrer–Zeitung, 1963). (*Britain's Blunder: An Objective Study of the Second World War, Its Cause, Conduct, and Consequence* [London? 1953?].)

677. G[eorge] R[acey] Jordan, *Sowjets siegen durch Spione. Roosevelt hat der Sowjet-Union die Atombombe ausgeliefert,* trans. by Heinrich Härtle (Göttingen: Schütz, [1960]). (*From Major Jordan's Diaries* [New York: Bookmailer, 1953].)

678. Helmut Steinberg, *pseud.* [i.e., Heinrich Härtle], "Roosevelt—ein weltgeschichtliches Verhängnis," in Jordan (XI/677), pp. 207–219.

679. George N. Crocker, *Schrittmacher der Sowjets. Das Schicksal der Welt lag in Roosevelts Hand,* trans. by Dietrich Niebuhr (Tübingen: Schlichtenmayer, [1960]). (*Roosevelt's Road to Russia* [Chicago: Regnery, 1959].)

680. Indeed, so rapidly has revisionist literature increased in Germany in the past few years, and so important has it become to nationalists, that the time appeared opportune to attempt a first survey of twentieth-century history from the nationalist-revisionist viewpoint. This task was accomplished by a high school teacher, Walther Reitenhart, who in a slim brochure summarized the "findings" of Hoggan, A. J. P. Taylor, Frau von Ribbentrop, Nicoll, Tansill, Walendy, Barnes, d'Argile, Sündermann, and Glasebock: *Kriegsschuldforschung entlastet Deutschland. Ein Überblick,* Beihefte zur Deutschen Hochschullehrer–Zeitung, no. 2 ([Tübingen:] Deutsche Hochschullehrer–Zeitung, 1964).

681. Russell Grenfell, *Bedingungsloser Hass? Die deutsche Kriegsschuld und Europas Zukunft,* trans. by Egon Heymann (Tübingen: Schlichtenmayer, 1954). (*Unconditional Hatred. German War Guilt and the Future of Europe* [1st world ed., 3d printing; New York: Devin-Adair, 1954].)

682. Charles C. Tansill, *Die Hintertür zum Krieg. Das Drama der internationalen Diplomatie von Versailles bis Pearl Harbor,* trans. by Hans Steinsdorff (Düsseldorf: Droste, [1957]). (*Back Door to War: The Roosevelt Foreign Policy 1933–1941* [Chicago: Regnery, 1952].)

683. Freda Utley, *Die kostspielige Rache,* trans. by Egon Heymann (Hamburg: Nölke, [1950]). (*The High Cost of Vengeance* [Chicago: Regnery, 1949].)

684. Utley, *Arabische Welt—Ost oder West? Vom neuen Schauplatz des kalten Krieges,* trans. and introd. by Peter Kleist (Göttingen: Plesse, [1958]). (*Will the Middle East Go West?* [Chicago: Regnery, 1957].)

685. F[rederick] J[ohn] P[artington] Veale, *Der Barbarei entgegen. Wie der Rückfall in die Barbarei durch Kriegsführung und Kriegsverbrecherprozesse unsere Zukunft bedroht,* trans. by Ursula Michaelsen, introd. by Paul Leverkuehn (Hamburg: Nölke, [c. 1951]). (*Advance to Barbarism* [Appleton, Wis.: Nelson, 1953].) Leverkuehn, incidentally, was one of the defense attorneys in the General Staff and Manstein trials and later became CDU Bundestag deputy. A second edition of Veale's book appeared in 1962 at the Priester Verlag in Wiesbaden.

686. Veale, *Verschleierte Kriegsverbrechen* (Wiesbaden: Priester, [c. 1959]). (*Crimes Discreetly Veiled* [London: Cooper, (1958)].) Veale's latest book, *Schuld und Sühne* (Tübingen: Schlichtenmayer, 1964), came to my attention too late to be included here.

687. Charles Bewley, *Hermann Göring* ([Göttingen:] Göttinger Verlagsanstalt, [1954]).

688. Paul Rassinier, *Die Lüge des Odysseus* (Wiesbaden: Priester, [c. 1959]). After the original appearance of the book in France, Rassinier is reported to have been expelled from the Socialist Party and to have been forced to vacate his seat in the National Assembly.

689. Oddly enough, this was the man who, according to Walter Laqueur, "was sent by the Hoover Foundation to cover the Auschwitz trial in Frankfurt!" See "Nazism and the Nazis," *Encounter,* XXII, 4 (April, 1964), 42.

690. Paul Rassinier, *Zum Fall Eichmann: Was ist Wahrheit?—oder—Die unbelehrbaren Sieger* (Leoni: Druffel, [1963]). (*Le véritable procès Eichmann ou les vainqueurs incorrigibles* [Paris, 1962].)

691. J. G. Burg, *Schuld und Schicksal: Europas Juden zwischen Henkern und Heuchlern* (Munich: Damm, 1962).

692. We might also mention here Franz Josef Scheidl, *Israel, Traum und Wirklichkeit* (Munich: Schild, 1962), which was banned because of its anti-Semitic and pro-Soviet bias. Actually Scheidl vehemently denies such a bias and insists that his opposition is exclusively limited to political Zionism, i.e., to Jewish chauvinism. Instead, Scheidl appeals to antinationalist, liberal, and humanist Judaism and calls for the evacuation of Israel, its return to the Arabs, and the assimilation of all Jews all over the world.

Chapter XII. The Ideas and Literature of Nationalism (II): Dissemination

1. *Der Weg (El Sendero)* (Buenos Aires: Dürer Verlag).

2. Brunner (VII/49), pp. 338–339.

3. *Ibid.,* p. 366.

4. Because of the difference in occupation status and, hence, in occupation policy, the formation of specifically Nazi or philo-Nazi publishing firms occurred in Austria about three years earlier than in Germany. In Austria the process of commercially organizing the denazified authors (insofar as a writing ban had not been imposed on them by a denazification tribunal) began as early as 1947. In that year the Stocker Verlag in Graz resumed operations, and the Otto Müller Verlag in Salzburg began publication of the propaganda materials of the nationalist opposition chief, A. H. Kraus. Shortly thereafter the SD's counterintelligence officer, SS Major Wilhelm Hoettl, a prominent Nuremberg witness and, under the pseudonym Walter Hagen, the author of *The Secret Front* (*Die geheime Front: Organisation, Personen und Aktionen des deutschen Geheimdienstes* [Stuttgart: Veritas, 1952]), established the Nibelungen Verlag in Linz and became part owner of the Pilgram Verlag in Salzburg. Only now, after the formation of the German Federal Republic in 1949 and the concomitant relinquishing of some of the Allies' more stringent occupation control functions, (including licensing of pub-

lishers) was it possible to found publishing firms in Germany with the intent of promoting anti-Allied, antidemocratic, and nationalist authors. In December, 1949, the Ludendorff enthusiasts were able to reopen their publishing house Hohe Warte. This was followed in February, 1950, by the establishment of the Plesse Verlag in Göttingen, from which Leonhard Schlüter separated himself a year later to found his own enterprise, the Göttinger Verlagsanstalt. These were also the most active years of two publishers closely identified with the then growing SRP: Hans Siep and Gutenberg Verlag, both of Hamburg. By 1952, with the founding of Druffel Verlag at Leoni in Upper Bavaria and Kurt Vowinckel's resumption of operations in Heidelberg, the conditions of the times and the expiration or amnesty of denazification bans on publishing or writing produced a sharp increase in the number of publishers available to "nonconformists."

5. As literary production knows no political frontiers, our list will include also those five Austrian publishers whose works occupy a significant place in the total picture of German nationalist literature. For the same reason the source of the most uncompromising Nazi writings in Buenos Aires, the Dürer Verlag, is here included.

6. This firm, owned and run by one Ludwig Leher, evidently prides itself on the support of such people as A. J. App, of Philadelphia, the Chicago German-Amercian Rightists Arthur Koegel and H. Fischer, and the well-known German radical nationalist in New York, Frederick C. Weiss, important middleman for the distribution of anti-Semitic and Nazi literature. For App, Weiss, and Koegel, see Forster and Epstein (VII/40), pp. 53, 201 ff., 231. Caution is required, for this is a slipshod and unreliable book.

7. As pointed out in the previous chapter, Cramer's Combat SS accounts and the books of his star author, Otto Skorzeny, were confiscated shortly after their publication in 1963. In the autumn of 1963 Cramer went on trial on the charge of distributing literature designed to endanger the state. After six weeks the trial was prorogued until May, 1965. Before it could be resumed, however, Cramer, his family, and 21,000 copies of his impounded stock disappeared without leaving a trace. Kubala (XI/371), p. 5.

8. See above, XI/53.

9. Thus on January 9, 1953, Wolfgang Sarg, SRP editor and fanatical chief of Natinform, wrote to his deputy: "Herr Vowinckel is fully and entirely on our side . . . collaborates closely with Natinform . . . and is my publisher for the Göring biography." And in a confidential report of a secret Natinform meeting, January 16–19, 1953, Vowinckel's relation to Sarg is characterized as follows: "[Sarg] receives from Vowinckel packages with clothes, shoes, victuals, and at regular intervals also financial contributions, which invariably amount to DM 50–100."

10. Johann Philipp Palm, a bookseller, was executed in 1806 for distributing a patriotic anti-Napoleonic pamphlet called *Germany in its Deep Humiliation*. The parallel to which Burri wished to draw attention by the name of his firm reveals his intentions. Incidentally, a monument to Palm graces the main square of the little Austrian town of Braunau, the birthplace of Adolf Hitler.

11. In 1965, helpless under growing financial and legal pressures (not least those applied by his erstwhile friends Oberländer and Ziesel), Schlichtenmayer committed suicide. "Schlichtenmayer: Pleite von rechts," *Der Spiegel,* XIX, 22 (May 26, 1965), 91–92.

12. *Bulletin on German Questions* (London), X, 235/236 (May 15, 1959), 15.

13. *Studien von Zeitfragen, Presse- und Buchspiegel,* no. VIII-IX (September 29, 1962), p. 5.

14. See above, XI/520.

15. See above, XI/66.

16. See above, XI/478.

17. See above, XI/12.

18. See above, XI/311.

19. See above, XI/421.

20. See above, XI/415, 417.

21. See above, XI/225, 226.

22. For a background story on the operation of C. Bertelsmann, see *Der Spiegel,* XI, 30 (July 24, 1957), 32–41.

23. See above, XI/644.

24. From a confidential report of a conversation between Kleist, Vowinckel, the information agent E. A. Schmidt, and the deputy Natinform chief, Heidelberg, February 11, 1953.

25. See Helmut Sündermann's remonstrance against what he called an entirely arbitrary and unwarranted presumption by the *Börsenblatt. Nation Europa,* V, 10 (October, 1955), back cover.

26. Rosenberg (XI/26). While Schütz in the preface admitted that "a few formal and stylistic" corrections were made and assured the reader that these corrections had not altered "the meaning of the presentation or its evaluation," the Göttingen historian Hans–Günther Seraphim, in a close comparison between the Plesse text and the original of Rosenberg's memoirs, found in 109 pages of text no fewer than 350 omissions, changes, and additions. Many of the alterations were suppressions of Rosenberg's criticisms of Hitler and National Socialism, making Rosenberg "a kind of chief witness for a harmless but stout-hearted Nazism." *Frankfurter Allgemeine Zeitung,* September 20, 1956. The alterations were the handiwork of Heinrich Härtle, whose interpretive skill we admired in his *Nietzsche and National Socialism* (XI/540).

27. Cf. "Die Bücherstürmer von Frankfurt," *Deutscher Aufbruch* (Munich), V, 11 (October–November, 1955), and Dieter Vollmer, "Ein Akt der Selbsthilfe," *Nation Europa,* V, 11 (November, 1955), back cover.

28. [Club republikanischer Publizisten,] *CrP-Information,* August, 1956.

29. From a confidential report of a discussion with Krüger in Germersheim, April 16, 1953.

30. From the first catalogue, *"Ziele-Aufbau-Arbeit."*

31. Except possibly for Karl–Heinz Priester's quaint "welcome" with which he introduced his *D.E.N. Bücherdienst* and which ended with "You

will understand that we refuse to supply obscene literature and writings which are the symbols of the alien-controlled spirit of the age."

32. "Rechtsradikalismus in der Bundesrepublik: Ein Erfahrungsbericht," *Aus Politik und Zeitgeschichte* (Supplement to *Das Parlament*), B 20/60, May 16, 1962.

33. *Ibid.*, p. 241.

34. Oberländer and von Machui have edited *Meilensteine.* Also see above, VI/144, 162; XI/439.

35. See above, XI/644 and nearby text.

36. Hahn-Butry, who had been publishing the news service *Bundeswehr Korrespondenz,* has since 1962 been producing *Die Europäische Sicht.* In addition, he publishes *Afrika Bulletin, Afrika Schnellbrief,* and *Écho de l'Afrique et de l'Europe.*

37. See above, VI/6.

38. See below, Chapter XVIII, Section G.

39. The change in name seemed advisable when the newly founded National Democratic Party superseded the German Reich Party.

40. The magazine initially established "editorial offices" in Sweden, the Netherlands, and Switzerland. With Per Engdahl and Paul van Tienen filling the first two positions, respectively, an intimate connection to the European Social Movement was assured. In Switzerland the "editorial office" was in the charge of Hans Oehler, who in 1947 had been convicted of treason and sentenced to two years' penal servitude. The charges had grown out of Oehler's presence in October, 1940, at a conference in Munich of the heads of all Swiss pro-Nazi organizations. The purpose of the conference had been to attempt a merger of these groups into one solid Nazi bloc, to maximize the effectiveness of German pressure on Switzerland. (See *The Wiener Library Bulletin* [London], IV, 3–4 [May–July, 1950], 21.) Oehler, incidentally, also prepared the first German translation of Maurice Bardèche. Engdahl, van Tienen, and Oehler were joined at the beginning of the second year of publication by Erich Kernmayr, who in those days was still heading up the so-called Gmunden Circle of Nazi activists, and by the Danish Nazi, Captain Erik Laerum.

41. See Dieter Lechner, "Ein gefährlicher Schwärmer und seine Hintermänner," *Frankfurter Rundschau,* December 10, 1957.

42. See above, VII/9. This aspect of *Nation Europa's* financial background was revealed by the testimony of one of Naumann's collaborators, Heinz Siepen, who had been arrested with Naumann and five others in January, 1953. See above, text near V/63 and V/89. See the Wiener Library's summary of impounded Naumann documents, "The Naumann Plot: Evidence from the Impounded Documents," *The Wiener Library Bulletin* (London), VII, 3–4 (May–August, 1953), 20.

43. More recently Gerhard Frey, the ambitious and successful publisher of *German National News and Soldiers' News,* and the nationalist publishers Schütz (Plesse) and Sündermann (Druffel) have acquired 7.84 per cent of the shares. (But cf. Hans Frederik, *Die Rechstradikalen* [Munich-Inning:

Humboldt, [1965?]), p. 55.) Originally also over a half-dozen foreigners from Sweden, Switzerland, Canada, Belgium, and the United States, subscribed DM 12,000. The American backers were the inevitable Arthur Koegel and his fellow Chicagoan Otto Jaeckel, with two shares each. The editor in chief, Ehrhardt, held some twenty shares of the sixty-three and remained solely responsible for the make-up, direction, and contents of the journal. In January, 1954, the stockholders organized a separate entity called The Friends of *Nation Europa* for the purpose of gaining additional financial support either directly or through greatly expanded readership. The society as a corporate entity also became a stockholder, with two shares. The Swedish engineer Carl E. Carlberg, a Nordic-folkish sectarian who contributed the notion of a gymnic, spiritual, and biological renewal of the decadent and subverted West, was the single largest foreign shareholder, with four shares. (For Carlberg's "political philosophy" see his "Dreizehn Thesen" [V/52]. Cf. Carl E. Carlberg, "Der gymnische Gedanke," *Der Weg* [Buenos Aires], VI, 5 [May, 1952], 337–340.) Carlberg died in 1962. In his will he left his apartment in Stockholm to the Carlberg Foundation, the front for a secret society which he had founded and whose military training and caches of arms, explosives, and poison led in May, 1965, to sensational police raids and arrests. Initial reports suggested collaboration between the Swedish Nazis and the Egyptian Embassy in Stockholm. (W. Bauer-Heyd, "Arbeiten Schwedens Nazi für Ägypten? Experten sprechen von regelmässigen Berichten an die Stockholmer Botschaft," *Süddeutsche Zeitung* [Munich], no. 114 [May 13, 1965], p. 5.)

44. See above, XI/4.

45. *Nation Europa,* V, 5 (May, 1955), 3.

46. *Ibid.,* pp. 3–4.

47. For the published exchange of letters see *Vierteljahrshefte für Zeitgeschichte,* III, 2, (April, 1955), 223–225. For an open letter in rebuttal to Rothfels' letter of January 25, 1955, see *Nation Europa,* V, 3 (March, 1955), 70–72.

48. Cecile von Goetz, "Baruchistan?" *Nation Europa,* IV, 11 (November, 1954), 17.

49. *Ibid.,* p. 15.

50. *Ibid.,* p. 21.

51. See *Für die Demokratie,* I (IX), 7 (August, 1960), 7. The editor, however—Ehrhardt himself—has been convicted, albeit on charges of insulting the president of the Bundestag. At that time, in 1957, he was handed a three months' suspended sentence. For the *corpus delicti,* the insulting open letter to Eugen Gerstenmaier, see *Nation Europa,* VI, 5 (May, 1956), end cover.

52. *Klüter Blätter,* III, 1 (1952), quoted in Weber (XI/602), p. 13.

53. Wulf (III/13), p. 373.

54. See [Club republikanischer Publizisten,] *CrP-Information,* September, 1956, p. 20.

55. See the letter reproduced in Wulf (III/13), p. 245. Cf. Strothmann (XI/567), p. 105.

56. Quoted in *Die Brücke,* III, 10 (September 3, 1956), 2.

57. Paul F. Douglass, *God among the Germans* (Philadelphia: University of Pennsylvania Press, 1935), p. 49.

58. The truculently antidemocratic, antirepublican, fiercely nationalist and authoritarian-monarchist orientation of the Protestant ministry (with few exceptions) had prepared the field for the Nazis all too well. This process was similar to that which had hollowed out and delivered up to the Nazis other bourgeois and upper-bourgeois institutions and classes. See Bracher *et al.* (III/36), pp. 326–348. Theologians of the Glaubensbewegung Deutsche Christen argued that divine revelation did not exhaust itself with the appearance of the historical Jesus but continued to act in history and that Hitler, therefore, must be a divinely ordained savior whose deeds and program are to be accepted as new revelation. To these churchmen "gospel and National Socialism are . . . the two pillars of the German Evangelical Church." "Christ," they insist, "has come to us through Adolf Hitler." This shameful and disastrous chapter in the history of German Protestantism can now be followed in the careful study of Günther van Norden, *Kirche in der Krise. Die Stellung der evangelischen Kirche zum nationalsozialistischen Staat im Jahre 1933* (Düsseldorf: Presseverband der evangelischen Kirche im Rheinland, 1964).

59. Under the leadership of Hauer, Johann von Leers (Hitler's Number One anti-Semite—see above, VII/175, 176), Hans F. K. Günther ("Race-Günther," so called—see above, XI/518-520), Hermann Wirth (the racist mythologist of "Atlanticism"), and Count Ernst Reventlow (one of the earliest folkish Hitlerites), the German Faith Movement represented a merger of a variety of folkish, neopagan, "Teutonic" religions, including the League of Free Religious Congregations of Germany (Bund der freireligiösen Gemeinden Deutschlands) and Ludwig Fahrenkrog's Germanic Faith Fellowship (Germanische Glaubensgemeinschaft, GGG).

60. For the orientation and goals of the German Faith Movement after the break with Hauer, see Schloz (XI/104).

61. Quoted in Henri Lichtenberger, *The Third Reich,* trans. by K. S. Pinson (New York: Greystone, 1937), p. 192.

62. This conviction Hitler had brought home from the war where the experience of the *union sacrée* had, in the words of Lichtenberger, "given birth in the hearts of many to the hope that the dream of an interconfessional and *national church,* so often entertained by generous and tolerant souls, would now become a realized fact. Catholic and Protestant had fought side by side in the trenches. They felt that their common love of the German fatherland . . . was deeper than the confessional differences which separated them. . . . All Germans—Catholics, Lutherans or Calvinists—would be able to kneel, without distinction before the 'German God' " (Lichtenberger [XII/61], p. 190). Hitler's second lesson on the importance of not exacerbating religious differences came from his native Austria, where pan-German nationalism had ruined its chances with the devoutly Catholic peasantry and the lower middle class by permitting its reverence for the Protestant "mother country" and its violent opposition to the Catholic, antinationalist, polyglot

dynasty of the Habsburgs to betray it into a fanatical "Away-from-Rome" movement.

63. In *Mein Kampf* Hitler wrote: "For a political leader the religious teachings and institutions of his people should remain above attack. The movement resolutely refuses to take up any position with regard to the problems that are outside its political work or do not present a fundamental interest for this work. The mission of the movement is not in the nature of a religious reform, but in the nature of a political reorganization of our people." (Quoted in Birger Forell, "National Socialism and the Protestant Churches in Germany," in Maurice Baumont *et al.* [III/31], p. 811.) And point 24 of the "irrevocable" Nazi Party program said: "We envisage the liberty of all religious confessions within the State in so far as they do not threaten its integrity and in so far as they do not violate German customs and the morality of the Germanic race. The Party as such represents the point of view of a positive Christianity, without binding itself on the confessional plane to a particular church" (*ibid.*, p. 812).

64. *Within* the party, however, the attitude toward Christianity was dictated more by Rosenberg and hence was far more ideological. Without rejecting Christianity outright, Rosenberg stressed the fundamental incompatibilities between the Christian and the genuinely Germanic mentality and viewed the diverse orthodox creeds as irreconcilable enemies of a unified folk. Yet even he did not want to exterminate the churches, but merely to end "spiritual conflicts" by creating one "co-ordinated" church and by grafting onto it the Nazi outlook and way of life.

65. Waldemar Gurian, *Hitler and the Christians* (New York: Sheed and Ward, 1936), pp. 59–60.

66. Douglass (XII/57), p. 63. Such faithfulness was apparently not highly appreciated in Tübingen, the seat of Hauer's postwar group. There, among the (as usually misnamed) League for Freedom of Religion and Conscience (Bund für Glaubens- und Gewissensfreiheit, BGG), Böhme's "Unitarians" were contemptuously referred to as "the paltry appendix of Hauer's God-believers." (From a confidential report of June 6, 1952, on the BGG.) Of course, such scorn ill became the once mighty Hauer. He who at the peak of his fortune had been the authoritarian Führer of several hundred thousand members of the German Faith Movement now counted all of forty-nine souls in his BGG. And even these were not all true believers. Only twenty-six of them came from the Faith Movement. Three were former Ludendorffians, four were "nondenominational" Nazis, and seven were Communists! Despite such highly irregular composition and the group's derision, Böhme came to speak before it on the "Unitarian World View," an address, we are told, which contained little information but a great deal of "turgid word music and home-made lyrics" (*ibid.*).

67. From a handbill, dated Hameln, May 28, 1949, and Hanover, May 29, 1949, and signed by Albert Heuer, Dr. H. Böhme, Prof. Dr. G. v. Frankenberg, Dr. W. Goegginger, Fritz Hermann, Dr. G. Krüger, and Dr. G. Pick. The actual founding took place in October, 1949, in Wiesbaden.

68. *Ibid.*

69. *Ibid.*

70. *Ibid.* Initially, the German People's League for Religious Freedom, which in the preamble of its bylaws called itself an "association of free-thinking, free-religious, and free-believing societies and of free-minded personalities and groups," consisted of the then ninety-year-old League of Free Religious Congregations of Germany, which, as we have seen, had been a part of Hauer's German Faith Movement, the German Free Thinkers' Association (Deutscher Freidenker Verband, under Hermann Graul), Böhme's "German Unitarians," a Club for Free-believing Ceremonials (Verein für freigläubige Feiergestaltung, under Fritz Hermann, of Hamburg), the Germanic Faith Fellowship of the painter and old Hauer ally Ludwig Fahrenkrog, the Society for Life Science (Gesellschaft für Lebenskunde, under the old fanatical Ludendorffian Herbert Frank, of Duisburg), and an Independent Society for the Cultivation of Recent Science and Art (Unabhängige Gesellschaft zur Pflege junger Wissenschaft und Kunst) under the then editor of the important *Welt am Sonntag,* Klaus Besser. (This last group soon disbanded, and Frank's association merged and became a Society for Religious Freedom and Life Science [Gesellschaft für Geistesfreiheit und Lebenskunde, under Arnold Pollmann, of Duisburg].) Finally, the German Monist League (Deutscher Monistenbund) also joined the German People's League.

71. Of the former, the then editor of *Welt am Sonntag,* Klaus Besser, is an excellent example. Brought up in a folkish atmosphere, Besser had been a radical Ludendorffian who even after the war "was the first who again became active and performed—albeit only objective (*sachlich*)—work which could also have served the promotion of ML's [Mathilde Ludendorff's] religious teachings" (Besser's letter to Paul Fink [Göttingen], July 22, 1950). Later Klaus Besser became a liberal-democrat who was profoundly concerned to maintain an open market place for all ideas, religions, and ideologies. When he, together with his wife, brother, and some of their friends, including some Ludendorffians, organized in October, 1946, the Independent Society for the Cultivation of Recent Science and Art, it was his intention to contribute to a new cultural flowering "through liberation from dogmatic thinking" and to "cultivate the new paths in science and art which could lead these fields out of the confinement produced by racist, nationalist, and religious prejudices" (Unabhängige Gesellschaft zur Pflege junger Wissenschaft und Kunst, *Gesellschaftsvertrag,* paragraph 3, "Richtlinien für die Arbeit," Peine, October 27, 1946). In the same vein he wrote: "Brought up in the 'folkish' spirit, I had earlier always thought that everything that was said about Germany in foreign countries had its origin in ill-will and hatred. Only today do I see how often they were right. There is a strong tendency in the German to refuse to admit defeats, mistakes, and faulty action. He invariably first blames others for his fate" (Letter to Paul Fink [Göttingen], July 22, 1950). Or again: "I see in the budding of new nationalist tendencies a great danger for German politics. Today's situation is damned similar to that of 1932, and if everyone is not on guard at his place, then doubtlessly we'll experience a suprising turn similar to that of 1933, only that this one would very likely

end very much more quickly with a renewed collapse" (letter to Albert Heuer [Westerfeld, near Hanover], March 29, 1950). Cf. similar sentiments in Besser's letters to M. Gerstenberg (Göttingen), April 2, 1950, to H. J. Koch (Stuttgart-Degerloch), January 4, 1950, and to Herbert Frank (Duisburg-Meiderich), n.d., but evidently between March 19, and March 26, 1950.

On the other hand, there were in Besser's Independent Society unreconstructed Ludendorff fanatics, like the engineer Herbert Frank, leader of the small Society for Life Science, who had been dictatorially expelled from the Ludendorff organization for having dared to criticize the High Priestess. ("Erklärung" of "28 Hartungs 1949" [!] signed by Dr. Mathilde Ludendorff, Karl von Unruh, and Franz Baron Karg von Bebenburg. See also Frank's twenty-one-page "defense" entitled "In Defense of my Honor—after twenty years' activity on behalf of German God-Cognition," end of March, 1949.) Frank insisted that Ludendorff's struggle to "remove the spiritual-intellectual Judaization of our racial comrades and [to remove] other alien influences" was a glorious vindication of freedom of the spirit (letter to Albert Heuer, March 8, 1950). To condemn Mathilde Ludendorff, Frank argued, would be a betrayal of freedom of opinion because "the Ludendorff Weltanschauung is extraordinarily close to our liberal intentions and search for truth" (letter of Frank to Heuer, March 12, 1950). While the unintentional irony of that judgment in the light of Ludendorff's enormities will become fully clear only after we have come to analyze that movement in a subsequent section, some inkling of it can even now be provided by quoting briefly one other passage from one of Frank's letters: "I profess even today the view that in a German country and in the German people only German essence should be cultivated and that the foreign infiltration of other spiritual goods hampers the highest unfolding of culture. Everywhere in nature one can observe the striving after species-purity in all the diversity of the several species" (letter to Heuer, March 25, 1950).

72. See *Die Brücke,* III, 10 (September 3, 1956), 2.

73. Quoted in Weber (XI/602), p. 22.

74. *Ibid.,* p. 21.

75. *Ibid.*

76. Bracher *et al.* (III/36), 302.

77. *Ibid.,* pp. 856–857.

78. Kurt Fischer, *Herbert Böhme* (Munich, 1937), pp. 3-4, 15-16; quoted in Wulf (III/13), p. 373.

79. Quoted in Eric A. Peschler, "Faschimus unter der Tarnkappe," *Die Andere Zeitung* (Hamburg), no. 36 (September 6, 1956), p. 11.

80. Peschler, "Nun singen sie wieder," *Kontakte,* II, 2–3 (September–October, 1952), 18; reprinted from *Abendzeitung* (Munich), August 21, 1952.

81. Peschler (XII/79).

82. *Feinde der Demokratie* (Lower Saxony), III, 7 (April–May, 1954).

83. See above, VI/86–91, and below, XV/74 and nearby text.

84. When Hitler awarded him the Goethe medal, Burte thanked Hitler with words "which revealed anew his strong attachment of the Führer." On

that occasion the then chancellor of the University of Freiburg apostrophized the laureate with "You pointed out the dangers . . . the inundation by the Jews (*Verjudung*). . . . Before your eyes there arose the symbol of the all-embracing renascence of our people, the Swastika." And a Swiss observer, describing the elaborate Nazi pageant in honor of Burte, wrote: "It is nonsense to wish to celebrate Burte as poet without seeing at the same time the consequence of his political thought in the totalitarian state, to wish to eliminate from his poetry Burte's mania for blond hair and his Jew hatred. Burte's glorification of Adolf Hitler cannot be removed from his entire thinking, his entire work and from his poetry." All quoted in *Feinde der Demokratie* (Lower Saxony), VIII, 8 (June–July, 1959), 28–29.

85. Quoted in Weber (XI/602), p. 21.

86. See above, V/60.

87. *Deutsche Presse Agentur* (*dpa*), *Inf.* 1626 (November 30, 1955).

88. Cf. above, X/165.

89. In the autumn of 1963 Seidenfaden became the center of a controversy which ended in painful countermeasures against the DKEG. The occasion was a speech of Seidenfaden's before the Frankfurt Cultivation Center, in which he sharply attacked the late Bert Brecht, the Communist dramatist and probably Germany's greatest recent literary figure. This led to vehement counterattacks by the *Frankfurter Allgemeine Zeitung* and *Frankfurter Rundschau,* which loudly objected to the fact that the Cultivation Center of the DKEG was meeting on the premises of the civic adult education center. The city thereupon promptly rescinded its permission for the DKEG's use of the hall. When the nationalist press came to Seidenfaden's assistance with scathing attacks on the "opinion terror" of the "licensed" press, an otherwise obscure incident became the occasion for a major confrontation of the democratic and nationalist forces on a problem of cultural significance. See *Studien von Zeitfragen, Analysen, Berichte, Informationen zum nationalen Nonkonformismus,* X, 5 (November 13, 1963), 5–6.

90. In previous years, the laureates had been the folkish, anti-Semitic Hitler admirer Hermann Burte, the former Nazi poet Wolfgang Schwarz, an erstwhile colleague of Böhme's in the culture and propaganda apparatus of the SA, and the nationalist novelist Hans Heyck.

91. Quoted in *Die Brücke,* III, 10 (September 3, 1956), 4.

92. *Landeszeitung für die Lüneburger Heide,* June 25, 1957.

93. Initially the congress was thought of as analogous to the Mayors' Meeting (Deutscher Städtetag) or the German County Meeting (Deutscher Landgemeindetag): hence, it was at first called German Cultural Meeting (Deutscher Kulturtag).

94. Members of nationalist youth organizations were much in evidence, as were prominent members of the DRP, the DG, the BHE, and CSU. Colonel Walther Dahl, of the Reichsverband der Soldaten (RdS), spoke, as did August Haussleiter.

95. Ernst Rose, *A History of German Literature* (New York: New York University Press, 1960), p. 292.

96. Timmel is a leading figure in the Working Association of Liberal

Academicians' Associations (Arbeitsverband der freiheitlichen Akademikerverbände), a misleading name for extreme Right-wing groups, and is president of the Ring of Associations Loyal to the Folk (Ring volkstreuer Verbände). He is prominently involved in the South Tyrolian ethnic struggle. Timmel's "folk-loyalty" organization apparently so impressed Böhme that he, in turn, set about in December, 1964, to form a Working Circle (Arbeitskreis) of Associations Loyal to the Folk. Consisting of such "folk-loyal" groups as Aktion Oder-Neisse (AKON), Emergency Association of Former RAD Members (Notgemeinschaft ehemaliger RAD–Angehöriger), League of Patriotic Youth (Bund heimattreuer Jugend, BHJ), Stahlhelm, DRP, German Club (Deutscher Klub), DKEG, Comradeship (Kameradschaft), and Friends of the Good Film (Freunde des Guten Films), the Working Circle determined to cultivate the memory of Germany's fallen heroes, maintain connections to the "brothers in South Tyrol" and fight against pornography in books and films. These and similar aims were to be presented to a wider public in the course of the Working Circle's first public demonstration on the occasion of Bismarck's one hundred fiftieth birthday, April 1, 1965.

97. In recognition of outstanding service to the cause of folkdom, Böhme also initiated the award of a South Tyrolian wine pitcher. The first award, in 1961, went to Roland Timmel. In the following year, the signal honor was bestowed on Hans Krüger, then CDU deputy and president of the peak association of the Provincial Associations of Germans expelled from East and Southeast Europe. In 1963 Krüger became Erhard's Expellee Minister, but he soon resigned when malodorous details of his Nazi past became known (see below, XVII/149).

98. See "Hans Venatier" Sonderdruck: *Nation Europa,* n.d. Cf. *Deutscher Informationsdienst,* no. 798 (March 2, 1959).

99. See "Aus der Arbeit des deutschen Kulturwerkes," *Studien von Zeitfragen, Analysen, Berichte, Informationen zum nationalen Nonkonformismus,* XI, 7 (July 16, 1964), 5.

100. Grimm (XI/140), p. 53.

101. *Ibid.,* p. 54.

102. Hinrichs died in 1956, aged seventy-seven.

103. See *Der Informationsdienst,* no. 189 (July 12, 1952), p. 4.

104. *Studien von Zeitfragen, Analysen und Berichte,* IX, 13 (July 19, 1962), 2. According to the DRP organ *Reichsruf,* Holle Grimm's call had beckoned, among others, Colin Jordan from England, Jean Thiriart from Belgium, Gil Murgaza from Spain, R. Logger of the Netherlands, Conrad Meier-Jensen from Denmark, Steinböck from South Africa, and Konrad Windisch from Austria.

105. Dr. R., "Dichtertag in Lippoldsberg," *Cellesche Zeitung,* July 22, 1955.

106. See, for example, the venomous attack on the "House Ludendorff" by the conservative-authoritarian writer Martini (III/4) and the equally spirited, documented defense by Edmund Reinhard, one of the true believers ("Zwei Welten: Trifft das Haus Ludendorff eine rechtliche oder auch nur

eine politische Verantwortung für den faschistischen Gewaltstaat und dessen Rassenpolitik?" unpublished typescript; Dresden, April, 1948).

107. Nazi literature of the early nineteen-thirties provides innumerable examples of the hostility between the NSDAP and the Ludendorffs. *Pars pro toto,* we might cite Hjalmar Kutzleb, the Nazi literary critic: "A suffragette of equally mediocre talent both as author and thinker, marries a name before which the globe once trembled, places it on an advertising sign and sells under that trade mark all kinds of insane hogwash (*Bafel*) which otherwise would have gathered mildew in her desk. Mathilde, the product of decayed metropolitan enlightenment, dabbles in religion; she who doesn't know a word of Greek, abuses the Evangelists; she, who is childless, offers unctuous platitudes about the rearing of children; she who has no notion about the ultimate questions of the Ego and transcendence, pastes together a 'Weltanschauung.' . . . If any hidden satanic power had plotted to devalue permanently through ridicule the name of the greatest German military leader, that plot could hardly have succeeded more fully, than what is actually happening." (*Die Neue Literatur,* XXXIV, 12 [December, 1933] 723.)

108. The epitome of this "sellout" came, of course, with Hitler's efforts to mollify the Catholic clergy in preparation for a Concordat with the Holy See. In his Reichstag speech on March 23, 1933, Hitler even went as far as to say that "the government sees in both Christian confessions the most important factors for the maintenance of our folkdom." Nuremberg Document 3387-PS, "Hitler's assurance, given in his Reichstag speech, 23 March 1933, to respect treaties concluded between the Christian churches and the component states of the German Reich (Exhibit USA-566)," *Trial of the Major War Criminals* (Nuremberg: 14 November 1945—1 October 1946) (Nuremberg: 1948), XXXII, 251–252.

109. Letter of Franz Baron Karg von Bebenburg to Herbert Frank, October 11, 1947.

110. See the documents assembled by Herbert Frank in his typescript of March, 1949, entitled "Zur Wahrung meiner Ehre. (Nach 20 jährigem Wirken für die deutsche Gotterkenntnis)." Most of the countervailing evidence came from an intimate friend of Colonel General Ludwig Beck, Colonel Robert Holtzmann, chairman of a Land organization of the Ludendorffian Tannenberg League and, until 1936, General Ludendorff's representative in Berlin.

111. Klaus Besser, "Kulturpolitische Auswirkungen der Werke des Hauses Ludendorff. Zum Urteil über Frau Dr. Mathilde Ludendorffs ideologische Stellung zum Nationalsozialismus," typescript, n.d., but very likely end of February–beginning of March, 1950.

112. Cf. letter of Klaus Besser to Paul Fink, July 22, 1950.

113. See *Der Rechtsstreit vor den Verwaltungsgerichten über die Verbotsverfügung der Innenminister der deutschen Länder gegen Bund für Gotterkenntnis (Ludendorff), Verlag Hohe Warte in Pähl/Obb.* Dokumente der Gegenwart, no. 8 (Pähl/Obb.: Von Bebenburg, 1963). For technical legal reasons, courts in Baden-Württemberg, Saarland, Bremen, and Schleswig-

Holstein and two administrative regions of North Rhine–Westphalia later lifted the ban again. In Bavaria an appeals court sustained the lower court and upheld the continued suppression of the Ludendorff organization and publishing firm.

114. Letter of Klaus Besser to Paul Fink, July 30, 1950.

115. See above, XI/673.

116. Joachim Henrich, "Unser gemeinsames Anliegen," reproduced in *Die Brücke,* III, 12 (October 15, 1956), Annex, p. 1.

117. Joachim Henrich, "Der Auftrag unserer Generation," *Allgemeine Deutsche Lehrerzeitung* (Frankfurt), n.s., XIV, 19 (November 1, 1961).

118. *Ibid.*

119. See above, Chapter X, Section H.

120. At about that time Schranz himself organized a very similar group which he called League for a Rule of Law State (Bund für Rechtsstaatlichkeit). Its objective was to wage war against the inequality of rights which, according to the league, was being perpetuated in Bonn as long as war criminals were still being prosecuted or held in jail and as long as Germany's rightful national claims in South Tyrol, Alsace, and other irredenta remained unacknowledged. Schranz was a member of the league's advisory council, as was the notorious Rightist Rudolf Aschenauer. (See above, VII/69 and below, XIII/30–32, XV/65, XVI/55).

121. For details on the discussion and resolutions passed by the Working Circle, see *Feinde der Demokratie* (Lower Saxony), VIII, 3–4 (March–April, 1959), 31–34, and *Studien von Zeitfragen, Analysen und Berichte,* VIII, 16–17 (November 20, 1961), 4–5.

122. See above, VII/86 and nearby text.

123. See above, XI/685, 686.

124. "A Congress of 'Young Europeans,'" *The Wiener Library Bulletin,* (London), XIII, 5–6 (1959), 55, and *Studien von Zeitfragen, Analysen und Berichte,* VIII, 16–17 (November 20, 1961), 6–7.

125. See text at reference VII/76.

126. *Studien von Zeitfragen, Analysen und Berichte,* VIII, 16–17 (November 20, 1961), 3.

127. Quoted in *The Wiener Library Bulletin* (London), XVII, 1 (January, 1963), 9.

128. Quoted *ibid.*

129. One of the Swedish delegates, Rütger Essén, a friend of Sven Hedin and editor of *Fria Ord,* was deported by German authorities as undesirable. (*Bulletin on German Questions* [London] XV, 337 [July 22, 1963], 12.) Essén, incidentally, is an important stockholder of *Nation Europa.*

130. Ehrhardt saw some form of unification as necessary for the white man's self-defense and survival in the face of the world revolution of the colored races, but he rejected the Gaullist conception of "fatherlands" as too "statist" and inadequately folkish.

131. The three cofounders were Otto Behnke, Gustav Melcher, and Gerhard Ohnesorg.

132. "Restoring Historical Truth," *The Wiener Library Bulletin* (Lon-

don), XV, 1 (1961), 4. A very similar "research" organization had been started as long ago as February, 1954, by Herbert Grabert and the former Combat SS officer Werner Vormfelde. They called their group Research Fellowship of the National Opposition (Forschungsgemeinschaft der Nationalen Opposition) (*Feinde der Demokratie* [Lower Saxony] III, 5 [February, 1954]). This formation had been preceded in October, 1953, by a Historical Society—League for the Establishment of Historical Truths (Historische Gesellschaft—Bund zur Feststellung geschichtlicher Wahrheiten), which the fanatical Friedrich Lenz had organized, but which appeared to have been stillborn. (See *Das Ziel* [Hanover], II, 24 [October 31, 1953], 2.) In January, 1957, the Federal Association of Former Internees and Victims of Denazification (Bundesverband der ehemaligen Internierten und Entnazifizierungsgeschädigten) also called for a Working Fellowship for Research in Historical Facts (Arbeitsgemeinschaft zur Erforschung historischer Tatsachen) (*Der Ring* [Düsseldorf], IV, [January, 1957], 6). And in the following year a Society for Contemporary History (Gesellschaft für Zeitgeschichte) was formed in Munich. Its president was Peter Kleist, and the executive board consisted of H. B. von Grünberg, the last Nazi chancellor of the University of Königsberg and DRP leader; Hans W. Hagen, a Goebbels protégé and later cultural editor of "national Bolshevik" papers (see above, VI/209 and nearby text) and of the *Reichsruf*; and Theodor Baur, another prominent DRP official. (*Deutscher Informationsdienst,* no. 758 [August 18, 1958].)

133. Quoted in "Restoring Historical Truth," (XII/132).

134. *Ibid.*

135. See above, text at XI/671–673. The misuse of the name of the great German historian, whose plea for objectivity makes the linking of his name with that of Hoggan even more ironic, drew scathing rebukes from German historians. The president of the German Historical Society, Professor Karl Erdmann, called it an insult to the memory of Ranke. See *Der Spiegel,* XVIII, 20 (May 13, 1964), 28.

136. *Ibid.,* p. 32.

137. *Ibid.,* p. 33. According to *Der Spiegel,* the former Düsseldorf Gauleiter Friedrich Karl Florian, though not a member, also maintains friendly relations to the society.

138. See above, XI/424.

139. See above, VIII/92; and below, XVII/155, 156. The group also organized the more political and extreme-Right bourgeois German Circle 1958 (Deutscher Kreis 1958) as a counterweight to the SPD's anti-atomic weapons campaign and to its supporters among broad sections of the intelligentsia. The founding committee of the German Circle 1958 consisted of Becher, Ziesel, the Munich attorney Alfred Seidl (who, as defense counsel of SS Colonel Walter Huppenkothen, the Canaris enemy, successfully employed the Nazi argument that the German Resistance movement contributed to England's decision to declare war on Germany in 1939), and the elitist-authoritarian journalist and author Winfried Martini (whom many consider one of the foremost experts on the "Jewish Question"). Also on the com-

mittee were the Right-wing Catholic political science professor and former chairman of the Occidental Academy, Friedrich August von der Heydte; the old Nazi author Heinrich Zillich; the Minister for Food in von Papen's and Schleicher's "cabinets of barons," Baron Magnus von Braun (the father of the rocketeer Wernher); the Catholic conservative (and at one time philo-Nazi) theologian Michael Schmaus; the Right-wing CSU deputy Count Georg Henckel von Donnersmarck; the conservative Austrian art historian Hans Sedlmayr (author of *The Lost Center*); and the Hamburg physicist Pascual Jordan, an enthusiast for nuclear brinkmanship and a CDU politician on the party's far Right, to boot. The main target of the German Circle's vituperations and hysterical accusations (reminiscent of McCarthy-type smear tactics) is the "left intelligentsia," which has allegedly monopolized the communications media and is preparing Germany for a sellout to the Bolsheviks.

140. See above, III/36, and text at reference XI/445.

141. See above, XI/540 and XII/26.

142. See above, text at references XI/245–250. After Kolbenheyer's death Reichenberger became honorary chairman of the GfP.

143. See above, XII/9.

144. See above, VII/69, XII/120; and below, XV/65, XVI/55.

145. See above, XI/4.

146. See above, text at references XI/490–493.

147. See above, VI/172 and text at XI/532.

148. Petri is a member of Deutsche Studentenschaft, a dueling fraternity. In 1963 he became deputy chairman of the GfP.

149. *Parlamentarisch–Politischer Pressedienst,* 2/2911 (November 29, 1955).

150. *Bulletin on German Questions* (London), XV, 335–336 (July 1, 1963), 18. For Hoggan's book, see above, XI/671. Cf. *Studien von Zeitfragen. Analysen, Berichte, Informationen zum nationalen Nonkonformismus,* V/1964 (May 15, 1964), 2–3.

151. Reproduced in *Studien von Zeitfragen, Analysen und Berichte,* IX, 8 (May 24, 1962), 5.

152. *Ibid.,* p. 2.

153. *Ibid.,* pp. 5–10.

154. A measure of the effectiveness of the GfP and the various other societies for the propagation of "historical truth," whose revisionist campaign has an impact far beyond the narrow confines of radical nationalism and penetrates deep into the bourgeois conservative circles of the CDU-CSU, is a brief report of two recent conferences organized by the conservative Evangelical Academy (Tutzing). The conferences dealt with the causes of the First and Second World Wars. The report ends as follows: "It is interesting to note a certain development. At the first discussion 38 per cent held a democratic view, 60 per cent were undecided, 2 per cent were Right-extremists. At the second discussion, 15 per cent took a democratic view, 80 per cent were undecided, and 5 per cent were Right-extremists." *Bulletin on German Questions* (London), XVI, 358/359 (June 29, 1964), 3.

CHAPTER XIII: PARTY POLITICS (I): THE SOCIALIST REICH PARTY (SRP)

1. Büsch and Furth (IV/3).

2. The raids had been ordered for the purpose of seizing incriminating documents which were to provide the evidential basis for the state's case against the SRP before the Constitutional Court.

3. See above, text following reference IV/56.

4. For Gericke's later political activity, see below, XVII/127.

5. See above, X/144 and nearby text.

6. After completion of the organizational task, Remer turned the Land chairmanship over to Walter Schmüser, of Rendsburg.

7. Two weeks after the Priester secession, the decimated NDP followed Leuchtgens into a merger with the Lower Saxon Land organization of the DKP-DRP.

8. See above, VII/12.

9. Weber accused Priester of having broken the agreement with Dorls and of using the interim period of the "working association" to build up the NDP at the expense of SRP forces in the northern parts of Hesse.

10. In the middle of 1951, the Baden-Württemberg SRP was divided into a Land Württemberg organization under the former DP member Willi Mellin and a Land Baden branch under Karl Theodor Förster.

11. Report of the deputy chairman of Natinform, August 28, 1953.

12. The signs of an internal crisis which eventually manifested strongly disintegrative tendencies became first visible in the autumn of 1951. A number of factors appear to have contributed. At first it was a crisis of confidence, precipitated by the question of the expense allowances for Diet deputies. In the Diet elections of 1951 the SRP had vigorously campaigned on a promise to reduce the allowances and to re-establish "old Prussian thrift." The monies saved were to be used to relieve the housing shortage. Once elected, the sixteen SRP deputies voted promptly and unanimously for an *increase* in allowances. As this had been a lively issue in the campaign, the voters' reaction to this betrayal of their trust made itself felt in a number of subsequent by-elections. (In Wiesmoor not a single SRP candidate was elected. In Wolfsburg the SRP lost 40 per cent of its votes in three weeks!) Indeed, cases of self-dissolution of entire local and district chapters were not unknown. This difficulty was followed by resignations from the parliamentary Fraktion and shortly thereafter by the unmasking of the Bundestag Deputy Richter/Rössler as a fraud. Not much later, the party organizations of Cuxhaven and Varel became involved in criminal suits, and Remer had to defend himself in a number of widely publicized and damaging lawsuits. To this were added personal enmities among the leadership corps which kept the party's "honors court" working at full capacity. Morale seemed shattered. Even dues were no longer paid regularly.

13. SRP meetings and rallies were systematically disturbed by democratic parties and associations which closely collaborated in this enterprise. The government did its part by disbanding meetings, prohibiting speakers from appearing, and, above all, by stipulating that parties which did not have

parliamentary representation on the Federal or the state level must present 200 signatures on behalf of every candidate. When the SRP pointed out that it *did* have parliamentary representation, namely the Bundestag Deputy Fritz Dorls, the Election Commission ruled that a deputy who had been elected on another ticket and only afterwards shifted his party allegiance did not constitute representation within the meaning of the election law.

14. Diepholz 33 per cent, Bremervörde 33 per cent, Lüneburg-Land 30 per cent, and Hadeln 28 per cent.

15. Aurich 29 per cent, Lüneburg-Stadt 28 per cent, Verden 28 per cent, Rotenburg 28 per cent, Zeven 26 per cent, Emden-Stadt 24 per cent, Celle-Stadt 23 per cent, Jever 21 per cent, Wittmund 20 per cent, Holzminden 19 per cent, Cuxhaven-Stadt 18 per cent.

16. North Württemberg and North Baden.

17. For the Guelph-monarchist political tradition in the "flatland" of Lower Saxony, see below, Chapter XVII, Section B.

18. See Ludwig Arps, "Das unruhige Dorf," *Deutsche Zeitung und Wirtschaftszeitung* (Stuttgart), no. 60 (July 28, 1951), p. 3.

19. See Robert Botzat, "Niedersachsen greift gegen die SRP nicht durch," *Die Neue Zeitung* (Munich), October 17, 1951.

20. The Land government of Lower Saxony did not place its employees before the alternative of resigning either from the SRP or from their official post. Rather, it demanded, as a condition of continued employment, a loyalty declaration. The SRP executive committee thereupon publicly informed all its members that as far as the party's short- and long-range goals went, the required declaration could be signed in good conscience without any reservations.

21. See above, VI/79 and nearby text.

22. See above, VII/39, and below XV/78.

23. Only if absolutely necessary was the SRP prepared to participate in an anti-Marxist government, and then only with an "expertise minister" (*Fachminister*) who was neither in the party leadership nor in the parliamentary party; that is, with a man who was not publicly or closely identified with the party.

24. See above, IV/71 and nearby text.

25. According to a published interview with knowledgeable members of the WAV, Loritz maintained that his negotiations with Dorls had been specifically and explicitly sanctioned by his WAV colleagues. (*Der Informationsdienst,* no. 115 [September 26, 1951], p. 1). Oddly enough, Loritz' conception of the "activists" who have to be united to fight against the twin evils of Communism and the "inept old parties" included in the first place "the former Resistance fighters of the Third Reich [and] also those convinced anti-Nazis who are neither Marxist, nor Communist, nor capitalist" (*ibid.*). The joint phalanx of WAV and SRP was, according to Loritz, to declare war especially on two power groups: the "Tauroggeners" and the old Nazis (*ibid.* p. 2).

26. See Count Westarp's consideration of this point as reported by Botzat (XIII/19).

27. When SRP forces were suspected of being implicated in an attempt on Adenauer's life, Count Westarp, whose relative moderation and loyalty declarations had earned him the suspicion of the more hot-blooded SRP enthusiasts, disavowed such methods "as long as other means of opposition are available." But then this "moderate" leader added, "However, should the SRP be seriously hindered in the execution of its opposition, then it would have to restudy its entire attitude toward acts of violence." Reported in *Die Neue Zeitung* (Munich), April 3, 1952.

28. See below, XV/85.

29. The purely tactical camouflage nature of the self-dissolution was underlined by the fact that the SRP's executive board was never authorized, and was "constitutionally" incompetent, to declare the dissolution. Indeed, according to Westarp the enlarged party council, the SRP's highest legislative body, had before the trial specifically decided not to bring about its own dissolution, regardless of the trial's outcome. (See *Hamburger Echo,* September 23, 1952, and *Die Neue Zeitung* [Munich], September 24, 1952.) Nor was there any doubt in the minds of the party leaders themselves as to the significance of the "dissolution." On September 12, 1952, the SRP deputy Ernst–Wilhelm Springer concluded a *"Sonderrundschreiben"* to his followers: "I remain with comradely greetings and with the shout: The SRP is dead! Long live the SRP!" (Quoted in the *"Schnellbrief"* of the Lower Saxon Minister of the Interior of October 24, 1952.)

30. See above, VII/69, XII/120; and below XV/65, XVI/55.

31. Concerning Aschenauer's American contacts, see Forster and Epstein (VII/40), pp. 215 ff.

32. See Aschenauer's letter to the editor to that effect in *Der Spiegel,* VI, 34 (August 20, 1952), 34. See also Haussleiter's public attack on Aschenauer in which Haussleiter alleged that the latter "travels through Germany with the assertion that he is a kind of official trustee of the outlawed SRP." (See below, XV/65.)

33. On Colonel Gümbel's other political activities, see above, VIII/39.

34. "Wenn das Verbot kommt," *Der Spiegel,* VI, 33 (August 13, 1952), 7.

35. See *Die Welt* (Hamburg), August 15, 1952; cf. *Hannoversche Presse* of the same date.

36. According to an (unpublished) interview with Hans Hill, Westarp had vainly asked Dorls to submit himself to a party "trial" in order to prove the inaccuracy of the *Spiegel* report. When Dorls refused to do so, Westarp resigned both his party offices and his Lower Saxon diet seat. At the same time, the party council and the executive board expressed their confidence in Remer and Dorls and expelled Westarp "for subversive activity." Dorls' reluctance to prove publicly the falsity of the *Spiegel* exposé was quite understandable in view of his private admission that 80 per cent was correct and 20 per cent a bit vague. According to Werner Körper, the SRP's Land chairman of Rhineland-Palatinate, the "activities" complained of were Westarp's unauthorized negotiations with Bonn, which he carried on behind the backs of Dorls, Remer, and the rest. The object of the discussions at the

time was to suggest to the coalition partners in Bonn that only increased propagandistic efforts on the part of the SRP could counter a potentially dangerous chess move which the SPD in Lower Saxony was allegedly preparing. Westarp suspected that the Lower Saxon SPD would copy its sister organization in the southwest where it succeeded in toppling a CDU government by breaking the FDP out of the coalition. Evidence of preparations along similar lines in Lower Saxony was seen in the alleged appointment as Secretary of State of a former member of Goebbels' Propaganda Ministry for the sole purpose of taking up contact with the FDP and (other) distinctly Rightist parties. Apprised of this "danger from the Left," Bonn had supposedly agreed to partial concessions to Westarp. From a confidential report of an interview with Körper, n.d., but evidently from the middle or end of September, 1952.

37. See, for example, the detailed findings of the *Oberverwaltungsgericht für die Länder Niedersachsen und Schleswig-Holstein* in the case of the "Freie Wählergemeinschaft e.V., Bad Pyrmont," II OVG-A 230/52, September 14–16, 1953.

38. From a *"Schnellbrief"* of the Lower Saxon Minister of the Interior of October 24, 1952.

39. *Das Urteil des Bundesverfassungsgerichts vom 23. Oktober 1952 betreffend Feststellung der Verfassungswidrigkeit der Sozialistischen Reichspartei,* published by the members of the *Bundesverfassungsgericht* (Tübingen: 1952), p. 5.

40. See the Minister's *"Schnellbrief"* of October 24, 1952.

41. See the Minister's *"Schnellbrief"* of October 29, 1952.

42. For a partial list of SRP candidates and other Nazis who managed to obtain council seats over the lists of the "respectable" parties, see *Hannoversche Presse,* November 15, 1952.

43. See, for instance, the challenge before the *Oberverwaltungsgericht* of the so-called Independent Bloc for Justice and Order (Unabhängiger Block für Recht und Ordnung) in Celle. Its chairman, Joachim Schrader, argued, *inter alia,* that on his list only nine were former members of the SRP, whereas there were twenty-one SRP men on other "respectable" lists in Celle. *Feinde der Demokratie* (Lower Saxony), II, 5 (February–March, 1953).

44. Förster's letter to the former executive secretary of the SRP, Fritz Heller, December 5, 1952.

45. Förster's letter to Remer, December 5, 1952.

46. From an interview with Hans Hill (Hanover), n.d., but very probably August or early September, 1952.

47. Letter of Sarg to his deputy, September 18, 1952. This pessimistic estimate is contradicted by the SRP Land Chairman of Rhineland-Palatinate, Werner Körper: "Except for a disappearingly small number of people, the SRP now [i.e., in September–October, 1952] stands in all of its old vigor. There is a particularly close unity among the entire leadership corps." From the confidential report of a discussion with Körper, n.d., but very evidently from the end of September or beginning of October, 1952.

48. From a letter of Meyer to Dr. Andreas Binder, February 9, 1953.

49. Eventually Meyer followed his own advice; in November, 1953, he was elected to the executive committee of the DRP Land organization of Lower Saxony.

50. According to Werner Körper, Meissner's German Bloc (DB) was also taken into consideration, but Meissner was considered too shrewd to lend himself easily to the SRP's game. Moreover, Remer and Dorls possessed evidence to the effect that Meissner was working for the Federal Office for the Protection of the Constitution. From a confidential interview with Körper, n.d., but evidently from the middle or end of September, 1952.

51. "Körper remarked that the SRP . . . could absorb (*in sich auffangen*) the DG; that, to be sure, is a wish which he as yet does not care to express" (*ibid.*).

52. Lower Saxon Minister of the Interior, Press Office, *Presse Information* no. 7/53, March 20, 1953.

53. Rumors also had it that the diet deputies of the League of Germans Loyal to Their Homeland (Bund heimattreuer Deutscher, BHD), Dr. Fritz Schulz, Horst Büchler, and Josef Erbacher, intended to form a parliamentary group, German Community, to which the former SRP deputy Franz Kewer would accede. (*Braunschweiger Zeitung,* September 14, 1952.) Cf. below, XVII/138, 139.

54. *Frankfurter Allgemeine Zeitung,* November 17, 1952.

55. With von Lobenthal's removal, the *Correspondence of the German Community* (*Korrespondenz der Deutschen Gemeimschaft, KdG*) a news service he had hitherto edited, also ceased publication. He now turned out an economic newsletter, *Wirtschaftsführer Briefe,* a task for which he had gathered a deal of practical experience as quondam editor of Hjalmar Schacht's financial information service. See *Deutsche Presse Agentur* (*dpa*), *Inf.* 2131 (December 1, 1952).

56. From a confidential report of a discussion with Körper on December 2, 1952. In the matter of concealment, Werner Körper approved of Dorls's clever reticence, for the latter, despite his disappearance from the public scene, had managed to keep all the strings in his hands. By the same token, Körper complained about Remer's lack of caution and feared that he might yet experience legal difficulties because of it.

57. Letter of the former SRP district leader Hugo Jungmann to August Haussleiter, January 11, 1953.

58. The reasons were clearly detailed by Jungmann. A prohibition of the entire party could come only from the Federal Constitutional Court in Karlsruhe. In view of the then developing conflict between the Administration and the Court, such an eventuality appeared unlikely. A ban by the Lower Saxon Minister of the Interior appeared also improbable. Since the Federal elections were still nine months away, the Minister would have no reason to proceed with the precipitous haste which the communal election in November had made necessary and which had resulted in legal challenges by the excluded electoral associations and in months of litigation. The most important reason, however, was the changed political picture in Lower Saxony. In the communal elections the bans had been largely motivated by the general fear

that the mushrooming electoral associations might destroy the position, in the communes and districts, of the SPD and the bourgeois parties. Now, on the contrary, outlawry of the DG would make an electoral victory of the bourgeois parties inevitable, an eventuality which the ruling SPD would certainly do its best to prevent. Hence, SRP strategists expected the SPD to be most uninterested in such a ban. (Jungmann's letter to Haussleiter, January 11, 1953.)

59. From a confidential report of a discussion with Werner Körper, January 14, 1953.

60. *Ibid.*

61. Letter of Bavarian Land diet Deputy Dr. Renate Malluche to Wolfgang Kaden (a radically nationalist law student at Göttingen University who was later to become Land chairman of the DG), February 5, 1953. Incidentally, ten years later the then forty-six-year-old Dr. Malluche married August Haussleiter, age fifty-eight.

62. To what extent the decisions of an SRP attorneys' conference contributed to the new sense of self-confidence is difficult to say. The conference was called by Dorls and Remer to take place in the home of the former Nazi Mayor of Düsseldorf, Carl Haidn. The initial date of February 6, 1952, had to be postponed. The purpose of the meeting was evidently to assess the legal ramifications of SRP activity in and through the DG. (Confidential discussion memorandum of the deputy chairman of Natinform with Werner Körper, February 6, 1952.)

63. At a meeting in Lüneburg on March 10, 1953, for example, the large crowd was welcomed by a former SRP man who had appeared on the list of one of the suppressed electoral associations, and the speakers' table was graced by such notables as the former Nazi *Regierungspräsident* and later SRP provincial Leader, Kurt Matthaei, the SRP district chief Hugo Jungmann, the former SRP functionary Hans Retzlaff, and the local SRP leader Gerhard von Kusserow. Kurt Matthaei, incidentally, must not be confused with the former SRP executive secretary and *Reichsjugend* leader, Walter Matthaei.

64. *Feinde der Demokratie,* (Lower Saxony) II, 6 (March–April, 1953).

65. See the press release of the Ministry of the Interior, *Presse Information,* no. 7/53, March 20, 1953. Cf. also the press release of April 2, 1953, entitled "Der Niedersächsische Minister des Innern weist Erklärung der 'Deutschen Gemeinschaft' zurück." A few weeks later the Social Democratic government of Hesse followed Lower Saxony's lead and, in turn, banned the DG in its territory.

66. Confidential report of a discussion with Krüger, April 16, 1953.

67. See above, text near XII/29.

68. Confidential report (XIII/66).

69. See above, text at XIII/24, 25. Cf. "Das Hintergründige in Herrn Loritz," *Das Ziel* (Hanover), II, 10 (July 25, 1953), 2, and "Herr Loritz dementiert . . . ," *ibid.,* II, 8 (July 11, 1953).

70. *Feinde der Demokratie* (Nordmark), no. 5 (June 15, 1953), p. 46.

71. See above, IV/73.

72. See above, IX/122–124 and nearby text.

73. *Deutsche Presse Agentur* (*dpa*), Landesdienst Nord, July 14, 1953.

74. *Deutscher Informationsdienst,* no. 294 (August 4, 1953), p. 3.

75. On these points, see the July 25, 1953, report in *Feinde der Demokratie* (Nordmark), no. 6 (August 20, 1953), p. 8, and *Deutscher Informationsdienst,* no. 294 (August 4, 1953), p. 3.

76. From reports of Krüger's speech at the first Frankfurt meeting of the DAV on July 17, 1953.

77. From a report of a campaign meeting of the DRP, August 26, 1953, in Worms we have the following description: "In [the restaurant] 'Reichskanzler' there sat beside Körper and his ladies, eighteen men, all of them confidential agents of the SRP from Stuttgart, Rastatt, and the Palatinate. Körper made a speech defending himself [and apologizing] for the occurrences [that took place in the course] of going over from the SRP to the DG, the DAV and now the DRP."

78. The top SRP leaders, except for Gerhard Krüger, also disappeared from the political scene: Fritz Dorls returned to his home town in Westphalia, where he was said to have begun an unexciting career as watchman in a factory. Otto Ernst Remer had escaped after his conviction on libel charges, but returned in 1954 after an amnesty had eliminated the sentence against him. He found employment with an agricultural machinery manufacturer and appeared in the news only sporadically in connection with arms deals with Arab states. In 1959 Remer was again arrested, a suspicion of tax fraud having been added to police interest in his Near Eastern business transactions. Though released at that time, he was rearrested three years later on the tax charges. Remer avoided trial by escaping to the Near East, where—according to some sources of unknown reliability—he joined his former SRP colleague Ernst-Wilhelm Springer in a gun-running enterprise. The same sources also reported a meeting in Beirut at which Remer, Springer, Léon Degrelle, and the Eichmann aide Alois Brunner alias George Fischer (cf. above, VII/173) supposedly considered the founding of an international Nazi party. In the spring of 1963 Remer was back in Germany. The court now convicted him and sentenced him to three weeks in jail and a moderate fine. The fourth SRP leader, the fraudulent Richter/Rössler, left Germany after his release from prison to find support, comfort, and employment in Egypt's Nazi colony. Yet, apparently disappointed in his sanguine hopes, Rössler eventually returned to Essen, where he accepted a position with a commercial firm. Finally, Count Wolf Westarp also has hung up his political gloves and is said to be earning his living as a businessman. (See Willbrand [XI/321], pp. 24–25.) For Krüger's later brief career in the DRP and the secessionist Deutsche Freiheits-Partei (DFP), see below, Chapter XVI, Section D.

CHAPTER XIV: PARTY POLITICS ON THE EXTREME RIGHT (II)

1. See above, Chapter IV.

2. It may be recalled in this connection that Leonhard Schlüter, the chairman of the Lower Saxon Land party, who had resigned his office in protest against the hypocritical last-minute lifting of the British ban on his political activities immediately prior to the federal elections in September, 1949, subsequently left the party altogether because he felt that the original goal of negotiating with other parties for the purpose of constructing a large nationalist-conservative opposition bloc was being sidetracked by the new influx of radicals into the DRP. See above, IV/56 and nearby text.

3. Letter of Hermann Klingspor to Heinrich Hellwege, chairman of the directorate of the DP, September 12, 1949. See below, Chapter XV, Section B.

4. *Rundschreiben* of the Zonal DKP-DRP party executive, no. VIII/49 (August 16, 1949). But see below, text near XV/6–8.

5. See letters of Klingspor to Hellwege, September 12, 22, 30, October 6, 26, November 19, 1949, January 21, 1950, and letters of Hellwege to Klingspor, September 29, October 28, November 3, 1949, January 9, 1950. Letters of Carl Lauenstein (plenipotentiary of the DP directorate) to Klingspor, October 11, November 1, 1949. Letter of Klingspor to Lauenstein, October 14, 1949.

6. Letter of Emil Bierbrauer, chairman of the District Essen, to Klingspor, September 26, 1949. Cf. also *Rundschreiben,* no. 11/49 (September 30, 1949).

7. Letter of Ludwig Schwecht, chairman of the District Düren, to Klingspor, October 1, and Klingspor's answer of October 4, 1949.

8. For this purpose a negotiating team was named, consisting of Richter, Miessner, Hermann von Lüninck, Steuer, Walter Harckensee, and Klingspor. Minutes of the meeting of the Parteileitung in Wuppertal on September 1, 1949.

9. Von Thadden's letter to Klingspor, September 7, 1949. For further details on the items agreed upon at Giessen, see a memorandum by Klingspor, typescript, undated, but very likely written shortly after January 5, 1950. Also cf. *Rundschreiben,* no. 10/49 (September 15, 1949).

10. This is precisely what Leuchtgens did, much to the puzzlement of many of his voters who had not been privy to the plans hatched at Giessen.

11. It was to consist of Karl Schäfer and Erich Teuscher for the former NDP, Lothar Steuer and a member of the Lower Saxon branch (Richter suggested Anton Mainzer) for the former DKP-DRP, and Klingspor as chairman.

12. See *Rundschreiben,* no. 1/50 (January 16, 1950).

13. *Rundschreiben,* no. 10/49 (September 15, 1949).

14. Invitation and agenda sent to Mainzer, Teuscher, Schäfer, dated November 19, 1949.

15. *Rundschreiben,* no. 5/49 (December 6, 1949).

16. Letter of Klingspor to Leuchtgens, December 16, 1949.

17. Letter of Miessner to Dietrich Korsch, chairman of the District Watenstedt-Salzgitter, December 11, 1949, forwarded by von Thadden on December 19, 1949.

18. See *Neuer Vorwärts* (Hanover), January 20, 1950.

19. See, for instance, the letter to Klingspor (December 23, 1949) of the reasonably moderate nationalist Anton Mainzer, in which he expressed the fear of many Lower Saxon party members that the DRP in Lower Saxony might be bereft of all competitive political chances by the machinations of reactionary circles.

20. Telegram of Leuchtgens to Klingspor, December 22, 1949.

21. Letter of Klingspor to Leuchtgens, December 23, 1949.

22. Von Thadden's report on Miessner's strategy meeting in his letter to Klingspor, December 29, 1949.

23. The meeting was attended by Franz Richter, Anton Mainzer, Johannes Guth, of Brunswick (executive secretary of the Land party), Heinz Frommhold, Otto Laun (district cochairman of Harburg), Heinz Billig, of Bad Pyrmont, Dietrich Korsch, of Watenstedt, Hannes Kaiser, also of Brunswick, Kurt Jaeger, of Hanover, and Walter Kniggendorf.

24. Von Thadden himself was kept informed of the matters discussed by Mainzer and Frommhold. Mainzer had assured him that he would not participate in Miessner's plot to wrest the party leadership from Klingspor and to usurp that position either directly or by using Richter as his front man.

25. Memorandum by Klingspor, no date, but evidently written between the fifth and eleventh of January, 1950. Cf. Klingspor's typescript summary of events leading to the rupture of the DKP-DRP (no date, very likely written in the last week of January, 1950). Cf. further *Rundschreiben,* no. 1/50 (January 16, 1950).

26. Of interest in this connection is a detailed letter of Klingspor to Thomas Dehler (dated June 28, 1955), in which the former commented at length on the motives and machinations of Herwart Miessner.

27. In a letter to Klingspor of January 5, 1950.

28. According to the declaration, Leuchtgens and Teuscher would see to it that the Joint Delegates' Convention be held in Göttingen as planned; that the bylaws and program which had been worked out by the interim executive board on November 27, 1949, be accepted unanimously if possible, and without much discussion and parliamentary sparring, in any case; that the executive committee be kept to a small number, excluding from it members of the parliamentary party; that the party headquarters remain in the close vicinity of the party's chairman and not be merged with the Fraktion's office in Bonn; and, finally, that an appropriate resolution be passed by the convention condemning the Bundestag members for interfering with the functions of the Parteileitung and for having consistently disregarded its decisions.

29. Rolf Hermann, district chairman of Kassel, had been a founding member in 1948 of the Deutsche Block in Kassel. This extremist group—loosely associated with Karl Meissner's DB in Bavaria—participated in the local elections despite constant harassment by the Military Government in

the form of temporary injunctions and even the arrest of two of its leaders. It gathered an astonishing 8 per cent of the votes cast and captured five councilmanic seats. When the DB was outlawed by the American authorities, the five city councilors joined the FDP to avoid the loss of their mandates. Shortly thereafter, Hermann joined the NDP. Interview with Karl Meissner, April 17, 1957. Cf. *Der Informationsdienst,* no. 55 (February 26, 1951).

30. Von Thadden's report to Klingspor, January 16, 1950.

31. The weakness of the entire Lower Saxon Land organization, and, a fortiori, of those of its parts for which Miessner and friends pretended to speak, is starkly described by the chairman of the Brunswick district organization, Hannes Kaiser (letter to Franz Richter, January 7, 1950). According to him, the Land organization was still in an embryonic state, and its birth seemed dubious. Of 75 political districts, only 43 had any kind of DRP organization, and most of these were little more than paper organizations, consisting of a chairman, a vice-chairman, and a treasurer. In only six or nine districts were there any really promising beginnings. The Land headquarters was in no better shape. There was not even enough money for postage, mimeographing, etc. Even as late as January 1950, the DRP had no officially printed program or statement of principles, nor did it have a newspaper or information bulletin. Dues were paid fitfully, if at all, speaker's information was unavailable, and work among the youth hardly visible.

32. Report of Hans Heinrich Zisseler to Klingspor, January 16, 1949.

33. Von Thadden's letter to Klingspor, January 16, 1949.

34. *Ibid.*

35. The sentiment among district chairmen can be gathered from a letter of the chairman of the District Ammerland, H. Planert, to Klingspor (January 20, 1949), in which Planert gives his reasons for preferring a party split to the continued existence of the DKP-DRP. As the strength of a district organization of the DRP was often greater than that of an entire Land organization of the DKP, "we cannot be expected to suffer the indignity of continued tutelage by the DKP or to accept the imposition of a DKP program." "We don't want a renewal of the NSDAP," wrote Planert, "but we want its good parts," and although he himself never became a member of the Nazi Party, as a *Jungdeutschnationaler* prior to 1933 he "recognized the positive features" of Nazism. "With Steuer's ideas we'd be committing suicide here. We've got to compete with the SRP. We can't imagine why you should have delegated your powers to a man like Steuer, of all people. With his ideas we wouldn't dare to face our voters. We'd cease being a Rightist party and would become an association for the maintenance of conservatism. The DNVP is dead and cannot be revived. Such Land organizations [of our party] as Hamburg and Schleswig-Holstein are a liability to us here in Lower Saxony."

36. Von Thadden's letter to Klingspor, January 16, 1950.

37. Telegram to Klingspor, January 15, 1950, signed by Zisseler, Hans Barkhausen, Otto Meesmann, Jaeger, and Schlüter. Schlüter had in the meantime re-entered the DRP, which he had left in September, 1949, in protest against the "national-Bolshevik" activity of Dorls, Krüger, Remer, and

company. (Cf. above, XIV/2.) Cf. also Zisseler's letter to Klingspor of January 16, 1950.

38. Report of participant observers from the DKP at Kassel (Frau von Bannert, Padberg, and Wilhelm Piepenbrink) to the DKP delegates' convention at Hamm, January 29, 1950.

39. The other members were Erich Teuscher, Rolf Hermann, Rudolf Hafer, and Müller von Hagen from the NDP; and Hans-Heinrich Scheffer, Hermann Krüger-Imhoff, and Hannes Kaiser from the DRP.

40. *Der Informationsdienst,* no. 15 (October 4, 1950).

41. See "National-Sozialismus: Rechter Flügel stark," *Der Spiegel,* IV, 2 (January 14, 1950), 5.

42. Cf. *Propaganda Rundschreiben,* no. I/51 (January 30, 1951).

43. Klingspor's letter to von Thadden, April 21, 1950. Cf. *Propaganda Rundschreiben,* no. XIV/50 (November 23, 1950), 3.

44. See above, VII/39, and below, XV/78.

45. Letter of Klingspor to Johann Kühl, business manager pro tempore of the Land organization of Schleswig-Holstein (DKP), reproduced in *Rundschreiben,* no. 6/50 (March 15, 1950), from the Parteileitung of the Nationale Rechte.

46. Letter of Leuchtgens to Klingspor, April 5, 1950.

47. Götzendorff had joined Loritz prior to the 1949 election and entered the Bundestag with the twelve-man WAV delegation. (See above, text near IV/145.) Inordinately ambitious and unscrupulous, Götzendorff now disassociated himself from Loritz to prepare the ground for a major organizational coup against him. In November, 1949, the thirty-six-year-old Götzendorff announced the founding of a so-called Bloc of Expellees (Block der Heimatvertriebenen), later Fighting Bloc of Expellees, with which he hoped to undermine (in the Bavarian Land elections of 1950) the basis of both the WAV and the German Community–BHE coalition. See *SPD Pressedienst,* P/IV/174 (November 23, 1949). Cf. *Der Informationsdienst,* no. 22 (October 31, 1950) and no. 30 (November 23, 1950).

48. *Die Tat* (Zurich), January 16, 1951.

49. Cf. *Der Informationsdienst,* no. 30 (November 23, 1950).

50. The federal government presented at that time no danger as the applicable provision of the Basic Law, Article 21, required action by the Federal Constitutional Court, which had yet to be constituted.

51. Deutscher Bundestag, Verhandlungen des deutschen Bundestages, 1. Wahlperiode, *Stenographische Berichte,* 7. Sitzung (September 22, 1949), pp. 80, 81.

52. *Ibid.,* pp. 81, 82.

53. *Ibid.,* p. 85.

54. *Frankfurter Rundschau,* October 7, 1949; cf. *Die Welt* (Hamburg), October 7, 1949.

55. See *Rundschreiben,* no. 5/50 (March 4, 1950). Not all facts alleged there by Klingspor are correct.

56. See *Rundschreiben an alle Kreisverbandvorsitzende* by acting Land Chairman Anton Mainzer, April 4, 1950.

57. Most of them came from the Brunswick district organization. Their leaders were the executive secretary, Johannes Guth, of Brunswick; Rolf Nehring, chairman of the District Watenstedt-Salzgitter; his colleague Dietrich Korsch; and Walter Karstädter, also of Brunswick.

58. *Rundschreiben* of the chairman of the Land organization Lower Saxony (Anton Mainzer) of April 17, 1950. Cf. *Braunschweiger Zeitung,* April 18, 1950.

59. See below, XVII/115. In a report on a discussion (on December 16, 1949) with Miessner and Richter, Erich Teich, the DRP official who later was to join the "national-Bolshevik" circles around the FeS (see above, text near VI/179-183), aptly described Miessner's outlook when he quoted him as having said: "I'm no idealist; I'm an economist. If by going to Bonn I couldn't improve on my job as senior counselor in the Ministry of Finance, the whole work in Bonn would be senseless." (Von Thadden sent a copy of this report to Klingspor on December 19, 1949.)

60. Leuchtgens had earlier pleaded in vain with Klingspor to rejoin the DRP to help him reassert conservative principles in that party. When Klingspor underscored the quixotic nature of such notions, Leuchtgens (who had been completely isolated both in the Fraktion and in the party) recognized the hopelessness of his situation and resigned. (Leuchtgens' letter to Klingspor, April 5, 1950.) For the DP's Hesse party organization, see *Die Neue Zeitung* (Munich), March 10, 1952. See below, XVII/16–18 and nearby text.

61. On the proceedings at this conference at Hamm on January 29, 1950, see *Rundschreiben* (Nationale Rechte), no. 3/50 (February 1, 1950) and no. 4/50 (February 25, 1950); cf. *Der Informationsdienst,* no. 5 (February 26, 1951).

62. On the question of party finances, see U. W. Kitzinger, *German Electoral Politics: A Study of the 1957 Campaign* (Oxford: Clarendon, 1960), Chapter X. On CDU finance in nonelection years, see Arnold J. Heidenheimer, "German Party Finance: The CDU," *American Political Science Review,* LI, 2 (June, 1957), 369–385. On the continuing difficulties created by dubious methods of party finance, see R. W. Miller, "Recent Efforts toward Legal Regulation of Political Parties in Western Germany," *Papers of the Michigan Academy of Science, Arts, and Letters,* XLVII (1962), 299–310.

63. Letters from Klingspor to von Thadden, March 28, 1950, and to Leuchtgens on the following day. Also Klingspor's letter to von Thadden, April 21, 1950.

64. To add insult to injury, the chairman of the DRP's new Land organization was a former member of the NR's leadership group who had betrayed his own party and made a special deal with Richter behind Klingspor's back. Cf. Anton Mainzer's *Rundschreiben* to all district chairmen, April 4, 1950, and *Rundschreiben,* no. 2/52 (February 23, 1952), of the "Parteileitung, Vereinigte Rechte (Nationale Rechte)."

65. See above, Chapter V, Section C; and below, Chapter XVII, Section C.

66. Taking part in these negotiations were Richter and von Thadden for

the DRP; the indefatigable party founder Joachim von Ostau (who had in the meantime founded a National Union), Haussleiter, Spindler, and Canon Goebel for the German Community (DG); and Klingspor for the NR. The DG and the NR refused to join von Ostau. (For details on this renewed unsuccessful attempt at a rally, see *Deutsche Presse Agentur* (*dpa*), *Inf.* 546 [May 5, 1950], p. 2.) The National Union was founded shortly after the federal election (August 28, 1949) in Dortmund, at first as an Interest Association for the Formation of a National Union, with a view toward serving as a common platform for a large rally of the National Opposition which hopefully would be organized in time to participate in the Land elections in June, 1950, in North Rhine–Westphalia. The program had the old characteristic features of all of von Ostau's ventures: the Reich within frontiers which correspond to the basic principles of international law, the end to any discrimination against former Nazis, solidarity of all estates and occupations, a profit-sharing scheme, the representation of corporations alongside of political representation, the popular election (for a very long term) of the chief of state, and neutralism. The leading members of the new organization included, besides von Ostau, Fritz Unterberg (Duisburg) and E. Schneider (Cologne) as chairman and vice-chairman, respectively; von Ostau's old follower, Wolfgang Kölpin (Bad Godesberg); former SPD Land diet deputy Ernst Arnds (Castrop-Rauxel); expellee leader, ex-Communist, and former candidate for the Land diet on the FDP ticket Friedrich Kopatschek; H.B. Tschierschke (Recklinghausen); and Count Lutz von Schwerin-Krosigk (Essen). After considerable political activity, especially in the Ruhr district, the new group fell apart with the resignation of the last two. See "Bericht über die Dortmunder Tagung am 28. August 1949" (signed by von Ostau), "Zehn richtungsweisende Grundsätze für die Bildung der 'Nationalen Union,' " "Satzung." (All three documents are mimeographed.) Cf. *Deutsche Presse Agentur* (*dpa*), *Inf.* 94 (January 23, 1950), p. 2; *Neuer Vorwärts* (Hanover), December 8, 1950, p. 5. After the failure of this venture, von Ostau sought to construct yet another political base from which he could participate in the 1950 Land elections. This was the Bloc of National Unification (Block der nationalen Einigung, BNE) which von Ostau and Kopatschek founded in May 1950. (See *Die Neue Zeitung* [Munich], May 19, 1950, p. 6.) When that venture did not yield the desired returns, von Ostau joined with Karl-Heinz Priester's NDP (in Hesse) and Feitenhansl's VU (in Bavaria) to form a National Democratic Reich Party (Nationaldemokratische Reichs–Partei) to which also the tiny Hamburg League of Independents under Topp acceded. (*Deutsche Presse Agentur* (*dpa*), *Inf.* 65 [August 6, 1950].) This was by no means von Ostau's last political enterprise. It was followed in 1954 by a National Democratic Party of Germany (Nationaldemokratische Partei Deutschlands, NPD), which in turn gave way in 1957 to the monarchist People's Movement for Emperor and Reich (Volksbewegung für Kaiser und Reich). See above, VI/129; and below, XVI/180.

67. Letter of Steuer to Bertram Schumacher, August 15, 1950. The emphasis of the word "unconditionally" is supplied by the present writer.

68. *Rundschreiben* of Land organization of NR (North Rhine–West-

phalia), May, 1950; letters of Klingspor to Land executive committee of April 11, April 17, and May 5, 1950. Also minutes of the meeting of the Land executive committee on May 29, 1950.

69. Letter of Bertram Schumacher to Klingspor, December 4, 1950.

70. Klingspor's letter to Schumacher, December 9, 1950.

71. These were the Communist Party, the Center Party, and the Radical Social Freedom Party (Radikalsoziale Freiheits–Partei) (which fights for the realization of Silvio Gesell's economic theory).

72. Especially in East Westphalia, where it obtained in excess of 5 per cent of the votes.

73. At a Land party convention on May 22, 1950, the NR had nominated its candidates. The first three places went to Lothar Steuer, Wilhelm Piepenbrink, and Hans Joachim von Rohr-Demmin. The latter, a wealthy Pomeranian landowner, president of the Pomeranian Land League, and prominent German National (DNVP) Deputy in the Prussian Diet, played a considerable role in the last years of the Weimar Republic. In 1933 he joined his party chief, Hugenberg, in Hitler's first cabinet as State Secretary in Hugenberg's Reich Ministry of Nutrition and Agriculture. On the question of von Rohr's part in bringing about Chancellor Brüning's fall and that of Schleicher, see Bracher (III/7), pp. 512, 697. Cf. above, VI/219.

74. Thus, within the government district Detmold, the DRP could more than double the figures achieved by the DKP in the previous year. In this government district several Land districts (e.g., Detmold and Höxter) gave in excess of 10 per cent of the votes to the DRP. Within these *Landkreise* in not a few of the smaller towns more than 20, 25, and even 30 per cent voted for the DRP (e.g., Bentrup, Hakedahl, Hedderhagen, Heesten, Niederschönhagen, Trophagen in Detmold, and Drenke, Rothe, Beller, Hagedorn, Born, Eilversen, in Höxter). See Statistisches Landesamt Nordrhein-Westfalen, *Die Wahlen in Nordrhein-Westfalen in den Jahren seit 1948* (Düsseldorf: 1952).

75. To the fastidious Klingspor, the DRP, in accepting the support of such unsavory characters as Kniggendorf or Götzendorff, had placed itself beyond the pale. He was shocked beyond words when the DRP's treasurer admitted that the party caucus in the Bundestag clung to the criminally convicted Götzendorff merely because it thereby attained the minimum number necessary to be eligible for an extra DM 750 per month. See Klingspor's *Rundschreiben,* no. 1/51 (January 26, 1951).

76. Negotiations looking toward the establishment of a NR Land organization in Lower Saxony initially involved Klingspor, Steuer, Meesmann, and Schlüter. The designation of a chairman occasioned considerable difficulty, if we are to believe Schlüter's description of the events. Zisseler appeared very skeptical regarding the chances of success for an independent party and was not certain that he cared to be involved. Meesmann was willing to take the chairmanship eventually, but begged to be allowed to remain relatively in the background until a pending business venture had been concluded. Under these circumstances, Steuer and Klingspor begged Schlüter to take over the new Land organization; Schlüter reluctantly agreed to accept the chairmanship, but only on a temporary basis.

77. *Einladung* dated December 27, 1950. In the *Einladung* (invitation) the NR described itself as the bearer of those ideas which had once made Germany a united, free, and respected country. In foreign policy, the invitation pointed out, the key problem was to free not only Germany but all of Europe from the threats and tutelage under which it suffered at the time. The founding committee which sent out the invitation consisted of Klingspor as party leader, Leonhard Schlüter, and H. H. Zisseler. At Hanover, Schlüter was elected chairman. The executive board consisted of Zisseler, Hans Barkhausen, H. J. Otto, Heinrich Behr, Harald Zühlsdorf, and Heinrich Rathert. (*Rundschreiben,* no. 1/51 [January 26, 1951].) Rathert was at that time still district chairman in the DRP.

78. See *Rundschreiben,* no. 2/51 (April 25, 1951). Actually, according to Schlüter two of the members of the NR's executive committee, Behr and Otto, advised their party faithfuls in the districts of Harburg and Stade to vote for the FDP and, indeed, refused to participate in the NR's electoral campaign.

79. See above, Chapter V, Section C; and below, Chapter XVII, Section C.

80. Adolf von Thadden later accused the DRP's executive secretary, Ewald Gaul, of having betrayed party interests to the FDP and of being thus largely responsible for the failure of the negotiations.

81. See *Propaganda Rundschreiben,* no. V/1951 (May 23, 1951).

82. Letter of Klingspor to Schlüter, May 4, 1951. Even before the elections of May, 1951, Klingspor sought to moderate Schlüter's noisy nationalism. At that time he requested Schlüter not to use the provocative colors black-white-red for campaign purposes. Rejecting that request, Schlüter shot back: "Mr. Klingspor, I have noticed in the meantime that you as a former member of the German People's Party and exponent of Stresemann's policies also feel yourself attacked by my sharp words against the incompetent parties (*Versagerparteien*) outside of the nationalist coalition of 1933. It would appear that you are even today incapable of leaping over your own party political shadow of yore." Open letter (mimeographed) of Leonhard Schlüter to Hermann Klingspor, June 26, 1951, p. 3.

83. Standard speech for DRP speakers, April 26, 1951. Shortly before inner power struggles eliminated the DRP's executive secretary Johannes Guth from the party, he was reported to have made public speeches in which he described as one of the most important German tasks the "vindication of the honor of the Combat SS." The Federal Republic, Guth maintained, "was not worth shedding a drop of blood for." If it had to be defended, then the ramparts should be manned by the 86 per cent of the Bundestag deputies who managed to have stayed out of the war and by the Resistance fighters and former concentration-camp inmates. As to German guilt, in the light of the atrocities committed in Korea, "we deny that anyone has any right to speak of crimes against humanity in Germany." *Die Neue Zeitung* (Munich), January 8, 1951, and *Deutsche Presse Agentur* (*dpa*), *Inf.* 33 (January 6, 1951).

84. After the expulsion of Richter/Rössler, the vice-chairman Schäfer had moved into the chairmanship. In March, 1951, however, he resigned his

post and was followed by Colonel Hans-Heinrich Scheffer, a "moderate," as these things went in the DRP, and, at any rate, an honorable man. *Der Informationsdienst,* March 16, 1951.

85. Schlüter's open letter of June 26, 1951, p. 12.

86. For the DSP and Gereke, see above, Chapter VI, Section E. The RP was formed by those former functionaries and members of the DRP who were expelled in the spring of 1950 on suspicion of preparing the take-over of the party. The intrigue was essentially one of Kniggendorf's many moves either to seize the party as a whole or, failing that, to split it and carry a major part of it with him into the SRP. See *Propaganda Rundschreiben,* no. VII/50 (August 1, 1950).

87. See *Propaganda Rundschreiben,* no. III/1950 (June 13, 1950). For Goebel, see above, IV/7, VIII/53, XIV/63.

88. See *Propaganda Rundschreiben,* no. VII/50 (August 1, 1950).

89. *Ibid.*

90. *Ibid.,* no. III/1950 (June 13, 1950).

91. *Ibid.,* no. V/1951 (May 23, 1951).

92. *Ibid.*

93. *Ibid.,* no. VIII/1950 (August 18, 1950).

94. It is dubious that the SRP leaders had any clear idea of the measures then taken or of their relation to the class structure, political support, or ideology of the Nazi movement. For these relationships, see Arthur Schweitzer's excellent *Big Business in the Third Reich* (Bloomington: Indiana University Press, 1964).

95. In a letter only two days after the startling election of May 6, 1951, Klingspor already warned the DRP chairman Scheffer to make all necessary preparations to be ready should new elections be called subsequent to the outlawing of the SRP.

96. *Propaganda Rundschreiben,* no. V/1951 (May 23, 1951).

97. *Ibid.*

98. *Ibid.,* no. VIII/50 (August 18, 1950).

99. *Ibid.,* no. XIII/50 (November 11, 1950).

100. Standard speech for DRP speakers, April 26, 1951. On "co-ownership," see above, VIII/59.

101. Such as the districts Gifhorn, Helmstedt, Hameln-Stadt, Watenstedt-Salzgitter, and Wilhelmshaven.

102. See Niedersächsisches Amt (VI/146).

103. See *Propaganda Rundschreiben,* no. V/1951 (May 23, 1951).

104. Klingspor's letter to Schlüter, May 4, 1951, Schlüter's answer of May 8, 1951; Meesmann's letter to Klingspor of May 8, 1951, Zisseler's letter to Klingspor of May 9, 1951, Scheffer's letter to Klingspor of May 15, 1951, Klingspor's letter to Scheffer of June 1, 1951, Scheffer's letters to Klingspor of June 10 and 20, 1951, Scheffer's letter to Schlüter, June 18, 1951, and Schlüter's open letter to Klingspor of June 26, 1951.

105. See report on the meeting of the temporary Land executive committee of the NR in Lower Saxony, June 10, 1951. Klingspor and Steuer attended that meeting ex officio. Cf. also Klingspor's report to all members

of the executive committee, district chairmen, and co-workers of the NR in Lower Saxony, June 19, 1951.

106. The executive committee consisted at that time of Hans Zisseler, Barkhausen, H. J. Otto, Behr, Rathert, Lothar Neumann, and Natzsch. The last two had joined the committee on June 10, 1951, and Neumann became its acting chairman.

107. Minutes of the executive committee meeting of June 10, 1951.

108. Klingspor's report on the "Schlüter case" to the executive committee, all district leaders, and co-workers of the NR in Lower Saxony, dated June 19, 1951.

109. The invitation to join the FDP Fraktion was extended to Schlüter by the highly respected liberal Mayor of Göttingen and chairman of the Fraktion, Hermann Föge, on May 13, 1951. (*Der Spiegel,* IX, 25 [June 15, 1955].) For Schlüter's exploits in the FDP see below, Chapter XVII, Section C.

110. Scheffer's letter to Klingspor, June 20, 1951.

111. Letter of Lothar Neumann to Klingspor, August 7, 1951. Cf. *aide-mémoire* on the conference of leading NR officials called by Neumann on September 9, 1951.

112. Thus, for instance, in the beginning of November, the entire local (*Ortsgruppe*) organization in Hameln, under the leadership of Schlüter's close friend, the young and dynamic Krebs, went over to the SRP after, as he said, the "reactionary basis of the NR" had been revealed to him and after he had discovered that the much emphasized differences between the SRP and the DRP-NR were lies. See letter of Lothar Neumann to Klingspor, November 12, 1951. The author of the letter did nothing to reconcile the logical difficulties of Krebs' reported position.

113. Letter of Zisseler to Klingspor, October 24, 1951. On November 16, 1951, Zisseler took the next step after having sounded the possibility of a Land-level "working association": he called together Meesmann and Günther Schwendy (NR), Scheffer and Jaeger (DRP), and Oeltze von Lobenthal and Thomas (from the DG) for a discussion of the problem of a "working association" embracing NR, DRP, and DG, at first on the Land level, but looking toward merger on the federal level in the unspecified future. (Zisseler's letter to Klingspor of November 19, 1951.) Klingspor saw no objections to the maintenance of close contact with the DG of Lower Saxony. He warned, however, against agreements on the federal level because of the great differences among the various Land organizations. Also on that level one would have to deal with August Haussleiter, whom Klingspor could not accept as a suitable partner. (Klingspor's answer to Zisseler, November 26, 1951.)

114. Klingspor's report concerning an *Arbeitsgemeinschaft* (working association) with the DRP, dated June 25, 1951.

115. *Rundschreiben,* no. 4/51 (November 16, 1951). Also Klingspor's letter to Scheffer of the same date.

116. On Früchte, see Schlüter's open letter to Klingspor of June 26, 1951, pp. 9–10. In September, 1951, Früchte left the DRP and in December,

1952, resigned from the Diet. Ewald Gaul, the DRP's former manager, charged in the course of a press conference that the DRP's opportunistic endorsement of the fraudulent Jürgen Früchte had led to numerous resignations from the party. *Deutsche Presse Agentur* (*dpa*), *Inf.* 1031 (July 17, 1951).

117. Klingspor's letter to Scheffer, November 16, 1951.

118. *Rundschreiben,* no. 5/51 (December 5, 1951), of the Party Directorate (Parteileitung) of the NR.

119. The party's statement provides no indication that any thought was given to the economic consequences of these demands. One looks in vain for a discussion of the consequences, for instance, for the net growth of the economy if scarce capital resources are invested in such unproductive and expensive items as private housing. Indeed, no one apparently thought to ask who might be able to afford the homes, as long as their construction devours the capital necessary for the rebuilding and expansion of the industrial base on which the growth of the economy and, hence, ultimately the prosperity of the people, depend.

120. See *Propaganda Rundschreiben,* no. XI/51 (December 13, 1951), report on the delegates' conference of the National Right in Recklinghausen on December 1, 1951, and a DRP handbill of October, 1952, entitled "Deutschland braucht keine Programme, Deutschland braucht Männer und Frauen mit klarer Zielsetzung." Cf. *Rundschreiben,* no. 51 (January 26, 1951), of the Party Directorate of the National Right.

Chapter XV: The Quest for a United Nationalist Opposition

1. *Rundschreiben der Zonenleitung,* no. XI/47 (September 15, 1947), p. 1.

2. Letter of Hellwege to Jäger, September 5, 1947.

3. *Rundschreiben der Zonenleitung,* no. XI/47 (September 15, 1947). Cf. Letter of Jäger to Zone Council, September 10, 1947.

4. Adolf Dedekind, Hellwege's adjutant, sought to persuade DRP district organizations in Dortmund and Oberhausen, behind their party leadership's back, to bolt to the DP. See "Zusammenfassende Feststellung zu der Angelegenheit DP-Ewers (Lübeck)," attached to *Rundschreiben,* no. XII/47 (October 21, 1947). See also letter of Hans Ewers to Jäger, October 15, 1947.

5. See *Rundschreiben* of the chairman of the Zone Council to the members of the apostate Regional Association of Lübeck, November 7, 1947.

6. Two days before the meeting von Thadden, in a letter to Klingspor, confided how nice it would be if these very important talks were to succeed. He described the DRP's relation to the DP as excellent and hoped that the Guelphs among the DP leadership would not be put off by the outcry of the SPD and the British Military Government that the DP was swinging into the

DRP's nationalist line. Von Thadden reminded Klingspor that the DRP had contested the by-election in Wolfsburg under the DP label.

7. Such as, for example, a memorandum of von Thadden's of June 3, 1949, a *Rundschreiben* of Jäger's (no. VIII) of August 16, 1949, and a message of his, just a few days before his sudden death, addressed to the delegates' conference of the North Rhine–Westphalian DKP-DRP which met at Essen on August 27, 1949.

8. Letter of Klingspor to Hellwege, September 12, 1949.

9. On September 12, 1949, Klingspor, who had taken over the chairmanship of the DKP-DRP after Jäger's sudden death and the lapse of his own British-imposed "activities prohibition," inquired of Hellwege if he wished to begin again where they had left off in June. A meeting was arranged in Bonn on September 18 and was attended by Hellwege, Hans-Christoph Seebohm, and Lauenstein for the DP and by Klingspor and von Lüninck for the DKP-DRP.

10. Klingspor's letter to Hellwege, October 26, 1949.

11. The interim agreements, incidentally, had said nothing about the equality of the parties, about merging the entire parties rather than just selected parts, or about the distribution of top positions on a fifty-fifty basis.

12. The answer to his insistence that fusion negotiations could proceed only on the level of the party chiefs, Klingspor was not to receive in the form of a letter from Hellwege. On the contrary, Hellwege purposely procrastinated. The answer came in a flood of most disquieting reports from the DKP-DRP's district organizations. The Essen organization, for instance, had learned from a plenipotentiary of the DP that its executive board had rejected the notion of a DP–DKP fusion. Assuming the truth of the report, the Essen organization of the DKP-DRP (pursuant to an earlier decision of its membership) had thereupon voted to join the DP. Almost simultaneously word arrived from the Land chairman of Schleswig-Holstein, the former German National politician Eldor Borck, that the Land executive committee of the DP informed the DKP that merger on the all-party level was quite out of the question and that only individual members of the DKP would be permitted to transfer to the DP. On September 30, 1949, the DP's Number Two man, Seebohm, personally supervised the formation of a DP Land organization in North Rhine–Westphalia which consisted exclusively of those district organizations which had recently left the DKP-DRP. See letter of Emil Bierbrauer, chairman of the district organization of Essen, to Klingspor, September 26, 1949, and Klingspor's letter to Hellwege, September 30, 1949. Cf. also *Rundschreiben,* no. 11/49 (September 30, 1949). See letter of Ludwig Schwecht, chairman of the district Düren, to Klingspor, October 1, 1949.

13. Klingspor's letters to Schwecht, October 4, 1949, and to Hellwege of September 29, October 6, November 3, November 19, 1949, and January 21, 1950, and Hellwege's letters to Klingspor of October 28, November 3, 1949, and of January 9, 1950. On the pre-election deals between the DRP's Lower Saxon Land organization under von Thadden and the DP, according

to which the DP would underwrite the campaign expenditures of three district DRP candidates and place three additional DRP candidates on the DP Land list in return for DRP support of the DP in all the districts, see minutes of the meeting of the DRP executive committee of January 15, 1950, and von Thadden's letter to all district chairmen of January 16, 1950.

14. See *Der Informationsdienst,* no. 19 (October 18, 1950).

15. Friedrich Erbe, "Vierzehn Jahre Wahlen in Westdeutschland (1946–1960)," in Erwin Faul, ed., *Wahlen und Wähler in Westdeutschland* (Villingen: Ring, [1960]), p. 57.

16. *Ibid.,* p. 58.

17. See *Der Informationsdienst,* no. 20 (October 23, 1950).

18. For signs of increasing estrangement, see *Der Informationsdienst* no. 22 (October 31, 1950); no. 26 (November 11, 1950); no. 28 (November 15, 1950); no. 33 (December 4, 1950). Finally, after the campaign in the federal by-elections in Donauwörth, Haussleiter opened fire with personal attacks against Oberländer, accusing him of toadyism, opportunism, and betrayal. Oberländer returned the fire in the form of a libel suit. See *ibid.,* no. 82 (May 31, 1951).

19. Under the chairmanship of Oeltze von Lobenthal, the DG Land organization was founded in Lower Saxony in the spring of 1950 and immediately sought to come to an agreement with the newly founded Union of Expellees and Patriots, a local forerunner of the BHE. The DG's negotiating team consisted of Lobenthal, Boch, Fromme, van Eyck, and Krahl. After the split-up of the Tatgemeinschaft freier Deutscher, its Lower Saxon branch under Dr. König and Krahl joined the DG. See K. K. Krebs, *Rundschreiben* no. 2 (*Deutsche Gemeinschaft Niedersachsen*) (June 30, 1950).

20. Of course, this was not the first occasion for such discussions. As long ago as May, 1950, when the newly founded DRP decided to challenge its former party colleagues of the DKP in the North Rhine–Westphalian Land election, von Thadden negotiated with August Haussleiter and the expellee leader Canon Georg Goebel (see above, XIV/66). Goebel's Interest Group of Eastern Refugees had formed the North Rhine–Westphalian part of the Tatgemeinschaft freier Deutscher, which had merged in April, 1950, into the German Community (see above, VIII/55, 56), but which felt incapable of contesting the Landtag elections. These negotiations ended with an electoral alliance between the DRP and Goebel's eastern refugees. At that time the general secretary of the North Rhine–Westphalian Land organization of the DG, Heinrich Lindner, strongly objected to Haussleiter's presumption in entering into such an agreement in the name of the Land organization. Cf. also *Der Informationsdienst,* no. 18 (June 30, 1950), and the protocol of a meeting of the directorate of the DG in Frankfurt, on May 23, 1950, in *Deutsche Presse Agentur* (*dpa*), *Inf.* 69 (June 9, 1950). The quotations that follow in the text are taken from Deutsche Gemeinschaft, "Das Nationale Manifest der Deutschen Gemeinschaft" (broadside, Munich, November 18, 1951).

21. Klingspor's letter to H. H. Zisseler, November 26, 1951. The "unalterable program" of the DG breathed the spirit of the Conservative Revolu-

tion and exhibited more than just traces of that other "unalterable program" of twenty-five points—the program of the NSDAP—whose aim was also the rebirth of Germany "in German spirit and in German freedom." Haussleiter's first demand was the destruction of "uncontrollable party cliques" and the "anonymous and totalitarian party bureaucracies" as well as the "corroding materialist spirit of the interest groups in our public life." He raised the old conservative demand for local self-government and a corporate form of representation and rejected the particularism of the states in favor of an "organic structuring of tribes and regions." The cultural role of the state was to fight against nihilism in the "intellectual and cultural life." Haussleiter then proclaimed "the law of national solidarity in regard to all the victims of the Second World War, the expellees and the seriously disabled, those who have suffered damages through the war and the prisoners of war, and in regard to everyone whom the Morgenthau Plan has robbed of his material existence." In opposition to the "exploitation, control and tutelage of our economy by foreigners," the DG demanded an "active economic policy in favor of the middle classes and the artisans," as well as a "German *Marktordnung*" for the farmer and the "liberation of the worker" through "co-ownership" which vouchsafes the "organic unity of capital and labor in the plant community." Deutsche Gemeinschaft (XV/20).

22. Scheffer's letter to Klingspor, December 16, 1951.

23. Scheffer's letter to Klingspor, December 29, 1951.

24. The first discussion took place on January 20, 1952, in Düsseldorf. Von Thadden and Steuer also attended. (Scheffer's letter to Klingspor, January 16, 1952.)

25. Klingspor's letter to Scheffer, December 22, 1951.

26. Klingspor's letter to Scheffer, February 22, 1952.

27. See above, VI/86-89, 91, and nearby text.

28. See above, VI/189.

29. From an interview with Jungnickel, Bonn, May 26, 1957.

30. See above, text near VI/70 and VI/107.

31. See above, V/39.

32. See above, VIII/55.

33. See above, VI/189.

34. See above, VIII/95.

35. See below, text at XVII/70.

36. See above, VI/209.

37. See above, XIV/109, and below, XVII/75 and nearby text.

38. Cerff had been chief of the radio section of the Hitler Youth, a key position in the Nazis' indoctrination program. After his transfer to the Ministry of Propaganda he soon came into conflict with Goebbels, whom he accused of inadequate ideological purity. On May 22, 1943, Goebbels noted in his diary: "I had a sharp conflict with Cerff. . . . Cerff takes a somewhat super-national-socialistic attitude. If he had his way music, for instance, would be made only on lyres." Louis P. Lochner (II/1), p. 390.

39. See above, V/96 and nearby text.

40. Griesmayr, Hess, and Cerff met at the Frankfurt home of Albert

Smagon. Smagon began his political career, as did Brehm, as a member of the nationalist-revolutionary Aufbruch circle in the Sudetenland. His faithfulness to the cause was later rewarded with the post of Nazi District Leader and Counselor in Bratislava (Slovakia). In the postwar period he became an important Witiko League member, a staff member of the East-financed *Deutsche Nationalzeitung,* founder of the Expellees' Publishers Association, and manager (*Verlagsleiter*) of the *Ost-West Kurier* (Frankfurt). See below, text near XVII/164.

41. Von Sivers, a Baltic German, the chairman of the DG in Württemberg, is a professor of economics at the Stuttgart Polytechnic, and Schwandtner, a member of the DG's executive board, owns a textile business. Colonel Rumrich, also a member of the DG's executive board, had been a Land diet deputy for the DG and was later to join the DP, which ran him as a Bundestag candidate in the federal election of 1953. Before 1945 von Sivers had been a professor of economics at the then newly founded Reich University of Poznan (Posen), whose task it was to have been—in the words of the college "politruk" Hanns Streit— "to form [part of] a consolidated East wall of German spirit which will forever vigilantly prevent any Slav inroads." Von Sivers contributed his part to the "consolidation" of the Teutonic wall. See in this connection Max Weinreich (V/23), pp. 126–131, especially p. 128.

42. Yet only a few months later, Wilhelm Wesemeyer, member of the anti-Semitic, anti-Christian Ludendorff sect and representative in the Bonn-Godesberg area of the FeS, alleged that von Thadden was actively working for the FeS and was contributing several articles on contemporary topics to the FeS's press in the hope, presumably, of improving his chances for reelection to the Bundestag. From a report of an interview with Wesemeyer, Bad Godesberg, April 14, 1953.

43. In this connection, Hess suggested Wilhelm Meinberg as chairman of a unified nationalist rally, as a man on whom the ANG members could agree. Meinberg had entered radical, ultranationalist politics at the age of twenty as a member of the Völkischer Schutz- und Trutzbund (Folkish League for Defense and Offense), one of the most uncompromisingly folkish, anti-Semitic, and radical fighting leagues of the early nineteen-twenties. He was also the founder of the first Stahlhelm group in the Ruhr region. In 1929, Meinberg joined the Nazi Party, became one of its top agrarian experts, was elected in 1932 to the Prussian Diet on the Nazi ticket, and went to the Reichstag in the following year. In the Third Reich, Meinberg, the Prussian State Councilor with the assimilated SS rank of general, became the Number Two man in the Ministry of Nutrition and Agriculture and after a falling out with his old friend, the "blood and soil" theoretician and Minister R. W. Darré, became director of the Hermann Göring Works in Salzgitter. Although a convinced National Socialist, Meinberg had retained a reputation for probity and even moderation.

44. See above, XIV/47.

45. According to the Meissner plan, leadership of the working association would lie in the hands of the leaders of the DB, DU, and DRP, and—

accepting a suggestion of Jungnickel's—in those of Wilhelm Meinberg. Each of the four major divisions of the National Bureau, such as Organization, Propaganda, Administration, and General Management, was to be directed by one of the four party leaders. The country, finally, was to be divided into three sections, each under the control of one of the participating groups. Something like this scheme was in fact eventually worked out, in lieu of the unified organization which could not be realized. The various organizations represented at the ANG meetings were to form themselves into Land Working Associations under the direction of a regional co-ordinator. For Bavaria, Herbert Böhme was designated as co-ordinator, and the participating groups were DP, DU, DB, and possibly DG. In Baden-Württemberg, Naumann's friend and DU official Josef Mahlberg was to take over the direction of the local branches of the DG and DU. Hess was asked to co-ordinate the activities of the DU, DB, and DRP in Rhineland-Palatinate. Smagon was to work with DU and DRP in Hesse. For North Rhine–Westphalia, Klingspor was designated; the co-operating groups were to be the Nationale Rechte and an insignificant splinter under Sepp Schelz which called itself War Generation (Kriegsgeneration). In Lower Saxony the DRP and the League of Germans Loyal to Their Homeland (Bund heimattreuer Deutscher, BHD) were to co-ordinate their activity under the direction of H.-H. Scheffer. Wolf Schenke was given supervision over Hamburg, and in Schleswig-Holstein, Werner Boll was asked to guide the joint undertakings of DRP and DB.

46. Meissner's recalcitrance was partly motivated by the fact that the DB's uncompromisingly militant and radical rhetoric and its widely reported strong-arm tactics (see above, IV/93) appeared to Meissner's single-minded fanaticism and megalomaniac imagination to be producing "unbelievable successes." (Interview with K. Meissner, Hamburg, April 17, 1957.) To the less sanguine observer, these "successes," while symptomatic, perhaps, hardly appear to justify Meissner's disproportionate exhilaration. In the 1950 Land diet elections, the DB was able to register such scattered successes as the 20 per cent support in the little town of Wunsiedel, 10 per cent in Bayreuth, over 12 per cent in Coburg, and 17 per cent in the Town District of Neustadt bei Coburg. In fact, in all of Upper Franconia, the DB was able to increase its share of the vote from 0.4 per cent to 4.9 per cent in a matter of two years. In the meantime, the DB had also been able to get a foothold in North Germany. Lübeck in particular seemed hospitable to Meissner's brand of radicalism, and in 1951 the DB emerged from the election as that city's fourth largest party. In the surrounding villages, DB candidates found themselves sometimes supported by as many as 70 per cent of the electors. This "wave of success" lasted into 1952. In the Bavarian communal elections of that year, the DB share in Neustadt b. Coburg rose to 27 per cent, in Bayreuth to almost 13 per cent, in Kulmbach to 13.5 per cent, and in Marktredwitz to 10.6 per cent. But in all of Bavaria the DB gathered only 0.6 per cent of the votes, albeit on the basis of having provided no more than 411 out of a total of over 137,000 candidates for city, county, township, and village councils. Bayerisches Statistisches Landesamt, Beiträge zur Statistik Bayerns, no. 182, *Kommunalwahlen in Bayern am 30. März, 1952,* pp. 9,

22, 28; *ibid., Wahl zum Bayerischen Landtag am 26. November 1950,* pp. 71–94.

47. Letter to von Thadden, October 27, 1952.

48. Von Sivers, who feared that the current rapprochement of his Württemberg DG to Haussleiter's Bavarian party might be jeopardized by the hostility of the ANG, insisted that Haussleiter was willing to co-operate with the ANG. To the great amusement of all present, Griesmayr demonstrated this "willingness" by reading a letter from Haussleiter in which the latter invited the ANG to accept the DG's "National Manifesto" and to "work along the guidelines and by-laws of the DG."

49. From an interview with Rudolf Jungnickel, May 26, 1957.

50. Sterzing, BHE district chairman of Oldenburg, once defined the BHE as "the advance guard against the insolence (*Gemeinheit*) of those who were lucky enough to win." For additional information on Dr. Schulz and his political activity, see above, VI/145; and below, XVII/138, 139.

51. Letter of Klingspor to Scheffer, January 29, 1953.

52. See above, V/89 and nearby text.

53. Letter of Klingspor to Scheffer, January 29, 1953.

54. *Ibid.*

55. At Friedberg, we may recall, the DRP representative von Thadden still argued for the acceptance of the Contractual Agreement as a *fait accompli.*

56. "Richtsätze der DRP," *Das Ziel* (Hanover), II, 2 (February, 1953), 3 (Sonderbeilage).

57. *Ibid.* Actually Scheffer could not attend the convention because of ill-health. His prepared address was read by von Thadden. Probably the warmest audience response was evoked by Dr. Fritz Schulz, who gave relatively free rein to his speciality: anti-labor union rabble rousing.

58. "Deutsche Reichs-Partei, Kerntruppe der nationalen Sammlung," *Das Ziel* (Hanover), II, 2 (February, 1953), 1.

59. Rather than admit the inadequate organizational and financial basis which would not allow the DRP to contend seriously in the communal elections, the party executive pretended that the election law, admittedly unfavorable for the DRP, so favored the SPD that the public interest demanded an alliance of all "anti-Marxist" forces. Therefore (the DRP told its friends), the party would enter its own ticket only in a few places, such as Göttingen and Celle. In other areas, DRP candidates would run on other lists. See *Propaganda Rundschreiben,* no. II/1952 (October 16, 1952).

60. Letter of W. Rempel to Albert Gnade, November 11, 1952.

61. Letter of Zisseler to Klingspor, March 3, 1953. Indeed, according to Viktor Wehrmann, a leader of the DRP's Wilhelmshaven organization, by 1953 the party's membership had shrunk to one-tenth of its 1950 figure. From a report of a secret discussion in Oldenburg on May 3 and 4, 1953.

62. Letter of Zisseler to Klingspor, June 23, 1953. As we have seen, many of the Electoral Associations were banned as illegal SRP successor organizations. Of course, not all were either led or infiltrated by SRP followers. In some of them, the SRP played an insignificant part or none at all. Letter of Zisseler to Klingspor, March 3, 1953.

63. The following account is based on *Propaganda Rundschreiben,* no. I and II (February 15 and June 20, 1953), of the DRP's executive propaganda section as well as on private correspondence between some of the principal actors involved. Special reference will be made only to the materials obtained from the correspondence.

64. The meeting was also attended by the DSB chief, Karl-Heinz Priester, and by Dr. Fritz Schulz and Josef Erbacher, the spokesman for the newly formed League of Germans Loyal to Their Homeland (BHD). See above, XIII/53; and below, XVII/138, 139.

65. Cf. above, VII/69; and below, XVI/55. In view of Aschenauer's "unusual" connections, it is not surprising under the circumstances which obtained in Right-extremist circles after the war that he would be suspected of being the tool of the government with the commission to infiltrate radical circles and to guide them into an acceptance of Adenauer's foreign policy. (Confidential report of a talk in Kaiserslautern with Martin Peters, quondam chairman of the SRP's "honor court," March 12, 1953.) That the government did not scruple to use more or less unregenerate Nazis and anti-Semites for its own purposes, we have already had several occasions to demonstrate. Obviously suspecting something of that sort, Haussleiter wrote to Aschenauer after the latter's resignation from the DG: "If you came to us to win over to the Adenauer course, national men and national youth, then of course you were bound to suffer shipwreck in our [organization]." At the same time Haussleiter attacked Aschenauer publicly without mentioning his name when he wrote: "There is a man of substance who has become known by his activity in the postwar period. He travels around, introduces himself as a particular confidant of the Office for the Protection of the Constitution, demonstrates persuasively his connections to the Office of the Federal Chancellor, and travels through Germany with the assertion (*Versicherung*) that he is a kind of official trustee of the outlawed SRP and that it is his responsibility to see to it that the SRP does not get drawn into the Eastern undertow. He exults over the 'National Rally' for which he can procure the necessary millions, if one is to believe him. . . . But now comes the big secret: Group after group which accepts his tempting offers is declared a SRP successor organization . . . discussion partner after discussion partner of the great man is being arrested. Only he himself remains unscathed, shadowy wanderer between two worlds. His commission is as unfathomable as are his financial sources." ("Menschen verlieren ihr Gesicht," *Die Deutsche Gemeinschaft* [Munich], III, 4 [February, 1953], 2.) To this Aschenauer answered: "As a free German citizen I . . . held the view that it was necessary to overcome the consequences of the occupation policies and to remove existing political resentments and the tensions which appeared between the generations. . . . Furthermore I mentioned that in my opinion there is also in Bonn growing awareness [of the importance of] not letting the young generation be drawn into national-Bolshevik or Bolshevik currents." From a letter to Haussleiter of January 15, 1953, reproduced in *Deutscher Informationsdienst,* no. 292 (July 27, 1953), pp. 3–4. Cf. *ibid.,* no. 296 (August 11, 1953), and *Vorwärts* (Cologne), March 25, 1955. Incidentally, Aschenauer is the man who some years earlier had played a role in pro-

moting inadvertently the career of the Junior Senator from Wisconsin, Joseph McCarthy. It was Aschenauer, then lawyer for a number of Malmédy war criminals appealing against their conviction on grounds that their confessions had been extorted from them by unfair, and even brutal, means, who indirectly supplied McCarthy with much of the accusations against the American interrogation and prosecution staff. Senator McCarthy's guest appearance in 1949 on the Armed Services Subcommittee investigating the charges of improper handling of the German Combat SS prisoners at Schwäbisch-Hall and Dachau first brought him to the attention of the larger public. Incomprehensively, and without the slightest shred of corroborative evidence, American students of McCarthyism and the Malmédy investigations rely on an alleged "Army Intelligence" report and on each other in calling Aschenauer "a member of a Communist spy ring" and "a German Communist" (Jack Anderson and Ronald W. May, *McCarthy, the Man, the Senator, the "ism"* [Boston: Beacon, 1952], pp. 162, 246), "a notorious Communist agent" (James Rorty and Moshe Decter, *McCarthy and the Communists* [Boston: Beacon, 1954], p. 63), "a Communist agitator" (Richard H. Rovere, *Senator Joe McCarthy* [New York: Harcourt, Brace, 1959], p. 112, fn.) and a "left-wing agitator" (Richard Gallagher, *Malmédy Massacre* [New York: Paperback Library, 1964], p. 137). The probative value of these characterizations cannot be rated highly when gauged by the reliability of these authors in other matters. Thus, the Munich attorney Rudolf Aschenauer appears as living in Frankfurt (Anderson and May, p. 162), and even as Aschenhauer (Rorty and Decter, *loc. cit.*). Worse yet Rorty and Decter baldly assert that Aschenauer "admitted that he had worked up the whole case in defense of the SS (*sic*) men, that he had manufactured all the charges." This last revelation (again unsubstantiated) is made in the face of Aschenauer's sworn testimony before a subcommittee of the Senate Armed Services Committee in Munich, which included the following exchange: "MR. CHAMBERS [on the Committee staff]: Have you made any effort to verify or co-ordinate the accuracy of the statements? DR. ASCHENAUER: Yes. MR. CHAMBERS: Are you convinced that these statements are accurate and truthful? DR. ASCHENAUER: In general, I would say yes." Anderson and May take a similarly cavalier attitude toward facts. In their eagerness to expose McCarthy as a liar, they themselves take startling liberties with the principles of fair and full reporting. To McCarthy's testimony (under oath) that he had "had *no contact* with Aschenauer of any kind" (p. 162: emphasis is Anderson and May's), the authors juxtapose two excerpts from Aschenauer's testimony: "Q: Where are you submitting the affidavits? . . . A: For example to McCarthy. . . ." and "Q: Why did Diefenthal send this letter to you, Dr. Aschenauer, to be transmitted to Senator McCarthy? A: So that Senator McCarthy is informed about the various statements that had been made" (pp. 162–163). What Anderson and May suppressed in the first question was an intervening response of Aschenauer's: "SENATOR BALDWIN [Chairman of the Subcommittee]: Where are you submitting the affidavits? DR. ASCHENAUER: I have not submitted it yet, but I shall. SENATOR BALDWIN: Where do you intend to submit it? . . . . DR.

ASCHENAUER: For example, to McCarthy. . . ." In short, Aschenauer merely *intended—planned*—to submit materials to McCarthy. Whether he actually did in this case or not was never ascertained. Anderson and May's second quotation is equally unfairly separated from the context, for four exchanges after the apparent (and to McCarthy, damaging) "admission" that Aschenauer transmitted Combat SS defense materials to the Senator, we find that Aschenauer typically did not send it directly to McCarthy. "MR. CHAMBERS: Why did you send this to Mr. Finucane, instead of to Senator McCarthy, as requested by Diefenthal? DR. ASCHENAUER: Because I am in easier correspondence with the National . . . Council for Prevention of War than I am with Senator McCarthy." This indirect procedure of supplying McCarthy with German accusations against the U.S. Army was again emphasized by Aschenauer in the same hearings when he said: ". . . but usually when I have sent material about Malmédy process across, it was said that it was submitted to the Senate Committee or to one of the individual Senators, and for me it was easier to send this to the National Council for Prevention of War than send it to a Senator." (*Malmédy Massacre Investigation,* Hearings on S. Res. 42, U.S. Senate Subcommittee of the Committee on Armed Services, 81st Cong., 1st sess., part 2. [Washington: 1949], pp. 1453, 1459, 1460, 1464.) Cf. Rudolf Aschenauer, *Um Recht und Wahrheit im Malmédy-Fall* (Nuremberg: n.p., February, 1950). I wish to thank Mr. Jerome L. Merin for having initially brought Aschenauer's role in the Malmédy massacre investigation to my attention.

66. See Aschenauer's letter to the directorate of the DG, January 14, 1953, quoted in *Deutscher Informationsdienst,* no. 292 (July 27, 1953), p. 1.

67. Letters of von Thadden to Aschenauer of December 18, 1952, and January 7, 1953, and of Aschenauer to von Thadden of December 29, 1952, paraphrased in *Propaganda Rundschreiben,* no. I/1953 (February 15, 1953), of the DRP propaganda section. On January 14, 1953, Aschenauer wrote to Haussleiter and the party directorate: "It is in my view intolerable that I, on the one hand, carry on with your explicit consent, difficult negotiations in the North and Northwest, with the goal of a comprehensive agreement, but that you, on the other hand, tolerate, or even promote an activity on the part of the DG which is totally irreconcilable with the negotiations." *Deutscher Informationsdienst,* no. 292 (July 27, 1953), p. 2. With Haussleiter's full agreement, Aschenauer had informed the highest Land authorities: "In the Land Lower Saxony . . . the German Community will not become active as a political organization and will not be established" (*ibid.*).

68. Priester's letters to Wolfgang Kaden, November 6, 1952, and December 18, 1952. In the summer of 1966, the then 36-year-old Kaden drowned in the Baltic Sea.

69. "Today I received a letter from one of my comrades in Wiesbaden who writes: 'In the meantime, K.-H. Priester was once again creating a hubbub (*Schaumschlagen*) around here. . . . That'll be again a nice little bankruptcy. He is calling himself the representative of the true Germany! He's corporatively joined with Haussleiter, whereupon 50 per cent of the people quit the German Community. Three years ago he had also corporatively joined with the SRP; the bankruptcy followed half a year later. . . .' Unfor-

tunately it is a fact that this man has played, or rather still plays, a sad role in Hesse." Letter of Herbert Bischoff to Gnade of December 30, 1952.

70. Letter of Dr. Malluche to Kaden, February 5, 1953.

71. For Schönborn see above, VI/116, VII/151.

72. The "founding" took place in the course of a meeting in Gnade's home. Priester's letter to Kaden, December 18, 1952.

73. According to Meissner, tentative agreements reached in the course of these discussions were to be submitted by the three party leaders to their appropriate party organs for ratification. To Meissner's amazement, the two groups most directly responsible for, and interested in, the interparty talks, the DU and DRP, rejected the worked-out organizational plans.

74. From an interview with Meissner, April 17, 1957.

75. From an interview with Jungnickel, May 26, 1957.

76. For Meinberg's background see above, XV/43.

77. The two most flamboyant operations were border demonstrations at the Zonal border near Lübeck and Coburg, replete with torches, burning of the border barriers, illegal crossings, brave declarations and manifestos. The Lübeck rally took place in December, 1952, and the demonstration in Coburg was planned for the anniversary of the founding of the German Empire, January 18, 1953.

78. See above, VII/39. Hedler's initial acquittal, in February, 1950, by a court two of whose three judges had been former Nazis, was one of the first of a long series of judicial scandals which directed public attention to the political complexion of the postwar German bench. (See below, Chapter XVIII, Section D.) In March, 1950, Hedler joined the DRP, whose Bundestag deputies had shocked decent opinion by providing Hedler a hero's welcome. In June, 1951, the state appealed from the lower court (*Landesgericht*) decision and, ironically enough, on July 20, 1951, obtained a reversal of the earlier verdict. Hedler was sentenced to nine months in jail and was burdened with the entire costs of the trial. Subsequent appeals by Hedler failed, and on October, 1952, he was promptly arrested and began serving his sentence. After resigning from the DRP, Hedler (in January, 1952) launched his own party in partnership with the equally notorious ex-DRP deputy Günther Götzendorff. The new party was called National Reich Party (NRP) and established district organizations in North Rhine–Westphalia, Schleswig–Holstein, and Lower Saxony. Reports also mentioned negotiations with Karl Meissner, but nothing came of them. The NRP demanded the reconstruction of a sovereign German Reich "within its historic frontiers," rejected "attempts to force upon us constitutions which do not correspond to our essence and to our kind," repudiated any notion of collective guilt, called for the vacating of all judgments rendered by denazification tribunals, insisted that the honor of the German soldier be re-established and that the one-sided verdicts against war criminals be repealed, demanded the return of all military and civilian prisoners in Allied custody as well as of all those accused of "supposed war crimes," and proposed an occupational chamber as "a counterweight to a parliament of political parties." Hedler, furthermore, called for the reintroduction of a labor service and demanded a "German socialism which does

not create any class differences, but rather removes them." ("Leitsätze der Nationalen Reichs–Partei [NRP].") In a flyer headed "German men and women! German youth!" Hedler hardly bothers to conceal his unreconstructed Nazism. With intentional reference to his pre-1945 model he writes: "Germany, awake! Remember your past! Think of the deeds of your fathers. . . . Germany for the Germans: may this call sound throughout all German lands. . . . Neither the SPD nor the CDU nor any of the other licensed parties can pull you out of the muck (*Dreck*). . . . This only German men can do, . . . but not cowards and knaves without a fatherland (*vaterlandslose Gesellen*). . . . Where is the international court with German membership which is to judge the crimes committed against Germans? . . . Do not think that we will ever become soldiers, either voluntarily or under compulsion, unless Germany—at last—immediately receives full sovereignty and unless a decent peace treaty is signed which takes account of Germany's honor and returns all territories in the West and in the East that have been robbed and stolen from us." Within a few months, most of the local branches, especially in North Rhine–Westphalia, had abandoned the Hedler party for the Right-radical district organizations of the DP. On Hedler see *Deutsche Presse Agentur* (*dpa*), *Inf.* 271 (February 12, 1952); *Politisches Archiv* (Berlin-Grunewald), WRP/039; *Feinde der Demokratie* (Nordmark), no. 1 (October 14, 1952), pp. 14–15; and no. 4 (February 12, 1953) and 5 (June 24, 1953), pp. 19–20; a report of an interview with Ernst Falkenroth, of Hagen, erstwhile executive secretary of the NRP, August 26, 1952.

79. See "Die Sammlung vollzogen," *Das Ziel* (Hanover), II, 6 (June, 1953), 1. Cf. "Aufruf zur Bildung eines Blocks nationaler Kräfte!" (leaflet, Frankfurt, May 3, 1953).

80. Hertel became a Nazi district leader as early as 1929 and was awarded the golden party badge. His early radical activity brought him the friendship of the Vehmic murderer Edmund Heines, who himself fell victim to political murder in the "blood purge" of June, 1934. Hertel had known Werner Naumann as a student in the early thirties. Later, when Hertel became an editor of the *Völkischer Beobachter,* he again worked closely with the then Under Secretary of the Propaganda Ministry. In 1945, Hertel joined Naumann's battalion of militia that offered last-ditch resistance in the area around Hitler's bunker. See *Feinde der Demokratie* (Lower Saxony), II, 8 (June, 1953), and Federal Republic of Germany, Ministry of the Interior, "Verfassungswidrigkeit der Deutschen Reichs-Partei" (6342 Aa-1138 III/53, September 14, 1953), p. V (3.b).

81. The Reichsblock's "presidium" consisted of Alexander Andrae, Konrad Böhm, Rolf Büsser, former SS General Georg Ebrecht, Rudolf Jungnickel, Horst-Günther Kosche, Wilhelm Meinberg, Ulrich Ortmann, Hans Stürtz, Adolf Wolf, and Herbert Wolff. See "Die Sammlung vollzogen" (XV/79), p. 1. By June, 1953, Hedler had again turned his back on the Reichsblock since "all those who were there at work were a bunch of gangsters," as he ungraciously was to remark later on. (From a confidential report of a discussion with Hedler, June 24, 1953.)

82. "Einig gegen die 45er," *Das Ziel* (Hanover), II, 7 (July, 1953), 1.

83. See *Frankfurter Allgemeine Zeitung,* November 17, 1952.

84. Open letter of the diet deputies Ernst Ullrich, Martin Thellmann-Bidner, and Paul Wuellner, reproduced in *Der Informationsdienst,* no. 242 (January 24, 1953), p. 1.

85. An enthusiastic Nazi, Noack had been Inspector General of the League of National Socialist German Jurists (Bund Nationalsozialistischer Deutscher Juristen, BNSDJ). His early and unstinting support of Hitler was rewarded soon after 1933 with a vice-presidency of the Reich Chamber of Jurists, a Superior Judgeship, and membership in the Academy of German Law. Finally he obtained a professorship at the University of Halle and later at Berlin. His claim to fame rested largely on such articles as "National Socialist Policies in the Area of the Law" (*Juristische Wochenschrift,* 1934) and "The de-Judaization of the German Legal Profession" (*ibid.,* 1938), in which he wrote: "In the course of centuries the Jewish spirit penetrated deeply into the juristic life of the people. It will take long, systematic, and arduous work to eradicate the last influence and consequences. A disease, an epidemic, can be effectively fought only by discovering and destroying the bacillus. A weed can be exterminated only by removing its roots." (See *Hamburger Echo,* March 12, 1952.) Noack's new edition of the *Commentaries to the Statutes of the Legal Profession,* to replace the earlier work of a Jewish attorney, also exhibited his preoccupation with "the racially alien members of the legal profession." (See the letters to the editor of the *Frankfurter Allgemeine Zeitung* of Professor Siegfried A. Kaehler, on August 15, 1952, and of Attorney Erich List, on August 22, 1952.) Cf. also Noack's disingenuous attempt to "prove" that the Third Reich was the only truly, authentically democratic government then extant, in "Führer und Volk als Grundlagen deutscher Demokratie" in Noack and Walz (XI/35), pp. 5–32. On March 1, 1953, Noack, together with his attorney friend Karl Heinz Knipphals, of Kiel, founded the German Solidarity (Deutsche Solidarität) and carried on fusion negotiations with the DRP, DB, DG, Priester's DSB, the Nationale Rechte, and a large number of other Right-extremist splinters. After the first optimism over the chances of becoming the rallying point of former SRP voters and other radical forces, the German Solidarity—as so many of the sleepwalkers on the Right lunatic fringe of the new German political spectrum—was rudely awakened from its dreams by the new electoral law and promptly hurried into an alliance with the National Rally. (See *Feinde der Demokratie* [Lower Saxony], II, 8 [June, 1953]; III, 2 [October–November, 1953]; *Feinde der Demokratie* [Nordmark], no. 5 [June 24, 1953], pp. 27–29; and *Deutscher Informationsdienst,* no. 300 [August 26, 1953].) The German Solidarity recruited itself largely from the membership of Haussleiter's Schleswig-Holstein organization and of the former SRP. As no one besides the party founders had the slightest expectations that the German Solidarity could do more than increase the splintering on the extreme Right and by its very appearance rob the parties on that side of the political spectrum of every vestige of credibility, suspicions arose that the launching of the German Solidarity had been planned by those who wished to destroy the possibility of a united National Opposition party. (See in this respect the

letter of Rudolf Karl Dinter to the Stahlhelm regional leader Karl Smets, April 15, 1953.) On the other hand, Noack and his German Solidarity were also accused by professional anti-Communists of swimming in Pankow's wake. (See Friedrich Victor Risse and Lothar Greil's *Alarm,* I, 4 [August 1, 1955], 2.)

86. Haussleiter, with characteristic braggadocio, claimed the accession of sixty-nine independent electoral groups. See *Feinde der Demokratie* (Nordmark), no. 6 (August 20, 1953), p. 9. According to one report these splinter and electoral groups included the Association of Bavarians Damaged by Occupation Policies (Besatzungsgeschädigte), Non-Party Electoral Association of Bayreuth, Airborne Infantry Association, Communal Electoral Association of Salzgitter, League of Expellees—Upper Palatinate, Working Association of German Farmers, Youth League Eagle, Middle Class Bloc—Upper Franconia, League of German Socialists, German Middle Party, German National People's Party, National Working Circle of Cologne, and a number of local electoral associations. See Waldemar Schweitzer's article in *Länder-Informationsdienst* (*lid*) (Stuttgart), no. 630, and *Politisches Archiv* (Berlin-Grunewald), WRS lf/017.

87. *Die Neue Zeitung* (Munich), July 13, 1953. As mentioned above, Hedler had earlier withdrawn from the forces forming the Reichsblock. Having also rejected the WAV in Bavaria, and coyly—if only halfheartedly—repulsed the advances of the SRP people in Württemberg, Hedler came to see in Haussleiter "the only man who has any possibility of getting a few candidates through. Especially a man from Stuttgart-Vaihingen is very interested and hard at work to get Hedler into the DG." (From an interview memorandum of June 24, 1953.) The mysterious man from Vaihingen was no doubt the former SRP, and later DG, functionary, Willi Mellin.

88. See *Frankfurter Allgemeine Zeitung,* July 20, 1953; *Wirtschafts–Zeitung* (Stuttgart), July 22, 1953; *Die Neue Zeitung* (Munich), July 23, 1953 (article by Wolf-Dieter Barchewitz); *Feinde der Demokratie* (Lower Saxony), II, 9 (July, 1953). See above, text following XI/59.

89. See, for instance, the typical complaints of Zisseler in the letters quoted above, XV/61, 62.

90. Klingspor's discussion memorandum for the NR's executive board meeting in Recklinghausen, October 10, 1953.

91. Minutes of the meeting of the Political Executive (*Politische Leitung*) of the VR in Bonn (*Bundeshaus*), on April 1, 1953.

92. The North Rhine–Westphalian organization of the DP consisted primarily of former members and functionaries of Klingspor's old German Conservative Party who had seceded during (or shortly after) the latter's frustrating, and ultimately futile, fusion negotiations with Hellwege in the weeks following the first Bundestag election in August, 1949. (See above, XV/12. See letter of Ludwig Schwecht to Klingspor, October 1, 1949, and of Klingspor to Schwecht of October 4 and to Hellwege of October 6, 1949.) They were soon dismayed to see Hellwege's acceptance not only of Bonn's democratic institutions but also of the specific policies of the Adenauer government. They favored instead the formation of a National Opposition bloc

which would rally all nationalist forces to the Right of Adenauer. Against the wishes of the DP's national party high command, its North Rhine–Westphalian organization persisted in negotiating with the FDP and the NR and even joined them on common lists in the local elections of November, 1952. At first merely annoying, these discussions appeared downright dangerous to the Hellwege moderates when the sensational disclosures following the Naumann arrests threatened the democratic credibility of anyone who had ever had any dealings with the North Rhine–Westphalian FDP. Taking the Naumann scandal as a pretext, Hellwege stole a march on his intraparty rivals on the oppositionist Right: in an unusual—and legally probably questionable—procedure, Hellwege dissolved the entire North Rhine–Westphalian Land organization, expelled its leaders, and suspended its membership. The expelled DP functionaries and most of the district organizations under the leadership of Schwecht, Felicitas von Einem, and Hannes Flossdorf now called themselves Independent German Party (Unabhängige Deutsche Partei, UDP) and continued their discussions with the radical Right. It is worth pointing out, however, that personal and organizational differences counted almost as heavily as political controversies in bringing about the clash between the North Rhine–Westphalian DP and the federal party executive. For while it is quite true that the ultraconservative Hellwege had no stomach for neo-Nazi radicalism, he was not above distinguishing opportunistically between those radical nationalists with whom he was willing to work for the sake of the strength of the party and those he felt free to anathematize publicly. Thus, for instance, he saw no pressing reason to disband the Hesse organization, "some of whose executive board members," in the words of Klingspor, "might readily have had to share Naumann's fate had they happened to have lived in the British Zone of Occupation." Moreover, the Lower Saxon SPD thought it had persuasive evidence to prove that the DP, at one time or another, had thought of toppling the SPD government with the help of the subversive SRP. Also, ironically enough, Hellwege's triggerman in the summary "execution" of the North Rhine–Westphalian organization, Wilhelm Rosenthal, the former executive secretary of the DKP-DRP's Land organization, was the very man who only two years earlier had tried to undermine the electoral alliance between the NR and the FDP by engineering a partnership with the discredited Joachim von Ostau and the notorious Nazi radical and fraud Richter/Rössler. (For Rosenthal's many other machinations, see Klingspor's letter of accusation to the Land executive of North Rhine–Westphalia of June 17, 1950, and the minutes of the Land executive committee meetings at Recklinghausen of January 1, 1951, and of December 2, 1951.) In connection with Hellwege's remarkably selective intolerance of radical nationalists, it should be recorded that he showed little squeamishness in accepting into his Bavarian organization notorious political freebooters from Loritz' WAV and men whose political experience was limited to subverting the Czechoslovak republic as Hitler's vanguard in Henlein's party or as members of the so-called *Kameradschaftsbund*. See above, VI/209; and below, text at XVII/20–23. Cf. Vereinigte Rechte (Nationale Rechte), Parteileitung, *Rundschreiben,* no. 1/53 (February 27, 1953).

93. This hostility was, of course, limited to the secessionist leaders. As for the rank and file DP members, the NR was actively engaged in enticing them into its fold. (Letter of the party executive of the Vereinigte Rechte [Nationale Rechte] to the NR district chairmen in Dortmund, Bielefeld, Cologne, Paderborn, Mühlheim, Moers, Düsseldorf, Bensberg, Wiedenfeld, Witten, Recklinghausen, Bochum, and Rheinberg, of March 2, 1953.)

94. It was this dislike which was partly at the bottom of Klingspor's reluctance to merge with the DRP before the election as long as there was still a chance to attach the UDP to the NR.

95. More accurately, the working association of the NR and UDP which had been concluded on April 16, 1953, in Cologne was again dissolved, and the attempt to negotiate a merger broken off. See Vereinigte Rechte (Nationale Rechte), Landesverband Nordrhein-Westfalen, *Rundschreiben* no. 3/53 (April 20, 1953). Eventually Flossdorf and Mrs. von Einem made a deal with the BHE. This move was unacceptable to the groups around Schwecht and Karl Freitag. They joined the FDP. (Klingspor [XV/90].)

96. Steuer's letter to von Thadden, misdated May 26, 1953 (very likely June 26).

97. In the elections of 1949 the electoral district Wilhelmshaven-Friesland had given the DRP almost 24 per cent of all votes cast and made it the second strongest party. (For an analysis of the 1949 election in Wilhelmshaven, see above, Chapter IV, Section B.)

98. Letter of Steuer to von Thadden, July 4, 1953. Two weeks after this letter, an information service announced that Dr. Heinrich Kunstmann, the later chairman of the DRP, and chief of the Hamburg sanatorium in which Inge Dönitz worked as a nurse, was discussing Frau Dönitz' candidacy with the Admiral's counsel, Otto Kranzbühler. Supposedly, Inge's acceptance was to depend on Kranzbühler's assessment of the consequences of that candidacy for the imprisoned Admiral. Despite Mrs. Dönitz' denial that she intended to run on the DRP ticket, rumors persisted that she had not only been offered the candidacy but even accepted. According to the same source, Mrs. Dönitz was persuaded by Vice Admiral Ruge, the later chief of the new German navy, not to run in the election lest she inadvertently create new problems for her incarcerated husband. See *Feinde der Demokratie* (Nordmark), August 20, 1953, pp. 1–2.

99. "Wahlgesetz zum zweiten Bundestag und zur Bundesversammlung vom 8. Juli 1953," *Bundesgesetzblatt,* no. 32 (Bonn: July 10, 1953), part I, par. 9, sec. 4, p. 472.

100. *Ibid.,* par. 25, sec. 2, p. 473.

101. *Ibid.,* par. 34, sec. 1, p. 474.

102. *Ibid.,* par. 26, sec. 1 and 2, p. 473.

103. *Ibid.,* par. 34, sec. 4.

104. Letter of von Thadden to Klingspor, June 29, 1953: ". . . electoral law has turned out to be totally disadvantageous for us. . . . I've gotten over the first shock."

105. Steuer's letter to von Thadden, July 4, 1953.

106. Letter of von Thadden to Klingspor, June 29, 1953. Von Thad-

den's scheme would have required the withdrawal of the FDP and BHE candidates in favor of the DRP nominee, a wealthy farmer who could count on the support of former SRP voters without ever having himself been a member of the SRP.

107. *Ibid.* Cf. also "Einig gegen die 45er" (XV/82).

108. Steuer's letter to von Thadden, July 4, 1953.

109. Letter of Klingspor to von Thadden, October 27, 1952.

110. See "Die Hintergründe des Nau-Nau," *Das Ziel* (Hanover), II, 2 (February, 1953), 1; "Kirkpatrick missachtet menschliche Grundrechte" and "Vizekanzler ignoriert Naumann–Fall," *ibid.*, II, 3 (March, 1953), 2; "Naumanns Hieroglyphen," *ibid.*, II, 4 (April, 1953), 4; "Mehr Anstand, Herr Adenauer!" *ibid.*, II, 5 (May, 1953), 1; "Kein Material gegen Naumann," *ibid.*, II, 7 (July 4, 1953), 2; "Hans Grimm an Heuss," *ibid.*, II, 9 (July 18, 1953), 1; etc.

111. Letter of Klingspor to von Thadden, June 16, 1953.

112. Letter of Steuer to von Thadden, July 4, 1953.

113. "DRP gegen 'Ermächtigungsgesetz,'" *Das Ziel* (Hanover), II, 8 (July 11, 1953), 1.

114. *Ibid.*

115. "Naumann aus der Haft entlassen," *Das Ziel* (Hanover), II, 11 (August 1, 1953), 1.

116. "More widely known" would probably be more correct. A public opinion survey of August, 1953, which asked "Do you know who Dr. Werner Naumann is?" disclosed that only 37 per cent of the respondents (57 per cent of the males, but only 22 per cent of the females) could accurately identify Naumann, that 32 per cent (26 per cent men and 37 per cent women) recognized the name but did not know who he was, and that 30 per cent (16 per cent of the men and 41 per cent of the women) failed to recognize even the name. Noelle and Neumann (II/4), p. 195.

117. "My friends who know me also know that my views differ greatly from those which official places are pleased to attribute to me. I have never been in favor of the notion of restoration, but I know that our people will continue to live only insofar as it clings to the values which once had made Germany great and respected. Even as I am capable of changing, still I am not rootless." So Naumann, at a press conference in Hanover on August 12, 1953, as reported in *Das Ziel* (Hanover), II, 13 (August 15, 1953), 2.

118. "Die Kandidaten der DRP," *Das Ziel* (Hanover), II, 12 (August 8, 1953).

119. In the course of an interview on October 20, 1953, Naumann "rejected in general all these politicians because they have had years to build something, but they have never gotten beyond their original cadres of members and have accomplished nothing of positive value. On the contrary, Priester, Haussleiter, Meissner, and Hedler, etc., are responsible for the fragmentation of the National Opposition. In particular, Dorls has done an exemplary job in this respect."

120. "Dr. Naumann told me he had had no intention at all to engage in

public politics this early, but was forced into it by Kirk Patrick's (*sic!*) challenge." From a confidential interview report, October 20, 1953.

121. At his press conference in Hanover on August 12, 1953, Naumann gave four reasons for accepting the DRP candidacy: (1) His fellow candidates were not party hacks (*Funktionäre*) but "personalities well known throughout Germany," in whose character and mental qualities he had great confidence. (2) "The goals and platform of the DRP correspond to the demands and wishes of every true patriot." (3) Refusal to run would only have strengthened those forces which seek to prevent the organization of a unified nationalist rally. (4) His own experience had taught him that arbitrariness and terror would soon threaten every independent German unless immediate steps were taken in defense of his civic rights. From the official press "handout" of the DRP.

122. A public-opinion survey of February, 1953, asked whether or not Naumann's arrest by the British should be sharply protested. Only 20 per cent saw no cause for a protest. Forty-seven per cent said that a more or less sharp protest was in order, and 33 per cent "didn't know." Noelle and Neumann (II/4), p. 277.

123. In the course of his introduction of Werner Naumann to the electors of Diepholz, Hans Hertel, DRP district chairman of Nienburg, said that "Naumann was not the candidate of a party, but rather the above-party representative of national Germany in its fight against every arbitrariness, the freedom fighter No. 1." "Dr. Werner Naumann klagt an," *Das Ziel* (Hanover), II, 13 (August 15, 1953), 2.

124. For Rudel see above, VI/204.

125. See above, Chapter XI, Section B/II/a and Chapter XII, Section B/II.

126. Rudel (VI/204), p. 260.

127. For Meinberg's background, see above, XV/43.

128. Though an early and fervent supporter of the Nazis, Kunstmann, as a devout Christian, later came into conflict with the NSDAP over the latter's church policies and especially over its euthanasia program. See Erdmann Franke's eulogy, "Pioneer eines neuen Nationalismus," *Studien von Zeitfragen. Analysen, Berichte, Informationen,* Sondermaterial B/1964 (March 26, 1964), 3–5.

129. Nationale Rechte, Landesverband Nordrhein-Westfalen, *Wahlkampfrundschreiben,* no. 3 (August 18, 1953).

130. At the NR's Land executive board meeting in Düsseldorf on August 1, 1953, Klingspor also reported on his abortive negotiations with the BHE. An alliance with that party was out of the question, in view of its demand that NR candidates must first become members of the BHE and must sign a written promise to resign their seat should they ever deviate from the BHE party line. At the same meeting there was also unanimous condemnation of the DRP plan to "go it alone." Klingspor was delegated to remind the DRP executive that the alliance agreement did not permit the partners to make such basic decisions without reference to the other partner and that if

the DRP persisted in its course, the NR would be forced to condemn publicly the hopelessness and irresponsibility of the venture. Needless to say, the time for legalistic debaters' points was long gone, if indeed it ever existed in the relations between the two uneasy partners. For the NR's abortive attempts to come to terms with the BHE and the North Rhine–Westphalian Land organization of the DP, or rather its secessionist wing, the Independent DP (UDP), and for an account of the FDP's reluctance to accept NR candidates on its electoral list, see Klingspor (XV/90).

131. Klingspor and Steuer had told von Thadden and Scheffer, when the latter apprised them of their plans to run Naumann, that the NR would under no circumstances agree to campaign for and with him, regardless of whether or not the NR succeeded in entering an election alliance. (*Ibid.*)

132. On December 12, 1953, a FDP committee accepted Klingspor's offer of joining the FDP and recommended approval to the FDP's Land executive committee. On the following day the executive granted the fusion and hailed the accession of the NR. *Rundschreiben,* no. 5/53 of the NR-*Parteileitung,* December 18, 1953.

133. See *Rundschreiben,* no. 1/54 (January 6, 1954), the *"Einladung"* to the Delegates' Convention in Recklinghausen on January 24, 1954, of January 15, 1954, and *Rundschreiben,* no. 2/54 (February 2, 1954). Cf. *Feinde der Demokratie* (North Rhine–Westphalia), no. 1 (March 15, 1954), p. 19, and the "Sonderdruck" produced by Lothar Steuer for the Land diet election in North Rhine–Westphalia of June 27, 1954. Here Middelhauve and Klingspor explained the absorption of the National Right by the FDP as in the interests of all nationalists and appealed openly and fervently for their votes in the name of a "national rally." Klingspor and Steuer became members of the FDP's Land executive committee. Steuer and several of his friends from the National Right entered the Land diet, which promptly elected Steuer vice-chairman. Lothar Steuer died in May, 1957, at the age of sixty-four. In the fall of 1965, the eighty-year-old Klingspor resigned from the FDP's Land executive committee on the ground of age. (Letter of Klingspor to the author, November 30, 1965.)

134. See Rudel (VI/204), pp. 37–38, 163, 219–220.

135. In the previous year, the anti-Young Plan referendum concerning the "Law against the Enslavement of the German People," which had brought together for the first time all elements of the National Opposition against Weimar, clearly indicated the direction of sentiment in Diepholz. While the support for this Nationalist-Nazi referendum did not quite reach 14 per cent in all of Germany and even in Lower Saxony barely exceeded 19 per cent, Diepholz achieved the dubious fame of being one of the two districts in which a majority voted with the German Nationals, Stahlhelm, and Nazis.

136. In that election, only Ammerland outdid the good people of Diepholz in their devotion to the Nazis.

137. Ostermann had left the SRP and joined the FDP as early as January, 1952. This, however, could not prevent his ouster from the Landtag when the Constitutional Court voided the seats of all SRP deputies in the following October. See Niedersächsischer Landtag (VI/138), pp. 38, 44.

138. According to *Das Ziel* (Hanover), II, 15 (August 29, 1953). *Der Spiegel* published an election prediction by the political advisor of the British High Commissioner. The British official predicted 30 per cent of the national popular vote each for the CDU and SPD and 12 to 15 per cent for the DRP. The major losses were anticipated to be sustained by the DP and FDP, which, together, were not expected to attract more than 12 to 15 per cent of the vote.

139. Anticipating legal chicanery of one sort or another, Naumann had painstakingly read his speeches lest an extemporaneous remark in an unguarded moment provide the government with a pretext and legal handle to outlaw the DRP. (*Deutsche Presse Agentur* [*dpa*], *Inf.* 1253 [August 28, 1953], p. 2.) After Naumann's speaking ban had gone into effect, some of the meetings for which he was scheduled were addressed instead by Peter Kleist.

140. For details of the denazification procedure and its legally very questionable basis, see "Naumann-Entnazifizierung: Wahlanfechtung möglich," *Der Spiegel,* VII, 36 (September 2, 1953), 9–10. See *Das Ziel* (Hanover), II, 16 (September 5, 1953), 1–3.

141. After the election Naumann thought that had he been released from prison six weeks earlier, and had the DRP not been threatened with official suppression, the DRP would have been able to send at least twenty-five to thirty deputies to Bonn. From a report of an interview with Naumann, October 20, 1953.

142. See Rudel (VI/204), pp. 38, 49–52, 232–233. Von Thadden had earlier called Perón to ask his permission for Rudel's participation in the election campaign, while Dorls, on the other hand, had reportedly flown to Argentina to persuade Rudel not to participate in the campaign on the DRP ticket. See *Feinde der Demokratie* (Nordmark), no. 6 (August 20, 1953), p. 6.

143. Rudel (VI/204), pp. 234–254.

144. *Ibid.,* p. 242. After two days of campaigning through Bavaria, Rudel concluded: "If I tally up the results of my trip down here in Bavaria, I can hardly believe that they'll permit me to continue to speak unhindered. . . . An image of my activity here will have been created [at the Office for the Protection of the Constitution] which might lead to undemocratic and illegal measures against us" (*ibid.,* p. 246).

145. "Einstweilige Verfügung gegen Adenauer," *Das Ziel* (Hanover), II, 18 (September 19, 1953), 1.

146. Federal Republic of Germany (XV/80). The governments "case" rested ostensibly on the concentration of former Nazi and SRP functionaries and members among the leading men of the DRP and on excerpts from campaign speeches in which they sought to vindicate parts of the Nazi regime and heaped abuse on the Federal Republic and its policies. "Bonner Wahlmanöver," *Das Ziel* (Hanover), II, 16 (September 15, 1953).

147. On the legal battle between Adenauer and the DRP, in which the latter carried away a clear moral victory—albeit a full year after the election —see "Wenn niemand davon spricht," *Der Spiegel,* VIII, 44 (October 27, 1954), 13–14. For the beginnings see *Süddeutsche Zeitung* (Munich), Sep-

tember 2, 1953, and *Frankfurter Allgemeine Zeitung* of the same date. See also the September, 1953, issues of the party paper *Das Ziel.*

148. "Das sind 'freie Wahlen,' " *Das Ziel* (Hanover), II, 16 (September 6, 1953), 2.

149. For detailed analyses of the 1953 elections, see Hirsch-Weber and Schütz (VIII/135), especially pp. 163–188.

150. The CDU increased its percentage share of the total vote since the first federal election from 31 to 45 per cent, while the share for the FDP declined from almost 12 to 9.5 per cent, that of the German Party (DP) from 4 to 3.2 per cent, the regional Bavarian Party lost over half of its electors and declined from 4.2 to 1.7 per cent, and the oppositional Catholic Center Party lost no fewer than 70 per cent of its voters, slipping from 3.1 to 0.8 per cent of the total vote cast.

151. See Schleswig-Holstein, Statistisches Landesamt, "Ergebnis zur Kreistagswahl vom 29.4.1951 umgerechnet auf die Wahlkreiseinteilung der Bundestagswahl vom 14.8.1949," *Sonderdienst* (published August 17, 1953), and "Die Bundestagswahl am 6. September 1953" (published September 9, 1953).

152. See Statistisches Landesamt Baden-Württemberg, Statistik von Baden-Württemberg, vol. 8, *Die Wahl zur Verfassungsgebenden Landesversammlung von Baden-Württemberg am 9. März 1952,* and vol. 11, *Die Wahl zum zweiten Bundestag der Bundesrepublik Deutschland am 6. September, 1953.*

153. From an interview with Karl Meissner, April 17, 1957.

154. The German Bloc never recovered from the organizational and electoral disasters of 1953. By 1957 Meissner announced that the DB would no longer contest elections, but as an "anti-Bolshevik cadre organization" would continue its propagandistic and ideological work in the "preparliamentary" area. With its folkish Weltanschauung and notions of an "organic socialism" and its vision of a partyless "folk state" with unequal, graduated suffrage, the DB reflects more faithfully than most other "ideological cadre organizations" its roots in the folkish sector of the Conservative Revolution.

155. According to the Natinform chief Wolfgang Sarg, the influx into the DP from the SRP was largely the result of the publicity which the police seizure of Richter's files received. The search had been ordered because there was substantial evidence that Richter's DP organization was being massively infiltrated by the SRP. From a confidential report of a discussion with Sarg on January 19, 1953. Cf. below, XVII/19.

156. There is even indirect evidence that some SRP groups in Lower Saxony proposed to vote for the SPD on the ground that the first order of business remained the toppling of the CDU. Where this could be done with Rightist support, all well and good; where only the SPD was strong enough to defeat the CDU candidate, SRP support would have to go to the hated "Reds."

157. See Niedersächsisches Amt für Landesplanung und Statistik, Veröffentlichungen: Series F, XIV, 2, *Die Kommunalwahlen in Nieder-*

sachsen am 9. November 1952 (Hanover: 1953). Cf. (VI/146). For the Rhineland-Palatinate, see below, XV/162, and nearby text.

158. "Das Ergebnis der 'freien Wahlen,'" *Das Ziel* (Hanover), II, 17 (September 12, 1953), 1.

159. "So musst du wählen!" *ibid.*, 16 (September 5, 1953), 4.

160. For a catalogue of complaints which the DRP later made the basis for an unsuccessful suit to void the elections on grounds of illegal interference and abrogation of the civil liberties of free speech, assembly, and press, see "Deutschland wacht auf," *Das Ziel* (Hanover), II, 15 (August 29, 1953), 1, and "Das sind 'freie Wahlen'" (XV/148); cf. "Wahlanfechtung durch DRP," *ibid.*, II, 17 (September 12, 1953), 2. A typical example of the obstacles placed in the way of DRP campaigning is reported by an eyewitness in the Palatinate. The DRP rented a hall in Worms for DM 200 and inundated the surrounding countryside with placards announcing a rally. Despite the fact that the meeting had not been officially prohibited, local police pasted over the announcements, misleading the interested public into assuming that the meeting had been canceled. When the "rally" took place as planned (the date was August 28, i.e., nine days before election day), there were in the hall a scattering of some fifty people, about eight of whom were local police in mufti, including the police chief of Worms. The fifty also included reporters from the local press and a stenotypist who took down everything that was said. When Rudolf Jungnickel, the chairman of the meeting, announced that he was turning it into an internal party discussion and asked non-DRP members to remove themselves, one of the policemen declared that the police would not leave. From a report of August 28, 1953.

161. In two districts, Alzey and AGB Oppenheim, the DRP received 13.4 per cent of the votes. In Worms 10.9 per cent voted for the DRP. In Kirchheimbolanden, 8 per cent; in the city district Zweibrücken, 7.7 per cent; in Landau/Pfalz, 6.7 per cent; in the Land district Zweibrücken, 6.1 per cent; in Pirmasens, 5.7 per cent; and in the districts Bergzabern and Bingen the tally was 5.2 per cent and 5 per cent, respectively.

162. See Statistisches Landesamt Rheinland-Pfalz, Statistik von Rheinland-Pfalz, vol. 29, *Die Wahl zum zweiten Bundestag am 6. September 1953 in Rheinland-Pfalz* (Bad Ems: 1953), and Statistik von Rheinland-Pfalz, vol. 24, *Die Kommunalwahlen am 9. November 1952 in Rheinland-Pfalz* (Bad Ems: 1953).

163. From a confidential report of a visit to Körper and his family on January 13, 1953.

164. See confidential report of an eyewitness, August 28, 1953. Incidentally, the primary reason for the reluctance to support the DRP appeared to have been a deep suspicion of Adolf von Thadden. The known fact, sedulously broadcast by Haussleiter, that von Thadden had worked for the Polish Intelligence Service continued to make the rounds in nationalist circles long after its innocuousness had been proved in court. When it no longer sufficed, it was replaced by another story, according to which von Thadden had an agreement with Adenauer to the effect that the DRP would be allowed to

become the reservoir of all Rightist groups, but would fully support Adenauer's policies. (From a report of an interview with the SRP functionary Erich Schirschin, November 23, 1952.) Werner Körper, in the course of a postelection discussion with his old friend Naumann, asked him bluntly: "Tell me, what's going to happen with the DRP? Can one trust von Thadden in the light of his questionnaire? What's Hess doing in the Palatinate? . . . What kind of mission has he got?" It is only fair to point out that the SRP's suspicion of the DRP was reciprocated by Naumann, despite his eagerness, in the last stages of the campaign, for contacts to such men as Werner Körper and other regional SRP leaders. After the election, when he began to work out plans for a reorganization of the DRP, Naumann felt that "any infiltration [of the reorganized party] was out of the question because he rejects that obsolete ideology (*alte Gedankengut*) . . . men who work in the manner of the SRP (*SRP-Allüren*) could not be considered as collaborators." (From a confidential report of an interview with Naumann on October 20, 1953.)

165. Limited to precisely those districts in Upper and Middle Franconia from which the DB and DG received such support as they could ever boast of (leaving out of account the very modest "successes" of the DG in Suabia), the DRP did not succeed in more than three cases (in the Land districts Kulmbach and Bayreuth and in the city of Nuremberg) in enlarging its inheritance from the German Bloc and the German Community.

166. Only in the cases of Kulmbach, Bayreuth, Schwabach, Fürth, and Regensburg, where the DB or BHE-DG had previously received 14, 10, 8.4, 7, and 5 per cent, respectively, was there something like a direct transfer of votes to the DRP, with losses in the last three districts not exceeding 20 per cent.

167. See Bayerisches Statistisches Landesamt (XV/46), no. 163, 182; and no. 193, *Zweite Bundestagswahl in Bayern am 6. September 1953.*

168. Public-opinion polls and objective economic statistics for the years prior to 1953 readily explain why Right-extremists in those years had every right to be optimistic about their future political potential. The polls reflect not only the general discontent but the dangerously low esteem in which the majority of the people held their democratic institutions and the men who guided them. Also, the unemployment figures, which had been rising only slowly since 1946, took a dramatic leap upward after the currency reform of 1948 and reached their zenith in the winter 1951–1952, with over one and a half million men out of work.

169. This becomes perfectly clear from the DRP's election manifesto in the 1953 election. Here the first nine of the twenty-two platform planks concerned themselves with foreign policy. Cf. "Deutschland den Deutschen: Das Ziel der Deutschen Reichs-Partei," *Das Ziel* (Hanover), II, 15 (August 29, 1953), 3–4.

170. "Die Bilanz," *Das Ziel* (Hanover), II, 15 (August 29, 1953), 3.

171. See above, Chapter VI, Section D.

Chapter XVI: The National Opposition Between the Front Lines

1. "300,000 freie Deutsche," *Das Ziel* (Hanover), II, 17 (September 12, 1953), 1.

2. Werner Kugler, "DRP, Lucht & Co.," *Die Brücke,* II, 11 (November, 1955), 1–5.

3. Naumann had warned von Thadden before the election that nothing would ever come of the DRP unless it began after the election to organize anew from the ground up. Von Thadden had agreed with that. (From a confidential report of an interview with Naumann, October 20, 1953.) According to Kugler, the day after the election (September 7, 1953) a conclave in Naumann's home, including Adolf von Thadden and Erwin Stolz, decided on Scheffer's dismissal (on the ground of incompetence) and on the personnel of the party leadership. At a meeting of the Parteileitung in Würzburg on October 17/18, 1953, Scheffer and General Andrae openly criticized the candidacy of Naumann, which had provoked the government into massive, and in the end fatal, countermeasures. At the same time they could not prevent the premature calling of the delegates' convention for November 29, to take place in Göttingen. Before that date, the anti-Scheffer *Fronde* had to force Scheffer to resign. They did this at a renewed meeting of the Parteileitung, November 14, which had been scheduled ostensibly to prepare for the delegates' convention. The hatchet man was Otto Hess, the Land chairman of Rhineland-Palatinate, who had been one of those present at the secret Naumann meeting. Open attacks on Scheffer forced the latter ultimately to offer his resignation. (A week earlier, on November 7, 1953, in Oldenburg, Scheffer had already been dismissed as Lower Saxon Land chairman. By a vote of 24 to 21, City Councilor Walter Liebehenz, of Göttingen, beat Scheffer for the post. Hellmuth Koch, of Eschede, became first vice-chairman and Otto Karl Harnack of Wesermünde, second vice-chairman. For other top party posts see *Das Ziel* [Hanover] II, 26 [November 14, 1953], p. 3.)

4. See above, XV/81 and nearby text.

5. While the very popular Meinberg and Andrae were voted in with 99 and 95 votes out of 101, respectively, von Thadden barely nosed out Scheffer on the second ballot with a mere 60 votes. Naumann's opinion of von Thadden is in this connection of some interest. Naumann was said to have been at first quite suspicious of von Thadden because of the latter's lack of discretion. After better acquaintance with von Thadden and his family, Naumann was favorably impressed: "He will be put to work in ways appropriate to his abilities." Naumann called von Thadden "a typical East Elbian Junker with saucy (*schnodderig*) manners, too young and immature, who first will have to gather experience in the social area." From a report of an interview with Naumann, October 20, 1953, p. 4.

6. See above, XV/80.

7. The three other members of the advisory council were Rolf Büsser, another Reichsblock alumnus, who became treasurer; Hans Haack, the Nazi Attorney-General of Hamburg and legal counsel to ex-Gauleiter Kaufmann, in charge of legal matters; and Lilli Nolden, ex-SRP activist and assistant

of Princess Elisabeth Isenburg, whose charitable Silent Help (Stille Hilfe) devoted itself exclusively to war criminals and their families. For a complete listing of the membership of the enlarged executive committee, which includes the chairmen of the Land organizations, see *Freies Nachrichten Büro* (*fnb*), no. 47 (December 5, 1953), p. 4.

8. "Das Gewissen des deutschen Volkes," *Das Ziel* (Hanover), II, 29 (December 5, 1953), 2.

9. See *Der Reichsruf* (*Süddeutsche Ausgabe des Organs "Das Ziel" der DRP* [*Reichsblock*]), III, 1 (January 9, 1954); *Das Ziel* (Hanover) III, 3 (January 23, 1954); and others.

10. "DRP: Partei des Reiches—Partei der Zukunft," *Reichsruf* (Hanover), III, 19 (May 15, 1954), 1.

11. The government had done its best to propagate that notion. DRP leaders—accurately, we believe—attributed a goodly share in the party's electoral defeat to the success of the government's insinuations.

12. "DRP: Partei des Reiches—Partei der Zukunft," in *Unser Weg, Unser Ziel: Politische Grundsatzerklärungen der Deutschen Reichs Partei, Vorträge gehalten auf dem Parteitag, 8. und 9. Mai 1954* (Hanover: 1954), p. 6.

13. *Ibid.*, p. 7.

14. *Ibid.*, pp. 10–11.

15. *Ibid.*, p. 13.

16. *Ibid.*, p. 11.

17. *Ibid.*, pp. 10, 12.

18. On the notion of the army as the "School of the Nation" and its role in German history, see now the magistral work of Reinhard Hoehn, *Die Armee als Erziehungsschule der Nation. Das Ende einer Idee* ([Bad Harzburg:] Verlag für Wissenschaft, Wirtschaft und Technik, 1963). Hoehn, originally a professor of law and political science, became in 1936 the first chief of the SD (Security Service), which in those early days consisted of twenty young men, many of them drawn from the universities. One of them, Ohlendorf, the bright young man whom Hoehn had hired, achieved international notoriety for his central part in the murder of some 90,000 people. In 1937 Hoehn was dismissed through the intervention of Julius Streicher. "Extracts from the Testimony of Defendant Ohlendorf," *Trials of War Criminals before the Nürnberg Military Tribunals under Control Council Law No. 10* (Nuremberg: October, 1946–February, 1948), IV, 227 ff.

19. *Unser Weg* (XVI/12), p. 39.

20. *Ibid.*, p. 45.

21. *Ibid.*, pp. 40–41.

22. *Ibid.*, p. 38.

23. *Ibid.*, p. 75.

24. *Ibid.*, p. 79.

25. *Ibid.*, p. 91.

26. *Ibid.*, p. 92.

27. *Ibid.*, p. 16.

28. *Ibid.*, p. 13.

29. *Ibid.*, pp. 13–14.

30. *Ibid.*, p. 14.

31. "DRP zur Politik der Zeit" (mimeographed), May, 1954.

32. *Ibid.*

33. Hertel, a close friend of Werner Naumann, had hitherto been organizational chief of the DRP and editor of its paper.

34. Manns was an "old guard" Nazi who had first joined the NSDAP in 1923, the SA even a year earlier. (His full membership in both is dated from 1926.) Eleonore von Wangenheim, SRP executive board member, wrote Lower Saxon SRP executive board member Gerhard Heinze on December 5, 1951: "I have known Manns since 1932; we were, after all, already comrades in the earliest period of struggle. Today I still esteem his beliefs; he has remained faithful to the cause!" (Exhibit 262 quoted in the opinion of the Federal Constitutional Court, in the Socialist Reich Party case [1BvB 1/51], October 23, 1952, [XIII/39], p. 46.) Before joining the DRP, Manns had been editor of several SRP organs.

35. Hans Hertel, "Niedersachsen–Grundstein zum neuen Reich!" *Reichsruf* (Hanover), Sonderausgabe Niedersachsen-Wahl, IV, 15 (April 9, 1955), 5. (Emphasis in the original.)

36. See, for example, "Kommt der totale Konfessionskrieg," *Reichsruf* (Hanover), III, 10 (March 13, 1954), 1; or "Kulturkampf tobt in Bayern," *ibid.*, (March 20, 1954), 2.

37. For the nature of that German Socialism, see the repeated articles in the *Reichsruf* by the party's expert on labor and social problems, Willi Reich–Mummenhoff. Typical are his serialized "The Marxist DGB in Crisis" in the August, 1954, issues of the paper, and his "Radicalization of the Marxist Labor Union" (November 5, 1954). For the nature of German Socialism see above, Chapter VI, Section B. For an extended treatment of "Artisan" and "Middle Class Socialism" in the Third Reich and its later fate, see Schweitzer (XIV/94). Cf. Lebovics (VI/13).

38. *Reichsruf* (Hanover), IV, 15 (April 9, 1955), 5–6.

39. The school-law issue appeared to have wrought the greatest changes in the general voting pattern in Lower Saxony in 1955. In the Protestant regions, large contingents of electors punished the DP for its close association with the CDU by switching to the FDP, which, like the DRP (and of course the SPD) stood for a radical separation of church and state and fought the growing influence of the Catholic clergy. In the Catholic (the western) districts of the Land, former Center Party voters discovered that they could push their school and church programs more effectively through the CDU and abandoned the Center Party. At the same time, however, Protestant voters who had hitherto given their ballot to the CDU left it in droves, causing a decline of CDU returns even in areas where it had captured former Center Party voters. That this led to a disproportionate increase in Catholic influence within the CDU was clear. See in this connection the election analyses of Josef Schmidt, Hanover (unpublished manuscript in the author's possession).

40. They were occupied by the first six candidates listed on the party's

Land list, as no DRP candidate came even close to winning a direct seat. These were, in order, Georg Joel, the old Nazi Prime Minister of Oldenburg and former Deputy Gauleiter; Bruno Moeller, a shipyard director who had been removed by the British because of his strong Nazi ties; Hildegard von Rheden, a former leader of the Nazi women's organization; Hans Hertel; von Thadden; and Scheffer.

41. See above, Chapter VI, Section F.

42. Quoted in *Feinde der Demokratie* (Lower Saxony), IV, 1 (September–October, 1954), 33.

43. See above, VI/223.

44. See above, Chapter VI, Section F.

45. See above, text at VI/224. These embarrassing rumors and political indiscretions forced the DRP executive committee into a public denial. It admitted that "leading DRP politicians are constantly being accosted by people from the *Nation*. But it is out of the question that there are any agreements, arrangements, or any kind of collaboration" (*Politik und Wirtschaft,* June 3, 1955). The allegation of financial support from then freely flowing East German funds was, according to August Haussleiter (*Die Deutsche Gemeinschaft* [Munich], no. 15 [August, 1956]) and the Club republikanischer Publizisten (*CrP-Information,* March, 1957, p. 26) officially proven in the course of a libel suit which Haussleiter started against the DRP district chairman Förster. At the same time, von Thadden wrote to Paul Lüth, former head of the industry- and government-financed anti-Communist vigilante "youth organization" Bund Deutscher Jugend, close associate of men whom U.S. Army Intelligence had hired to organize an anti-Soviet guerrilla unit (see above, X/14 and nearby text), and later publisher of a nationalist information service: "Haussleiter's statement that the DRP was not independent but was receiving money from both the East and big industrialists close to Bonn has also been subject to a court trial in which it was established that this constituted an insult and that Haussleiter could not prove his accusations" (letter of January 31, 1957). See also the tendentious "inside story" account of Werner Kugler in *Die Brücke,* II, 6 (June 13, 1955; Nachtrag), 1–2.

46. See above, Chapter V, Section C, and below, Chapter XVII, Section C. The massive infiltration of the FDP (which became a matter of public scandal following the revelations in the Naumann affair) had been the result of its efforts to halt or to counterbalance the rapid dwindling of its liberal electors by opening the door wide to former or present Nazis and other ultra-Rightists. A few months prior to the arrest of the Naumann circle, Gerhard Krüger, cofounder of the SRP and one of its spokesmen before the Federal Constitutional Court, had sought to demonstrate to the court that the SRP was not the only party anxious to garner the active organizational participation and votes of former or present Nazis. To support this contention, the truth of which even the most casual acquaintance with postwar German political campaigning readily confirms, Krüger requested that the Court call as witness (among others) the former Nazi leader of Krüger's home town. Hermann Schwertfeger was to testify, if Krüger had his way, that the former

Nazi District Leader of Peine was systematically recruiting former Nazi functionaries for the organizational construction of the FDP. (*Deutsche Opposition* [Cuxhaven], July 10, 1952.) Naturally the Court was not inclined to embarrass Mr. Adenauer's coalition partners and rejected the request. Krüger's *tu quoque,* however, hit the mark squarely.

47. In order to solve the FDP's financial problems, the Land executive secretary, Horst Huisgen, had organized a Society for the Promotion of the Lower Saxon Economy (Gesellschaft zur Förderung der niedersächsischen Wirtschaft) and promptly placed it in charge of the former Nazi Mayor of Kattowitz, Hans Tiessler, who, in turn, surrounded himself with ex-NSDAP, Hitler Youth, or SS enthusiasts. Freiberger had been one of them. Cf. V/104.

48. Freiberger's resignation came amidst persistent rumors of certain financial irregularities in Lower Saxony which have never been completely cleared up.

49. One of the more prominent DNP leaders was Dr. Andreas Binder, who, it may be remembered, had become Lower Saxon Land chairman of Haussleiter's German Community (DG) in order to preside over the transfer of the underground SRP organization to the DG. (See above, text near XIII/55.) The new party's program prominently featured such demands as restitution payments to all those who had been harmed by Allied or German postwar regimes, constitutional changes which would replace the federal with a unitary political structure and would greatly increase the executive powers of the head of state, and the reintroduction of the death sentence for treason and other crimes. "Programm der Deutschen Nationalpartei von 1954" (leaflet; [Hanover, December 6, 1954]).

50. That this spatial proximity alone would have provided ample opportunity for meetings with such *Nation* editors as the national-neutralist Gottfried Griesmayr and his friend Fritz Brehm, both of whom were at that time knee-deep in BHE politics in Bavaria, goes without saying. For Griesmayr and Brehm see above, V/39, VI/79, VI/209, VI/219. Cf. *Feinde der Demokratie* (Lower Saxony), IV, 3 (January, 1955), 22; and IV, 4 (February–March, 1955), 25.

51. *Deutsche Presse Agentur* (*dpa*), *Inf.* 1217 (August 24, 1955), p. 3. It might be said here in passing that the *Nation,* which had actively supported the DNP for the diet election and had ignored the DRP, urged all national voters to cast their ballots for the DRP once it had become clear that the DNP would fail to get the required signatures. See Kugler (VI/79).

52. Joel had guided the Land organization with little distinction since Hertel's resignation in June, 1955. That Freiberger was the party leadership's choice became evident when Wilhelm Meinberg had to intervene in a very turbulent meeting to browbeat the noisy opposition. One other personnel change, though little regarded or little known at the time, deserves mention as contributing significantly to the trend of the developments in the following two years. The former SRP journalist Adolf Manns, who had held the editorship of the party organ for a year, was quietly replaced after the Land election by the strongly neutralist Gerhard Bednarski, who edited at the same time *Der Ruf—Hannoversches Echo,* an expellee paper with close contact to

the BHE and the League of Expelled Germans (BvD). Under Bednarski, *Der Ruf* became stridently nationalist with strong neutralist overtones. (See above, VI/112.)

53. The election of the popular Meinberg as the party's chairman came off without a hitch. The first and second vice-chairmanships went to Dr. Heinrich Kunstmann and to Adolf von Thadden. The latter had to win his place in the only contested election. He beat his rival, the former national and Lower Saxon Land chairman, Colonel Hans–Heinrich Scheffer, by forty votes. The treasury again went to Rolf Büsser, of Hanau; the legal department, to the former Nazi Attorney-General Hans Haack, of Hamburg. The women's department was again placed in the hands of Lilli Nolden. New in the inner circle were the publisher (Plesse Verlag, Göttingen) and former SS officer Waldemar Schütz, who had moved into the Land diet as Hans Hertel's successor; Karl Pollak, the DRP official from Bayreuth; and Dr. Andreas Binder, the former DG Land chairman who had come into the DRP with Freiberger's German National Party. The enlarged executive board consisted of these nine members of the executive committee, the Land chairmen, ex officio, and eight additional members. These latter were General Andrae; Hans B. von Grünberg, Naumann confidant and last Nazi chancellor of the University of Königsberg; Frau Hildegard von Rheden, diet deputy and former Nazi women's leader; Herbert Bangemann, a former SRP functionary who appeared in the number eight slot on the DRP Land list in the 1955 election; Erwin Stolz, SRP-alumnus, manager and later chief of organization of the party, assistant to von Thadden and Naumann's lieutenant; Frau Theodora Mehlis; Carl-H. Hey, quondam SRP functionary, in charge of the organization of the North Rhine–Westphalian party and editor in chief of *Der deutsche Arbeiter,* the organ of the nationalist, far-Right, formerly SRP-related German Employee's Association (Deutscher Arbeitnehmer Verband, DAV); and Heinz Schimmerohn, SRP sympathizer and functionary of the German National Party. See *Die Brücke,* II, 10 (October, 1955), 1; and 11 (November, 1955), 4; *Feinde der Demokratie* (Lower Saxony), V, 1 (October–November, 1955), 34; *Deutscher Informationsdienst,* no. 513 (October 28, 1955). For Schimmerohn's past see *Oberverwaltungsgericht* (XIII/37), p. 32.

54. Adolf von Thadden, "Aussenpolitik für ganz Deutschland," Parteitag der Deutschen Reichs-Partei, Hannover, 24./25.9.55, (mimeographed), pp. 10–11. It is interesting to note that the *Reichsruf* did not reprint the text of von Thadden's speech. It was independently printed through the financial contributions of "unnamed donors" and added as a supplement to the *Reichsruf* issue of October 22, 1955. Cf. *Feinde der Demokratie* (Lower Saxony), V, 1 (October–November, 1955), 37.

55. Almost the entire December 3–4, 1955, meeting of the party executive board in Frankfurt was devoted to "eastern" infiltration and subversion in the ultranationalist sector of German politics. (See *Die Brücke,* II, 12 [December, 1955], 6.) The main speaker on that occasion was the notorious Rudolf Aschenauer (see above, VII/69, XV/65), whose role in postwar ultranationalist circles has at times been said to be Bonn's and the CSU's

watchdog against nationalist-neutralist infiltration and infection. Aschenauer's presence at the Frankfurt meeting was reported by Karl Staudinger, *pseud.* [i.e., August Haussleiter], *Zwischen Yorck und John. Folgen der deutschen Bewusstseinsspaltung* (Frankfurt: Joachim Henrich, [January, 1957]), p. 18. For the publisher of this tract, see above, text at XII/116–117.

56. See von Thadden's article in *Reichsruf* (Hanover) V, 4 (January 28, 1956). The Land resolution was accepted by the national party executive committee, which met in Oldenburg at the time of the Land convention, as a valid expression of the foreign-policy program of the national Party. More than that, the national party executive also placed itself squarely behind von Thadden's speech at the Land convention, which appeared in form of a long article in the party organ and in which von Thadden elaborated on the demands briefly outlined in the resolution. Waldemar Schütz, the new press chief, saw to it that 100,000 copies of that issue of the paper were distributed.

57. See Kunstmann's letter to Eberhard Taubert, former anti-Jewish and anti-Communist propaganda expert in the Goebbels ministry and lay member of the dreaded extrajudicial People's Courts, February 15, 1957. After the war Taubert became deputy chairman of the government-subsidized anti-Communist vigilante group People's League for Peace and Freedom and consultant to the Ministry for all-German Questions. In 1955, Taubert, that former virulent anti-Semite, was forced to resign from the league under public pressure. See above, VI/6.

58. Heinrich Kunstmann, "Der Kommunismus als Heilslehre," Parteitag der Deutschen Reichs–Partei, Hannover, 24./25.9.55, pp. 8, 9.

59. See Fritz René Allemann, *Bonn ist nicht Weimar* (Cologne: Kiepenheuer & Witsch, 1956), pp. 302–314.

60. See *Die Welt* (Hamburg), January 31, 1956. In 1957 Friedrich Jarschel, Otto Strasser's press chief, alleged that the DRP had received DM 25,000 for the 1955 Land election in Lower Saxony from the Society for the Promotion of the Lower Saxon Economy, Freiberger's old organization. *Deutscher Informationsdienst,* no. 710 (December 18, 1957), p. 2.

61. Herbert Freiberger, "Nur eine Lösung: Bündnisfreiheit Deutschlands," *Reichsruf* (Hanover), V, 26 (June 30, 1956), 3–4.

62. *Ibid.,* p. 3.

63. "Freiberger telegraphiert an Sorin," *ibid.,* p. 1.

64. Letter of von Thadden to Paul Lüth, January 31, 1957.

65. See "Die DRP will jetzt 'hoffähig' werden," *Hannoversche Presse,* September 9, 1956.

66. See Volker von Hagen, "Ohne Rudel und ohne Naumann," *Die Welt* (Hamburg), no. 207 (September 4, 1956), p. 3. Cf. the reprint from *Die Brücke,* "Die aussichtsreichste nationale Gruppierung," *Reichsruf* (Hanover), V, 40 (October 6, 1956), 2. The election of the new executive committee and enlarged executive board was also transacted quietly and failed to furnish those sensations which some had expected of it. It neither revealed the fine Florentine hand of Werner Naumann in the background nor permitted a glance behind the scenes where—rumor had it—bitter struggles for leadership and for ideological direction were being fought out. Meinberg

was re-elected chairman with an overwhelming majority. Kunstmann became his deputy, a new office created by appropriate changes in the bylaws. The eight-man executive committee contained this time in the descending order of the number of votes that elected them, Rolf Büsser (238 votes out of a total of 254), Herbert Freiberger (235), Hugo Jungmann (224), Waldemar Schütz (213), Adolf von Thadden (211), Erwin Stolz (195), Karl Pollak (187), Hans Haack (171). The members of the extended executive board, in addition to the Land chairmen ex officio, were: Alfred Schütze, an officer of the Berlin DRP (which had only recently made headlines through unauthorized overtures to the East Germans and subsequent purges in its ranks) (236), H. B. von Grünberg (219), Heinz Schimmerohn (214), Herbert Bangemann (212), H.-G. Kosche (the vice-chairman of the Bavarian Land organization) (208), Hildegard von Rheden (204), Werner Gebhardt (former North Rhine–Westphalian executive secretary of the SRP) (191), C.-H. Hey (179), Lilli Nolden (171), and Heinrich Stulle (a former DP district chairman who formed in 1954 a Landwirte Partei which he led into the DRP in February, 1956) (169). (See *Rundschreiben,* 11/56 [Parteileitung], September 9, 1956.) Only the resignation of General Andrae on the grounds of age permitted the suspicion that the teamwork of the national party leadership had not been entirely exemplary, a suspicion which in the following year was confirmed by a widely publicized, scathing denunciation of the DRP leadership by Andrae.

67. See "Unser Standort in einer zweigeteilten Welt" in Deutsche Reichs–Partei, Parteileitung, *Das ganze Deutschland soll es sein! Referate gehalten auf dem Parteitag der DRP, Wiesbaden,* September 1, 2, 1956 (Hanover), pp. 19–27.

68. "Faktor des Ausgleichs zwischen Ost und West," *Reichsruf* (Hanover), V, 36 (September 8, 1956), 3.

69. "Unser Standort" (XVI/67), p. 26.

70. "Landesvorstand Niedersachsen: Keine Hilfeleistung für die CDU," *Reichsruf* (Hanover), V, 46 (November 17, 1956), 6.

71. Here the all-German wind was blowing stronger than ever, after the party crisis which ended with the withdrawal from the party of its two federal ministers, Theodor Oberländer and Waldemar Kraft.

72. Letter of von Thadden to Paul Lüth, January 24, 1957.

73. See above, VI/102 and nearby text. Oskar Meerwarth, owner of an export-import business, was the most consistent and the biggest advertiser in the *Nationale Rundschau* which, otherwise, was remarkably free of advertising copy.

74. Cf. "Landesgemeinschaft Baden-Württemberg geschlossen für klaren Kurs," *Die Deutsche Gemeinschaft* (Munich), VII, 21 (1st December edition, 1956), 4.

75. See "Statt Sektierertum eine massvolle Politik," *Reichsruf* (Hanover), V, 45 (November 10, 1956), 2. Cf. "Zusammenschluss der nationalen Kräfte im Süd-West-Staat," *ibid.,* V, 51/52 (December 22, 1956), 8.

76. See *Die Brücke,* III, 15 (December 1, 1956), 7.

77. For Heinemann and his All-German People's Party (Gesamtdeutsche Volkspartei, GVP) see above, VI/79.

78. See *Die Brücke,* IV, 2 (January 15, 1957), 4.

79. In his letter to Erich Kernmayr of February 11, 1957, Adolf von Thadden denied that Albrecht had spoken of a "German front" or had demanded the inclusion of Communists: "Rather, he spoke silly and harmless rubbish, adding 'And don't forget the Left!' "

80. Haussleiter, on the other hand, insisted that no more than twenty-four DG members had followed Meerwarth and Mellin and resigned from the DG. See *Deutsche Gemeinschaft* (Munich), VII, 21 (1st December edition, 1956).

81. "Gruss den DG-Kameraden!" *Reichsruf* (Hanover), V, 45 (November 10, 1956), 3. Cf. *Die Brücke,* IV, 2 (January 15, 1957), 2, 4. We might mention here in passing that a not dissimilar attempt to force the DG into some kind of electoral coalition with the DRP was also made in Bavaria. In December, 1956, Bertold Fortmeier, who belonged neither to the DG nor to the DRP, oragnized a so-called Working Circle for the Unification of the National Parties (Arbeitskreis für die Vereinigung der Nationalen Parteien). In its organizing committee were, among others, the former Goebbels publicist and later cultural editor in several of the nationalist-neutralist, East-financed papers, Hans W. Hagen, who since the spring of 1956 had been writing for the *Reichsruf,* and the notorious Colonel Ludwig Gümbel (see above, VIII/39). On January 27, 1957, the Arbeitskreis held a meeting in Munich in which participated representatives of the DRP, DG, German Bloc (DB), Priester's German Social Movement (DSB), Strasser's German Social Union (DSU), some "free election groups," and a large contingent of nationalists without party attachment. Among the latter was also Herbert Böhme. The DRP claimed the working circle resolved to participate in the forthcoming national election in the ranks of the DRP without giving up for the present at least the several party affiliations. This rally effort also foundered on the rocks of mutual suspicions and failed to move either Haussleiter or Strasser into closer collaboration. (From a confidential "Bericht über die Tagung am 27.1.57" and "Das Wahlfieber greift um sich: Richtigstellung von ein paar faustdicken Falschmeldungen," *Die Deutsche Gemeinschaft* [Munich], VIII, 3 [1st February ed., 1957], 2. Cf. *Die Brücke,* IV, 3 [February, 1957].) Of the better-known nationalist figures at the Munich meeting there were Meinberg, von Thadden, Priester, Herbert Böhme, Friedrich Klein of Priester's DSB, and Andreas Mang of the Peasants' and Middle Class Party. Haussleiter had refused to attend, but the DG was represented.

82. Under the pseudonym Staudinger (XVI/55), Haussleiter, with some outside assistance, argued in *Zwischen Yorck und John* (*Between Yorck and John*) that disappointment and frustration have made the originally Western nationalists and conservative Rightists ripe for infiltration by agents of the East. This tendency has been supposedly especially marked among Protestants who fear the growing Counterreformation in Adenauer Germany. In his megalomaniac delusion, Haussleiter sees the entire game as

essentially an attempt to grind down the most important nationalist organization that can still control and roll back the Eastern trend, his own DG. Obsessed by paranoid fears, Haussleiter combines truths, half-truths, and untruths into a seamless web of intrigue centering around the DRP, and involving the SRP, the "national-Bolshevik" constructions described above in Chapter VI, and, of course, the Stuttgart National Working Fellowship. The brochure was designed to crush the smoldering spirit of rebellion inside the DG which, if allowed to go unchecked, might well have endangered Haussleiter's leadership. An attempt was made to have Paul Lüth (see above, XVI/45) publish the booklet on the eve of the Stuttgart meeting of December 16, 1956. Protracted discussions and Lüth's eventual refusal to become involved delayed its appearance until the end of January, 1957. (See von Thadden's letter to N. J. Ryschkowsky, January 24, 1957, and cf. Rolf Büsser's memorandum on a discussion [concerning the pamphlet] with Paul Lüth at Offenbach, February 15, 1957.) According to Dr. Kunstmann, the brochure had been at least partially financed by the government-subsidized People's League for Peace and Freedom. (See Kunstmann's letters to Eberhard Taubert, the league's former deputy chairman, of February 15 and March 12, 1957, and Taubert's reply of March 3, 1957. For Taubert and the league, see above, VI/6, XVI/57.)

83. His first step was a whirlwind tour to such key nationalist publicists and distributors of nationalist literature as Erich Kernmayr, at that time still editor of the influential *German Soldiers' News* (*DSZ*), and Karl-Heinz Priester. This he followed up with a successful application for a temporary court injunction against further distribution and the seizure of the still undistributed copies of the brochure. The third step was the quickest and widest possible dissemination of the news of the court injunction to dissuade editors and commentators from dealing with the material until a court had decided the truth value of the pamphlet's serious allegations.

84. Letter of von Thadden to Erich Kernmayr, February 11, 1957. Despite this letter, the next issue of the *DSZ* failed to carry a "counter-explanation." Instead it brought an inconspicuous notice (p. 5) of the DRP's national executive board meeting in Kassel, February 2–3, 1957. The board determined "that collaboration with, or membership in, the League for German Unity and National Questions of Defense was irreconcilable with membership in the DRP." The board also strictly prohibited any collaboration with the League of Germans. Immediate expulsion from the DRP was threatened to anyone disregarding these warnings and prohibitions. It will be remembered that the League for German Unity was the East-financed Nehring-Ebrecht instrument for the infiltration of nationalist groups and the spread of the Tauroggen mythology (see above, VI/226 and nearby text). As a further measure to brake a development that could clearly have disastrous consequences, the DRP party leadership prohibited the district organizations from selling or distributing the East-financed *Nationale Rundschau*. (Previously, the DRP had stanchly denied that any district organizations peddled the paper.) See *Die Brücke*, IV, 5 (March, 1957), 5. Cf. *Reichsruf* (Hanover), VI, 6 (February 9, 1957), 6.

85. See *Politisch-Parlamentarischer Pressedienst,* no. 71/57 (July 1, 1957), p. 2.

86. The negotiations were begun by national BHE chairman Friedrich Wilhelm von Kessel and Meinberg and later continued by Frank Seiboth and Erwin Feller for the BHE and von Thadden and Freiberger for the DRP. Rumor had it that on June 24, 1957, von Thadden agreed to von Kessel's suggestion that the six Lower Saxon DRP diet members join the BHE Fraktion as guests (*Hospitanten*) to endanger the DP-CDU majority in the parliamentary committees. In return, the BHE would guarantee the DRP five top places on its Land lists in the federal election. The final approval of this agreement was to have been given on June 27. On that day, BHE chairman von Kessel was said to have gone to see Adenauer. After that, the BHE publicly declared its lack of interest in any agreement with the DRP! Adenauer's patronage power had apparently been too much to withstand. (See [Club republikanischer Publizisten,] *CrP-Information,* August, 1957.) Cf. Sch., "DRP ging zum BHE: Gute Plätze auf BHE-Listen gesucht," *Die Deutsche Gemeinschaft* (Munich), VIII, 5/6 (2d March–1st April ed., 1957), 2.

87. Newspapers spoke of an FDP offer to the DRP of the second and fifth place on its Lower Saxon Land list. This offer, was, however, tied to certain conditions. One was the exclusion of Freiberger (who was a FDP renegade); the other, the incorporation of the DRP into the FDP after the election. Both were unacceptable. ([Club republikanischer Publizisten,] *CrP-Information,* September, 1957, quoting *Die Welt* [Hamburg], August 13, 1957.)

88. See above, XI/539-551 and nearby text. See also *Deutsche Informationen* (Bonn), 18/II (May 16, 1957), p. 4.

89. Adolf von Thadden, "Zum Parteitag der DRP in Köln," *Reichsruf* (Hanover), VI, 26 (May 11, 1957), 1.

90. "Die Pressekonferenz der DRP in Köln," *Reichsruf* (Hanover), VI, 22 (June 1, 1957), 8.

91. Kunstmann's speech was prominently featured on the *Reichsruf*'s front page, to the exclusion of all other addresses at the congress.

92. Heinrich Kunstmann, "Wir fordern inneren Frieden," *Reichsruf* (Hanover), VI, 22 (June 1, 1957), 2.

93. "Die Pressekonferenz" (XVI/90).

94. Quoted in *Die Brücke,* IV, 18 (October 15, 1957), 1, 2.

95. A few days after the Kassel meeting, however, Meinberg admitted that he strove for a fusion (*Zusammenschluss*) of the smaller parties which could represent a "national bloc," besides the CDU and the SPD. See *Frankfurter Allgemeine Zeitung,* September 25, 1957.

96. The anti-Meinberg rebellion had been planned by Freiberger and the Land chairmen of Baden-Württemberg (Heinz von Arndt), Bavaria (Horst-Günther Kosche), Hamburg (Hugo Jungmann), and Hesse (Max Rinke). The fall of Meinberg and von Thadden was to have been followed by the formation of a triumvirate "directorium" consisting of Freiberger, Kosche, and Jungmann. In the heated controversy which followed Kosche's

motion to expel von Thadden, the latter accused Freiberger of what he had so earnestly denied in his letter to Erich Kernmayr eight months earlier; namely, that Freiberger had maintained "closest relations" to the *Nationale Rundschau* and was even "financially dependent" (presumably on that East-subsidized paper). (See *Die Brücke,* IV, 22/23 [January 15, 1958], 1, footnote 1.) Rudolf Krüger, the Land chairman of North Rhine–Westphalia, had apparently informed Kunstmann of these "closest relations." Freiberger promptly brought a slander suit against Krüger (*ibid.,* p. 1). In his February 11, 1957, letter to Kernmayr, von Thadden had written: "A collaboration Freiberger–Henn is entirely out of the question (*davon ist doch keine Rede*)."

97. Quoted in *Die Brücke,* IV, 18 (October 15, 1957), 2. Cf. *Deutscher Informationsdienst,* no. 697 (October 26, 1957), pp. 2–3.

98. Kurt Döring, "Führungskrise in der Deutschen Reichspartei," *Frankfurter Allgemeine Zeitung,* September 27, 1957.

99. In the balloting for the deputy chairmanships (a change in the by-laws had created the post of a second deputy chairman) Kunstmann was narrowly defeated. Otto Hess, the former Land chairman of Rhineland-Palatinate and party organizer, became first deputy chairman. The second deputy chairmanship went to Waldemar Magunia, "old guard" Nazi (he entered the Party in 1921), former member of Erich Koch's East Prussian Gau headquarters and later General Commissar of the Kiev District. Into the Parteileitung were elected Waldemar Schütz (with 415 out of 480 votes); H.-H. Scheffer (381); H. G. Schroeter, a lawyer and deputy chairman (later acting chairman) of the Lower Saxon Land organization (364); H.-G. Kosche (350); Erwin Stolz (325); Hans Schikora, a former regional SRP leader from Rhineland-Palatinate (298); Heinrich K. Kunstmann (295); Hildegard von Rheden (215). To the enlarged executive board (in addition to the Land chairmen ex officio) were elected Georg Joel (320); former SS General Lothar Debes (319), von Grünberg (315), Stulle (305), Rolf-Dieter Spieler (301), Gebhardt (265), Herbert Bangemann (263), Anneliese Brandes (262), Carl-Herbert Hey (240), Lilli Nolden (237). See "Parteivertretertag in Kassel-Wilhelmshöhe," *Reichsruf* (Hanover) VI, 44 (November 2, 1957), 8.

100. "Im alten Tritt," *Frankfurter Allgemeine Zeitung,* October 29, 1957.

101. The exculpation rests on the argument that men like Hagen were writers, not intelligence agents, and that therefore they could not have penetrated the elaborate camouflage under which the East-oriented wirepullers operated. And, in any case, they had been promised freedom to write without interference from their employers!

102. *Reichsruf* (Hanover), VI, 46 (November 16, 1957), 8.

103. CDU Deputy Alois Scherf, in his speech in the diet on November 21, 1957, charged that the FDP-BHE Fraktion "had not a single time gotten in touch" with its coalition partner. (Niedersächsischer Landtag, Dritte Wahlperiode, *Stenographischer Bericht,* 52. Sitzung, November 21, 1957 [Hanover], col. 2948.) The FDP delegation chairman, Heinz Müller (Osterode) denied that and offered to furnish proof of his attempts to get in touch with

the DP-CDU Fraktion (*ibid.*, col. 2936). The FDP Deputy Winfrid Hedergott could say without contradiction from the DP-CDU that the latter had been informed of FDP-BHE intentions on Saturday, November 2, before the final agreement with the DRP had been signed and sealed (*ibid.*, col. 2967). What clearly was involved here was the question of *when* the FDP-BHE Fraktion informed the DP-CDU. It is true that the former were correct in insisting that they had informed their coalition partners technically before the final agreement with the DRP had been ratified. The DP-CDU were right in feeling that they had been placed before a *fait accompli* because they had heard about the impending agreement with the DRP only in the last moment; throughout the preceding weeks the fact that these negotiations were going on had been carefully kept from them.

104. *Ibid.*, col. 2967.

105. It will be remembered also that the Freiberger forces had threatened to expel von Thadden at the Kassel meeting of the DRP executive committee on the pretext that he had exceeded his authority when he suggested to his fellow DRP deputies that they join the BHE Fraktion. Cf. XVI/86.

106. When FDP Deputy Hedergott sought to blunt the DP-CDU argument that the DRP was seeking to occupy the thirteenth committee seat and thus grasp a powerful key lever through which it could wield disproportionate power, he pointed out that the thirteenth seat was unnecessary to block the DP-CDU, but failed to mention the tactical advantage of being able to frustrate it by mere abstention. This did not by any means constitute a key weapon, but it was a tactical advantage which might explain the eagerness of the FDP-BHE to welcome the DRP deputies in their ranks. For Hedergott's argument, see Niedersächsischer Landtag (XVI/103), col. 2966. The only other possibility was that the accession of the DRP deputies to the BHE Fraktion might have made it possible for the latter to break its parliamentary coalition with the FDP and gain sole control over the two committee seats.

107. In a round letter of November 9, 1957, sent to all Land and district organizations, Stolz admitted that negotiations between the FDP-BHE Fraktion and DRP deputies had been going on since the first week in October, that is, at a time when the party executive committee under Freiberger's sway had specifically prohibited Meinberg and von Thadden from engaging in such discussions and had forced their resignation over this issue.

108. Niedersächsischer Landtag (XVI/103), col. 2950.

109. Niedersächsischer Landtag, Dritte Wahlperiode (XXIV. Tagungsabschnitt), *Stenographischer Bericht,* Ausserordentliche (51.) Sitzung, November 19, 1957 (Hanover), cols. 2918–2919.

110. Kurt Döring, "Niedersachsen neigen zum Grundsätzlichen," *Frankfurter Allgemeine Zeitung,* November 9, 1957.

111. See Hans Henrich, "Schwarz-rotes Welfen Team," *Frankfurter Rundschau,* November 14, 1957.

112. Only in Hamburg did it seem for a while as though a major party split were developing. There, efforts to achieve some kind of nationalist-neutralist rally had been under way since the beginning of 1957. The initial

impulse had come from Otto Strasser's German Social Union (DSU), but it was soon dissipated when ultranationalist and folkish purists, like, for insance, Karl Meissner's German Bloc (DB), refused to collaborate with Strasser as long as he maintained connections to individuals and groups suspected of East orientation. (The stumbling block was a so-called Brandenburg-Gate Circle under the leadership of Lieutenant Colonel H. Kardel, a holder of the Knights Cross. A warmly encouraging notice in the *Reichsruf,* VI, 7 [February 16, 1957], 1, marking the founding of that circle, had to be revoked by von Thadden [*ibid.,* VI, 8 (February 23, 1957), 4] with the excuse that it had been inadvertently published while he, the responsible editor in chief, was out of town.) After the national election, during the period of Meinberg's and von Thadden's temporary banishment from the leadership of the DRP, these efforts culminated in the formation (by Hamburg representatives of the DRP, DSU, and DB) of a Working Fellowship of the National Opposition (Arbeitsgemeinschaft der nationalen Opposition) under the chairmanship of the former SRP functionary and present DRP Land chairman of Hamburg, Hugo Jungmann. The Working Fellowship was formally founded on November 6, 1957, the day on which the Fraktion arrangement between the DRP and the FDP-BHE brought down the Lower Saxon government. Five days later, the DRP executive committee, now again under the leadership of Meinberg and von Thadden, declared an emergency in its Hamburg Land organization, promptly expelled Jungmann from the party, and suspended the entire Hamburg executive board. Jungmann, who, along with Freiberger, was known as one of the chief opponents of the DRP's new "bourgeois course," now consciously set about organizing the anti-Meinberg wing of the DRP, the DB, and DSU into a counterparty which, in contrast to the DRP, as he saw it, would be the instrument of a clear ideology, possessed of impressive symbolism, and employ a tight organizational scheme with unified and rigorous doctrinal and organizational training. (Jungmann succeeded in December, 1957, in staging a meeting of functionaries of various DRP Land organizations. He sought to obtain their agreement to the formation of a new organization which would use the Hamburg Arbeitsgemeinschaft of the DSU, DB, and DRP as a model.) The plan miscarried: Strasser disapproved of the Hamburg DSU chairman Willi Henneberg; moreover, the anticipated exodus from the DRP did not materialize. By March, 1958, nothing was left of Jungmann's grandiose scheme except a small group of DRP dissidents under his leadership and that of the former vice-chairman, Waldemar Magunia. With the help of a totally insignificant Folk-Social Movement (Volkssoziale Bewegung), which the little-known Hanoverian cabaret artist Hans Jähde had organized in 1956, Jungmann and Magunia formed the Free Socialist People's Party (Freie Sozialistische Volkspartei). In its program, Jungmann's strongly "German socialist" proclivities, which had brought him into sharp conflict with the conservative nationalist elements in the DRP, and his radical neutralism found ample expression. For the DRP crisis that led to the Jungmann expulsion and for the formation of the Free Socialist People's Party, see *Die Brücke,* IV, 22/23 (January 15, 1958), 2–3.

113. Quoted in Gesellschaft zum Studium von Zeitfragen, *Analysen und Berichte,* V, 13 (May 21, 1958), 6.

114. *Ibid.,* pp. 3–4.

115. Kernmayr made the journey in the company of his publisher, the DRP executive board member Waldemar Schütz, of the Göttingen publishing house Plesse.

116. In June, 1958, the Lower Saxon Land executive committees of the FDP and BHE, pretending to have discovered that the Detmold resolutions of the DRP had so altered the latter's political line that no further collaboration was possible, ordered their Landtag Fraktionen to cancel the guest arrangement with the six DRP deputies. In view of the clear continuity, if not to say identity, of the DRP's political position as it found expression in the resolutions adopted at Detmold, this was purely a pretext for a retreat from an increasingly vulnerable and costly position. Considering future political possibilities in Lower Saxony, the DRP guests had become a liability. The expulsion from the joint Fraktion doubtless constituted a blow to the DRP's attempt to receive the grooming necessary for eventual political acceptance as the bona fide Right-extreme wing of the parliamentary spectrum. At the same time, the DRP's larger goal of forming the nucleus for a nationalist Third Force had long since vanished, and the severance of ties to the bourgeois parties, whose anti-Adenauer reliability had never been great, was bound to contribute to the internal pacification of resentments which were still rankling in many DRP faithfuls.

117. Reproduced in Gesellschaft zum Studium von Zeitfragen, *Analysen und Berichte,* V, 20–21 (December, 1958), 4.

118. *Ibid.,* p. 13.

119. Such as, for instance, in the old demands for an end to defamation of former Nazis and to the war-crimes trials and for restitution to former Nazis whom the Allies and Bonn had aggrieved. An entire paragraph was even devoted to express the party's distaste for the "loathsome self-accusations of undignified (*würdelos*) Germans to the effect that Germany alone was responsible for both World Wars" and for "the irresponsible falsification of German history for cheap political purposes." *Ibid.,* p. 5.

120. Such generalizations as "Service for the community and self-discipline in the people's community should dominate our social life" or "it is the task of the woman to be mother to her children. Only in emergency and in response to a genuine vocational call should she be a second breadwinner" are cases in point. *Ibid.,* p. 6.

121. Conservatism also suffused the section dealing with the "peasantry." There the DRP stressed that "agriculture is not a trade" and that "in the peasantry lies the necessary counterweight to the metropolitan thinking of the Western world which is oriented toward immediate success. Hence the maintenance of the peasant family takes precedence over the necessary rationalization" (*ibid.,* p. 9).

122. *Ibid.,* p. 11.

123. *Ibid.,* pp. 7–8.

124. Land diets were to be indirectly elected through the city and county councilors; a Reich council, modeled after Bismarck's Federal Council and consisting of representatives of the Land presidents, was to be the highest executive Reich organ. The Reich president would be elected for seven years by a Reich assembly made up of the chairmen of local and district assemblies. The Reich assembly, which could be convened by the president or a third of its membership for extraordinary sessions, had the right to veto decisions of the Reichstag.

125. See, for instance, the outright apologia for the Hitler Reich in "Das Ende des Hitlerismus," *Reichsruf* (Hanover) VII, 19 (May 10, 1958), 1–2, where the limits of constitutionality were observed only by use of the most transparent tricks of argumentation.

126. In 1955, the DRP, under Hess's leadership, had contested the Land diet elections in an electoral coalition with the German Party. As in 1953 the DRP alone had received 45,000 votes (or 2.5 per cent of the total) and the DP, another 19,700 (or 1.1 per cent), the combined forces, campaigning under the label of a Free Electoral Association (Freie Wähler Gemeinschaft, FWG), potentially represented about 65,000 voters. The election results, however, looked different. The combined forces of DRP and DP were able to gather no more votes than the DRP had managed to capture in 1953 all by itself. Compared to the accumulated DRP and DP votes in 1953, the FWG lost 57 per cent of them in the government district Koblenz; 40 per cent in the previous "stronghold," the government district Rhine-Hesse; almost two-thirds in the government district Montabaur. Only in the largest district, the Palatinate, could the FWG improve upon the combined 1953 DRP and DP votes, and then only by 4 per cent. In that southern, more industrial, and Protestant part of the Land, the FWG gathered 4.6 per cent of the popular vote, and certain districts of that region showed a well above average affinity for the FWG. Thus, the county Frankenthal gave almost 9 per cent of its votes to the DRP-DP. In the city district Landau, it was 8.3 per cent; in the city of Neustadt, 7.7 per cent; in Neustadt county, 5.9 per cent. In Kusel, 5 per cent; Rockenhausen, 6.1 per cent; and in the district of Kirchheimbolanden, even 12 per cent of all votes went to the FWG. Hence, when, four years later, observers were shocked to find the district Neustadt voting 7 per cent DRP, Frankenthal 11 per cent, and the districts Kirchheimbolanden, Kusel, Rockenhausen, and Zweibrücken even between 11 per cent and 18 per cent, they eagerly sought for "specific reasons" to explain what they believed was a sudden massive reassertion of radical nationalism.

127. Conspicuous by his absence was only Werner Körper, the former SRP Land chairman who, as we saw, worked feverishly after the outlawry of the SRP to salvage the organization and with this aim maintained constant contact, not only to the national SRP leaders, but also to Gustav Heinemann, Helene Wessel (see above, VI/79), Naumann, von Thadden, General Ramcke, Dr. Fritz Schulz, Haussleiter, Griesmayr, and Hess. (On Körper's activities, see the confidential reports of discussions with him, his family, and fiancé of December 3, 1952, February 6, 1953, April 17, 1953, and August 28, 1953. Copies in the possession of the author.)

128. According to the Electoral Law, those parties which are represented in a Land diet by at least five deputies need not collect signatures to place their candidates on the ballot. All others have to submit 200 valid signatures in support of a candidate in each electoral district and an additional 2,000 signatures to be granted the all-important Land-list privileges. (*Bundesgesetzblatt,* Part I, no. 21 [May 9, 1956], par. 19, sec. 2; par. 21, sec. 2; par. 28, sec. 1.) In Bremen, with its 100-seat chamber, the overcoming of the 5 per cent clause would have also meant a minimum of five seats—enough to avoid the costly, time- and energy-consuming collection of signatures in 1961. (By the use of the d'Hondt system, this is not quite literally true. Thus, for instance, in 1955 the Communist Party in Bremen, which achieved just 5 per cent of the valid votes, received only four seats. See Bremen, Statistisches Landesamt, "Die Wahl zur Bremischen Bürgerschaft am 9. Oktober 1955 im Lande Bremen," pp. 3–5.)

129. Thus the party congress passed a resolution demanding an end to the trials of Nazi criminals, which no doubt represented the sentiments of the DRP electors more correctly than the party program of Munich. "These trials do not involve guilt and expiation, crime and punishment; they involve exclusively the resumption of collective accusations against the German people, in order to soften them up for the demands of the peace treaty of tomorrow. . . . We demand an end to this mischief, which is grist for the mill of Communist world propaganda and of all Germanophobes." Quoted in *Studien von Zeitfragen, Analysen und Berichte,* VI, 13 (October 21, 1959), 13–14. At the party congress Meinberg was again re-elected, with 388 out of 392 votes. The election became a massive demonstration of gratitude for the seriously ailing chairman, as everyone knew that this was the last time that he would run. In the light of the real power relationship within the leadership group, the election of the first deputy chairman was of far greater actual importance. Otto Hess was re-elected as the man who actually had guided the party in the past year. The second deputy chairmanship went to Dr. H. K. Kunstmann. The members of the executive committee were: Stolz, Hans Schikora, Hans Bernhard von Grünberg, Adolf von Thadden, Waldemar Schütz, Conrad Lüddecke-Stielau, and Hildegard von Rheden. Onto the extended executive board were elected: H. Bangemann, Heinrich Stulle, Heinz Schimmerohn, C.-H. Hey, Oskar Lutz (an old "folkdom fighter" of the German minority in Estonia and "honorary" SS officer), Arthur Wagner (a Bavarian party official), the gynecologist Dr. H. Fikentscher, and Hans Biegel and Karl-Heinz Schürmann (both members of the Rhineland-Palatinate leadership).

130. DRP officials pretended to be pleased at the threefold increase in the vote over the devastating national election of 1957, when the DRP received about 5,500 votes, or 1.4 per cent. They did not permit their joy to be dimmed by the thought that in 1951 the SRP in its first (and only) campaign in Bremen moved into the city parliament with eight men, on the basis of 8 per cent of the popular vote, and that even in the otherwise catastrophic 1953 elections, the DRP received over 10,000 votes, or 3 per cent of the total votes cast. In 1955, the DRP had formed an electoral coalition with the BHE

and with such splinters as the so-called German Solidarity (DS) and an Emergency Association of the Middle Class (Notgemeinschaft des Mittelstandes). The result was that the BHE, which two years earlier, campaigning alone, had received 3.2 per cent of the votes (11,600), now was supported by only 2.9 per cent of the voters (10,600).

131. For an investigation and interpretation of these reactions, see Peter Schönbach, *Reaktionen auf die antisemitische Welle im Winter 1959/1960,* Frankfurter Beiträge zur Soziologie, Sonderheft 3 ([Frankfurt:] Europäische Verlagsanstalt, [c. 1961]).

132. *DRP-Pressedienst* (Hanover), "Erklärung des Vorsitzenden der Deutschen Reichs-Partei, Wilhelm Meinberg, vor der Bundes-Pressekonferenz am 30. 12. 1959 in Bonn."

133. Oddly enough, these prudent cautions were almost immediately thrown to the wind. For although Meinberg was right when he surmised that the DRP membership of two swastika smearers was surely not enough to bring the party before the Constitutional Court, he was pushing his luck when he approved plans to hold a Rhineland-Palatinate Land convention on January 16, 1960, in Kaiserslautern, the scene of one of the DRP triumphs of the previous year. This started a series of legal moves by the state government which ten days later led to the ban of the Land organization by the state Ministry of the Interior, on the ground that the Palatinate DRP was, in point of leading personnel, a successor organization of the outlawed Socialist Reich Party. However justified these charges were substantively, the administrative suppression of a political party without a trial, even without hearings, was hardly worthy of a constitutional regime. Eleven months later the Superior Administrative Court recognized this and rescinded the ban. In the meantime the DRP had built up a new cadre organization, taking care to steer clear of previously exposed SRP members.

134. This took the form first of inducing the city to withdraw an earlier agreement to make available a city-owned hall. When a court injunction stopped this attempt, the Labor Union Federation planned counterdemonstrations and mass participation in (and virtually swamping) the public committee sessions of the DRP and its plenary meetings. The city thereupon prohibited both the DRP congress and the counterdemonstrations. The court again stepped in to force the city to allow the DRP to meet. Thereupon both the DGB and DRP received permission to hold their gatherings.

135. "Pfiffe am Waldkater," *Der Spiegel,* XIV, 30 (July 20, 1960), 23–25.

136. "Die Demokratie im 'demokratischen Laufstühlchen,' " *Stuttgarter Zeitung,* July 12, 1960.

137. The first deputy chairmanship went to Oskar Lutz, the former Baltic folk enthusiast who had been a diet deputy of the BHE, but had switched his allegiance primarily because he was attracted by the DRP's uncompromising neutralism. The second deputy chairmanship went to the former SRP official Werner Gebhardt. The former chairman, Wilhelm Meinberg, was asked to continue to serve as a member of the executive committee. The rest of the party executive consisted of the old stand-bys von

Thadden, Hess, Schütz, Lüddecke-Stielau, and Schikora, who were joined by the former executive board member Schimmerohn. The chairman of the North Rhine–Westphalian party, Udo Diekelmann, was added as a new member. The enlarged party executive board consisted of H. B. von Grünberg, the party ideologist, who was "demoted" from the executive committee, and the old board members along with Frau von Rheden, Bangemann, Stulle, Hey, Fikentscher, Wagner, and Biegel. New members were Emil Maier-Dorn, of Augsburg, and Hans Votsch, of Darmstadt, who together with Bernhard Brünsing tried to appeal to workers through a newsletter. See *Bulletin on German Questions* (London), XII, 268/269 (September 15, 1960).

138. In the balloting for the chairmanship, von Thadden defeated his predecessor, H.-H. Scheffer, by a narrow margin.

139. The successful challenger was Prince Hubertus zu Löwenstein, the Right-wing anti-Nazi historian. See *Deutscher Informationsdienst,* no. 797 (February 24, 1959).

140. Beyond that, the identity of the interior pages of the *German Weekly* with those in the *Reichsruf* was further testimony that the closest possible parallelism between the two sister publications was planned and, so far as possible, provided for.

141. *Deutscher Informationsdienst,* no. 790 (January 16, 1959).

142. *Ibid.,* no. 842 (October 14, 1959).

143. Quoted in *Studien von Zeitfragen, Presse- und Buchspiegel,* VII, 12/13 (October–November, 1960), 4–5.

144. Quoted *ibid.,* VII, 8/9 (August, 1960), 6.

145. Quoted *ibid.,* VII, 12/13 (October–November, 1960), 5.

146. Quoted *ibid.,* p. 6.

147. Quoted *ibid.,* p. 5.

148. Quoted *ibid.,* p. 7.

149. See above, XVI/118 and nearby text.

150. Quoted in *Studien von Zeitfragen, Presse- und Buchspiegel,* VII, 12/13 (October–November, 1960), 4–5.

151. Quoted *ibid.,* pp. 8–9.

152. Quoted in *Studien von Zeitfragen, Analysen und Berichte,* VIII, 18–19 (December 12, 1961), 3.

153. *Bulletin on German Questions* (London), XIII, 285–287 (June 15, 1961), 13.

154. The Party Program is reproduced in its entirety in *Studien von Zeitfragen, Analysen und Berichte* VIII, 8/9 (June 21, 1961).

155. See above, XVI/133.

156. *Der Spiegel,* XV, 43 (October 18, 1961), 92.

157. "Hilfe aus Afrika," *Der Spiegel,* XV, 45 (November 1, 1961), 40–41.

158. After the outlawry of the SRP, its functionaries, as we have seen, opened negotiations with all kinds of personalities in the extremist groups to reconnoiter the possibilities of establishing some organizational form in which the old SRP voters could be held together. In this connection, Werner Körper, the SRP chief of the embryonic Palatinate organization, took up

contact with (among others) Gottfried Griesmayr and Otto Hess. By February, 1953, these talks were broken off. "Körper learned from Remer about negotiations of Hess with the BHE. Thereupon all connections to Hess were severed. Körper is of the opinion that Hess is merely a front for some kind of official bureau, with the task of gaining an overview over the Rightist groups." (From a confidential report on a conversation with Körper on February 5, 1953. Report is dated February 6, 1953.) On December 30, 1952, one Walter Geiss (or Giess), one of the members of the subversive and later outlawed Natinform apparatus, warned members about Hess: "Investigations are not yet completed. Still one can say with some certainty that [Hess] is an opponent, and collaboration with him is out of the question." Moreover, it will be remembered that in 1955 Hess, then chairman of the Rhineland-Palatinate Land organization of the DRP, entered into an electoral alliance with the DP and fought the elections under the title of Free Electoral Association. To the purists, such collaboration with the DP was heinous treason to the cause and altogether unforgivable. For the DP, many of whose members, to be sure, were radical nationalists, indistinguishable ideologically from the purists, had fatally sinned when it became Adenauer's most faithful satellite organization.

159. The new executive committee consisted of: Schütz, von Grünberg, Schimmerohn, Lüddecke-Stielau; the former SRP functionary and von Thadden's deputy in Lower Saxony, Walter Seetzen; Gerhard Woitschell, of Wiesbaden; Kunstmann's general secretary, Walter Kupka; and Emil Maier-Dorn, of Augsburg. Into the expanded executive board were elected Hildegard von Rheden, Biegel, Votsch, Wagner, Stulle, plus Udo Diekelmann, the Land chairman of North Rhine–Westphalia; Werner Roesch, Bavarian DRP official; Werner Kärcher, the DRP boss of Rhine-Hesse; and Willi Mellin, the former SRP and DG Land chairman and coleader of the anti-Haussleiter rebellion in Baden-Württemberg in 1956–1957.

160. Cf. *Reichsruf* (Hanover), XI, 3 (January 20, 1962). For a listing of the personalities and districts which left the DRP in the first few days after the Frankfurt meeting, see *Studien von Zeitfragen, Analysen und Berichte,* VIII, 18–19 (December 12, 1961), 9.

161. *Ibid.,* pp. 3–4.

162. Kunstmann was promptly elected chairman and Lutz, again, his deputy. The second deputy post was given to Hans Jähde, chairman of the Volkssoziale Bewegung, which joined the DFP, as did a Hamburg League of the New Order (Bund Neue Ordnung), a local organization of former SRP people. (For Jähde, see above, XVI/112.) The executive committee consisted of Gebhardt; Scheffer, the former Lower Saxon and national DRP chairman; Högelow, of Bielefeld; and Günther Proksch, the former DRP regional director of Upper Bavaria. To the wider executive board belonged Hans Schikora, the former SRP chief Gerhard Krüger, Arthur Wagner, Ingeborg Gebauer, Hans-Joachim Röhr, Arnold Neugeborn, and Horst Grüll. See *Studien von Zeitfragen, Analysen und Berichte,* IX, 1 (January 26, 1962), 3.

163. For the complete text of the Action Program and for the speeches

of Kunstmann and Schikora, which for their amazing democratic mimicry are worth reading, see *ibid.*, pp. 6–9. At the end of 1962, the DFP organized its first party congress in Düsseldorf, where a "Düsseldorf Manifesto" was debated and eventually adopted. In November, 1963, the party's second congress took place in Dortmund. There the DFP's leaders gave renewed expression to the party's will to become a parliamentary mass party and to be satisfied neither with ideological propaganda and enlightenment of public opinion nor with order, elite, or cadre conceptions of political organization. Substantively, reunification stands, of course, here, too, in the center of DFP demands. Rejecting the proto-Gaullist policies of the DRP and the latter's attempt to form bourgeois nationalist circles to the Right of the CSU (especially in the GDP/BHE and the former DP) into a large "national-democratic" bloc, the DFP comes much closer to the conceptions of Haussleiter's DG. (See below, XVI/184.) Thus, in foreign policy, the DFP sees German reunification as a precondition for a pan-European rally. At the same time, the DFP, unlike the DG, tends to approve of the ultimate formation of a "Europe of Fatherlands." The DRP's Gaullist solution the DFP sees basically as designed to perpetuate German division and the formation of a "Carolingian" Europe. In June, 1965, the DFP changed its name to Action Fellowship for an Independent Germany (Aktionsgemeinschaft für ein unabhängiges Deutschland, AGUD).

164. Günther Proksch, "Nationale Opposition, nationale Politik und Deutsche Freiheits Partei," in Otto Strasser, ed., *Ziel und Weg der Nationalen Opposition,* Schriften für Deutschlands Erneuerung, no. 1 (Munich: [Deutsche Freiheit, pref. October 9, 1962]), p. 22.

165. See *Studien von Zeitfragen, Analysen und Berichte,* IX, 11–12 (June 27, 1962), 5.

166. Speech of the DRP Saar chairman Willy Kallert, reproduced in *Reichsruf* (Hanover), XI, 2 (January 13, 1962), and quoted in *Studien von Zeitfragen, Analysen und Berichte,* IX, 2–3 (February 23, 1962), 9. Indeed, by 1963, "modernists" or "reformers" within the DRP leadership (such as, for instance, the new chairman of the Hesse Land organization, Gerhard Woitschell) reportedly agitated for a change in party label to "National-democratic Union" and for drastic modification of the nationalist-traditionalist symbolism which the DRP had hitherto consistently employed. See, *ibid.*, X, 1 (August 6, 1963), 6–7.

167. Adolf von Thadden, *Wille und Weg des nationalen Deutschland. Eine Rede des Frankfurter Parteitags der DRP, 1962* (Hanover: Reichsruf, 1962), p. 23.

168. Reproduced in *Studien von Zeitfragen, Analysen und Berichte,* IX, 1 (January 26, 1962), 6.

169. See above, XVI/150.

170. See above, text near XVI/26.

171. Von Thadden (XVI/167), pp. 20–21, 23.

172. Quoted in *Studien von Zeitfragen, Analysen, Berichte, Informationen zum nationalen Nonkonformismus,* XI, 1 (January 9, 1964), 6.

173. *Ibid.*, p. 6.

174. *Ibid.,* p. 12.

175. Thus, the *German Weekly*'s trio of Härtle, Kleist, and Kernmayr labored constantly to show that collaboration with the United States was merely the lesser of two gigantic evils and must not in any case lead to any relaxation in the continuous struggle against American influence in German life and thought.

176. Cf. the report on the DRP's annual congress on September 20–22, 1963 in Karlsruhe-Durlach in *Studien von Zeitfragen, Analysen, Berichte, Informationen zum nationalen Nonkonformismus,* X, 3A (Sonderdienst, October 3, 1963), 2–6.

177. This was dramatically manifested by the sharp decline in attendance at the annual party congress. At the Northeim congress of December, 1961, 532 delegates took their seats. In Frankfurt, in June, 1962, 432 delegates attended. In September, 1963, in Karlsruhe, only 356 conferees, representing probably no more than 6,000 party members, were duly seated.

178. *Studien von Zeitfragen, Analysen, Berichte, Informationen zum nationalen Nonkonformismus,* A/1964 (Sondermaterial, February 4, 1964). Here it is important to point out that the DFP's participation in the Schleswig-Holstein alliance in no way represented a retreat from its anti-Gaullist, quasi-neutralist conviction. Its leadership went to some pain to make this perfectly clear when it declared: "There, too, discussions were held not to bring about a rally for a rally's sake, but to produce a clarification of viewpoints. . . . There is no [possibility of] coalition with those 'nationalists' who are characterized by an ideological [*geistigen*] line which runs from Strauss to von der Heydte, Ziesel, Oberländer, Kern, Peter Kleist, Ehrhardt, [and] von Thadden. These forces are further removed from the DFP than those Social Democrats who are disappointed by the 'new look' of their party, or than those FDP electors who are similarly disappointed by Mende's continual giving-in." Quoted *ibid.,* XI, 3 (April 3, 1964), 3.

179. "Neue Parteigründung geplant," *Süddeutsche Zeitung* (Munich), no. 286 (November 28–29, 1964), p. 2.

180. Despite NDU support for the new party, the most prominent NDU leader, Joachim von Ostau (see above, VI/129 and XIV/66), was not elected to the NPD executive board. (See *Studien von Zeitfragen, Analysen, Berichte, Informationen zum nationalen Nonkonformismus,* XI, 13–14 [December 11, 1964], 2–7.) The party chairmanship went to the cement manufacturer Friedrich Thielen, the Land chairman of the Bremen DP. His three deputies were a GDP official and ex-Nazi, Wilhelm Gutmann, von Thadden, and the Hesse DRP leader and (like Gutmann) 1931-member of the Nazi Party, Wilhelm Fassbender. The presidium included the DRP leaders von Grünberg, Hess, and Schütz, the GDP politician and 1931-Nazi alumnus Otto Theodor Brouwer, and Georg Körner, an "old [Nazi] fighter" (vintage 1929). The executive committee consisted of Frau Elfriede Bläsing, Wilhelm Höft, Eberhard von Hauff, Wilhelm Kuhlmann, Karl Knüpper, Emil Maier-Dorn, Prince Karl of Salm, Heinz Schimmerohn, Frau Gertraud Winkelvoss.

181. For a reproduction of the party program see *Deutscher Informationsdienst,* XV, 1120 (December 19, 1964), 3–4.

182. In the Land election of April, 1964, the tattered GDP/BHE, with the support of the local DRP, garnered 1.8 per cent of the votes. One should recall that in the previous Land election of 1960 the GDP/BHE had still been able to get 8.2 per cent of the votes. In the Bundestag election of 1961 support for the GDP/BHE had shrunk to 2.8 per cent.

183. The federal elections of September, 1965, and the Bavarian communal elections of March, 1966, seem to bear out this expectation. In gathering over 600,000 votes (2 per cent of the total vote) in 1965, the NPD did somewhat better than had been generally predicted, considering its still rudimentary organizational base. In Bavaria, on the communal level, and in such old nationalist strongholds as Bayreuth, Erlangen, Passau, and Nuremberg, the NPD received 10.6, 9.5, 9.2, and 7.5 per cent of the votes respectively. That is about the same percentage as such parties as the DG or the DB were able to capture in the first five or six postwar years in the same regions. (Cf. above, XV/46. For the Bavarian elections see Philip Shabecoff, "Party Called Neo-Nazi Gains in Bavarian Elections," *New York Times,* March 15, 1966, p. 14, cols. 4–6.) The trend foreshadowed by these elections was maintained in the Hesse Land election of November 6, 1966, and confirmed two weeks later in the Bavarian Land election of November 20, 1966. In Hesse the NPD won 8 per cent of the vote and 8 out of 96 diet seats. In Bavaria close to 10 per cent opted for the nationalist party, thus sending the NPD into the diet with 15 mandates out of a total of 204 seats. (Philip Shabecoff, "German Rightists Make Gain in Vote," *ibid.,* November 7, 1966, p. 1, col. 2; p. 12, cols. 4–6. Thomas J. Hamilton, "German Rightists Obtain 15 Seats in Bavarian Vote," *ibid.,* November 21, 1966, p. 1, col. 8; p. 5, cols. 4–6.) Incidentally, on December 4, 1965, the DRP was officially dissolved and merged integrally with the NPD.

184. That wing, reacting strongly against the "soft" approach to the menace of "atheistic Communism" in Washington and, to its utter consternation, even in the Vatican, has moved closer to the nonclerical bourgeois-nationalist Right, which continues to agitate for a militant anti-Communism, an independent German nuclear capability, and "massive retaliation."

185. "Clerical" circles of the CDU have publicly "pointed with concern" to the political tendencies on the CSU's extreme Right and have magnified the "danger" and misinterpreted it for political reasons of their own. Thus an information service close to the CDU wrote: "Bonn fears a nationalist wave in the Federal Republic. When the division of Germany becomes hardened by international treaties. Anticipated trend of that nationalism: (*a*) against further close collaboration with the West, (*b*) inclination toward a massive neutralism. Through which the Federal Republic might succumb to the Communist pull. . . . Background: Active efforts at rallying Rightist groups are continuing. In all parts of the federal territory. Could lead to a basic change in party alignment." Cited in *Studien von Zeitfragen, Analysen, Berichte, Informationen zum nationalen Nonkonformismus,* X, 4 (October 21, 1963), 4.

186. By 1961, these had been reduced to one, August Haussleiter's miniscule German Community (DG). Insisting that a shared past on the Right wing of German politics no longer provides a meaningful basis for

future activity, the DG has consistently opposed the DRP's attempts to form a neo-Harzburg bloc to the Right of the CSU. To the DG, the bourgeois-national DP and the GDP/BHE (the DRP's potential partners) have put themselves beyond the pale by their years of collaboration with the CDU. A rally of the remaining fragments to the Right of the CDU-CSU could be little else but the machinations of a "Bonn front organization." To the ego-maniacal Haussleiter, coalitions and rallies have (as we have noted) always been unacceptable (especially since his bad experiences in 1953–1954). Instead of "rallies," the DG has preferred to operate with the image of "crystallization," in which it invariably sees itself as the crystallizing agent, into whose framework the others are to fit themselves. An equally wide chasm separates the DRP's economic and social bourgeois conservatism from the DG's self-conscious anti-Marxist, *petit-bourgeois* "socialism," which calls for the destruction of the power of finance capitalism and the nationalization of key industries. In foreign policy the DG opposes the DRP's Gaullism with a vision of a proto-Austrian solution of reunification through German neutrality and rejects Gaullist atomic policies from the position of a principled "nationalist pacifism." In a close association with de Gaulle's France, Haussleiter sees a suicidal provocation of the two continental superpowers which can lead only to a Russian–Anglo-Saxon encirclement of the West European "bloc" and thus, ultimately, to disaster. Also, unlike both the DRP and the DFP, the DG rejects any pan-European conception and even argues that the possibility of realizing its preferred plan of reunification through absolute neutrality is far greater than that of any rival scheme, as both the U.S. and the U.S.S.R. will recognize it as a practical way of preventing the formation of an independent "Third Force" Europe. These propositions were approved anew at the DG's party congress in Karlsruhe at the end of September, 1963. There, frequent and laudatory references to Nasser and Ben Bella as appropriate examples for the solution of the most outstanding German social and economic problems led one observer to characterize the DG's social program as "Nasserism from above and Poujadism from below." (See *ibid.,* III A/1963 [Sonderdienst, October 3, 1963], 8.) In persisting, like the DRP and the DFP, in viewing itself as a potential mass party, the DG, as a self-conscious Weltanschauung party, banks on an eventual revulsion among the German electorate against the de-ideologizing of postwar German politics. In the face of the DRP's determined effort to amass conservative nationalist votes under the NPD label in the 1965 elections, the DG joined the former DFP under the name Action Group of Independent Germans (Aktionsgemeinschaft unabhängiger Deutscher, AUD). The leadership of the electoral alliance was in the hands of August Haussleiter; a former nationalist-neutralist Bundestag deputy (FDP), Hermann Schwann; and the editor of the DFP organ *Freie Nation,* Oskar Lutz. The AUD's showing in the election was even more disastrous than the usual Haussleiter debacles. With 53,000 votes or 0.2 per cent of the total, the AUD polled fewer than 10 per cent of the votes garnered by the rival NPD.

CHAPTER XVII. RENAZIFICATION OR RESTORATION?

1. From the testimony of Michael Heinze-Mansfeld before the Investigation Subcommittee of the Forty-Seventh Committee of the German Bundestag, December 18, 1951. Bundestag, *Stenographisches Protokoll über die 3. Sitzung des 47. Ausschusses, Untersuchungsausschuss gemäss Drucksache Nr. 2680 (Personalpolitik Ausw. Amt) am 18. Dezember 1951.*

2. This generally conservative mood also conditioned the thinking about the Nazi catastrophe and the lessons to be drawn from it. Instead of seeing Hitler's seizure of power as the culmination of fourteen years of persistent undermining of democratic institutions and of the prestige of the Republic by all of its enemies on the extreme Right (of whom the Nazis were only relative latecomers in any politically effective sense)—that is, instead of blaming the failure of Weimar democracy on the absence of democrats among the decisive elites of bureaucracy, army, industry, and the learned professions—postwar anti-Nazis all too often blame Weimar's failure on an excess of democracy, seeing in Nazism an essentially populist revolt of the masses. They all too frequently blame "the most democratic constitution" for Hitler's success, claiming that his rise to power had been thoroughly legal and proper in a formal way. They overlook that Hitler's seizure of power contradicted in every particular the democratic rules of the game and was made possible only by the connivance of authoritarian reactionaries who thought to "use" him for their own political purposes. The conservative reaction against what are thought to have been excesses of populism has led to a search for social models from a long dead, preindustrial past. The writings of economic romantics like Wilhelm Roepke, who shares the Spengler and Ortega y Gasset thesis that "mass" democracy must end in Caesarism and who recommended reversing the direction of industrialization to return to the craftsman and the direction of urbanization to return to the solidarity of neomedieval organic ties in a village community, were widely discussed in these German circles. There has also been a religious revival as the response to the Nazi horrors among German intellectuals who have always mistrusted and never understood the common cradle of Western freedom, the rationalist Enlightenment. Unable to free themselves from their romantic aversion against the Enlightenment, and misinterpreting the rise of totalitarianism as the product of rationalism and materialism, of individualism and socialism, German bourgeois "democrats" have tended to look toward the social doctrines of the Christian churches and rediscovered the social gospel of Pope Pius XI.

3. The social and political functions of the ideology of anti-Communism in the West, and especially in West Germany, have unfortunately not received the attention of Western social scientists that they deserve. Quite naturally, they have attracted a great deal of attention among Communist scholars, but their accounts are far too doctrinaire, schematic, and polemical to be of much use. A good introduction to work done in this area in East Germany and the Soviet Union is the symposium that Leo Stern published under the title *Der Antikommunismus in Theorie und Praxis des deutschen Imperialismus* ([Halle: Martin-Luther-Universität Halle-Wittenberg,] 1963)

and the bibliographies there included. Cf. Otto Heinrich von der Gablentz, who writes: "Everything was overshadowed by the fight against Communism and the Soviet Union. But Bolshevism was the heir of the 'revolution.' In the face of this fight, National Socialism appeared to many merely as an episode. Supported by powerful foreign allies and armed with the great tradition of the struggle against the revolution, those forces [like] the propertied bourgeoisie, the bureaucracy, and the churches, which during the Weimar period had been unable to deal with National Socialism, now grew strong." "Reaktion und Restauration," in *Zur Geschichte und Problematik der Demokratie. Festgabe für Hans Herzfeld* (Berlin: Duncker & Humblot, [c. 1958]), p. 71.

4. When a representative sample of Germans was asked to express approval or disapproval of the statement "Politics today is for me far too materialistic. Everyone is only out to earn money. What we lack is ideals that could arouse enthusiasm," half agreed with it. Of course the sentiments of this half do not permit valid inferences concerning their actual behavior. See Rudolf Walter Leonhardt, *X-mal Deutschland* (6th ed.; Munich: Piper, 1962), pp. 392–400.

5. See Helmut Schelsky, "Über das Restaurative in unserer Zeit," *Frankfurter Allgemeine Zeitung,* April 9, 1955.

6. From the foreword of Bauer's volume of lyrics, *Mein blaues Oktavheft* (Hamburg: Tessloff, 1955), quoted in Kurt Roschmann, "Exemplarischer Fall einer Emigration," *Deutsche Rundschau,* LXXXI, 12 (December, 1955), 1320–1323.

7. Eugen Kogon, "Beinahe mit dem Rücken an der Wand," *Frankfurter Hefte,* no. 9/1954, quoted in Nemitz (X/289), p. 39. Kogon exemplifies the discontent of many intellectuals and their discomfort in the face of Germany's postwar development. See in this connection the excellent and critical little book of Paul Noack, *Die Intellektuellen: Wirkung, Versagen, Verdienst* (Munich: Olzog, [c. 1961]), especially pp. 88–96. How far more complex the problem is to which Kogon referred than the situation as depicted in most laments over "renazification" can be gauged by comparing Kogon's statement with that, for instance, of the news magazine *Der Spiegel,* which, in 1965 at the time of the great debate on the extension of the statute of limitation for Nazi murderers, wrote: "The Nazis did not go underground in 1945; they returned to their bourgeois occupations. [Nazi] Party members voted, [Nazi] Party members moved into the parliaments and governments of the Federal Republic. Ribbentrop's diplomats occupied desks in Bonn's Foreign Office; Hitlerite generals, barely returned from Russian captivity, put on the Bundeswehr uniforms. In Kiel the euthanasia professor Heyde, under the alias Sawade, submitted expert testimony to the Land government. Last year, at the euthanasia trial in Lüneburg, when a Hanover lawyer appeared as a witness who had handled requests for mercy in the Führer's chancellory and was asked by the judge: 'And you, too, probably joined the Party in 1933?,' the witness was indignant at being regarded as an opportunist. He answered, the hand raised in outrage: 'No, no, your Honor, earlier, much earlier.' Above all, the judiciary and the police were suffused with Nazis. National

Socialists in leading positions undertook to help guard the liberal order of the Federal Republic. The Attorney-General Wolfgang Immerwahr Fränkel, who has in the meantime been pensioned, exceeded at times the Bloody Judge Freisler in point of rigor as member of the Reich Prosecutors Office during the war. The SA man Joachim Loesdau was elected Federal Judge only last month. And in the 'Security Group Bonn' of the Federal Criminal Office, which has the task of protecting the Federal Republic against traitors and spies, there are police officers [who were former members of] the Mobile Killing Unit 9, which during the war murdered at least 11,000 Lithuanian and Russian Jews." "Verjährung: Gesundes Volksempfinden," *Der Spiegel,* XIX, 11 (March 10, 1965), 33.

8. Reifferscheidt (II/25).

9. Wilhelm Korspeter, *Die Demokratie im Spiegel der Bundesrepublik* (Vortrag gehalten am 1. und 2. März 1952 auf der Jahreshauptversammlung des Ortsvereins Hannover der SPD), *passim.*

10. These political and social ideals are also widely shared by the *petite bourgeoisie,* as well as by the "true believers" of yesteryear, and constitute what are generally called "the good parts of National Socialism."

11. See Georg Weippert, "Die Ideologien der 'Kleinen Leute' und des 'Mannes auf der Strasse,' " in his *Jenseits von Individualismus und Kollektivismus. Studien zum gegenwärtigen Zeitalter* (Düsseldorf: Schilling, 1964), pp. 148–173.

12. Cf. Stammler (X/126), pp. 63–68.

13. From a letter of J. H. von Ostau to Wolfgang Müller, October 12, 1949. Cf. Ebsworth (II/33), p. 35. Royalist enthusiasm even prompted an invitation to the then Princess Elizabeth of Great Britain, heavy with child, to spend the period of confinement in "her" ancestral castle in Brunswick and to be brought to bed with the heir to both crowns in the land of his forefathers! (Two years after the completion of the present chapter, there was published Hermann Meyn's *Die Deutsche Partei. Entwicklung und Problematik einer national-konservativen Rechtspartei nach 1945* [Düsseldorf: Droste, (1965)]. It successfully traces the tension and conflict between the DP's monarchist-conservative base in Lower Saxony and the radically nationalist and even national socialist elements in the party apparatuses of the other Länder.)

14. Cf. *Hannoversche Presse,* May 17, 1949. In August, 1947, the nationalist anti-Guelph forces inside the NLP succeeded in founding a party youth organization, Bund junger Deutscher, in which the influence of the Hitler Youth and especially the Combat SS quickly became dominant. Notions of "training a leadership elite" and demands for a "virile German policy" were here common. The Guelph wing of the DP was clearly uneasy about these developments and tried to dissociate itself from the BjD.

15. At a party congress in Kassel at the end of 1951, Seebohm, although Federal Minister, did not scruple to declame with great pathos: "We bow with reverence before every symbol of our nation—I say emphatically, before every symbol—under which German men have sacrificed their lives for their fatherland," an unmistakable reference to the then raging debate over the

federal government's ban on war decorations that bore the swastika emblem. As recently as June, 1964, "Seebohm was chastised by Chancellor Erhard . . . after he delivered a militant speech at an annual Sudeten-German expellee rally in Nuremberg. He asserted that the Munich Agreement of 1938 remained a legally binding compact and demanded the return of Sudeten-German lands to the Sudeten-Germans." Arthur J. Olsen, "Goldwater in Touch with Right Wing in Germany," *New York Times,* July 15, 1964, p. 21, col. 3. Cf. below, Section D.

16. Leuchtgens, it will be remembered, had merged the remaining parts of the National Democratic Party (after his split with Karl-Heinz Priester) with the rebellious Lower Saxon DRP under the leadership of the radical trio, Miessner, Richter, and Kniggendorf. It was not long before Leuchtgens, who had entered the first Bundestag as a FDP candidate, found it impossible to work within the DRP delegation and left it to attach himself to the DP Fraktion. Cf. above, XIV/60.

17. *Die Neue Zeitung* (Munich), March 10, 1952.

18. "Das ist die Deutsche Partei," published by the executive committee of the SPD, Bonn, August, 1953, p. 27. In this company should also be mentioned the old Nazi District Leader Fritz Fuchs, who did not bother to proclaim his attachment to democracy. In July, 1953, Leuchtgens, who after the unsuccessful local elections had been kicked upstairs as honorary chairman, was expelled from the party (along with eleven others), supposedly because of his opposition to what he called "the neo-Fascist course which has been steered for months under Schranz and executive board member Fritz Fuchs." At that time, Derichsweiler, who had become chairman of the party, declared his solidarity with the group of expelled functionaries and his unwillingness to go along with the trend of "restoration." Shortly before the 1953 election he resigned to run for the FDP. Eventually Derichsweiler returned to the DP, via the FVP, and again became chairman of the Hesse organization. (See *Die Neue Zeitung* [Munich], July 23, 1953, and *Feinde der Demokratie* [Nordmark], no. 6 [August 20, 1953], pp. 13–14.) Fuchs, incidentally, went over to the DRP, where he became second chairman of the Hesse Land organization.

19. One of the documents that fell into the hands of the police, and which appeared to reflect Richter's ideological training, contained the following: "These types of traders were people without land, who called themselves God's chosen people. Whoever had eyes to see could recognize the spider's web that was spun around the entire world. . . . That which gained shape in 1933 bordered on the miraculous. . . . The German people created an order for itself." (*Feinde der Demokratie* [Lower Saxony], II, 4 [February, 1953].) To what extent the DP official Richter was also involved in the formation of a so-called Defense Force Right (Abwehrdienst Rechts) is not clear. That organization was created by members of the League for Truth and Justice, together with former SRP members and members of the organization for "victims of denazification," for the purpose of identifying and harassing all those who had collaborated in the formulation and operation of the denazi-

fication procedure. Richter became DP city councilor of Oldenburg. (*Ibid.*, II, 5 [March, 1953].) Cf. above, XV/155.

20. See above, VI/79, 209, 217 (and nearby text), 219; and text at XV/36. Cf. below, text at XVII/158.

21. A nephew of Heinrich Held, the Bavarian Minister President in the Weimar period.

22. From a memorandum by Adolf von Thadden on a meeting of Right-extremist organizations on August 6–7, 1952, at Friedberg/Hesse. Later, Paul Schmidt, von Ribbentrop's chief interpreter, became Land chairman of the Bavarian DP.

23. Quoted in Roland Delcour, "Néonazis, Parti des Réfugiés et Parti Allemand," *Allemagne d'Aujourd'hui,* May–September 1957, p. 85.

24. *Feinde der Demokratie* (Lower Saxony) II, 7 (April–May, 1953). One of the DP district business managers, Willi Reupke, NSDAP member since 1931, police officer and SS leader and founder of a so-called German Anti-Marxist Front (Deutsche Antimarxistische Front, DAF), contributed to the 1953 campaign by massive defamation of the SPD chief Erich Ollenhauer, for which a court jailed him for a half a year. See *Hannoversche Presse,* August 25, 1953, and *Feinde der Demokratie* (Lower Saxony) III, 6 (March, 1954).

25. *Feinde der Demokratie* (Lower Saxony), II, 9 (July, 1953).

26. Ehrich later became a high official (*Regierungsdirektor*) of the Lower Saxon Land representation in Bonn and in 1963, by now a member of the FDP, he returned to Hanover as personal assistant to the Minister of Education, the archconservative former DP politician, political theorist, and ambassador Hans Mühlenfeld, who had also switched to the FDP.

27. Schneider, who at one time favored collaboration with the SRP, became general secretary of the DP and later its national chairman.

28. Quoted in [Club republikanischer Publizisten,] *CrP-Information,* September, 1957.

29. In the 1957 national election, for instance, there appeared among the DP candidates: Hans Westerholt (Oldenburg), Labor Service leader in the Nazi regime; Georg Körner (North Rhine–Westphalia), Labor Front leader; Wilhelm Jürgensen (Schleswig-Holstein), "folkdom fighter" and active worker in the Nazi Foreign Organization (AO), whom the Danes interned for over four years; Gerhard Teuschert (Hamburg), Nazi official in the Rosenberg Ministry; Richard Duckwitz (Bremen), Nazi Mayor of Bremen between 1944 and 1945; Heinrich Ahlers (Bremen), for nine years official of the German Labor Front; Theodor Kaiser, official of the corporative estate of carpenters; Erich Stolleis (Rhineland-Palatinate), Lord Mayor of Ludwigshafen under the Nazis; Heinrich Krämer (Rhineland-Palatinate), division chief in the Nutrition Estate; Benno Graf (Bavaria), official in the Nazified Folk League for Germandom Abroad (VDA); Johann Deininger (Bavaria), Land farmers' leader and Nazi Reichstag deputy. From *Feinde der Demokratie* (Lower Saxony) VI, 10 (September–October, 1957).

30. In May he also resigned from the Landtag parliamentary party.

31. In Lower Saxony the GDP lost over two-thirds of the votes which DP and BHE separately collected in the 1957 elections and just under two-thirds as compared to the 1959 diet elections.

32. In 1918 a similar attempt had foundered on the opposition of Gustav Stresemann.

33. Allemann (XVI/59), p. 284.

34. In the light of later intraparty controversies, Allemann is perfectly correct when he emphasizes that the seemingly clear Left-Right or democracy-nationalism split in the FDP was rendered more complex by a vertical pro- and anti-NATO policy split. Thus the nationalist Land organizations can be divided into those, like Hesse under August Martin Euler, which saw in the nationalist rally a means to support Adenauer's foreign policy from the extreme Right wing, and those, like North Rhine–Westphalia under the Hitler Youth leaders around Middelhauve, and Siegfried Zoglmann's party paper *Deutsche Zukunft,* which fanned nationalist resentments against the Western Allies. A similar split among the liberal-democratic parts of the FDP pitted the Berlin supporters of Adenauer's foreign policy against the southwestern FDP under the venerable Reinhold Maier, who voiced serious reservations to the unflinching West-integration course of the government. During the crucial foreign-policy debate following the 1953 election, the liberal–nationalist split largely disappeared behind the "support-for-Adenauer" and "opposition-to-Adenauer" controversy. This development made possible the staggering "coup" in North Rhine–Westphalia which saw the former Hitler Youth leaders in control of the FDP Land organization make common front with the "Marxists" of the SPD to topple the left-CDU government of Karl Arnold. See above, Chapter XVI, Section B. In Allemann (XVI/59), see pp. 283–285. Cf. below, XVII/106.

35. The "national rally" was, of course, partly an attempt by the FDP to inherit the former SRP electors who had become "politically homeless" after the outlawing of their party. All other parties, except the SPD, made more or less similar efforts, however distasteful it may have been to the purists among their members.

36. FDP (V/61), p. 10.

37. From a confidential report dated April 9, 1953.

38. "Am Telephon vorsichtig," *Der Spiegel* VII, 19 (May 6, 1953), 7. For another defense of Middelhauve's thesis of "a duty toward the 'Right,' " see excerpts from his address to the Rhein-Ruhr Club of March 4, 1953, in *Feinde der Demokratie* (Nordmark), no. 5 (June 24, 1953), p. 12.

39. How best to deal with the masses of former Nazis was of course the subject of endless debate in the early postwar years. For a good example see Schleswig-Holsteinischer Landtag (VI/188), pp. 178, 186.

40. For Rudel's denial of the alleged plot see his *Zwischen Deutschland und Argentinien* (VI/204), p. 207.

41. From testimony of one of Middelhauve's close friends, as reproduced in *Feinde der Demokratie* (Nordmark), no. 5 (June 24, 1953), p. 2.

42. Krüger in a discussion with Karl Smets. Confidential report, April 16, 1953.

43. "Am Telephon vorsichtig" (XVII/38).

44. *Ibid.*, p. 8.

45. See above, Chapter V, Section C.

46. In the spring of 1964 Sir Ivone died, age sixty-seven.

47. *I.K.B.—Information, Kommentare, Berichte.*

48. See above, text near V/63, and V/89.

49. In the middle of November, 1952, Bo Järborg, the Berlin correspondent of the influential Swedish paper *Dagens Nyheter,* reported on the rising concern of the Allies, but especially the British, over the long-observed preparations of a Nazi leadership cadre around Werner Naumann for a comeback which British counterintelligence feared might be timed to occur after the ratification of the Bonn Treaties. (*Deutsche Presse Agentur* [*dpa*], *Inf.* 2038 [November 17, 1952].) Two weeks later, Drew Middleton reported from Bonn on the resignation from the FDP's National Economic Policy Committee of its chairman Hans Ilau. Ilau quit because of a "trend toward the 'perniciousness' of reactionary nationalism" within the FDP. "These forebodings," wrote Middleton, "are shared to a considerable degree by officials of the French and British High Commissions and they are beginning to circulate among United States officials." Middleton was even able to identify the area of greatest Allied concern. "According to the same source, Achenbach maintains close political contact with a number of former officials of the National Socialist regime, including a former high official of Dr. Joseph Goebbels' Propaganda Ministry, two former Gauleiters and a former SS-*Obergruppenführer.* These men have not yet emerged to play an overt role in current politics." ("German Quits Unit Wooing Ex-Nazis," *New York Times,* November 29, 1952, p. 5, col. 1.)

50. From an unpublished analysis of German public reaction to the Naumann arrests by Paul Freedman, n.d. (but very likely February or March, 1953). See the bitter attack of Lothar Steuer in *Politischer Brief Nr. 28,* Vereinigte Rechte (VR), February–March, 1953. For the guessing game in Great Britain see *Deutsche Presse Agentur* (*dpa*), *Inf.* 105 (January 21, 1953). For some discussion of the "economic motives," see "Der Mufti lässt grüssen," *Der Spiegel,* VII, 5 (January 28, 1953), 5–6.

51. FDP (V/61), p. 1.

52. *Ibid.*

53. *Ibid.*, p. 4.

54. *Ibid.*, p. 12.

55. *Ibid.*, p. 12.

56. *Ibid.*, p. 13.

57. *Ibid.*, p. 14.

58. *Ibid.*

59. *Ibid.*

60. In 1963 Döring died suddenly at the age of forty-three.

61. See above, Chapter XIV, Sections B and C.

62. For the following account of the Lower Saxon situation in 1952-53 the author is relying heavily on an unpublished manuscript by Josef Schmidt (Hanover), August 11, 1953: Shortly before the Land party convention in the beginning of 1951, at which the Land executive board was to be elected, party headquarters sent to the Hanover district bureau sixty-three new applications for membership. This seemed curious, as membership was granted by the district organization and only reviewed by the Land headquarters. (Freie Demokratische Partei [FDP], Landesverband Niedersachsen, "Satzung," adopted November 3, 1951, par. 3, secs., 2, 4.) Made suspicious by this unusual procedure, the liberals in Hanover began to check the applicants and discovered that most had been sent by Miessner. Action on applications was delayed until after the convention. The first invasion had been successfully stopped, and the newly elected executive board contained no Stegner-Huisgen people.

63. The liberals had warned their members that continued weak attendance at business meetings and elections might lead to a sudden snap vote being won by the increasing number of former DRP members whom Miessner had been sluicing into the Hanover organization and who invariably attended in full force, came early, and voted late. The warning was heeded.

64. Miessner started his second wave of infiltration again prior to the annual party meeting. This time he did not repeat the previous year's mistake and sent his DRP friends singly, rather than in a group. But the Hanover bureau, still under the control of the liberals, screened the applicants and filed the applications of twenty-five of the forty whom Miessner had sent, pending "the clarification of the over-all situation in the FDP."

65. On the day of the election for district party officers, a truckload of young people would arrive, identify themselves as bona fide members who had been admitted by the regional office, and proceed to outvote the old, lethargic, liberal-democratic members who rarely bothered to attend these internal election meetings in strength. By the time the democrats woke up to what had happened, they found their district organization run by officers of the Stegner-Huisgen persuasion.

66. That much was certain from such evidence as the telephone tapes of a conversation of Huisgen with Naumann and of two letters of Huisgen to Kaufmann (May 20, 1952, and May 31, 1952) in which Huisgen arranged for a meeting between Kaufmann, Scheel, Stegner, and himself on May 24, 1952, at "a quiet, remote place outside Hanover," and gave the former Gauleiter details on the confidential decisions taken at a main committee meeting of the national party on May 17, 1952. In addition, the sensational intelligence report, on the basis of which the British were said to have arrested Naumann and his friends, was at that time given widest publicity. (See above, [V/12].) It asserted that Stegner was planning the formation of a National Opposition party which would comprise "the Right wing of the FDP and DP, as well as the smaller extreme Rightist groups." (See above, text at XV/35.) It is curious that Alfred Onnen, a friend of Stegner's and member of the three-man Committee of Inquiry, should try to deny that Stegner was implicated. On May 30, 1953, Onnen wrote to the liberal-

democratic Mayor of Göttingen, Hermann Föge, one of the notables of the Lower Saxon FDP, "As a member of the three-man committee and after a discussion with Chancellor Adenauer . . . I am obliged to tell you that the Chancellor has explicitly told me that the Lower Saxon FDP is to be viewed as being consolidated and that Chairman Artur Stegner and his Land organization are not implicated in the Naumann affair. On the contrary, Stegner has accomplished valuable work. This [the Chancellor said] was also the view of the British High Commissioner." In a public declaration (undated but evidently between May 30 and June 6, 1953) Onnen did not scruple to connect the shortly to be submitted report of the Committee of Inquiry with the statement that Stegner and the Lower Saxon FDP were not implicated in the Naumann affair. We know, of course, that the committee's report dealt only with the situation in North Rhine–Westphalia and did not even mention Lower Saxony, let alone cleanse it of all suspicion of complicity.

67. Stegner promptly dismissed the officers of the Hanover district organization and replaced them with a provisional commissar. The liberal officers locked their headquarters, and Stegner countered by attaching the bank account of the district treasury.

68. It was not a moment too soon, for in the beginning of August, Stegner called a district meeting in Hanover, which showed that the infiltrators, who even in the spring of 1953 had numbered no more than 89, had by now increased to 253, including practically the entire DRP district organization. This was the handiwork of Miessner and of the "commissar" whom Stegner had put in charge of the district organization two short months earlier. As the liberals had boycotted this meeting, except for a few observers who were promptly shouted down when they tried to speak, the radical nationalists and Harzburg Frontists could demonstratively consummate their conquest of one of the Lower Saxon FDP's last liberal strongholds by the election of Stegner's cat's-paw and fifth-column chief, Herwart Miessner, to the district chairmanship.

69. The report itself had been widely publicized in the form of a *Spiegel* article months before Naumann mounted his attack against the FDP ("Verschwörung wider den Geist," *Der Spiegel,* VII, 20 (May 13, 1953), 5–6. On the authorship of the report, see above, V/12.

70. British intelligence report (V/12), p. 15, par. 38. Cf. above, text at XV/35.

71. A new three-man committee of inquiry was formed to investigate, this time, the Lower Saxon party, including its books. In November, Stegner announced that he would not seek re-election at the next party convention.

72. "FDP-Führungswechsel in Hannover angekündigt," *Die Welt* (Hamburg), November 26, 1953; *Deutsche Presse Agentur* (*dpa*), *Inf.* 133 (November 27, 1953), pp. 2–3; "Neue Krise in der FDP," *Hamburg Echo,* January 14, 1954; *Deutsche Presse Agentur* (*dpa*), *Inf.* 6 (January 15, 1954), p. 3, and *Inf.* 7 (January 17, 1954), p. 2.

73. While the Liberal League received initially a great deal of sympathy from the liberals in Bonn and a change in the bylaws was contemplated to accommodate it, the FDP now took the position that the members of the

Liberal League had in effect resigned from the party when they resigned from the Land organization and that they would have to reapply to the (by now Nazified) district branch if they wanted to re-enter the FDP. Members of the Liberal League who were also deputies in the Land diet were informed that they would have to apply for readmission in their district on pain of being expelled from the parliamentary party.

74. During the chance absence of Hermann Föge, the Lower Saxon FDP's most prominent liberal and chairman of its Fraktion, Schlüter had himself elected onto the Land committee in Föge's stead. The job of that committee was the making up of the Land list, which had hitherto always been the task of the party convention. Of course, Schlüter and his friends made certain that Föge would not be placed on the ticket. (See Föge's statement in *Göttinger Tageblatt,* June 6, 1955.)

75. See above, III/56–57, IV/18, XIV/76. It may be recalled that Schlüter had entered the Land diet in 1951 under obscure circumstances which convinced many people, including the thoroughly honest Hermann Klingspor, that the ambitious Schlüter would let few scruples stand in his way, once he had determined his goals. No sooner had he reached the diet on the combined Land lists of the Deutsche Reichs–Partei and the Nationale Rechte (NR) than Schlüter abandoned the DRP-NR and joined the parliamentary party of the FDP, first as guest and subsequently as full-fledged member.

76. The importance of that committee is due to the states' exclusive legislative competency in the field of education and the historically conditioned political prime importance of the struggle over church-and-state and church-and-school issues.

77. *Frankfurter Allgemeine Zeitung,* May 28, 1955.

78. These moves can be conveniently followed in the detailed feature article in *Der Spiegel,* IX, 24 (June 15, 1955), 12–24.

79. This is all the more true as none of the cases in which Schlüter was involved could be fully clarified, the British authorities at the time having quashed most of the court procedures. A committee of inquiry which the diet appointed in June, 1955, to investigate the entire Schlüter case and which reported in February, 1956, heard expert testimony of the Minister of Justice and studied the available files on the activity of the quondam police chief. From the available evidence the committee concluded that "the image of the personality of Deputy Schlüter, as it emerges from a study of the files, must arouse most serious doubts about entrusting to him the office of Minister of Education in the Land Lower Saxony." Niedersächsischer Landtag (III/56), p. 664. This will be referred to below (XVII/110) as "Diet Report (III/56)."

80. *Feinde der Demokratie* (Lower Saxony), IV, 6 (June 1, 1955), sec. III, 1–2.

81. Berg (XI/79).

82. See above, XI/264.

83. See above, XI/73, XI/411.

84. See above, XI/174.
85. See above, XI/687.
86. See above, XI/140.
87. See above, XI/442.
88. Rainer Taeppe, *Das Ende des Fortschritts. Konservative Perspektiven* ([Göttingen:] Göttinger Verlagsanstalt, [c. 1956]).
89. Franz von Papen, *Europa was nun? Betrachtungen zur Politik der Westmächte* ([Göttingen:] Göttinger Verlagsanstalt, [1954]).
90. See above, XI/232.
91. Artur Stegner, *Die Überwindung des Kollektivismus* ([Göttingen:] Göttinger Verlagsanstalt, [1953]).
92. See above, XI/231.
93. See above, XI/219–220.
94. For some of these, see above, XI/188, XI/639, XI/641.
95. Not unnaturally, it was this more than any other aspect of the case that exercised the emotions of the dismissed university instructors. See "Der Göttinger Protest ein historisch-politisches Ereignis?" *Deutsche Hochschullehrer-Zeitung,* III, 4/6 (April–June, 1955), 9–11. That journal, under the editorship of Herbert Grabert, is the organ of the Forschungshilfe. See also Grabert's answer to a letter from the United States, "Über die Göttinger Protestaktion," *ibid.,* III, 7/12 (July–December, 1955), 18–19.
96. "Ein Feuer soll lodern" (III/56), p. 21.
97. "FDP chairman Dehler declared to our correspondent: 'I would have intervened ruthlessly, if I had had the feeling that considerable material was available against Schlüter. But until now nothing concrete has been shown me. That's why I cannot do anything against the right of the FDP parliamentary party in the Lower Saxon diet to determine who from their midst is to be a Minister. . . . If no concrete and serious objections against Schlüter are before them, the Lower Saxon FDP cannot let itself be forced to its knees by an extraparliamentary power.' " *Die Welt* (Hamburg), June 1, 1955.
98. *Deutsche Presse Agentur* (*dpa*), *Landesdienst Niedersachsen,* May 25, 1955.
99. *Ibid.,* May 27, 28, 30, June 1, 3, 1955; *Braunschweiger Zeitung,* May 27, 1955; *Hannoversche Presse,* May 28, 1955; *Norddeutsche Zeitung* (Hanover), May 31, 1955; *Nordsee Zeitung* (Bremerhaven) June 2, 1955. On the other hand, such organizations as the ultranationalist German Saar League and the Academy for Public Administration and Economics in Göttingen, as well as individual officers of the German Association of Classical Philologists and of the Lower Saxon Land organization of the German Teachers' Association congratulated Schlüter on his assumption of office. (*Cellesche Zeitung,* May 31, 1955; *Deutsche Presse Agentur* (*dpa*), June 2, 1955.) The action of the Academy for Public Administration and Economics becomes readily understandable if one remembers that its director was Karl Siegert, one of the authors of Schlüter's publishing house and one of those professors who were removed from their university position in 1945

because of their radical attachment to National Socialism. Siegert was the author in the Third Reich of a volume entitled *Jewry in the Code of Criminal Procedure* (*Das Judentum im Strafverfahrensrecht*).

100. *Deutsche Presse Agentur* (*dpa*), *Landesdienst Niedersachsen,* May 27, 1955.

101. *Goslarsche Zeitung,* June 1, 1955.

102. *Cellesche Zeitung,* May 28, 1955.

103. *Die Zeit* (Hamburg), June 2, 1955.

104. *Rheinischer Merkur* (Koblenz), June 3, 1955.

105. *Frankfurter Allgemeine Zeitung,* June 3, 1955. For a very similar view see also *Weser-Kurier* (Bremen), June 2, 1955, and P.M., "Ein erfreuliches Zeichen politischer Reife," *Vorwärts* (Cologne), VIII, 22 (June 3, 1955), 2.

106. A year later, the Adenauer attempt to harness local party organizations to his chariot was to lead to one of his most serious defeats, when the North Rhine–Westphalian FDP struck at the Chancellor by toppling the CDU government of Karl Arnold in an unprecedented coalition with the SPD. In 1955, however, the Lower Saxon DP was not the FDP, and Hellwege was no "Young Turk." See the analysis of Arnold J. Heidenheimer, "Federalism and the Party System: The Case of West Germany," *American Political Science Review,* LII, 3 (September, 1958), 809–828. Cf. above, XVII/34.

107. "Ein Feuer soll lodern" (III/56), p. 20.

108. P.M. (XVII/105). Cf. Eric A. Peschler, "Der Fall Schlüter—ein Sympton," *ibid.*

109. "Ein Feuer soll lodern" (III/56), p. 22.

110. Diet Report (III/56), pp. 667–669. The surprising and hopeful aspect of the report, which so candidly recorded Hellwege's weakness in the face of inexorable demands from Bonn, was the unanimity of the seven committee members, four of whom were members of the coalition parties.

111. Cf. the scathing article by Maria Meyer-Sevenich, SPD member of the Lower Saxon diet and member of the committee of inquiry, "Dr. Adenauers Verantwortung für den 'Fall Schlüter,'" *Vorwärts* (Cologne), February 17, 1956, p. 5. Cf. also "Das Ende eines Skandals" (XI/182), the reproduction of the oral reports by CDU Deputy Fratzscher and SPD Deputy Maria Meyer-Sevenich in submitting the committee of inquiry report to the diet, pp. 23–32.

112. The chairman of the Hamburg FDP, Willy Rademacher, insisted afterward that the FDP executive had not backed up Schlüter but had merely taken a position on the objections against Schlüter as a person. See *Deutsche Presse Agentur* (*dpa*), *Landesdienst Niedersachsen,* June 2, 1955.

113. Anonymous (Otto Schmidt-Hannover?), *Die Grosse Hetze* (III/56), p. 264.

114. This gambit had been taken up early by the ultranationalist and reactionary press. It also played a major part in the pro-Schlüter campaign of the papers friendly to the coalition partners. Thus on May 28, 1955, the *Cellesche Zeitung* wrote: "This example [i.e., a newspaper strike of the DGB]

is now being imitated, so that it is not difficult to recognize the wirepullers behind that action. One should not forget that all the professors who are now 'flaunting their indignation' have come into office within the nine-year administration period of the SPD that has just now come to a close. It is no secret that during that period in office, high positions were filled only with persons who had the correct party [membership] card. . . . The current 'spontaneous action' does not lack the embarrassing aftertaste that it is a command performance which had been arranged long ago." On May 30, 1955, the official party organ of the CDU, *Deutschland-Union-Dienst,* accused the SPD of having instigated the protest actions against Schlüter. (See *Goslarsche Zeitung,* June 1, 1955; cf. also the *Cellesche Zeitung* for that date and for June 2, 1955.)

115. The reader may recall that it had been Miessner who, together with Richter and Kniggendorf, engineered the split of the then DKP-DRP in January, 1950, and who found himself, shortly thereafter, outmaneuvered by von Thadden and by Schlüter, whose warning against Miessner's radicalism contributed substantially to Miessner's defeat in the executive board election of the new DRP. (See above, text following XIV/39.) Miessner had been able to take partial revenge in the spring of 1951 when he, by that time a ranking member of the FDP's Hanover organization, scuttled negotiations for an electoral alliance between the FDP and the Lower Saxon National Right (NR), led by Schlüter. (See above, text following XIV/79.) Now, four years later, the implacable Miessner saw his chance to cash the still outstanding balance of his revenge on Schlüter.

116. See Klingspor's letter to Dehler, June 7, 1955.

117. Letter of Klingspor to Dehler, June 28, 1955.

118. In the winter of 1952–1953, after the leaders of the outlawed SRP had agreed to use August Haussleiter's German Community (DG) as a front organization in Lower Saxony, Haussleiter sought to obtain Schnuhr's services in building local DG groups. Hugo Jungmann, a former regional leader of the SRP, cautioned Haussleiter: "Herr Schnuhr, to be sure, had not belonged to the SRP, but rather belonged to the founders of the BHE. All the same, in several meetings he spoke out for the SRP. Hence he is being regarded as a wirepuller of the SRP. This point of view of Herr Borowski [Lower Saxon Minister of Interior] does not seem to me correct, as Herr Schnuhr has not yet been able to arrive at a clear decision, and because of this he is, in wide circles, being treated very cautiously. Herr Schnuhr has further told me he wishes to watch the development of the Erbacher group and the Heinemann-Wessel Party before making a decision. Under these circumstances it is inadvisable, for the time being, to give Herr Schnuhr the mission to organize the DG in this area." (Letter of Jungmann to Haussleiter, January 11, 1953.) For "the Erbacher group" see below, XVII/139. For the Heinemann-Wessel Party, see above, VI/79.

119. Quoted in Jenke (V/85), p. 195.

120. This program is identical with those of the various interest associations of the "victims of denazification" (e.g., Bundesverband der ehemaligen Internierten und Entnazifizierungsgeschädigten, which was outlawed in April,

1959; Soziales Hilfswerk für ehemalige Zivilinternierte; Interessengemeinschaft der Entnazifizierungsgeschädigten; Arbeitsgemeinschaft der Verbände, Vereinigungen und Kameradschaften der Entnazifizierungsgeschädigten und ehemaligen Internierten) with which Wetzel was in close contact. In December, 1957, Wetzel, together with the FDP Deputy Otto Dowidat and the chairman of the Legal Committee of the Bundesverband, Peter Schell, organized a Committee for Internal Legal Pacification (Ausschuss für inneren Rechtsfrieden), to which were to belong not only the former internees and denazified persons but also all the other associations of groups that had restitution claims against the government, such as the HIAG and other veterans' associations. The committee's main function was to draft a bill which Dowidat was to introduce in the Bundestag and which would, if passed, eliminate once and for all many of the disabilities still imposed on former Nazis and compensate them for injustices or damages suffered.

121. Otto Wetzel, *Vertrauliche Mitteilungen für alle "Ehemaligen"* (Cologne: Wetzel, 1957), p. 5.

122. *Ibid.*, pp. 11–12.

123. *Ibid.*, p. 13.

124. *Ibid.*, p. 17.

125. *Ibid.*, pp. 18–19. Eight years later, prior to the federal election of 1965, Wetzel, thoroughly disillusioned by the FDP, which, he thought, had become a "party of the system," counselled the "former ones" to vote for the oppositionist National-Democratic Party. *Bulletin on German Questions* (London), XVII, 392 (October 20, 1965), 6.

126. Wetzel (XVII/121), p. 28.

127. After the 1957 election, the small nationalist splinter group which Bernhard Gericke had built up in Wolfsburg joined the FDP. The reader may remember Gericke as one of the original founders of the SRP and its first ideologist, who in October, 1950, resigned from the party in protest against what he called "the unmistakable restoration and resuscitation of nationalist and National Socialist ideology." ([XIII/39], p. 46.) Gericke proclaimed a "new socialism," and the SRP leaders promptly accused him of wishing to divest the "socialism" of the SRP of its folkish ties. After the separation, Gericke founded the National Labor Party (Nationale Arbeiter Partei). It was this group that he led into the Lower Saxon FDP.

128. For the liberal-democratic FDP organization of East Friesland (Emden), one of the last remaining strongholds of liberalism in the Lower Saxon party, the FDP Fraktion's "guest agreement" with the DRP in the autumn of 1957 and the consequent bursting of the bourgeois coalition was the last straw. Under the leadership of the most respected members of the Emden party, the liberal-democrats resigned from the FDP to form a Liberal Working Circle.

129. See above, XVI/116.

130. In the Land elections of North Rhine–Westphalia in 1962 the FDP suffered renewed defeat and slipped to an ominous 7 per cent of the popular vote.

131. To what embarrassment the FDP's remarkable hospitality vis-à-

vis the "former ones" has repeatedly led can be exemplified by a recent example; namely, the choice, in the spring of 1964, of the Federal Minister of Justice, Ewald Bucher, an important member of the FDP's Left wing, as his party's nominee for the presidency of the Federal Republic. For Bucher, whose dedication to democratic principles at that time was not in doubt, was known to have been an enthusiastic member of the Hitler Youth, where he earned its gold badge. The fact that the FDP continuously pointed out that Bucher's Nazi activities lay in the distant past and that Germany's internal health required finally an end to the constant search for skeletons in the closets of decent people could neither prevent the wide public discussion of the case nor mitigate the sour taste left by the tactlessness of proposing a presidential candidate with an active, indeed enthusiastic, Nazi past.

132. See Erich Reigrotzki, *Soziale Verflechtungen in der Bundesrepublik: Elemente der sozialen Teilnahme in Kirche, Politik, Organisationen und Freizeit* (Tübingen: Mohr (Siebeck), 1956), p. 143.

133. This development was also hastened by the proven inadequacy of the various thinly camouflaged "emergency associations" and "free electoral associations" which had gained local importance in community and other elections.

134. *Frankfurter Allgemeine Zeitung,* December 16, 1957. Among others, Asbach intended to appoint Combat SS Major Peter Fink housing administrator and hired former SS leader Gerhard Gutjahr as manager. Of twenty-one BHE district chairmen, twelve were ex-SS men, as were six members of the executive. See *Deutscher Informationsdienst,* no. 716 (January 18, 1958), p. 4. In 1964, the authorities for the prosecution of Nazi crimes at Ludwigsburg began finally to investigate Asbach's wartime activity in Poland.

135. John Dornberg, *Schizophrenic Germany* (New York: Macmillan, 1961), pp. 154–155.

136. Hanns von Krannhals, *Der Warschauer Aufstand 1944* (Frankfurt: Bernard & Graefe, 1962), p. 321.

137. This did not keep him from becoming, between 1939 and 1945, an agricultural expert for the Nazi organization for occupied territories, Reichsland.

138. From a confidential report on an interview between Körper and the deputy chairman of Natinform, February 5, 1953. Dr. Schulz was said to have contributed DM 5,000.

139. A few days later, Schulz was joined by the BHE Diet Deputies Josef Erbacher and Horst Büchler, who (together with the former SRP Deputy Franz Kewer and the two DRP representatives Hans-Heinrich Scheffer and Wilhelm Schüler) formed a new parliamentary group. In July, 1952, Schulz announced the formation of a so-called League of Germans Loyal to their Homeland (Bund heimattreuer Deutscher, BHD) as an interim solution until a great national rally movement could get started. The BHD was apparently meant as a possible later reservoir for the SRP, whose outlawry was then already predictable. Schulz, together with Remer, Dorls, Körper, Haussleiter, and von Thadden, was said to have made three separate

attempts (in Hanover, Bonn, and Heidelberg) on behalf of a National Rally Movement. (For the Heidelberg meeting of September 1–2, 1952, see above, text near XV/50.) We are told that von Thadden withdrew from these efforts at that time and that Schulz had become untrustworthy because he was suspected of driving an automobile of the Ministry for All-German Affairs and of being in its pay. (From a confidential report of a discussion with Körper, Germersheim, February 5, 1953.) The BHD's press chief was the ubiquitous former Strasser representative Bruno Fricke. (See above, VI/136.) In October, 1952, the ex-SRP Deputy Kewer lost his seat, along with all the other SRP deputies, and in the following March, Schulz and Büchler joined the DRP, only to resign again in September, 1953, after the disastrous election. Erbacher remained for a while the only parliamentary representative of the BHD. He too tried his hand at the business of inheriting the outlawed SRP. His vehicle was an "electoral association" which he had founded together with former SRP functionaries and Rudolf Aschenauer the ultra-Rightist attorney and adviser to the suffragan bishop of Munich. (See above, VII/69, XII/120, XV/65, XVI/55.) Courts ordered the prompt dissolution of the "electoral association" as a patent front organization. Erbacher continued his association with Aschenauer in the joint production of a Right-radical journal *Deutsche Blätter*. Later Erbacher joined the German Party (DP), for which he ran in the 1953 election. When that attempt failed, he joined the radicalized Lower Saxon FDP, on whose ticket he won another term in the diet in 1955. He also won a seat in the Hanover city council. (Niedersächsischer Landtag (VI/138), pp. 10–13.) Cf. also *Der Informationsdienst,* no. 124 (October 31, 1951), pp. 1–2.

140. Reinhart Holt, "Wenn die Heimatvertriebenen wüssten . . ." *Echo der Woche* (Munich), March 15, 1952, p. 4. See early data in *Das Deutsche Führerlexikon 1934/1935* (XI/40), p. 483.

141. Stuckart was present at the notorious Wannsee Conference of January, 1942, when government officials and SS chiefs discussed plans for the "final solution of the Jewish question." At that conference Stuckart's contribution was a suggestion to sterilize all "mixed breeds." He was convicted in the Wilhelmstrasse trial in April, 1949, but was prematurely released from prison for reasons of health.

142. *Feinde der Demokratie* (Nordmark), no. 2 (November 15, 1952), and no. 3 (December 8, 1952), pp. 10–11. As county chairman of the BHE, Schepmann was in 1952 promptly elected to the city council of Gifhorn. Four years later, the SA chieftain became deputy mayor, thanks to a cynical coalition agreement with the local SPD leadership. Only when Schepmann was re-elected deputy mayor in 1961, but this time with the equally opportunistic assistance of the CDU, did the self-righteous howls of anguish from the SPD lead to embarrassing headlines that forced his eventual resignation. See "SA marschiert," *Der Spiegel,* XV, 21 (May 17, 1961), pp. 30–32.

143. Cf. above, V/63, VIII/88. For Hunke's early career, see *Das Deutsche Führerlexikon 1934/1935* (XI/40), p. 207.

144. Cf. above, V/107.

145. See [Club republikanischer Publizisten,] *CrP-Information,* May 1957, p. 43.

146. To the utter consternation of many, Krumey's nine-month-long trial on charges of complicity in mass murder ended on February 3, 1965, with a virtually suspended sentence. Sentenced to five years, Krumey received credit for his years of pretrial detention. His codefendant Otto Hunsche was acquitted altogether. Cf. below, XVIII/66.

147. Oberländer also became chairman of the notorious League for the German East (Bund deutscher Osten), the ideological center for the Teutomaniacal *Drang nach Osten.*

148. In the debate of December 1, 1960, as quoted by Oberländer in a letter to *Der Spiegel,* XVIII, 5 (January 29, 1964), 19.

149. The literature on the Oberländer affair, which dragged on for years, is enormous. A thorough study of it repays the effort only from the point of view of its capacity to reveal the temper and quality of German public morality. For a brief but readily accessible English summary of the facts and devious moves in that scandal, see *Bulletin on German Questions* (London), XI, 258 (April, 1960), 11–12; 260 (May 1, 1960), 9–11; XII, 263 (June 15, 1960), 17; 264 (July 1, 1960); XIII, 308 (May 1, 1962); and Dornberg (XVII/135), pp. 130–135. For partisan Oberländer-defense literature, see above, XI/437, XI/439–440. But not all nationalists defended the Minister. He has been attacked by Right-extremists, charging him with opportunism for his democratic rhetoric. See H. B. von Grünberg, "Oberländer, der grosse Kanoniker der Demokratie," *Reichsruf* (Hanover), VII, 6 (February 8, 1958), 4. In December, 1963, Bonn's massive restoration produced a renewed ministerial scandal. Erhard's Minister of Expellees, Hans Krüger, whose intimate connection with the Nazi Party, in which he held a variety of official positions, was fully known to his party colleagues prior to his appointment, was forced to resign his post when East German propaganda disclosed that he had also been a member of one of Hitler's dreaded *Sondergerichte,* the "special courts," and trapped Krüger in self-contraditions and lies. (See "Es kam auf ihn zu," *Der Spiegel,* XVIII, 1/2 [January 8, 1964], 20; "Einfach durchhalten," *ibid.,* XVIII, 4 [January 22, 1964] 19–20; "Amtsvertrieben," *ibid.,* XVIII, 5 [January 29, 1964], 18–19.) Krüger's orientation (apart from his Nazi past) was no secret to anyone in German politics. In 1962 Herbert Böhme's radically folkish German Cultural Work in the European Spirit, which annually awards a South Tyrolian wine pitcher in recognition of extraordinary service to the cause of "folkdom," made its second award to Hans Krüger. (See above, XII/97.) Krüger, to be sure, managed both in 1962 and in 1963 to be unavoidably absent from Böhme's festivities. (See *Studien von Zeitfragen, Analysen, Berichte, Informationen zum nationalen Nonkonformismus* X, 4 [October 21, 1963], 10.)

150. S., "Oberländers Gefolgschaft," *Die Zeit* (Hamburg), May 6, 1954.

151. See *Feinde der Demokratie* (Lower Saxony), III, 7 (April–May, 1954), and *Welt der Arbeit,* quoted in *Bulletin on German Questions*

(London), XII, 263 (June 15, 1960), 17. According to these sources, the men appointed to these positions were Werner Ventzki, Georg Goldschmidt, Hans Georg Schlicker, Werner Essen, and Georg Krischker. A similar development took place on the Land level when another Bavarian BHE leader, Walter Stain, the former chief of the Sudetenland Hitler Youth, became State Minister of Labor in both CDU- and SPD-led coalition cabinets. The new Minister promptly filled all available places in his table of organization with old Nazi friends. The former editor in chief of the Silesian Nazi press, the BHE Deputy Reinhold Kolarczyk, became his press chief, and the former deputy Gauleiter, SA General Fritz Kollner, holder of the gold badge of the Nazi Party, became a ministerial division chief.

152. See Boehm (IV/7), p. 564. For the history of these groups and of their contribution to the rise of Nazism in Czechoslovakia, see also Luža (V/94), pp. 62–109. In other areas of his concern, Luža is, unfortunately, not a reliable guide. Though generally informative and balanced, he abandons all objectivity when he minimizes the officially tolerated—if not instigated—anti-German terrorism in the first few weeks after the liberation. This is, of course, not to belittle Luža's great merit in demolishing the extravagant claims and legends assiduously cultivated by Sudeten German chauvinists.

153. Boris Čelovsky, "The Transferred Sudeten Germans and their Political Activity," *Journal of Central European Affairs,* XVII, 2 (July, 1957), 134, footnote 32. Cf. Luža (V/94), pp. 63–67.

154. How well they have succeeded emerges from the fact that the 600-man Witiko League holds twelve of the thirty seats on the Sudeten German Council (Sudetendeutscher Rat), the foreign-policy body of the Regional Association, composed of ten Sudeten members of the Bundestag, ten delegates of the Regional Association, and ten co-opted members, presumably (at least symbolically) representative of the 1.9 million expelled Sudetenlanders in the Bonn Republic. For the bitter disagreements between the group around the late Rudolf Lodgman von Auen and the folkish (Witiko) group of Brehm, Brand, Hermann Hönig, and Josef Böhm that accompanied the formation of the Sudeten German Council on April 3, 1955, see *Deutscher Informationsdienst,* no. 462 (April 19, 1955), pp. 1–2. The folkish group tried to prevent it. They complained of being kept in the dark about the council's foreign policy discussions and sharply criticized Lodgman von Auen's contact to Otto von Habsburg. The former was a member of the Abendländische Akademie, a center of authoritarian, antiliberal, anti-Bolshevik, corporative, Christian conservatism which maintained close ties to Otto von Habsburg's Centro Europeo de Documentación in Madrid and Salzburg.

155. After the war, Becher entered the Bavarian legislature as a member of Haussleiter's German Community (DG), later became chairman of the parliamentary party of the BHE, executive secretary of the Sudeten German Council, and chief of the Sudeten German Press Service. Cf. above, XII/139.

156. Small wonder, in view of sentiments such as these: "As theater, press, schools, and, above all, those occupations which, like the art business,

have half commercial, half artistic character to start with, were to a great extent in the hands of men of an alien race, it is easy to understand that a general dejudaization is the first precondition for the reconstruction of Sudeten German cultural life." Quoted in *Der Spiegel,* XVIII, 44 (October 28, 1964), 60. For Becher's more recent views on the concentration-camp trials, see *ibid.* Cf. above, VIII/92; XII/139.

157. According to Institute for International Politics and Economics, ed., *Beware—German Revenge-Seekers Threaten Peace* (Prague: Orbis, 1959), Appendix 4, pp. 74–78, after the Nazi annexation of the Sudetenland, Brand became Gau manager for the Four Year Plan. But cf. Luža (V/94), p. 65, footnote 11. See above, text at V/94–95.

158. See above, VI/79, VI/209, VI/217 (and nearby text), VI/219; text at XV/36 and at XVII/20.

159. The first executive committee consisted of Walter Brand, Fritz Brehm, and Walter Zawadil. Between 1953 and 1956 Frank Seiboth, Albert Smagon, and Konstantin Höss led the league. After 1956 it has been Höss, Smagon, and Walter Becher. (Boehm [IV/7], p. 565.) On the political backgrounds of Rightist Sudeten German Regional Association and Witiko League leaders, see also Hans Jaeger, "Sudeten Irredenta," *The Wiener Library Bulletin* (London), XVII, 3 (July, 1963), 36, and Kurt Nelhiebel, *Die Henleins gestern und heute. Hintergründe und Ziele des Witikobundes* (Frankfurt: Röderberg, 1962).

160. See above, text near X/81–82.

161. See above, text near VIII/85.

162. Thus, to insure themselves of trained leadership cadres in the future, the Regional Associations have formed an Association of Expellee and Refugee German Students (Vereinigung heimatvertriebener und geflüchteter deutscher Studenten, VHDS) and, more specifically, the Sudeten German Regional Association, supports a Society of Sudeten German Students (Gesellschaft Sudetendeutscher Studenten). Such Witiko spokesmen as Franz Böhm, the former president of the Nazi Party Tribunal in the Sudetenland, Hermann Raschhofer, one of Hitler's legal experts (see above, XI/440), and the former foreign minister in Hitler's Slovak puppet government, Ferdinand Durcansky, seek to keep alive in the student group the nationalist-folkish ideals of the old Kameradschaftsbund.

163. In 1953 there were 320 expellee publications. (K.-Dieter Brodmann, "Die Presse der deutschen Heimatvertriebenen," in *Die Deutsche Presse 1954; Zeitungen und Zeitschriften* [Berlin: Duncker & Humblot, 1954], p. 606.) By 1956 the number of publications had risen to 350, including 22 weeklies, 65 biweeklies, 187 monthlies, 23 bimonthlies, and 50 quarterlies. The most important of the papers under Witiko influence in the early nineteen-fifties was Frank Seiboth's *Wegweiser für Heimatvertriebene* (Frankfurt), which in 1953 had a circulation of 120,000. Among its editors were Franz Wittek, Ernst Frank, and Gerhard Bednarski. At that time the *Volksbote* (Munich), published by Fritz Hoppe, edited by Franz Gaksch and Carl Prochaska, which featured articles by such extreme conservatives as Emil Franzel, had a readership of 70,000. Albert Smagon and Paul

Stadtler's *Ost-West Kurier* (Frankfurt) boasted a circulation of 55,000 to 60,000 (cf. *ibid.,* pp. 608 and 653), and Karl Jungschaffer and Erich Maier's *Vertriebenen Anzeiger* attracted 28,500 readers in 1953. Among "Witiko papers" must also be counted the even more blatantly nationalistic *Sudetendeutsche Zeitung* (Munich), which the Right-extremist *Deutsche National–Zeitung und Soldaten–Zeitung* took over in 1963, and a *Mitteilungs- und Informationsdienst für Vertriebenenfragen* (*MID*) under the editorship of Erich Maier. In later years Jungschaffer's *Münchner Sudeten Echo,* with a circulation of 10,000 in 1961, and Walter Becher's *Sudetendeutscher Artikeldienst* must be added to this list. To be sure, according to *Die Deutsche Presse 1961* (X/107), not only has the number of expellee papers decreased in recent years (*ibid.,* table 20, pp. 108*–109*) but their circulation has also declined. Thus the *Ost-West Kurier* was down to 49,000 and the *Volksbote* even to 28,400. The *Vertriebenen Anzeiger* had in 1961 a circulation of 25,000.

164. See above, text at VI/212; and XV/40.

165. *Süddeutsche Zeitung* (Munich), April 18, 1959, and *Welt der Arbeit* (Cologne), April 10 and 17, 1959. See above, Chapter XII, Section A/I.

166. In competition at first with the official organ of the Sudeten German Regional Association, *Sudetendeutsche Zeitung* (*SZ*), *Der Sudetendeutsche* was eventually merged with the *SZ.* At the end of 1963 *Der Sudetendeutsche* was re-established as the forum of the ultranationalist wing of the Witiko League, but this time under the aegis of the Right-extreme *Deutsche National–Zeitung und Soldaten–Zeitung* which had entered the expellee field in the previous year when it absorbed the *Schlesische Rundschau.* The political orientation of the new *Der Sudetendeutsche* is guaranteed by a staff that includes the old SdP politician and Nazi functionary Rudolf Steffen, the extremely nationalist priest Emmanuel J. Reichenberger (see above, VII/49; XI/245-250), the folkish literature professor Herbert Cysarz (see above, text near XII/151-153) and the Right-wing BHE politician Walter Stain (see above, XVII/151). (See *Studien von Zeitfragen, Analysen, Berichte und Informationen zum nationalen Nonkonformismus,* XI, 1 [January 9, 1964], 7–8.) Its circulation probably does not exceed 4,000 by far. In 1964 the *Deutsche National–Zeitung und Soldaten-Zeitung* extended its activity within the Sudeten German Regional Association by the purchase of the *Teplitz-Schönauer Anzeiger.* This massive movement of extreme Rightist forces within the Association had led its former chairman, the late SPD deputy Wenzel Jaksch, to speak of "infiltration." For Karmasin, see Luža (V/94), p. 165, footnote 35.

167. See above, Chapter XII, Section A/I.

168. Ernst Frank, a Witiko member, is the organizer of the Friends of E. G. Kolbenheyer and of folkish gymnastic organizations. In this latter capacity he has been publishing since 1950 a bimonthly journal entitled *Sudetendeutscher Turnerbrief,* which in 1960 had a circulation of 2,000. Ernst Frank also has the distinction of being the brother of Karl Hermann Frank, the former Secretary of State under the figurehead Reich Protector of

Bohemia and Moravia. As such, K. H. Frank became the undisputed boss of the occupied country, especially as he was chief of police of the protectorate and ranking SS officer, to boot. In May, 1946, Karl Hermann Frank was publicly hanged near Prague.

169. See above, Chapter XII, Section A/I.

170. See above, XVII/151.

171. "Don't we see how out of the East madness (*Tollwut*!) advances toward us? Does the world know that there [in the East] where our ancestors prayed and erected their houses of worship, a persecution of Christians has raged during the last fifteen years . . . the likes of which cannot again be found in all of history including Nero? . . . We are in the front line, the vanguard fighters to break the yoke of Bolshevist colonialism over Eastern Europe." Thus the First Speaker of the Sudeten German Regional Association, the Federal Minister for Transport, Hans-Christoph Seebohm, in Stuttgart (1958), Munich (1959), and in Bonn. "Das Mysterium," *Der Spiegel,* XV, 21 (May 17, 1961) 37.

172. Walter Brand, "Zehn Jahre Witiko-Bund, Rückblick auf die Tätigkeit und Ausblick auf die Aufgaben," in *Die Marbacher Vorträge 1958. Beiträge des Witiko-Bundes zu Fragen der Zeit* (Frankfurt: Heimreiter, [c. 1959]), VI, 219–220.

173. Brand, *Bewältigung der Vergangenheit, Bewältigung der Zukunft.* Vortrag auf der Jahrestagung des Witiko Bundes, 13. Oktober 1963, Dinkelsbühl. Erweiterte Fassung (Frankfurt: Heimreiter, [c. 1963]), pp. 7–8. In a footnote (p. 8) we are expressly told that the long and enthusiastic applause of the six hundred attending members clearly indicated their total agreement with Brand's views.

174. *Ibid.,* pp. 9–10.

175. *Ibid.,* p. 17.

176. *Ibid.,* p. 18.

177. *Ibid.,* p. 23.

178. *Ibid.,* pp. 23–29. The level of argumentation of Brand's counter-indictment is characterized by his analogy between the financial deal through which was secured the release of the captured invaders from Castro's jails and the "Jews against trucks" negotiations at the end of the war. "Why," asks Brand, "is *the German people in its totality*" being held responsible for the latter, when no one cried out against the inhuman cynicism of the former. Apart from the facts that no one has ever blamed *all* Germans for top-secret negotiations about which even Hitler was kept in the dark, and that Castro's cynical blackmail was roundly and loudly condemned in many quarters, the Witiko League appeared incapable of perceiving the moral difference between a "deal" involving captured armed insurrectionists who could legitimately have been sentenced to death by a court-martial and one involving Himmler's innocent victims whose death even the perverted Nazi law never made an attempt to justify.

179. *Ibid.*, p. 33.

180. Quoted in Jenke (V/85), p. 221.

181. In reliance on this treaty, the Witiko League and others stipulate

that any acceptable future settlement must include not only the return of the Sudeten Germans to their homeland but also the "return" of that homeland to the Reich. While there is never any suggestion in these demands of the use of force or of a reconquest, the Czechs and other Eastern neighbors or near neighbors of Germany see in them evidence of a revanchist, belligerent nationalism. For Minister Seebohm's recent espousal of the doctrine of the legality of the Munich Agreement, see above, XVII/15.

182. Jenke (V/85), p. 221.

183. "Das Mysterium" (XVII/171), p. 37.

184. See Dean Gülzow's speech reported in *Frankfurter Rundschau,* September 30, 1960.

185. "Das Mysterium" (XVII/171), pp. 36, 39.

186. Walter Heinrich, "Hat der Westen eine Idee?" in *Beiträge des Witiko Bundes zu Fragen der Zeit* (Frankfurt/Main, 1957), p. 16, quoted in Jenke (V/85), p. 222.

187. In the summer of 1963 attempts were reported to form a Working Association of National Organizations (Arbeitsgemeinschaft nationaler Verbände), that was to include such widely differing nationalist groups as the Witiko League, the All-German Party (GDP), the social-conservative DRP, the social-radical DG, the radically folkish antidemocratic German Bloc (DB) and its semi-independent youth group, Youth League Eagle. *Bulletin on German Questions* (London), XV, 338/339 (August 15, 1963), p. 8.

188. *Feinde der Demokratie* (Lower Saxony) VIII, 8 (June–July, 1959).

Chapter XVIII. State and Society in a Period of Restoration

1. Karl W. Deutsch in Roy C. Macridis and Robert E. Ward, eds., *Modern Political Systems: Europe* (Englewood Cliffs [New Jersey]: Prentice-Hall, 1963), p. 385.

2. Nemitz (X/289), p. 40.

3. Though not necessarily only the dictatorship of the party. For an excellent analysis of the alliance system underlying the Nazi regime and its changes through the years, see Schweitzer (XIV/94).

4. See the excellent study by John H. Herz, "Political Views of the West German Civil Service" (X/289).

5. Richard Hiscocks, *Democracy in Western Germany* (London: Oxford University Press, 1957), p. 204.

6. *Parlamentarisch-Politischer Pressedienst,* April 15, 1955.

7. The law provided for the recognition of pension claims of former Nazi officials except those who had been placed in denazification Group I, Major Offenders, and those former Gestapo officials who were still in office on May 1, 1945.

8. Many of the most dubious applications of the law were given wide publicity by the German Labor Union Federation (DGB) and the associa-

tions of former anti-Nazi Resistance fighters and of victims of Nazism. In the public exposure of a most dubious development, the parliamentary interpellations of the SPD and some of the more liberal dailies and weeklies played important roles.

9. See above, XI/442, 444.

10. "Küsst die Faschisten," *Der Spiegel,* X, 8 (February 22, 1956), 15–16. Cf. Max Kukil, "Es ist Zeit: Bundesrepublik werde hart!" *Vorwärts* (Cologne), February 17, 1956, p. 3.

11. For a large number of other examples, the reader might readily consult John Dornberg (XVII/135), pp. 43 ff., or better yet, *Feinde der Demokratie* (Lower Saxony), V, 6 (March–April, 1956), 20–23; VII, 9 (July, 1958), 10–21; VII, 9A (July–August, 1958), 8–10; VII, 9B (August, 1958), 2–4.

12. *Allgemeine Wochenzeitung der Juden* (Düsseldorf), July 9, 1954.

13. Quoted in Helmut Hammerschmidt and Michael Mansfeld, *Der Kurs ist falsch* (Munich: Desch, 1956), pp. 48–49.

14. "Das Unrecht der Wiedergutmachung," broadcast on November 9, 1954, reproduced *ibid.,* pp. 50–51.

15. Schaeffer's opposition to generosity in the discharge of Germany's moral debt was nothing new. As early as 1952 his intransigence in the course of the original Israeli-German reparations negotiations led to the dramatic resignation of the two German negotiators, Franz Böhm and Otto Küster, who publicly charged their government with hypocrisy. For a short but exceedingly well-informed account of the legal and technical provisions of German indemnification and reparations, see Hilberg (II/9), pp 738–759.

16. American Jewish Congress, Commission on International Affairs, *The German Dilemma: An Appraisal of Anti-Semitism, Ultra-Nationalism and Democracy in West Germany* (New York: n.p., 1959), pp. 51–52. Cf. Hendrik G. van Dam, "Reparation in the Federal Republic," in Stahl (VIII/137), pp. 287–289.

17. In fairness it must be stressed, however, that a determined effort by the Adenauer administration greatly speeded up the indemnification process from 1960 on. By December 31, 1961, decisions had been reached in 68 per cent of the 2.8 million claims, 73 per cent of them favorable to claimants. Up to that date, a total of 11.5 billion marks had been paid out. (See van Dam [XVIII/16], pp. 287–289.) Unfortunately, experts in the restitution field and interested parties, such as the Conference of Jewish Material Claims Against Germany, under Kurt Grossmann, and the American Federation of Jews from Central Europe, under Curt Silbermann, thought to have discovered in the new Erhard government a reversion to attitudes in matters of restitution characteristic of the period prior to 1960. See *Bulletin on German Questions* (London), XVI, 358/359 (June 29, 1964), 3.

18. The unpopularity, especially of the restitution agreement with Israel, was dramatically demonstrated when Adenauer's Bundestag supporters—usually remarkable for their painstaking attention to the Chancellor's every whim—balked when they received the final version of the agreement. Of the 143-man CDU Fraktion, 60 deserted their leader, as did over half of

all the coalition deputies. Had it not been for the full support of the opposition party's 125-man Fraktion, Adenauer, and with him (in this instance) Germany's slowly recovering international credit, would have been dealt a staggering setback.

19. Certain courses of studies have once again become practically preconditions for specific positions in the upper Civil Service and in the economy, and the influence on the university students of those controlling the jobs has grown correspondingly. Especially through the restored fraternity system, the old upper-bourgeois cliques of conservative academicians are again playing a disproportionate role in preventing major reforms toward a more egalitarian educational system. (See above, Chapter X, Section G.) See in this connection Karl-Heinz Diekershoff, *Der Einfluss der Beamtenverbände auf die Gestaltung des Pesonalvertretungsgesetzes vom 15.8.1955. Eine Studie zur Verbandsproblematik in der parlamentarischen Demokratie* (Diploma thesis, University of Cologne, 1961), cited in Wildenmann (II/5), p. 137, and Wildenmann's own discussion (pp. 130–150), as well as the sources cited there.

20. Von der Gablentz (XVII/3), pp. 74–75.

21. John H. Herz in Gwendolen M. Carter and John H. Herz, *Major Foreign Powers* (4th ed.; New York: Harcourt, Brace, and World, 1962), p. 436.

22. See above, Chapter VIII, Section B.

23. Carter and Herz (XVIII/21). Rudolf Wildenmann puts it even more apocalyptically: "The Federal Republic stands at the crossroads. One direction into which it could develop politically and socially is toward a quasi-authoritarian, rigid governmental structure in the disguise of a parliamentary party democracy, politically one-sided with a 'conservative' civil service, i.e., one adapted to that form of government and deeply influencing it, and an opposition to which would be conceded the role [of carrying on] 'decent,' but for participation in government 'not really adequate,' politics. The other direction which [the Federal Republic] can take is [toward] a fully developed parliamentary form of government with a well-developed opposition, in which the Civil Service, as a highly qualified consultative body with a profoundly democratic value orientation, could unfold itself." And with regard to the "quasi-authoritarian" alternative Wildenmann writes: "That such a conception could be taken seriously all the way up to Ministers of the federal government reflects in a sense the real situation." Wildenmann (II/5), pp. 149–150.

24. This still appears to be the case, despite massive evidence that a doctrinaire class-conflict view of politics in Germany is being increasingly abandoned. An opinion study in 1960 of class solidarity and party voting disclosed that fewer than 20 per cent of the sample were insisting that workers must vote for Socialist and middle-class voters for "bourgeois" parties. A majority of respondents believed that both workers and middle-class people might vote for either Socialist or "bourgeois" parties, depending on the concrete situation or issues. Indeed, over 60 per cent of middle-class respondents agreed that on principle they could not see why a "bourgeois"

should not vote for a labor party, if the conditions warranted it. (Seymour Martin Lipset, "The Changing Class Structure and Contemporary European Politics," *Daedalus,* Special Issue, Winter, 1964, p. 283.) That this evidence for "de-ideologization" or presumed "class homogenization" emerges from essentially "hypothetical" or "academic" questionnaire situations which imply nothing as to actual behavior is unfortunately all too often forgotten. Thus, in actual practice the German bourgeois voter, especially the professional, the civil servant, and the employer, in only five to ten cases out of one hundred ever finds any conditions which might warrant his support of an "unbourgeois" candidate. Cf. the sophisticated analysis of electoral fluctuations and the role of the floating vote in Germany by Erwin Faul, "Soziologie der westdeutschen Wählerschaft," in Erwin Faul, ed., *Wahlen und Wähler in Westdeutschland* (Villingen: Ring, [1960]), pp. 135–315, but especially p. 313. Faul agrees that voting switches have so far predominantly taken place among the non-Socialist parts of the electorate, but he feels that there exists "at least a certain disposition" on the part of non-Socialist voters to support the SPD. Naturally, our reference to the middle-class floating vote must not be thought to imply that its absence *alone* has prevented the SPD from seriously challenging CDU predominance. In this connection the voting behavior of the skilled workers is far more crucial.

25. In 1949 Adenauer promptly created an entirely superfluous Ministry for Bundesrat Affairs when he needed an appropriate, yet sufficiently innocuous post for DP chief Hellwege. In 1953 no sounder reasons led to the formation of a Ministry for Family Affairs. The massive creation in that year of four Ministers for Special Tasks, so called, was also not designed to enhance the prestige of the cabinet. Similar liberties with cabinet posts became standard operation when in 1955–1956 incumbents were retained even after their parties had gone into opposition and in later cabinet reshuffles when functional areas were redivided to provide additional patronage plums. The formal framework within which Adenauer's political style could in this respect unfold itself most completely was provided by Articles 64 and 65 of the Basic Law. Article 64 gives the Chancellor the exclusive right to appoint and dismiss the ministers. Article 65 deals with the Chancellor's exclusive competence in setting out the general lines of policy.

26. Adenauer's preference for executive action by experts and distrust of legislative oversight revealed themselves luminously in the course of a heated Bundestag debate when Adenauer attacked a critic of his Saar treaty with France, an FDP deputy who happened to have been a lawyer and notary With his voice quivering with rage, the imperious Chancellor shouted: "There is one thing more I want to tell you. Whoever approaches international law problems on the basis of thirty years' experience as a notary had better keep away from them!" ("Wir sind das Feigenblatt," *Der Spiegel,* IX, 11 [March 9, 1955], 14.) In what self-respecting legislature would a speaker get away with impugning the intellectual capacity of a colleague without immediate rebuke from the House? And where but in Germany would a civil lawyer be considered professionally unprepared to interpret a treaty—the specific task, presumably, of the international lawyer?

27. See Thilo Vogelsang's "Introduction" to Hermann Pünder's *Politik in der Reichskanzlei: Aufzeichnungen aus den Jahren 1929–1932,* Schriftenreihe der Vierteljahrshefte für Zeitgeschichte, no. 5 (Stuttgart: Deutsche Verlags-Anstalt, 1961.)

28. See *Frankfurter Rundschau,* April 21 and 24, 1950.

29. They formed themselves into no less reactionary organizations of their own, many of which permitted the ceremonial wearing of a sword.

30. *Frankfurter Rundschau,* September 1, 3, 4, 5, 6, 1951.

31. *Ibid.,* November 16, 17, 20, 22, 23, 24, 1951.

32. The dislike of Luther and his protégés was not limited to the old, aristocratic, conservative Foreign Office hands, but extended even to such bright young Nazis as Peter Kleist. See his *Die europäische Tragödie* (XI/533), pp. 40–42.

33. Luther was only aping his master. In 1935 Hitler had complained to Rauschning: "I told those Father Christmases that what they were up to was good enough for quiet times, when they can all go their sleepy way, but not good enough for creating a new Reich." Quoted in Paul Seabury, *The Wilhelmstrasse* (Berkeley, Los Angeles: University of California Press, 1954), pp. 30–31.

34. "Only caution and a sense of timing distinguished their approach to these 'historical tasks' [i.e., German territorial expansionism] from that of the Nazi leadership." *Ibid.,* p. 39.

35. *Ibid.,* pp. 162–163.

36. *Ibid.,* p. 163.

37. *Ibid.,* p. 103. Of the 120 officials of the "higher service" stationed in Berlin (i.e., not including the diplomats at foreign posts), at least 71 were already Party members in August, 1940. Of these 50 were pre-Nazi career officers. Of the 22 (out of 120) who were not Party members, 11 had applied for membership, but had been rejected for such varied reasons as inadequate activism, excessive arrogance, etc. Of the nine division chiefs in the Foreign Office in 1940, only one (Friedrich W. O. Gaus, chief of the legal division) was not a career official, turned Nazi.

38. *Ibid.,* p. 164.

39. *Ibid.,* p. 168.

40. For a readily available selection of these Foreign Office documents, see Poliakov and Wulf (II/39), pp. 9–168. In a foreword to this section of the book, the coauthors say: "The documents of this chapter demonstrate the extent to which even officials of the diplomatic service between 1939 and 1945 were mobilized for Hitler's war against the Jews. Of course, like in any war, the fighting enthusiasm of the individuals varied greatly. There were enthusiastic vanguard fighters like the Legation Councilors Franz Rademacher and Eberhard von Thadden in Berlin, the Legation Councilor Carltheo Zeitschel in Paris and Under Secretary of State Martin Luther. But there were also more phlegmatic battlers like Otto Abetz, Sonnleithner and Rudolf Rahn, or 'involuntary recruits' like Ambassador [Hans Georg] von Mackensen, State Secretary von Weizsäcker and Minister [Baron Konstantin] von Neurath. In one way or another everyone had a hand in it, so long as he

served in the German Foreign Service." A considerably larger selection of documents, though still only a fraction of all the documents introduced in the trial of von Weizsäcker, G. A. Steengracht von Moyland, W. Keppler, E. W. Bohle, E. Woermann, K. Ritter, O. von Erdmannsdorff, and E. Veesenmayer, can be found in *Trials of War Criminals before the Nuernberg Military Tribunals under Control Council Law No. 10* (Nuernberg: October, 1946–April, 1949), Vols. XII, XIII, XIV.

41. The role of the so-called "Peace Bureau" in Stuttgart or the Evangelical Relief Association as way stations on the comeback trail of these men proved of particular importance. See above, Chapter V, Section B.

42. The CDU members were: Erich Köhler, Eugen Gerstenmaier, Josef-Ernst Prince Fugger. Gerstenmaier and von Fugger had been members of the Kreisau Resistance Circle and were sentenced to long prison terms after the failure of the July 20 plot. The SPD members were: Hermann Brill, a Buchenwald alumnus who in 1939 was sentenced to twelve years' imprisonment; Fritz Erler, who in 1939 received ten years for illegal political activity; and Willi Birkelbach, who in 1942, after years of imprisonment, was sent to the Penal Military Unit 999.

43. "Das Wort hat der Bundestag," *Frankfurter Rundschau,* no. 244 (October 21, 1952), p. 3.

44. *Ibid.*

45. Hammerschmidt and Mansfeld (XVIII/13), p. 28.

46. *Ibid.,* p. 29.

47. *Ibid.*

48. This and the following account is taken from the essay "Deutsche Richter" in Dahrendorf (X/227), pp. 176–196, and from Walther Richter, "Die Richter der Oberlandesgerichte der Bundesrepublik: Eine berufs- und sozialstatistische Analyse," in Heinz-Dietrich Ortlieb, ed., *Hamburger Jahrbuch für Wirtschafts- und Gesellschaftspolitik* (Tübingen: Mohr (Siebeck), 1960), V, 241–259. Richter modifies the widely accepted definitions of German social strata suggested by Janowitz (X/227), counting the second highest civil-service rank (*Beamte des gehobenen Dienstes*) not among the upper middle class. This permits Richter to say (p. 259) that "the majority of judges do not derive from the *Grossbürgertum,* but from the *Mittelbürgertum* and *Kleinbürgertum.*" Janowitz does not use the category *Grossbürgertum.*

49. Dahrendorf (X/227), p. 182.

50. The public service in Germany can be viewed as the reservoir from which substantial and decisive portions of practically all elites derive. It is this sociological function of breeding elites which gave (and gives) this "estate" such an extraordinary status in state and society. Its political orientation and ethos are of crucial importance since not only half of all judges, but also roughly half of all full professors and teachers and a third of all university students, come from families of civil servants.

51. On July 10, 1957, and March 10, 1958.

52. This is the title of an English-language brochure published by the East German Government on the press conference of October 21, 1958. It

contains the opening speech of Albert Norden, member of the Politburo of the Central Committee of the SED, and excerpts from official court records illustrating the former activity of 450 judges of Hitler's People's Courts and Special Courts and of 150 former military judges who, the committee charged, were occupying important positions in the Bonn judiciary.

53. *Ibid.*, p. 8.

54. Cf. Wolfgang Koppel, ed. (for the Organizing Committee of the Document Exhibit "Ungesühnte Nazijustiz" in Karlsruhe), *Ungesühnte Nazijustiz. Hundert Urteile klagen ihre Richter an* ([Karlsruhe:] no publisher, August, 1960).

55. Poland and Czechoslovakia, which, together with Denmark, had co-operated in earlier publications of incriminating documents through the Committee for German Unity, made similar offers.

56. As a consequence of this failure, Ossip Flechtheim, of the Freie Universität Berlin, was able to assert as late as 1964 that 83 per cent of the judges on the Federal Court of Justice had been members of the Nazi Party.

57. *The Bulletin* (Bonn), July 17, 1962, p. 5 (emphasis mine).

58. To be sure, the government of Rhineland-Palatinate explained that there were hardly any serious cases in the Land and that, in any case, negotiations with incriminated officials which had taken place even before the law was passed had resulted in a number of voluntary resignations. See "Notausgang für Hitlers Richter," *Freiheit und Recht* (Düsseldorf), VIII, 7 (July, 1962), 18.

59. Ausschuss für Deutsche Einheit und Vereinigung Demokratischer Juristen Deutschlands, *Von der Reichsanwaltschaft zur Bundesanwaltschaft. Wolfgang Fränkel, neuer Generalbundesanwalt. Eine Dokumentation* (n.p., n.d.).

60. Gerd Wilcke, "Some Ex-Nazis Quit Courts on Bonn Deadline," *New York Times*, July 3, 1962.

61. "Bonn Sifts Charges on Aide's Nazi Past," *ibid.*, July 6, 1962. In December, 1964, a new and similar scandal penetrated into the newspapers. On promptings from the president of the Luxembourg parliament, the State Attorney-General of Rhineland-Palatinate, Leonhard Drach, was suddenly "discovered" to be a convicted war criminal. After the war he had been found guilty by a Luxembourg court of having sent a number of Luxembourgers to their death for minor infractions when he was prosecuting attorney of the German occupiers. Sentenced to a total of thirty-five years, Drach had been amnestied in 1954. Three years later Drach was back in the German judiciary service and was rapidly promoted. When this case came to the attention of a former SPD Minister of Rhineland-Palatinate, he charged that "there exists in the judiciary of Rhineland-Palatinate 'a shocking camaraderie with war criminals.'" Walter Schallies, "Ein Schlag ins Gesicht der Luxemburger . . . ," *Süddeutsche Zeitung* (Munich), no. 22 (January 26, 1965), p. 3.

62. "Ex-Nazi Prosecutor Is Accused by Bonn," *New York Times*, July 20, 1962. To be sure, the proceedings never went beyond the preliminary stages. In September, 1964, the superior provincial court in Karlsruhe dis-

continued them on the ground that it had no proof that Fränkel was aware at the time of the invalidity of the laws which he applied to send people to their death for minor infractions.

63. Huppenkothen was accused of having contributed substantially to the conviction of the anti-Nazi military intelligence chief Admiral Wilhelm Canaris and of his deputy, the Resistance leader General Hans Oster.

64. Thirteen former SD, Gestapo, and SS agents had been indicted for the murder of 5500 Lithuanian Jews, but only ten men went on trial. Three had committed suicide while awaiting trial.

65. See H. G. van Dam and Ralph Giordano, eds., *KZ-Verbrechen vor deutschen Gerichten* ([Frankfurt:] Europäische Verlagsanstalt, [1962]).

66. At the same time, a swelling chorus of criticism has greeted the remarkable leniency of many of the sentences German courts have imposed on Nazi criminals. This became especially embarrassing when the sentences for murder committed by the Nazis were compared with those handed down in more "conventional" murder trials. Thus, the German Coordinating Council of the Society for Christian-Jewish Cooperation pointed out "that in jury trials mass murders and crimes of violence of the National Socialist period are treated differently than other murder cases." Also, Hermann Veit, SPD opposition leader in the Land diet of Baden-Württemberg, in a widely reported speech in July, 1963, scathingly indicted German courts for their leniency in cases of Nazi crimes. Veit placed part of the blame for this unhealthy state of affairs on the "many witnesses [who] suddenly find themselves in a position where they no longer can remember anything," and partly on the state secretaries and other high officials who despite their Nazi past are back in office, and who now loudly protest that they had "known nothing about it." ("Diese Bestien," *Der Spiegel,* XVII, 30 [July 24, 1963], 26.) In his reply, the minister of justice of Baden-Württemberg, Wolfgang Haussmann, argued that the reason for the relatively low rate of life sentences (16%) lies in the very scrupulosity of German criminal procedure which appropriately distinguishes between first degree murder and accessory to murder. Most of the Nazi defendants had committed murder on higher orders and thus are considered merely accessories under German law. In addition, sixteen and more years after the perpetration of the crimes the courts are no longer able in many cases to determine whether the degree of the defendant's autonomy or of initiative which he brought to the execution of the atrocities was sufficient for a charge of first degree murder, rather than for the lesser charge of accessory to murder. These and other explanations offered by the several ministries of justice hardly sufficed to allay the widespread consternation that followed the sentencing—after a nine-month-long trial—of Hermann Krumey and Otto Hunsche, both charged with complicity in the murder of 300,000 people. On February 3, 1965, the court acquitted Hunsche and gave Krumey five years. Even that sentence was suspended in actual practice as Krumey was given "credit" for the five years he had spent in pre-trial detention.

In the course of the debate on the German handling of Nazi crimes, speakers for the CDU and the All German Party (GB/BHE) typically stressed the importance of leniency for mitigating circumstances, while vociferously denouncing the crimes. (See *The Wiener Library Bulletin* [London], XVIII, 1 [January, 1964], 1.) Altogether, by January 1, 1964, the Western Allies had convicted 5,025 Nazi defendants, 806 of whom were sentenced to death. 486 death sentences were actually carried out, the remaining 320 were commuted. All of the 320 convicts were later released, many of them long before the termination of their reduced sentences. Indeed, as early as the end of 1954, all but six of 4,539 Nazi criminals convicted by the Western Allies had been freed. Until January 1, 1964, the German judiciary had handled 12,882 cases arising from the Nazi period. Of these 5,445 trials resulted in convictions (42%), 4,033 in acquittals (31%). In 689 cases (5.5%) it never came to a trial; in 2,563 cases (20%) a trial was begun but was discontinued on orders from the court, 2,122 of them falling either under amnesty or the statute of limitations. Another 152 cases (1.5%) were not completed for other reasons. Of the 5,445 convictions, 88 (or 1.6%) resulted in death sentences or, after the abolition of capital punishment, in life terms. 5,243 of the convicted criminals (or 96%) were sentenced to varying prison terms, shorter than life. 114 convictions (or 2.4%) resulted merely in fines. See Bundesjustizministerium, *Die Verfolgung nationalsozialistischer Straftaten im Gebiet der Bundesrepublik Deutschland seit 1945* (Bonn: n.p., July, 1964).

67. Dietrich Strothmann, "Kriminelle Kriminalisten? Gestern SS-Sturmbannführer—heute Polizeidirektor," *Freiheit und Recht* (Düsseldorf), VIII, 7 (July, 1962), 14.

68. National Council of the National Front of Democratic Germany, Documentation Center of the State Archives Administration of the German Democratic Republic, *Brown Book, War and Nazi Criminals in West Germany: State, Economy, Administration, Army, Justice, Science* ([Dresden:] Zeit im Bild, [pref. 1965]). M. Oppenheimer, ed. (for the Presidium of the Association of Victims of the Nazi Regime [VVN]), *Die unbewältigte Gegenwart. Eine Dokumentation über Rolle und Einfluss ehemals führender Nationalsozialisten in der Bundesrepublik Deutschland* (Frankfurt: Vereinigung der Verfolgten des Naziregimes, [pref. June 30, 1962]). The extent of "renazification," in the sense of filling important public positions with previous Nazis, moved the political scientist Ossip Flechtheim, of the Otto Suhr Institut in Berlin, to issue a public warning: "In the meantime restoration and renazification, especially in the ministerial bureaucracy, in the police inclusive of the [Office for the] Protection of the Constitution, and in the judiciary have celebrated veritable triumphs. To give only a few examples that are possibly not even the most extreme: Of the forty-eight judges of the Federal Administrative Court, forty have been members of the NSDAP. The personnel divisions (as well as the divisions of the Federal Ministry of the Interior dealing with civil-service laws) are staffed almost exclusively with former [Nazi] Party members. The State Secretaries Globke, Vialon, Hopf and others were most eager servants of the Third Reich. The Greater German General Foertsch, who had been sentenced to twenty-five years as a war criminal, . . . has become Inspector General of the Bundeswehr. In

Aachen, Bonn, Mönchen-Gladbach, Cologne, Krefeld, Düsseldorf, Essen, Dortmund, and Gelsenkirchen the chiefs of the criminal police are exclusively former SS colonels. The director of the criminal police of North Rhine–Westphalia is also a former SS colonel." Reproduced in *Deutscher Informationsdienst,* XV, 115 (November 1, 1964), 7.

69. In actual fact, the number of out-and-out criminals with doctor's degrees and professorial titles as they appeared in the doctors' trials, in the jurists' trials, and in the Einsatzgruppen cases was considerable.

70. Hans Thieme, "Hochschullehrer klagen an," *Deutsche Universitäts-Zeitung,* VIII, 7 (April 7, 1953), 3.

71. *Ibid.,* p. 5.

72. As one letter-writer to the editor of the *New York Times* put it, ". . . for example, at the University of Cologne, a friend of mine, one of the few professors with an anti-Nazi record, is for that reason ostracized by his colleagues." Letter of Hans Koningsberger, *New York Times,* February 9, 1964, sec. 4, p. 10, col. 5.

73. From "Das Judentum in der Rechtswissenschaft," p. 66, quoted in *Dokumentation, Judenmörder und Kriegsverbrecher am Hebel der Bundesrepublik* (Berlin [East]: November, 1956). This documentation is a propaganda tract of the Committee for German Unity, an arm of the East German government. Despite the obviously self-serving purpose of the committee's efforts and the hypocritical nature of its ringing accusations, the facts presented, except for such details as dates, etc., are reliable.

74. See Seraphim's "Die geschichtlichen Lösungsversuche der Judenfrage" (Munich: 1943), also quoted *ibid.* In this connection see also Seraphim's contribution to the festivities attendant upon the official opening of the first branch (in Frankfurt) of the *Hohe Schule* for National Socialism, March 26–27, 1941. On that occasion Seraphim spoke on "the ethnographic and economic problems of a total European solution [*europäische Gesamtlösung*] of the Jewish question." See Poliakov and Wulf (V/23), pp. 141, 144.

75. "Das Ende des Parteienbundesstaates," *Juristische Wochenschrift 1934,* no. 4, p. 195, quoted in *Dokumentation* (XVIII/73), p. 22.

76. *Verfassung* (Hamburg: 1936), p. 160, quoted *ibid.*

77. *Verfassung,* p. 63, quoted *ibid.*

78. *Verfassung,* p. 60, quoted *ibid.*

79. *Bau und Gefüge des Reiches* (Hamburg: 1941), pp. 51–52, 13, quoted *ibid.* For additional English-language excerpts from the juristic-political works of E. R. Huber, see Poliakov and Wulf (V/23), pp. 340–341, and University of Colorado (XI/650), pp. 62–65, 74–77.

80. See above, XI/214–220 and nearby text.

81. Ursula Maria Martius, "Videant consules . . . ," *Deutsche Rundschau,* LXX, 11 (November, 1947), 99.

82. "Das Judentum in der Kriminalpsychology" (Berlin: 1936), pp. 61, 88, quoted in *Dokumentation* (XVIII/73), p. 25.

83. Former Nazi professors are, of course, not the only academicians who reject the moral implications of the Nazi experience. A recent case in

point was the Hamburg psychologist Peter Hofstätter, who prior to 1945 served as an army psychologist and as a forensic pathologist and between 1949 and 1956 taught at the Massachusetts Institute of Technology and at Catholic University (Washington, D.C.). In the summer of 1963 Hofstätter contended that as Hitler had declared war on the Jews and as the executioners wore uniforms as "soldiers" in this "war" of extermination, their actions could not be likened to plain murder. This quaint analogy between genocide and war and between murder squads and soldiers hardly provoked any passionate response, but eventually drew a scathing rebuttal from Count Johann Adolf Kielmansegg, the new commander of the NATO forces in Central Europe, who quite rightly saw in Hofstätter's absurdity a dastardly attack on the honor of the soldier. (See *Bulletin on German Questions* [London], XV, 340 [September 9, 1963], 12; XV, 341/342 [October 8, 1963], 15.)

While this book was in press, an apparently exhaustive series of catalogues of former Nazi professors in today's German universities came to my attention. Unfortunately its findings could not be incorporated into our account. The booklets by Rolf Seeliger, *Braune Universität,* nos. 1-4 (Munich: Seeliger, 1964-1966) give the professors' present positions, quotations from their Nazi works, and their own comments on their past.

84. On the German press, the periodical *Publizistik* (Bremen) frequently contains useful materials, as does the yearbook of the Berlin Institut für Publizistik. For critical commentaries see especially Walter Hagemann, *Dankt die Presse ab?* (Munich: Isar, 1957), and (most important for the following section) Albert Schiefer, "Die Presse der Phrasen," *Die Europäische Zeitung* (Bonn), IV, 12 (December 19, 1956), 3. See also a discussion of the reaction which that article provoked, "Die Schlacht im falchen (*sic!*) Saal" *ibid.,* V, 2 (February 20, 1957), 10. For the early years, see Henry P. Pilgert, *Press, Radio, and Film in West Germany 1945–1953* (Historical Division, Office of the Executive Secretary, Office of the U.S. High Commissioner for Germany, 1953). (In the Bibliography, below, listed under U.S. Department of State.)

85. Faced with ruinous losses in circulation, some regional papers even went so far as to permit in their local news sections a political point of view in opposition to the editorial policy represented by the rest of the paper.

86. Schiefer (XVIII/84) maintains that the postlicense press had a readership in excess of two million, while Pilgert ([XVIII/84], p. 47) counts only 1.3 million as of autumn 1951. This uncertainty in press statistics is due to the absence, until 1952, of any agency corresponding to the American Audit Bureau of Circulation. The implication of this argument is flatly contradicted by the official American position (Pilgert, p. 47) that the new postlicense publications have signally "failed to effect a large scale shift of readers from old to new papers." Pilgert sees the reason for this failure (1) in the absence of appeal of the local press for expellees, (2) in the lack of attachment to the traditional local papers of persons under thirty-five on the (erroneous) assumption that the *Heimatblatt* type of newspaper vanished after Hitler's seizure of power, (3) in the capacity of regional papers to meet

the competition by producing "local" editions, and (4) in the higher quality of the regional (i.e., licensed) press. (Pilgert, pp. 47–48.) By 1960 the 970 papers with a circulation below 20,000 had almost six million readers, or 29 per cent of the total. See *Die Deutsche Presse 1961* (X/107), p. 87*, Table 5.

87. See above, Chapter XII, Section B/I.

88. See above, XI/424.

89. In 1960, 63 of these central editorial offices serviced 758 newspapers with a combined circulation of 5 million, which represented 46 per cent of the 1,686 then existing newspapers and 24 per cent of the total circulation of 20.5 million. *Die Deutsche Presse 1961* (X/107), p. 25* (cf. also Table 13, pp. 96*–97*).

Chapter XIX: Conclusion

1. Werner Naumann, Goebbels' second-in-command, once very acutely described the NSDAP as follows: "The NSDAP was an accumulation of the most diverse forces, which were all attempting to influence the shaping of the Third Reich. Its [the NSDAP's] capacity to integrate (*Fassungsvermögen*) extended from Schacht to Ley. Idealists and opportunists, dutiful officials and convinced socialists, enterprising captains of industry and artists of marked individuality, representatives of liberalism and followers of collectivist views, were held together in it by strong leadership. The most diverse groups struggled in this party for the realization of their demands from the first day of its existence. The period of its activity was too short for the imposition of a uniform type. For that reason, also, the bracket which had held them all together broke when the leadership collapsed in 1945." "Wo stehen die ehemaligen Nationalsozialisten?" in Naumann (V/1), p. 159.

2. This was more wittily expressed by a German observer of the postwar scene: "There were Nazis, and there still are Nazis; but as long as Nazism is not an art style, one should not speak of Neo-Nazism."

3. "Das politische Doppelleben des deutschen Volkes: Die Wahrheit," *National-Zeitung* (Basel) September 5, 1947, quoted in *Deutsche Rundschau* (Stuttgart Ausgabe), LXXIII, 11 (November, 1947), 127–128.

4. See Rudolf Pechel, "Die Deutschen in Europa," *Deutsche Rundschau,* LXXV, 8 (August, 1949), 673–679.

5. See Rupert Breitling, *Die Verbände in der Bundesrepublik* (Meisenheim am Glan: Hain, 1955), pp. 97–98.

6. Of course, the Nazi regime, the war, and the postwar dislocations have greatly contributed to the weakening of the old status structures.

7. Cf. P. G. J. Pulzer, "West Germany and the Three Party System," *The Political Quarterly,* XXXIII, 2 (October–December, 1962), 414–426.

8. Seymour Martin Lipset, "Some Social Requisites of Democracy: Economic Development and Political Legitimacy," *American Political Science Review,* LIII, (March, 1959), 86.

9. Cf. Gabriel A. Almond and Sidney Verba, *The Civic Culture: Political Attitudes and Democracy in Five Nations* (Princeton [N.J.]: Princeton University Press, 1963), pp. 246 ff.

10. Juan J. Linz Storch de Grazia, *The Social Bases of West German Politics* (Ph.D. dissertation, Columbia University, 1959), p. 108.

11. These generalizations are borne out by Almond and Verba ([XIX/9], pp. 495 ff.), who suggest that in the case of Germany important deviations from the "civic culture" provide a political culture which is incongruent with a stable democratic political system. The deviations, in Almond and Verba's terminology, are an imbalance between a strongly marked "subject" orientation toward the polity and an only weakly developed participation-orientation; between very high competency in dealing with, and faith in, administrative output and very low competency and faith in political claim input; between a highly pragmatic appreciation of output and system effectiveness and a disconcerting absence of general system affect, independent of output satisfactions.

12. Lipset (XIX/8), p. 87.

13. Seymour Martin Lipset, *The First New Nation. The United States in Historical and Comparative Perspective* (New York: Basic Books, [c. 1963]), p. 238. Lipset's contention that "ascriptive, elitist values are far from dead in West Germany" is supported by Heinz Hartmann, *Authority and Organization in German Management* (Princton [N.J.]: Princeton University Press, 1959), pp. 11, 242.

14. Almond and Verba (XIX/9), pp. 152–153: "Now we discover that German feelings about the specifically political aspects of their governmental system tend to be negative, and that this negativism tends to be most marked among the educated middle and upper middle classes. In other words, it is precisely among these elements which in most democratic countries tend to support democratic processes that contemporary German democracy appears to have least support. . . . Perhaps both factors are present: a sense of discomfort over the disorderliness and lack of dignity of democratic politics, and anxiety about any kind of political involvement, based on the Nazi trauma."

15. But cf. Werner Feld, *Reunification and West German–Soviet Relations* (The Hague: Nijhoff, 1963), especially pp. 23, 177, 180.

16. Plessner (I/1).

17. F. S. C. Northrop, "European Political Experience Since World War II," in his *The Complexity of Legal and Ethical Experience: Studies in the Method of Normative Subjects* (Boston: Little, Brown, 1959), pp. 125–142. Cf. also Northrop's *European Union and United States Foreign Policy* (New York: Macmillan, 1954), Chapters VII, VIII.

APPENDIXES

NOTE:

One of the characteristics of nationalist organizations and periodicals has been their transience. Many of them vanish after a short life, only to reappear, some weeks or months later, under a different name. Hence, a considerable number of the groups and journals listed in the Appendixes were or are practically identical in personnel and sponsorship, and most of them are defunct.

Because of the frequently brief and obscure existence of extreme Rightist associations and publications, an absolutely complete catalogue cannot be ensured. The following lists do, however, include almost all the West German nationalist organizations and periodicals (outside of West Berlin and the Saarland) that had appeared prior to 1965, with four major, intentional exceptions.

From these Appendixes the following categories have been omitted: (1) The hundreds of military tradition associations and their information bulletins; (2) the scores of nationalist student fraternities and their house organs; (3) the countless more or less camouflaged nationalist (*ad hoc*) electoral associations that appear in town, county, and state elections; and (4) the innumerable mimeographed bulletins that almost all youth groups produce for their members.

For purposes of alphabetization, initial German definite articles have not been taken into account in the Appendixes.

APPENDIX A

Nationalist Parties and Organizations

I. Parties and Other Political Groups

Aktion "Die Ehemaligen"
Aktion 61
Aktion Oder-Neisse (AKON)
Aktion Wiedervereinigung (AWV)
Aktionsgemeinschaft für ein unabhängiges Deutschland (AGUD) (*See also* Deutsche Freiheits-Partei)
Aktionsgemeinschaft Nürnberg
Arbeitsgemeinschaft der Kriegsgeneration
Arbeitsgemeinschaft der Nationalen Opposition
Arbeitsgemeinschaft Deutsche Bauern
Arbeitsgemeinschaft ehemalige Schwarze Front
Arbeitsgemeinschaft für deutsche Politik (Bad Nauheim)
Arbeitsgemeinschaft für deutsche Politik (Hanover, Munich)
Arbeitsgemeinschaft [für] Nationale Politik (ANP)
Arbeitsgemeinschaft für Recht und Wirtschaft
Arbeitsgemeinschaft für unabhängige Politik
Arbeitsgemeinschaft für Wehrfragen
Arbeitsgemeinschaft Nation Europa
Arbeitsgemeinschaft Nationale Rechte
Arbeitsgemeinschaft Nationaler Gruppen (ANG)
Arbeitsgemeinschaft Nationaler Kreise (ANK)
Arbeitsgemeinschaft Nationaler Verbände
Arbeitsgemeinschaft vaterländischer Verbände
Arbeitsgemeinschaft zur Wiedererrichtung des deutschen Arbeitsdienstes
Arbeitskreis Deutschland der Europäischen Nationale
Arbeitskreis für die Vereinigung der Nationalen Parteien
Arbeitskreis für Nationale Politik
Arbeitskreis für Wiedervereinigung und Neutralität
Arbeitskreis volkstreuer Verbände
Arbeitsring "Aktion Wiedervereinigung"
Arbeitsring für Wahrheit und Gerechtigkeit
Bayerischer Bauernbund

Bayerischer Rechtsblock
Bewegung Reich
Block der Heimatvertriebenen (*See also* Kampfblock der Heimatvertriebenen)
Block der nationalen Einigung (BNE)
Block der Unabhängigen
Block der vaterländischen Einigung
Brandenburger Tor-Kreis
Bruderschaft
Bruderschaft Deutschland
Bürgerpartei
Der Bund (Katakombe Scheinwerfer)
Bund der Europäer
Bund der Europäer—Junges Europa
Bund der Frontsoldaten
Bund der Unabhängigen
Bund Deutsche Erneuerung
Bund deutscher Erneuerung (*See also* Bund für deutsche Erneuerung)
Bund deutscher Nation
Bund deutscher Solidaristen
Bund deutscher Sozialisten
Bund einiges Deutschland
Bund freier Soldaten
Bund für deutsche Einheit (und nationale Wehrfragen)
Bund für deutsche Erneuerung (BDE) (*See also* Deutsche Soziale Union)
Bund für Deutschlands Erneuerung, Deutsche Soziale Union (*See also* Deutsche Soziale Union)
Bund für Wahrheit und Recht
Bund heimattreuer Deutscher (BHD)
Bund nationaler Europäer
Bund Neue Ordnung
Christlich-Nationale Volks-Partei
Christlich-Soziale Deutschland-Partei (CDP)
Dachverband der Nationalen Sammlung
Demokratische Föderalistische Partei Europas (DFPE)
Deutsch-Arabische Gemeinschaft (DArG)
Deutsch-Arabische Gesellschaft (Weinheim)
Deutsch-Arabisches Hilfswerk
Deutsch-Nationale Front
Deutsch-Nationale Sammlung (DNS)
Deutsch-Nationale Volks-Partei (DNVP) (1949)
Deutsch-Nationale Volks-Partei (DNVP) (1962)
Deutsch-Sozialistische Partei (DSP)
Deutsche Aktionsgemeinschaft
Deutsche Arbeiter Partei
Deutsche Aufbau Partei (DAP)
Deutsche Aufbauvereinigung (DAV)

Der Deutsche Block (DB)
Deutsche demokratische Aufbau Partei
Deutsche Freiheitsbewegung
Deutsche Freiheits-Partei (Brunswick, 1953)
Deutsche Freiheits-Partei (DFP) (1962)
Deutsche Gemeinschaft (DG)
Deutsche Gruppe
Deutsche Idealisten Partei
Deutsche Konservative Partei (DKP)
Deutsche Konservative Partei—Deutsche Rechts-Partei (DKP-DRP)
Der Deutsche Kreis
Deutsche Landvolk Partei (DLP)
Deutsche Mittelpartei
Deutsche National-Partei von 1954 (DNP)
Deutsche Notgemeinschaft
Deutsche Partei Europas
Deutsche Partei für Freiheit und Recht
Deutsche Rechts-Partei (DRP) (1946)
Deutsche Rechts-Partei (DRP) (1959)
Deutsche Rechts-Partei (Konservative Vereinigung) (DRP[KV]) (*See also* Deutsche Rechts-Partei [1946])
Deutsche Reichsbewegung—Europa Nationale
Deutsche Reichs-Partei (DRP)
Deutsche Reichs-Partei—Nationale Rechte (DRP-NR)
Deutsche Sammlung
Deutsche Sammlungsbewegung
Deutsche Solidarität
Deutsche Soziale Bewegung in der Europäischen Sozialen Bewegung (DSB)
Deutsche Soziale Einigung
Deutsche Soziale Partei (DSP)
Deutsche Soziale Union (DSU) (*See also* Bund für Deutschlands Erneuerung)
Deutsche Soziale Volks-Partei (DSVP)
Deutsche Sozialistische Friedensfront
Deutsche Sozialistische Front
Deutsche Sozialistische Volks-Partei
Deutsche Staatspartei
Deutsche Unabhängigkeits Bewegung (DUB)
Deutsche Union (DU)
Deutsche Vaterländische Partei (DVP)
Deutsche völkische Gemeinschaft (DVG)
Deutsche Volksbewegung
Deutsche Volkspartei (DVP)
Deutsche Werkgemeinschaft
Deutscher Arbeitnehmer Verband (DAV)
Deutscher Bauern- und Mittelstandsbund
Deutscher Freiheitsbund

Deutscher Freiheitsorden
Deutscher Kampfverband unabhängiger Soldaten (DKUS)
Deutscher Rat zur Förderung der europäischen Gemeinschaft
Deutscher Ring für Wiedervereinigung und Neutralität
Deutscher Saarbund—Volksbund für die Wiedervereinigung Deutschlands
Deutscher Volksdienst
Deutschland-Rat (DR)
Die Dritte Front
DSU-Zentralisten
Europa-Afrika Union (Eura)
Europa Freiwillige Süd
Europa-Front
Europäische Front Deutschland
Europäische Neu-Ordnung (ENO)
Europäische Soziale Bewegung (ESB) (*See also* Deutsche Soziale Bewegung)
Europäische Verbindungsstelle (EVS)
Europäische Volksbewegung (EVB)
European Liaison Service
Freie Soziale Union
Freie Sozialisten Deutschlands (FSD)
Freie Sozialistische Partei (FSP)
Freie Sozialistische Volks-Partei (FSVP)
Freiheits-Partei
Freikorps Deutschland
Freisozialistischer Mittelstandsbund
Freunde der Erneuerung Deutschlands
Freundeskreis der nationalen Jugend
Freundeskreis vaterländischer Jugend
Friedenskorps West
Führungsring ehemaliger Soldaten (FeS)
Gemeinschaft der Kriegsgeneration (GKG)
Gemeinschaft unabhängiger Deutscher (GuD)
Gemeinschaft volkstreuer Verbände
Gesamtdeutsche Arbeitsgemeinschaft
Gesamtdeutsche National-Partei
Gesamtdeutsche Union (GU)
Graue Front, Unabhängiger Soldatenbund Deutschlands
Interessengemeinschaft Deutsche Rechts-Partei
Junge Partei
Junges Europa (JE)
Jungeuropäischer Arbeitskreis
Kampfblock der Heimatvertriebenen (*See also* Block der Heimatvertriebenen)
Kampfbund für Wahrheit und Recht
Komitée Deutscher Osten
Der Kreis, Vereinigung für Ehre und Recht

Kriegsgeneration
Kyffhäuserbund
Landwirte Partei
Leserkreis National-Zeitung
Mitteleuropäische Reichs-Union
Mittelstandsblock Oberfranken
Mittelstandspartei
Nationaldemokratische Partei (NDP)
Nationaldemokratische Partei Deutschlands (NPD) (1954)
Nationaldemokratische Partei Deutschlands (NPD) (1964)
Nationaldemokratische Reichs-Partei
Nationale Arbeiter-Partei
Nationale Arbeitsgemeinschaft
Nationale Demokratisch-Sozialistische Arbeiter Partei (NDSAP)
Nationale Deutsche Arbeiter Partei (NDAP)
Nationale Einheitspartei Deutschlands (NED)
Nationale Opposition e.V.
Nationale Partei Deutschlands (NPD)
Nationale Rechte (NR) (*See also* Deutsche Rechts-Partei)
Nationale Reichs-Partei (NRP)
Nationale Sammelbewegung (-partei)
Nationale Sammlung
Nationale Sammlungsbewegung (NSB)
Nationale Sammlungsbewegung Baden-Württemberg
Nationale Solidarität Deutschlands (NSD)
Nationale Union
Nationale Volks-Partei (NVP)
Nationale Volkspartei Deutschlands
Nationaler Arbeitskreis Köln
Nationaler Block
Nationaler Kameradschaftskreis (NKK)
Nationales Informations Bureau (Natinform)
Nationaleuropäische Deutschland Partei (Hamburg) (NEDP)
Nationalpolitisches Forum
Nationalsoziale Demokraten
Nationalsoziale europäische Bewegung
Neubürger Partei (Deutsche Rechts-Partei)
Neubürgerbund
Neue Europäische Ordnung (NEO)
Neue Partei
Neutrale-Deutsche Soziale Union (NDS-Union)
Notgemeinschaft des deutschen Volkes (NDV)
Notgemeinschaft deutscher Bauern
Notgemeinschaft Deutschlands
Notgemeinschaft reichstreuer Verbände
Ost-West Partei
Partei der guten Deutschen

Partei der Kriegsgeschädigten
Partei für Einigkeit und Recht und Freiheit
Partei für Volksselbstbestimmung
Rat zur Förderung der europäischen Gemeinschaft
Rechtssozialistische Deutsche Arbeiter Partei
Reichsblock
Reichsorden
Reichssozialistische Deutsche Arbeiter Partei (RSDAP)
Reichsverband der Soldaten (RdS)
Sammlung zur Tat (SzT)
Schleswig-Holsteinische Bauern- und Landvolkpartei
Schutzbund ehemaliger deutscher Soldaten (BdS)
Selbstbestimmungs-Partei
Soziale und Nationale Opposition (SNO)
Sozialistische Reichs-Partei (SRP)
Sozialistische Volks-Partei
Sozialorganische Ordnungsbewegung Europas (SORBE)
Sozialpolitische Gesellschaft
Stahlhelm, Bund der Frontsoldaten
Tatgemeinschaft freier Deutscher (TfD)
Traditionsgemeinschaft "Der Stahlhelm"
Unabhängige Arbeiter-Partei (UAP) (1962)
Unabhängige Deutsche Gemeinschaft (UDG)
Unabhängige Deutsche Partei (UDP)
Unabhängige Deutsche Rechts-Partei (UDRP)
Unabhängige Freiheitspartei Deutschlands (UFD)
Unabhängige Reform-Partei (URP)
Unabhängige Vereinigung Neue Politik (UVNP)
Union des Mittelstandes
Vaterländische Partei
Vaterländische Union (VU)
Verband deutscher Soldaten (VdS)
Vereinigte deutschsoziale Arbeiter-Partei
Vereinigte Rechte (VR)
Vereinigte Rechte (Nationale Rechte)
Vereinigung Deutsche Nationalversammlung (VDNV)
Vereinigung zur Überwindung parteipolitischer Gegensätze
Völkisch-soziale Bewegung (Völkisches Zentrum)
Volk gegen Krieg
    Saarbund)
Volksbund für die Wiedervereinigung Deutschlands (*See also* Deutscher
Volksfront
Volkssoziale Bewegung (Deutschlands)
Volkssozialistische Freiheits-Partei
Werkgemeinschaft der schaffenden Deutschen
Wirtschaftliche Aufbauvereinigung (WAV)
Zusammen

II. *Folkish and Folkish-Religious Organizations*

Arbeitsgemeinschaft für Lebenskunde
Arbeitskreis für völkische Gemeinschaft
Arbeitsring deutscher Gemeinschaften zur Pflege und Erneuerung von Art und Gattung (ARDG)
Artgemeinschaft
Biologisch-Weltanschauliche Ganzheitsgemeinschaft
Bund freireligiöser Gemeinden Deutschlands
Bund für deutsch-völkische Erneuerung
Bund für Glaubens- und Gewissensfreiheit
Bund für Gotterkenntnis (L)
Deutschblütiger Bund der Rächer Arabiens
Deutsche Ganzheit (*See below,* A/IV)
Deutsche Gesellschaft für Erbgesundheitspflege
Deutsche Gobineau Gesellschaft
Deutsche Tatgemeinschaft guten Willens
Deutsche Unitarier Religionsgemeinschaft
Deutscher Freidenker-Verband
Deutscher Volksbund für Geistesfreiheit
Deutschgläubige Gemeinschaft
Freundeskreis "Vergangenheit und Zukunft im gegenwärtigem Leben"
Gemeinschaft der Freyen (Goden-Orden)
Germanische Glaubensgemeinschaft (GGG)
Gesellschaft der Schillerfreunde
Gesellschaft für Deutschtum
Gesellschaft für Geistesfreiheit und Lebenskunde
Gesellschaft für Lebenskunde
Gotenbund, Grossgermanische Bewegung
Indogermanischer Schutzverband
Kampfbund für Glaubens- und Gewissensfreiheit
Ludendorff-Bewegung
Neugeistiger Kreis der Deutschen
Neu-germanisch-deutsche Bewegung Deutschlands
Nordische Glaubensgemeinde
Reichsflagge—Bund völkischer Frontkämpfer
Ring 1926
Schutz- und Trutzbund der völkischen Deutschen
Unitarische Freie Religionsgemeinschaft
Verein für freigläubige Feiergestaltung
Volksbund für Geistesfreiheit

III. *Interest Groups*

Arbeitsgemeinschaft für Verbände, Vereinigungen und Kameradschaften der Entnazifizierungsgeschädigten und ehemaligen Internierten
Arbeitskreis zur Wahrung der Interessen der ehemaligen Waffen-SS

Ausschuss für inneren Rechtsfrieden
Besatzungsgeschädigte Bayerns
Block der Kriegs- und Nachkriegsgeschädigten
Bund der Notgemeinschaft ehemaliger RAD-Angehöriger
Bund für Rechtsstaatlichkeit
Bundesverband der Entnazifizierungsgeschädigten
Deutsche Kriegsopfer-Kameradschaft
Deutscher Kriegsopfer Verband
Geschädigten Vereinigung (Hamburg)
Hessischer Interniertenverband
Hilfsgemeinschaft auf Gegenseitigkeit der Soldaten der ehemaligen Waffen-SS (HIAG)
Hilfswerk der ehemaligen Freiwilligenverbände
Hilfswerk ehemaliger Internierter und Entnazifizierungsgeschädigter
Interessengemeinschaft der Entnazifizierungsgeschädigten
Kameradschaft Hessen ehemaliger Internierter und Entnazifizierungsgeschädigter
Kameradschaftshilfe ehemaliger Internierter
Kampfbund für Freiheit und Recht
Notgemeischaft der Heimatvertriebenen und Kriegsgeschädigten (NG)
Notgemeinschaft der Währungsgeschädigten
Schutzgemeinschaft geschädigter Angehöriger ehemaliger nationaler Verbände
Soziales Hilfswerk für Zivilinternierte
Stille Hilfe
Unpolitische Interessengemeinschaft ehemaliger politischer Internierter (UIG)
Verband der Flieger- und Währungsgeschädigten
Verband der Internierten
Verband der vertriebenen Beamten aus dem Osten
Verein deutsch-empfindender Fliegergeschädigten
Vereinigung der ehemaligen Internierten und Entnazifizierungsgeschädigten
Vereinigung ehemaliger Internierter in Moosburg

IV. *"Research" Organizations and Ideological Clubs*

Arbeitsgemeinschaft zur Erforschung historischer Tatsachen
Arbeitskreis für geistige Erneuerung
Bochumer Kreis
Deutsche Ganzheit—Weltanschauung Urstoff Arbeitsgemeinschaft
Deutsches Kulturwerk Europäischen Geistes (DKEG)
Forschungsgemeinschaft der Nationalen Opposition
Gesellschaft für freie Publizistik (GfP)
Gesellschaft für soziale Forschung
Gesellschaft für Zeitgeschichte
Gesellschaft zur Förderung geschichtswissenschaftlicher Forschung

Historische Gesellschaft—Bund zur Feststellung geschichtlicher Wahrheiten
Jungeuropäischer Arbeitskreis
Komitée zum Schutz der Bürger gegen Diffamierung durch die Linkspresse
Komitée zur Wiederherstellung der geschichtlichen Wahrheit
Kulturagentur Bloch
Studiengesellschaft für staatspolitische Öffentlichkeitsarbeit
Studiengruppe zur Förderung geistiger Erkenntnisse

V. *Monarchist, Conservative, and "Anti-Communist" Organizations*

Abwehrdienst Rechts
Antikommunistische Aktion
Bund der Preussen
Counter-Cominform-Organisation (CCO)
Deutsche Antimarxistische Front
Deutsche Kaiser-Partei
Deutscher Heimatschutz (DHS)
Deutscher Kreis 1958
Internationale Demokratische Kampf-Liga (INDEKAI)
Kaiserliche Reichsbewegung
Kampfbund gegen Kommunismus
Konservative Partei
Monarchistische Partei Deutschlands (MPD)
Nachbarschaftsbewegung
Preussenbund
Stosstrupp gegen bolschewistische Zersetzung
Tradition und Leben
Traditionsbund Reich und Preussen
Volksbewegung für Kaiser und Reich
Volksbund für Frieden und Freiheit (VFF)
Volksbund für Krone und Reich
Witiko Bund

APPENDIX B

Nationalist Youth Groups

Alt-Wandervogel—deutsche Jugendschaft
Arbeitsgemeinschaft deutscher Jugend (AdJ)
Arbeitsgemeinschaft vaterländischer Jugendverbände
Arbeitskreis junger Monarchisten (AJM)
Art-Jugend
Bismarck-Jugend
Block junger Deutscher (BjD)
Der Bund
Bund der Reichspfadfinder
Bund Deutscher Afrika-Jugend
Bund Deutscher Jugend (BDJ)
Bund deutscher Jungen
Bund heimattreuer Jugend (BHJ)
Bund junger Deutscher
Bund nationaler Jugend
Bund nationaler Studenten (BNS)
Bund vaterländischer Jugend (BVJ)
Deutsche Adlerjugend
Deutsche Arbeiter Jugend
Deutsche Bündische Pfadfinderschaft
Deutsche Freiheitsjugend
Deutsche Freischar
Deutsche Jugend (DJ)
Deutsche Jugend im Verband deutscher Soldaten
Deutsche Jugendkraft (DJK)
Deutsche Jungenschaft
Deutsche Jungkameradschaft
Deutsche Jungkonservative
Deutsche Pfadfinderschaft
Deutsche Pfadfinderschaft (1950)
Deutsche Reichsjugend (DRJ)
Deutsche Reichsjugend (1955)
Deutsche Reichsjungenschaft
Deutsche Unitarier Jugend
Deutsche Zugvögel

Deutscher Bund
Deutscher Jugendbund
Deutscher Jugendbund Kyffhäuser
Deutscher Jugendbund Steuben
Deutscher Jugendsturm
Deutscher Jungsturm
Deutscher Mädchenwanderbund
Deutscher Mädelbund
Deutscher Pfadfinderbund
Deutscher Pfadfinderbund von 1911
Deutscher Schülerkreis
Deutscher Wanderbund
Deutsches Jugendkorps
Deutschgläubige Jugend
Deutschsozialistischer Jungsturm
Deutschvolkjugend
Deutsch-Wandervogel
Fahrende Gesellen
Fallschirmjäger Jugend
Fränkischer Jugendsenat
Freie Pfadfinderschaft
Freier Demokratischer Studentenbund
Freiheitlich-Deutscher Studentenbund
Gau Ferdinand von Schill
Gau Hohenstaufen
Gefährtenschaft
Gesamtdeutsche Jugend
Graue Reiter
Hanseaten Jugend
Hansische Jungenschaft
Der Horst
Jugend der Deutschen Sozialen Bewegung
Die Jugend der Soldaten
Jugendbund Adler (JBA)
Jugendbund Die Goten
Jugendkorps Scharnhorst (*See also under* Scharnhorst)
Jugendsozialwerk Hessen
Jugendverbindungsstelle Aachen
Jungdeutsche Adler
Jungdeutsche Bewegung
Jungdeutsche Freischar
Jungdeutsche Kameradschaft
Jungdeutsche Volkschaft Thule
Jungdeutschlandbund
Junge Adler
Junge Adler, Deutsche Jugendbewegung
Junge Adler 1947

Junge deutsche Freiheitsfront
Junge Deutsche Gemeinschaft
Junge Europäische Legion (JEL)
Junge Gemeinschaft
Junge Graue Front
Junge Kameradschaft
Junge Nation
Junge Nation Deutschland
Jungenschaft
Jungenschaft im Bund
Jungkameradschaft
Jungnationaler Bund
Jungstahlhelm
Jungsturm Hannover
Jungwandervogel 1956
Kameradschaft deutscher Jugend
Kameradschaft deutscher Jungen
Kameradschaftsring nationaler Jugend[verbände] (KNJ)
Kampfbund deutscher Jugend (KDJ)
Kampfbund Germania
Lübecker Jugendkorps 1912
Marine-Jugend
Nationale Deutsch-Jugend
Nationale deutsche Jugend (der DSU)
Nationale Jugend Deutschlands
Nationale Jugendgemeinschaft [Deutschlands]
Nationale Pfadfinder
Nationaler Jugendbund
Nationaler Studentenbund
Nationales Jugendkorps
Nationaljugend Deutschlands
Neue Deutsche Jungenschaft
Nordischer Mädelbund
Pfadfinderschaft Nation Europa
Reichjugend
Reichsfront
Reichsjugend
Reichsjugend—unabhängiger Jugendbund
Reichsjugendkorps
Reichsjugendkorps Scharnhorst (*See also* Jugendkorps Scharnhorst)
Reichsorden
Ring deutscher Fahrtenbünde
Ringpfadfinder
Scharnhorst—Bund deutscher Jungmannen
Schillerbund deutscher Jugend
Schiller-Jugend
Die Schwalben

Solidarische Studenten
Sozialistische Reichsjugend
Sturmvaganten
Tatgemeinschaft
Trucht
Unabhängige vaterländische Jugendverbände der Bundesrepublik Deutschland
Unitarier Jugend
Vaterländischer Jugendbund
Vertriebenen Jugend
Völkische Reichsjugend
Waldläuferbund
Wandervogel
Wiking Jugend
Wikinger
Zugvogel—deutscher Fahrtenbund

APPENDIX C

Nationalist Newspapers, Periodicals, Youth Publications, and Information Services

I. *Newspapers and Periodicals*

Alarm—im Dienste der Wahrheit und Aufklärung (Munich)
Alte Kameraden (Karlsruhe)
Die andere Seite (Hanover) (*See also under* Deutsche Blätter)
Die Anklage—Organ der entrechteten Nachkriegsgeschädigten (Bad Wörishofen, Berlin)
Argumente—Deutsche Stimme (Oberhausen)
Argumente und Dokumente (Bochum)
Aufbruch (Munich)
Der Aufmarsch (Bad Godesberg, Sieg-Kreis)
Der Ausweg (Hamburg)
Der Bauhüttenbrief (Wolfratshausen/Munich)
Beiträge zur politischen Neuordnung (Hamburg)
Blätter für organische Politik (Ulm)
Brot und Freiheit—Sozialrevolutionärer Monatsbrief (Frankfurt)
Die Bruderschaft (Hanover)
Bruderschaft Deutschland (Hamburg)
Deutsch-Nationale Zeitung
Deutsche Arbeit (Munich)
Deutsche Arbeit—Deutscher Dienst (Munich) (*See also* Deutsche Arbeit)
Der deutsche Arbeiter (Duisburg)
Deutsche Arbeiter Zeitung (Hamburg)
Der Deutsche Beobachter (Hamburg)
Das Deutsche Blatt (Rottach/Tegernsee)
Deutsche Blätter—Die andere Seite (Hanover)
Der Deutsche Dienst—Deutsche Politik (Essen) (*See also* Deutsche Arbeit—Deutscher Dienst)
Das Deutsche Echo (Lochham)
Deutsche Freiheit (Munich)
Die Deutsche Gemeinschaft—Das Kampfblatt der deutschen Freiheitsbewegung (Munich)

Deutsche Hochschullehrer-Zeitung (Tübingen)
Deutsche Monatshefte für Politik & Kultur
Deutsche Nachrichten (Hanover) (*See also under* Reichsruf)
Deutsche Nationalzeitung—unabhängige Wochenzeitung (Munich)
Deutsche National-Zeitung und Soldaten-Zeitung (Munich) (*See also under* Deutsche Soldaten-Zeitung)
Deutsche Opposition—Neue Folge der Deutschen Wacht (Cuxhaven)
Deutsche Politik
Deutsche Reichszeitung für sozialistische Politik und Reichseinheit (Bückeburg)
Der deutsche Soldat (Eichstätt)
[Die] Deutsche Soldaten-Zeitung (Munich) (*later* Deutsche Soldatenzeitung und National-Zeitung, *then* Deutsche National-Zeitung und Soldaten-Zeitung)
Deutsche Solidarität (Kiel)
Der Deutsche Sozialist (Osterrode)
Deutsche Stimme (Hamburg)
Der Deutsche Vorwärts—unabhängiges Kampfblatt (Hamburg)
Deutsche Wacht—Stimme der Sozialistischen Reichs-Partei (Oldenburg)
Der Deutsche Weg (Hanover)
Deutsche Wirklichkeit (Hamburg)
Deutsche Wochen-Zeitung (Hanover)
Das Deutsche Wort (Cologne)
Die Deutsche Zukunft (Düsseldorf)
Deutscher Anzeiger (Munich)
Deutscher Aufbruch (Munich)
Deutscher Beobachter (Hagen/Westphalia)
Deutscher Beobachter (Hamburg)
Deutscher Freiheitsorden (Bad Mergentheim)
Deutscher Ruf (Hamburg)
Deutsches Echo (Göttingen)
Der Deutschland-Brief—Kampfschrift für das Reich und die deutsche Lebensfreiheit (Berchtesgaden)
Deutschland-Echo (Frankfurt)
Die Europäische Nationale (Wiesbaden)
Europaruf—Organ der abendländischen Erneuerung (Zurich-Munich-Salzburg)
Fackel (Frankfurt?)
Das Florett (Bückeburg)
Das Flugblatt—Streitschrift für eine deutsche Politik
Der Fortschritt (Düsseldorf)
Das Forum—Mitteilungsblatt der Studiengruppe zur Förderung geistiger Erkenntnisse
Frankfurter Echo—Mitteilungen der National-Demokraten
Das Freie Deutsche Wort (Frankfurt)
Das Freie Forum (Neustadt)
Die Freie Meinung (Düsseldorf)

Freie Meinung (Villingen)
Freie Nation (Velen)
Der Freie Sozialist (Cologne)
Freies Deutschland—Die Dritte Kraft (*See also* Brot und Freiheit)
Freiheit und Ordnung (*See also under* Brot und Freiheit)
Der Freiheitsbote (Marburg/Lahn)
Freiheitsbriefe für Deutschlands Erneuerung (Wiera/Treysa)
Freiheits-Echo (Neustadt/Weinstrasse)
Der Freiwillige (Osnabrück)
Der Frontsoldat (Bonn)
Der Frontsoldat erzählt (Flensburg)
Der Führungsring ehemaliger Soldaten (Munich)
Das Fundament (Munich)
Gemeinschaft und Politik—Zeitschrift für soziale und politische Gestalt (Bad Godesberg, Bellnhausen/Gladenbach)
Der Gemeinschaftsbote (Homberg/Alsfeld)
Gesamtdeutsche Warte (Hamburg)
Das Gewissen—Freiheit und Ordnung (Ulm)
Das Imperium—Nation Europa–Nation Arabien (Bad Godesberg)
Die Information—Blätter für den politisch und wirtschaftlich Interessierten (Hanover)
Kameradschaftsbrief [der Deutschen Gemeinschaft] (Hanover)
Klüter-Blätter—Deutsche Sammlung aus europäischem Geiste (Lochham)
Der Konservative Bote (Hamburg)
Kurierdienst (Hamburg)
Kyffhäuser (Wiesbaden)
Luftwaffen Ring (Detmold)
Meilensteine (Limburg/Lahn)
Militärpolitisches Forum (Neumünster)
Monatsblätter für deutsche Politik (Cologne)
Die Nation—Die Stimme Deutschlands (Munich)
Nation Europa—Monatsschrift im Dienste der europäischen Erneuerung (Coburg)
Der Nationaldemokrat (Friedberg)
Nationale Rundschau (Karlsruhe)
Nationaler Beobachter (Hamburg)
Nationalpolitisches Forum (Neumünster) (*See also* Militärpolitisches Forum)
Neue Politik (Hamburg)
Das Neue Reich (Hanover) (*See also under* Deutsche Wochen-Zeitung)
Der Neue Ruf (Hanover, Brunswick)
Neue Weltschau (Stuttgart)
Neutrales Deutschland
Notweg—unabhängige Monatszeitschrift der ehemaligen Berufssoldaten (Detmold)
Nürnberg Ruf
Das offene Wort (Cologne)

Opposition und Ziel (Cologne)
Ost-West Kurier (Frankfurt)
Phalanx des Reiches—Blätter für Grossraumpolitik, Demographie und Ethnologie (Bad Godesberg)
Politik im Gespräch (Hamburg)
Das Reich (Bückeburg)
Reichsbote (Varel)
Reichsruf (Hanover) (*later* Deutsche Nachrichten)
Die Reichszeitung für nationale Opposition und deutsche Selbstbehauptung (Neuhaus)
Rheinisch-Westfälische Nachrichten (Düsseldorf)
Der Ring (Düsseldorf, Wuppertal)
Der Ruf (Brunswick) (*later* Der Neue Ruf)
Ruf und Echo (Nachbarschaft, Hanover)
Ruhr-Arbeiter-Zeitung (Bochum)
Saat und Ernte—Zeitung für heimatverbundene Politik, Wirtschaft und Kultur (Neustadt/Weinstrasse)
Die Sammlung (Cologne)
Scheinwerfer (Stuttgart)
Schlesische Rundschau (Munich)
Das Signal—Sprachrohr zur Sammlung der Nationalen Opposition (Hamburg)
Soldat im Volk (Cologne)
Die Sozialistische Freiheit
Der Staatsbürger—Monatsschrift der Entnazifizierungsgeschädigten, Internierten und Entrechteten (Hanover)
Der Stahlhelm (Bonn)
Die Stimme (Artgemeinschaft)
Das Suchlicht (Coburg)
Der Sudetendeutsche (Hamburg)
Teplitz-Schönauer Anzeiger (Munich)
Das Tribunal (Munich)
Vaterland (Wuppertal)
Die Vernunft (Munich)
Das Volk (Cologne)
Volkseuropa (Kehl/Rhine)
Der Weg nach vorn (Cologne)
Weg und Ziel
Wegwarte
Werkbrief
Der Widerstand (Kiel)
Wiking-Ruf (Hameln)
Wir Bauern (Dannenberg)
Zeitschrift für Geopolitik—Monatshefte für deutsches Auslandswissen (Bellnhausen)
Das Ziel (Hanover) (*later* Reichsruf, *then* Deutsche Nachrichten)
Die Zweite Reformation (Karlsruhe)

II. *Youth Publications*

Adler der Nordmark
Der Adlerführer (Memmingen)
Allzeit bereit (Assmannshausen)
Die Anderen (Munich)
Argumente der jungen Generation (Oberhausen)
Audi-Max (Bielefeld)
Der Bismärcker (Berlin)
Blätter aus St. Georg (Hamburg)
Bundschuh
Der Deutsche Ruf (Wiesbaden)
Deutscher Jugenddienst
Deutscher Studenten-Anzeiger (Hanover)
Deutschland Ruft (Hanover)
Drachenboot—Stimme der Wiking Jugend
Düssel Echo (Düsseldorf)
Die Ehrenwache (Bonn)
Erkenntnis und Tat (Hördt)
Der Fahrende Gesell
Fanal—Stimme der Wikinger (Cologne)
Die Fanfare (DJB Kyffhäuser, *later* BDJ, Essen)
Die Fanfare (Oldenburg)
Jugend in der Herausforderung
Jugendbrief
Junge Front (Berlin)
Die Junge Kameradschaft
Junger Beobachter (Assmannshausen)
Junges Forum (Hamburg)
Der Kompass (Munich)
Die Kompassnadel (Bonn)
Der Kornett
Das Lagerfeuer
Der Lotse
Mein Standpunkt (Westerstede)
Nachrichten aus der Nationalen Jugend (Brunswick)
Der Neue Aufbruch (Hanover)
Der Neue Weg
Der Nordpfeil
Die Peitsche (Bamberg)
Der Pfeil (Munich)
radikal (Wiesbaden)
Rütlischwur (Herne)
Der Scharnhorstjunge (Düsseldorf)
Schwarzer Reiter (Cuxhaven)
Das Schwert (Lochham)
Stimme der Wikinger (Cologne) (*See also* Fanal)

Student im Volk
Sturmruf (Nuremberg)
Der Trommler (Nuremberg)
Unsere Arbeit (Memmingen)
Unsere Generation
Unsere Sprache (Überdissen)
[Der] Widerhall (Lochham)
Der Wildpfad

III. *Folkish-Religious Periodicals*

Antworten an unsere Freunde (Pähl)
Deutsch-Unitarische Blätter (Cologne)
Eekboom Blätter (Hamburg)
Erbe und Verantwortung—Eugenische Rundschau
Erzieher Briefe (Stuttgart)
Forschungsfragen unserer Zeit
Freies Menschentum
Der Freireligiöse (Ludwigshafen)
Füllhorn (Stuttgart)
Die Geistesfreiheit (Mannheim)
Germanenglaube
Glaube und Tat (Worms)
Licht und Leben (Hamburg)
Licht und Weg (Mannheim)
Mensch und Mass (Pähl)
Nordische Zeitung (Düsseldorf)
Der Quell—Zeitschrift für Geistesfreiheit (Pähl)
Ring der Treue (Hamburg)
[Der] Soldat im Kampf für Wahrheit, Recht und Freiheit (Rendsburg, Hanover)
Unitarisches Mitteilungsblatt (Frankfurt)
Volkswarte (Pähl)

IV. *Monarchist-Nationalist Periodicals*

Botschaft (Frankfurt)
Kaiser und Reich (Wetter/Ruhr)
Tradition und Leben (Cologne)

V. *Information Services*

Afrika- [und] Orient-Information[en] (Bad Godesberg)
Akon-International (Aachen)
Anmerkungen—Presseinformation der Gesamtdeutschen Union (Brunswick)
anticominform press (Bad Godesberg)
Anti-Komintern Dienst (Bad Godesberg)
Arbeitsgemeinschaft deutscher Journalisten—Pressedienst

Aussprache—Mitteilungsblatt der Arbeitsgemeinschaft Nationale Politik (ANP)
Bonner Mitteilungen der Bundestagsabgeordneten der Deutschen Rechts-Partei
Bundeswehr Korrespondenz (Bonn)
Deutsche Informationen (Bonn)
Deutsche Kommentare [am Rio de la Plata] (Buenos Aires, Coburg)
Deutsche Politik—Redner- und Informationsdienst des Deutschen Block
Das Deutsche Reich (Landesverband Bayern, SRP)
Deutscher Beobachter (Northeim, DB)
Deutscher Ruf (Hamburg)
Deutscher unabhängiger Zeitungsdienst (DUZ) (Düsseldorf)
Dienst aus Hamburg (DaH)
Dokumentation der Woche (Munich)
Die Drahtschere
DRP-Informationsdienst
Druffel Verlagsmitteilungen (Leoni)
DSU-Nachrichten (Dortmund)
Europa Briefe (Ulm)
Europa Korrespondenz
Europa von Morgen—Ständedemokratischer Solidaristischer Pressedienst (Berlin)
Die Europäische Nationale (Wiesbaden)
Die europäische Sicht (Heimersheim/Ahr)
FR-Briefe
Freies Nachrichten Büro (fnb)
Freikorps Deutschland Mitteilungsblatt
Das ganze Deutschland
Gegen den Strom (Stockdorf/Starnberg)
HIAG-Informationsbrief (Munich)
Inform—Informationsdienst der Deutschen Freiheits-Partei (Hanover)
Die Information
Informationen für Kultur, Wirtschaft und Politik—Monatsschrift der Freien Sozialen Union (Hamburg)
Informations- und Pressedienst der Sammlung zur Tat (Villingen)
Informationsblätter der Europäischen Volksbewegung (Kehl/Rhine)
Informationsblatt Nordrhein-Westfalen (SRP)
Informationsblatt Württemberg-Baden (SRP)
Informationsbrief (Düsseldorf, Bonn) (Stahlhelm)
Informationsbrief der Dritten Front
Informationsbrief, Kreisverband Stade (SRP)
Informationsdienst, Bund Deutscher Jugend
Informationsdienst der Kriegsgeneration
Informationsdienst zum Afrika Problem (Munich)
Inter-Europa-Information, Deutsches Afrika-Orient Büro (Bad Godesberg)
Kommentare, Berichte, Informationen (Düsseldorf)

Kommentare zu Politik und Wirtschaft (Siegburg) (Deutschnationale Volks-Partei)
Korrespondenz der Deutschen Gemeinschaft (KdG) (Brunswick)
Kulturdienst der Gesamtdeutschen Arbeitsgemeinschaft (Hamburg)
Kurzberichte zum Zeitgeschehen (kbz) (Schwetzingen, Coburg)
Mitteilungs- und Informationsblatt für Rheinland-Pfalz (SRP)
Mitteilungsblätter—Bund der Frontsoldaten
Mitteilsungsblätter des Stuttgarter Arbeits- und Aussprachekreises für soziale Verständigung
Mitteilungsblatt der Dritten Front (Hamburg)
Natinform Informationen (Oldenburg)
Natinform Pressedienst (Oldenburg)
Niedersächsische Nachrichten—Landesverband Niedersachsen SRP
Nordische Kultur Information (Bad Godesberg)
Politische Briefe (Siegen/Westphalia)
Politischer Sonderdienst—Deutsche Gemeinschaft (Munich)
Pressedienst für undoktrinäre Politik (Hamburg)
Pressekorrespondenz der Nationaldemokratischen Partei (NDK) (Wiesbaden)
Realpolitik (Hamburg)
Der Rotstift (Munich)
Rundbriefe für deutsche Erneuerung (Frankfurt)
Scharnhorst Mitteilungen (Heidelberg)
sic (Hamburg)
Der Sprechabend—Richtlinien für die politische Monatsarbeit (Munich, DB)
SRP-Brief, Rheinland-Pfalz
Strasser Briefe (Frankfurt)
Strasser Vorschau auf Weltpolitik und Zeitgeschehen (Munich) (*See also* Vorschau)
Südoldenburger Vorposten, Kreisverband Vechta (SRP)
Unabhängiger Deutscher Zeitungsdienst
Vertrauliche Briefe der Gesellschaft zum Studium von Zeitfragen (Offenbach)
Völkischer Dienst für Volksstaat und Volkssozialismus (Hamburg)
Vorschau—Politische Korrespondenz von Otto Strasser (Frankfurt) (*See also* Strasser Vorschau)
Die Wahrheit, Schleswig-Holstein (SRP)
Weltkampf—der Antikomintern Brief (Bad Godesberg)
Wirtschaftsführer Briefe (Brunswick)
Ziel und Weg (Frankfurt)

BIBLIOGRAPHY

For reasons of practicality this Bibliography is limited exclusively to those items which are referred to in the Notes. Moreover, as no useful purpose would be served by a detailed account of the unpublished correspondence on which substantial parts of the present work are based, the Bibliography, unlike the Notes, lists merely the names of the letter writers and does not include the names of the recipients or the dates. Finally, to respect the privileged anonymity of certain sources, confidential reports are identified only by dates and subject matter.

For purposes of alphabetization, the German definite article at the beginning of a title has not been taken into account.

The Bibliography is organized according to the following scheme:

A. PRIMARY SOURCES

I. Published Sources

1. BOOKS AND BROCHURES
2. ARTICLES
   (a) *Signed Articles*
   (b) *Unsigned Articles*
3. DOCUMENTS
   (a) *Collections of Documents and Reference Works*
   (b) *Government Documents*
   (c) *Party Documents*

II. Unpublished Sources

1. BROCHURES AND ARTICLES
2. PARTY DOCUMENTS
3. CORRESPONDENCE

B. SECONDARY SOURCES

I. Published Sources

1. BOOKS AND BROCHURES
2. ARTICLES
   (a) *Signed Articles*
   (b) *Unsigned Articles*

II. Unpublished Sources

1. BOOKS AND ARTICLES
2. CONFIDENTIAL REPORTS

A. PRIMARY SOURCES

I. Published Sources

1. BOOKS AND BROCHURES

App, Austin J. *Der erschreckendste Friede der Geschichte,* Trans. by E. J. Reichenberger. Salzburg: Hellbrunn, 1950. (*History's Most Terrifying Peace.* San Antonio: Boniface Press, 1946.)

Aschenauer, Rudolf. *Landsberg: Ein dokumentarischer Bericht von deutscher Seite.* Munich: Arbeitsgemeinschaft für Recht und Wirtschaft, 1951.

———. *Um Recht und Wahrheit im Malmédy-Fall.* Nuremberg: n.pub., February, 1950.

———. *Zur Frage einer Revision der Kriegsverbrecherprozesse.* Nuremberg: [Aschenauer,] September 1, 1949.

Asenbach, W. von, *pseud.* [i.e., Johann von Leers?]. *Adolf Hitler, sein Kampf gegen die Minusseele. Eine politisch-philosophische Studie aus der Alltagsperspektive.* Buenos Aires: Editorial Prometheus, n.d.

Assmann, Kurt. *Deutsche Schicksalsjahre—Historische Bilder aus dem 2. Weltkrieg und seiner Vorgeschichte.* Wiesbaden: Brockhaus, 1950.

Augier, Marc. *Götterdämmerung: Europa 1945.* Leoni: Druffel, 1956.

Backhaus, Hugo C., *pseud.* [i.e., Herbert Grabert]. *Volk ohne Führung.* [Göttingen:] Göttinger Verlagsanstalt, [1955].

———. *Wehrkraft im Zwiespalt. Zur Psychologie des Besiegten.* [Göttingen:] Göttinger Verlagsanstalt, [c. 1952].

Bärwolf, Adalbert. *Da hilft nur beten.* Düsseldorf: Muth, 1956.

Bardèche, Maurice. *Nürnberg oder die Falschmünzer.* Wiesbaden: Priester, 1957.

———. *Die Politik der Zerstörung: Nürnberg oder Europa.* Göttingen: Plesse, 1951.

———. *Der Weg nach vorn.* Göttingen: Plesse, [1951?].

Barényi, Olga von, *pseud.* [i.e., Olga Gerstberger]. *Prager Totentanz.* Munich: Schild, 1959.

———. *Der tote Briefkasten.* Munich: Schild, 1960.

Barnes, Harry Elmer, ed. *Entlarvte Heuchelei. (Ewig Krieg um ewigen Frieden.) Revision der amerikanischen Aussenpolitik seit Franklin Delano Roosevelt.* With the collaboration of William Henry Chamberlin, William L. Neumann, Frederick R. Sanborn, and Charles C. Tansill; preface by Herbert Grabert; trans. by Marie Adelheid Princess Reuss zur Lippe. Wiesbaden: Priester, 1961. (*Perpetual War for Perpetual Peace. A Critical Examination of the Foreign Policy of Franklin Delano Roosevelt and Its Aftermath.* With the collaboration of W. H. Chamberlin, Percy L. Greaves, Jr., George A. Lundberg, George Morgenstern, W. L. Neumann, F. R. Sanborn, and C. C. Tansill. Caldwell [Idaho]: Caxton, 1953.)

Bartz, Karl. *Als der Himmel brannte: Der Weg der deutschen Luftwaffe.* Hanover: Sponholtz, 1955.

———. *Die Tragödie der deutschen Abwehr.* Salzburg: Pilgram, 1955.

Baumbach, Werner. *Zu spät? Aufstieg und Untergang der deutschen Luftwaffe.* 2d rev. ed. Munich: Pflaum, [1949].

Baur, Hans. *Ich flog Mächtige der Erde.* Kempten im Allgäu: Pröpster, 1956.

Beitl, Richard. *Wörterbuch der deutschen Volkskunde.* Stuttgart: Kröner, 1956.

Bekker, Cajus, *pseud.* [i.e., Hans-Dieter Berenbrok]. *Augen durch Nacht und Nebel. Die Radar-Story.* 2d imp. ed. [Oldenburg, Hamburg:] Stalling, [1964]. (Title of the first edition: *Radar Duell im Dunkel.*)

———. *Flucht übers Meer. Ostseedeutsches Schicksal 1945.* 2d rev., enl. ed. [Oldenburg, Hamburg:] Stalling, [1964]. (Title of the first edition: *Ostseedeutsches Schicksal 1944/45.*)

———. *Kampf und Untergang der Kriegsmarine.* Hanover: Sponholtz, [c. 1956].

———. *. . . und liebten doch das Leben. Die erregenden Abenteuer deutscher Torpedoreiter, Froschmänner und Sprengbootpiloten.* Hanover: Sponholtz, [c. 1956].

———. *Die versunkene Flotte: Deutsche Schlachtschiffe und Kreuzer, 1925–1945.* Oldenburg: Stalling, [1961].

Berg, Rudolf, *pseud.* [i.e., Dietrich Klagges]. *Angeklagter oder Ankläger?* [Göttingen:] Göttinger Verlagsanstalt, [1954].

Berka, Günther. *Gibt es eine oesterreichische Nation?* Eckartschriften, no. 7. Vienna: [Österreichische Landsmannschaft,] 1961.

Beumelburg, Werner. *Hundert Jahre sind wie ein Tag.* Oldenburg: Oldenburger Verlag, [1950].

———. *Jahre ohne Gnade: Chronik des zweiten Weltkrieges.* Oldenburg: Stalling, [c. 1952].

———. *Nur Gast auf dunkler Erde.* Oldenburg: Stalling, 1951.

Bewley, Charles. *Hermann Göring.* [Göttingen:] Göttinger Verlagsanstalt, [1954].

Bilanz des zweiten Weltkrieges: Erkenntnisse und Verpflichtungen für die Zukunft. Oldenburg: Stalling, [c. 1953].

Blunck, Hans Friedrich. *Lebensbericht.* Vol. 1: *Licht auf den Zügeln* (1953); Vol. 2: *Unwegsame Zeiten* (1952). Mannheim: Kessler, 1952–1953.

Boehm, Hermann, *Norwegen zwischen England und Deutschland.* Lippoldsberg: Klosterhaus, 1956.

Boehm, Max Hildebert. *Die deutschen Grenzlande.* Berlin: Hobbing, 1925.

———. *Das eigenständige Volk.* Göttingen: Vandenhöck & Ruprecht, 1933.

———. *Ruf der Jungen. Eine Stimme aus dem Kreise von Moeller van den Bruck.* 3d ed. Freiburg i. Br.: Urban, 1933.

Böhme, Herbert. *Bekenntnisse eines freien Mannes.* Munich: Türmer, 1960.

Borchmeyer, [Josef,] ed. *Hugenbergs Ringen in deutschen Schicksalsstunden. Tatsachen und Entscheidungen in den Verfahren zu Detmold und Düsseldorf, 1949–1950.* Detmold: Maximilian, 1951.

Borries, Kurt. *Deutschland im Kreise der europäischen Mächte.* Stuttgart: Silberburg, 1962.

Bräutigam, Otto. *Überblick über die besetzten Ostgebiete während des 2. Weltkrieges.* Mimeographed. Tübingen: Institut für Besatzungsfragen, 1954.

Brand, Walter. *Bewältigung der Vergangenheit, Bewältigung der Zukunft.* Vortrag auf der Jahrestagung des Witiko Bundes, 13. Oktober 1963, Dinkelsbühl. Erweiterte Fassung. Frankfurt: Heimreiter, [c. 1963].

Brehm, Bruno. *Am Rande des Abgrunds. Von Lenin bis Truman.* Graz: Stocker, 1950.

———. *Heimat in Böhmen.* Salzburg: Pilgram, [1951].

———. *Schatten der Macht. Ein Buch vom Gift der Welt.* Graz: Stocker, [1949].

———. *Die Throne stürzen.* Munich: Piper, [1951].

———. *Das zwölfjährige Reich.* (1) *Der Trommler* (1960), (2) *Der böhmische Gefreite* (1960), (3) *Wehe den Besiegten allen* (1961). Graz: Stocker (later, Styria), 1960–1961.

Bruder, Herbert. *Ich komme wieder. Ein deutscher Soldat erzählt.* Leoni: Druffel, [c. 1958].

Brüning, Heinrich. *Die Vereinigten Staaten und Europa. Ein Vortrag gehalten im Rhein-Ruhr-Klub, Düsseldorf.* Stuttgart: Deutsche Verlags-Anstalt, [1954].

Brunner, Heinz. *Geblieben aber ist das Volk. Ein Schicksal, für alle geschrieben.* Graz, Göttingen: Stocker, [1954?].

Buchrucker, Ernst. *Die Ehre des Soldaten. Deutsches Soldatentum in europäischer Wehrmacht?* Stollhamm: Rauschenbusch, 1953.

Burg, J. G. *Schuld und Schicksal. Europas Juden zwischen Henkern und Heuchlern.* Munich: Damm, 1962.

Burgdörfer, Friedrich. *Bevölkerungsdynamik und Bevölkerungsbilanz.* Munich: Lehmann, 1951.

Burri, Franz. *Deutsches Südtirol. Selbstbestimmung—Autonomie—Rückgliederung.* Lindau: Palm-Schriften, [1961].

Busch, Fritz Otto. *Das Geheimnis der "Bismarck."* Hanover: Sponholtz, [1950].

———. *Tragödie am Nordkap. Der Untergang des Schlachtschiffes "Scharnhorst."* Hanover: Sponholtz, [1952].

Busch, Harald. *So war der U-Boot Krieg.* Bielefeld: Deutsche Heimat, 1952.

Clauss, Max Walter. *Der Weg nach Jalta. Präsident Roosevelts Verantwortung.* Heidelberg: Vowinckel, 1952.

Crocker, George N. *Schrittmacher der Sowjets. Das Schicksal der Welt lag in Roosevelts Hand.* Trans. by Dietrich Niebuhr. Tübingen: Schlichtenmayer, [1960]. (*Roosevelt's Road to Russia.* Chicago: Regnery, 1959.)

D'Argile, René, Jacques Ploncard d'Assac, *et al.*, eds. *Das Geheimnis um die Ursachen des 2. Weltkrieges.* Wiesbaden: Priester, 1958.

Dauthage, Heinrich, *pseud. Brennendes Land—Land am Brenner.* Vienna: Typographische Anstalt, 1961.

Degrelle, Léon. *Die verlorene Legion.* Göttingen: Plesse, 1952.

Dethleffsen, Erich, and Karl Heinrich Helfer. *Soldatische Existenz morgen.* Bonn: Schimmelbusch, 1953.

Der deutsche Soldat in der Armee von morgen. Wehrverfassung, Wehrsystem, Inneres Gefüge. Munich: Isar, 1954.

Diels, Rudolf. *Der Fall Otto John. Hintergründe und Lehren.* [Göttingen:] Göttinger Verlagsanstalt, [1954].

Dietl, Gerda-Louise, and Kurt Herrmann, eds. *General [Eduard] Dietl. Das Leben eines Soldaten.* Rev. by Max Dingler. Munich: Münchner Buchverlag, [1951].

Dörfler, Peter. *Apollonia Trilogie. Roman eines Geschlechts.* (I) *Die Lampe der törichten Jungfrau.* (II) *Apollonias Sommer.* (III) *Um das kommende Geschlecht.* Hamm: Grote, 1952.

Dokumente zum 2. Weltkrieg: Alliierte Kriegsverbrechen und Verbrechen gegen die Menschlichkeit. Buenos Aires: Dürer, 1954.

Domizlaff, Hans. *Es geht um Deutschland.* Hamburg: Dulk, 1952.

Dornberger, Walter. *V-2: Der Schuss ins Weltall. Geschichte einer grossen Erfindung.* Esslingen: Bechtle, [c. 1958].

Drascher, Wahrhold. *Schuld der Weissen?* Tübingen: Schlichtenmayer, 1960.

———. *Die Vorherrschaft der weissen Rasse.* Stuttgart: Deutsche Verlags-Anstalt, 1936.

Dwinger, Edwin Erich. *Es geschah im Jahre 1965.* Salzburg: Pilgram, 1957.

———. *General Wlassow. Eine Tragödie unserer Zeit.* Freiburg i. Br.: Dikreiter, [1951].

———. *Die verlorenen Söhne: Eine Odyssee unserer Zeit.* Salzburg: Pilgram, 1956.

———. *Wenn die Dämme brechen. . . .* Frankfurt-Überlingen: Dikreiter, 1950.

———. *Zwischen Weiss und Rot. Die russische Tragödie 1919–1920.* Jena: Diederich, 1930.

Ehrhardt, Arthur. *Der Junker und der deutsche Traum: Die Wiedergründung des Reiches durch Otto von Bismarck.* Leoni: Druffel, 1959.

Ehrich, Emil. *Die Auslandsorganisation der NSDAP.* Schriften der Deutschen Hochschule für Politik, II. Der organisatorische Aufbau des Dritten Reiches, no. 13. Berlin: Junker und Dünnhaupt, 1937.

Eich, Hermann. *Die unheimlichen Deutschen.* Düsseldorf: Econ, 1963. (*The Unloved Germans.* Trans. by Michael Glenny. New York: Stein and Day, [c. 1965].)

Eichler, Richard W. *Der gesteuerte Kunstverfall. Ein Prozess mit 129 Bildbeweisen.* Munich: Lehmann, [1965].

———. *Können, Künstler, Scharlatane*. 2d enl. ed. Munich: Lehmann, [1960].

Eisen, Heinrich. *Bahnhof Russkinaja meldet sich nicht*. Darmstadt: Röhrig, 1955.

———. *Der Schienenwolf*. Darmstadt: Röhrig, 1956.

———. *Die verlorene Kompanie*. Freiburg: Dikreiter, 1953.

Emsen, Kurt van, *pseud.* [i.e., Karl Strünkmann]. *Adolf Hitler und die Kommenden*. Leipzig: Lindner, 1932.

Engdahl, Per. *Vasterlandets förnyelse* (The Defense of the West). Malmö: Bok och Tidskrift, 1951. 2 vols.

Erfurth, Waldemar. *Der finnische Krieg 1941–1944*. Wiesbaden: Limes, 1950.

———. *Die Geschichte des deutschen Generalstabes von 1918–1945*. 2d ed. Göttingen: Musterschmidt, 1960 [c. 1957].

Ernst, Paul. *Der Zusammenbruch des deutschen Idealismus*. Munich: Müller, 1918.

———. *Der Zusammenbruch des Marxismus*. Munich: Müller, 1919.

Ernst, Robert. *Rechenschaftsbericht eines Elsässers*. 2d ed. Berlin: Bernard & Graefe, [1954].

Ernsthausen, Adolf von. *Wende im Kaukasus*. Landser am Feind, no. 2. Heidelberg: Vowinckel, 1958.

———. *Die Wölfe der Lika*. Landser am Feind, no. 5. Heidelberg: Vowinckel, 1959.

Esche, Harold. *Die Ausplünderung des deutschen Ostens*. Rosenheim: Inngau, Lang, n.d.

Esteban-Infantes, Emilio. *Blaue Division: Spaniens Freiwillige an der Ostfront*. Trans. by Werner Haupt. Leoni: Druffel, [1958].

Ettighofer, Paul C. *44 Tage und Nächte. Der Westfeldzug 1940*. Stuttgart: Veritas, 1953.

Euringer, Richard. *Die Sargbreite Leben. Wir sind Internierte*. [Hamm:] Grote, [c. 1952].

Falkenbach, F. H., *pseud.* [i.e., Friedrich Heiss], ed. *Mitten durch unser Herz*. Munich: Andermann, 1956.

Fechter, Paul. *Geschichte der deutschen Literatur*. Gütersloh: Bertelsmann, 1952.

Feder, Gottfried. *Der deutsche Staat*. 3d ed. Munich: Deutschvölkische Verlagsbuchhandlung, 1924.

Fernau, Joachim. *Deutschland, Deutschland über alles. . . . Von Arminius bis Adenauer*. Oldenburg: Stalling, 1952.

Feurstein, Valentin. *Irrwege der Pflicht 1938–1945*. Munich, Wels: Welsermühl, 1964.

Flex, Walter. *Der Wanderer zwischen beiden Welten*. Munich: Beck, [1938?].

Frank, Ernst. *Heimat ohne Vaterland*. Frankfurt: Heimreiter, [c. 1958].

———. *Leidenschaftliches Egerland*. 5th ed. Frankfurt: Heimreiter, 1954.

Frank, Hermann. *Landser, Karst und Skipetaren: Bandenkämpfe in Albanien*. Heidelberg: Vowinckel, 1957.

Frank Wolfgang. *Die Wölfe und der Admiral. Triumph und Tragik der U-Boote.* Oldenburg: Stalling, 1953.

———, and Bernhard Rogge. *Schiff 16: Die Kaperfahrt des Schweren Hilfskreuzers "Atlantis" in den sieben Weltmeeren.* Oldenburg: Stalling, 1955.

Fraschka, Günter. *Aufstand in Warschau: General Bor kämpft für die Freiheit seines Volkes. 1. August 1944.* Rastatt/Baden: Pabel, 1960.

———. *Fertigmachen zum Erschiessen: Zwischen Willkür und Gewissen. 8 Kriegsgerichtsfälle.* Rastatt/Baden: Pabel, 1959.

———. *Gnade für Paris: Frankreichs Hauptstadt zwischen den Fronten.* Rastatt/Baden: Pabel, 1959.

———. *Das letzte Aufgebot: Vom Sterben der deutschen Jugend.* Rastatt/Baden: Pabel, 1960.

———. *. . . mit Schwertern und Brillianten: Aus dem Leben der 27 Träger der höchsten deutschen Tapferkeitsauszeichnung.* Rastatt/Baden: Pabel, 1958.

———. *Prag, die blutige Stadt. Der Aufstand vom 5. Mai 1945.* Rastatt/Baden: Pabel, 1960.

———. *20. Juli 1944. Ein Bericht.* [Rastatt/Baden:] Pabel, [c. 1961].

Fried, Ferdinand, *pseud.* [i.e., Ferdinand Friedrich Zimmermann]. *Das Abenteuer des Abendlandes.* [Düsseldorf, Cologne:] Diederich, [c. 1950].

———. *Der Aufstieg der Juden.* Goslar: Blut und Boden, [c. 1937].

———. *Die soziale Revolution: Verwandlung von Wirtschaft und Gesellschaft.* Leipzig: Goldmann, [c. 1942].

———. *Der Umsturz der Gesellschaft.* Stuttgart: Deutsche Verlags-Anstalt, [1950].

Friessner, Hans. *Verratene Schlachten.* Hamburg: Holsten, [1956].

Frisch, Sepp. *Die Saar bleibt deutsch. Zur Heimkehr der Saar. Ein Rückblick 1680–1955.* Leoni: Druffel, 1956.

Fritzsche, Hans. *Es sprach Hans Fritzsche.* Nuremberg: Thiele, [1949].

Geouffre de la Pradelle, Raymond de, Jean de Pange, *et al. Verjagt—beraubt—erschlagen. Die Austreibung aus den alten deutschen Grenzmarken. Schicksal und Völkerrecht.* Wiesbaden: Priester, [c. 1961].

Gheorghe, Jon. *Automatic Arrest.* Leoni: Druffel, 1956.

Glasebock, Willy. *War Deutschland am 2. Weltkrieg allein schuld?* [Niederpleis/Siegburg:] Ring, 1963.

Grabert, Herbert. *Hochschullehrer klagen an. Von der Demontage deutscher Wissenschaft.* 2d enl. ed. [Göttingen:] Göttinger Verlagsanstalt, [1953, c. 1952].

———. *Krise und Aufgabe des völkischen Glaubens.* Berlin: Nordischer Verlag, 1937.

———. *Der protestantische Auftrag des deutschen Volkes.* Stuttgart: Gutbrod, 1936.

———. *Die völkische Aufgabe der Religionswissenschaft.* Stuttgart, Berlin: Truckenmüller, 1938.

———, *et al.*, eds. *Friedrich Grimm: Ein Leben für das Recht. Tatsachen und Dokumente zur Erinnerung an das Wirken eines grossen Anwalts und Patrioten.* Tübingen: Deutsche Hochschullehrer-Zeitung, 1961.

Graff, Sigmund. *Goethe vor der Spruchkammer oder Der Herr Geheimrat verteidigt sich.* Göttingen: Plesse, 1951.

———. *Von S.M. zu N.S. Erinnerungen eines Bühnenautors (1900–1945).* Munich, Wels: Welsermühl, [c. 1963].

Greil, Lothar. *Die Lüge von Marzobotto.* Munich: Schild, 1959.

———. *Die Wahrheit über Malmédy.* Munich: Schild, 1958.

Greiner, Helmut. *Die oberste Wehrmachtsführung 1939–1945.* Wiesbaden: Limes, 1952.

Grenfell, Russell. *Bedingungsloser Hass? Die deutsche Kriegsschuld und Europas Zukunft.* Trans. by Egon Heymann. Tübingen: Schlichtenmayer, 1954. (*Unconditional Hatred. German War Guilt and the Future of Europe.* 1st world ed., 3d printing. New York: Devin-Adair, 1954.)

Griesmayr, Gottfried. *Bolschewistische Weltrevolution—Gespenst oder Wirklichkeit?* Politikum Reihe, no. 9. Stuttgart: Fink, 1962. (Republished in 1964 under the title *Weltrevolution und deutsche Frage.*)

———. *Ist Wiedervereinigung überhaupt noch möglich?* Stuttgart: Fink, 1962.

———. *Der politische Weg der Kriegsgeneration.* Schriftenreihe der Deutschen Union. Berlin: Hess, 1950.

———. *Unser Glaube. Bekenntnis eines jungen Deutschen.* Berlin: Nordland, [1941].

Grimm, Friedrich. *Generalamnestie als völkerrechtliches Postulat.* (Lecture.) Cologne, Opladen: Westdeutscher Verlag, 1951.

———. *Nun aber Schluss mit Rache und Vergeltung: Eine ernste Betrachtung zehn Jahre nach dem Zusammenbruch.* [Göttingen:] Göttinger Verlagsanstalt, [1955].

———. *Politische Justiz, die Krankheit unserer Zeit.* Bonn: Bonner Universitätsdruckerei Gebr. Scheur, 1953.

———. *Unrecht im Rechtsstaat. Tatsachen und Dokumente zur politischen Justiz, dargestellt am Fall Naumann.* Tübingen: Deutsche Hochschullehrer-Zeitung, 1957.

Grimm, Hans. *Answer of a German: An Open Letter to the Archbishop of Canterbury.* Trans. by Lynton Hudson. Dublin: Euphorion, 1952.

———. *Erkenntnisse und Bekenntnisse.* 2d ed. [Göttingen:] Göttinger Verlagsanstalt, [1956].

———. *Die Erzbischofschrift: Antwort eines Deutschen.* Göttingen: Plesse, 1950.

———. *Volk ohne Raum.* Lippoldsberg: Klosterhaus, [1956].

———. *Warum—woher—aber wohin? Vor unter und nach der geschichtlichen Erscheinung Hitler.* Lippoldsberg: Klosterhaus, 1954.

Die grosse Hetze. Der niedersächsische Ministersturz. Ein Tatsachenbericht zum Fall Schlüter. [Göttingen:] Göttinger Verlagsanstalt, [1958].

Grosser, J[ohannes] F[ranz] G[ottlieb], ed. *Die grosse Kontroverse. Ein Briefwechsel um Deutschland.* Hamburg: Nagel, [c. 1963].

Grünberg, Hans Bernhard von. *Bewältigung der Vergangenheit.* Schriftenreihe der DRP. Hanover: Reichsruf, 1960.

———. *Vom neuen Reich.* Schriftenreihe der DRP. Hanover: Reichsruf, 1959.

Gründel, E. Günther. *Die Sendung der jungen Generation, Versuch einer umfassenden revolutionären Sinndeutung der Krise.* Munich: Beck, 1932.

Guderian, Heinz. *Erinnerungen eines Soldaten.* Heidelberg: Vowinckel, 1951.

———. *Kann Westeuropa verteidigt werden?* Göttingen: Plesse, [1950].

———. *Panzer–marsch! Aus dem Nachlass des Schöpfers der deutschen Panzerwaffe.* Edited by Oskar Munzel. [Munich:] Schild, 1956 [c. 1955].

———. *So geht es nicht! Uberlegungen zur Wiederbewaffnung.* Heidelberg: Vowinckel, 1951.

Günther, Hans, F. K. *Formen und Urgeschichte der Ehe.* 3d rev. ed. Göttingen: Musterschmidt, 1951.

———. *Frömmigkeit nordischer Artung. Ein Querschnitt durch das Indogermanentum von Benares bis Reykjavik.* 6th ed. Pähl: Von Bebenburg, 1963.

———. *Gattenwahl zum ehelichen Glück und erblicher Ertüchtigung.* 3d rev. ed. Munich: Lehmann, 1951.

Härtle, Heinrich. *Kriegsschuldlüge und Friedensvertrag.* Hanover: Reichsruf, 1959.

———. *Nietzsche und der Nationalsozialismus.* Munich: Eher, 1937.

Hagen, Hans W. *Durchbruch zur neuen Mitte. Drei Studien zur Überwindung der Kulturkrise.* Munich: Türmer, [1957].

———. *Zwischen Eid und Befehl: Tatzeugenbericht von den Ereignissen am 20. Juli 1944 in Berlin und "Wolfschanze."* Munich: Türmer, [1958].

Hahn, Assi. *Ich spreche die Wahrheit.* Esslingen: Bechtle, 1951.

Hammerstein, K. W., *pseud.* [i.e., Kurt Wentzel]. *Landsberg: Henker des Rechts.* Wuppertal: Abendland, 1952.

Hansen, Ernst Siegfried. *Disteln am Weg: Von der Besetzung Dänemarks bis zu den Bonner Erklärungen.* Bielefeld: Deutsche Heimat, [c. 1957].

———. *Kurier der Heimat. Das Spiel um Schleswig zwischen Kapitulation und Programm Nord.* Bielefeld: Deutsche Heimat, [c. 1955].

Harun-el-Raschid Bey, [Wilhelm]. *Aus Orient und Occident: Ein Mosaik aus buntem Erleben.* Bielefeld: Deutsche Heimat, 1954.

Hasemann, Richard. *Nasses Brot.* Pfullingen: Neske, 1952.

———. *Südrand Armjansk.* Pfullingen: Neske, 1952.

Hauer, Jakob Wilhelm. *Was will die deutsche Glaubensbewegung?* 3d ed., edited by Herbert Grabert. Stuttgart: Gutbrod, 1935.

Hausser, Paul. *Die Waffen-SS im Einsatz.* Göttingen: Plesse, 1952.

Hawemann, Walter. *Achtung, Partisanen! Der Kampf hinter der Ostfront.* Hanover: Sponholtz, [c. 1953].

Hecht, Günther. *General Wlassow.* Limburg/Lahn: Zeitbiographischer Verlag, 1961.

Heiber, Helmut, ed. *Das Tagebuch von Joseph Goebbels 1925/26*. Stuttgart: Deutsche Verlags-Anstalt, [1961].

Heinrichsbauer, August. *Der Ruhrbergbau in Vergangenheit, Gegenwart und Zukunft*. Essen: Glückauf, 1948.

———. *Schwerindustrie und Politik*. Essen: West, 1948.

Helbok, Adolf. *Deutsche Volksgeschichte. Wesenszüge und Leistungen des deutschen Volkes*. Tübingen: Deutsche Hochschullehrer-Zeitung, 1964.

Hennig, E[dwin]. *Ganzheit und Einzelwesen im Lichte des Entwicklungsgedankens*. Lecture given at Stuttgart, October 13, 1935. Tübingen: Heine, 1935.

———. *Das naturwissenschaftliche Weltbild der Gegenwart*. Durchbruch-Schriftenreihe, no. 6. Stuttgart: Durchbruch-Verlag Bühler, [pref. 1937].

———. *Zeitgeschichtliche Aufdeckungen. Ein Beitrag zur Erforschung der jüngsten Vergangenheit*. Munich: Türmer, [1964].

Herbert, Edmund, *pseud.* [i.e., Edmund Gleede and Mathias Kluchen]. *Wir sprechen Hitler frei*. Lüneburg: Arbeitsgemeinschaft 33, [1953].

Herda, Helmut. *Die Schuld der Anderen*. Augsburg: Kraft, [1953].

Hermann, Hans-Georg, *pseud.* [i.e., Hermann Schaefer]. *Verraten und Verkauft*. Fulda: Fuldaer Verlagsanstalt, 1958.

Hess, Ilse, *England–Nürnberg–Spandau: Ein Schicksal in Briefen*. Leoni: Druffel, 1952.

———. *Gefangener des Friedens: Neue Briefe aus Spandau, 1952–1955*. Leoni: Druffel, 1956.

Hesse, Fritz. *Das Spiel um Deutschland*. Munich: List, 1953.

Heusinger, Adolf. *Befehl im Widerstreit: Schicksalsstunden der deutschen Armee 1923–1945*. Tübingen: Wunderlich, 1950.

Hierl, Konstantin. *Gedanken hinter Stacheldraht*. Heidelberg: Vowinckel, 1953.

———. *Im Dienst für Deutschland, 1918–1945*. Heidelberg: Vowinckel, 1954.

———. *Schuld oder Schicksal? Studie über Enstehung und Ausgang des zweiten Weltkrieges*. Heidelberg: Vowinckel, 1954.

Hiess, Joseph. *Glasenbach: Buch einer Gefangenschaft*. 2d ed. Wels: Welsermühl, [1956].

———. *Wir kamen aus Glasenbach: Buch einer Heimkehr*. Wels, Munich: Welsermühl, [1957].

Hoggan, David L. *Der Erzwungene Krieg. Die Ursachen und Urheber des 2. Weltkrieges*. 4th ed., trans. by M. E. Narjes and Herbert Grabert. [Tübingen:] Deutsche Hochschullehrer-Zeitung, 1963 [c. 1961].

———. *Frankreichs Widerstand gegen den 2. Weltkrieg. Die französische Aussenpolitik von 1934–1939*. Trans. by Institut für deutsche Nachkriegsgeschichte. Tübingen: Deutsche Hochschullehrer-Zeitung, 1964.

Hotzel, Curt, ed. *Deutscher Aufstand. Die Revolution des Nachkrieges*. Stuttgart: Kohlhammer, 1934.

Hove, Alkmar von. *Achtung, Fallschirmjäger! Eine Idee bricht sich Bahn*. Leoni: Druffel, [c. 1954].

Hover, Gerd. *Der Fall Schmeisser ohne Schminke.* Oberammergau: Roeder, 1956.
———. *Von Liebknecht über Hitler zum Warschauer Pakt.* Oberammergau: Widar, n.d.
———. *Von der Reichswehr zum ersten Bundeswehr "Deserteur."* Oberammergau: Widar, n.d.
Hudal, Alois. *Die Grundlagen des Nationalsozialismus.* Leipzig, Vienna: Günther, 1937.
———. *Rom, Christentum und deutsches Volk.* Innsbruck: Tyrolia, 1935.
Huter, Franz. *Südtirol. Tausendjährige Heimat.* 3d rev. ed. Innsbruck, Vienna, Munich: Tyrolia, [1964].
Jaeckel, Ernst. *Dämon Gold.* Düsseldorf: Strunk, [1952].
Jerk, Wiking. *Endkampf um Berlin.* Buenos Aires: Dürer, 1947.
Jester, Werner. *Im Todessturm von Budapest 1945.* Landser am Feind, no. 7. Heidelberg: Vowinckel, 1960.
Johst, Hanns. *Gesegnete Vergänglichkeit.* Frankfurt: Pandion, [c. 1955].
Jordan, G[eorge] R[acey]. *Sowjets siegen durch Spione. Roosevelt hat der Sowjet-Union die Atombombe ausgeliefert.* Trans. by Heinrich Härtle. Göttingen: Schütz, [1960]. (*From Major Jordan's Diaries.* New York: Bookmailer, 1953.)
Jünger, Ernst. *Der Kampf als inneres Erlebnis.* Berlin: Mittler, 1940.
Jungnickel, Rudolf. *Gewissen und Gewalt.* Coburg: Veste, 1954.
———. *Ich will euch sagen was Not tut. Rede eines jungen Deutschen.* Frankfurt am Main: Hilbert, 1948.
———. *Sammlung der Jugend.* n.p., n.d.
Karge, Hermann. *Mensch und Volk: Eine naturphilosophische Betrachtung.* Uelzen (Hanover): Klatte, 1953.
Keller, Paul Anton. *Väterheimat zwischen Drau und Sann. Ein Buch der Erinnerung.* Vienna: Wancura, [1956].
Kemmerich, Parzival. *Im Vorfeld von Stalingrad. Tagebuchblätter.* Munich: Türmer, [1964].
Kempka, Erich. *Ich habe Hitler verbrannt.* Munich: Kyrburg, [1950].
Kern, Erich, *pseud.* [i.e., Erich K. Kernmayr]. *Algerien in Flammen: Ein Volk kämpft um seine Freiheit.* 2d imp. ed. Göttingen: Plesse [1958].
———. *Das andere Lidice: Die Tragödie der Sudetendeutschen.* Wels: Welsermühl, [1950]. [Klagenfurt:] Kaiser, [1950].
———. *Buch der Tapferkeit.* Leoni: Druffel, [1953].
———. *Deutschland im Abgrund.* Göttingen: Schütz, [c. 1963].
———. *Der Dorn im Fleische. Roman der Fremdenlegion.* Wels: Welsermühl, [1955].
———. *General von Pannwitz und seine Kossaken.* [Im Blick zurück, vol. 18.] Lizenz des Plesse-Verlags, Göttingen. Neckargemünd: Vowinckel, [1963].
———. *Das goldene Feld.* [Munich-Lochhausen:] Schild, [1957].
———. *Das grosse Kesseltreiben: Bleibt der deutsche Soldat vogelfrei?* 2d enl. ed. Göttingen: Plesse, [c. 1960].

———. *Der grosse Rausch: Russlandfeldzug 1941–1945*. Waiblingen: Leberecht, 1950 [c. 1948].

———. *Das harte Leben (Auszüge aus einem Tagebuch 1947 bis 1950)*. Wels: Welsermühl, [c. 1950].

———. *Die letzte Schlacht. Ungarn 1944–45*. Göttingen: Schütz, [c. 1960].

———. *Menschen im Netz*. Wels: Welsermühl, 1958.

———. *Opfergang eines Volkes. Der totale Krieg*. Göttingen: Schütz, 1962.

———. *Stadt ohne Gnade. Ein Roman um Berlin*. Wels: Welsermühl, [c. 1959].

———. *Der Tag des Gerichts*. Munich: Türmer, [1961].

———. *Die Uhr blieb stehen*. Wels: Welsermühl, [1953].

———. *Verrat an Deutschland. Spione und Saboteure gegen das eigene Vaterland*. Göttingen: Schütz, 1963.

———. *Von Versailles zu Adolf Hitler: Der schreckliche Frieden in Deutschland*. Göttingen: Schütz, 1961.

———. *Weisser Mann, toter Mann? Ostasien im Umbruch—Ein Augenzeugenbericht*. Starnberg, Wels: Welsermühl, [1955].

Kernmayr, Hans Gustl. *Wir waren keine Banditen*. Düsseldorf: Bourg, 1952.

Kesselring, Albert. *Gedanken zum zweiten Weltkrieg*. Bonn: Athenäum, 1955.

———. *Soldat bis zum letzten Tag*. Bonn: Athenäum, 1953.

Kiel, Heinz. *Canaris zwischen den Fronten*. Bremerhaven: Hermann, 1950.

Kindermann, Heinz, and Dietrich, Margarete. *Lexikon der Weltliteratur*. 3d ed. Vienna: Humboldt, [1951, c. 1950].

Klagges, Dietrich. *Die Lage des Nationalismus*. Bad Harzburg: [Klagges,] 1962.

Kleist, Peter. *Auch Du warst dabei. Ein Buch des Ärgernisses und der Hoffnung*. Heidelberg: Vowinckel, 1952.

———. *Chruschtschow 50 km vor Hamburg*. Göttingen: Plesse, [c. 1959].

———. *Deutschland, Europa und der Ost-West-Konflikt*. Hanover: National, 1961.

———. *Die europäische Tragödie*. Göttingen: Schütz, [c. 1961].

———. *Südafrika. Land für Weiss und Schwarz*. Göttingen: Schütz, 1963.

———. *Zwischen Hitler und Stalin. 1939–1945*. Bonn: Athenäum, 1950.

Koch, Hubert. *Der Väter Land. Deutsche Heimat zwischen Weichsel und Memel*. Leer: Rautenberg & Möckel, 1953.

Koellreutter, Otto. *Der deutsche Führerstaat*. [Tübingen: Mohr, 1934.]

———. *Die Entnazifizierung—eine Sünde wider Recht und Ehre*. Landau: Vollmer, [1954].

———. *Der nationale Rechtsstaat. Zum Wandel der deutschen Staatsidee*. Recht und Staat in Geschichte und Gegenwart, no. 89. Tübingen: Mohr (Siebeck), 1932.

———. *Über Schuld und Aufgabe der geistigen Führungsschicht im deutschen politischen Leben der Gegenwart*. [Göttingen:] Göttinger Verlagsanstalt, [c. 1955].

———. *Vom Sinn und Wesen der nationalen Revolution.* [Tübingen: Mohr, 1933.]

———. *Das Wesen der Spruchkammern und der durch sie durchgeführten Entnazifizierung.* [Göttingen:] Göttinger Verlagsanstalt, [c. 1954].

Kolbenheyer, Erwin Guido. *Die Bauhütte. Grundzüge einer Metaphysik der Gegenwart.* New rev. ed. Munich: Langen-Müller, 1940.

———. *Menschen und Götter.* Darmstadt: Wittich (for the Kolbenheyer Association), 1956.

Konsalik, Heinz G. *pseud.* [i.e., Heinz A. M. Günther]. *Sie fielen vom Himmel. Roman einer Generation.* Darmstadt: Schneekluth, [1958].

Krätschmer, Ernst Günther. *Die Ritterkreuzträger der Waffen-SS.* Göttingen: Plesse, [c. 1957].

Kraft, Zdenko von. *Verwirrung oder Verfall? Ein Buch vom Ungeist der Zeit.* Graz, Stuttgart: Stocker, 1964.

Krüger, Gerhard. *Das unzerstörbare Reich.* Hamburg: Gutenberg, [c. 1952].

Kubizek, August. *Adolf Hitler, mein Jugendfreund.* Graz: Stocker, 1953.

Kuenheim, Dietrich von, ed. *Sowjet-Agenten überall.* Oberammergau: Widar, 1955.

Langenbucher, Hellmuth, ed. *Ins Herz hinein: Ein Hand- und Lesebuch für Feier und Besinnung in Schule und Haus.* Vol. I: *Geleit durch das Jahr, Tage und Wochen.* Bad Reichenhall: Neue Schule, Leitner, [c. 1957].

Leemann, A[lbert] C[onrad]. *Ursitte im Urstoff. Die grosse Versöhnung.* Wels, Munich: Welsermühl, 1962.

———. *Der Urstoff in der Urgestalt.* Zurich: Thomas, 1952.

———. *Die Wiedergeburt des Abendlandes.* Wels, Munich: Welsermühl, 1962.

Leers, Johann von. *Reichsverräter.* Buenos Aires: Dürer, [c. 1947]. 2 vols.

Lenz, Friedrich. *Der ekle Wurm der deutschen Zwietracht. Politische Probleme rund um den 20. Juli 1944.* 2d ed. Heidelberg: Lenz, [1953].

———. *Stalingrad, der "verlorene" Sieg.* Heidelberg: Lenz, 1956.

———. *Unser Kanzler Ollenhauer und seine Palladine.* Heidelberg: Lenz, [1957].

———. *Zauber um Dr. Schacht.* Heidelberg: Lenz, 1954.

Lippert, Julius. *Lächle . . . und verbirg die Tränen. Erlebnisse und Bemerkungen eines "Kriegsverbrechers."* Leoni: Druffel, [1955].

Lochner, Louis, P., ed. *The Goebbels Diaries, 1942–1943.* New York: Doubleday, 1948.

Lossberg, Bernhard von. *Im Wehrmachtsführungsstab.* Hamburg: Nölke, 1949.

Lotze, Karl-Heinz. *. . . und es saust der Frack. Luftjagd über die Normandie und in der Reichsverteidigung 1944/45.* Landser am Feind, no. 12. Neckargemünd: Vowinckel, 1961.

Ludwig, Gerhard. *Massenmord im Weltgeschehen. Bilanz zweier Jahrtausende.* Stuttgart: Vorwerk, 1951.

Lusar, Rudolf. *Die deutschen Waffen und Geheimwaffen des zweiten Weltkrieges und ihre Weiterentwicklung.* Munich: Lehmann, 1956.

Lutz, Hermann. *"Verbrecher-Volk" im Herzen Europas?* Tübingen: Schlichtenmayer, 1959. (*German-French Unity: Basis for European Peace.* Chicago: Regnery, 1957.)

Mann, Thomas. *Betrachtungen eines Unpolitischen.* Berlin: Fischer, 1919.

———. *Friedrich und die grosse Koalition.* Sammlung von Schriften zur Zeitgeschichte, no. 5. Berlin: Fischer, 1915.

Mannhardt, Johann W. *Der Faschismus.* Munich: Beck, 1925.

———. *Hochschulrevolution.* Hamburg: Hanseatische Verlagsanstalt, 1933.

Manstein, Erich von. *Aus einem Soldatenleben 1887–1939.* Vol. I. Bonn: Athenäum, 1959.

———. *Verlorene Siege.* Vol. II. Bonn: Athenäum, 1955.

Marhefka, Edmund. *Die Herren dieser Welt und das Problem der Macht.* Berlin: Maximilian, 1962.

Martell, Bernhard. *Aufstand des Abendlandes. Eine politische Provokation.* Schweinfurt: neues forum, [1961].

Mayen, Jan. *Alarm—Schnellboote! Zwischen Kanal und Kaukasusküste; ein Tatsachenbericht vom Einsatz der kleinen Boote.* Oldenburg: Stalling, [c. 1961].

Meister, Jürg. *Der Seekrieg in den osteuropäischen Gewässern 1941–1945.* Munich: Lehmann, 1958.

Meyer, Konrad. *Nahrungsraum und Übervölkerung: Ein Weltproblem der Gegenwart.* [Göttingen:] Göttinger Verlagsanstalt, [1953].

Miessner, Herwart. *Um die Sicherung des Berufsbeamtentum.* [Göttingen:] Göttinger Verlagsanstalt, [1953].

Mildenberger, Helmut. *Heimweh hinter Stacheldraht.* Buenos Aires: Dürer, 1951.

Miltschinsky, Viktor. *Kärnten wehrt sich!* Eckartschriften, no. 9. Vienna: [Österreichische Landsmannschaft], 1962.

Möller, Eberhard Wolfgang. *Chicago oder der Mann der auf das Brot trat.* Hamburg: Holsten, 1963.

———. *Der Führer.* Edited by Baldur von Schirach. Munich: Zentralverlag der NSDAP, Eher, [c. 1938].

Möller-Witten, Hans. *Männer und Taten: Ritterkreuzträger erzählen.* Munich: Lehmann, 1958.

Moeller van den Bruck, Arthur. *Das Dritte Reich.* 4th ed. Hamburg: Hanseatische Verlagsanstalt, 1931.

———. *Das Recht der jungen Völker: Aus dem politischen Nachlass.* Edited by Hans Schwarz. Berlin: Der Nahe Osten, 1932.

———. *Sozialismus und Aussenpolitik.* Edited by Hans Schwarz. Breslau: Korn, 1933.

———, Heinrich von Gleichen, and Max Hildebert Boehm, eds. *Die neue Front.* Berlin: Paetel, 1922.

Moengal, W., *pseud. Mögen wir auch untergehen.* Vienna: Europäischer Verlag, 1962.

Mosley, Sir Oswald. *The Alternative.* Ramsbury (Wilts.): Mosley Publications, 1947.

———. *Ich glaube an Europa. Ein Weg aus der Krise. Eine Einführung in das europäische Denken.* Trans. by Heinrich Härtle. Lippoldsberg: Klosterhaus, [c. 1962]. (*Europe—Faith and Plan: A Way Out from the Coming Crisis and an Introduction to Thinking as a European.* London: Euphorion, 1958.)

Münchhausen, Börries Frh. von. *Das dichterische Werk in 2 Bänden.* (1) *Das Baladenbuch;* (2) *Das Liederbuch.* Stuttgart: Deutsche Verlags-Anstalt, 1955–56.

Nadler, Josef. *Geschichte der deutschen Literatur.* Vienna: Günther, 1951.

Naumann, Werner. *Nau-Nau gefährdet das Empire?* Edited by Karl Heinrich Peter. Göttingen: Plesse, 1953.

Neesse, Gottfried. *Staatsdienst und Staatsschicksal.* Hamburg: Holsten, 1957.

Nicoll, Peter H. *Englands Krieg gegen Deutschland. Die Ursachen, Methoden und Folgen des zweiten Weltkriegs.* Tübingen: Deutsche Hochschullehrer-Zeitung, 1963. (*Britain's Blunder: An Objective Study of the Second World War, Its Cause, Conduct, and Consequence.* [London? 1953?].)

Nieland, Friedrich. *Wieviele Welt-(Geld-) Kriege müssen die Völker noch verlieren? Offener Brief an alle Bundesminister und Parlamentarier.* Hamburg–Wellingsbüttel: n.p., 1957.

Noack, Erwin, and G. A. Walz. *Deutsche Demokratie.* Berlin: Deutscher Rechtsverlag, 1938.

Nowak, Josef. *Mensch auf den Acker gesät. Kriegsgefangen in der Heimat.* Hanover: Sponholtz, 1956.

Nowotny, Rudolf, ed. *Walter Nowotny: "Tiger vom Wolchowstroj"—"Fliegerwunder aus Österreich." Berichte aus dem Leben meines Bruders.* Leoni: Druffel, 1957.

Oscar, Friedrich. *Über Galgen wächst kein Gras: Die fragwürdige Kulisse der Kriegsverbrecherprozesse im Spiegel unbekannter Dokumente.* Brunswick: Erasmus, [1950].

Oven, Wilfred von. *Mit Goebbels bis zum Ende.* Buenos Aires: Dürer, 1949. 2 vols.

Pabst, Helmut. *Der Ruf der äussersten Grenze: Tagebuch eines Frontsoldaten.* Edited by Hermann J. Meyer. Tübingen: Schlichtenmayer, 1953. (*The Outermost Frontier: A German Soldier in the Russian Campaign.* Trans. by A. and E. Wilson. London: Kimber, [c. 1957].)

Panzermeyer, *pseud.* [i.e., Kurt Meyer]. *Grenadiere.* [Munich-Lochhausen:] Schild, [c. 1957].

Papen, Franz von. *Europa was nun? Betrachtungen zur Politik der Westmächte.* [Göttingen:] Göttinger Verlagsanstalt, [1954].

[Peter, Karl-Heinz, ed.] Archiv Peter für historische und zeitgeschichtliche Dokumentation. *Spiegelbild einer Verschwörung: Die Kaltenbrunner-Berichte an Bormann und Hitler über das Attentat vom 20. Juli 1944. Geheime Dokumente aus dem ehemaligen Reichssicherheitshauptamt.* Stuttgart: Seewald, [c. 1961].

Petersson, Ingo, *pseud.* [i.e., F. E. Porsch]. *Ein sonderlicher Haufen: Die Saga vom Sturmbatallion 500.* Landser am Feind, no. 4. Heidelberg: Vowinckel, 1959.

Pfeffer, Karl Heinz. *Begriff und Wesen der Plutokratie.* Berlin: Junker & Dünnhaupt, 1940.

———. *Die deutsche Schule der Soziologie.* Leipzig: Quelle & Meyer, 1939.

———. *England: Vormacht der bürgerlichen Welt.* Hamburg: Hanseatische Verlagsanstalt, 1940.

———. *Der englische Krieg ist auch ein jüdischer Krieg.* Munich: Eher, 1943.

———. *Handwörterbuch der Politik.* Darmstadt: Leske, 1956.

———. *Das Judentum im osteuropäischen Raum.* Essen: Essener Verlagsanstalt, 1938.

Picht, Werner. *Wiederbewaffnung.* Pfullingen: Neske, 1954.

Picker, Henry, ed. *Hitlers Tischgespräche im Führerhauptquartier, 1941–1942.* Bonn: Athenäum, 1951.

Plassmann, Josef Otto. *Deutsches Land kehrt heim: Ostmark und Sudetenland als germanischer Volksboden.* Berlin: Ahnenerbe, 1939.

———. *Princeps und Populus: Die Gefolgschaft im ottonischen Staatsaufbau nach den sächsischen Geschichtsschreibern des 10. Jahrhunderts.* [Göttingen:] Göttinger Verlagsanstalt, [1954].

Plettenberg, Malte. *Guderian: Hintergründe des deutschen Schicksals von 1918–1945.* Düsseldorf: abz, 1950.

Pohl, Brigitte. *Fastnacht der Dämonen. Erlebnisse einer Wienerin.* Leoni: Druffel, [1963].

Polonius, *pseud. Keine Angst vor Sowjetrussland.* Heidelberg: Vowinckel, 1951.

Pongs, Hermann. *Im Umbruch der Zeit: Das Romanschaffen der Gegenwart.* [Göttingen:] Göttinger Verlagsanstalt, [1954]. A new edition appeared under the title: *Romanschaffen im Umbruch der Zeit. Eine Chronik von 1952 bis 1962.* 4th rev. enl. ed. [Tübingen:] Deutsche Hochschullehrer-Zeitung, 1963.

Priester, Karl-Heinz. *Deutschland, Ost-West Kolonie oder gleichberechtigt in einem freien Europa?* Schriftenreihe "Die Europäische Nationale," no. 1. Wiesbaden: Die Europäische Nationale, 1951.

———. *Die 12 Punkte-Forderung der NDP an die deutsche Bundesregierung und die Herren Oberkommissare und ihre Begründung. Originalbericht über die Wiesbadener NDP-Versammlung am 27. Oktober, 1949 in der Bose Aula zu Wiesbaden.* N.p., n.d.

Priller, Josef. *Geschichte eines Jagdgeschwaders.* Heidelberg: Vowinckel, 1956.

Raeder, Erich. *Mein Leben.* Tübingen: Schlichtenmayer, 1957. 2 vols.

Ramcke, H. Bernhard. *Fallschirmjäger—damals und danach.* Frankfurt: Lorch, 1951.

Raschhofer, Hermann. *Der Fall Oberländer. Eine vergleichende Rechtsanalyse der Verfahren in Pankow und Bonn.* Tübingen: Schlichtenmayer, 1962.

Rassinier, Paul. *Die Lüge des Odysseus.* Wiesbaden: Priester, [c. 1959].

———. *Zum Fall Eichmann: Was ist Wahrheit?—oder—Die unbelehr-*

baren Sieger. Leoni: Druffel, [1963]. (*Le véritable procès Eichmann ou Les vainqueurs incorrigibles*. Paris: 1962.)

Rauschning, Hermann. *Deutschland zwischen West und Ost*. Berlin: Christian, [1950].

———. *Ist Friede noch möglich?* Heidelberg: Vowinckel, 1953.

———, *et al. Mitten ins Herz. Über eine Politik ohne Angst*. Berlin: Henssel, 1955.

Der Rechtsstreit vor den Verwaltungsgerichten über die Verbotsverfügung der Innenminister der deutschen Länder gegen Bund für Gotterkenntnis (Ludendorff), Verlag Hohe Warte in Pähl/Oberbayern. (Darstellung und Würdigung der Tätigkeit von BfG und VHW im Hinblick auf Art. 9, Abs. 2 GG durch das Bundesamt für Verfassungsschutz.) Dokumente der Gegenwart, no. 5. Pähl: Von Bebenburg, 1963.

———. (Beweismittelband 3 des Bundesamtes für Verfassungsschutz.) Dokumente der Gegenwart, no. 6. Pähl: Von Bebenburg, 1963.

———. Dokumente der Gegenwart, no. 8. Pähl: Von Bebenburg, 1963.

Reed, Douglas. *Der grosse Plan der Anonymen*. Zurich: Thomas, 1952.

Reichenberger, Emmanuel J. *Europa in Trümmern. Das Ergebnis des Kreuzzuges der Alliierten*. 4th ed. Graz: Stocker, 1954 [c. 1950].

———. *Rettung Europas?* Munich: Tribunal, 1960.

———. *Wider Willkür und Machtrausch. Erkenntnisse und Bekenntnisse aus zwei Kontinenten*. Graz: Stocker, 1955.

Reinhard, Severin, *pseud*. [i.e., René Sonderegger]. *Spanischer Sommer*. Affoltern a. Albis (Switz.): Aehren, [c. 1948].

Reitenhart, Walther. *Kriegsschuldforschung entlastet Deutschland. Ein Überblick*. Beihefte zur Deutschen Hochschullehrer-Zeitung, no. 2. [Tübingen:] Deutsche Hochschullehrer-Zeitung, 1964.

Reitsch, Hanna. *Fliegen—mein Leben*. Stuttgart: Deutsche Verlags-Anstalt, [c. 1951].

Remer, Otto Ernst. *20. Juli 1944*. Hamburg: Deutsche Opposition, 1951.

Rendulic, Lothar. *Gefährliche Grenzen der Politik*. Munich, Salzburg: Pilgram, 1956.

———. *Gekämpft, gesiegt, geschlagen*. Wels, Heidelberg: Welsermühl, 1952.

———. *Glasenbach–Nürnberg–Landsberg. Ein Soldatenschicksal nach dem Krieg*. Graz: Stocker, 1953.

———. *Soldat in stürzenden Reichen*. Munich: Damm, 1965.

———. *Weder Krieg noch Frieden. Eine Frage an die Macht*. Wels, Munich: Welsermühl, 1961.

Ribbentrop, Annelies von. *"Verschwörung gegen den Frieden." Studien zur Vorgeschichte des zweiten Weltkrieges*. Leoni: Druffel, 1962.

Ribbentrop, Joachim von. *Zwischen London und Moskau. Erinnerungen und letzte Aufzeichnungen*. Leoni: Druffel, 1953.

Rieker, Karlheinrich. *Ein Mann verliert einen Weltkrieg. Die entscheidenden Monate des deutsch-russischen Krieges 1942–1943*. Frankfurt: Fridericus, [c. 1955].

Risse, Friedrich Victor. *Eroberungspolitik der Kreml-Machthaber 1954/1955.* [Munich: Risse, 1955.]

———. *So zersetzt Moskau den Westen.* [Munich:] Internationale Demokratische Kampfliga, [1954].

Ritter, Gerhard. *Staatskunst und Staatsräson. Das Problem des "Militarismus" in Deutschland.* Munich: Oldenbourg, 1954.

Roeder, Guido. *Im Morgenrot der Weltrevolution.* 2d ed. Oberammergau: Widar, 1955.

Roeder, Manfred. *Die rote Kapelle.* Hamburg: Siep, n.d.

Röhrs, Hans Dietrich. *Mit Arztbesteck und Sturmgewehr. Zwischen Tatra und Teiss 1944/45.* Neckargemünd: Vowinckel, 1961.

Rohden, H. D. Herhudt von. *Die Luftwaffe ringt um Stalingrad.* Wiesbaden: Limes, 1950.

Rosenberg, Alfred. *Letzte Aufzeichnungen. Ideale und Idole der nationalsozialistischen Revolution.* Göttingen: Plesse, 1955.

Rudel, Hans-Ulrich. *Aus Krieg und Frieden. Aus den Jahren 1944–1952.* Göttingen: Plesse, 1953.

———. *Dolchstoss oder Legende?* Brochure. N.p., n.d., but very likely Buenos Aires, 1951.

———. *Es geht um das Reich.* Buenos Aires: Dürer, [1952].

———. *Trotzdem.* Preface by the author's parents. Waiblingen (Wttbg.): Leberecht, [pref. September, 1950]; also Buenos Aires: Dürer, [c. 1949].

———. *Von den Stukas zu den Anden. Am höchsten Vulkan der Erde.* Leoni: Druffel, 1956.

———. *Wir Frontsoldaten zur Wiederaufrüstung.* Brochure. N.p., n.d.

———. *Zwischen Deutschland und Argentinien. Fünf Jahre in Übersee.* Göttingen: Plesse, [1954?].

Rumpf, Hans. *Das war der Bombenkrieg.* Oldenburg: Stalling, 1961.

Salomon, Ernst von. *Der Fragebogen.* Hamburg: Rowohlt, 1951.

Sanden, Heinrich, *pseud.* [i.e., Helmut L. Sündermann]. *Europa ohne Phrase.* Leoni: Druffel, 1953.

Schäfer, Wilhelm. *Der deutsche Gott. Fünf Briefe an mein Volk.* Munich: Müller, 1923.

———. *Die dreizehn Bücher der deutschen Seele.* Munich: Müller, 1925 [c. 1922].

Schaeffer, Heinz. *U-977: 66 Tage unter Wasser.* Wiesbaden: Limes, 1950.

Schaumburg-Lippe, Prinz Friedrich Christian zu. *Dr. G. Ein Porträt des Propagandaministers.* Wiesbaden: Limes, 1963.

———. *Souveräne Menschen. Kleine Lebensregeln—grossgeschrieben.* Leoni: Druffel, [1954].

———. *Zwischen Krone und Kerker.* Wiesbaden: Limes, 1952.

Schild, Hermann, ed. *Mit offenem Visier. Aus den Lebenserinnerungen eines deutschen Rechtsanwalts, Professor Dr. Friedrich Grimm.* Leoni: Druffel, [1961].

Schilling, Wilhelm. *Über die Verantwortung für die Demontage deutscher Wissenschaft.* [Göttingen:] Göttinger Verlagsanstalt, [1953].

Schirach, Henriette von. *Der Preis der Herrlichkeit.* Wiesbaden: Limes, 1956.

Schlamm, William S. *Die Grenzen des Wunders.* [Zurich:] Europa, [1959]. (*Germany and the East-West Crisis. The Decisive Challenge to American Policy.* New York: McKay, [1959].)

Schloz, Wilhelm. *Kampf und Ziel der Deutschen Glaubensbewegung.* Durchbruch–Schriftenreihe, no. 1. Stuttgart: Durchbruch–Verlag Bühler, [1937?].

Schmahl, Eugen, and Wilhelm Seipel. *Entwicklung der völkischen Bewegung.* Giessen: Roth, [1933].

Schmidt, Paul. *Statist auf diplomatischer Bühne, 1923–1945.* Bonn: Athenäum, 1949.

Schmidt-Hannover, Otto. *Umdenken oder Anarchie: Männer–Schicksale–Lehren.* [Göttingen:] Göttinger Verlagsanstalt, [1959].

Schmidt[-Wodder], Johannes. *Von Wodder nach Kopenhagen, von Deutschland nach Europa. Mein politischer Werdegang.* Flensburg: Wolff, [c. 1951].

Schwabe, Hans B. *Deutschland in seiner tiefen Erniedrigung. Das deutsche Reich—eine europäische Wirklichkeit.* Lindau: Palm–Schriften, [1961].

Schwarzbauer, Heribert. *Menschen ohne Angesicht.* Graz, Vienna, Stuttgart: Stocker, 1950.

Schweiger, Herbert. *Wahre Dein Antlitz. Lebensgesetz, Politik und die Zukunft des deutschen Volkes.* Munich: Türmer, [1963].

Siegert, Karl. *Represalie, Requisition und höherer Befehl: Ein Beitrag zur Rechtfertigung der Kriegsverurteilten.* [Göttingen:] Göttinger Verlagsanstalt, [1953].

Silling, Victor, *pseud.* [i.e., Artur von Machui]. *Die Hintergründe des Falles Oberländer.* Gross Denkte/Wolfenbüttel: Grenzland, Rock, [c. 1960].

Skorzeny, Otto. *Geheimkommando Skorzeny.* Hamburg: Hansa, 1950. (*Skorzeny's Secret Missions: War Memoirs of the Most Dangerous Man in Europe.* Trans. from the French by Jacques Le Clercq. New York: Dutton, 1950.)

———. *Lebe gefährlich.* Niederpleis/Siegburg: Ring, 1963.

———. *Wir kämpften—wir verloren.* Niederpleis/Siegburg: Ring, 1963.

Sluyse, Willem. *Die Jünger und die Dirnen.* Buenos Aires: Dürer, [1954].

Sondermann, Gustav. *Arzt—Kasse—Volksgesundheit.* Munich: Lehmann, 1952.

Sontag, Franz [*pseud.* Junius Alter]. *Nationalisten. Deutschlands nationales Führertum der Nachkriegszeit.* Leipzig: Koehler, 1930.

Soucek, Theodor. *Wir rufen Europa: Vereinigung des Abendlandes auf sozialorganischer Grundlage.* Wels, Starnberg: Welsermühl, 1956.

Spann, Othmar. *Der wahre Staat: Vorlesungen über Abbruch und Neubau der Gesellschaft.* Leipzig: Quelle & Meyer, 1921.

Spengler, Oswald. *Preussentum und Sozialismus.* Munich: Beck, 1920.

Spindler, Gert P. *Der Leistungsstaat.* Düsseldorf: Komet, 1948.

———. *Mitunternehmertum.* Lüneburg: Metta Kinau, Wolf & Taeuber, 1951.

———. *Neue Antworten im sozialen Raum. Leitbilder für Unternehmer.* Düsseldorf, Vienna: Econ, [c. 1964].

Springer, Hildegard, *pseud.* [i.e., Hildegard Fritzsche], ed. *Das Schwert auf der Waage: Hans Fritzsche über Nürnberg.* Heidelberg: Vowinckel, 1953.

Stahmer, Heinrich Georg. *Japans Niederlage—Asiens Sieg. Aufstieg eines grösseren Ostasien.* Bielefeld: Deutsche Heimat, 1952.

Staudinger, Karl, *pseud.* [i.e., August Haussleiter?]. *Zwischen Yorck und John. Folgen der deutschen Bewusstseinsspaltung.* Frankfurt: Joachim Henrich, [January, 1957].

Stegner, Artur. *Die Überwindung des Kollektivismus.* [Göttingen:] Göttinger Verlagsanstalt, [1953].

Steguweit, Heinz. *Der Jüngling im Feuerofen.* Bonn: Vink, 1952.

Steinberg, Helmut, *pseud.* [i.e., Heinrich Härtle]. *Marxismus–Leninismus–Stalinismus: Der geistige Angriff des Ostens.* Hamburg: Holsten, 1955.

Steiner, Felix. *Die Armee der Geächteten.* Göttingen: Plesse, [c. 1963].

———. *Die Freiwilligen. Idee und Opfergang.* Göttingen: Plesse, [1958].

———. *Von Clausewitz bis Bulganin: Erkenntnisse und Lehren einer Wehrepoche.* Bielefeld: Deutsche Heimat, 1956.

———. *Die Wehridee des Abendlandes.* Frankfurt: Parma, 1951.

Stering, Erich von. *Jeder war ein Stück von uns. Leben und Kampf einer Kompanie . . . von Attika nach Serajewo.* Landser am Feind, no. 3. Heidelberg: Vowinckel, 1959.

———. *Wir tragen die Fahne. Panzerjagd in Süddeutschland 1945.* Landser am Feind, no. 10. Neckargemünd: Vowinckel, 1961.

Steuer, Lothar. *Hugenberg und die Hitler Diktatur.* Detmold: Maximilian, 1949.

Strasser, Otto. *Aufbau des deutschen Sozialismus.* 2d enl. imp. ed. With the Hitler–Strasser discussion as an appendix ("Anlass der Trennung"). Prague: Grunov, [pref. 1936].

———. *Deutschland und der 3. Weltkrieg.* Munich: Deutsche Freiheit, 1961.

———. *Deutschlands Erneuerung.* Buenos Aires: Trenkelbach, [1946].

———. *Dr. Otto Strasser, der unbeugsame Kämpfer für ein freies Deutschland.* Frankfurt: [Strasser,] 1955.

———. *Europa von Morgen: Das Ziel Masaryks.* Zurich: Weltwoche, 1939.

———. *Exil.* Munich: Deutsche Freiheit, 1958.

———. *Germany Tomorrow.* Trans. by Eden and Cedar Paul. London: Cape, [1940].

———. *History in My Time.* Trans. by Douglas Reed. London: Cape, [1941].

———. *Hitler and I.* Boston: Houghton Mifflin, 1940. (*Hitler und Ich.* Konstanz: Asmus, 1948.)

———, ed. *Ziel und Weg der Nationalen Opposition.* Schriften für Deutschlands Erneuerung, no. 1. Munich: [Deutsche Freiheit, pref. October 9, 1962].

Strassner, Peter. *Verräter: Nationalkomitée "Freies Deutschland"—Keimzelle der DDR.* Munich: Schild, 1960.

Sündermann, Helmut L. *Alter Feind—was nun? Wiederbegegnung mit England und Engländern.* Leoni: Druffel, 1956.

———. *Das Dritte Reich: Eine Richtigstellung in Umrissen.* Leoni: Druffel, 1959.

———. *Das Erbe des falschen Propheten. Moskaus Kampf um Deutschland von Lenin bis heute—und morgen?* Leoni: Druffel, 1957.

———. *Die Pioniere und die Ahnungslosen. Skizzen amerikanischer Vergangenheit und Gegenwart.* Leoni: Druffel, [1960].

———. *Potsdam 1945: Ein kritischer Bericht.* Trans. of the Conference Minutes by Peter Erlau. Leoni: Druffel, 1962.

Taeppe, Rainer. *Das Ende des Fortschritts, konservative Perspektiven.* [Göttingen:] Göttinger Verlagsanstalt, [c. 1956].

Tansill, Charles Callan. *Die Hintertür zum Krieg. Das Drama der internationalen Diplomatie von Versailles bis Pearl Harbor.* Trans. by Hans Steinsdorff. Düsseldorf: Droste, [1957]. (*Back Door to War. The Roosevelt Foreign Policy 1933–1941.* Chicago: Regnery, 1952.)

Teske, Hermann. *Der silberne Spiegel: Generalstabsdienst unter der Lupe.* Heidelberg: Vowinckel, 1952.

Thadden, Adolf von. *Wille und Weg des nationalen Deutschland. Eine Rede des Frankfurter Parteitags der DRP, 1962.* Hanover: Reichsruf, 1962.

Thiriart, Jean. *Un empire de 400 millions d'hommes: l'Europe.* Brussels: Sineco, 1964.

Thorwald, Jürgen. *Wen sie verderben wollen. Bericht des grossen Verrats.* Stuttgart: Steingrüben, [1952].

Uhlig, A. Werner. *Atom—Angst oder Hoffnung? Die Lehren des ersten Atommanövers der Welt.* Munich: Isar, 1955.

University of Colorado, Department of Philosophy, eds. *Readings on Fascism and National Socialism.* Denver: Swallow, n.d.

Utley, Freda. *Arabische Welt—Ost oder West? Vom neuen Schauplatz des kalten Krieges.* Trans. and introd. by Peter Kleist. Göttingen: Plesse, [1958]. (*Will the Middle East Go West?* Chicago: Regnery, 1957.)

———. *Die kostspielige Rache.* Trans. by Egon Heymann. Hamburg: Nölke, [1950]. (*The High Cost of Vengeance.* Chicago: Regnery, 1949.)

Veale, F[rederick] J[ohn] P[artington]. *Der Barbarei entgegen. Wie der Rückfall in die Barbarei durch Kriegsführung und Kriegsverbrecherprozesse unsere Zukunft bedroht.* Trans. by Ursula Michaelsen, introd. by Paul Leverkuehn. Hamburg: Nölke, [c. 1951]. (*Advance to Barbarism.* Appleton [Wis.]: Nelson, 1953.)

———. *Schuld und Sühne.* Tübingen: Schlichtenmayer, 1964.

———. *Verschleierte Kriegsverbrechen.* Wiesbaden: Priester, [c. 1959]. (*Crimes Discreetly Veiled.* London: Cooper, [1958].)

Venatier, Hans. *Der Boss und seine Narren.* Düsseldorf: Muth, [c. 1956].

———. *Der Major und die Stiere.* Düsseldorf: Bourg, [c. 1953].

Vesper, Will, ed. *Deutsche Jugend. 30 Jahre Geschichte einer Bewegung.* Berlin: Holle, [1934].

———. *Die Ernte. Unvergängliches Gedicht aus 8 Jahrhunderten deutscher Lyrik.* Burg Stettenfels/Heilbronn: Hünenburg, [c. 1958].

———. *Das harte Geschlecht.* Graz, Göttingen: Stocker, 1952.

———. *Die Neue Literatur.* Vols. 34–42. Leipzig: Avenarius, 1933–1941.

———. *Seltsame Flöte: Hundert Geschichten aus verzauberter Welt.* Burg Stettenfels/Heilbronn: Hünenburg, [1958].

Vogel, Karl. *M-AA 509: Elf Monate Kommandant eines Internierungslagers.* Memmingen: Vogel, 1951.

Vollmer, Dieter. *Vom Wesenhaften.* Göttingen: Plesse, 1955.

Vom Hellweg, Fritz. *Rheinwiesen 1945.* Wuppertal-Vohwinkel: Huth, 1951.

Waffen-SS im Bild. 2d ed. Göttingen: Plesse, [c. 1957].

Wahl, Karl. *". . . es ist dast deutsche Herz." Erlebnisse und Erkenntnisse eines ehemaligen Gauleiters.* Augsburg: Wahl, 1954.

Walendy, Udo. *Wahrheit für Deutschland: Die Schuldfrage des zweiten Weltkrieges.* Vlotho/Weser: Volkstum und Zeitgeschichtsforschung, 1964.

Wartenberg, Hermann. *Die Front geht mitten durchs Herz.* Bielefeld: Uhlenburg, [c. 1953].

———. *Spähtrupp.* Göttingen: Plesse, 1955.

Waser, Bert. *Demokratische Wahrheiten. Betrachtungen eines simplen Zeitgenossen.* Lindau: Palm-Schriften, [1964].

Wecker, Gero. *Die Letzten von Prag.* Freiburg i. Br.: Dikreiter, [1953, c. 1952].

Welsperg, Wolfgang von, *pseud.* [i.e., Manfred von Ribbentrop]. *Süd Tirol: Kampf für Recht und Volkstum.* 2d ed. Hamburg: Hutten, 1962 [c. 1959].

Westphal, Siegfried. *Heer in Fesseln: Aus den Papieren des Stabschefs von Rommel, Kesselring und Rundstedt.* Bonn: Athenäum, 1950.

Wetzel, Otto. *Vertrauliche Mitteilungen für alle "Ehemaligen."* Cologne: Wetzel, [1957].

Wick, Günther. *Wandlungen des Marxismus.* Lindau: Palm-Schriften, [1963].

Winnig, August. *Europa-Gedanken eines Deutschen.* Berlin: Eckart, 1952.

Wirth, Hermann. *Was ist deutsch?* Vienna: Editio Totius Mundi, 1956.

Woltereck, Heinz, ed. *Erbkunde, Rassenpflege, Bevölkerungspolitik: Schicksalsfragen des deutschen Volkes.* Leipzig: Quelle & Meyer, 1935.

Wulle, Reinhold. *Geschichte einer Staatsidee.* Berlin: NBD—Nationaler Bücherdienst, 1935.

———. *Die Grossen 5—Aufstand gegen Versailles.* "Das abc des NBD" Series, no. 1. Berlin: NBD—Nationaler Bücherdienst, n.d.

Yowev, Stefan, *pseud. Bricht der Weltkommunismus zusammen?* Tübingen: Schlichtenmayer, 1961.

———. *Die kommunistische Weltbewegung in der Krise.* Duisdorf/Bonn: Studiengesellschaft für Zeitprobleme, n.d.

Zerkaulen, Heinrich. *Zwischen Nacht und Tag. Erlebnisse aus dem Camp 94.* Munich: Mühlberger, 1951.

Ziegler, Hans Severus. *Adolf Hitler aus dem Erleben dargestellt.* Göttingen: Schütz, 1964.

———. *Entartete Musik. Eine Abrechnung.* Düsseldorf: Völkischer Verlag, n.d.

———. *Praktische Kulturarbeit im Dritten Reich: Anregungen und Richtlinien für die künftige Volkserziehung.* Nationalsozialistische Bibliothek, no. 22. 3d impr. ed. Munich: Zentralverlag der NSDAP, 1934.

———. *Wende und Weg. Kulturpolitische Reden und Aufsätze.* Weimar: Fink, 1937.

Ziesel, Kurt. *Dankt das Abendland ab? Ein Vortrag der in Wien nicht stattfinden durfte.* Eckartschriften, no. 11. Vienna: [Österreichische Landsmannschaft,] June, 1963.

———. *Der deutsche Selbstmord. Diktatur der Meinungsmacher.* [Velbert-Kettwig:] blick + bild Verlag für politische Bildung, [1963].

———. *Die Geister scheiden sich. Die interessantesten Leserbriefe und wesentlichsten Pressestimmen.* Munich: Lehmann, [1959].

———. *Die Literaturfabrik. Eine polemische Auseinandersetzung mit dem Literaturbetrieb im Deutschland von heute.* [Vienna, Cologne:] Wancura, [c. 1962].

———. *Die Pressefreiheit in der Demokratie. Eine kritische Untersuchung.* Munich: Lehmann, [1962].

———. *Der rote Rufmord. Eine Dokumentation zum kalten Krieg.* [Tübingen: Schlichtenmayer, 1961.]

———. *Das verlorene Gewissen. Hinter den Kulissen der Presse, der Literatur und ihrer Machtträger von heute.* Munich: Lehmann, [c. 1958].

———. *Die verratene Demokratie.* Munich: Lehmann, 1960.

Zischka, Anton. *Afrika—Europas Gemeinschaftsaufgabe Nr. 1.* Oldenburg: Stalling, 1951.

———. *Asien. Hoffnung einer neuen Welt.* Oldenburg: Stalling, 1950.

———. *Englands Bündnisse. Sechs Jahrhunderte britische Kriege mit fremden Waffen.* Leipzig: Goldmann, 1940.

———. *Frieden in einer reicheren Welt.* Oldenburg: Stalling, 1956.

———. *Welt in Angst und Hoffnung.* Oldenburg: Stalling, 1955.

2. ARTICLES

(a) *Signed Articles*

Amaudruz, Guy A. "Von der Notwendigkeit einer europäischen Rassenpflege," *Der Weg,* VI, 5 (May, 1952), 329–336.

Amberger, Heinz. "Wir und Europa," *Burschenschaftliche Blätter,* LXVII, 6 (June, 1952), 173.

[Aschenauer, Rudolf.] "Die Bauhütten–Philosophie Kolbenheyers in der Krise unserer Zeit," *Die andere Seite,* III, 3 (July, 1952), 6–9.

———. "Hans Grimms 'Antwort eines Deutschen' im Kreuzfeuer der Kritik," *Die andere Seite, Informationsdienst,* no. 7 (November, 1950), pp. 7–8.

Basso. "Die Vergangenheit, die Zukunft und wir," *Wiking-Ruf,* II, 3 (January, 1952), 3.

Baudissin, Count Wolf. "The New German Army," *Foreign Affairs,* XXXIV (October, 1955), 1–13.

Beck-Broichsitter, Helmut. "Der Kernpunkt," *Die Bruderschaft* (Rundschreiben an den Freundeskreis, Hanover), August, 1950, pp. 2–5.

Becker, Frédéric G. "Eine deutsch-französische Europa-Front muss entstehen um den Europa–Gedanken auf die rechte Bahn zu bringen!" Address of June 17, 1956, in "Sonderdruck," *Ziel und Weg* (Frankfurt), June, 1956.

———. "Die Europäische Volksbewegung im Kampf mit der 'Europa-Heuchelei,' " *Europaruf* (Zurich, Munich, Salzburg), I, 8/9 (September 15, 1957), 2.

Benestad, Michael. "Vom Bergfried aus gegen den Bolschewismus!" *Wiking-Ruf,* I, 1 (November, 1951), 14.

Berg, Gunnar. "Brücke der Liebe," *Nation Europa,* IV, 6 (June, 1954), 61–64.

Blunck, Hans Friedrich. "Vom Wandervogel zur SA," in Will Vesper, ed., *Deutsche Jugend.* Berlin: Holle, [1934]. Pp. 1–7.

Brand, Walter. "Zehn Jahre Witiko-Bund; Rückblick auf die Tätigkeit und Ausblick auf die Aufgaben," in *Die Marbacher Vorträge 1958. Beiträge des Witiko-Bundes zu Fragen der Zeit.* Frankfurt: Heimreiter, [c. 1959]. VI, 219–220.

Carlberg, Carl E. "Dreizehn Thesen," *Nation Europa,* IV, 12 (December, 1954), 42–43.

———. "Der gymnische Gedanke," *Der Weg,* VI, 5 (May, 1952), 337–340.

Dörfler, Anton. "Ruf aus der Ostmark," *Die Neue Literatur,* XXXIX, 12 (December, 1938), 665.

Dr. R. "Dichtertag in Lippoldsberg," *Cellesche Zeitung,* July 22, 1955.

Drowe. "Der Hecht im Karpfenteich," *Widerhall,* III, 4 (October, 1952), 10–12.

Düpow, Otto Karl. "Bonner Schützenhilfe in Algerien," *Deutsche Freiheit* (Munich), no. 5 (March 1, 1956), p. 5.

Egmont, Gunnar. "Nasser Asphalt in Österreich," *Europaruf* (Zurich, Munich, Salzburg), III, 8 (August, 1959), 1–2.

Ehrhardt, Arthur. Open letter to Dr. Eugen Gerstenmaier. *Nation Europa,* VI, 5 (May, 1956), end cover.

———. Open letter to Professor Hans Rothfels. *Nation Europa,* V, 3 (March, 1955), 70–72.

Engdahl, Per. "Demokratie—Diktatur—Korporativismus," *Nation Europa,* II, 1 (January, 1952), 21–26.

Exul foederatus, *pseud.* "Nationale Emigration," *Nation Europa,* III, 7 (July, 1953), 45–48.

Feld, C. "Kann man mit den Sowjets verhandeln?" *Rundbrief* (FeS), I, 7 (May, 1952), 1–2.

Fischer, Josepha. "Jugendverbände und Jugendbewegung in der Geschichte der katholischen Jugendführung," in Will Vesper, ed., *Deutsche Jugend.* Berlin: Holle, [1934]. Pp. 360–375.

Frank, Ernst. "Der Lebens- und Schaffensweg E. G. Kolbenheyers," *Der Bauhütten Brief,* II, 2 (1956), 7–13.

Franke-Gricksch, Alfred. "Europa, Aufmarsch– oder Kraftfeld," *Die Bruderschaft* (Hanover), January, 1950, p. 4.

Freiberger, Herbert. "Nur eine Lösung: Bündnisfreiheit Deutschlands," *Reichsruf* (Hanover), V, 26 (June 30, 1956), 3–4.

Führungsring ehemaliger Soldaten. "Was denkt das Volk über den Verteidigungsbeitrag?" *Rundbrief,* I, 7 (May, 1952), 5–6.

G. T. "Subventionierte Tradition," *Der Heimkehrer* (Göppingen), IV, 3 (March, 1953), 2.

Girgensohn, Walter. "Pharisäer!" *Der Stahlhelm* (Bonn), XXIII, 7 (July, 1956), 5.

Gisl. "Rasse und Wurzelgrund," *Widerhall,* III, 3 (September, 1952), 18–21.

———. "Was wäre denn Weihnachten . . ." *Widerhall,* V, 1 (January, 1954), 2–5.

Goebbels, Joseph. "Mitkämpfer von der Standarte," *Nationalsozialistische Briefe,* no. 23 (September 1, 1926).

Goetz, Cecile von. "Baruchistan?" *Nation Europa,* IV, 11 (November, 1954), 15–21.

Grimm, Friedrich. "Die Krankheit unserer Zeit," *Der Adlerführer,* VI, 4 (1957), 1–2.

Grosser, Johannes F. G. "Strafprozess gegen Bonn," *Der Deutsche Weg* (Hanover), II, 16 (first half of April, 1952), 1–2.

Gruenagel, Fritz. "Vom Schwund des Ehrbegriffes," *Burschenschaftliche Blätter,* LXVII, 8/9 (August–September, 1952), 266–273.

Grünberg, H. B. von. "Oberländer, der grosse Kanoniker der Demokratie," *Reichsruf* (Hanover), VII, 6 (February 8, 1958), 4.

Hagen-Michel, *pseud.* [i.e., J. F. G. Grosser]. "Politische Umtriebe," *Der Deutsche Weg* (Hanover), II, 15 (end of March, 1952), 2.

Hausser, Paul. Open letter to the Federal Minister of Defense, Franz Josef Strauss. *Der Freiwillige,* II, 5 (May, 1957), 7–8.

———. "SS–Verfügungstruppe und Wehrmacht," *Der Freiwillige,* I, 2 (February, 1956), 3–4.

———. "Die Waffen-SS antwortet," *Wiking-Ruf,* I, 2 (December, 1951), 1.

———. "Wissenschaft oder Spekulation," *Der Freiwillige,* I, 9 (September, 1956), 4.

Heberer, Gerhard. "Woher kommen wir?" *Der Weg,* VI, 7 (July, 1952), 466–471.

Heide, K. Book review of Hans Fritzsche, *Das Schwert auf der Waage. Widerhall,* V, 2 (February, 1954), 17–18.

———. Book review of Edmund Herbert, *Wir sprechen Hitler frei. Widerhall,* IV, 11/12 (November–December, 1953), 30–31.

Hein, Gerd. Letter to Editor, *Welt am Sonntag* (Hamburg), December 11, 1951.

———. "Sondernummer," *Rundbrief* (FeS), April, 1952.

Henrich, Joachim. "Der Auftrag userer Generation," *Allgemeine Deutsche Lehrerzeitung* (Frankfurt), n.s., XIV, 19 (November 1, 1961).

———. "Unser gemeinsames Anliegen," *Die Brücke,* III, 12 (October 15, 1956), Annex, 1.

Herold, Lutz. "Europa, Schau nach Süden!" *Europaruf* (Zurich, Munich, Salzburg), III, 10 (October, 1959), 5–6.

Hertel, Hans. "Niedersachsen—Grundstein zum neuen Reich!" *Reichsruf* (Hanover), Sonderausgabe Niedersachsen-Wahl, IV, 15 (April 9, 1955), 5–6.

Hoggan, David L. Letter to the editor of the *American Historical Review,* LXVIII, 3 (April, 1963), 914.

———. Reply to G. L. Weinberg's book review of *Der erzwungene Krieg, American Historical Review,* LXVIII, 3 (April, 1963), 914–915, and further rebuttal, LXIX, 1 (October, 1963), 303.

Hohlbaum, Robert. "Deutsche Burschenschaft von Heute," *Burschenschaftliche Blätter,* LXVII, 5 (May, 1952), 129–131.

Hover, Gerd. "Verschwörung gegen die Freiheit," *Nation Europa,* VI, 9 (September, 1956), 67–72.

Jarschel, Friedrich. "Das falsche Eurafrika," *Deutsche Freiheit* (Munich), no. 6 (March 15, 1957), p. 5.

Juergens, H. "Enttäuschte Hoffnungen," *Der Notweg* (Detmold), III, 11 (November, 1951), 7.

Kern, Erich, *pseud.* [i.e., Erich K. Kernmayr]. "Die Kriegsgeneration in der Sackgasse," *Der Freiwillige,* II, 4 (April, 1957), 3–6.

Kitzing, Erich. "Um die Studentin," *Burschenschaftliche Blätter,* LXVII, 7 (July, 1952), 232.

Kniggendorf, Walter. "Otto Ernst Remer: Das Problem des Untertan," *Florett,* n.d.

Krueger, J. "Verwoerds starke Hand," *Europaruf* (Zurich, Munich, Salzburg), III, 10 (October, 1959), 8.

Kunstmann, Heinrich. "Wir fordern inneren Frieden," *Reichsruf* (Hanover), VI, 22 (June 1, 1957), 1–2.

Littmann, Arnold. "Die bündische Jugend von 1925–1933," in Will Vesper, ed., *Deutsche Jugend.* Berlin: Holle, [1934]. Pp. 121–187.

Manteuffel, Hasso von. "Der Staat und wir," *Nordwest Zeitung* (Oldenburg), August 1, 1951, p. 1.

Marais, Kowie. "Die eurafrikanische Gemeinschaft," *Europaruf* (Zurich, Munich, Salzburg), II, 1 (January 1, 1958), 2.

Meinke, Henning. " 'Aufgaben' der deutschen Jugend," *Der Widerhall,* II, 10 (end of January, 1952), 7–9.

———. "Wir sind noch zu moralisch," *Der Widerhall,* II, 11 (end of February, 1952), 1–5.

Mende, Hinnerk. "Ein Brief aus Köln," *Widerhall,* III, 1 (July, 1952), 18–19.

Merten, Inge. "Mitten aus dem Geschehen. Tagebuchblätter," in Raymond de Geouffre de la Pradelle, Jean de Pange, *et al., Verjagt–beraubt–erschlagen. Die Austreibung aus den alten deutschen Grenzmarken. Schicksal und Völkerrecht.* Wiesbaden: Priester, [c. 1961]. Pp. 175–271.

Minet, Auguste. "Manifest an die europäische Nation," (leaflet), [1961].

Moeller van den Bruck, Arthur. "Der Wanderer ins Nichts," in Karl Radek *et al.*, eds., *Schlageter, eine Auseinandersetzung*. Berlin: Vereinigung Internationale Verlags-Anstalten, 1923.

Morgenbrod, Horst. "Tätigkeitsbericht" (Deutsch-Arabische Gesellschaft, *Rundbrief,* no. 3/37), *Afrika- und Orient-Informationen,* I, 11 (June, 1957), 4.

[Nehring, Joachim.] "Der Alte und der neue Prokonsul," *Der Scheinwerfer,* no. 35, 1949.

Noack, Erwin. "Führer und Volk als Grundlagen deutscher Demokratie," in Erwin Noack and G. A. Walz, *Deutsche Demokratie*. Berlin: Deutscher Rechtsverlag, 1938. Pp. 5–32.

Observer, *pseud.* "Wird jetzt die 08/15 Suppe angerührt?" *Wiking-Ruf,* V, 8 (August, 1956), 12–13.

Ortlepp, Hellmut. "Deutschland," *Schwarzer Reiter,* no. 6 (Gilbert [October], 1951), p. 2.

Otto, Wolfgang. "Die geheimnisvollen 'deutschen Landsknechte im Orient,' " *Deutsche Soldaten–Zeitung* (Munich), II, 45 (November 6, 1952), 3–4.

Peham, Friedrich. "Europas Jugend zur Vereinigungsidee," *Europaruf* (Zurich, Munich, Salzburg), I, 4 (April 15, 1957), 2.

Priester, Karl-Heinz. "Landesverrat gegen die Reichsregierung ist kein Landesverrat!" *Die Europäische Nationale* (Wiesbaden), VI, 66 (July, 1956), 9.

Proksch, Günther. "Nationale Opposition, nationale Politik und Deutsche Freiheits–Partei," in Otto Strasser, ed., *Zie und Weg der Nationalen Opposition*. Schriften für Deutschlands Erneuerung, no. 1. Munich: [Deutsche Freiheit, pref. October 9, 1962]. Pp. 15–24.

Putzer, F. H. "Weg zur Klärung," *Der Notweg* (Detmold), III, 12 (December, 1951), 2.

R. A. "Die Windfahne," *Widerhall,* III, 3 (September, 1952), 11–12.

Reich-Mummenhoff, Willi. "Die marxistische DGB in der Krise," *Reichsruf* (Hanover), III, 32 (August 14, 1954), 3.

———. "Radikalisierung der marxistischen Gewerkschaft," *Reichsruf* (Hanover), III, 44 (November 5, 1954), 3.

Reichenberger, Emmanuel J. "Wachet auf und wecket einander!" *Der Weg,* VI, 5 (May, 1952), 357–360.

Rethel, L. "Totengräber des Bauerntums," *Wir Bauern,* I, 26 (June 29, 1952), 2–3.

Ringe (Ministerialrat). "Versorgung der Wehrmachtsangehörigen," *Der Notweg* (Detmold), III, 11 (November, 1951), 6–7.

Risse, Friedrich Victor. "Im Zwielicht des geteilten Vaterlandes," *Deutsche Soldaten–Zeitung* (Munich), VII, 2 (February, 1957), 5.

Ross, Colin. "Die Vereinigten Staaten und Sowjetrussland als wesensverwandte Herrschaftsformen," *Widerhall,* III, 3 (September, 1952), 12–13.

Roth, Franz. "Fehlschüsse," *Der Stahlhelm* (Bonn), XXIII, 6 (June, 1956), 2.

Ruttner, Manfred. "Was bedeutet uns Kolbenheyer?" *Der Bauhütten Brief,* II, 3 (1956), 4–7.

S. "Die reformatorischen Leistungen der ehemaligen Waffen-SS," *Wiking-Ruf,* IV, 7 (July, 1955), 10–12.

———. "Die Waffen-SS als Teil der ehemaligen Kriegswehrmacht. Eine Antwort an das Institut für Zeitgeschichte," *Wiking-Ruf,* IV, 6 (June, 1955), 13–15, 18.

Sch. "DRP ging zum BHE: Gute Plätze auf BHE-Listen gesucht," *Die Deutsche Gemeinschaft* (Munich), VIII, 5/6 (2d March–1st April ed., 1957), 2.

Schäfer, Wilhelm. "Die deutsche Judenfrage. Eine Rede in Berlin," in his *Der deutsche Gott. Fünf Briefe an mein Volk.* Munich: Müller, 1923. Pp. 213–266.

Schmidt, Siegfried. "Die nationalen und völkischen Jugendverbände," *Erkenntnis und Tat,* VII, 5/6 (May–June, 1956), 15, 17.

Schumann, Gerhard. "Lieder der Umkehr," *Der Ruf* (Munich), I, 2 (September 1, 1945), 12.

Schwarzenborn, F. Book review of Gottfried Griesmayr, *Der politische Weg der Kriegsgeneration, Der Weg,* VI, 3 (March, 1952), 222.

Smidt, Udo. "Sinn und Sendung evangelischer Jugendführung," in Will Vesper, ed., *Deutsche Jugend.* Berlin: Holle, [1934]. Pp. 345–359.

Smitmans, Klaus C. "Gerechtigkeit für die Waffen-SS," *Wiking-Ruf,* I, 2 (December, 1951), 14.

Sörensen, Wolf. "Die Stimme der Ahnen," *Widerhall,* IV, 7 (July, 1953), 8–12.

Sorrel. Letters to Editor of *Welt am Sonntag* (Hamburg), November 26, 1951; January 2 and 16, 1952.

———. "Soldatenverbände im Umbruch," *Der Notweg* (Detmold), III, 11 (November, 1951), 3.

Soucek, Theodor. "Droht eine Weltwirtschaftskrise?" *Europaruf* (Zurich, Munich, Salzburg), II, 5 (May 1, 1958), 1.

Steidl, Rudolf. "Sondernummer," *Deutsche National–Zeitung,* August, 1955.

Steinberg, Helmut, *pseud.* [i.e., Heinrich Härtle]. "Geist und Tat: Zum 50. Geburtstag von H. W. Hagen," *Reichsruf* (Hanover), VI, 27 (May 18, 1957), 5.

———. "Roosevelt—ein weltgeschichtliches Verhängnis," in G. R. Jordan, *Sowjets siegen durch Spione. Roosevelt hat der Sowjet-Union die Atombombe ausgeliefert.* Trans. by Heinrich Härtle. Göttingen: Schütz, [1960]. Pp. 207–219.

Stössel, Harald. "Deutschlands General–Aufgabe: Afrika," *Bergische Wochenpost* (Wuppertal), no. 8 (February 25, 1956).

Thadden, Adolf von. "Unser Standort in einer zweigeteilten Welt," in *Das ganze Deutschland soll es sein! Referate gehalten auf dem Parteitag der DRP (Wiesbaden, 1.–2. September, 1956).* Hanover, pp. 19–27.

———. "Zum Parteitag der DRP in Köln," *Reichsruf* (Hanover), VI, 26 (May 11, 1957), 1.

Uhlig, A. W. "Lärm macht in Deutschland keinen Eindruck. Notwendige

Bemerkungen zu dem neuen Feldzug gegen 'Neo-Nazismus,' " *Deutsche Soldaten–Zeitung* (Munich), II, 11 (March 13, 1952), 1.

Vesper, Will. "Paul Ernst," *Die Neue Literatur,* XXXIV, 6 (June, 1933), 313.

———. "Unsere Meinung," *Die Neue Literatur,* XXXIV, 4 (April, 1933), 229–238.

Voigt, Horst. "Die Bruderschaft—Gesinnungsgemeinschaft und Orden," *Die Bruderschaft* (Hanover), January, 1950, p. 18.

———. "Bruderschaft und Deutsche Union," *Die Bruderschaft* (Hanover), August, 1950, p. 11.

Vollenweider, Erwin. "Europa, hilf dir selbst," *Europaruf* (Zurich, Munich, Salzburg), I, 8/9 (September 15, 1957), 3.

Vollmer, Dieter. "Ein Akt der Selbsthilfe," *Nation Europa,* V, 11 (November, 1955), back cover.

Wangemann, E. "Brief an einen scheidenden Kameraden," *Wiking-Ruf,* III, 10 (October, 1954), 8.

Wilken, M. "Grundlagen unserer Stahlhelm-Arbeit: Gedanken zur Giessener Botschaft," *Der Stahlhelm* (Bonn), XXI, 5 (May, 1954), 1.

Windisch, Konrad. "Wo bleiben die Taten? Einmal muss das Recht wieder Recht werden," *Der Adlerführer,* VI, 4 (1957), 5–7.

Wittkemper, W. "Das grosse Spiel beginnt. . . . Augen auf!" *Widerhall,* III, 4 (October, 1952), 13–15.

Ziemssen, Dietrich. " 'Wir' in Vergangenheit, Gegenwart und Zukunft," *Wiking-Ruf,* III, 6 (June, 1954), 5–6.

Ziesel, Kurt. "Kurt Ziesels Antwort an Jan A. van der Made," *Nation Europa,* VIII, 5 (May, 1958), 65–66.

(b) *Unsigned Articles*

"Abkommen zwischen den Jugendverbänden 'Jugendbund Adler,' 'Wikingjugend' und 'Bund heimattreuer Jugend,' Wien," *Unsere Arbeit,* III, 2 (1955), 3.

"Abrechnung mit Herrn Euler," *Der Nationaldemokrat* (Friedberg), II, 3 (April 1, 1949), 2.

"Afrika Farblichtbilder Vorträge: 'Kornkammer Nordafrika,' " *Afrika- und Orient-Informationen,* I, 11 (June, 1957), 17.

"An die deutschen Arbeiter," *Der Nationaldemokrat* (Friedberg), no. 9 (June, 1948), p. 1.

"Andere Aktion 'Frieden mit Israel,' " *Widerhall,* III, 3 (September, 1952), 8–9.

"Atlantik Pakt," *Der Nationaldemokrat* (Friedberg), II, 3 (April 1, 1949), 1.

"Der Atlantik Pakt und wir!" *Der Nationaldemokrat* (Friedberg), II, 4 (April 15, 1949), 1–2.

"Auf uns kommt es an," *Deutscher Beobachter* (Hamburg), I, 1 (June 8, 1951), 1–2.

"Aus dem Parteileben; Bericht über den Delegiertentag der Deutschen Rechten," *Der Konservative Bote* (Hamburg), II, 4/5 (May 15/31, 1948), 10–11.

"Die aussichtsreichste nationale Gruppierung," *Reichsruf* (Hanover), V, 40 (October 6, 1956), 2.

"Befehlsausgabe? Stab oder Front?" *Deutscher Beobachter* (Hamburg), I, 2 (June 22, 1951), 2.

"Die Bilanz," *Das Ziel* (Hanover), II, 15 (August 29, 1953), 3.

"Bonner Wahlmanöver," *Das Ziel* (Hanover), II, 16 (September 5, 1953), 1.

"Die Bücherstürmer von Frankfurt," *Deutscher Aufbruch* (Munich), V, 11 (October–November, 1955), 4.

"Das sind 'freie Wahlen,'" *Das Ziel* (Hanover), II, 16 (September 5, 1953), 2.

"Das war die Stunde der Hiag: 10,000 Kameraden in Minden," *Der Freiwillige,* I, 9 (September, 1956), 3–8.

"Deutsche Reichs-Partei, Kerntruppe der nationalen Sammlung," *Das Ziel* (Hanover), II, 2 (February, 1953), 1.

"Deutschland den Deutschen: Das Ziel der Deutschen Reichs-Partei," *Das Ziel* (Hanover), II, 15 (August 29, 1953), 3–4.

"Deutschland wacht auf," *Das Ziel* (Hanover), II, 15 (August 29, 1953), 1.

"Deutschland zwischen Ost und West," *Der Nationaldemokrat* (Friedberg), II, 4 (April 15, 1949), 1.

"Dr. Werner Naumann an den NWDR," *Das Ziel* (Hanover), II, 10 (July 25, 1953), 3.

"Dr. Werner Naumann klagt an," *Das Ziel* (Hanover), II, 13 (August 15, 1953), 2.

"300,000 freie Deutsche," *Das Ziel* (Hanover), II, 17 (September 12, 1953), 1.

"DRP gegen 'Ermächtigungsgesetz,'" *Das Ziel* (Hanover), II, 8 (July 11, 1953), 1.

"DRP: Partei des Reiches—Partei der Zukunft," *Reichsruf* (Hanover), III, 19 (May 15, 1954), 1.

"Ein Gespräch über den Kanal hinweg," *Der Widerhall,* II, 12 (March, 1952), 6–9.

"Ein Urteil der politischen Justiz?" *Die Europäische Nationale* (Wiesbaden), IV, 49 (November 1, 1954), 4.

"Ein Wort zur Versöhnung," *Neue Politik,* I, 43/44 (December 24, 1956), 3–4.

"Eine Schlacht für den Frieden!" *Der Nationaldemokrat* (Friedberg), II, 5 (beginning of May, 1949), 2.

"Einig gegen die 45er," *Das Ziel* (Hanover), II, 7 (July 4, 1953), 1.

"Einige Arbeitshinweise für die Winterarbeit," *Die Junge Front,* I, 1 (September–October, 1956), 18.

"Einigung nun auch in Bayern," *Deutsche Soldaten–Zeitung* (Munich), II, 13 (March 27, 1952), 7.

"Einstweilige Verfügung gegen Adenauer," *Das Ziel* (Hanover), II, 18 (September 19, 1953), 1.

"Das Ende des Hitlerismus," *Reichsruf* (Hanover), VII, 19 (May 10, 1958), 1–2.

"Das Ende eines Skandals. Der Bericht des 6. Parlamentarischen Untersuchungsausschusses," *Du und Dein Landtag, Parlamentsberichte der SPD Fraktion im Niedersächsischen Landtag,* no. 22 (February, 1956), pp. 23–32.

"Die Engländer haben diese Tatsache gewusst," *Widerhall,* III, 3 (September, 1952), 7–8.

"Die entscheidende Stunde versäumt . . . ," *Die Europäische Nationale* (Wiesbaden), VI, 71 (December, 1956), 4.

"Entscheidung im Bonner Farbenstreit," *Burschenschaftliche Blätter,* LXVII, 5 (May, 1952), 169.

"Entschliessung," *Der Nationaldemokrat* (Friedberg), II, 8 (middle of July, 1949), 1.

"Das Ergebnis der 'freien Wahlen,' " *Das Ziel* (Hanover), II, 17 (September 12, 1953), 1.

"Erklärung des Vorsitzenden der Deutschen Reichs-Partei Wilhelm Meinberg vor der Bundes-Pressekonferenz am 30.12.1959 in Bonn," *DRP-Pressedienst* (Hanover).

"Erklärung des Vorstandes des Bundesverbandes der Soldaten der ehemaligen Waffen-SS zum Kollektiv Begriff 'SS,' " *Der Freiwillige,* VI, 6 (June, 1961), 6–7.

"Faktor des Ausgleichs zwischen Ost und West," *Reichsruf* (Hanover), V, 36 (September 8, 1956), 3.

"Freiberger telegraphiert an Sorin," *Reichsruf* (Hanover), V, 26 (June 30, 1956), 1.

"Führertum in der Sackgasse," *Der Widerhall,* II, 14 (May, 1952), 9–12.

"Gedanken über Südtirol," *Der Adlerführer,* VI, 4 (1957), 4.

"Generalfeldmarschall Kesselring beim Stahlhelm in München," *Der Stahlhelm* (Bonn), XXI, 1 (January, 1954), 4.

"Gereke's 'Konserven Geschäft!' " *Der Deutsche Weg* (Hanover), II, 16 (first half of April, 1952), 5.

"Das Gewissen des deutschen Volkes," *Das Ziel* (Hanover), II, 29 (December 5, 1953), 2.

"Gleichberechtigung im Sterben!" *Deutscher Beobachter* (Hamburg), I, 2 (June 27, 1951), 1.

"Der Göttinger Protest ein historisch-politisches Ereignis?" *Hochschullehrer-Zeitung,* III, 4/6 (April–June, 1955), 9–11.

"Der grosse Prüfstein," *Deutsche Soldaten–Zeitung* (Munich), II, 41 (October 9, 1952), 1.

"Gruss den DG-Kameraden!" *Reichsruf* (Hanover), V, 45 (November 10, 1956), 3.

"Hans Grimm an Heuss," *Das Ziel* (Hanover), II, 9 (July 18, 1953), 1.

"Hans Venatier," Sonderdruck. *Nation Europa,* n.d.

"Herr Loritz dementiert . . . ," *Das Ziel* (Hanover), II, 8 (July 11, 1953), 1.

"Die Hintergründe des Nau-Nau," *Das Ziel* (Hanover), II, 2 (February, 1953), 1.

"Das Hintergründige in Herrn Loritz," *Das Ziel* (Hanover), II, 10 (July 25, 1953), 2.

"Ihr, unsere Opfer," *Widerhall,* IV, 11/12 (November–December, 1953), 1–6.

"Im Zeichen des Erfolges," *Rechts heran! DRP-Nachrichten,* February 7, 1949, p. 3.

"In Konstanz wird es sich entscheiden," *Wir Bauern,* I, 26 (June 29, 1952), 1–2.

"In Memoriam Pestbeule," *Der Nationaldemokrat* (Friedberg), II, 8 (July, 1949), 1.

"Jenseits der Ideologien," *Neue Politik,* II, 21 (May 25, 1957), 13–14.

"Kampfspruch," *Unsere Arbeit,* V, 4 (1957), 1.

"Die Kandidaten der DRP," *Das Ziel* (Hanover), II, 12 (August 8, 1953), 1.

"Kein Material gegen Naumann," *Das Ziel* (Hanover), II, 7 (July 4, 1953), 2.

"Kirkpatrick missachtet menschliche Grundrechte," *Das Ziel* (Hanover), II, 3 (March, 1953), 2.

"Kommt der totale Konfessionskrieg," *Reichsruf* (Hanover), III, 10 (March 13, 1954), 1.

"Kulturkampf tobt in Bayern," *Reichsruf* (Hanover), III, 11 (March 20, 1954), 2.

"Landesgemeinschaft Baden-Württemberg geschlossen für klaren Kurs," *Die Deutsche Gemeinschaft* (Munich), VII, 21 (1st December edition, 1956), 4.

"Landesvorstand Niedersachsen: Keine Hilfeleistung für die CDU," *Reichsruf* (Hanover), V, 46 (November 17, 1956), 6.

"Mehr Anstand, Herr Adenauer!" *Das Ziel* (Hanover), II, 5 (May, 1953), 1.

"Menschen verlieren ihr Gesicht," *Die Deutsche Gemeinschaft* (Munich), III, 4 (February, 1953), 2.

"Musste das sein?" *Der Notweg* (Detmold), III, 11 (November, 1951), 1–2.

"Nationalismus-Antinationalismus," *Der Pfeil,* VII, 8 (1956), 1–2.

"Naumann aus der Haft entlassen," *Das Ziel* (Hanover), II, 11 (August 1, 1953), 1.

"Naumanns Hieroglyphen," *Das Ziel* (Hanover), II, 4 (April, 1953), 4.

"Organischer Aufbau," *Deutsche Soldaten–Zeitung* (Munich), II, 13 (March 27, 1952), 6.

"Parität nur durch Marktordnung" (editorial), *Wir Bauern,* I, 29 (July 20, 1952), 1–2.

"Parteidiktatur," *Der Nationaldemokrat* (Friedberg), II, 8 (July, 1949), 2.

"Personalgutachterausschuss am Werk," *Deutsche Soldaten–Zeitung* (Munich), V, 9 (September, 1955), 2.

"Die Pressekonferenz der DRP in Köln," *Reichsruf* (Hanover), VI, 22 (June 1, 1957), 8.

" 'Preussens Gloria' auf US–Schalmeien!" *Deutscher Beobachter* (Hamburg), I, 3 (June 27, 1951), 2.

"Der Prozess gegen Erwin Schönborn," *Die Deutsche Gemeinschaft* (Munich), VIII, 15 (2d September ed., 1957), 4.

"Quantität und Qualität," *Der Widerhall,* II, 14 (May, 1952), 13–14.
"Realer Wille zur Not-Wende," *Der Widerhall,* II, Sonderfolge (end of September–beginning of October, 1951), 1–2.
"Rendsburg, ein Meilenstein," *Der Freiwillige,* V, 11 (November, 1960), 7.
"Richtsätze der DRP," *Das Ziel* (Hanover), II, 2 (February, 1953), 3.
"Die Ruhe zeigt unsere Stärke," *Wir Bauern,* I, 25 (June 22, 1952), 1–2.
"Rund um den Stahlhelm," *Das Ziel* (Hanover), II, 27 (November 21, 1953), 2.
"Die Sammlung vollzogen," *Das Ziel* (Hanover), II, 6 (June, 1953), 1.
"Schluss jetzt," *Deutscher Beobachter* (Hamburg), I, 1 (June 8, 1951), 1.
"So musst du wählen!" *Das Ziel* (Hanover), II, 16 (September 5, 1953), 4.
"Statt Sektierertum eine massvolle Politik," *Reichsruf* (Hanover), V, 45 (November 10, 1956), 2.
"Sudetendeutsche Jugend einst und jetzt," *Sudetendeutsche Jugend,* no. 9 (1956).
"Die Treue ist das Mark der Ehre!" *Der Stahlhelm* (Bonn), XXIII, 7 (July, 1956), 5.
"Über die Göttinger Protestaktion," *Deutsche Hochschullehrer-Zeitung,* III, 7/12 (July–December, 1955), 18–19.
"Um Recht und Ehre," *Der Freiwillige,* VI, 5 (May, 1961), 4–8.
"Verhöhnung der Verfassung," *Europaruf* (Zurich, Munich, Salzburg), IV, 6 (June, 1960), 3.
"Verleumdungsaktion des 'Grünwalder Kreises' gescheitert," *Reichsruf* (Hanover), VI, 19 (May 11, 1957), 2.
"Vertrauen zu wem?" *Deutscher Beobachter* (Hamburg), I, 2 (June 22, 1951), 1–2.
"Vizekanzler ignoriert Naumann–Fall," *Das Ziel* (Hanover), II, 3 (March, 1953), 2.
"Volksstaat oder Parteienstaat?" *Neue Politik,* II, 10 (March 9, 1957), 3–4.
"Vor einem Verfahren gegen Schlüter," *Reichsruf* (Hanover), VI, 6 (February 9, 1957), 3.
"Wahlanfechtung durch DRP," *Das Ziel* (Hanover), II, 17 (September 12, 1953), 2.
"Das Wahlfieber greift um sich: Richtigstellung von ein paar faustdicken Falschmeldungen," *Die Deutsche Gemeinschaft* (Munich), VIII, 3 (1st February ed., 1957), 2.
"Die Wahrheit über Landsberg," *Informationsdienst "Die Deutsche Gemeinschaft,"* Sonderdruck, 1951.
"Der Weg der Nationalen Opposition," *Deutscher Beobachter* (Hamburg), I, 2 (June 22, 1951), 12.
"Wer ist August Haussleiter?" *Die Deutsche Gemeinschaft* (Munich), VIII, 12 (1st August ed., 1957), 3.
"Wer jetzig Zeiten leben will," *Unsere Arbeit,* V, 4 (1957), 1.
"Wer lügt—Leuchtgens oder Euler?" *Der Nationaldemokrat* (Friedberg), II, 5 (beginning of May, 1949), 2.
"Wer schürt eigentlich gegen wen?" *Deutsche Soldaten–Zeitung* (Munich), II, 49 (December 4, 1952), 2.

"Der 'Westen' und die deutsche Freiheit," *Burschenschaftliche Blätter,* LXVII, 8/9 (August–September, 1952), 291.

"Wir sind für einander bestimmt!" *Wir Bauern,* I, 27 (July 6, 1952), 1–2.

"Wirwarr in den deutschen Parteien!" *Der Nationaldemokrat* (Friedberg), II, 4 (April 15, 1949), 2.

"Wo steht der deutsche Soldat?" *Deutscher Beobachter* (Hamburg), I, 1 (June 8, 1951), 1–2.

"Ziel und Weg des 'Reich Ordens,' " *Der Informationsdienst,* no. 186 (July 1, 1952), p. 5.

"Der 'Zufall' führt Regie!" *Die Europäische Nationale* (Wiesbaden), VI, 62 (February, 1956), 7–8.

"Zum Bonner Grundgesetz," *Der Nationaldemokrat* (Friedberg), II, 2 (March, 1949), 1.

"Zur Auflösung der LDP," *Der Nationaldemokrat* (Friedberg), II, 3 (April 1, 1949), 2.

"Zur Bundestagswahl!" *Der Nationaldemokrat* (Friedberg) II, 8 (July, 1949), 2.

"Zur Klärung!" *Der Stahlhelm* (Bonn), XXI, 2 (February, 1954), 1.

"Zusammenschluss der deutschen Rechten," *Der Konservative Bote* (Hamburg), II, 6/7 (June 15/30, 1948), 1.

"Zusammenschluss der nationalen Kräfte im Süd-West-Staat," *Reichsruf* (Hanover), V, 51/52 (December 22, 1956), 8.

3. DOCUMENTS

(a) *Collections of Documents and Reference Works*

Addressbuch des deutschsprachigen Buchhandels 1955. Frankfurt: Buchhändler-Vereinigung, n.d.

Anschriften deutscher Verlage und ausländischer Verlage mit deutschen Auslieferungen. IX. Jg. (1959). Marbach/Neckar: Schillerbuchhandlung Hans Banger.

Ausschuss für Deutsche Einheit und Vereinigung Demokratischer Juristen Deutschlands. *Von der Reichsanwaltschaft zur Bundesanwaltschaft. Wolfgang Fränkel, neuer Generalbundesanwalt. Eine Dokumentation.* N.p., n.d.

Bayerische Akademie der Wissenschaften. Historische Kommission, ed. *Neue deutsche Biographie.* Vol. IV. Berlin: Duncker & Humblot, 1959.

Committee for German Unity (German Democratic Republic). *Dokumentation: Judenmörder und Kriegsverbrecher am Hebel der Bundesrepublik.* Berlin (East), November, 1956.

———. *Murderers at Large in West Germany.* [Berlin: Neues Deutschland, 1958.]

Dam, Hendrick G. van, and Ralph Giordano, eds. *KZ-Verbrechen vor deutschen Gerichten.* [Frankfurt:] Europäische Verlagsanstalt, [1962].

Degener, Hermann A. L. *Degeners Wer ist's?* 10th ed. Berlin: Degener, 1935.

———, ed. *Wer ist's?* 8th ed. Leipzig: Degener, 1922.

———, ed. *Wer ist's?* 9th ed. Berlin: Degener, 1928.

Deutsche Bibliographie Zeitschriften 1945–1952. Frankfurt: Buchhändler-Vereinigung, 1958.

Das Deutsche Führerlexikon 1934/35. Berlin: Stollberg, 1934.

DIVO. *Basic Orientation and Political Thinking of West German Youth and Their Leaders, 1956. Report on a Nationwide Survey.* Mimeographed, 1956.

Franz, Günther. *Die politischen Wahlen in Niedersachsen 1867 bis 1949.* 3d enl. ed. With Appendix: "Die Wahlen 1951 bis 1956." Bremen-Horn: Dorn, 1957.

Habel, Walter, ed. *Wer ist wer?* Das deutsche *Who's Who?* 11th ed. of *Degeners Wer ist's?* Berlin-Grunewald: arani, [c. 1951].

———. *Wer ist wer?* Das deutsche *Who's Who?* 12th ed. of *Degeners Wer ist's?* Berlin-Grunewald: arani, [c. 1955].

———. *Wer ist wer?* Das deutsche *Who's Who?* 13th ed. of *Degeners Wer ist's?* Berlin-Grunewald: arani, [c. 1958].

———. *Wer ist wer?* Das deutsche *Who's Who?* 14th ed. of *Degeners Wer ist's?* Vol. 1: Bundesrepublik Deutschland und Westberlin. Berlin-Grunewald: arani, [c. 1962].

Hofer, Walther, ed. *Der Nationalsozialismus: Dokumente 1933–1945.* Rev. ed. [Frankfurt:] Fischer Bücherei, [c. 1957].

Institut für Publizistik der Freien Universität Berlin. *Die Deutsche Presse 1954: Zeitungen und Zeitschriften.* Berlin: Duncker und Humblot, 1954.

———. *Die Deutsche Presse 1956: Zeitungen und Zeitschriften.* Berlin: Duncker und Humblot, 1956.

———. *Die Deutsche Presse 1961: Zeitungen und Zeitschriften.* Berlin: Duncker und Humblot, 1961.

Jacobsen, Hans-Adolf, ed. *1939–1945: Der zweite Weltkrieg in Chronik und Dokumenten.* 5th ed. Darmstadt: Wehr und Wissen, 1961.

Koppel, Wolfgang, ed. *Ungesühnte Nazijustiz. Hundert Urteile klagen ihre Richter an.* For the Organizing Committee of the Document Exhibit "Ungesühnte Nazijustiz." [Karlsruhe:] n.p., August, 1960.

Kürschners Deutscher Literatur-Kalender 1952. LII. Jg. Berlin: De Gruyter, 1952.

Kürschners Deutscher Literatur-Kalender 1963. LIV. Jg. Berlin: De Gruyter, 1963.

Mehnert, Klaus, and Heinrich Schulte, eds. *Deutschland-Jahrbuch 1953.* Essen: Rheinisch-Westfälisches Verlagskontor, [c. 1953].

Neumann, Erich Peter, and Elisabeth Noelle, eds. *Antworten.* 2d ed. Allensbach am Bodensee: Verlag für Demoskopie, 1955.

Noelle, Elisabeth, and Erich Peter, Neumann, eds. *Jahrbuch der öffentlichen Meinung 1947–1955.* 2d corr. ed. Allensbach am Bodensee: Verlag für Demoskopie, [c. 1956].

Oppenheimer, M., ed. (Präsidium der Vereinigung der Verfolgten des Naziregimes [VVN]). *Die unbewältigte Gegenwart. Eine Dokumentation über Rolle und Einfluss ehemals führender Nationalsozialisten in der Bundesrepublik Deutschland*. Frankfurt: Vereinigung der Verfolgten des Naziregimes, [pref. June 30, 1962].

Poliakov, Léon, and Josef Wulf. *Das Dritte Reich und seine Denker*. Berlin: arani, 1959.

———. *Das Dritte Reich und seine Diener, Dokumente*. Berlin-Grunewald: arani, 1956.

Pross, Harry, ed. *Die Zerstörung der deutschen Politik, Dokumente 1871–1933*. [Frankfurt:] Fischer Bücherei, [c. 1959].

Ruhm von Oppen, Beate, ed. *Documents on Germany under Occupation 1945–1954*. London: Oxford University Press, 1955.

Schnabel, Reimund, ed. *Macht ohne Moral: Eine Dokumentation über die SS*. Frankfurt: Röderberg, 1957.

Wulf, Josef. *Literatur und Dichtung im Dritten Reich*. [Gütersloh:] Mohn, [c. 1963].

(b) *Government Documents*

Allied Control Council. Directive No. 24. Berlin, January 12, 1946.

———. Directive No. 38. Berlin, October 12, 1946.

Baden-Württemberg. Statistisches Landesamt. Statistik von Baden-Württemberg, Vol. 8. *Die Wahl zur Verfassungsgebenden Landesversammlung von Baden-Württemberg am. 9. März 1952*. N.p., n.d.

———. ———. ———, Vol. 10. *Die Wahl zum ersten Bundestag der Bundesrepublik Deutschland am 14. August 1949*. Stuttgart, 1953.

———. ———. ———, Vol. 11. *Die Wahl zum zweiten Bundestag der Bundesrepublik Deutschland am 6. September 1953*. Stuttgart, 1953.

———. ———. ———, Vol. 24. *Die Landtagswahl vom 4. März 1956 in Baden-Württemberg*. Stuttgart, 1956.

———. ———. Statistische Berichte. Reihe: Wahlstatistik, no. II-W-4/53. *Die Gemeinderats- und Kreistagswahlen in Baden-Württemberg am 15. November 1953*. 23 March 1954.

———. ———. *Die Wahl der Gemeinderäte und Gemeindeverordneten in Baden-Württemberg am 11. November 1956*. BIII 3, 18 December 1956.

Bavaria. Bayerischer Landtag. *Stenographischer Bericht über die Verhandlungen des Bayerischen Landtags*. Vols. II (no. 37, November 28, 1947); III (no. 93, December 1, 1948); V (nos. 128, November 9, 1949; 136, December 16, 1949; 137, January 17, 1950).

———. Bayerisches Statistisches Landesamt. *Statistisches Jahrbuch für Bayern 1947*. XXIII, [pref. Munich, 1948].

———. ———. Beiträge zur Statistik Bayerns, no. 147. *Die Wahlen in den Gemeinden und Kreisen Bayerns 1946 und 1948*. [Pref. June, 1949.]

———. ———. ———, no. 150. *Die erste Bundestagswahl in Bayern am 14. August 1949*. [Pref. March, 1950.]

———. ———. ———, no. 163. *Wahl zum Bayerischen Landtag am 26. November 1950*. [Pref. April, 1951.]

———. ———. ———, no. 182. *Kommunalwahlen in Bayern am 30. März, 1952.* [Pref. February, 1953.]

———. ———. ———, no. 193. *Zweite Bundestagswahl in Bayern am 6. September 1953.* [Pref. February, 1954.]

———. ———. ———, no. 203. *Kommunalwahlen in Bayern am 18. März 1956.* [Pref. February, 1957.]

———. ———. "Wahl zum Bayerischen Landtag am 28. November 1954," by Richard Schachtner, *Zeitschrift des Bayerischen Statistischen Landesamts,* LXXXVII, 3/4 (1955), 146–160.

Bremen. Statistisches Landesamt. *Statistische Berichte (Statistischer Dienst),* A 12/3 (Reihe: Bevölkerung, Folge II), October 6, 1956.

———. ———. *Statistische Mitteilungen aus Bremen.* XI, 4 (1956).

———. ———. "Die Wahl zur Bremischen Bürgerschaft am 9. October 1955 im Lande Bremen."

Federal Republic of Germany. Bundestag. *Bericht des Untersuchungsausschusses* (44. Ausschuss), *Verhandlungen des deutschen Bundestages,* 1. Wahlperiode, Anlagen, *Drucksache Nr. 2274.*

———. ———. *Stenographisches Protokoll über die 3. Sitzung des 47. Ausschusses, Untersuchungsausschuss gemäss Drucksache Nr. 2680 (Personalpolitik Ausw. Amt) am 18. Dezember 1951.*

———. ———. "Tätigkeitsbericht des Personalgutachterausschusses für die Streitkräfte" (December 6, 1957), 3. Wahlperiode, *Drucksache Nr. 109.*

———. ———. *Verhandlungen des deutschen Bundestages,* Erste Wahlperiode, *Stenographische Berichte,* 7. Sitzung (September 22, 1949); 148. Sitzung (June 7, 1951); and 235. Sitzung (October 23, 1952), 10799–10834.

———. ———. ———, Zweite Wahlperiode, *Drucksache Nr. 1619* (July 13, 1955).

———. ———. ———, ———, *Stenographischer Bericht,* 30. Sitzung (May 21, 1954); 116. Sitzung (March 12, 1956); 139. Sitzung (April 12, 1956).

———. Bundesverfassungsgericht. ["Urteil] in dem Verfahren über den Antrag der Bundesregierung auf Feststellung der Verfassungswidrigkeit der Sozialistischen Reichspartei." 1 BvB 1/51. October 23, 1952.

———. ———. *Das Urteil des Bundesverfassungsgerichts vom 23. Oktober 1952 betreffend Feststellung der Verfassungswidrigkeit der Sozialistischen Reichspartei.* Tübingen, 1952.

———. "Bundeswahlgesetz vom 7. Mai 1956," *Bundesgesetzblatt,* no. 21 (May 9, 1956), part I, pp. 383–407. Bonn.

———. "Gesetz zur Regelung der Rechtsverhältnisse der unter Artikel 131 des GG fallenden Personen" (May 11, 1951). *Bundesgesetzblatt,* no. 22, May 13, 1951. Bonn.

———. Ministry of Justice. *Die Verfolgung nationalsozialistischer Straftaten im Gebiet der Bundesrepublik Deutschland seit 1945.* Bonn: n.p., July, 1964.

———. Ministry of the Interior. "Verfassungswidrigkeit der Deutschen

Reichs-Partei" (6342 Aa-1138 III/53, September 14, 1953). Mimeographed, notarized copy.

———. "Wahlgesetz zum ersten Bundestag und zur ersten Bundesversammlung der Bundesrepublik Deutschland vom 15. Juni 1949," *Bundesgesetzblatt,* June 17, 1949, pp. 21–23. Bonn.

———. "Wahlgesetz zum zweiten Bundestag und zur Bundesversammlung vom 8. Juli 1953," *Bundesgesetzblatt,* no. 32 (July 10, 1953), part I, pp. 470–491. Bonn.

German Democratic Republic. National Front of Democratic Germany. National Council. Documentation Center of the State Archives Administration of the German Democratic Republic. *Brown Book. War and Nazi Criminals in West Germany: State, Economy, Administration, Army, Justice, Science.* [Dresden:] Zeit im Bild, [pref. 1965].

———. ———. ———. *White Book on the American and British Policy of Intervention in West Germany and the Revival of German Imperialism.* N.p., [1951].

German Reich. (Third Reich.) Geheime Staatspolizei, Polizeistelle München. "Die illegale monarchistische Bewegung in Bayern," by Regierungsrat Wentz. Munich: October 1939. In *Deutscher Informationsdienst,* no. 294 (August 4, 1953), p. 5.

———. ———. Volksbund für das Deutschtum im Ausland. *Dienstanweisungen und Mitteilungen des VDA-Gauverbandes Oberdonau.* Sonderbeilage, Linz: [1944].

———. (Weimar.) Reichstag. Bureau des Reichstags. *Reichstags-Handbuch, II. Wahlperiode, 1924.* Berlin, 1924.

Hesse. *Gesetz- und Verordnungsblatt für Gross-Hessen.* Nos. 7–23 (March 15, 1946—August 4, 1946). Wiesbaden.

———. *Gesetzes-Sammlung.* Gesetz zur Befreiung von Nationalsozialismus und Militarismus (May 29, 1947—October 9, 1947). Pp. 63–76. Stuttgart and Wiesbaden.

———. Hessischer Landtag, Zweite Wahlperiode, *Stenographischer Bericht über die 32. Sitzung* (October 8, 1951), 1294–1296; *42. Sitzung* (March 18, 1952), 1709–1726.

———. Hessisches Ministerium für Politische Befreiung. *Amtsblatt.* I, 1/2 (January 15, 1947) to III, 63 (August 9, 1949). Wiesbaden.

———. ———. *Rundverfügungen,* nos. 1–60 (April 26, 1946–December 28, 1946). Wiesbaden.

———. Hessisches Statistisches Landesamt. Beiträge zur Statistik Hessens, no. 52. *Die Kommunalwahlen in Hessen: Ergebnisse der Gemeindewahlen und Kreiswahlen vom 4. 5. 1952.* September, 1952.

———. ———. ———, no. 64. *Hessen wählt zum zweiten Bundestag: Das amtliche Ergebnis der Wahl zum zweiten Bundestag in Hessen am 6. September 1953.* November, 1953.

———. ———. ———, no. 72. *Die Wahl zum hessischen Landtag am 28. November 1954.* March, 1955.

———. ———. ———, no. 86. *Die Kommunalwahlen in Hessen: Ergeb-*

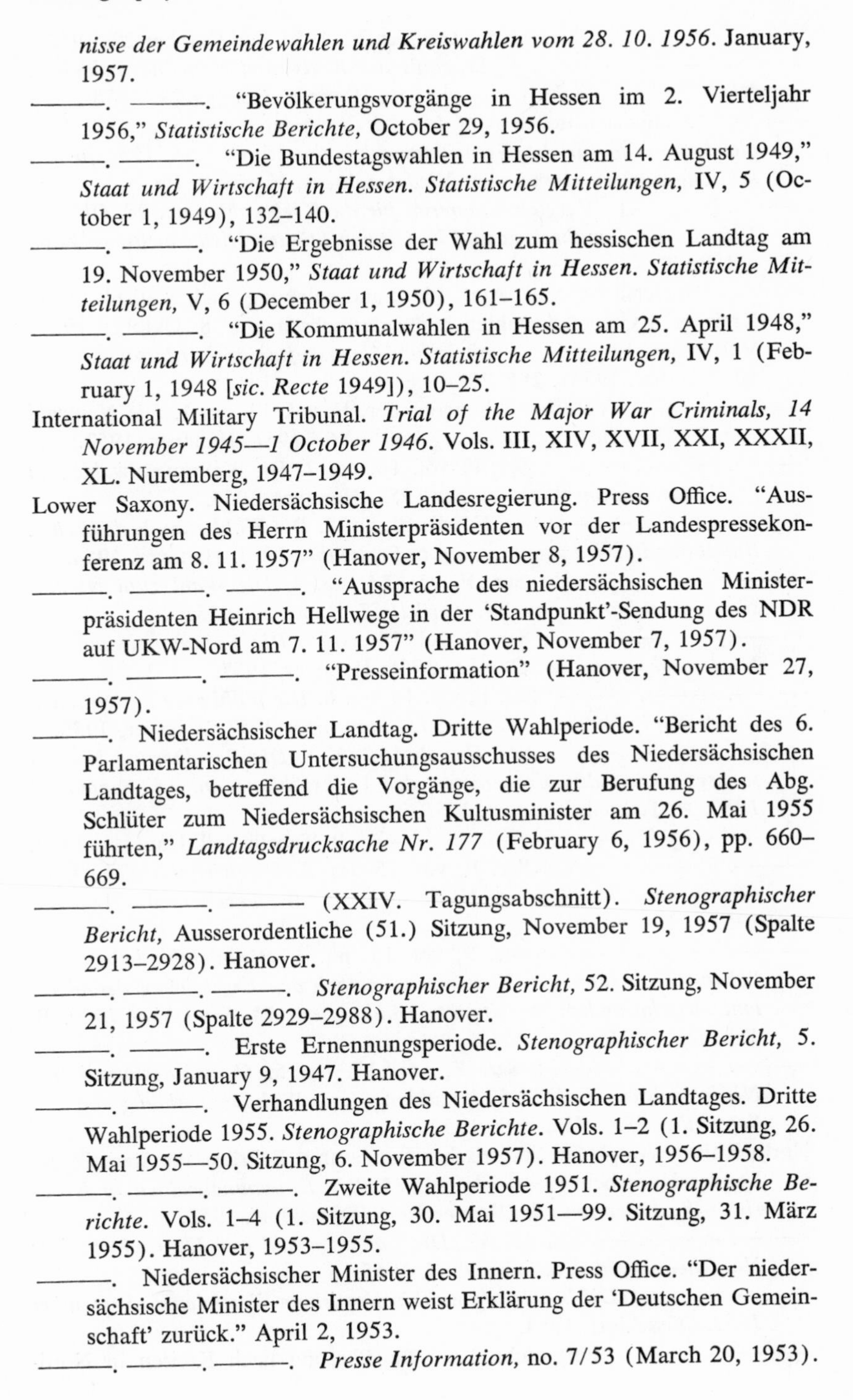

nisse der Gemeindewahlen und Kreiswahlen vom 28. 10. 1956. January, 1957.

———. ———. "Bevölkerungsvorgänge in Hessen im 2. Vierteljahr 1956," *Statistische Berichte,* October 29, 1956.

———. ———. "Die Bundestagswahlen in Hessen am 14. August 1949," *Staat und Wirtschaft in Hessen. Statistische Mitteilungen,* IV, 5 (October 1, 1949), 132–140.

———. ———. "Die Ergebnisse der Wahl zum hessischen Landtag am 19. November 1950," *Staat und Wirtschaft in Hessen. Statistische Mitteilungen,* V, 6 (December 1, 1950), 161–165.

———. ———. "Die Kommunalwahlen in Hessen am 25. April 1948," *Staat und Wirtschaft in Hessen. Statistische Mitteilungen,* IV, 1 (February 1, 1948 [*sic. Recte* 1949]), 10–25.

International Military Tribunal. *Trial of the Major War Criminals, 14 November 1945—1 October 1946.* Vols. III, XIV, XVII, XXI, XXXII, XL. Nuremberg, 1947–1949.

Lower Saxony. Niedersächsische Landesregierung. Press Office. "Ausführungen des Herrn Ministerpräsidenten vor der Landespressekonferenz am 8. 11. 1957" (Hanover, November 8, 1957).

———. ———. ———. "Aussprache des niedersächsischen Ministerpräsidenten Heinrich Hellwege in der 'Standpunkt'-Sendung des NDR auf UKW-Nord am 7. 11. 1957" (Hanover, November 7, 1957).

———. ———. ———. "Presseinformation" (Hanover, November 27, 1957).

———. Niedersächsischer Landtag. Dritte Wahlperiode. "Bericht des 6. Parlamentarischen Untersuchungsausschusses des Niedersächsischen Landtages, betreffend die Vorgänge, die zur Berufung des Abg. Schlüter zum Niedersächsischen Kultusminister am 26. Mai 1955 führten," *Landtagsdrucksache Nr. 177* (February 6, 1956), pp. 660–669.

———. ———. ——— (XXIV. Tagungsabschnitt). *Stenographischer Bericht,* Ausserordentliche (51.) Sitzung, November 19, 1957 (Spalte 2913–2928). Hanover.

———. ———. ———. *Stenographischer Bericht,* 52. Sitzung, November 21, 1957 (Spalte 2929–2988). Hanover.

———. ———. Erste Ernennungsperiode. *Stenographischer Bericht,* 5. Sitzung, January 9, 1947. Hanover.

———. ———. Verhandlungen des Niedersächsischen Landtages. Dritte Wahlperiode 1955. *Stenographische Berichte.* Vols. 1–2 (1. Sitzung, 26. Mai 1955—50. Sitzung, 6. November 1957). Hanover, 1956–1958.

———. ———. ———. Zweite Wahlperiode 1951. *Stenographische Berichte.* Vols. 1–4 (1. Sitzung, 30. Mai 1951—99. Sitzung, 31. März 1955). Hanover, 1953–1955.

———. Niedersächsischer Minister des Innern. Press Office. "Der niedersächsische Minister des Innern weist Erklärung der 'Deutschen Gemeinschaft' zurück." April 2, 1953.

———. ———. ———. *Presse Information,* no. 7/53 (March 20, 1953).

———. ———. "Schnellbrief," October 24, 1952, and October 29, 1952.

———. ———. *Vorläufiges Ergebnis der Kreis- und Gemeindewahlen in Niedersachsen am 28. Oktober 1956.* Hanover, October 29, 1956.

———. [Niedersächsisches Amt für Landesplanung und Statistik?] *Vergleichsmaterial für die Gemeindewahlen am 28. Oktober 1956 in den kreisangehörigen Gemeinden Niedersachsens.* N.p., n.d. Pp. 5.

———. [———?] *Vergleichsmaterial für die Kreiswahlen am 28. Oktober 1956 in den Landkreisen und kreisfreien Städten Niedersachsens.* N.p., n.d. Pp. 9.

———. Niedersächsisches Amt für Landesplanung und Statistik. "Die Kreis- und Gemeindewahlen in Niedersachsen am 28. Oktober 1956: Vorläufiges Ergebnis," *Statistische Monatshefte für Niedersachsen,* X, 10 (October, 1956), 285–287.

———. ———. Veröffentlichungen: Ser. F, vol. 14, no. 1. *Die Neuwahl zum Niedersächsischen Landtag am 6. Mai 1951.* Hanover, 1952.

———. ———. ———: Ser. F, vol. 14, no. 2. *Die Kommunalwahlen in Niedersachsen am 9. November 1952.* Hanover, 1953.

———. ———. ———: Ser. F, vol. 14, no. 3. *Die Wahl zum 2. deutschen Bundestag in Niedersachsen am 6. September 1953.* Hanover, 1954.

———. ———. ———: Ser. F, vol. 14, no. 4. *Die Wahl zum Niedersächsischen Landtag am 24. April 1955.* Hanover, 1955.

———. ———. ———: Ser. F, vol. 14, no. 5. *Die Kommunalwahlen in Niedersachsen am 28. Oktober 1956.* Hanover, 1957.

———. ———. ———: Ser. F, vol. 14, no. 6. *Die Wahl zum 3. deutschen Bundestag in Niedersachsen am 15. September 1957.* Hanover, 1958.

———. ———. ———: Ser. F, vol. 15, no. 1. *Die Bevölkerung Niedersachsens nach den Ergebnissen der Volkszählung am 13. September 1950.* A. Textteil. Hanover, 1955.

———. ———. ———: ———. ———. B. Tabellenteil. Hanover, 1953.

———. ———. ———: Ser. F, vol. 15, no. 2. *Die wirtschaftliche Gliederung der Bevölkerung Niedersachsens.* B. Tabellenteil. Hanover, 1953.

———. ———. ———: Ser. F, vol. 15, no. 4. *Die nichtlandwirtschaftlichen Arbeitsstätten in Niedersachsen nach den Ergebnissen der nichtlandwirtschaftlichen Arbeitsstättenzählung am 13. September 1950.* B. Tabellenteil. Hanover, 1953.

———. ———. ———: Ser. F, vol. 15, no. 5. *Gemeindestatistik für Niedersachsen. Teil 1: Volkszählung und Wohnungszählung am 13. September 1950.* Hanover, 1952.

North Rhine–Westphalia. Statistisches Landesamt. Beiträge zur Statistik des Landes Nordrhein-Westfalen, no. 73. *Die Kommunalwahlen in Nordrhein-Westfalen am 28. Oktober 1956.* Düsseldorf, 1957.

———. ———. ———, no. 47. *Die Landtagswahl am 27. Juni 1954 in Nordrhein-Westfalen.* Düsseldorf, 1955.

———. ———. *Die Bundestagswahl in Nordrhein-Westfalen, 6. September 1953.* Düsseldorf, 1954.

———. ———. "Fortgeschriebene Bevölkerung nach Kreisen in Nord-

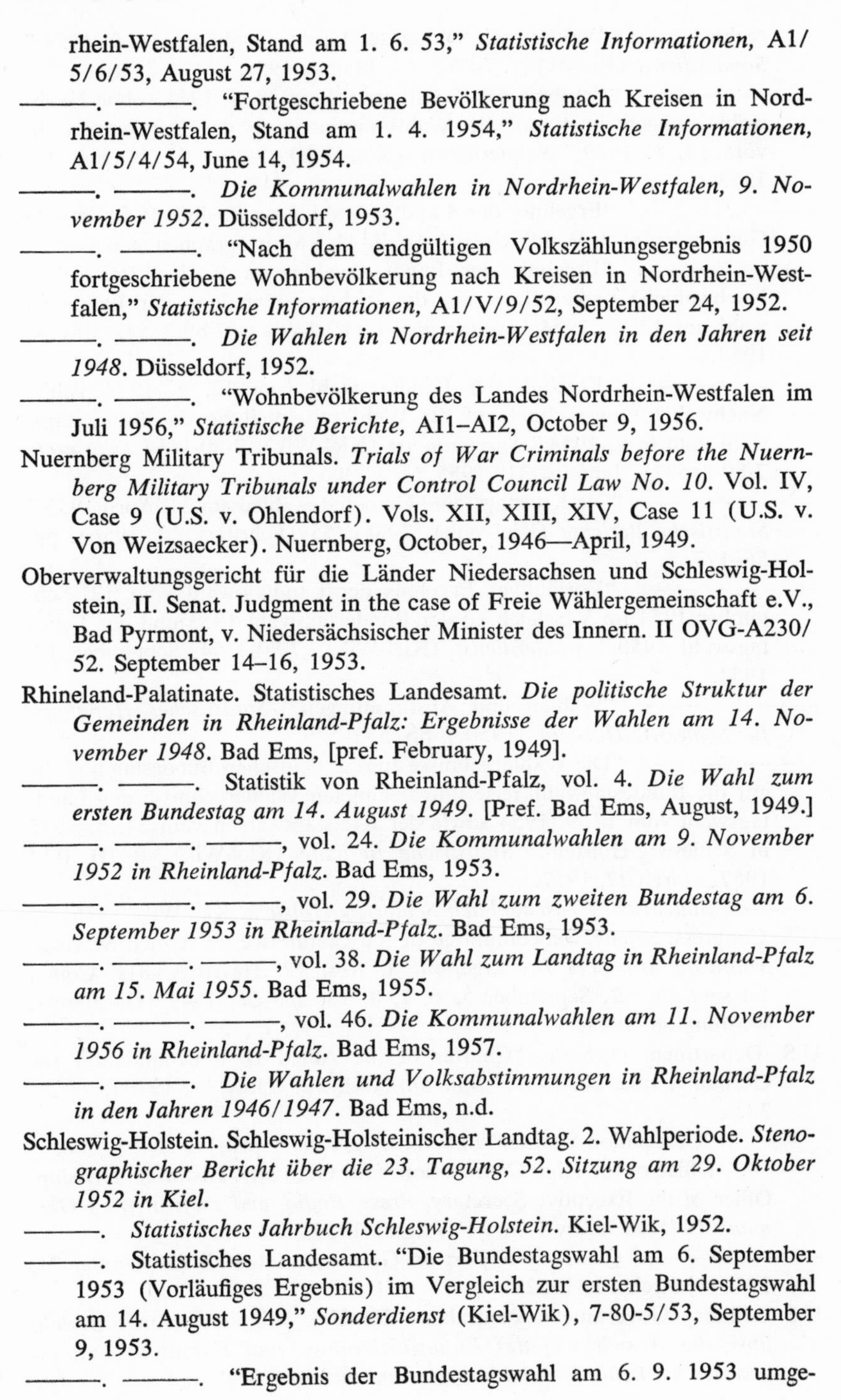

rhein-Westfalen, Stand am 1. 6. 53," *Statistische Informationen*, A1/5/6/53, August 27, 1953.

———. ———. "Fortgeschriebene Bevölkerung nach Kreisen in Nordrhein-Westfalen, Stand am 1. 4. 1954," *Statistische Informationen*, A1/5/4/54, June 14, 1954.

———. ———. *Die Kommunalwahlen in Nordrhein-Westfalen, 9. November 1952*. Düsseldorf, 1953.

———. ———. "Nach dem endgültigen Volkszählungsergebnis 1950 fortgeschriebene Wohnbevölkerung nach Kreisen in Nordrhein-Westfalen," *Statistische Informationen*, A1/V/9/52, September 24, 1952.

———. ———. *Die Wahlen in Nordrhein-Westfalen in den Jahren seit 1948*. Düsseldorf, 1952.

———. ———. "Wohnbevölkerung des Landes Nordrhein-Westfalen im Juli 1956," *Statistische Berichte*, AI1–AI2, October 9, 1956.

Nuernberg Military Tribunals. *Trials of War Criminals before the Nuernberg Military Tribunals under Control Council Law No. 10*. Vol. IV, Case 9 (U.S. v. Ohlendorf). Vols. XII, XIII, XIV, Case 11 (U.S. v. Von Weizsaecker). Nuernberg, October, 1946—April, 1949.

Oberverwaltungsgericht für die Länder Niedersachsen und Schleswig-Holstein, II. Senat. Judgment in the case of Freie Wählergemeinschaft e.V., Bad Pyrmont, v. Niedersächsischer Minister des Innern. II OVG-A230/52. September 14–16, 1953.

Rhineland-Palatinate. Statistisches Landesamt. *Die politische Struktur der Gemeinden in Rheinland-Pfalz: Ergebnisse der Wahlen am 14. November 1948*. Bad Ems, [pref. February, 1949].

———. ———. Statistik von Rheinland-Pfalz, vol. 4. *Die Wahl zum ersten Bundestag am 14. August 1949*. [Pref. Bad Ems, August, 1949.]

———. ———. ———, vol. 24. *Die Kommunalwahlen am 9. November 1952 in Rheinland-Pfalz*. Bad Ems, 1953.

———. ———. ———, vol. 29. *Die Wahl zum zweiten Bundestag am 6. September 1953 in Rheinland-Pfalz*. Bad Ems, 1953.

———. ———. ———, vol. 38. *Die Wahl zum Landtag in Rheinland-Pfalz am 15. Mai 1955*. Bad Ems, 1955.

———. ———. ———, vol. 46. *Die Kommunalwahlen am 11. November 1956 in Rheinland-Pfalz*. Bad Ems, 1957.

———. ———. *Die Wahlen und Volksabstimmungen in Rheinland-Pfalz in den Jahren 1946/1947*. Bad Ems, n.d.

Schleswig-Holstein. Schleswig-Holsteinischer Landtag. 2. Wahlperiode. *Stenographischer Bericht über die 23. Tagung, 52. Sitzung am 29. Oktober 1952 in Kiel*.

———. *Statistisches Jahrbuch Schleswig-Holstein*. Kiel-Wik, 1952.

———. Statistisches Landesamt. "Die Bundestagswahl am 6. September 1953 (Vorläufiges Ergebnis) im Vergleich zur ersten Bundestagswahl am 14. August 1949," *Sonderdienst* (Kiel-Wik), 7-80-5/53, September 9, 1953.

———. ———. "Ergebnis der Bundestagswahl am 6. 9. 1953 umgerechnet auf die Wahlkreiseinteilung der Landtagswahl am 12. 9. 1954," *Sonderdienst* (Kiel-Wik), 7-80-3/54, May 4, 1954.

———. ———. "Ergebnis der Kreistagswahl am 29. 4. 1951 (ohne Nachwahl) umgerechnet auf die Wahlkreiseinteilung der Bundestagswahl vom 14. 8. 1949," *Sonderdienst* (Kiel-Wik), 7-80-3/53, August 17, 1953.

———. ———. "Ergebnis der Landtagswahl vom 9. Juli 1950 in den Gemeinden nach Wahlkreisen," Az. 7–32. (Mimeographed, n.d.)

———. ———. "Ergebnis der Landtagswahl vom 9. 7. 1950 (ohne Nachwahlen) umgerechnet auf die Wahlkreiseinteilung der Landtagswahl am 12. 9. 1954," *Sonderdienst* (Kiel-Wik), 7-80-2/54, May 4, 1954.

———. ———. "Ergebnis der Landtagswahl vom 12. 9. 1954 (ohne Nachwahl) umgerechnet auf die Wahlkreiseinteilung der Bundestagswahl vom 6. 9. 1953," *Sonderdienst* (Kiel-Wik), 7-80-1/55 (*sic; recte* 7-80-8/54?), January 31, 1955.

———. ———. "Die Kreistags- und Gemeindewahlen am 24. April 1955," *Statistische Berichte* (Kiel-Wik), 7-80-6/55 (February 20, 1956), pp. 56–177.

———. ———. "Vorläufiges Ergebnis der Landtagswahl vom 12. September 1954 im Vergleich zu der Bundestagswahl 1953 und der Landtagswahl 1950," *Sonderdienst* (Kiel-Wik), 7-80-4/54, September 13, 1954.

———. ———. "Wahlen und Abstimmungen," *Statistisches Handbuch für Schleswig-Holstein,* [1950?], pp. 535–549.

———. ———. "Die Wahlergebnisse zum 2. deutschen Bundestag und die auf die Bundestagwahlkreise umgerechneten Wahlergebnisse der Landtagswahl vom 12. 9. 1954 sowie der Kreistagswahlen vom 24. 4. 1955 in Schleswig-Holstein," *Statistische Berichte* (Kiel-Wik), B III 1-1/1957, March 22, 1957.

———. *Statistisches Taschenbuch Schleswig-Holstein.* Kiel-Wik, 1956.

U.S. Congress. Senate. Subcommittee of the Committee on Armed Services. *Malmédy Massacre Investigation, S. Res. 42.* Hearings, 81st Cong., 1st sess. Part 2, September 5, 6, 7, 8, 13, and 28, 1949 (Germany). Washington, 1949.

U.S. Department of State. "Charter of the Allied High Commission for Germany, June 20, 1949," *Bulletin,* XXI, 523 (July 11, 1949), 25-28, 38.

———. "Occupation Statute," *Bulletin,* XX, 511 (April 17, 1949), 500.

———. Office of the High Commissioner for Germany. Historical Division. Office of the Executive Secretary. *Press, Radio, and Film in West Germany 1945–1953,* by Henry P. Pilgert. 1953.

———. ———. *Quarterly Report on Germany.* 1st–10th (September 21, 1949—March 31, 1952).

U.S. Military Government. Zentralamt der U.S. Militärregierung. *Bericht über die Auswirkung des Entnazifizierungs- und Entmilitarisierungsgesetzes bei Behörden und in Privatunternehmen.* N.P., n.d.

U.S. Office of the Chief Counsel for the Prosecution of Axis Criminality. *Nazi Conspiracy and Aggression, Opinion and Judgment.* Washington: Government Printing Office, 1947.

(c) *Party Documents*

Arbeitsgemeinschaft parteiloser freier Wähler, Villingen, [Karl Steinfeld]. *Die dritte Idee: Volk steh auf zur Tat!* Broschürenreihe Sammlung zur Tat, no. 1, [Villingen/Schwarzwald, 1949].

Arbeitskreis für die Vereinigung der Nationalen Parteien. [Bertold Fortmeier, Krailling.] "Bericht über die Tagung am 27. 1. 57."

Beratungsstelle für die Aufstellung unabhängiger Kandidaten. "Merkblatt für die Aufstellung unabhängiger Kandidaten bei der Bundestagswahl am 14. August 1949."

Bruderschaft Deutschland. Landesverband Hamburg. "Einladung," May 29, 1952.

———. ———. Open Letter, April, 1952.

Buchkameradschaft Scharnhorst. "Ziele—Aufbau—Arbeit." Leaflet, n.d.

Bund Nationaler Studenten (BNS). "Satzung," n.p., n.d.

Deutsche Aufbau Partei (DAP). "Programm." N.p., n.d.

———. Hauptvorstand. Der 1. Vorsitzende. *Rundschreiben,* nos. 2 and 3, January and February, 1946.

Deutsche Gemeinschaft (DG). Landesverband Niedersachsen. *Rundschreiben,* no. 2, June 30, 1950.

———. "Das Nationale Manifest der Deutschen Gemeinschaft." Leaflet. Munich, November 18, 1951.

Deutsche Jugend. [Alfons Höller.] "Aufruf an die deutsche Jugend." Mimeographed, n.d.

Deutsche Jugend im VdS. Landesmark Niedersachsen. "Arbeitsordnung und grundsätzliche Bestimmungen." Mimeographed, n.d.

———. ———. *Jugendbrief,* 11/56 (November 15, 1956), and 12/56 (December 15, 1956).

Deutsche Konservative Partei (DKP). [Joachim von Ostau and Reinhold Wulle.] *Rundschreiben,* no. 4, May, 1946.

Deutsche Konservative Partei—Deutsche Rechts–Partei (DKP-DRP). British Zone. [Later Nationale Rechte. Parteileitung.] *Rundschreiben,* nos. 1/50–6/50 (January 16, 1950—March 15, 1950).

———. Interessengemeinschaft Nordrhein-Westfalen der Kreisverbände. *Rundschreiben,* nos. 2–11, March 3—September 30, 1949.

———. Parteileitung. *Rundschreiben,* nos. VIII–XI (August 16—September 30, 1949).

Deutsche Nationalpartei von 1954 (DNP). "Programm der Deutschen Nationalpartei von 1954—DNP." Leaflet. N.p., n.d. [Hanover, December 6, 1954.]

Deutsche Rechts–Partei (DRP). Party program of April, 1949.

———. *Rechts heran! DRP-Nachrichten,* February 7, 1949.

———. Die Bundestagsabgeordneten. *Bonner Mitteilungen,* no. 3, January 15, 1950.

———. Interessenvertretung für das Land Niedersachsen. *Rundschreiben,* nos. V/49–VII/49 (March 22—April 25, 1949).
———. Landesverband Niedersachsen. *Rundbrief.* Pro/1, October 22, 1949.
———. ———. *Rundschreiben,* no. 2/V/49, September, 1949.
———. [F. L. Schlüter.] *Nachrichten für die Kreisverbände Niedersachsens.* January 17, 1949.
Deutsche Rechts–Partei (Konservative Vereinigung) (DRP[KV]). *Rundbrief,* nos. 1 (August, 1946), 4 (November, 1946), and 5 (December, 1946).
———. *Rundbrief—Mitteilungsblatt der DRP(KV),* nos. 8/47–11/47 (April 30—July 30, 1947).
———. *Rundschreiben,* nos. I/48–XIV/48 (February 6—November 23, 1948).
———. Zonenrat. *Rundschreiben,* nos. I/47–XII/47 (January 23–October 21, 1947).
———. Zonenratgeschäftsstelle. *Rundbrief,* July 23, 1946.
Deutsche Reichs Jugend. "An die deutsche Jugend." N.p., n.d.
———. *Deutschland ruft.* N.p., n.d.
———. Münchow, Herbert. "Offener Brief an den Oberbürgermeister der Stadt Flensburg, Herrn Fritz Drews," February 18, 1951. Mimeographed.
———. Schneekloth, Wilhelm. "Warum Jugendgruppen?" Handbill, n.d.
Deutsche Reichs–Partei (DRP). "DRP zur Politik der Zeit." Mimeographed leaflet, May, 1954.
———. "Kein lebensfähiges Deutschland ohne gesunde Landwirtschaft!" Leaflet, Bundestag election 1957.
———. "Leitsätze der Deutschen Reichs–Partei: Nationale und soziale Grundideen einer kommenden Bewegung." September, 1955.
———. *Satzung.* Hanover: Laschke, n.d.
———. *Unser Weg, unser Ziel: Politische Grundsatzerklärungen der Deutschen Reichs–Partei. Vorträge gehalten auf dem Parteitag, 8. und 9. Mai 1954.* Hanover, 1954.
———. "Wählen, aber wen?" Leaflet, 1957.
———. "Wiedervereinigung durch Adenauer?" Handbill, [September,] 1954.
———. "Wiedervereinigung in Frieden und Freiheit." Leaflet, Bundestag election, 1957.
———. Kreisverband Kassel-Stadt (Land). [A. Gebauer.] "Aufruf zur Unterschriftsammlung," n.d.
———. Landesverband Niedersachsen. "Deutschland braucht keine Programme, Deutschland braucht Männer und Frauen mit klarer Zielsetzung." Leaflet, October, 1952.
———. ———. Parteileitung. News release. Hanover, April 17, 1950.
———. Parteileitung. "Das ganze Deutschland soll es sein!" Leaflet, Bundestag election, 1957.

———. ———. *Das ganze Deutschland soll es sein: Referate gehalten auf dem Parteitag der DRP*. Wiesbaden, September 1 and 2, 1956.

———. ———. *Rundschreiben,* 11/1956 (September 9, 1956).

———. Press Office. News releases. Hanover, February 21 and June 15, 1957.

Deutsche Soziale Partei (DSP). Open letter of Günther Gereke to his supporters, May 8, 1951. Mimeographed.

Deutsche Union (DU). "Grundsätze der Deutschen Union," n.d.

———. "Resolution," n.d.

———. "Was will die Deutsche Union?" N.d.

Deutsche Volksbewegung–Sammlung zur Tat. Der vorbereitende Ausschuss. "Einladung," Brunswick, October 21, 1949.

Deutscher Gewerkschaftsbund. Landesbezirk Niedersachsen. *Der Fall Schlüter: Presseübersicht.* I (May 31, 1955) and II (June 6, 1955).

Deutscher Jugendbund Kyffhäuser im Kyffhäuserbund. Landesmark Niedersachsen. "Satzung." Hanover, October 10, 1955.

Deutscher Volksbund für Geistesfreiheit. Leaflets. Hameln, May 28, 1949 and Hanover, May 29, 1949.

Druffel Verlag. *Druffel–Mitteilungen.* Autumn, 1956.

———. "Warum die Hess Briefe und die Ribbentrop-Memoiren beschlagnahmt wurden." Leaflet, n.d.

Europa Akademie. "Einladung und Programm-Vorschau für die Europa-Akademie in Saalfelden bei Salzburg, in der Zeit vom 13. bis 19. Juli 1956."

Europäische Soziale Bewegung (ESB). Organizational Committee. [Reporter: Bengt–Olov Ljungberg.] Report on the Organization, in "Rechtsradikalismus in Europa (II)," *Hamburger Brief II,* no. 89, Sondermaterial, September 9, 1956.

———. Program Committee. "Die Vorschläge des Programmausschusses," *Harburger Brief,* Sondermaterial, Appendix 4, [September 1956?].

Europäische Volksbewegung (EVB). "Aktiv für Gesamt-Europa." Leaflet, n.d., but probably 1955.

———. "Europäer aufgewacht!" Leaflet, n.d., but probably 1955.

Freie Demokratische Partei (FDP). Landesverband Niedersachsen. "Satzung." Adopted November 3, 1951.

Freikorps Deutschland. "Deutsche Männer, deutsche Jugend!" Leaflet, n.d.

———. "Hans-Ulrich Rudel zu der Frage: Wo steht die deutsche Jugend heute?" Leaflet, n.d.

Friedenskorps West. [Rudolf Jungnickel.] "Deutsche Männer! Deutsche Jugend!" Leaflet, Christmas 1950, New Year's 1951.

Führungsring ehemaliger Soldaten (FeS). [Gerd Hein; Hanns Baier; Max Schrank.] Open letter to members of the Bundestag, September 26, 1951. Flier.

Gemeinschaft unabhängiger Deutscher (GuD). Gerhard Krüger. "Wichtige nachträgliche Mitteilung." Handbill. Bisperode, July 8, 1949.

Movimento Sociale Italiano (MSI). "Das Programm des Italienischen Neo-

Faschismus," *Hamburger Brief,* Sondermaterial, Appendix 1, [September, 1956?], pp. 1–2.

Nationaldemokratische Partei (NDP). Landesleitung Hessen. "Bekanntmachung," October 15, 1949.

Nationaldemokratische Partei Deutschlands. "Erklärung," Friedberg, June 21, 1946.

———. "Programm der Nationaldemokratischen Partei Deutschlands," Friedberg, October 18, 1945 (Mil. Gov. Info. Control License No. US-W-2061).

Nationale Einheitspartei Deutschlands (NED). [J. von Ostau.] "Delegiertentagung in Bad Godesberg." Handbill, April 17, 1947.

Nationale Rechte (NR). Landesverband Niedersachsen. Landesvorstand. "Rundschreiben," June 19, 1951.

———. Landesverband Nordrhein-Westfalen. *Rundschreiben,* nos. 9/50–11/50 (May 13–23, 1950).

———. ———. *Wahlkampfrundschreiben,* no. 3, August 18, 1953.

———. Parteileitung. *Rundschreiben,* nos. 1/51–1/54 (January 26, 1951—January 6, 1954).

———. ———. Der Vorsitzende. *Rundschreiben,* nos. 1/49 (October 27, 1949), and 5/49 (December 6, 1949).

———. [Steuer, Lothar.] *Politischer Brief,* no. 10 (June, 1951).

Nationale Reichs–Partei (NRP). [Wolfgang Hedler.] "Deutsche Männer und Frauen! Deutsche Jugend!" Leaflet, n.d.

Nationales Informationsbüro Deutschland (Natinform). "Bücherliste," no. 3/52, [October 4, 1952?].

———. Press Office. "Natinform-Archivbericht," September 13, 1952.

———. ———. "Natinform-Artikeldienst," September 13, 1952.

———. ———. *Natinform-Pressedienst,* nos. 27 (September 13, 1952), and 30 (September 24, 1952).

Northern League for Pan-Nordic Friendship. "Aims and Principles." Sausalito, Calif., and Dunfermline, Scotland. Leaflet, n.d.

Notgemeinschaft des deutschen Volkes (NDV). [Joachim H. von Ostau.] "Aus der Vergangenheit lernen: Was will die 'Notgemeinschaft des deutschen Volkes (NDV)'? Zur vorbereitenden Tagung am 5. Februar 1949 in Goslar." Printed broadside, February 1, 1949.

Ostau, Joachim H. von. "Mitteilung." Printed flier, June 14, 1948.

———. "Mitteilung an alle Gesinnungsfreunde." Printed flier, July 16, 1948.

———. "Offene Antwort." Printed flier, n.d.

Reichsblock. "Aufruf zur Bildung eines Blocks nationaler Kräfte!" Leaflet. Frankfurt, May 3, 1953.

Rudman, Ray K. Illustrated leaflets: "Future Jewish Plans," "Jewish Esthers and Money," "Die 'Protokolle v Wyse v Sion' (Joodse Geheime Planne)," "Torch Commandoes!" (No. BN-72/18/3/52), "21st Century Atrocities" (No. 1/11/7/49).

Sozialdemokratische Partei Deutschlands (SPD). Parteileitung. "Arbeitsgemeinschaft demokratischer Kreise," *Rundschreiben,* no. 42 (May 6, 1953).

Der Stahlhelm e.V., Landesverband Gross-Hamburg. "Verrat im Stahlhelm!" Leaflet. Hamburg, December 17, 1953.

Unabhängige Gesellschaft zur Pflege junger Wissenschaft und Kunst. "Gesellschaftsvertrag." Peine, October 27, 1946.

Unabhängige Vaterländische Jugendverbände der Bundesrepublik Deutschland. "Einladung . . . zu der . . . in Verbindung mit der Arbeitsgemeinschaft Demokratischer Kreise in Bückeburg stattfindenden *Staatspolitischen Tagung. . . .*" Wiesbaden, October 10, 1956.

Vereinigte Rechte (VR). *Politischer Brief,* no. 28 (February–March, 1953).

Vereinigte Rechte–Deutsche Reichs-Partei (VR-DRP). Parteileitung. Propaganda Department. *Propaganda Rundschreiben,* no. II/1952 (October 16, 1952).

Vereinigte Rechte (Nationale Rechte). Parteileitung. *Rundschreiben,* nos. 6/52 (June 11, 1952), 1/53 (February 27, 1953), and 3/53 (April 20, 1953).

Vorbereitender Ausschuss zur Herbeiführung der Generalamnestie. "Aufruf zur Unterstützung der überparteilichen Aktion zur Herbeiführung der Generalamnestie." Essen, February, 1952.

II. Unpublished Sources

1. BROCHURES AND ARTICLES

Goetz, Cecile von. "Dr. Strasser, the Coming Man in Germany," typescript, n.d.

Leuchtgens, Heinrich. "Der Entwurf einer Verfassung des Deutschen Reiches," typescript, n.d.

Sarg, Wolfgang. "Die politische Konzeption der Deutsch-Amerikaner: ein Interview," typescript, September 18, 1952.

Spindler, Gert P. "Dürfen uns die Flüchtlinge lästig sein?" Typescript, n.d.

———. "Eigentum und soziale Frage," typescript, n.d.

———. "Krise der menschlichen Beziehung," typescript, n.d.

———. "Sozialisierung? Mitunternehmertum!" Typescript, n.d.

Wulle, Reinhold. "Betrachtungen eines Unpolitischen," mimeographed typescript, July, August (Part B), 1946.

———. "Christliches Abendland: Vergangenheit oder Aufgabe," n.d.

———. "Höre, Herr . . . ," typescript, n.d.

2. PARTY DOCUMENTS

Altenberg Conferences, June 2/3, July 21/22, and July 28/29, 1951. Minutes.

Bruderschaft. Beck-Broichsitter, Helmut, and Gerhardt Boldt, "Stellungnahme," photostat of typescript.

Bund für Gotterkenntnis (L). Frank, Herbert. "Zur Wahrung meiner Ehre. (Nach 20 jährigem Wirken für die deutsche Gotterkenntnis)." Typescript, Duisburg-Meiderich, end of March, 1949.

———. Ludendorff, Mathilde, Karl von Unruh, and Franz Baron Karg von Bebenburg. "Erklärung," typescript, January 28, 1949.
———. Reinhard, Edmund. "Zwei Welten: Trifft das Haus Ludendorff eine rechtliche oder auch nur eine politische Verantwortung für den faschistischen Gewaltstaat und dessen Rassenpolitik?" Typescript, Dresden, April, 1948.
Deutsche Gemeinschaft (DG). Direktorium. Meeting, Frankfurt, May 23, 1950. Minutes.
Deutsche Konservative Partei (DKP). Delegiertentagung, June 27, 1946. Minutes.
———. [Bannert, Frau von; Padberg; and Piepenbrink.] Delegiertentagung, Hamm, January 29, 1950. Report.
———. Klingspor, Hermann. Detailed *aide-mémoires* on the telephone conversation with Heinrich Leuchtgens of December 22, 1949, and on the events on and before January 5, 1950.
———. Schmidt-Hannover, Otto. "Ansprache an die Konservativen von Schleswig-Holstein," Stadthalle, Rendsburg, April 30, 1946.
Deutsche Konservative Partei–Deutsche Aufbau Partei (DKP–DAP). Fusion negotiations, March 21, 1946. Minutes.
Deutsche Konservative Partei–Deutsche Rechts-Partei (DKP–DRP). Parteileitung. Meeting at "Wuppertaler Hof," Wuppertal-Barmen, September 1, 1949. Minutes.
Deutsche Rechts–Partei (Konservative Vereinigung) (DRP[KV]) "Einladung zur Delegiertentagung in Düsseldorf [November 23–24, 1946]." Typescript, November 9, 1946.
———. Landesverband Nordrhein-Westfalen. "Resolution," typescript, April 24, 1949.
———. ———. Der Vorsitzende [Hermann Klingspor]. "Rundbrief an alle Kreisverbände," March 31, 1947.
———. "Protokoll der Delegiertentagung," Düsseldorf, November 23–24, 1946.
———. "Richtlinien für die Parteiorganisation," n.d.
———. Zonen Delegiertentagung, June 27, 1946. Minutes.
———. Zonenrat. Agenda for the Hanover Meeting of November 18, 1947.
———. ———. Der Vorsitzende [Hermann Klingspor]. "Rundschreiben" to the members of the Bezirkverband Lübeck, November 7, 1947.
Deutsche Reichsjugend. "Vorläufiger Arbeitsplan," mimeographed typescript, n.d.
———. "Vorläufige Satzungen," mimeographed typescript, n.d.
———. [Wilhelm Schneekloth.] "Warum Jugendgruppen?" Mimeographed handbill.
Deutsche Reichs–Partei (DRP). Kunstmann, Heinrich. "Der Kommunismus als Heilslehre." Address at the Parteitag of the DRP, Hanover, September 24/25, 1955.
———. Propaganda Abteilung. [A. von Thadden.] *Propaganda Rundschreiben,* nos. III/50–II/53 (June 13, 1950—June 20, 1953).

———. Rheden, Hildegard von. "Die politische Verantwortung der Frau." Address at the Parteitag of the DRP, Hanover, September 24/25, 1955.

———. Scheffer, Hans-Heinrich. "Wehrpolitik in unserer Sicht." Address at the Parteitag of the DRP, Hanover, September 24/25, 1955.

———. Thadden, Adolf von. "Aussenpolitik für ganz Deutschland." Address at the Parteitag of the DRP, Hanover, September 24/25, 1955.

Deutsche Soziale Partei. Depositions from police interrogations of: Wilhelm Assling (Dannenberg, August 6, 1952), Anneliese Bahn (Dannenberg, August 6, 1952), Heinrich Busch (September 16, 1952), Elisabeth Coers (Hanover, July 27, 1952), Otto Dennstedt (Dannenberg, August 6, 1952), Wilhelm Karl Gerst (Bonn, September 9, 1952), Johannes F. G. Grosser (Frankfurt, August 2 and September 17, 1952), Richard Henke (Frankfurt, September 16, 1952), Fred Henrich (Frankfurt, September 11, 1952), Hermann Korte (Lebbin, July 31, 1952), Artur von Machui (September 12, 1952), Wolfgang Meerstein (Frankfurt, September 11, 1952), Hubert Michel (Frankfurt, September 12, 1952), Katja Maria Pelka (Hanover, July 24, 1952), Christa Schauss (Hanover, July 27, 1952), Helene Schneider (Frankfurt, September 16, 1952), Marcel Schulte (Frankfort, September 15, 1952), Heinrich Siemer (Hanover, August 27, 1952), Lieselotte Ulrich (Hanover, August 7, 1952).

Deutscher Block (DB). Landesverband Bayern. Delegiertentagung, Vohenstrauss, Oberpfalz, June 21, 1949. Minutes.

Freie Demokratische Partei. [Fritz Neumayer, Thomas Dehler, Alfred Onnen.] "[Vertraulicher Bericht an] den Gesamtvorstand der Bundespartei über die Lage im Landesverband Nordrhein-Westfalen . . ." Bonn, June 5, 1953.

Junge Partei. [Alexander Braun.] "Grundsatz Entwurf," typescript, November 1, 1951.

Nationale Rechte (NR). Landesverband Niedersachsen. Gründungsausschuss. "Einladung [for the founding meeting in Hanover, January 6, 1951]," December 27, 1950.

———. ———. Landesvorstand. "Einladung zu einer Tagung des Landesvorstandes und der Kreisverbände in Hannover am 22. Juli 1951," July 12, 1951.

———. ———. ———. Minutes of the meeting of September 9, 1951.

———. ———. Sitzung des vorläufigen Landesvorstandes, June 10, 1951. Report.

———. Landesverband Nordrhein-Westfalen. Landesvorstand. Minutes of the meetings of March 29, 1950, January 1, 1951, December 2, 1951, August 1, 1953, October 10, 1953.

———. Parteileitung. "Einladung," November 19, 1949.

———. ———. "Einladung zu einer Vertretersitzung der Kreisvereine Nordrhein-Westfalen am Sonntag den 19.3.1950 . . . in Dortmund . . . ," Siegen, March 4, 1950.

Nationale Reichs–Partei (NRP). "Leitsätze der Nationalen Reichs–Partei (NRP)!" N.d.

Nationales Informationsbüro Deutschland (Natinform). *Aide-mémoire* of a discussion between Peter Kleist, Kurt Vowinckel, and E. A. Schmidt. February 11, 1952.

———. [Baron, A. F. X., Wolfgang Sarg.] "Gesetze der Natinform," Oldenburg, January 20, 1953.

———. ———. "Treueerklärung," Oldenburg, January 20, 1953.

———. [Baron, A. F. X., Wolfgang Sarg, Karl Smets.] "Entscheidungen der Natinformkonferenz vom 16.–19. Januar 1953," Oldenburg, January 17, 1953, together with "Anlage," Oldenburg, January 18, 1953.

———. ———. "Resolution," Oldenburg, January 20, 1953.

———. [Hoffmann, Heinz.] "Organisationsplan," Appendix 5 to letter of July 21, 1952.

———. ———. "Zweck und Ziel des Natinform," Appendix 2 to letter of July 21, 1952.

———. Main Office, South. Memorandum, July 9, 1953.

———. Minutes of the conference between A. F. X. Baron and Wolfgang Sarg, Oldenburg, January 16–19, 1953.

Naumann Case. Prosecution documents. Multilith copies.

Notverband des Deutschen Volkes (NDV). [Joachim H. von Ostau.] "Was bezweckt die NDV?" Typescript, [January, 1949?].

Richter, Dr. Franz, *pseud.* [i.e., Fritz Rössler]. "Lebenslauf," photostat of manuscript, February 12, 1947.

Sammlung zur Tat—Europäische Volksbewegung (Deutschland). "Beschluss des Aktionsausschusses," Worms, June 6, 1949.

———. "Die Generallinie," typescript, March 26, 1949.

———. *Informationsschreiben* (*Rundschreiben*), no. 1 (n.d.), no. 2 (April 15, 1949).

———. "Satzung," typescript, May 5, 1949.

———. Aktionsausschuss. "Protokoll der Sitzung," typescript, Cologne, May 8, 1949.

———. ———. "Die 10 Thesen," typescript, Villingen/Schwarzwald, March 13, 1949.

———. Nordrhein-Westfalen. Vorbereitender Ausschuss. "Gründungskonference der SzT in Köln," typescript, Cologne, September, 1949.

Schmidt-Hannover, Otto. "Memorandum," December 13, 1946.

———. "Redeverbot für Schmidt-Hannover," mimeographed, n.d.

———. "Vernebelung," typescript, n.d.

Sozialistische Reichs–Partei (SRP). Raoul Nahrat. "In kameradschaftlicher Verbundenheit . . . ?" Mimeographed typescript, July, 1952.

Tatgemeinschaft freier Deutscher. "Grundprogramm," n.d.

———. Minutes of Staff Meetings of April 19, 1951, June 20 and 27, 1951, July 4 and 25, 1951, August 19, 1951, and October 10, 1951.

Vereinigte Rechte (VR). "Rundschreiben (vertraulich)," April 5, 1952.

———. Politische Leitung. Minutes of the meetings of January 8, April 1, May 18, June 20, October 7, 1952, and January 25, April 1, July 4, 1953.

Vereinigte Rechte (Nationale Rechte) (VR/NR). Parteileitung. Letter to the "Kreisverbände Nordrhein-Westfalen," March 2, 1953.

3. CORRESPONDENCE*

Alfoldi, Géza
Andrae, Alexander
Baron, Anthony F. X.
———, and Wolfgang Sarg
Bauer, Hans
———, Peter Thoma, and Karl E. Naske
Beck-Broichsitter, Helmut
Besser, Klaus
Bierbrauer, Emil
Bischoff, Herbert
Borchmeyer, Josef
Braun, Alexander
Brown, E. G.
Bruhn, Helmut
Crüwell, Ludwig
Dethleffsen, Erich
Dietz, Werner
Dinter, Rudolf Karl
Draeger, Helmuth
Dücker-Plettenberg, Count Georg
Erler, Fritz
Ewers, Hans
Förster, Karl Theodor
Frank, Herbert
Franke-Gricksch, Alfred
Frommhold, Heinz
Giess, H.
Groeben, Peter von der
Heberer, Gerhard
Hellwege, Heinrich
Heubaum, Karl-Heinz
Hoffmann, Heinz
Huxley-Blythe, Peter J.
Jäger, Wilhelm
Jungmann, Hugo
Kaiser, Hannes
Karg von Bebenburg, Franz Baron
Klingspor, Hermann
Kögler, Theodor
Koelpin, Wolfgang
Koller, Karl
Kunstmann, Heinrich
Kurth (Göttingen)
Lademacher, Siegfried
Lauenstein, Carl
Leuchtgens, Heinrich
Lüninck, Hermann Baron von
Mainzer, Anton
Malluche, Renate
Manrique, R.
Manteuffel, Hasso von
Meesmann, Otto
Meyer, Heinrich
Miessner, Herwart
Milde, Harald
Natinform, Main-Office, South
Neumann, Lothar
Ossenkop, Gertrude
Ostau, Joachim H. von
Planert, H.
Priester, Karl-Heinz
Ramcke, H. Bernhard
Rau, Hek, *pseud.* [i.e., H. E. Krause]
Read-Jahn, F. W.
Rempel, W.
Richter, Franz, *pseud.* [i.e., F. Rössler]
Riggert, Ernst
Rombach, Wilhelm
Sarg, Wolfgang
Scheffer, Hans-Heinrich
Schlüter, Franz Leonhard
Schmidt, Helmut
Schneyder, Erich
Schnitzler, Elisabeth
Schudnagis, Walter
Schumacher, Bertram

* Only those persons are here listed whose letters have actually been referred to in the Notes. For the names of the recipients and the dates of these letters, see the specific references.

Schwecht, Ludwig
Simon, Carl
Smets, Karl
Sontag, Franz
Spindler, Gert P.
Spohrmann, Walter
Steinfeld, Karl
Steuer, Lothar
Suleck, Paul
Szekely, Johann
Taubert, Eberhard
Teich, Erich
Thadden, Adolf von
Thoma, Peter
Wulle, Reinhold
Zisseler, H. H.

B. SECONDARY SOURCES

I. Published Sources

1. BOOKS AND BROCHURES

Actuel Service. *Das Organisationsnetz der antidemokratischen Kräfte in der Bundesrepublik*. Mimeographed typescript. Copenhagen: n.d.

Allemann, Fritz René. *Bonn ist nicht Weimar*. Cologne: Kiepenheuer & Witsch, 1956.

Almond, Gabriel A., and Sidney Verba. *The Civic Culture: Political Attitudes and Democracy in Five Nations*. Princeton (N.J.): Princeton University Press, 1963.

Altmann, Rüdiger. *Das Erbe Adenauers*. 3d ed. Stuttgart-Degerloch: Seewald, [1960].

American Jewish Congress, Commission on International Affairs. *The German Dilemma: An Appraisal of Anti-Semitism, Ultra-Nationalism, and Democracy in West Germany*. New York: n.p., 1959.

Anderson, Jack, and Ronald W. May. *McCarthy, the Man, the Senator, the "Ism."* Boston: Beacon, 1952.

Arendt, Hannah. *The Origins of Totalitarianism*. New York: Harcourt, Brace, 1951.

Atkins, Henry G. *German Literature through Nazi Eyes*. London: Methuen, [1941].

Baeyer-Katte, Wanda von. *Das Zerstörende in der Politik. Eine Psychologie der politischen Grundeinstellung*. Heidelberg: Quelle & Meyer, 1958.

———, *et al. Autoritarismus und Nationalismus—ein deutsches Problem?* Politische Psychologie, Schriftenreihe, vol. II. [Frankfurt:] Europäische Verlagsanstalt, [c. 1963].

Baumont, Maurice, *et al.*, eds. *The Third Reich*. New York: Praeger, 1955.

Benoist-Méchin, Jacques G. P. M. *History of the German Army since the Armistice*. Trans. by Eileen R. Taylor. Zurich: Scientia, 1939.

Berendsohn, Walter A. *Die humanistische Front: Einführung in die deutsche Emigranten-Literatur*. Part I (Von 1933 bis zum Kriegsausbruch 1939). Zurich: Europa, [c. 1946].

Berges, Wilhelm, and Carl Hinrichs, eds. *Zur Geschichte und Problematik der Demokratie. Festgabe für Hans Herzfeld*. Berlin: Duncker & Humblot, [c. 1958].

Bischoff, Ralph F. *Nazi Conquest through German Culture.* Cambridge (Mass.): Harvard University Press, 1942.

Blücher, Count Viggo. *Der Prozess der Meinungsbildung dargestellt am Beispiel der Bundestagswahl 1961.* Bielefeld: EMNID, 1962.

Blüher, Hans. *Die deutsche Wandervogelbewegung als erotisches Phänomen.* Berlin: Weise, 1912.

———. *Karl Fischers Tat und Untergang: Zur Geschichte der deutschen Jugendbewegung.* Bad Godesberg: Voggenreiter, 1952.

———. *Wandervogel. Geschichte einer Jugendbewegung.* 4th ed. Berlin: Weise, 1919. 2 vols.

Böse, Georg, ed. *Unsere Freiheit morgen: Gefahren und Chancen der modernen Gesellschaft.* [Düsseldorf:] Diederichs, [c. 1963].

Boldt, Gerhardt. *Die letzten Tage der Reichskanzlei.* Edited by Ernst A. Hepp. Hamburg, Stuttgart: Rowohlt, 1947.

Bolte, Karl Martin. *Sozialer Aufstieg und Abstieg. Eine Untersuchung über Berufsprestige und Berufsmobilität.* Stuttgart: Enke, 1959.

Borinski, Fritz, and Werner Milch. *Jugendbewegung: The Story of German Youth, 1896–1933.* German Educational Reconstruction no. 3/4. [London: German Educational Reconstruction, (pref. 1945).]

Bossenbrook, William T. *The German Mind.* Detroit: Wayne State University Press, 1961.

Bowen, Ralph H. *German Theories of the Corporative State.* New York: Whittlesey House, 1947.

Bracher, Karl D. *Die Auflösung der Weimarer Republik.* Schriften des Instituts für Politische Wissenschaft, no. 4. 2d ed., rev., enl. Stuttgart, Düsseldorf: Ring, 1957.

———, Wolfgang Sauer, and Gerhard Schulz. *Die nationalsozialistische Machtergreifung. Studien zur Errichtung des totalitären Herrschaftssystems in Deutschland 1933/34.* Cologne, Opladen: Westdeutscher Verlag, 1960.

Breitling, Rupert. *Die Verbände in der Bundesrepublik.* Meisenheim am Glan: Hain, 1955.

Brüdigam, Heinz. *Der Schoss ist fruchtbar noch. . . .* Frankfurt: Röderberg, [1964].

Buchheim, Hans. *Das Dritte Reich. Grundlagen und politische Entwicklung.* Munich: Koesel, 1958.

———. *SS und Polizei im NS-Staat.* Staatspolitische Schriftenreihe. [Duisdorf/Bonn: Studiengesellschaft für Zeitprobleme, c. 1964.]

Buchheit, Gert. *Soldatentum und Rebellion: Die Tragödie der deutschen Wehrmacht.* Rastatt: Grote, 1961.

Büsch, Otto, and Peter Furth. *Rechtsradikalismus im Nachkriegsdeutschland. Studien über die "Sozialistische Reichspartei" (SRP).* Schriften des Instituts für Politische Wissenschaft, no. 9. Berlin, Frankfurt: Vahlen, 1957.

Bunting, Brian. *The Rise of the South African Reich.* [Harmondsworth (Middlesex):] Penguin, [c. 1964].

Butler, Rohan D'O. *The Roots of National Socialism 1783–1933*. New York: Dutton, 1942.

Carlson, John Roy, *pseud.* [i.e., Arthur Derounian]. *Under Cover*. Philadelphia: Blakiston; New York: Dutton, [c. 1943].

Carr, Edward Hallett. *German-Soviet Relations between the Two World Wars, 1919–1939*. Baltimore: Johns Hopkins Press, 1951.

Carter, Gwendolen M., and John H. Herz. *Major Foreign Powers*. 4th ed. New York: Harcourt, Brace, and World, 1962.

Clay, Lucius D. *Decision in Germany*. New York: Doubleday, 1950.

Craig, Gordon A. *NATO and the New German Army*. Memorandum no. 8. Princeton (N.J.): Center of International Studies, Princeton University, October 24, 1955.

———. *The Politics of the Prussian Army, 1640–1945*. Oxford: Clarendon, 1955.

Crippen, Harlan R., ed. *Germany: A Self Portrait*. New York: Oxford University Press, 1942.

Cube, Walter von. *Ich bitte um Widerspruch*. Frankfurt: Frankfurter Hefte, 1952.

Dahrendorf, Ralf. *Gesellschaft und Freiheit: Zur soziologischen Analyse der Gegenwart*. Munich: Piper, 1962.

Danton, George H. *Germany Ten Years After*. Boston: Houghton Mifflin, 1928.

Davidson, Eugene. *The Death and Life of Germany*. New York: Knopf, 1959.

Deakin, Frederick William. *The Brutal Friendship: Mussolini, Hitler, and the Fall of Italian Fascism*. London: Weidenfeld and Nicolson, [c. 1962].

Delzell, Charles F. *Mussolini's Enemies, the Italian Anti-Fascist Resistance*. Princeton (N.J.): Princeton University Press, 1961.

Demeter, Karl. *Das deutsche Offizierkorps in Gesellschaft und Staat 1650–1945*. 2d rev., enl. ed. Frankfurt: Bernard & Graefe, 1962.

De Vries, Enno, *pseud. Neo-Nazismus in der Bundesrepublik*. Hamburg (mimeographed), 1956.

Doeberl, Michael, *et al.*, eds. *Das akademische Deutschland*. Berlin: Weller, 1930/31. 2 vols.

Donohoe, James. *Hitler's Conservative Opponents in Bavaria 1930–1945*. Leiden: Brill, 1961.

Dornberg, John. *Schizophrenic Germany*. New York: Macmillan, 1961.

Douglass, Paul F. *God among the Germans*. Philadelphia: University of Pennsylvania Press, 1935.

Duesterberg, Theodor. *Der Stahlhelm und Hitler*. Wolfenbüttel: Wolfenbütteler Verlagsanstalt, 1949.

Ebeling, Hans. *The German Youth Movement: Its Past and Future*. London: New Europe, 1945.

Ebsworth, Raymond. *Restoring Democracy in Germany*. London: Steven; New York: Praeger, 1960.

Edinger, Lewis J. *West German Armament*. Documentary Research Division, Research Studies Institute. Air University, 1955. [Maxwell Air Force Base, Ala.]

Ehrenthal, Günther. *Die deutschen Jugendbünde.* Berlin: Zentralverlag, 1929.

Eubank, Keith. *Munich.* Norman (Okla.): University of Oklahoma Press. [1963].

Fabricius, Wilhelm. *Die deutschen Corps.* 2d ed. Frankfurt: Deutsche Corpszeitung, 1926.

Faul, Erwin, ed. *Wahlen und Wähler in Westdeutschland.* Villingen: Ring, [1960].

Feld, Werner. *Reunification and West German–Soviet Relations.* The Hague: Nijhoff, 1963.

Feldman, Gene, and Max Gartenberg, eds. *The Beat Generation and the Angry Young Men.* New York: Citadel, [1958].

Fine, Benjamin. *German Schools on Trial.* New York: German Information Center, n.d.

Finke, Lutz E. *Gestatte mir Hochachtungsschluck: Bundesdeutschlands korporierte Elite.* Hamburg: Rütten & Loening, [c. 1963].

Fischer-Baling, Eugen. *Besinnung auf uns Deutsche.* Düsseldorf: Politische Bildung, 1957.

Flake, Otto. *Die Deutschen: Aufsätze zur Literatur und Zeitgeschichte.* Hamburg: Rütten & Loening, [c. 1963].

Forster, Arnold, and Benjamin R. Epstein. *Cross Currents.* New York: Doubleday, 1956.

Frederick, Hans. *Die Rechtsradikalen.* Munich-Inning: Humboldt, [1965?].

Friedrich, Julius [*pseud.?*]. *Wer spielte falsch? Hitler, Hindenburg, der Kronprinz, Hugenberg, Schleicher.* Hamburg: Laatzen, [October, 1949?].

Frischauer, Willi. *Himmler.* London: Odhams Press, 1953.

Fröhner, Rolf, *et al. Wie stark sind die Halbstarken? Beruf und Berufsnot, politische, kulturelle und seelische Probleme der deutschen Jugend im Bundesgebiet und Westberlin.* Bielefeld: von Stackelberg, 1956.

Gablentz, Otto H. von der. *Die Tragödie des Preussentums.* Munich: Hanfstaengl, 1948.

Gallagher, Richard. *Malmédy Massacre.* New York: Paperback Library, 1964.

Gallin, Mary Alice, O.S.U. *German Resistance to . . . Hitler.* Washington: Catholic University of America Press, 1961.

Geissler, Christian. *The Sins of the Fathers.* New York: Random House, 1962.

Geissler, Rolf. *Dekadenz und Heroismus. Zeitroman und völkisch-nationalsozialistische Literaturkritik.* Schriftenreihe der Vierteljahrshefte für Zeitgeschichte, no. 9. Stuttgart: Deutsche Verlags-Anstalt, [c. 1964].

Gerhard, Walter, *pseud.* [i.e., Waldemar Gurian]. *Um des Reiches Zukunft.* Freiburg i. Br.: Herder, [1932].

Gessler, Otto. *Reichswehrpolitik in der Weimarer Zeit.* Stuttgart: Deutsche Verlags-Anstalt, 1958.

Gimbel, John. *A German Community under American Occupation, Marburg, 1945–1952.* Stanford (Calif.): Stanford University Press, 1961.

Glaser, Hermann. *Spiesser–Ideologie. Von der Zerstörung des deutschen Geistes im 19. und 20. Jahrhundert.* 2d ed. Freiburg: Rombach, [c. 1964].

Glum, Friedrich. *Philosophen im Spiegel und Zerrspiegel. Deutschlands Weg in den Nationalismus und Nationalsozialismus.* Munich: Isar, 1954.

Gnielka, Thomas. *Falschspiel mit der Vergangenheit: Rechtsradikale Organisationen in unserer Zeit.* Frankfurt: Frankfurter Rundschau, [c. 1960].

Gordon, Harold J. *The Reichswehr and the German Republic 1919–1926.* Princeton (N.J.): Princeton University Press, 1957.

[Graml, Hermann.] *David L. Hoggan und die Dokumente.* Sonderdruck, Vierteljahrshefte für Zeitgeschichte. Stuttgart: Deutsche Verlags-Anstalt, n.d. [1963].

Grosser, Alfred. *Die Bonner Demokratie.* [Düsseldorf:] Rauch, [c. 1960].

———. *Western Germany from Defeat to Rearmament.* Trans. by R. Rees. London: Ahern & Kerwin, 1955.

Grosshut, F. S. *Staatsnot, Recht und Gewalt.* Nuremberg: Glock & Lutz, [c. 1962].

Gruchmann, Lothar. *Nationalsozialistische Grossraumordnung: Die Konstruktion einer "deutschen Monroe-Doktrin."* Stuttgart: Deutsche Verlags-Anstalt, 1962.

Gumbel, E. J. *Vom Fememord zur Reichskanzlei.* Heidelberg: Schneider, 1962.

Gurian, Waldemar. *Hitler and the Christians.* New York: Sheed and Ward, 1936.

Habermas, Jürgen, L. von Friedeburg, C. Oehler, and F. Weltz. *Student und Politik.* Neuwied: Luchterhand, 1961.

Hagemann, Walter. *Dankt die Presse ab?* Munich: Isar, 1957.

Hagen, Walter, *pseud.* [i.e., Wilhelm Hoettl]. *Die geheime Front: Organisation, Personen und Aktionen des deutschen Geheimdienstes.* Stuttgart: Veritas, 1952.

Hammerschmidt, Helmut, and Michael Mansfeld. *Der Kurs ist falsch.* Munich: Desch, 1956.

Hannover, Heinrich. *Politische Diffamierung der Opposition im freiheitlich-demokratischen Rechtsstaat.* Dortmund-Barop: Pläne, 1962.

Harling, Wolf Christian von. *Deutschland zwischen den Mächten.* Hamburg: Holsten, 1962.

Hartenstein, Wolfgang, and Günter Schubert. *Mitlaufen oder Mitbestimmen.* Veröffentlichungen des Instituts für angewandte Sozialwissenschaft, Bad Godesberg, vol. II. Frankfurt: Europäische Verlagsanstalt, [1961].

Hartmann, Heinz. *Authority and Organization in German Management.* Princeton (N.J.): Princeton University Press, 1959.

Hartshorne, Edward Y., Jr. *The German Universities and National Socialism.* London: Allen & Unwin, 1937.

Harwick, Christian. *Deutschland zwischen Ja und Nein: Prognose unter dem Fallbeil.* Kreuzlingen: Neptun, 1951.

Hassel, Ulrich von. *Vom anderen Deutschland.* Zurich: Atlantis, 1946.

Haupt, Hermann, ed. *Quellen und Darstellungen zur Geschichte der deutschen Burschenschaft und der deutschen Einheitsbewegung.* Heidelberg: Winter, 1910–1940. 17 vols.

———, and Paul Wentzcke. *Hundert Jahre deutscher Burschenschaft.* Volume VII of *Quellen und Darstellungen zur Geschichte der deutschen Burschenschaft und der deutschen Einheitsbewegung.* Heidelberg: Winter, 1921.

Heer, Georg. *Geschichte der deutschen Burschenschaft.* Vols. VI, X, XI, XVI of *Quellen und Darstellungen zur Geschichte der deutschen Burschenschaft und der deutschen Einheitsbewegung.* Heidelberg: Winter, 1919–1939.

Heidenheimer, Arnold J. *Adenauer and the CDU.* The Hague: Nijhoff, 1960.

Helbig, Herbert. *Die Träger der Rapallo Politik.* Göttingen: Vandenhök & Ruprecht, 1958.

Herrmann, Wolfgang. *Der neue Nationalismus und seine Literatur.* Breslau: Städtische Volksbüchereien, 1933.

Hertzmann, Lewis. *DNVP, Right-Wing Opposition in the Weimar Republic, 1918–1924.* Lincoln (Nebr.): University of Nebraska Press, 1963.

Herzog, Robert. *Die Volksdeutschen in der Waffen-SS.* Studien des Instituts für Besatzungsfragen in Tübingen zu den deutschen Besetzungen im 2. Weltkrieg, no. 5. Tübingen, May, 1955.

Hilberg, Raul. *The Destruction of the European Jews.* Chicago: Quadrangle, 1961.

Hilger, Gustav, and Alfred G. Meyer. *The Incompatible Allies: A Memoir-History of German-Soviet Relations, 1918–1941.* New York: Macmillan, 1953.

Hippe, Ewald, ed. *Joachim Nehring—Neo-Nazismus? Der "Scheinwerfer" Prozess vor der Hauptspruchkammer München.* Munich: Hippe, 1950.

Hirsch-Weber, Wolfgang, and Klaus Schütz. *Wähler und Gewählte. Eine Untersuchung der Bundestagswahlen 1953.* Berlin: Vahlen, 1957.

Hiscocks, Richard. *Democracy in Western Germany.* London: Oxford University Press, 1957.

Hock, Wolfgang. *Deutscher Antikapitalismus. Der ideologische Kampf gegen die freie Wirtschaft im Zeichen der grossen Krise.* Foreword by Heinrich Rittershausen. Veröffentlichungen des Instituts für Bankwirtschaft und Bankrecht an der Universität Köln. Wirtschaftswissenschaftliche Reihe, vol. 9. Frankfurt: Knapp, [1960].

Hoehn, Reinhard. *Die Armee als Erziehungsschule der Nation. Das Ende einer Idee.* [Bad Harzburg:] Verlag für Wissenschaft, Wirtschaft und Technik, 1963.

Hofmann, Hanns Hubert. *Der Hitlerputsch: Krisenjahre deutscher Geschichte 1920–1934.* Munich: Nymphenburg, 1961.

Horne, Alistair. *Return to Power: A Report on the New Germany.* New York: Praeger, 1956.

Hornung, Klaus. *Der Jungdeutsche Orden.* Düsseldorf: Droste, 1958.

Hughes, H. Stuart. *Consciousness and Society: The Reorientation of European Social Thought 1890–1930.* New York: Macmillan, 1958.

Institute for International Politics and Economics, ed. *Beware: German Revenge-Seekers Threaten Peace.* Prague: Orbis, 1959.

Irving, David. The *Destruction of Dresden.* Introd. by Ira C. Eaker, Lt. Gen. USAF (Ret.). New York, Chicago, San Francisco: Holt, Rinehart & Winston, [c. 1963].

Ismay, Lord. *NATO: The First Five Years, 1949–1954.* [Paris? 1954?]

Jahn, Hans Edgar. *Für und gegen den Wehrbeitrag.* Cologne: Greven, 1957.

Jahn, Rudolf, ed. *Grenzfall der Wissenschaft: Herbert Cysarz.* Frankfurt: Heimreiter, 1957.

Jaide, Walter. *Eine neue Generation. Eine Untersuchung über Werthaltungen und Leitbilder der Jugendlichen.* 2d ed. Munich: Juventa, 1963 [c. 1961].

Jaspers, Karl. *The Question of German Guilt.* Trans. by E. B. Ashton. New York: Dial, 1947.

Jenke, Manfred. *Verschwörung von Rechts?* Berlin: Colloquium, 1961.

Jungkunz, Hans, and Winifried Kaeppner. *Gesetz zum Artikel 131 GG.* Stuttgart: Kohlhammer, 1959.

Kaufmann, Walter H. *Monarchism in the Weimar Republic.* New York: Bookman Associates, 1953.

Kempner, Robert M. W. *Eichmann und Komplizen.* Zurich: Europa, 1961.

Kén, Olaf. *Der halbe Partisan.* Kreuzweingarten/Rhld.: Zeitbiographischer Verlag, 1964.

Kitzinger, U. W. *German Electoral Politics: A Study of the 1957 Campaign.* Oxford: Clarendon, 1960.

Klein, K. K., F. W. Riedl, and R. Ursin. *Weltweite Wissenschaft vom Volk: Volk–Welt–Erziehung.* Vienna, Wiesbaden: Rohrer, 1958.

Klemperer, Klemens von. *Germany's New Conservatism: Its History and Dilemma in the Twentieth Century.* Princeton (N.J.): Princeton University Press, 1957.

Klönne, Arno. *Gegen den Strom: Bericht über den Jugendwiderstand im Dritten Reich.* 2d ed. Hanover, Frankfurt: Norddeutsche Verlagsanstalt O. Goedel, 1960.

———. *Hitlerjugend.* Hanover: Norddeutsche Verlagsanstalt O. Goedel, 1956.

Klose, Werner. *Generation im Gleichschritt.* [Oldenburg:] Stalling, [1964].

Knight-Patterson, W. M., *pseud.* [i.e., W. Kulski]. *Germany from Defeat to Conquest.* London: Allen and Unwin, 1945.

Knoll, Joachim H. *Führungsauslese im Liberalismus und Demokratie.* Stuttgart: Schwab, 1957.

Knütter, Hans-Helmuth. *Geistige Grundlagen und politische Richtung der "Deutschen Nationalzeitung und Soldaten-Zeitung." Dargestellt am Jg. 1961.* Sonderheft. *Für die Demokratie,* V (XIII), 4 (1964).

———. *Ideologien des Rechtsradikalismus im Nachkriegsdeutschland: Eine Studie über die Nachwirkungen des Nationalsozialismus.* Bonner Historische Forschungen, vol. 19. Bonn: Röhrscheid, 1961.

Kochan, Lionel. *The Struggle for Germany, 1914–1945.* Edinburgh: [Edinburgh] University Press, [c. 1963].

Kogon, Eugen. *Die unvollendete Erneuerung: Deutschland im Kräftefeld, 1945–1963. Politische und gesellschaftspolitische Aufsätze aus zwei Jahrzehnten.* [Frankfurt:] Europäische Verlagsanstalt, [c. 1964].

Kohn, Hans. *German History: Some New German Views.* Boston: Beacon, 1954.

———. *The Mind of Modern Germany.* New York: Scribner's, 1960.

Kolnai, Aurel. *The War Against the West.* Pref. by Wickham Steed. London: Gollancz, 1938.

Korspeter, Wilhelm. *Die Demokratie im Spiegel der Bundesrepublik.* Vortrag gehalten am 1. und 2. März 1952 auf der Jahreshauptversammlung des Ortsvereins Hannover der SPD.

Krannhals, Hanns von. *Der Warschauer Aufstand 1944.* Frankfurt: Bernard & Graefe, 1962.

Krebs, Albert. *Tendenzen und Gestalten der NSDAP: Erinnerungen an die Frühzeit der Partei.* Stuttgart: Deutsche Verlags-Anstalt, 1959.

Krieger, Leonard. *The German Idea of Freedom. History of a Political Tradition.* Boston: Beacon, 1957.

Krim, Seymour, ed. *The Beats.* Greenwich (Conn.): Fawcett Publications, 1960.

Kruck, Alfred. *Geschichte des Alldeutschen Verbandes, 1890–1939.* Wiesbaden: Steiner, 1954.

Krüger, Horst, ed. *Was ist heute links? Thesen und Theorien zu einer politischen Position.* Munich: List, [c. 1963].

Laqueur, Walter Z. *Nasser's Egypt.* London: Weidenfeld and Nicolson, [c. 1956].

———. *Russia and Germany: A Century of Conflict.* London: Weidenfeld and Nicolson, [c. 1965].

———. *Young Germany: A History of the German Youth Movement.* London: Routledge & Kegan Paul, 1962.

Lemberg, Eugen, and Friedrich Edding, eds. *Die Vertriebenen in Westdeutschland: Ihre Eingliederung und ihr Einfluss auf Gesellschaft, Wirtschaft, Politik und Geistesleben.* Kiel: Hirt, 1959. 3 vols.

Leonhardt, Rudolf Walter. *X-mal Deutschland.* 6th ed. Munich: Piper, 1962.

Lichtenberger, Henri. *The Third Reich.* Trans. by K. S. Pinson. New York: Greystone, 1937.

Liebe, Werner. *Die Deutschnationale Volkspartei 1918–1924.* Düsseldorf: Droste, 1956.

Lipset, Seymour Martin. *The First New Nation. The United States in Historical and Comparative Perspective.* New York: Basic Books, [c. 1963].

Litchfield, E. H., *et al. Governing Post-War Germany.* Ithaca (N.Y.): Cornell University Press, 1953.

Lougee, Robert W. *Paul de Lagarde 1827–1891: A Study of Radical Conservatism in Germany.* Cambridge (Mass.): Harvard University Press, 1962.

Luža, Radomír. *The Transfer of the Sudeten Germans. A Study of Czech–*

German Relations, 1933–1962. [New York:] New York University Press, 1964.

M. E. *Die deutsche "Konservative Revolution" des 20. Jahrhunderts*. Edited by Georg Held and Wilhelm Vershofen. [Wiesbaden: Necessitas, c. 1953.]

Macdonald, B. J. S. *The Trial of Kurt Meyer*. Toronto: Clarke, Irwin, 1954.

McGovern, William M. *From Luther to Hitler*. Boston: Houghton Mifflin, 1941.

Macridis, Roy C., and Robert E. Ward, eds. *Modern Political Systems: Europe*. Englewood Cliffs (N.J.): Prentice-Hall, 1963.

Martin, Hermann. *Demokratie oder Diktatur?* Berlin: Politik und Wirtschaft, 1926.

———. *Zehn Jahre Stahlhelm. Denkschrift*. Leipzig: [C. F. Fleischer], 1929.

Martini, Winfried. *Die Legende vom Hause Ludendorff*. Rosenheim: Inngau, Lang, 1949.

Maschmann, Melita. *Fazit. Kein Rechtfertigungsversuch*. Stuttgart: Deutsche Verlags-Anstalt, 1963.

Massing, Paul W. *Rehearsal for Destruction: A Study of Political Anti-Semitism in Imperial Germany*. New York: Harper, 1949.

Matthias, Erich, and Rudolf Morsey, eds. *Das Ende der Parteien 1933*. Düsseldorf: Droste, 1960.

Maurer, Emil H. *Der Spätbürger*. Bern, Munich: Francke, [c. 1963].

Meissner, Boris. *Russland, die Westmächte und Deutschland. Die sowjetische Deutschlandpolitik 1943–1953*. Hamburg: Nölke, 1953.

Meyer, Henry C. *Mitteleuropa in German Thought and Action 1815–1945*. The Hague: Nijhoff, 1955.

Meyn, Hermann. *Die Deutsche Partei. Entwicklung und Problematik einer national-konservativen Rechtspartei nach 1945*. Düsseldorf: Droste, [1965].

Mohler, Armin. *Die Konservative Revolution in Deutschland 1918–1932. Grundriss ihrer Weltanschauungen*. Stuttgart: Vorwerk, 1950.

Montgomery, John D. *Forced to Be Free: The Artificial Revolution in Germany and Japan*. Chicago: University of Chicago Press, 1957.

Mosse, George L. *The Crisis of German Ideology. Intellectual Origins of the Third Reich*. New York: Grosset & Dunlap, [c. 1964].

Müller-Marein, Josef. *Deutschland im Jahre 1. Panorama 1946–1948*. Hamburg: Nannen, 1960.

Naess, Arno, Jens A. Christophersen, and Kjell Kvalø. *Democracy, Ideology and Objectivity: Studies in the Semantics and Cognitive Analysis of Ideological Controversy*. Oslo: Oslo University Press; Oxford: Blackwell, 1956.

Namier, Sir Lewis. *In the Nazi Era*. London: Macmillan, 1952.

Nelhiebel, Kurt. *Die Henleins gestern und heute. Hintergründe und Ziele des Witikobundes*. Frankfurt: Röderberg, 1962.

Neumann, Franz. *Behemoth: The Structure and Practice of National Socialism 1933–1944*. New York: Oxford University Press, 1944.

Neumann, Sigmund. *Die deutschen Parteien. Wesen und Wandel nach dem Kriege*. Berlin: Junker und Dünnhaupt, 1932.

Neurohr, Jean F. *Der Mythos vom Dritten Reich*. Stuttgart: Cotta, 1957.

Neusüss-Hunkel, [Ermenhild]. *Die SS*. Hanover: Norddeutsche Verlagsanstalt O. Goedel, 1956.

Noack, Paul. *Die Intellektuellen: Wirkung, Versagen, Verdienst*. Munich: Olzog, [c. 1961].

Nolte, Ernst. *Der Faschismus in seiner Epoche*. Munich: Piper, [1963]. (*Three Faces of Fascism: Action Française, Italian Fascism, National Socialism*. Trans. by Leila Vennewitz. New York, Chicago, San Francisco: Holt, Rinehart and Winston, [1966].)

Norden, Günther van. *Kirche in der Krise. Die Stellung der evangelischen Kirche zum nationalsozialistischen Staat im Jahre 1933*. Düsseldorf: Presseverband der evangelischen Kirche im Rheinland, 1964.

Northrop, F. S. C. *European Union and United States Foreign Policy*. New York: Macmillan, 1954.

Obermann, Emil. *Soldaten, Bürger, Militaristen: Militär und Demokratie in Deutschland*. Stuttgart: Cotta, 1958.

Oertzen, Friedrich Wilhelm von. *Die Deutschen Freikorps 1918–1923*. 6th ed. Munich: Bruckmann, 1939.

Orb, Heinrich, *pseud*. *Nationalsozialismus: 13 Jahre Machtrausch*. 2d ed. Olten: Walter, 1945.

Ortlieb, Heinz-Dietrich, ed. *Hamburger Jahrbuch für Wirtschafts- und Gesellschaftspolitik*. V. Tübingen: Mohr (Siebeck), 1960.

Paetel, Karl O. *Das Bild vom Menschen in der deutschen Jugendführung*. Bad Godesberg: Voggenreiter, 1954.

———. *Jugendbewegung und Politik*. Bad Godesberg: Voggenreiter, 1961. (The second enlarged edition, 1963, bears the title *Jugend in der Entscheidung 1913, 1933, 1945*.)

Picard, Max. *Hitler in Ourselves*. Trans. by Heinrich Hauser. Chicago: Regnery, 1947.

Pinson, Koppel S. *Modern Germany*. New York: Macmillan, 1954.

Plessner, Helmut. *Die verspätete Nation. Über die politische Verführbarkeit des bürgerlichen Geistes*. 3d ed. Stuttgart: Kohlhammer, 1959.

Plumyène, J., and R. Lasierra. *Les Fascismes français 1923–1963*. Paris: Seuil, 1963.

Pollock, Friedrich, ed. *Gruppenexperiment*. Frankfurter Beiträge zur Soziologie, no. 2. [Frankfurt]: Europäische Verlagsanstalt, [c. 1955].

Pritzkoleit, Kurt. *Gott erhält die Mächtigen. Rück- und Rundblick auf den deutschen Wohlstand*. [Düsseldorf:] Rauch, [c. 1963].

Pross, Harry. *Jugend—Eros—Poiltik. Die Geschichte der deutschen Jugendverbände*. Bern: Scherz, 1964.

———. *Literatur und Politik*. Olten, Freiburg i. Br.: Walter, [1963].

———. *Vor und nach Hitler. Zur deutschen Sozialpathologie*. Olten: Walter, 1962.

Pünder, Hermann. *Politik in der Reichskanzlei. Aufzeichnungen aus den*

Jahren 1929–1932. Schriftenreihe der Vierteljahrshefte für Zeitgeschichte, no. 5. Stuttgart: Deutsche Verlags-Anstalt, 1961.

Puttkamer, Jesco Günther Heinrich von. *Irrtum und Schuld. Die Geschichte des National-Komitées "Freies Deutschland."* Neuwied: Michael, [c. 1948].

Raabe, Felix. *Die bündische Jugend. Ein Beitrag zur Geschichte der Weimarer Republik*. Stuttgart: Brentano, 1961.

Rapp, Adolf. *Der deutsche Gedanke*. Bonn: Schroeder, 1920.

Rauschning, Hermann. *The Conservative Revolution*. New York: Putnam, 1941.

———. *The Revolution of Nihilism*. New York: Alliance Book, Longmans, Green, 1939.

———. *The Voice of Destruction*. New York: Putnam, 1940.

Reed, Douglas. *Nemesis? The Story of Otto Strasser*. Boston: Houghton Mifflin, 1940.

———. *The Prisoner of Ottawa: Otto Strasser*. London: Cape, 1953.

Reichmann, Eva G. *Hostages of Civilization. The Social Sources of National Socialist Anti-Semitism*. Boston: Beacon, 1951.

Reigrotzki, Erich. *Soziale Verflechtungen in der Bundesrepublik: Elemente der sozialen Teilnahme in Kirche, Politik, Organisationen und Freizeit*. Tübingen: Mohr (Siebeck), 1956.

Reiss, H. S., ed. *Political Thought of the German Romantics 1793–1815*. Oxford: Blackwell, 1955.

Reitlinger, Gerald. *The House Built on Sand*. London: Weidenfeld and Nicolson, 1960.

———. *The SS, Alibi of a Nation, 1922–1945*. 2d rev. ed. London: Heinemann, 1957.

Richter, Hans Werner, ed. *Bestandsaufnahme: Eine deutsche Bilanz 1962*. Munich: Desch, 1962.

Richter, Werner. *Re-Educating Germany*. Chicago: University of Chicago Press, 1945.

Ritter, Gerhard. *Europa und die deutsche Frage*. Munich: Münchener Verlag (Graph. Kunstanstalt), 1948.

———. *The German Resistance: Carl Goerdeler's Struggle Against Tyranny*. Trans. by R. T. Clark. New York: Praeger, 1958.

Roessler, Wilhelm. *Jugend im Erziehungsfeld*. Düsseldorf: Schwann, 1957.

Rogge, O. John. *The Official German Report*. New York: Yoseloff, 1961.

Roloff, Ernst-August. *Bürgertum und Nationalsozialismus 1930–1933. Braunschweigs Weg ins Dritte Reich*. Hanover: Literatur und Zeitgeschehen, 1961.

Rorty, James, and Moshe Decter. *McCarthy and the Communists*. Boston: Beacon, 1954.

Rose, Arnold M., ed. *Human Behavior and Social Processes: An Interactionist Approach*. Boston: Houghton Mifflin, [c. 1962].

Rose, Ernst. *A History of German Literature*. New York: New York University Press, 1960.

Roth, Guenther, and Kurt H. Wolff. *The American Denazification of Germany: A Historical Survey and an Appraisal*. Studies in German-

American Postwar Problems, no. 1. Columbus (Ohio): Ohio State University, Department of Sociology and Anthropology, 1954.

Rothfels, Hans. *The German Opposition to Hitler*. Trans. by Lawrence Wilson. Chicago: Regnery, 1962 [c. 1948].

Rovere, Richard H. *Senator Joe McCarthy*. New York: Harcourt, Brace, 1959.

St. John, Robert. *The Boss*. New York: McGraw-Hill, 1960.

Saller, Karl. *Die Rassenlehre des Nationalsozialismus in Wissenschaft und Propaganda*. Darmstadt: Progress, [c. 1961].

Samuel, Richard, and R. Hinton Thomas. *Expressionism in German Life, Literature, and the Theatre (1910–1924)*. Cambridge: Heffer, 1939.

Sastamoinen, Armas. *Hitlers svenska förtrupper*. Stockholm: Federatius, 1947.

———. *Ny-nazismen*. Stockholm: Federatius, 1961.

Schechtman, J. B. *Postwar Population Transfers in Europe, 1945–1955*. Philadelphia: University of Pennsylvania Press, 1962.

Schelsky, Helmut. *Die skeptische Generation, eine Soziologie der deutschen Jugend*. Düsseldorf: Diederichs, 1957.

Scheurig, Bodo. *Freies Deutschland: Das Nationalkomitée und der Bund deutscher Offiziere in der Sowjetunion 1943–1945*. Munich: Nymphenburg, 1960.

Schönbach, Peter. *Reaktionen auf die antisemitische Welle im Winter 1959/1960*. Frankfurter Beiträge zur Soziologie, Sonderheft 3. [Frankfurt:] Europäische Verlagsanstalt, [c. 1961].

Schoeps, Hans Joachim. *Das andere Preussen*. Stuttgart: Vorwerk, 1952.

Schonauer, Franz. *Deutsche Literatur im Dritten Reich*. Olten, Freiburg i. Br.: Walter, 1961.

Schüddekopf, Otto-Ernst. *Die deutsche Innenpolitik im letzten Jahrhundert und der konservative Gedanke*. Braunschweig: Limbach, 1951.

———. *Linke Leute von rechts: Die revolutionären Minderheiten und der Kommunismus in der Weimarer Republik*. Stuttgart: Kohlhammer, [c. 1960].

Schweitzer, Arthur. *Big Business in the Third Reich*. Bloomington (Ind.): Indiana University Press, 1964.

Schwierskott, Hans-Joachim. *Arthur Moeller van den Bruck und der revolutionäre Nationalismus in der Weimarer Republik*. Göttingen: Musterschmidt, 1962.

Seabury, Paul. *The Wilhelmstrasse*. Berkeley, Los Angeles: University of California Press, 1954.

Sedar, Irving, and Harold J. Greenberg. *Behind the Egyptian Sphinx. Nasser's Strange Bedfellows: Prelude to World War III?* Philadelphia: Chilton, [1960].

Seeliger, Rolf. *Braune Universität*. Nos. 1–4. Munich: Seeliger, 1964–1966.

Sell, Friedrich C. *Die Tragödie des deutschen Liberalismus*. Stuttgart: Deutsche Verlags-Anstalt, 1953.

Semmel, Bernard. *Imperialism and Social Reform: English Social-Imperial Thought 1895–1914*. Cambridge (Mass.): Harvard University Press, 1960.

Sherwood, Robert E. *Roosevelt and Hopkins, an Intimate History.* Rev. ed. New York: Harper, [1948].

Shirer, William L. *The Rise and Fall of the Third Reich.* New York: Simon and Schuster, 1960.

Siemering, Hertha, ed. *Die deutschen Jugendverbände.* Berlin: Heymann, 1931.

Skuhr, Werner. *Die Stellung zur Demokratie in der deutschen Nachkriegsdiskussion über den "Demokratischen und Sozialen Rechtsstaat."* Berlin: Ernst-Reuter-Gesellschaft, Freie Universität, 1961.

Snell, J. L. *Wartime Origins of the East-West Dilemma over Germany.* New Orleans: Hauser, 1959.

Snyder, Louis L. *German Nationalism: The Tragedy of a People.* Harrisburg (Penna.): Stackpole, 1952.

Sonnemann, Ulrich. *Das Land der unbegrenzten Zumutbarkeiten.* [Reinbek/Hamburg:] Rowohlt, [1963].

Sontheimer, Kurt. *Antidemokratisches Denken in der Weimarer Republik. Die politischen Ideen des deutschen Nationalismus zwischen 1918 und 1933.* 2d ed. [Munich:] Nymphenburg, [1964, c. 1962].

Sozialdemokratische Partei Deutschlands (SPD). Der Vorstand. *Das ist die Deutsche Partei.* Bonn: August, 1953.

———. ———. *Ich bin Generalmajor Remer.* N.p., n.d.

———. ———. *Partisanen gegen Bezahlung.* N.p., n.d.

———. ———. *Das wahre Gesicht der FDP.* Bonn: N.pub., July, 1953.

Speier, Hans. *German Rearmament and Atomic War.* Evanston (Ill.): Row, Peterson, 1957.

———. *Social Order and the Risks of War.* New York: Stewart, 1952.

———, and W. Phillips Davison. *West German Leadership and Foreign Policy.* Evanston (Ill.): Row, Peterson, [1957].

Stahl, Walter, ed. *The Politics of Postwar Germany.* New York: Praeger, 1963.

Stern, Fritz. *The Politics of Cultural Despair: A Study in the Rise of the Germanic Ideology.* Berkeley, Los Angeles: University of California Press, 1961.

Stern, Leo, ed. *Der Antikommunismus in Theorie und Praxis des deutschen Imperialismus. Zur Auseinandersetzung mit der imperialistischen deutschen Geschichtsschreibung.* Sonderband, Wissenschaftliche Zeitschrift der Martin-Luther-Universität Halle-Wittenberg. [Halle: Martin-Luther-Universität Halle-Wittenberg], 1963.

Stirk, Samuel D. *The Prussian Spirit.* London: Faber & Faber, 1941.

Strasser, Bernhard P. *Gregor and Otto Strasser.* Külsheim/Baden: Stössel, June, 1954.

Strothmann, Dietrich. *Nationalsozialistische Literaturpolitik. Ein Beitrag zur Publizistik im Dritten Reich.* 2d impr. enl. ed. Bonn: Bouvier, 1963 [c. 1960].

Tenenbaum, Joseph. *Race and Reich.* New York: Twayne, 1956.

Thayer, Charles W. *The Unquiet Germans.* New York: Harper, [1957].

Tönnies, Norbert. *Der Weg zu den Waffen: Die Geschichte der deutschen Wiederbewaffnung 1949–1957*. Cologne: Markus, 1957.

Viereck, Peter. *Metapolitics: The Roots of the Nazi Mind*. New York: Capricorn Books, 1961.

Waite, Robert G. L. *Vanguard of Nazism: The Free Corps Movement in Post-War Germany 1918–1923*. Cambridge (Mass.): Harvard University Press, 1952.

Waldman, Eric. *The Goose Step Is Verboten: The German Army Today*. Glencoe (Ill.): Free Press, [c. 1964].

Weinreich, Max. *Hitler's Professors: The Part of Scholarship in Germany's Crimes against the Jewish People*. New York: Yiddish Scientific Institute—YIVO, 1946.

Weinstein, Adelbert. *Armee ohne Pathos. Die deutsche Wiederbewaffnung im Urteil ehemaliger Soldaten*. Bonn: Köllen, 1951.

Weippert, Georg. *Jenseits von Individualismus und Kollektivismus. Studien zum gegenwärtigen Zeitalter*. Düsseldorf: Schilling, 1964.

Werner, Christian K. *Rechts—Links*. Bad Godesberg: Hohwacht, 1963.

Wiechert, Ernst. *Sämtliche Werke*. Vol. IX. Munich, Vienna, Basel: Desch, [1957].

Wildenmann, Rudolf. *Macht und Konsens als Problem der Innen- und Aussenpolitik*. Kölner Schriften zur Politischen Wissenschaft, vol. II. Frankfurt, Bonn: Athenäum, 1963.

Willbrand, Jürgen. *Kommt Hitler wieder? Rechtsradikalismus in Deutschland*. Donauwörth: Auer Cassianeum, [1964?].

Willis, F. Roy. *The French in Germany, 1945–1949*. Stanford (Calif.): Stanford University Press, 1962.

Wucher, Albert. *Eichmanns gab es viele*. Munich, Zurich: Droemersche Verlagsanstalt Th. Knaur Nachf., 1961.

Zeller, Eberhard. *Geist der Freiheit: Der zwanzigste Juli 1944*. 3d ed., enl. Munich: Rinn, [1956].

Zink, Harold. *The United States in Germany 1944–1955*. Princeton (N.J.): Van Nostrand, 1957.

2. ARTICLES

(a) *Signed Articles*

Abel, August. "Reinhold Wulle zum Gedächtnis," *Der Informationsbrief* (July, 1950), p. 8.

Abendroth, Wolfgang. "Das Problem der Widerstandstätigkeit der 'Schwarzen Front,'" *Vierteljahrshefte für Zeitgeschichte,* VIII, 2 (April, 1960), 181–187.

———. "Zur Funktion der Gewerkschaften in der westdeutschen Demokratie," *Gewerkschaftliche Monatshefte,* III, 11 (November, 1952), 641–648.

Allemann, Fritz René. "Adenauer's Eastern Policy," *Survey,* no. 44/45 (October, 1962), pp. 29–36.

Almond, Gabriel. "The Political Attitudes of German Business," *World Politics,* VIII, 1 (January, 1956), 47–62.

Arps, Ludwig. "Das unruhige Dorf," *Deutsche Zeitung und Wirtschaftszeitung* (Stuttgart), no. 60 (July 28, 1951), p. 3.

Ascher, Abraham, and Guenter Lewy. "National Bolshevism in Weimar Germany: Alliance of Political Extremes against Democracy," *Social Research,* XXIII, 4 (Winter, 1956), 450–480.

Auerbach, Hellmuth. "Die Einheit Dirlewanger," *Vierteljahrshefte für Zeitgeschichte,* X, 3 (July, 1962), 250–263.

Baldwin, Hanson W. "Germany's New Army," *New York Times,* October 14, 1957, p. 9, col. 3.

Barnes, Harry Elmer. Response to G. L. Weinberg's book review of David L. Hoggan's *Der erzwungene Krieg, American Historical Review,* LXVIII, 3 (April, 1963), 916–917, and further remarks, LXIX, 1 (October, 1963), 304, 306–307.

Bauer-Heyd, W. "Arbeiten Schwedens Nazi für Ägypten?" *Süddeutsche Zeitung* (Munich), no. 114 (May 13, 1965), p. 5.

Baum, W. "Marine, Nationalsozialismus und Widerstand," *Vierteljahrshefte für Zeitgeschichte,* XI, 1 (January, 1963), 16–18.

Baumann, Gerhard. "Psychologische Rückwirkungen in der Bevölkerung der Bundesrepublik beim Aufbau einer Gesamtverteidigung," *Wehrwissenschaftliche Rundschau,* XII, 3 (March, 1962), 123–139.

Bayer, Oswald. "Neonazismo en la Argentina" (*Comentario,* October–December, 1956), in *The Wiener Library Bulletin* (London), XI, 1–2 (January–April, 1957), 10.

Berghahn, Volker R. "Die Entwicklung der Mensur im Nachkriegsdeutschland," *Deutsche Universitäts-Zeitung,* XIX, 1 (January, 1964), pp. 12–18.

———. "Right Wing Radicalism in West Germany's Younger Generation," *Journal of Central European Affairs,* XXII, 3 (October, 1962), 317–336.

Bergmann, Walter H., *pseud.* [i.e., Walter Kniggendorf]. "Rechtsradikales Kabarett," *Das Freie Wort* (Düsseldorf), August 23, 1952, p. 5.

Bernhard, Ute. "Wie Jugendliche die Juden sehen," *deutsche jugend,* VIII, 2 (February, 1960), 69–73.

Bessel-Lorck, Lorenz. "Parolen des Rechtsradikalismus heute," in Wanda von Baeyer-Katte *et al., Autoritarismus und Nationalismus—ein deutsches Problem?* Politische Psychologie, Schriftenreihe, vol. II. [Frankfurt:] Europäische Verlagsanstalt, [c. 1963]. Pp. 50–60.

Blair, W. Granger. "Israeli Parties Ask Debate on Germans' Role in Cairo," *New York Times,* April 2, 1963, pp. 1, 8.

Bodensieck, Heinrich. "Nationalsozialismus in revisionistischer Sicht," *Aus Politik und Zeitgeschichte* (Supplement of *Das Parlament*) (Bonn), B 13/61 (March 29, 1961), pp. 175–180.

Boehm, Max Hildebert. "Gruppenbildung und Organisationswesen," in Eugen Lemberg and Friedrich Edding, eds., *Die Vertriebenen in Westdeutschland: Ihre Eingliederung, und ihr Einfluss auf Gesellschaft, Wirtschaft, Politik und Geistesleben.* Kiel: Hirt, 1959. II, 521–606.

Bohn, Helmut. "Die patriotische Karte in der sowjetischen Deutschlandpolitik," *Ost-Probleme,* VII, 38 (September 23, 1955), 40 (October 7, 1955), and 42 (October 21, 1955).

Botzat, Robert. "Niedersachsen greift gegen die SRP nicht durch," *Die Neue Zeitung* (Munich), VII, 244 (October 17, 1951).

Bracken, Helmut von. "Die deutsche Jugend von 1953 im Spiegel der Meinungsforschung. Zu der EMNID-Erhebung 'Die Jugend zwischen 15 und 24,' " *deutsche jugend,* II, 4 (April, 1954), 155–163.

Brauweiler, Heinz. "Der Anteil des Stahlhelm," in Curt Hotzel, ed., *Deutscher Aufstand. Die Revolution des Nachkriegs.* Stuttgart: Kohlhammer, 1934. Pp. 218–227.

Brodmann, K.-Dieter. "Die Presse der deutschen Heimatvertriebenen," in Institut für Publizistik an der Freien Universität Berlin, *Die Deutsche Presse 1954; Zeitungen und Zeitschriften.* Berlin: Duncker & Humblot, 1954. Pp. 605–606.

Broszat, Martin. "Die völkische Ideologie und der Nationalsozialismus," *Deutsche Rundschau,* LXXXIV, 1 (January, 1958), 53–68.

———. "Das sudetendeutsche Freikorps," *Vierteljahrshefte für Zeitgeschichte,* IX, 1 (January, 1961), 30–49.

Buchheim, Hans. "Die SS in der Verfassung des Dritten Reiches," *Vierteljahrshefte für Zeitgeschichte,* III, 2 (April, 1955), 127–157.

———. "Zu Kleists 'Auch Du warst dabei,' " *Vierteljahrshefte für Zeitgeschichte,* II, 2 (April, 1954), 177–192.

Büsch, Otto. "Geschichte und Gestalt der SRP," in Otto Büsch and Peter Furth, *Rechtsradikalismus im Nachkriegsdeutschland.* Berlin: Vahlen, 1957. Pp. 1–192.

Bussman, Walter. "Politische Ideologien zwischen Monarchie und Weimarer Republik," *Historische Zeitschrift,* CXC (1960), 55–77.

Carsten, F. L. "The Reichswehr and the Red Army 1920–1933," *Survey,* no. 44/45 (October, 1962), pp. 114–132.

———. "Stauffenberg's Bomb," *Encounter,* XXIII, 3 (September, 1964), 64–67.

Čelovsky, Boris. "The Transferred Sudeten Germans and their Political Activity," *Journal of Central European Affairs,* XVII, 2 (July, 1957), 127–149.

Cornides, Wilhelm. "Die Neutralitätslehre des Nauheimer Kreises," *Politisches Archiv,* VI, 8 (April 20, 1951), 3879–3892.

Croan, Melvin. "Reality and Illusion in Soviet-German Relations," *Survey,* no. 44/45 (October, 1962), pp. 12–28.

D. G. "Bündnis deutscher Republikaner," *Colloquium,* X, 11 (November, 1956).

———. "Nazismus in der Zange des Intellekts," *Colloquium,* X, 12 (December, 1956).

Dähnhardt, H., and Giselher Wirsing. "Die bündische Jugend," in Hertha Siemering, ed., *Die deutschen Jugendverbände.* Berlin: Heymann, 1931. Pp. 61–63.

Dahrendorf, Ralf. "The New Germanies: Restoration, Revolution, Reconstruction," *Encounter,* XXII, 4 (April, 1964), 50–58.

Dammers, Georg. "Gefährlich missbrauchte Freiheit," *Kontakte,* III, 6 (June, 1953), 14.

Davidson, Basil. "The Manteuffel Plan," *The New Statesman and Nation,* XL, 1008 (July 1, 1950), 6.

Dehio, Ludwig. "Um den deutschen Militarismus," *Historische Zeitschrift,* CLXXX (1955), 43–64.

Delcour, Roland. "Néonazis, Parti des Réfugiés et Parti Allemand," *Allemagne d'Aujourd'hui,* May–September, 1957, pp. 76–88.

Döring, Kurt. "Führungskrise in der Deutschen Reichspartei," *Frankfurter Allgemeine Zeitung,* September 27, 1957.

———. "Niedersachsen neigen zum Grundsätzlichen," *Frankfurter Allgemeine Zeitung,* November 9, 1957.

Drascher, Wahrhold. "Zur Soziologie des deutschen Seeoffizierkorps," *Wehrwissenschaftliche Rundschau,* XII, 10 (October, 1962), 555–569.

Ebeling, Hans. "Unvergessen: Theo Hespers. Katholische und freie Jugendbewegung im Widerstand gegen das NS-System," *Graue Blätter,* I, 1 (May, 1956), 12–14.

Edinger, Lewis J. "Post-Totalitarian Leadership: Elites in the German Federal Republic," *American Political Science Review,* LIV, 1 (March, 1960), 58–82.

Elten, J. A. "Die Brüder von der 'Bruderschaft,'" *Süddeutsche Zeitung* (Munich), no. 216 (September 19, 1950).

Engel, J. "Wer hat Angst vor dem bösen Wolf—sburg?" *Die Neue Zeitung* (Munich), V, 205 (September 2, 1949).

Eppe, Jürgen. "Generalangriff der Bundeswehr auf die deutschen Jugendverbände?" *Solidarität,* VIII (December 11, 1958), 187–189.

Erbe, Friedrich. "Vierzehn Jahre Wahlen in Westdeutschland (1946–1960)," in Erwin Faul, ed., *Wahlen und Wähler in Westdeutschland.* Villingen: Ring, [1960]. Pp. 17–111.

Erler, Fritz. "Über den Nazismus," *Neuer Vorwärts* (Hanover), November 23, 1951.

Euler, Heinrich. "Ulrich Noack—ein Leben aus freier Mitte," in *Ein Leben aus freier Mitte, Beiträge zur Geschichtsforschung.* Göttingen: Musterschmidt, 1961. Pp. vi–xxxii.

Fabricius, F. W. "Der Deutsche Pfadfinderbund," in Hertha Siemering, ed., *Die deutschen Jugendverbände.* Berlin: Heymann, 1931. Pp. 45–47.

Faul, Erwin. "Soziologie der westdeutschen Wählerschaft," in Erwin Faul, ed., *Wahlen und Wähler in Westdeutschland.* Villingen: Ring, [1960]. Pp. 135–315.

Flechtheim, Ossip K. "Parteien und Organisationen in der Bundesrepublik," *Gewerkschaftliche Monatshefte,* VIII, 5 (May, 1957), 259–269.

Foerster, Friedrich Wilhelm. "La position de l'Allemagne entre l'est et l'ouest. Les dangers de la reconstitution de l'armée allemande," *L'Année Politique et Économique,* XXX, 137 (June–July, 1957), 213–229.

Forell, Birger. "National Socialism and the Protestant Churches in Germany," in Maurice Baumont *et al.,* eds., *The Third Reich.* New York: Praeger, 1955. Pp. 811–831.

Foster, C. R., and George Stambuk. "Judicial Protection of Civil Liberties in Germany," *Political Studies,* IV, 2 (June, 1956), 190–194.

Franke, Erdmann. "Am Ende des Weges: Ein pathetischer Leerlauf im Nichts," Gesellschaft zum Studium von Zeitfragen, *Analysen und Berichte,* VI, 9 (August 14, 1959), 2–8.

———. "Pionier eines neuen Nationalismus," *Studien von Zeitfragen, Analysen, Berichte, Informationen,* Sondermaterial B/1964 (March 26, 1964), pp. 3–5.

———. "Vom Sinn und Unsinn guter Einsicht," *Studien von Zeitfragen, Analysen und Berichte,* VIII, 11 (August 2, 1961), 8.

Friesicke, Konrad. "Falschspiel mit der Jugend," *deutsche jugend,* VIII, 2 (February, 1960), 85–87.

Furth, Peter. "Ideologie und Propaganda der SRP," in Otto Büsch and Peter Furth, *Rechtsradikalismus im Nachkriegsdeutschland.* Berlin: Vahlen, 1957. Pp. 193–309.

Gablentz, Otto Heinrich von der. "Reaktion und Restauration," in Wilhelm Berges and Carl Hinrichs, eds., *Zur Geschichte und Problematik der Demokratie. Festgabe für Hans Herzfeld.* Berlin: Duncker & Humblot, [c. 1958]. Pp. 55–77.

Galatier-Boissière, J. "Bardèche ou la vérité n'est jamais bonne à dire," *Crapouillot,* no. 27 (1954), pp. 65–66.

Gatzke, H. W. "Russo–German Military Collaboration during the Weimar Period," *American Historical Review,* LXIII, 3 (April, 1958), 565–597.

Gembardt, Ulrich. "Gespräch ohne Partner?" *Deutsche Universitäts-Zeitung,* VIII, 2 (January 26, 1953).

Genz, Ekkehard. "Politische Träumer an Bonner Tischen," *Welt am Sonntag* (Hamburg), no. 39, September 30, 1951.

Gimbel, John. "American Denazification and German Local Politics 1945–1949: A Case Study in Marburg," *American Political Science Review,* LIV, 1 (March, 1960), 83–105.

Giovana, Mario. "New Fascists in Italy," *The Wiener Library Bulletin* (London), IX, 1–2 (January–April, 1955), 10.

Glaser, Jakob. "Im 'Stahlhelm' geht es rund . . ." *Welt der Arbeit* (Cologne), September 25, 1953, p. 2.

Goldschmidt, Dietrich. "Elitebildung in der industriellen Gesellschaft," *Die Neue Gesellschaft,* V, 1 (January–February, 1958), 34–41.

Gong, Walter. "Couleurstudenten 1961," *Die Zeit* (Hamburg), no. 22 (June 2, 1961), p. 7; no. 23 (June 8, 1961), p. 6; no. 24 (June 16, 1961), p. 8.

Gregor, James A. "Nordicism Revisited," *Phylon,* XXII (1961), 351–360.

Groote, Wolfgang von. "Bundeswehr und 20. Juli," *Vierteljahrshefte für Zeitgeschichte,* XII, 3 (July, 1964), 285–299.

Grossherr, Dieter. "Die Korporationen und die Demokratie," *Die Neue Gesellschaft,* III, 6 (November–December, 1956), 442–455.

Grote, Adolf. "Die beschönigte Katastrophe: Lage und Praxis der gegenwärtigen deutschen Geschichtsrevision," *Deutsche Rundschau,* LXXXII, 1 (January, 1956), 21–26.

Hagen, Rosemarie von dem. "Rousseau und die Problematik der Demokratie," *Deutsche Rundschau,* LXXVI, 3 (March, 1950), 157–166.

Hagen, Volker von. "Ohne Rudel und ohne Naumann," *Die Welt* (Hamburg), no. 207 (September 4, 1956), p. 3.

Halberstadt, Gerhard. "Schutz vor Schund," *deutsche jugend,* VIII, 3 (March, 1960), 117–123.

Hallgarten, G. W. F. "General Hans von Seeckt and Russia 1920–1922," *The Journal of Modern History,* XXI, 1 (March, 1949), 28–34.

Hamilton, Thomas J. "German Rightists Obtain 15 Seats in Bavarian Vote," *New York Times,* November 21, 1966, p. 1, col. 8; p. 5, cols. 4–6.

Hammerschmidt, Helmut. "Ist der Nationalsozialismus tot?" [Club republikanischer Publizisten,] *CrP-Information,* April, 1957, p. 37.

Heidenheimer, Arnold J. "Federalism and the Party System: The Case of West Germany," *American Political Science Review,* LII, 3 (September, 1958), 809–828.

———. "German Party Finance: The CDU," *American Political Science Review,* LI, 2 (June, 1957), 369–385.

Heigert, Hans. "Der Selbstmord der deutschen Studentenschaft," *Frankfurter Allgemeine Zeitung,* no. 80 (April 5, 1958).

Heilmann, Wolfgang. "Paul Ernst," *Neue Deutsche Biographie.* Berlin: Duncker & Humblot, 1959. IV, 630.

Hennemann, J. "Doch wieder Rasse-Günther?" *Welt am Sonntag* (Hamburg), no. 44 (November 4, 1951).

Henrich, Hans. "Schwarz-rotes Welfen Team," *Frankfurter Rundschau,* November 14, 1957.

Herlt, Rudolf. "Wer finanziert das Studium?" *Deutsche Universitäts-Zeitung,* VII, 13 (July 4, 1952), 14–16.

Herz, John H. "The Fiasco of Denazification in Germany," *Political Science Quarterly,* LXIII, 4 (December, 1948), 569–594.

———. "German Officialdom Revisited," *World Politics,* VII, 1 (October, 1954), 63–83.

———. "Political Views of the West German Civil Service," in Hans Speier and W. Phillips Davison, eds., *West German Leadership and Foreign Policy.* Evanston (Ill.): Row, Peterson, [1957]. Pp. 96–135.

Herzfeld, Hans J. "Zur neueren Literatur über das Heeresproblem in der deutschen Geschichte," *Vierteljahrshefte für Zeitgeschichte,* IV, 4 (October, 1956), 361–386.

Hippel, Ernst von. "Rousseaus Staatslehre als Mystik des Materialismus," *Neues Abendland,* VI, 7 (1950), 337–345.

Hirsch, Kurt. "Studentenverbindungen und ihre politische Bedeutung," *Textil-Bekleidung* (Düsseldorf), no. 10 (May 15, 1957), p. 3.

———. "Wohin segelt die Bundesmarine?" *Blätter für Deutsche und Internationale Politik,* no. 6 (June 20, 1958), pp. 425–432.

[Hitler, Adolf.] "Das politische Testament Adolf Hitlers vom 29. April 1945," in Hans-Adolf Jacobson, ed., *1939–1945. Der zweite Weltkrieg in*

Chronik und Dokumenten. 5th ed. Darmstadt: Wehr und Wissen, 1961. P. 532.

Hochhut, Rolf. "Der Klassenkampf ist nicht zu Ende," *Der Spiegel,* XIX, 22 (May 26, 1965), 28–44.

Hoffmann, Volkmar. "Stahlhelm Rebellion um Schwarz-Rot-Gold," *Schleswig-Holsteinische Volks-Zeitung* (Kiel), LXI, 82 (April 7, 1954), 7.

Holborn, Hajo. "Germany's Role in the Defense of Western Europe," *Proceedings of the Academy of Political Science,* XXVI, 2 (January, 1955), 156–167.

Holt, Reinhart. "Wenn die Heimatvertriebenen wüssten . . . ," *Echo der Woche* (Munich), March 15, 1952, p. 4.

Holz, Hans Heinz. "Die verschleierte Klassengesellschaft," in Horst Krüger, ed., *Was ist heute links? These und Theorien zu einer politischen Position.* Munich: List, [c. 1963]. Pp. 69–84.

I. B. "Politischer Schriftsteller oder Advokat?" *Studien von Zeitfragen, Presse- und Buchspiegel,* VIII, 8–9 (August–September, 1961), 2–3.

J. W. "Dürfen wir vergessen?" *Norddeutsche Zeitung* (Hanover), July 30, 1956.

Jaeger, Hans. "Sudeten Irredenta," *The Wiener Library Bulletin* (London), XVII, 3 (July, 1963), 36.

Janowitz, Morris. "Soziale Schichtung und Mobilität in Westdeutschland," *Kölner Zeitschrift für Soziologie und Sozialpsychologie,* X, 1 (1958), 1–38.

Jasper, Gotthard. "Über die Ursachen des zweiten Weltkrieges. Zu den Büchern von A. J. P. Taylor und David L. Hoggan," *Vierteljahrshefte für Zeitgeschichte,* X, 3 (July, 1962), 311–340.

Jensen, Kai. " 'SS-Treffpunkt Kairo'—eine dicke Ente!" *Die Brücke,* IV, 18 (October 15, 1957), 6–8.

Joesten, Joachim. "The Menace of Neo-Nazism," *New Germany Reports,* no. 15 (September, 1950), pp. 16–17.

Jordan, R. M. "Noch immer: Wolfgang Hedler," *Das Freie Wort* (Düsseldorf), n.d., probably beginning of March, 1950.

Kaehler, S. A. Letter to editor of *Frankfurter Allgemeine Zeitung,* August 15, 1952.

Kahn, Lothar. "The Swastika in German Novels," *The Wiener Library Bulletin* (London), XIV, 2 (1960), 29.

Kaiser, Carl C. "Der junge teutsche Reigen," *deutsche jugend,* IV, 5 (May, 1956), 207–212.

———. "Politische Meinungen der westdeutschen Jugend," *deutsche jugend,* V, 8 (August, 1957), 367–376.

———. "Zur politischen Grundhaltung der westdeutschen Jugend," *deutsche jugend,* VI, 1 (January, 1958), 21–27.

Kann, Robert A. "Wolfgang Menzel: Pioneer of Integral Nationalism," *Journal of the History of Ideas,* VI, 2 (April, 1945), 213–230.

Klaus, Roland. "Nicht gestern, Freund, morgen!" *Aus Politik und Zeitgeschichte* (Supplement of *Das Parlament*) (Bonn), December 28, 1958.

Klemperer, Klemens von. "Kommt ein viertes Reich? Zur Geschichte des Nationalbolschewismus in Deutschland," *Dokumente,* VIII, 2 (1952), 129–144. ("Toward a Fourth Reich? The History of National Bolshevism," *Review of Politics,* XIII, 2 [April, 1951], 191–210.)

Klönne, Arno. "Im alten Geist—ungebrochen weiter!" *Solidarität,* VI, 5 (May, 1956), 80.

———. "Jugendarbeit 'rechtsaussen,'" *Politische Studien,* IX, 101 (September, 1958), 617–625.

———. "Mit dem Rücken zur Wand," *Graue Blätter,* I, 1 (May, 1956), 7.

———. "Wir sind wieder völkisch," *Freie Presse* (Bielefeld), July 4, 1955.

Kluckhohn, Paul. "Die Konservative Revolution in der Dichtung der Gegenwart," *Zeitschrift für deutsche Bildung,* IX, 4 (1933), 177–190.

Kluke, Paul. "Nationalsozialistische Europaideologie," *Vierteljahrshefte für Zeitgeschichte,* III, 3 (July, 1955), 240–275.

Koch, Thilo. "Idealismus—ein deutsches Missverständnis," *Deutsche Rundschau,* LXXX, 4 (April, 1954), 362–365.

Koehl, Robert L. "Zeitgeschichte and the New German Conservatism," *Journal of Central European Affairs,* XX, 2 (July, 1960), 131–157.

Köhler, Wolfram. "Romanautor der Granaten in Kaffeehäuser warf," *Die Welt* (Hamburg), no. 103 (April 30, 1962).

Koningsberger, Hans. Letter to the editor of the *New York Times,* February 9, 1964, sec. 4, p. 10, col. 5.

Kubala, Wolfgang. "Mit dem Lastwagen voller SS-Bücher geflüchtet," *Süddeutsche Zeitung* (Munich), no. 106 (May 4, 1965), p. 5.

Kugler, Werner. "Angstpsychose von 'links bis rechts'?" *Die Brücke,* II, 6 (June 10, 1955), 1–5.

———. "DRP, Lucht & Co.," *Die Brücke,* II, 11 (November, 1955), 1–5.

Kukil, Max. "Es ist Zeit: Bundesrepublik werde hart!" *Vorwärts* (Cologne), IX, 7 (February 17, 1956), 3.

Kurth, Karl O. "In der Sicht des Auslandes," in Eugen Lemberg and Friedrich Edding, eds., *Die Vertriebenen in Westdeutschland: Ihre Eingliederung, und ihr Einfluss auf Gesellschaft, Wirtschaft, Politik und Geistesleben.* Kiel: Hirt, 1959. III, 513–530.

Laqueur, Walter Z. "Nazism and the Nazis," *Encounter,* XXII, 4 (April, 1964), 39–46.

Lechner, Dieter. "Ein gefährlicher Schwärmer und seine Hintermänner," *Frankfurter Rundschau,* December 10, 1957.

Lemberg, Eugen. "Der Wandel des politischen Denkens," in Eugen Lemberg and Friedrich Edding, eds., *Die Vertriebenen in Westdeutschland: Ihre Eingliederung, und ihr Einfluss auf Gesellschaft, Wirtschaft, Politik und Geistesleben.* Kiel: Hirt, 1959. III, 435–474.

Lemme, H. "Adler und Falken, Bund deutscher Jugendwanderer e.V.," in Hertha Siemering, ed., *Die deutschen Jugendverbände.* Berlin: Heymann, 1931. Pp. 88–89.

Lesser, J. "Loss to Learning?" *The Wiener Library Bulletin* (London), VIII, 1–2 (January–April, 1954), 8.

Lipset, Seymour Martin. "The Changing Class Structure and Contemporary

European Politics," *Daedalus* (special issue, Winter, 1964), pp. 271–303.

———. "Some Social Requisites of Democracy: Economic Development and Political Legitimacy," *American Political Science Review,* LIII, 1 (March, 1959), 69–105.

List, Erich. Letter to the editor of *Frankfurter Allgemeine Zeitung,* August 22, 1952.

Loock, Hans-Dietrich. "Zur 'Grossgermanischen Politik' des Dritten Reiches," *Vierteljahrshefte für Zeitgeschichte,* VIII, 1 (January, 1960), 37–63.

Ludemann, Peter F. "Hitler schützt for Torheit nicht," *Civis,* VI, 53 (May 15, 1959), 269–273.

———. "Schwarz-weiss-rot mit Schulterklappen," *Civis,* VI, 59 (November 15, 1959), 94–96.

Lüth, Paul. "Für jedes Wort stehe ich gerade," *Die Zeit* (Hamburg), no. 52 (December 25, 1952), p. 2.

Lütkemann, Wilhelm. "Wiedergewinnung der Solidarität," *Deutsche Universitäts-Zeitung,* VIII, 22 (November 20, 1953), 10.

M. F. "Die Argumente der starken Hand," *deutsche jugend,* II, 5 (May, 1954), 227–228.

M. K. "Wörterbuch der Völkerkunde," *Die Mahnung,* IV, 10 (May 15, 1957), 2.

Mansfeld, Michael. "Ich sehe diese würd'gen Peers . . ." (a six-part series), *Frankfurter Rundschau,* November 16, 17, 20, 22, 23, 24, 1951.

———. "Ihr naht euch wieder . . ." (a five-part series), *Frankfurter Rundschau,* September 1, 3, 4, 5, 6, 1951.

Martius, Ursula Maria. "Videant consules . . . ," *Deutsche Rundschau,* LXX, 11 (November, 1947), 99–102.

Maschner, Wilhelm. " 'Alter Feind, was nun?' " *Die Welt* (Hamburg), May 7, 1957.

Mau, Hermann. "Die deutsche Jugendbewegung," *Zeitschrift für Religion und Geistesgeschichte,* I (1948), 135–149.

Meier-Welcker, Hans. "Die Stellung des Chefs der Heeresleitung in den Anfängen der Republik," *Vierteljahrshefte für Zeitgeschichte,* IV, 2 (April, 1956), 145–160.

———. "Zur politischen Haltung des Reichswehr-Offizierkorps," *Wehrwissenschaftliche Rundschau,* XII, 7 (July, 1962), 407–417.

Menck, Clara. "Neue Burschenherrlichkeit? Die westdeutsche Nachkriegsuniversität und ihre Hörer," *Wort und Wahrheit,* IX, 2 (February, 1954), 117–125.

Meyer-Sevenich, Maria. "Dr. Adenauers Verantwortung für den 'Fall Schlüter,' " *Vorwärts* (Cologne), IX, 7 (February 17, 1956), 5.

Middleton, Drew. "German Quits Unit Wooing Ex-Nazis," *New York Times,* November 29, 1952, p. 5, col. 1.

Milatz, Alfred. "Das Ende der Parteien im Spiegel der Wahlen 1930 bis 1933," in Erich Matthias and Rudolf Morsey, eds., *Das Ende der Parteien 1933.* Düsseldorf: Droste, 1960. Pp. 743–793.

Miller, R. W. "Recent Efforts toward Legal Regulation of Political Parties in Western Germany," *Papers of the Michigan Academy of Science, Arts and Letters,* XLVII (1962), 299–310.

Miska, Peter. "Wir sind schon wieder so weit," *Frankfurter Rundschau,* April 26, 1950, p. 4.

———. "Der unbequeme Soldat," *Frankfurter Rundschau,* June 16, 1956, p. 23.

Molitor, Jan, *pseud.* [i.e., Josef Müller-Marein]. "Die Fallschirmjäger sind keine 'ohne-michler,' " *Die Zeit* (Hamburg), no. 31 (August 2, 1951).

Mommsen, Wilhelm. "Zur Bedeutung des Reichsgedankens," *Historische Zeitschrift,* CLXXIV (1952), 385–415.

Mouricou, F. "La Jeunesse allemande de l'ouest," *Allemagne d'Aujourd'hui,* July–October, 1957, pp. 180–194.

Napoli, J. F. "Denazification from an American's Viewpoint," *The Annals of the American Academy of Political and Social Science,* no. 264 (July, 1949), pp. 115–123.

Nemitz, Kurt. "Das Regime der Mitläufer; Soziologische Notizen zur Renazifizierung," *Die Neue Gesellschaft,* II, 3 (May–June, 1955), 39–45.

Niethammer, Lutz. "Hoggan auf Deutschlandfahrt," *Der Monat,* XVI, 190 (July, 1964), 81–90.

Northrop, F. S. C. "European Political Experience Since World War II," in his *The Complexity of Legal and Ethical Experience. Studies in the Method of Normative Subjects.* Boston: Little, Brown, 1959. Pp. 125–142.

Oberländer, Theodor. Letter to the editor of *Der Spiegel,* XVIII, 5 (January 29, 1964), 19.

Olsen, Arthur J. "Germany Remains the Key to Tensions Between East and West," *New York Times,* July 28, 1963, sec. 4, p. 3.

———. "Goldwater in Touch with Right Wing in Germany," *New York Times,* July 15, 1964, p. 21, col. 3.

———. "Rightists Honor Hitler Defender," *New York Times,* May 5, 1964, p. 9, col. 1.

Olzog, Günther. "Gefährdet die Bundeswehr die Demokratie?" *Politische Studien,* VIII, 96 (April, 1958), 227–232.

Opitz, G. W. "Zwischen Skepsis und Hoffnung," *Studien von Zeitfragen, Presse- und Buchspiegel,* X, 1 (January 31, 1963), 2.

P. M. "Ein erfreuliches Zeichen politischer Reife," *Vorwärts* (Cologne), VIII, 22 (June 3, 1955), 2.

Pachter, Henry M. "The Legend of the 20th of July 1944," *Social Research,* XXIX, 1 (Spring, 1962), 109–113.

Paetel, Karl O. "Das National Komitée 'Freies Deutschland,' " *Politische Studien,* VI, 69 (January, 1956), 7–26.

———. "Otto Strasser und die 'Schwarze Front,' " *Politische Studien,* VIII, 92 (December, 1957), 269–281.

Paulus, G. "Remer beschloss Politiker zu werden," *Braunschweiger Zeitung,* September 6, 1949, p. 8.

Pechel, Rudolf. "Die Deutschen in Europa," *Deutsche Rundschau,* LXXV, 8 (August, 1949), 673–679.

Peschler, Eric A. "Braune 'Europa Akademie,' " *Die Andere Zeitung* (Hamburg), no. 28 (July 12, 1956), p. 11.

———. "Der Fall Kurt Ziesel," *Die Andere Zeitung* (Hamburg), no. 39 (September 29, 1955), p. 6.

———. "Der Fall Schlüter—ein Symptom," *Vorwärts* (Cologne), VIII, 22 (June 3, 1955), 2.

———. "Faschismus unter der Tarnkappe," *Die Andere Zeitung* (Hamburg), no. 36 (September 6, 1956), p. 11.

———. "Hinter den Kulissen der bündischen Jugend," *deutsche jugend,* IV, 6 (June, 1956), 277–278.

———. "Naziverschwörung am Tegernsee," *Welt der Arbeit* (*Stimme der Arbeit aus Bayern*), IV, 8 (February 20, 1953).

———. "Nun singen sie wieder," *Kontakte,* II, 2–3 (September–October, 1952), 18.

———. "Schmutziger Lorbeer," *Welt der Arbeit* (*Stimme der Arbeit aus Bayern*), VII, 28 (July 13, 1956).

———. "Studentische Verbindungen Anno 1951," *Die Neue Zeitung* (Munich), VII, 189 (August 14, 1951), 6; 190 (August 15, 1951), 8; 195 (August 21, 1951), 6.

———. "Warum—woher—aber wohin?" *Mannheimer Morgen,* no. 292 (December 15, 1954), p. 8.

Plessner, Helmut. "Über Elite und Elitebildung," *Gewerkschaftliche Monatshefte,* VI, 10 (October, 1955), 602–606.

Plischke, Elmer. "Denazification Law and Procedure," *American Journal of International Law,* XLI (October, 1947), 807–827.

Podhoretz, Norman. "The Know-Nothing Bohemians," *Partisan Review,* Spring, 1958, pp. 308–309.

Pulzer, P. G. J. "West Germany and the Three Party System," *The Political Quarterly,* XXXIII, 2 (October–December, 1962), 414–426.

Raymond, Jack. "Nazi Peril Is Cited to U.S. House Unit," *New York Times,* November 24, 1951, p. 5, col. 5.

Reifferscheidt, Friedrich M. "1945 bis 1950: Triumph des Hindenburg-Deutschen," *Frankfurter Hefte,* VI, 2 (February, 1951), 90–100.

Richter, Hans Werner. "Strafanzeige . . . warum?" *Die Kultur* (Munich), May, 1956, p. 5.

Richter, Walther. "Die Richter der Oberlandesgerichte der Bundesrepublik: Eine berufs- und sozialstatistische Analyse," in Heinz-Dietrich Ortlieb, ed., *Hamburger Jahrbuch für Wirtschafts- und Gesellschaftspolitik.* V. Tübingen: Mohr (Siebeck), 1960. Pp. 241–259.

Ridder, Helmut. "Die veruntreute Freiheit," *Blätter für Deutsche und Internationale Politik,* no. 3 (March 25, 1960), pp. 223–227.

Ridley, F. "The Parliamentary Commissioner for Military Affairs in the Federal Republic of Germany," *Political Studies,* XII, 1 (February, 1964), 1–20.

Ritter, Gerhard. "The Historical Foundations of the Rise of National Socialism," in Maurice Baumont *et al.*, eds., *The Third Reich*. New York: Praeger, 1955. Pp. 381–416.

———. "The Military and Politics in Germany," *Journal of Central European Affairs*, XVII, 3 (October, 1957), 259–271.

Romoser, George K. "The Politics of Uncertainty: The German Resistance Movement," *Social Research*, XXXI, 1 (Spring, 1964), 73–93.

Roschmann, Kurt. "Exemplarischer Fall einer Emigration," *Deutsche Rundschau*, LXXXI, 12 (December, 1955), 1320–1323.

Rostocker, Rolf. "La Condemnation de la guerre dans le roman," *Documents (Revue des questions allemandes)*, XII (May–June, 1957), 521–527.

Rothfels, Hans, and Henry M. Pachter. "Forum—The German Resistance Movement," *Social Research*, XXIX, 4 (Winter, 1962), 481–488.

S. "Oberländers Gefolgschaft," *Die Zeit* (Hamburg), no. 18 (May 6, 1954).

S. R. "Ein Mann namens Rudolf Steidl," *Deutsche Zeitung und Wirtschaftszeitung* (Stuttgart), no. 34 (April 28, 1954), p. 13.

S-r. "Bruderschaft in West und Ost," *Frankfurter Rundschau*, March 3, 1951.

Schallies, Walter. "Ein Schlag ins Gesicht der Luxemburger . . . ," *Süddeutsche Zeitung* (Munich), no. 22 (January 26, 1965), p. 3.

Schallück, Paul. " 'Grünwalder Kreis ohne Maske,' " *Die Europäische Zeitung* (Bonn), IV, 8/9 (August 25, 1956), 13.

Schelsky, Helmut. "Über das Restaurative in unserer Zeit," *Frankfurter Allgemeine Zeitung*, April 9, 1955.

Schiefer, Albert. "Die Presse der Phrasen," *Die Europäische Zeitung* (Bonn), IV, 12 (December 19, 1956), 3.

Schiller, J. C. Friedrich von. "Das Deutsche Reich," Xenien (Musenalmanach für das Jahr 1797) in Julius Petersen and Gerhard Fricke, eds., *Schillers Werke*. Nationalausgabe. Weimar: Böhlaus, 1943. Vol. 1 (*Gedichte 1776–1799*), p. 320.

Schilling, Joachim. "Wir sind kein neuer Stahlhelm," *Die Neue Zeitung* (Munich), VII, 223 (September 22–23, 1951).

Schlömer, H. "Denkt die Burschenschaft noch völkisch?" *Civis*, II, 14 (February, 1956), 128–129.

Schmalfuss, Alex. "Standpunkt der Soldatenbünde," *Der Tagesspiegel* (Berlin), October 6, 1951, p. 2.

Schmidt, F. J. "Bruderzwist in der Bruderschaft," *Süddeutsche Zeitung* (Munich), no. 48 (February 27, 1951).

Schmidt, Heinrich. "Eine deutsche Geschichte," *Deutsche Universitäts-Zeitung*, VIII, 7 (April 7, 1953), 13.

Schmidt, Siegfried. "Überblick über die äussere Entwicklung der nationalen Jugendverbände," *Erkenntnis und Tat*, VII, 5/6 (May–June, 1956), 18–19.

Schreiber, Herrmann, and Karl Heinz Wocker. "Die unbewältigte Gegenwart; Ursachen der Anfälligkeit junger Menschen von heute für die Ideen von Gestern." *Stuttgarter Zeitung*, XVI (March 11, 1960), 3.

———. "Viele Wege führen nach rechts; Ursachen der Anfälligkeit junger Menschen von heute für die Ideen von Gestern." *Stuttgarter Zeitung*, XVI (March 10, 1960), 3.

Schumacher, H. "Die Fahrenden Gesellen e.V.," in Hertha Siemering, ed., *Die deutschen Jugendverbände.* Berlin: Heymann, 1931. Pp. 85–87.

Seraphim, Hans-Günther. "SS-Verfügungstruppe und Wehrmacht," *Wehrwissenschaftliche Rundschau,* V, 12 (December, 1955), 569–585.

Sethe, Paul. "Handeln wir zu langsam?" *Frankfurter Allgemeine Zeitung,* October 17, 1951.

Shabecoff, Philip. "German Rightists Make Gain in Vote," *New York Times,* November 7, 1966, pp. 1 (col. 2), 12 (cols. 4–6).

———. "Nazi SS Veterans Cheer Former General at Meeting," *New York Times,* October 25, 1965, pp. 1 (cols. 4–6), 17 (cols. 3–8).

———. "Party Called Neo-Nazi Gains in Bavarian Elections," *New York Times,* March 15, 1966, p. 14, cols. 4–6.

Sontheimer, Kurt. "Antidemokratisches Denken in der Weimarer Republik," *Vierteljahrshefte für Zeitgeschichte,* V, 1 (January, 1957), 42–62.

———. "Der Tatkreis," *Vierteljahrshefte für Zeitgeschichte,* VII, 3 (July, 1959), 229–260.

———. "Thomas Mann als politischer Schriftsteller," *Vierteljahrshefte für Zeitgeschichte,* VI, 1 (January, 1958), 1–44.

Soriat, Lucien. "Explication de la stabilité politique allemande," *Politique,* n.s., no. 13 (January–March, 1961), pp. 34–71.

Speidel, Hans. "Reichswehr und Rote Armee," *Vierteljahrshefte für Zeitgeschichte,* I, 1 (January, 1953), 9–45.

Spencer, Arthur. "National Bolshevism," *Survey,* no. 44/45 (October, 1962), pp. 133–152.

Spengemann, Walter. "Die missglückte Entnazifizierung," *Norddeutsche Zeitung* (Hanover), September 7, 1948.

Ssymank, Paul. "Geschichtlicher Überblick über deutsches Hochschulwesen und deutsches Studententum," in Michael Doeberl *et al.,* eds., *Das akademische Deutschland.* Berlin: Weller, 1931. II, 1–44.

Stammler, Eberhard. "Die politische Bildung und das Hakenkreuz," *deutsche jugend,* VIII, 2 (February, 1960), 63–68.

Stein, George H. "The Myth of a European Army," *The Wiener Library Bulletin* (London), XIX, 2 (April, 1965), 21–22.

Stern, Fritz. "The Political Consequences of the Unpolitical German," in *History 3.* New York: Meridian Books, [1960]. Pp. 104–134.

Stolz, Otto. "Neo-Nazis schaffen Querverbindungen," *Die Neue Zeitung* (Munich), V, 241 (October 14, 1949).

Strebin, F. "Autorität und Freiheit," *Aus Politik und Zeitgeschichte* (supplement of *Das Parlament*) (Bonn), January 13, 1960.

Strothmann, Dietrich. "Kriminelle Kriminalisten? Gestern SS-Sturmbannführer—heute Polizeidirektor," *Freiheit und Recht* (Düsseldorf), VIII, 7 (July, 1962), 14–15.

Struve, Walter. "Hans Zehrer as a Neoconservative Elite Theorist," *American Historical Review,* LXX, 4 (July, 1965), 1035–1057.

Stuckmann, H. "Dix jours dans la Bundeswehr," *Documents* (*Revue des questions allemandes*), XII (January–February, 1957), 36–38.

Sutton, John L. "The Personnel Screening Committee and Parliamentary

Control of the West German Armed Forces," *Journal of Central European Affairs,* XIX, 4 (January, 1960), 389–401.

Tabor, G. "Übersee Deutschtum und deutsche Politik," *Kölnische Rundschau,* December 13, 1948, p. 3.

Thieme, Hans. "Hochschullehrer klagen an," *Deutsche Universitäts-Zeitung,* VIII, 7 (April 7, 1953), 3–5.

Thoma, Peter. "Dr. Otto Strasser, die neutralistische Idee und der Neutralismus," *Die Sammlung* (Rundbrief der Sammlung zur Tat) (Cologne), no. 38, n.d. (probably January or February, 1961), pp. 9–12.

Thomas, Friedrich. " 'Bruder Studium' meidet die Politik," *Christ und Welt* (Stuttgart), no. 14 (March 31, 1960).

Thurnreiter, Toni. "Jugendfremde Politik," *Hessische Jugend,* no. 6/7 (1958), pp. 2–3.

Trevor-Roper, H. R. "The Germans Reappraise the War," *Foreign Affairs,* XXXI, 2 (January, 1953), 225–237.

Trischen, Theo. "Das fromme Märchen vom 'unpolitischen Stahlhelm,' " *Neue Ruhr Zeitung* (Essen), no. 38 (September 18, 1954), p. 1.

Union Internationale de la Résistance et de la Déportation. Comité international pour la lutte contre le neo-nazisme. "Les Arabes et le neonazisme." Brussels, April, 1965.

Vagts, Alfred. "Unconditional Surrender vor und nach 1945," *Vierteljahrshefte für Zeitgeschichte,* VII, 3 (July, 1959), 280–309.

Visurgius, *pseud.* "Ramcke macht Wirbel," *Weser-Kurier* (Bremen), October 27, 1952.

Voigt, Gerd. "Otto Hoetzsch—eine biographische Skizze," in Leo Stern, ed., *Der Antikommunismus in Theorie und Praxis des deutschen Imperialismus.* [Halle: Martin-Luther-Universität Halle-Wittenberg,] 1963. Pp. 142–156.

Volbracht, Adolf. "Dokumentation zum roten und braunen Faschismus," *Kontakte,* I, 8 (January, 1952), 9–10.

Volksbund für Frieden und Freiheit. Landesleitung Niedersachsen. "Wo steht heute der alte Marschierer?" n.d. (probably summer, 1951).

Voss, Theodor. Letter to the Editor of *Welt am Sonntag* (Hamburg), no. 40 (October 7, 1951).

W. L. R. "Rechts um!" *deutsche jugend,* IV, 1 (January, 1956), 38–39.

Wagner, Walter. "Politische Justiz in der Weimarer Republik: Der Feind von links," *Politische Meinung,* VI, 60 (1961), 48–61.

———. "Politische Justiz in der Weimarer Republik: Der Feind von rechts," *Politische Meinung,* VI, 58 (1961), 50–63.

Waite, Robert G. L. Book review of Maurice Baumont *et al.,* eds., *The Third Reich,* in the *American Historical Review,* LXI, 1 (October, 1955), 129–131.

Weinberg, Gerhard L. Book review of David L. Hoggan, *Der erzwungene Krieg,* in the *American Historical Review,* LXVIII, 1 (October, 1962), 104, and 3 (April, 1963), 917–918.

Weinland, Viktor H. "Wiedergeburt des Nationalsozialismus?" *Echo der Woche* (Munich), III, 76 (January 7, 1949), 2.

Weinsheimer, Lilo. "Diskussion über Kriegsbücher," *Aufwärts* (Giessen), no. 1 (1960), p. 4.

Weinstein, Adelbert. "Ein atlantischer General verlässt Washington," *Frankfurter Allgemeine Zeitung,* no. 51 (February 29, 1964).

Weippert, Georg. "Die Ideologien der 'Kleinen Leute' und des 'Mannes auf der Strasse,'" in his *Jenseits von Individualismus und Kollektivismus. Studien zum gegenwärtigen Zeitalter.* Düsseldorf: Schilling, 1964. Pp. 148–173.

Wenger, Paul Wilhelm. "Entnazifizierung am Ende," *Rheinischer Merkur* (Koblenz), no. 14 (April 2, 1949).

Weniger, Erich. "Das Korporationswesen als soziologisches Problem," *Die Sammlung* (Göttingen), VII, 2 (February, 1952), 125–131.

Wenzel, Walter. "Schluss mit der Ziesel-Reklame," *Die Andere Zeitung* (Hamburg), no. 21 (September 29, 1955), p. 6.

Werdau, Hermann. "Die Jünger der braunen und roten Diktatur," *PZ-Archiv,* February 5, 1952, pp. 38 ff.

Werner, Alfred. "Germany's New Flagellants," *The American Scholar,* XXVII, 2 (Spring, 1958), 169–178.

———. "Trotzky of the Nazi Party," *Journal of Central European Affairs,* XI, 1 (January–April, 1951), 39–46.

Werner, (Capt., ret.). "'Scharnhorst,' Bund deutscher Jungmannen e.V.," in Hertha Siemering, ed., *Die deutschen Jugendverbände.* Berlin: Heymann, 1931. Pp. 36–38.

Wesemann, Fried. "Die Totengräber sind unter uns: Aus den Dokumenten der Naumann-Affäre" (a five-part series), *Frankfurter Rundschau,* June 9, 10, 11, 12, 13, 1953.

Wewer, Heinz. "Die Hiag der Waffen-SS," *Frankfurter Hefte,* XVII, 7 (July, 1962), 448–458.

Whiteside, Andrew G. "The Nature and Origins of National Socialism," *Journal of Central European Affairs,* XVII, 1 (April, 1957), 48–73.

Wilcke, Gerd. "Bonn Urged to Curb Scientists Aiding Cairo in Missile Work," *New York Times,* April 3, 1963, p. 6.

———. "Germans Debate Brief for Hitler," *New York Times,* May 3, 1964.

———. "Some Ex-Nazis Quit Courts on Bonn Deadline," *New York Times,* July 3, 1962, p. 8, cols. 5–7.

Wilde, Harry. "Rudolf Diels—Porträt eines verkannten Mannes," *Politische Studien,* IX, 99 (July, 1958), 475–481.

Woerl, Rudolf. "Dunkle Wolken überm 'Lago di Bonzo,'" *Welt der Arbeit (Stimme der Arbeit aus Bayern),* IV, 29 (July 17, 1953).

Zimmermann, Friedrich. "Jugend und Politik," *Freiheit und Verantwortung,* no. 79 (1956).

Zink, Harold. "The American Denazification Program in Germany," *Journal of Central European Affairs,* VI, 4 (October, 1946), 227–240.

Zoller, Guido. "Die gleiche Blutgruppe," *Rheinischer Merkur* (Koblenz), no. 23 (June 6, 1952), p. 4.

(b) *Unsigned Articles*

"A Congress of 'Young Europeans,'" *The Wiener Library Bulletin* (London), XIII, 5–6 (1959), 55.
"A Vienne: En acquittant Verbelen un jury autrichien acquitte le Nazisme," *La Voix internationale de la résistance* (Brussels), VIII, 96 (February, 1966), 5–7.
"Abgeordnete rügen Zenker," *Die Welt* (Hamburg), April 19, 1956.
"Am Telephon vorsichtig," *Der Spiegel,* VII, 19 (May 6, 1953), 7.
"Amtsvertrieben," *Der Spiegel,* XVIII, 5 (January 29, 1964), 18–19.
"An den Staat heranführen," *Hannoversche Presse,* VI, 216 (September 15, 1951).
"Angebot der CDU," *Der Spiegel,* VII, 32 (August 5, 1953), 6.
"Auch ein Korrespondent," *Vorwärts* (Cologne), IX, 19 (May 11, 1956).
"aus dem hohlen bauch geholt," *Colloquium,* XI, 6 (June, 1957), 1.
"Aus der Arbeit des deutschen Kulturwerkes," *Studien von Zeitfragen, Analysen, Berichte, Informationen zum nationalen Nonkonformismus,* XI, 7 (July 16, 1964), 5.
"Austrian Blocks Leniency on Nazis," *New York Times,* February 18, 1966, p. 2, col. 5.
"Beschwerderecht: Bauch im Dreck," *Der Spiegel,* XVIII, 6 (February 3, 1964), 23–26.
"Blank gegen 'Diva,'" *Junge Stimme,* no. 13 (July 27, 1956).
"Bonn kritisiert Marineoffiziere," *Hamburger Allgemeine Zeitung,* April 19, 1956.
"Bücher von Rudolf Hess bleiben beschlagnahmt," *Die Welt* (Hamburg), May 4, 1957.
"Bürger in Uniform," *Der Spiegel,* X, 45 (November 7, 1956), 9–10.
"Bürger und Partisanen: Die Enthüllungen über den 'Technischen Dienst des BDJ,'" *Die Gegenwart,* November 8, 1952, pp. 727–731.
"Bürgerbräuromantik—Nationalbolschewismus unter dem Banner der nationalen Pflichterfüllung," *Christ und Welt* (Stuttgart), no. 51 (December 18, 1952).
"Call for Another Anschluss," *The Wiener Library Bulletin* (London), XVIII, 1 (January, 1964), 2.
"Ce 29 novembre, Verbelen, arrêté en 1962, sera jugé," *La Voix internationale de la résistance* (Brussels), VIII, 92–93 (October–November, 1965), 9.
"Die Demokratie im 'demokratischen Laufstühlchen,'" *Stuttgarter Zeitung,* July 12, 1960.
"Deutsch–Wandervogel," Gesellschaft zum Studium von Zeitfragen, *Analysen und Berichte,* VI, 11 (September 11, 1959), 12.
"Deutsche 'Berater' schüren in Kairo," *Welt am Sonntag* (Hamburg), no. 47 (November 23, 1952).
"Deutsche National–Zeitung: Sprachrohr des Volkes," *Der Spiegel,* XVII, 11 (March 13, 1963), 46–52.
"Diese Bestien," *Der Spiegel,* XVII, 30 (July 24, 1963), 26.

"Dokumentation über NS-Verbrechen," *Süddeutsche Zeitung* (Munich), no. 273 (November 13, 1964), p. 4.

"Die DRP will jetzt 'hoffähig' werden," *Hannoversche Presse,* September 9, 1956.

"Ein Reichsjugendführer verhaftet," *Frankfurter Allgemeine Zeitung,* June 26, 1957.

"Einfach durchhalten," *Der Spiegel,* XVIII, 4 (January 22, 1964), 19–20.

" 'Einiges war aber doch gut': Oberschüler diskutieren über den Nationalsozialismus," *Junge Stimme,* no. 7 (1958).

"Einmütigkeit im Bundestag: Raeder und Dönitz sind keine Vorbilder," *Hannoversche Presse,* April 19, 1956.

"Das Ende der Freikorps," *Welt der Arbeit (Stimme der Arbeit aus der Nordmark),* February 20, 1953, p. 7.

"Es kam auf ihn zu," *Der Spiegel,* XVIII, 1/2 (January 8, 1964), 20.

"Ex-Nazi Prosecutor Is Accused by Bonn," *New York Times,* July 20, 1962, p. 2, col. 1.

"Der Fall Schlüter" (editorial), *Deutsche Universitäts-Zeitung,* X, 11 (June 8, 1955), 3–4.

"Der falsche Fünfzehner," *Der Spiegel,* X, 33 (August 15, 1956), 11–14.

"FDP-Führungswechsel in Hannover angekündigt," *Die Welt* (Hamburg), November 26, 1953.

"Fregattenkapitän Kretschmer: 'Raeder ist unserer Kamerad,' " *Neue Ruhr Zeitung* (Essen), no. 120 (June 5, 1956), p. 2.

"Friessner: Den Blick vorwärts nach alter Soldatenart," *Die Welt* (Hamburg), October 20, 1951.

"Fröhliche Urständ!" *Deutsche Rundschau,* LXXVIII, 9 (September, 1952), 969.

"Geistlicher Rat teuer," *Der Spiegel,* III, 11 (March 12, 1949), 9–11.

"Generaloberst a.D. Friessner führt neuen Soldatenverband," *Die Welt* (Hamburg), October 9, 1951.

"Generaloberst a.D. Friessner tritt ab," *Die Welt* (Hamburg), December 11, 1951.

"German Insurers Bar Duel Claims," *New York Times,* May 7, 1961, p. 24, col. 1.

"German Teachers Irked by Contest," *New York Times,* August 15, 1965, p. 24, cols. 1–2.

"Geschäfte mit der Wiederbewaffnung?" *Feinde der Demokratie* (Lower Saxony), V, 4–5 (January–March, 1956), 53.

"The 'Hand of Paternalism,' " *The Wiener Library Bulletin* (London), XV, 3 (1961), 48.

"Hedlers Hitler Begeisterung," *Das Freie Wort* (Düsseldorf), n.d. (probably June, 1951).

"Heidelberg Sets Truce on Dueling," *New York Times,* December 7, 1961, p. 34, col. 3.

"Heye: Breitseite aus Bayern," *Der Spiegel,* XVIII, 46 (November 11, 1964), 38–39.

"HIAG der Waffen-SS: 'Durchbruch nach vorn,' " *Feinde der Demokratie* (Lower Saxony), VI, 7–8 (June–July, 1957), 33.

"Hilfe aus Afrika," *Der Spiegel,* XV, 45 (November 1, 1961), 40–41.

"Hilferufe an Otto Strasser," *Informationsdienst,* September, 1956.

"Hoggan Debunked," *The Wiener Library Bulletin* (London), XVII, 4 (October, 1963), 52.

"Hoggan: Einfach schön," *Der Spiegel,* XVIII, 20 (May 13, 1964), 28–35.

"Ich will mir den Mund nicht verbieten lassen," *Der Spiegel,* XVIII, 46 (November 11, 1964), 41–43.

"Im alten Tritt," *Frankfurter Allgemeine Zeitung,* October 29, 1957.

"Keine nazistische Verschwörung," *Weser–Kurier* (Bremen), October 27, 1952.

"Koalitions-Krise. Wir sind das Feigenblatt," *Der Spiegel,* IX, 11 (March 9, 1955), 8–19.

"Korporationsverbände werden erstmals aus dem Bundesjugendplan gefördert," *Informationen aus der Studentenschaft,* no. 2 (February, 1961), pp. 4–5.

"Küsst die Faschisten," *Der Spiegel,* X, 8 (February 22, 1956), 15–16.

"Kulissenwechsel," [Club republikanischer Publizisten,] *CrP-Information,* September, 1956, p. 14.

"Der Kurs gegen Adenauer," *Der Spiegel,* IV, 32 (August 10, 1950), 7–9.

"Landtagswahl in Baden-Württemberg," *Studien von Zeitfragen. Analysen, Berichte, Informationen zum nationalen Nonkonformismus,* XI, 4 (April 29, 1964), 7–8.

"Leiche im Auto," *Der Spiegel,* XI, 4 (January 23, 1957), 46.

"Marine Treffen: Die Luft ist raus," *Der Spiegel,* XVII, 26 (June 26, 1963), 37–39.

"Marinejugend," *Informationsdienst des Landesjugendringes Niedersachsen,* no. 62 (1956–1957), p. 5.

"Mobilizing the Fourth Reich," *The New Statesman and Nation,* XLII, 1065 (August 4, 1951), 116.

"Der Mufti lässt grüssen," *Der Spiegel,* VII, 5 (January 28, 1953), 5–6.

"Das Mysterium," *Der Spiegel,* XV, 21 (May 17, 1961), 37.

"Nach grossdeutschem Muster," *Der Spiegel,* VII, 6 (February 4, 1953), 5.

"Nagold: Solche Bengels," *Der Spiegel,* XVII, 51 (December 18, 1963), 25.

"Nagold: Tiefste Gangart," *Der Spiegel,* XVII, 46 (November 13, 1963), 52–59.

"National-demokraten: Auch die sind uns recht," *Der Spiegel,* IV, 3 (January 19, 1950), 10.

"Nau-Nau!" *Der Spiegel,* VII, 4 (January 21, 1953), 5–8.

"Naumann-Entnazifizierung: Wahlanfechtung möglich," *Der Spiegel,* VII, 36 (September 2, 1953), 9–10.

"The Naumann Plot: Evidence from the Impounded Documents," The *Wiener Library Bulletin* (London), VII, 3–4 (May–August, 1953), 20.

"Neo-nazistischer Verleger in Wien verhaftet," *Frankfurter Rundschau,* January 12, 1959.

"Neue Krise in der FDP," *Hamburger Echo,* January 14, 1954.
"Neue Parteigründung geplant," *Süddeutsche Zeitung* (Munich), no. 286 (November 28–29, 1964), p. 2.
"Neue Runde im Ringen um den Grafen Baudissin," *Neue Rhein Zeitung* (Cologne), August 15, 1956.
"Neue Wehrmacht im alten Geist?" *Deutscher Informationsdienst,* no. 452 (March 14, 1955).
"Notausgang für Hitlers Richter," *Freiheit und Recht* (Düsseldorf), VIII, 7 (July, 1962), 18.
"NS-Verbrechen: Ungleiches Recht," *Der Spiegel,* XVIII, 16 (April 18, 1964), 28–30.
"Offiziere: Griff nach den Sternen," *Der Spiegel,* XVII, 52 (December 25, 1963), 38–58.
"Pfiffe am Waldkater," *Der Spiegel,* XIV, 30 (July 20, 1960), 23–25.
"Polemik um 'nationale Studenten,'" [Club republikanischer Publizisten,] *CrP-Information,* March, 1957, p. 28.
"Die Problematik der Soldatenbünde," *Neuer Vorwärts* (Hanover), January 11, 1952.
"Raeder Ehrenmitglied des Marinebundes," *Hannoversche Presse,* June 4, 1956.
"Raeders Verzicht," *Hamburger Echo,* no. 90 (April 17, 1956).
"Rechtsradikale 'Reichsjugend' aufgelöst," *Internationaler Jugend Presse Dienst* (*ijpd*), VII, 237 (1957), 2.
"Rechtsradikalismus in der Bundesrepublik: Ein Erfahrungsbericht," *Aus Politik und Zeitgeschichte* (Supplement to *Das Parlament*) (Bonn), B20/60, May 16, 1962.
"Rechtsradikalismus in Europa" (a nine-part series), *Hamburger Brief,* II, 87, 89, 91, 94, 98 (September 1, 9, 19, 26, October 10, 1956) and III, 1, 9, 11/12, 14 (October 17, November 14, 23, December 1, 1956).
"'Reich und Revolution' (RR)," *Deutscher Informationsdienst,* XV, 1084 (February 3, 1964), 1–2.
"Remer am Nil," *Der Spiegel,* VII, 20 (May 13, 1953).
"Restoring Historical Truth," *The Wiener Library Bulletin* (London), XV, 1 (1961), 4.
"Richtungskämpfe in der Hiag," *Deutscher Informationsdienst,* no. 795 (February 11, 1959), pp. 1–3.
"Rudolf Jungnickels 'Papenheim'-Briefe und das 'Deutsche Manifest,'" *Die Brücke,* II, 3 (March, 1955), 5.
"SA marschiert," *Der Spiegel,* XV, 21 (May 17, 1961), 30–32.
"Scharfe Absage an politisierende Offiziere," *Süddeutsche Zeitung* (Munich), no. 229 (October 4, 1951), pp. 1–2.
"Scharnhorst, Gneisenau," *Frankfurter Allgemeine Zeitung,* April 19, 1956.
"Die Schlacht im falchen (*sic!*) Saal," *Die Europäische Zeitung* (Bonn), V, 2 (February 20, 1957), 10.
"Schlichtenmayer: Pleite von Rechts," *Der Spiegel,* XIX, 22 (May 26, 1965), 91–92.

"Schlüter: Ein Feuer soll lodern," *Der Spiegel,* IX, 24 (June 15, 1955), 12–24.

"Schmisse und Farben," *Junge Stimme,* no. 15 (August 6, 1960), p. 5.

"Seekrieg," *Der Spiegel,* XV, 6 (February 1, 1961), 3.

"70,000 junge Rechtsradikale," *Für die Demokratie,* I (IX), 1 (December, 1959—January, 1960), 25–26.

"Soldat im demokratischen Staat," *Politische Studien,* VI, 68 (December, 1955), 35–42.

"Soldaten vor der Entscheidung," *Hamburger Echo,* October 20, 1951.

"Soldatenverband wirbt auch um 'ungediente Jugend,'" *Frankfurter Rundschau,* September 12, 1951.

"SS et criminels de guerre au service de Nasser," *La Voix internationale de la résistance* (Brussels), VIII, 90–91 (August–September, 1965), 16; 92–93 (October–November, 1965), 18, 20.

"Die studentischen Korporationen," *Feinde der Demokratie* (Lower Saxony), III, 4 (January, 1954).

"Suchende Söhne," *Der Spiegel,* XVII, 29 (July 17, 1963), 30–31.

"Todesurteil als Lohn für Kameradschaft," *Deutsche Soldaten–Zeitung* (Munich), VI, 11 (November, 1956), 7.

"Treacherous Currents," *The Wiener Library Bulletin* (London), XII, 1–2 (1958), 6.

"Um den Begriff Neonazismus" (Letters between Arthur Ehrhardt and Professors Hans Rothfels and Theodor Eschenburg), *Vierteljahrshefte für Zeitgeschichte,* III, 2 (April, 1955), 223–225.

"Ungarische Exil-Faschisten," *Die Andere Zeitung* (Hamburg), no. 48 (November 29, 1956), p. 1.

"Untergrund-Bewegung Reich," *Die Wochen Zeitung* (Zurich), no. 18 (April 20, 1953).

"Verschwörung wider den Geist," *Der Spiegel,* VII, 20 (May 13, 1953), 5–6.

"Verzicht auf die Ehrenbürgerschaft," *Frankfurter Allgemeine Zeitung,* April 17, 1956.

"Vom Sinn und Unsinn guter Einsicht," *Studien von Zeitfragen, Analysen und Berichte,* VIII, 11 (August 2, 1961), 8.

"Von Mensuren hört man nichts," *Der Spiegel,* XI, 32 (August 7, 1957), 22–29.

"Das Vorleben des Herrn Münchow," *Flensburger Tageblatt,* March 1, 1950.

"Waffen-SS Hiag als politischer Stosstrupp?" *Feinde der Demokratie* (Lower Saxony), VIII, 1–2 (January, 1959), 3.

"Waffen-SS Hiag in der Krise," *Feinde der Demokratie* (Lower Saxony), V, 2 (November–December, 1955), 31–34.

"War Hitler ein Friedensfreund?" *Der Spiegel,* XVIII, 20 (May 13, 1964), 36–48.

"Was die Marinejugend will," *Junge Stimme,* no. 15 (August 9, 1958).

"Wenn das Verbot kommt," *Der Spiegel,* VI, 33 (August 13, 1952), 7.

"Wenn niemand davon spricht," *Der Spiegel,* VIII, 44 (October 27, 1954), 13–14.

"Wer in Bayern studiert," *Süddeutsche Zeitung* (Munich), no. 273 (November 13, 1964), p. 13.

" 'Wie beim alten Willem . . . ,' " *Hannoversche Presse,* VI, 260 (November 6, 1951), 2.

"Wir folgen der Fahne . . . ," *Informationen der Naturfreunde Jugend,* no. 10 (1955), pp. 7–8.

"Das Wort hat der Bundestag," *Frankfurter Rundschau,* October 21, 1952, 3.

"Ziesel—oder: Die verlorenen Massstäbe," *Feinde der Demokratie* (Lower Saxony), VII, 6–7 (May–June, 1958), 30–33.

"Zum ewigen Frieden," *Der Spiegel,* III, 35 (September 1, 1949), 8.

"Zum Problem der Waffen-SS Offiziere," *Deutscher Informationsdienst,* no. 604 (October 29, 1956), pp. 1–3.

"Zur Situation der nationalen Jugendverbände," *Die Brücke,* IV, 19 (October, 1957), 1–22.

"Zur Situation der nationalen Jugendverbände," Gesellschaft zum Studium von Zeitfragen, *Analysen und Berichte,* VI, 11 (September 11, 1959), 1–15.

"Zweimal Jugendring," *Die Andere Zeitung* (Hamburg), no. 29 (November 24, 1955), p. 3.

"12-Punkte Program des 'Stahlhelm,' " *Nordwest Zeitung* (Oldenburg), September 3, 1951.

II. Unpublished Sources

1. BOOKS AND ARTICLES

Besser, Klaus. "Kulturpolitische Auswirkungen der Werke des Hauses Ludendorff. Zum Urteil über Frau Dr. Mathilde Ludendorffs ideologische Stellung zum Nationalsozialismus." Typescript, [February–March, 1950].

Demokratische Gesellschaft, 1952. "Links und rechts im 'Führungsring.' " Mimeographed brochure, n.d.

Domandi, Mario. *The German Youth Movement.* Ph.D. dissertation. Columbia University, 1960.

Freedman, Paul. Report on the arrest of Werner Naumann. Typescript, [February, 1953?].

Griffith, William E. *The Denazification Program in the United States Zone of Germany.* Ph.D. dissertation. Harvard University, 1950.

Hill, Hans. "Interview with Wolf Count Westarp." Typescript, [August or early September, 1952?].

Hirsch, Kurt. "Rechtsradikale Literatur in der Bundesrepublik," Typescript, n.d.

Hoggan, David L. *The Breakdown of German-Polish Relations in 1939: The Conflict between the German New Order and the Polish Idea of Central Eastern Europe.* Ph.D. dissertation. Harvard University, 1948.

Jovy, Michael. *Deutsche Jugend und Nationalsozialismus. Versuch einer Klärung ihrer Zusammenhänge und Gegensätze.* Ph.D. dissertation. University of Cologne, 1952.

Lebovics, Herman. *A Socialism for the German Middle Classes: The Social*

Conservative Response to Industrialism, 1900–1933. Ph.D. dissertation. Yale University, 1965.

Linz Storch de Grazia, Juan J. *The Social Bases of West German Politics.* Ph.D. dissertation. Columbia University, 1959.

Lüth, Erich. "Die Beschmutzung des freien Wortes." Mimeographed brochure, May 2, 1958.

Müller, Wolfgang. "Geschichtliches Gutachten: War Major Remer schon am 20. Juli 1944 als Führer ein Drückeberger?" Typescript, June 1, 1952.

Pross, Harry. *Nationale und soziale Prinzipien in der bündischen Jugend.* Ph.D. dissertation. University of Heidelberg, 1949.

Schmidt, Josef. Political report. Typescript, August 11, 1953.

———. Report and analysis of the Lower Saxon Landtag elections. [May, 1955?]

Schudnagis, Walter. "Reichsjugend und Herbert Münchow." Typescript, [April, 1952?].

Weber, Alfred. *Im Schatten der braunen Utopie.* Unpublished book, typescript, 1952.

Zietlow, Fritz. "Eidesstattliche Erklärung." Typescript, April 15, 1951.

2. CONFIDENTIAL REPORTS

Note: To protect the sources of information, the following list identifies the reports merely by their subject matter and their dates, where known.

Abelli, Tullio. Discussion with Hamburg circle around Carl Tiso.

Bauverd, Jean-Maurice. Confidential mission for Arab countries.

Bund für Glaubens- und Gewissensfreiheit (BGG). June 6, 1952.

Deutsche Reichs–Partei (DRP). Election meeting in Worms, August 26, 1953.

Deutsche Union (DU). Founding meeting in Brunswick, January 24, 1949.

———. Situation report, March 25, 1950.

Diels, Rudolf. Discussions, April 7 and May 13, 1953.

Europäische Verbindungsstelle (EVS). Hanover meeting of January 24–26, 1954.

Falkenroth, Ernst. Discussion, August 26, 1952.

Hedler, Wolfgang. Discussion, June 24, 1953.

Jungnickel, Rudolf. Organization of the Filsen meeting of May 18, 1952.

Kapfer, Ludwig. Discussion, December 18, 1952.

Kögler, Theodor. Relation to the Gesamtdeutsche Volkspartei (GVP), March 9, 1953.

Körper, Werner. Discussions, September, October, December 2, 1952, and January 13, February 5, April 16, August 28, 1953.

Krüger, Gerhard. Discussion, April 16, 1953.

———. Meeting of the Deutsche Aufbauvereinigung (DAV), Frankfurt, July 17, 1953.

Laupheimer Circle. Meeting of Arbeitsausschuss with Deutsche Union (DU), Ulm, February 4–5, 1949.

———. Meeting, Bad Wimpfen, July 21, 1951.

Meissner, Karl. Report of St. Goar meeting, November 27, 1952.
Mischke, Gerhard. Discussion, April 9, 1953.
Müller-Schwaneck, Eric-Uwe (Eumsch). Discussion, August 18, 1952.
Münchow, Herbert. Discussion, October, 1951.
Natinform. Staff meeting, October 11–12, 1952.
———. Leaders' conference, January 16–19, 1953.
———. Staff meeting, February 11, 1953.
———. Planning session, May 3–4, 1953.
Nationale Partei Deutschlands (NDP). Situation report, June 26, 1952.
Naumann, Werner. Discussion, October 20, 1953.
Peters, Martin. Discussion, March 12, 1953.
Sarg, Wolfgang. Discussion, January 17, 1953.
Schirschin, Erich. Discussion, November 23, 1952.
Schmidt, Egon-Arthur. Discussion, February 11, 1953.
Sozialistische Reichs Partei (SRP). Meeting of August 28, 1953.
Suleck, Paul. Discussion, May 14, 1953.
Teich, Erich. Discussions, October 29, 1952, and January 21 and March 9, 1953.
———, and Wilhelm Wesemeyer. Discussion, April 14, 1953.
Vowinckel, Kurt. Discussion, February 12, 1953.

Indexes

Advice to the Reader

Throughout these Indexes, entries in the form "Abelli, Tullio, 212" refer the user to the given page of text (Volume I). Entries in the form "Abelli, Tullio, VII/10" refer the user to Note 10 of Chapter VII, in the section headed "Notes and References," pp. 999–1376 (Volume II).

For purposes of alphabetization, *initial* definite articles have not been taken into account. The German modified vowels (umlaut) ä, ö, ü have been alphabetized under ae, oe, ue.

List of Abbreviations

The most frequently cited parties and organizations as well as the names of the two German states and of five West German *Länder* appear in the sub-entries of the Indexes in the following abbreviated form:

ANG	Working Association of National Groups
ANP	Working Fellowship for Nationalist Politics
AvJ	Working Fellowship of Patriotic Youth Associations
AVNP	Working Circle for the Unification of the National Parties
AVS	Federal Office for the Protection of the Constitution
BdF	League of Front Line Soldiers
BdS	League of Former German Soldiers
BHE	Union of Expellees and Victims of Injustice
BNS	League of National Students
BRD	Federal Republic of Germany
B.-W.	Baden-Württemberg
CDU	Christian Democratic Union
CSU	Christian Social Union
DAP	German Reconstruction Party
DAV	German Reconstruction Association
DB	German Bloc
DDR	German Democratic Republic
DFP	German Freedom Party
DG	German Community
DGB	German Labor Union Federation
DKEG	German Cultural Work in the European Spirit
DKP	German Conservative Party
DKP-DRP	German Conservative Party–German Rightist Party
DP	German Party
DRP	German Reich Party
DRP (KV)	German Rightist Party (Conservative Association)
DSB	German Social Movement
DSP	German Social Party
DU	German Union
EDC	European Defense Community
ESB	European Social Movement
EVB	European People's Movement
EVS	European Liaison Center
FDP	Free Democratic Party
FeS	Leadership Circle of Former Soldiers
GDP	All-German Party
GfP	Society for Free Journalism
GuD	Fellowship of Non-party Germans
JBA	Youth League Eagle
JEA	Young European Working Circle
KB	League of Comradeship
KNJ	Comradeship Circle of National Youth [Associations]
L.S.	Lower Saxony
MSI	Italian Social Movement
NDP	National Democratic Party
NEO	New European Order
NK	National Fighting Fellowship
NLP	Lower Saxon Land Party
NPD	National Democratic Party of Germany (1964)
NR	National Right
N.R.-W.	North Rhine–Westphalia
NS	National Rally
NSDAP	National Socialist German Workers' Party
RB	Reich Bloc
R.-P.	Rhineland–Palatinate
S.-H.	Schleswig–Holstein
SORBE	Social Organic Order Movement of Europe
SPD	Social Democratic Party
SRP	Socialist Reich Party
SzT	Action Rally
VdS	Association of German Soldiers
VR	United Right
WAV	Economic Reconstruction Association

Index of Persons

Index of Subjects

Index of Places